THE BEST OF RIVER-TOWN SMALL-BALL

THE BEST OF RIVER-TOWN SMALL-BALL

(Revised Edition)

Doug Nachbar
Bloomington, MN

© 2016, 2023 by Doug Nachbar

All Rights Reserved. No part of this work may be copied or reproduced by any means available without the express written consent of the copyright holder. Mail requests for permission to use material to: Doug Nachbar, 7413 Landau Curve, Bloomington, MN 55438.

The Best of River-Town Small-Ball by Doug Nachbar. Special Limited Introductory Edition, 2016. Revised edition, 2023.

Published by Sand Creek Diamond Press, an imprint of C3 Marketing, Bloomington, MN 55438. Edited by Nancy Huber.

Permissions–We are grateful to the following for their permission to use excerpts from their copyrighted works:

Pat Devitt, Unpublished private memoirs.

Dolph Grundman and Nodin Press, LLC, *Jim Pollard, The Kangaroo Kid*, published in 2009.

Nathan Lewis and John Wiley & Sons, Inc., *Gold, The Once and Future Money*, published in 2007.

Tom Melchior, *Scott County Baseball*, 2008.

Kurt Menk, *The History of Arlington Baseball* and "Spirit of '76"–*Minnesota State Baseball Tournament Program Guide*.

Daniel A. Russell, Ph.D., Penn State University, "Why Aluminum Bats Can Perform Better Than Wood Bats," On-line article, 2006.

Marion Renault, Editor-in-Chief, *The Minnesota Daily*.

Curt Sampson, *Hogan*, published by Rutledge Hill Press in 1996.

We are likewise grateful for the availability of archived public domain publications such as *The Jordan Independent* and other weekly and daily newspapers, which we accessed at Minnesota State and county historical societies.

Cover Design by Rosi Back of Mankato, MN.

Interior Page Design by Traci Sabby of Westminster, CO.

"All That Glitters Is Not Gold."

— John Dryden

(Also attributed in various closely related forms to other renowned writers, including Geoffrey Chaucer and William Shakespeare.)

– CONTENTS –

PRE-GAME WARM-UP 1

Part I – The Game 19

Part II – The Players.. 67

- Introduction.. 69
- Donald "Tex" Erickson 83
- Jim Pollard 110
- Johnny Garbett 152
- John Freund 189
- Jim Stoll 227
- Pat Devitt... 255
- Fulton "Lefty" Weckman 279
- Jim Kubes.. 298
- Sherwood "Woody" Peters 317
- Jim "Jake" Harsh... 334
- Mark Hess 352

AFTERWORD.. 381

ACKNOWLEDGEMENTS 385

BIBLIOGRAPHY 389

x

PRE-GAME WARMUP

I see great things in baseball.
— Walt Whitman, 19th Century American Poet

Few boys have the privilege of growing up to play ball with their baseball heroes. I was fortunate, and as a result my visits beginning in 2012 to old teammate Frank Hilgers at his Kingsway apartment on the Lutheran Home's campus in Belle Plaine, Minnesota, took on some added dimension. Old ballplayers inevitably get around to talking about ballgames and other ballplayers when they get together. We would go there often over the next three years. We would go to the window often, too, and Frank would gaze out over the tree line on the horizon that fronts the Minnesota River bank. "God, I loved that river valley," Frank said more than once.

The Minnesota River joins the Mississippi River near historic Ft. Snelling in St. Paul, Minnesota, after a winding journey of 320 to 370 miles. It touches at least 20 counties, and we count the drainage of 37 counties within the basin through an area of 17,000 square miles, beginning near Ortonville on the state's western borders with North and South Dakota. It has an average flow rate of just over 4,400 cubic feet per second, drops in elevation from 960 ft. at its source to 640 ft. at its mouth. It is the largest tributary to the Mississippi River in Minnesota and has 13 distinct river tributaries to it, among which include the Chippewa, Cottonwood, Lac qui Parle, Redwood, Whetstone, and Yellow Medicine.

Smaller tributaries like Sand Creek, which neatly wraps around and defines the old ballpark just downstream from the waterfalls in Lagoon Park in Jordan, are more important here. The creek still sucks up foul balls hit behind home plate and down the first-base line. Ball shaggers had to roll up their jeans, navigate the creek and its rocks without slipping to grab bobbing baseballs before they became waterlogged and sank. If the quick-footed, hustling shaggers did their jobs during the games at Fairgrounds Park in Jordan, some balls could be saved and put back in use, at least for batting practice. It's the same creek that flooded nearly half the town's homes in May of 1960 after torrential local rains and the controlled outlet to Cedar Lake, was overwhelmed on a Friday night. The raging waters washed out a portion of Hwy 21, which separates the old native 30-inch-thick limestone block brewery building from the creek and the ballpark. Fairgrounds Park was flooded, of course, and rendered unusable for weeks until volunteer labor restored it to playable conditions.

It's the creek that empties into the Minnesota River in the river bottoms area now known as the "Louisville Swamp." One of eight designated "refuge units" within the Minnesota Valley National Wildlife Refuge, it is located behind Bryan Red Rock and the site of the Renaissance Festival off Hwy 169 just north of Jordan. The confluence of the creek and the river was a great walleye-fishing hole until we learned about the mercury and PCBs that polluted that fishery from the runoff of agricultural and industrial chemicals along the entire stretch of the river.

The sources say that Big Stone Lake is the headwaters of the Minnesota River, but a closer look at maps reveals that an inlet feeds the lake from a large watershed– a big swamp–on both sides of the Continental Divide there. That makes the south side of the swamp the headwaters to the Minnesota, and it makes the north side of the Laurentian Divide the headwaters to the Red River, which flows north into Canada.

Henry David Thoreau took a ride upriver in 1861 on a 160-foot-long steamship from St. Paul to as far as Redwood, noting in passing the last settlement on the way,

New Ulm, being of all German settlers. It was the year before Thoreau died, and the year before this river of life, teeming with wild game and fish that sustained a fairly large population of Indians, turned into a river of blood. He was impressed with the river, itself, and he wrote of the journey in a letter to his biographer, Mr. Sandborn, from Redwing, Minnesota, on July 25, 1861, recounting his impressions. Governor Alexander Ramsey was aboard, along with some other dignitaries and the annual payment in gold that was to be made to the Dakota Indians at Redwood, the Lower Indian Agency.

As Thoreau noted, the Minnesota winds through some of the richest farmland in the Upper Midwest, from Browns Valley in Traverse County downstream to Ortonville and Odessa in Big Stone County, through Redwood and Nicollet Counties and the city of New Ulm, named by German settlers after the beautiful old Ulm on the Danube River in Germany; on into Blue Earth County and the city of Mankato, where the sharp dogleg takes the river to the north and east through St. Peter; onward through the city and county of Le Sueur, then through Henderson and what is probably the deepest cut of the valley's banks; on through Belle Plaine and outside Jordan in Scott County on one side of the river, Sibley and Carver Counties on the other; through Carver, Chaska, then Shakopee, Prior Lake, Savage, Burnsville, Bloomington and to the confluence at Ft. Snelling with the Mississippi River.

The Minnesota River Valley was home to, and prime hunting and fishing for, various related Sioux Indian tribes until white settlers came. Attempts at coexistence failed repeatedly, as treaties were broken, land usurped, payments to Indians withheld, and Indians pushed out until, in 1862 in what is known as the Dakota (Sioux) Indian Uprising in some history books, superior white militia numbers and resources prevailed in battles fought near and in New Ulm. A kangaroo court of hearings condemned 303 Indians to death by hanging. President Lincoln's intervention commuted the sentences of all but 38 of the Indians and half-bloods. Their hanging in Mankato on December 26, 1862, is to this day the single, largest mass execution in the history of the United States. The Indian Wars that began in the Minnesota River Valley culminated in the massacre at Wounded Knee in 1890.

By then, baseball and the brewing of beer had taken hold in the Minnesota River Valley. Most of the towns in our tales are in the area of the Lower Basin of the Minnesota River–from New Ulm to Bloomington. They had breweries at one time or another. New Ulm still has a brewery, Schell's, and at least one ball club, the Brewers, who got shut out, 2-0, by Sobieski in the Class-C State Championship at Jordan in 2014. Bloomington has the Mall of America, the Minnesota Twins having moved to downtown Minneapolis. Rahr Malting is still in Shakopee, doing well with the resurgence of microbreweries and a lock on the business of the two remaining larger brewers, Budweiser and Miller. Cargill is bigger than ever in Savage. But Green Giant's old quarters in Le Sueur are shut down.

Pierre-Charles Le Sueur was reportedly the first European to visit the river. The Minnesota Territory and later the state were named for the river, and the town of Le Sueur, Minnesota, was named for the man. This river valley is notable as the origin and center of the vegetable canning industry in Minnesota. In 1903 Carson Nesbit

Cosgrove, an entrepreneur in Le Sueur, presided at the organizational meeting of the Minnesota Valley Canning Company, which was later renamed Green Giant. By 1930, the Minnesota River Valley had emerged as one of the country's largest producers of sweet corn. Green Giant had five canning factories in Minnesota, in addition to the original facility in Le Sueur. Today, after the same kind of consolidation that has occurred in every other industry as well, just the brand is managed. The vast facilities are boarded up. Hard to say whether the quality of the canned and frozen sweet corn, peas, and other vegetables has been altered, but the town of Le Sueur certainly has been.

Grain ports such as Port Cargill in Savage, the town named for the owner of the great harness racehorse, "Dan Patch," receive trucks hauling corn and soybeans from farmers selling their fall harvest or stored grains. The grains are weighed, purchased, and loaded onto river barges, which navigate the rest of the 14 miles of the Minnesota River that is dredged to a depth of nine feet to accommodate the barges, to the ports of Minneapolis and Saint Paul, and then down the Mississippi River to New Orleans. From there the beans and corn are loaded onto ocean-going vessels for shipment to ports around the world.

It wasn't long before I realized what they say about Alzheimer's is true: Frank might ask me five times in ten minutes how old "Nikki" was. He had told me to "hide her under your coat and bring her up," on the first visit with her in 2012 when the Golden Retriever was just a week removed from the litter and only eight weeks old. But after learning of her therapy dog ambitions and the house rules at Kingsway, we came with her on a leash to visit Frank on a regular basis. They bonded and lit up immediately in mutual affection on every subsequent visit.

Then I got a vague notion that maybe memory works like faith or physical conditioning. Maybe "working out" the memory could at least slow down the progressive nature of Frank's condition. It seemed that memory speaks well when encouraged and prompted. So, we talked about our days on the old baseball and softball diamonds with greater and greater detail. There was the context of the times, history, comparisons, connections, and the metaphorical nature of the games, too. We would come to call it "memory exercise" or "memory therapy," and we would learn that old catchers knew the game and the players better than the rest of us.

I asked Frank to tell me who he thought were the best ballplayers he had ever seen. The first three names came very quickly: "Jim Pollard, Tex Erickson, Johnny Garbett . . ." Knowing that "best" is difficult, if not impossible, to define objectively, we came up with a list by position, only to find out that some players excelled at more than one position. Then we tried to fill the three main categories of baseball with our best: pitching, defense, and hitting. Again, too many of our chosen were outstanding at more than one category. They were simply better ballplayers than the rest. We tried to limit our list to nine players and couldn't do it. Finally, we settled on the 12 ballplayers we thought were the best of the bunch that we had ever seen play. Our field covered players Frank had seen from the late 1940s on between us. Frank wanted to play, too, but I told him the list was his and that he couldn't make his own list. Indeed, the working title of our book was *The Best Ballplayers I Ever Saw* by Frank Hilgers. That soon became a subtitle that backed up *All That Glittered*, a reference to the Golden Age of Baseball, gold, and other things that glow. Then, before the printing presses warmed up, I learned that Frank couldn't be the author and there were other books by the same title already. So, we changed the title and scrubbed Frank's name from the cover.

Once we settled on our list, I went to work, interviewing, researching, reading, and writing the biographical profiles that make up the meat of this book along with a digestion of all the conversations with Frank. We reviewed together all the writing, sharing tears and cheers and making some adjustments. Themes emerged as hunches were confirmed and patterns became apparent: There really was a Golden Age of Baseball. It was defined best, we think, by the late Ernie Banks in a television interview April 23, 2014, on MSNBC's *Morning Joe* at Wrigley Field when asked what all this meant to him–baseball, the Cubs, the ballpark. "It's my life. It's my Bible," Ernie Banks, the late, Hall of Fame Cub shortstop and first baseman and an ordained minister, replied.

Baseball was life, and life was baseball everywhere, at all levels, and as kids we didn't discriminate the local from national heroes. Simply put, Jim Pollard played at Fairgrounds Park on Sunday night, and we would read about Mickey Mantle in the paper on Monday morning.

I had to scratch Bobby Kelly from Prior Lake, Bloomington, and, I think, Augsburg College, or the U of M. I couldn't locate him or anyone in his family to do justice to a profile on this great shortstop with the Prior Lake Jays from 1968 to 1976. So that made 11, 12 with Frank, but we had four other shortstops. Frank said that your shortstop was usually your best athlete on a team. He said that if a guy could play shortstop, he could play any other position as well. It also meant that our criteria for "best" included athleticism and an ability to play the whole game. Our best were complete ballplayers.

We saw some truly great ballplayers over the 60-year period in this Lower Basin of the Minnesota River Valley, and Frank's eye and appreciation for that greatness have always been better than most. I double-checked with Frank many ballplayers of different periods who didn't make the list against those who did. I counted three catchers on our list: Frank, Jim Stoll, and Jim Kubes. Lefty Weckman and Johnny Garbett were really good pitchers, as were Jim Stoll, Jim Kubes, Jim Pollard, Pat Devitt, and John Freund.

Jake Harsh was a "pure" first baseman, and the position was a natural for Jim Pollard, who, like John Freund, could play any position on the field and did when asked. Then, too, we had all those shortstops. Woody Peters played a great shortstop, as did Bobby Kelly, Mark Hess, and Tex Erickson. But John Freund, we learned, signed with the Chicago Cubs out of high school as a 17-year-old shortstop when he was compared to St. Louis Cardinal shortstop Marty Marion. Then, how long should the list be? The easiest thing to do is to appease and accommodate everybody in the interests of stroking everybody's ego. But if everybody makes any list of "Best Ballplayers," then the list is meaningless. You've watered it all down to the point where "best" becomes simply mediocre and you've got a telephone book for people to read. Our list is self-limiting, and many others are mentioned with distinction throughout the book. Every reader can make an argument for including or excluding anybody he or she wants from being on such a list as this. We also thought that they could make up their own list and put themselves first on their list. We make a good effort at presenting the reasons for our choices in the profiles. The discovery process has been most rewarding, for we have uncovered some gems that lend substantial weight to the regard with which we hold these great ballplayers. We hope the reader can share our enjoyment of reliving memories of and with profiled ballplayers and in hearing their stories about baseball and life.

Another reason for this book is that we heard once too often from a cohort of more contemporary ballplayers how "today's athletes are bigger, better, and faster than yesterday's." More than one of these modern-day players and fans said it directly and indirectly in the context of local ballplayers since, say, 1980 being better than anybody who ever played before. They seemed to think that history began in 1980. They denigrated those that had come before them. They put themselves or others of the modern day ahead of the likes of Jim Pollard, Tex Erickson, and Jim Stoll. They had never heard of John Freund or Johnny Garbett. They would have us look at just the numbers–the records and the appearances in state tournaments, the batting averages and homeruns. We marvel at the numbers they put up, but we all know, "The Devil's in the details."

Disparaging comments and denigrating innuendo were leaked by a more contemporary crowd about "those old guys like Tex Erickson," a reference to all levels of the Golden Age players and the authentic local legends. Could the modern-day school boy ballplayers in a diluted, post-expansion Major League Baseball day actually be better ballplayers than the sort that signed or turned down professional contracts right out of high school during the game's Golden Age? They were suggesting that amateur players were better than pros, that their Class-C and Class-B baseball and players could even be compared with the local Class-A and AA baseball and players of the Golden Age of the game. But then maybe they just didn't know any better because they weren't around for the Golden Age of Baseball. It was as true at the national level as it was at the local level. They missed it, and they called the era a "so-called" Golden Age because they couldn't respect anybody they couldn't see reflected in the mirror. Perhaps they just paid more attention to the numbers than is warranted. Somehow, an important connection with baseball's past had been broken. So, part of our task here is to straighten out the record for those who would manipulate it into something that suits them while forgetting, distorting, and revising history.

Baseball was Roger Kahn's beat. He began his journalism career in 1948 in the Big Apple; he covered baseball for the *New York Herald Tribune* in the early 1950s. *Sports Illustrated* selected his 1972 *Boys of Summer* as Number 2 in the magazine's 2002 list of the 100 best sports books of all time. He writes in *The Era*, a 1993 publication, that while athletes in general are bigger, stronger, and faster today than in years gone by, "baseball is not about bigger, stronger, and faster."

"Given a certain minimum standard," Kahn writes, "major league baseball is about timing, coordination, and hand-to-eye response." Writing in the early 1990s when Cardinal Ozzie Smith was the best-fielding shortstop in the game, Kahn argues that Smith, at 5-10 and 150 pounds, was actually 10 pounds lighter than Pee Wee Reese, the great-fielding shortstop of the Dodgers in the 1950s. The writer asks facetiously, "Are great fielding shortstops actually getting smaller?"

In the category of power hitting, Kahn mentions Jose Canseco, Mark McGuire, and Cecil Fielder as examples of big men at 6-4 to 6-6 and 240 to 260 pounds not being able to hit for the same distance as Mickey Mantle, who stood 5-11 and played at 190 to 200 pounds. "Are great sluggers growing bigger . . . and weaker?" Kahn asks. Then, too, why hasn't anyone ever been able to better Mantle's time of 3.1 seconds home to first base? What power hitter since has had Mickey Mantle's explosive speed? And why is it that the top two career leaders in triples at the Major League level played a century ago?

"An electronic timing device clocked balls fired by the Dodgers' Joe Black at 96 miles an hour one night in 1952," writes Kahn in *The Era*. "'Allie Reynolds,' Black says, 'was faster than me. When he was pushing it, he got up over one hundred.' Reynolds was big, but no giant, at six feet, 195 pounds." Most pitchers over the past 30 years seem to be at least that big or bigger. How many have thrown the ball any faster? Koufax was a little bigger at a reported 6-2 and 210 pounds, although he never looked it. We recall an article we can't resurrect saying the great lefthander had been clocked with a new radar gun at 105 mph in the early 1960s at the same time that Eddie Feigner's fast-pitch softball was measured at 120 mph, as was Bobby (The Golden Jet) Hull's slap shot in hockey. Lefty Weckman said that his coach, Dick Siebert, at the University of Minnesota, "always said that Bob Feller threw harder than anybody he'd ever seen." Siebert would have had as accurate of an eye for such things as anybody, having played Major League ball for 11 years, then playing a few more years in Minnesota's Class-A and AA "amateur" leagues, and then coaching the Gophers and scouting amateur players all over the state. A farm boy from Van Meter, Iowa, Feller, at 6 feet tall and 185 pounds, could bring it. Despite losing most of four years in the prime of his baseball career to military service during World War II, Feller won 266 games for the Cleveland Indians while racking up a boatload of strikeouts. You can't hit heat.

The "Feller fastball" was a topic of much discussion in baseball circles everywhere. On August 20, 1946, 31,000 people came to Griffith Stadium in Washington, D.C. to witness Feller, 21-8 at the time on his way to a 26-15 season. They were also treated to the best that science had to offer at the time in the way of a device called the "Lumiline Chronograph," to measure that fastball. With barely a warm-up stretch, Feller threw five pitches, the second ball the fastest recorded at 98.6 mph, the fifth hitting the device and demolishing it. Not bad for an old guy from a long-gone era in comparison to today's pitchers, all of whom, we are told on television, throw in the 90s. But there's one caveat: The Chronograph measured the ball at the plate as it passed through its sensors. Modern radar guns measure the baseball out of the pitcher's hand. The law of gravity doesn't bend to the wishes of youth or revisionist wannabes. Balls lose speed as they near the plate. "Some estimates put the [Feller] fastball at 101–103 mph, others as high as 107.6 mph," according to Robert Weintraub in his book, *The Victory Season*.

"My overall best player was Ronnie Beckman," Tom Melchior quotes the late Jordan Brewer Manager, Charlie Larca, in *Scott County Baseball* in all likelihood around 2005. "He's smarter than 75% of the guys who play in the major leagues." We have no way of knowing the truth of such statements. We don't have the network of close contacts with Major League ballplayers that Charlie Larca would have needed in order to make such a judgment call. Let's assume they are true. What we do know then is that 75 percent of the people in the stands, on the hillsides, and in the barber shops and bars during the game's Golden Age were likely to have been as smart as *anybody* who played the game after the Golden Age ended. Everybody knew baseball then, because "Baseball was life, and life was baseball." Moreover, there was a lot more to the game then. "Small ball," which was based on strong pitching and tight defensive play, smart base running and heads-up play, demanded execution of all the little things–because a solitary run, like a pre-inflationary gold-backed buck, was precious.

It's unfortunate that Charlie Larca isn't with us to argue further with our response to his claims and his attitude. But his legions of charges are still around now. They can continue to speak for and with their former manager, many of whom share his cock-o'-the-walk strut we used to see on Saturday mornings in Foghorn Leghorn as he left the henhouse. Larca-ism was a part of "Charlie Ball." We overheard them speak often with the same confidence as their manager. Not too many are around to speak for the old guys we heard denigrated and disparaged by those who never saw them play. Frank saw them all.

Perhaps the best example of Manager Larca getting it wrong is the way in which he talks about "Cooter" Stang in his interview for *Scott County Baseball*. For starters, we never knew, or knew of, a "Cooter" Stang. Bob Stang was known as "Cougar," and he earned the nickname as a result of his claiming he'd seen a mountain lion on the Minnesota River bottoms one Saturday morning while hunting fox squirrels among the tall, majestic oak and cottonwood trees with his 12-gauge shotgun. Probably also unknown to Charlie Larca and his charges is that Cougar had played some ball, too. Not that Bob Stang was a great baseball player, but he was a member of several Jordan Brewer teams during the 1950s. Known to even fewer folks is that "The Cat," as he was also known, was a good enough baseball player to have worked as a catcher on a U.S. Army team while serving country during the Korean War years of 1952-'53. His dugout companion and centerfielder on the team was none other than Willie Mays, who had been the National League Rookie of the Year in 1951 with the New York Giants after burning up the American Association for the AAA-Minneapolis Millers early in the year. Pretty fair company for anybody anywhere, but then Cougar was smart enough to have not blown that horn too often.

"Many of today's major leaguers could not have made any big league team in the 1950's," Kahn writes. He also writes that Willie Mays says that Jackie Robinson was the smartest ballplayer he ever saw and Stan Musial was the best hitter. But Leo Durocher, one of the best managers of all time, said Willie Mays was the best ball player he ever saw. As for pitchers, Frank and I sure liked Koufax, Gibson, Spahn, and Nolan Ryan, among others. But it's impossible to argue with the consensus of four Hall of Famers in Gary Graf's *And God Said, "PLAY BALL!"* Graf has two great hitters, Ted Williams and Joe DiMaggio, and two great pitchers, who typically never blow the horn of an arm other than their own, Dizzy Dean and Bob Feller, all in agreement that Satchel Paige was the best pitcher of all time. The warm climate winter leagues of California, Mexico, and the Caribbean were integrated. So were some barnstorming teams. Everybody played with and against everybody else. They would probably have experienced Satch at some time in the 1930s or 40's in California, then later when Bill Veeck brought him to Cleveland.

We heard the denigrating comments and innuendo about Jordan Brewer shortstop Tex Erickson from post-Golden Age ballplayers and their boosters. Their ignorance, spouted with authority and certainty, offended the sensibilities of those of us who had actually seen Tex play, for Tex Erickson was far more than "that scrawny, little, old man," as one saw him. They might as well have called Mother Teresa a whore, or Billy Graham a conman, as to discount Tex Erickson and his ability as a ballplayer. But here's the topper: They'd never even seen Tex play. We heard that one of the critics of the old guys had looked up his batting average and probably compared it with his own, noting in a crowd of baseball fans that theirs, with a metal bat, was .100 points higher in Class-C and Class-B action than Tex's career average playing real baseball with wood bats at the Class-A level. But by that criterion, batting average, if you didn't know baseball, you'd have to wonder how Brooks Robinson and Ozzie Smith ever made Major League Baseball's Hall of Fame.

How could they even think they were qualified to comment or compare? Suggesting that they and their generation were better than The Great Ones of "the greatest generation" was ludicrous. That Larca and his legions of ballplayers, which included some Class-A level hitters during the Metal Bat Era, ever wanted and chose to play at the Class-C level was the first clue. The blowing of their own horn in one way or another around the impressive numbers they put up in their day while denigrating "those old guys" speaks to a need to glow like gold, too. But the numbers never tell the whole story. Comparing the production and proficiency of hitting with metal to hitting with wood is a more preposterous idea, we've learned, than comparing the proverbial apples to oranges. When we had relayed to Lonsdale's legitimate legend, Jim Kubes, for example, what Arlington's Dave Hartmann had said about the metal bat meaning .100 points to his batting average in a summer, Kubes quickly added, "At least that much." These two men had played a great deal of baseball, as much or more ball than anybody ever, with much of it behind the plate as catchers. They hit balls with *both* wood and metal. They would know the difference and the clear advantage that metal bats gave to hitters. They would certainly know better than the bangers who only knew the clang of metal.

Tex Erickson played shortstop during the Golden Age of Baseball for the Jordan Brewers. John Freund was a really good shortstop and a great hitter, as well as an outstanding pitcher. Woody Peters was a great shortstop, as were Bobby Kelly of the Prior Lake Jays and Mark Hess, who made All-Conference for the University of Minnesota Gophers in the Big 10 in 1986. Independent of each other, Frank Hilgers and Ed Breimhorst, both of whom played with and against, or just watched, all of these great shortstops during their prime years and many others, too, echoed each other:

> "Tex Erickson is the best shortstop I ever saw play the game."

Both Frank and Ed had played a fair amount of the shortstop position in their day and had seen many shortstops both during and long after the time that Tex Erickson played. It is quite likely they know what they are talking about. Moreover, they couldn't have seen Tex at his best. They probably formed their opinion of him, at the earliest, in the late 1940s–10 years after he graduated from high school and four or five years after his baseball skills rusted for four years in the U.S. Navy during World War II.

Frank and I talked about the different eras of baseball and how those eras were defined. We talked about the ballplayers from every decade with which we had direct experience, going back into the late 1940s for Frank and as far forward as the mid-2000s. Because we had studied the game and its history since the time we were old enough to chew the gum that came with the trading cards we cherished, we talked about The Great Ones, too. We talked about Ty Cobb and Babe Ruth, and the records they set legitimately with their play in the first three or four decades of the 20th Century. We talked about how great a hitter Ted Williams was with the Red Sox and how Ruth filled The Stadium he is said to have built in New York with paying customers. If we had to choose one ballplayer around whom to build a team, DiMaggio was The Man. But if Mickey Mantle were available in our "draft," we would take him.

We saw many changes to the game that made huge differences in performance and both quality and style of play. Some of the most exciting aspects of the game have virtually disappeared–the steal of home and the inside-the-park homerun to name two. Triples are also becoming increasingly rare. The pennant race is as extinct as the two-bit beer at a ballpark.

We talked about how baseball fundamentals, for example, and the little things were paramount at one time, because of the significance of just one run. They seem to have become less and less important, as more and more offense has been generated from changes designed to excite and entertain disinterested fans. One run became insignificant after double-digit run scoring became the norm wherever metal bats were in use. But when the fundamentals are overlooked, as seems to have happened with the easy scoring of runs, the play gets sloppy and even more runs are scored without being earned. That's not good baseball. We think that this, like the rest of baseball, has some parallels with people and life.

We offer a scant bit of history and geography as simply broad context to our focus, which is more recent and on ballplayers who played in towns along the last leg of the Minnesota River–the dogleg, looking or traveling upriver from St. Paul and turning the corner at Mankato to New Ulm. This leg of the river, some 120 miles by water and 80 by highway, and the wider basin it drains, nurtured some of the best "amateur" baseball played anywhere, beginning later in the same century and peaking in quality with the Golden Age of Baseball. We put quotation marks around the word amateur, because the better ballplayers during this era were paid handsomely to play the game they loved and pay-for-play has always been the definition of professional. The river gave its name to various baseball leagues over the years: River Valley League, Minnesota River League, Minnesota Valley League, Valley Six League, to name a few. The leagues have changed in name and composition as well as class, or level, of play, too.

If you were a young boy like Frank Hilgers in the 1950s, you played ball every day all summer long in Jordan. Frank remembered playing "cork ball" and "wiffle ball" against garage doors, water pump houses, abandoned buildings, and in the backyards of friends' houses. But he remembered with greatest fondness playing real hardball at *The Ballpark*–"Fairgrounds Park," as the "Mini-Met" was known then, in pickup, as well as organized, community recreation games. You made the diamond's third base your home plate in the pickup games, so you could taste and feel the intoxicating thrill of hitting a ball that cleared the big, high fence on either side of the left field light tower. Just like Jim Pollard hit 'em. It was all such heady stuff then.

You used bats that were cracked in Jordan Brewer games or batting practice. With some black electrical or white athletic tape, and sometimes small nails or tacks you got from Joe Lunack, the shoemaker, the bats could be refurbished and put to use again by the kids. Sometimes, you had to saw off three or four inches from the business end of the bats in order to swing them.

You played at "being" Mickey Mantle or Ted Williams, and you envisioned yourself doing the great things that immortalized the ballplayers you liked and worshipped. You copied the batting stances of Jackie Robinson and Willie Mays. You tried switch-hitting the way The Mick did for the Yankees, and because he was said to "bone" his bats, you went to Pekarna's Meat Market for a big beef bone with which to bone your bat. You crouched in a coil at the plate like "Stan The Man" with the Cardinals, and you tried the basket catch that made "The Say Hey Kid" and the best centerfielder who ever lived a fan favorite. Fifty years after you couldn't wait to tear open the sports section of the *Minneapolis Tribune* to check the box scores and Willie's contributions at the plate for the Giants, you got goose bumps when you heard Bob Costas in an ESPN Special quote *L.A. Times* sports columnist Jim Murray on his defensive ability: "Willie Mays' glove was where triples went to die." With relative sloths flanking him in the Giant outfield at the cavernous Polo Grounds of New York, Mays was likely as not told by his first manager, Leo Durocher, to "take everything you can get." He got to everything. He played like a turbo-charged Kirby Puckett of the Minnesota Twins in a relatively small yard a generation later.

The son of Frank Sr., a very large local icon, who had starred in football and baseball at what was then St. Thomas College in St. Paul, "Junior," or "Butch," as he was known, would play hard at every game. He was expected at home to play hard, to excel, and to win. "I am my father's son," Frank would repeat often as he matured as a man. He would learn all aspects of the game from his father, soaking it all up like a sponge until his ball-playing mind and eye were one with those of his father, and Frank Sr. knew baseball very well.

Frank, like his father before him, was primarily a catcher. Lefty Weckman, who pitched for Dick Siebert and the University of Minnesota after turning down offers from Manager Walter Alston and the Los Angeles Dodgers upon graduating from high school in 1959, will tell you, "Frank Hilgers was as good as, or better than, any catcher I ever had with the Gophers or saw in the Big Ten or around the country then. I've never seen anybody ever who was even close to him all-around in amateur ball." And the Southern Minny, in which Weckman pitched for pay for two seasons for Owatonna, had some really good baseball.

Frank was good enough as a catcher in a Minnesota Twins tryout game at the Old Met to be offered a contract. He hit a homerun and a double off the fence in three at-bats, the only out a shot to the warning track. He would turn down the opportunity to chase every boy's dream then because he was 24 years old and feeding a wife and family of three kids in Jordan. He couldn't afford to take the pay cut from his job with the Metropolitan Mosquito Control District to pursue the dream of youth.

But it proved to himself that he was good enough. Not just a good baseball player, for baseball was life and life was baseball. It remained something he could draw strength from throughout life–that he really was good, and he knew that his father, who had died when Frank was just 16 years old, would be proud of him. Both were important–being good at whatever you do and knowing that your father was proud of you.

Playing ball, especially baseball, was in Frank's blood. Catching was in the DNA.

At his baseball-playing peak, Frank stood just under 6 feet 2 inches tall and carried 244 pounds. He was strong and fast, probably faster than any Major League catcher of his and maybe any day. Fast enough, we know, to have beaten the very quick, 150-pound Woody Peters, a shortstop, in a 100-yard foot race after the younger Peters had him by a couple of steps off the starting line at the Lagoon Park in Jordan.

"It took me 40 yards to drop the piano," Frank would say later in self-deprecating jest.

Weckman said he got sucked into a foot race against Frank, too. "There might have been one or two guys I couldn't beat on the Gopher baseball teams I played on," he said, "so I took Frank up on a bet for a beer or something at the Lagoon football park." He said that he, too, took a quick lead off the line, "So I thought I'd put him away at about midfield. But I couldn't. I couldn't lose him. When we crossed the 100-yard line, he was right on my tail, two steps behind, the same two steps I'd had on him after five yards. And he was carrying 240 or 250 pounds then."

Frank hit one of the two homeruns that are forever etched in the memory banks of Jordan baseball people who know the game's Golden Age in Brewer Town. Paul Sunder recounts for Tom Melchior in *Scott County Baseball* a towering 500-foot blast that Jim Pollard planted in the Phillips garden. But we recall another ball that the immortal Jim Pollard of Minneapolis Laker and Jordan Brewer fame hit when he assaulted the small rambler far over the left field fence and railroad tracks. It's hard to say today where the Phillips garden was, but the house hasn't moved. According to Dave Beckius, the house was owned by his father, Al, until 1961 when the he sold it to Ken Crane, the insurance man, and moved on top of the hill where the schools were later built. He'll vouch for the Jim Pollard homerun, and he said, "I'll show you the window he broke." His mother and father were enjoying the night, the crowd, and the game from their backyard, when Jim Pollard broke their bathroom window.

Nobody that we knew had ever bothered to actually measure the distance of either ball. We decided to finally do it, over 60 years after Pollard's blast, we'll say, in 1953, and over 50 years after Frank's howitzer in 1963.

In July of 2013 we counted 70 three-foot-long steps from the backside of the centerfield fence in Jordan, near where the 360-foot sign is on the ballpark side, to the center of the bridge that spans Sand Creek today. If those numbers are accurate, if Sand Creek is about as wide today as it was in the early 1960s, if the current bridge is about the same length as the bridge it finally replaced in 2013, and if the 360-foot sign on the center field fence is actually 360 feet from home plate and about the same distance from home plate today as the fence was over 50 years ago, then that would put Frank's shot at 570 feet–five feet short of the tape measure blast Babe Ruth hit out of Detroit's Briggs Stadium in 1921 and credited by the National Baseball Hall of Fame and the Guinness Book of World Records as *the longest homerun ever hit by a Major League baseball player*. After re-calculating things, they had taken away a 643-foot shot by Mickey Mantle in the same ballpark in 1961.

Everybody knows that those balls, the ones hit by Babe Ruth, Mickey Mantle, Jim Pollard, and Frank Hilgers with wood bats and unaided by anything outside of the laws of physics, natural diet, and athleticism, would have gone out of any park in the country, including Yellowstone.

Still, such inexact measurement bothered us, as did a question about the likely line of ball flight in comparison to the line our steps took. Similarly, we are sure that the long blasts by the likes of Babe Ruth and Mickey Mantle had as their basis the eyewitness reports of glassy-eyed sports writers in the press boxes of Major League stadiums. The precision of digital technology, lasers, and satellites wasn't available in the Big Leagues either, but five feet short of Ruth's monster homerun had to be reckoned with in some more accurate way then merely stepping it off.

We borrowed a "Measure Master" measuring wheel by Rolatape from a local farmer, and on August 21, 2013, we walked off 220 feet to the base of the old rambler from the corner of the left field fence where it reads 310 feet from home plate. "It hit that concrete square, bounced up, and broke the bathroom window," Dave Beckius said, pointing to the concrete housing of a cistern and the window. Subtract six feet, we figured, for the bounce, and that puts Jim Pollard's 1953 homerun for the Jordan Brewers at 530 feet–with a wooden bat.

Frank's towering blast had people talking about it for years . . . *It was a hot, humid Sunday night, August 4, 1963. Frank was having a good year at the plate. He was hitting over .400 just in the league play. He was playing third base tonight and batting cleanup, with Jordan High School's football coach, Bernie Riekena, behind the plate. But Ron Cap, the Robins pitcher had handcuffed Frank in his previous at bats. He was hitless on the night. It was a playoff game at Jordan's Fairgrounds Park. The Brewers had taken the first of the three-game series at New Prague on Wednesday night, 5-3. Win tonight and they would advance to the finals against Shakopee. Down 4-2 in the bottom of the ninth inning, two on and two out, the count 2-0 . . . Ron Cap did not want to go to 3-0 on Frank Hilgers. He didn't want to have to risk walking him and putting the winning run on first base. Not with Rotz Bush coming up next. Rotz had already gotten two hits on the night and seemed to be in his groove. Veteran catcher Tom Preston of New Prague thought Frank might even take a strike, so he called for a fastball. He knew they had to throw a strike. Oh-oh . . .* Picking it up from the August 8, 1963, *Jordan Independent* and the sports scribe disguised as the Brewer pitcher of record with a four-hitter on the night and the veteran slugger batting fifth in the order who happened to be in the on-deck circle at the time:

Cap wound up and delivered. At the crack of the bat the field looked like the gold rush of '49, as the park was mobbed with jubilant fans and players. Why? Hilgers had just smacked a 400-plus homer over the centerfield fence.

But neither the reporter, the players, nor most of the fans could see the other side of the barn and behind the massive elm trees that were there before the Dutch Elm epidemic hit. The white ball disappeared into the night and the heavens of lore as it cleared the towers, the trees, and the barn. Only the handful of young ball shaggers working the homerun alley along the tracks and the fewest of fans who had left the park early or who had jumped up along the left-field fence to catch the bottom half of the Brewer ninth had an idea of just how far that ball went. The reporter could only guess, and his guess of "400-plus" was accurate, but there was way more "plus" to the homerun than he could gauge. His birds-eye view of the shot was limited because he was down low on the field, the barn and trees obscuring his vision as the dark night swallowed the white ball above and behind the lights. Nobody had ever seen a ball hit that deep into the blue-black night at Fairgrounds Park.

Some said Frank Hilgers had hit a baseball farther than the ball the mighty Jim Pollard had hit. Others said that simply couldn't be. Nobody hit baseballs in Jordan farther than Jim Pollard. Not ever. Couldn't be done.

Frank's homerun off right-handed pitcher Ron Cap of New Prague cleared the picket fence near the flagpole that they would open for the Scott County Fair, so the trucks hauling the "Tilt-A-Whirl," the "Swings," the "Ferris Wheel," and "Merry-Go-Round" and other rides operated by the Stipes Shows could get into and out of Fairgrounds Park, and where the carny people could desecrate the local altar of baseball each summer for four days with their carnage of confidence games of chance: the "Diggers," the "Milk Bottles," the "Cats," the "Rifle Shooting," the "Balloons," and the "Free Throws" with a ballooned-up, slightly oblong-shaped basketball at an undersized hoop just a little higher than the regulation 10 feet and a little beyond the regulation 15 feet from a free-throw line.

Frank turned 225 pounds of 21-year-old thoroughbred thunder loose on a pitch in his wheelhouse. He got all of it–the ball coming down, everybody said, "on the bridge" that spans Sand Creek and the entrance to the park. It was a "walk-off" homerun before the expression had even been conceived. Somebody said it bounced into the creek, although the experienced shaggers couldn't find it. Legend has it, however, that the ball bounced hard in the middle of the bridge, cleared the creek, hit a railroad tie just right on second bounce, and came to rest against the sidewalk curb outside of Pekarna's Meat Market on Water Street.

Frank Pekarna noticed a baseball against the curb while enjoying a smoke in the cool of the morning the next day before returning to the back of the shop to cut up some pork for the family recipe of trademark sausage. He picked up the baseball and noticed the scuffmarks. It must have fallen out of a customer's car when they were coming into the shop, he thought. Frank Pekarna took the souvenir ball home and put it on the fireplace mantel in his living room, where it rested until his sons found it one day after school in the fall, maybe seven or eight years later, then lost it in a homerun derby game of their own in the back yard.

The Rolatape "Measure Master" wheel clicked off 145 feet to the inside corner of the bridge and 220 feet to an eyeballed "middle" of the bridge. That puts Frank's homerun at somewhere between 505 feet at the least, to 580 feet–50 feet longer than Pollard's, five feet longer than the mighty Babe's. Frank hit it, he said, with a 36-inch "Ted Williams" model Louisville Slugger fashioned in Louisville, Kentucky, at the Hillerich and Bradsby Company from tight-grained white ash that probably came from a tree in upstate New York or eastern Pennsylvania.

You would think that with all of the growing attention paid in the last 30 years to individual statistics, that somebody in Jordan, some blue-blooded baseball brat, would have measured the two historic homeruns. After all, both had been hit by authentic Jordan Brewer legends.

Performance-enhancing steroids and human growth hormone were unheard of during The Golden Age of Baseball. Weight rooms and personal trainers managing every lift and curl were equally rare. Natural athleticism and zealous ball-playing talent were celebrated by the ballplayers of this era and everyone else. They were gifts of the Creator not to be wasted.

We couldn't shake the gnawing disbelief in the numbers. Pollard's 530-foot blast to left, and Frank's 580-foot shot to center were impressive, to say the least. On August 30, 2013, we headed back to the ballpark, armed with a Bushnell Yardagepro rangefinder from the golf bag. We stood at home plate and focused on the 310-foot marker on the left-field fence. The rangefinder read 101 yards. Simple math gives you 303 feet, not the 310 posted on the fence. Then we focused on the 360 sign in straightaway centerfield. The rangefinder reported the same, and it showed 357 feet to the light tower, 348 feet to the flagpole.

Next, we went to the outside of the ballpark's perimeter, beginning in left field. We couldn't get a clear shot of the house, so we went to the house and had the same problem shooting back to the fence. That makes the Rolatape "Measure Master" wheel's number of 220 feet our number. Subtract the six feet for bounce, subtract seven feet for Jordan's fence fudge factor, and we give Jim Pollard credit for a 517-foot homerun.

Al and Teri Beckius weren't upset about the broken window, the homerun being of such historic perspective and Ruthian proportion in the 1950s that they were proud to have the ball in their possession. They kept the ball for years, and Al, the 6-2, 250 pound, oak-armed owner-operator of the Jordan Feed Mill, which last housed a family restaurant of that name and today still guards the entrance to the ballpark, was then Al Beckius's business, where he ground feed for farmers and loaded, two at a time, the 200-pound sacks of feed onto the backs of their pickup trucks, handling the burlap gunnysacks as though they were bags of popcorn at the movie theatre. Then he would return to his customers, farmers with time and an inclination to visit while in town, and when The Buzz was baseball, Al Beckius got PR mileage out of the Jim Pollard homerun that broke his bathroom window.

An issue lingered with the line of flight of Frank's homerun. We climbed the grandstands as high as we could to get as close of a straight-line view from home plate to the bridge as we could. We think that the ball cleared the fence somewhere between the light tower to the right of the 360-foot sign and the flagpole. Neither has ever been moved, we've been assured. We walked around to the outside of the ballpark near the light tower. The rangefinder gave us 183 feet to the light at the southeast corner of the bridge–from the fence between the light tower and the flagpole. We eyeballed an arbitrary "middle" of the bridge and from there took a reading back at the light at the corner of the bridge: 24 more feet. When you add up the numbers (353, 183, plus 24), you get 560 feet, 15 feet short of Babe Ruth's 1921 shot at Briggs Stadium in Detroit, 43 feet longer than Jim Pollard's homerun off the Al Beckius rambler on first bounce, and at least 27 feet longer than the creek-clearing blast over the right-field fence that you can read about in the profile on John Freund.[1]

"Frank hit 15 homeruns one year, maybe 1961 or '62 when I was in the service," Ed Breimhorst, a close friend and teammate of Frank's, said. "He'd have had 20 or 25 with a metal bat." You wonder, too, whether his historic shot over centerfield at Fairgrounds Park would have taken out on first bounce the large window in Pekarna's Meat Market rather than just rolling to a stop at the curb. Power hitting is why cleanup was his usual position in the batting order of every team on which he ever played.

Fred Kerber was a veritable "Brewer Killer" during the 1950s to early 60s. He won 102 games on the mound against just 19 losses between 1954 and 1963 for Shakopee–the most wins of any Shakopee pitcher in its history, while playing at a time when he had just half the number of starts he'd have had in the 1980s, for example. He went 15-0 pitching in 1955, according to Melchior, a record that Lowell Stark of Prior Lake says was 16-0. We think Stark's memory might be more accurate, because that same year, he went 8-0 on the mound for the American Legion team from Shakopee. Memory works better when clear associations can anchor things.

Sitting across the kitchen table from the 79-year-old Kerber in his home on a mid-April morning in 2014, he reminisced freely. He admitted to probably having given up the 500-foot blast to Jim Pollard in '53 or '54. He honored the memories of Rotz Bush in Jordan and his teammate, John Freund, in Shakopee as he praised their hitting. He remembered Frank Hilgers being "a really good hitter," as he sang the highest praise that any pitcher anywhere can ever sing of a hitter he's faced many times:

"He owned me," Fred Kerber said of Frank Hilgers.

Frank Hilgers behind the plate was the undesignated captain of the team. What made him a great catcher was his never-ceasing awareness of a hitter's strengths and weaknesses, his pitcher's capabilities and how much game he had left, as well as the overall game situation. You didn't count pitches thrown in those days. A good

---

[1] After reading a copy of the original edition of *The Best of River-Town Small Ball*, Tom ("Orangy") Breimhorst, former Jordan resident and Jordan Brewer, told us in a telephone conversation from his home in Indiana that he was an eyewitness to the homerun hit by Frank Hilgers in 1963 and that he actually saw the ball hit the Jordan Feed Mill building "about bridge-high" and bounce back into Sand Creek. He waded into the creek, found the ball and took it home. He had no reason to lie or to make up a tall take with us. So, on August 9, 2021, we went out to the back side of The Ballpark with a Bushnell Rangefinder again. We shot 83 yards (249 feet) from the fence to the flagpole, which is 347 feet, as noted, from home plate, to the building across the creek now housing The Feed Mill Restaurant. That's a total distance of 596 feet on a line as closely and conservatively as we can make it.

baseball man, like Frank Hilgers, simply knew when his pitcher had had enough. As a pitcher, you didn't need to play the continuous mental cat-and-mouse game with the hitters. You could very nearly shut down the mental part of pitching, save that energy, and trust that part to Frank's sense of things and his calling of a game. If you shook him off, he was likely to come out to the mound for a meeting. His agenda for the meeting was to convince you to give up on what you wanted to do in favor of what he knew you could do against a hitter he knew better than you. Frank knew his pitchers, and he knew hitters and baseball better than you would ever know.

Frank didn't like to waste breath or steps on a hot summer day. Nor did he appreciate having to dig balls out of the dirt or to have to hustle to the backstop to retrieve a wild pitch. God forbid that your shortstop should bobble a two-hop double-play ball, or an outfielder drop a fly ball or miss a cutoff man with a throw. The Captain was a perfectionist at the game, and he expected routine plays to be made. In fact, like his father before him, he demanded they be made.

I prodded Frank for his observations on the ballplayers that had left the best lasting impressions on him. They are the observations of a man who was one of the best all-around ballplayers to ever play in the Minnesota River Valley and a man who knew the game better than most. Our list is biased, we readily admit, from Jordan and the Minnesota River Valley area leagues and towns. After all, here is where we played and saw the most players the most often. But we know a really good ballplayer when we see him, even if we've only seen him a few times. We leave the comfort of our bias with several ballplayers, but we note that we never leave the watershed, the basin of the Lower Minnesota River, which is why all the towns are "river towns" in our stories. "Small ball" refers to the size of the river towns and to the prevailing style of baseball played during the Golden Age. Yet, there was nothing small about the game that Frank and the others played. They played large.

We hope that readers will enjoy the profiles and the connections to life, the sidebars and the vignettes. The Greater Reality, The Greater Truth, is formed by the stuff of legend and myth in the womb of community and the continuity of succeeding generations. It makes for good story. Moreover, you can learn something about pitching and hitting, and about history and community.

Ours is a short list, for Frank's eye was always a very discerning eye to which I deferred. I would learn from the research and interviews just how good his eye was. The profiles are presented in chronological order. We're always moving, like the river current. Our list is self-limiting, meaning that if just one or two more ballplayers were added, we would have had to consider adding another 50.

We celebrate the excellence in the ballplayers who make our short list of "The Best"–the crop of 24-Karat gold Greek gods whose glitter can't be tarnished with time, or denigrated by ignorance, denial, or lies. Truth be told, you can't manufacture gold with new technology, for then it's nothing more than the stuff of alchemy. It's little better than iron pyrite–fool's gold. It has the metallic luster and pale brass-yellow hue. But the resemblance to the real thing is just superficial.

PART I
THE GAME

It's my life. It's my Bible . . . It's my life.
—Ernie Banks, "Mr. Cub"

There was a Golden Age of Baseball, defined at best, we think, by the years 1947 to approximately 1970. Neither its beginning nor its ending was precise or simultaneous at all levels and locales. There was plenty of gold prior to 1947. Likewise, the gold only slowly ran out, beginning perhaps as early as 1957. Nobody hit a light switch to end it. This Golden Age is best recalled at the level of Major League Baseball because of the consistency of archived data. But it existed everywhere, at all levels, maybe beginning sooner or later in one place or at one level of ball, and ending sooner or later in others. We didn't define it. We discovered the claim and are delighted to have lived a part of it. It began with the end of World War II, Bill Starr notwithstanding, and the return of over eight million servicemen from multiple theatres of the world war. Many of them were ballplayers. They came home to play ball at many levels: big league, minor league, semi-pro, amateur and school ball, and in the streets and the backyards across America.

Everywhere, baseball was The Buzz, which was passed on via radio and print media, and word-of-mouth. The stars were America's heroes. This Golden Age coincided with the careers, in general, of Mickey Mantle and Willie Mays–both superstars in an era of many stars. It ended, in general, with the second wave of Major League expansion to 24 teams after comprising 16 teams, eight in each league, from 1901 until 1961. There was an overlapping of interest and participation, captured best perhaps in what former Cincinnati Red and Detroit Tiger Manager Sparky Anderson said about it. After managing in the Major Leagues for more than a decade, he said that it wouldn't matter to him if he were demoted to the minor leagues. "It's the same game," Anderson explained.

Expansion watered down the national pastime. Expansion diluted the quality of baseball everywhere. It cheapened the game at every level. But as with everything else in the society, the packaging got better while the product was lessened, hollowed out in a way that belied the packaging. The free agency that came with the end of the reserve clause in the standard contract meant big money to everyone. No longer were baseball players blue-collar workers in a flannel uniform. They would hold press conferences under spotlights wearing Armani suits, while fans would get hit for ever-increasing prices for tickets and refreshments.

Everything from the uniforms to the parks and the seating and to television helps to make baseball *look* good. Baggy, heavy wool uniforms, three-fingered minimalist gloves, and crownless caps with two-inch brims make yesterday's baseball players look funny by today's standards of dress and equipment. You couldn't help but notice the demise of baseball in the towns of the Minnesota River Valley. People stopped coming to the ballpark to watch a game. When a game drew a decent crowd, it just wasn't the same. The amps were down. In contrast, in 1950 when Jordan hosted Belle Plaine in a night game for the first time under the lights, in the totally rebuilt Fairgrounds Park, originally a WPA project, re-done with an entrepreneurial spirit and the classic business model, over 1,300 fans packed the little ballpark. Indeed, roughly 800 teams were packing their little parks all over the state that year, playing baseball in three distinct levels, or classes: AA, A, and B. Leagues along at least the Minnesota River Valley were wide open. Players in AA and A were paid. Some players, especially pitchers, were paid well. Competition was intense. It's interesting that Ty Cobb, probably one of the most intensely competitive players ever, the "Georgia Peach," who set more records than any man in baseball and who still holds many of them, including the highest lifetime batting average, .367, said, "The crowd makes the ballgame."

The crowds grew exponentially after World War II, both in numbers and intensity, according to David Halberstam in *The Winning Season*. The doubling of crowds in Major League Baseball tells the story of pre-war to post-war baseball attendance. But the numbers, as usual, don't tell the whole story. Intensity levels during The Golden Age of Baseball also pushed the needle off the charts at all levels of the game. Baseball, more than any other subject, was The Buzz.

Earlier in the 20th Century, when Babe Ruth was asked to explain how he hit homeruns, he might as well have been asked how to live: He said he took a strong grip and swung the bat as hard as he could, swinging right through the ball. "I swing big, with everything I've got. I hit big or I miss big. I like to live as big as I can." Fans everywhere sensed and appreciated that largesse.

In the 1950s, one to two thousand people would watch town team *league* baseball games at the ballparks. In 1948, over 7,500 fans saw Winsted beat Belle Plaine at Shakopee's Riverside Park for the Class-A State Championship. In 1959, nearly 3,000 watched Lefty Weckman of Jordan pitch Shakopee to a Class-B State Championship over highly favored Springfield at St. Cloud's Municipal Stadium. In 1969, over 2,600 fans appreciated Jim Stoll's performance at Jordan in the championship game, as Arlington beat one of the finest Class-B amateur baseball teams ever assembled–Herb Isakson's Minnesota Gopher-packed Prior Lake Jays. At the same Jordan ballpark in 2014, in the Class-C championship game, Sobieski's Tyler Jendro shut out a hard-hitting New Ulm team, 2-0, in front of an announced 562 fans.

A thousand fans in attendance for the championship game, the showcase of Minnesota's amateur baseball, is becoming a rare exception. Brownton, population 400, still put more than a thousand fans into its ballpark for a league game on a lazy Sunday afternoon in the 1960s, according to both Dave Hartmann from Arlington and Chuck Warner from Brownton.

It is a basic tenet of existence that when you get something for nothing, you don't value it as much as if you had worked to get it or paid for it with money earned honestly. In 2014, again, nearly 25 percent of the Class-C baseball teams in the state of Minnesota "made it to the state tournament." A 48-team field out of a total of maybe 224 teams looks to be headed in the direction of the old Bloomington Fire Department's Slow-Pitch Softball Tournament in the 1970s when something like 172 teams "qualified" for this fund-raising carnival of competition by sending their registrations along with a check and a red-stitch ball into the tournament officials.

"Baseball was life, and life was baseball" during this Golden Age. While it was just a game at one level of consciousness, it was war at another. Again, Ty Cobb: "I have observed that baseball is not unlike a war, and when you come right down to it, we batters are the heavy artillery."

It was an obsession, and everybody knew baseball. Jim Kubes played ball 250 days out of the year in the Lonsdale baseball park when he was growing up. Lefty Weckman hustled through his bread route for his father's bakery every morning, then headed to the ballpark for a game. Jim Stoll hit rocks with a broom handle every day after school. NBA Hall-of-Famer Jim Pollard would tear up his checks when he got beat on the mound with the Class-A Jordan Brewers in the early 1950s. Pat Devitt and his brother Ray took turns pitching tennis balls to each other in empty railroad cars in Prior Lake until it got too cold in the fall months to keep the heavy sliding door open to give them the light they needed.

Connections were an important part of the fiber and fabric of baseball. These connections included all of baseball, from Little League and the back yards to Cooperstown. They included the past with the present. You didn't denigrate the past and the old ballplayers. You respected and venerated them. Uniforms and numbers were "retired." Cooperstown was all about enshrining and memorializing The Great Ones. You don't tarnish what is great by including what is merely good. You don't gain entry to the halls of legendary status by expanding the size of the doorway, by changing conditions and criteria in order to accommodate. Ty Cobb was essentially the first inductee, because he garnered the most votes from the Baseball Writers Association of America, which voted in that first class. Yes, Cobb came ahead of Babe Ruth. The game is always bigger than any current star. The past informs the present. As Jim Stoll put it, the younger guys for the past 30 to 40 years have been playing on wall-to-wall carpeting and " . . . need to know how the rug got laid for them."

Pitchers have close relationships with their catchers. Shortstops and second basemen are "the keystone combination" because of their close relationship stemming from the all-important double play and from continually backing each other up. Umpires are connected to everybody and everything, because they make the calls that keep the game going–not unlike a beat cop in a large city or the police chief in a small town on a Friday night in the 1950s. Moreover–News Flash! –Every call is a judgment call! There are no subtleties or nuances in the black-and-white world that is a ball or a strike, a runner being safe or out. These nuances exist in the game, but they are inherent in the efforts expended to make the plays or to get the bat on the ball or in "taking something off of a pitch."

There have always been connections between the different levels of baseball. From Little League up through Major League Baseball, the game is at its roots the same. They influence each other, too, as Little League did with the gradual introduction of the protective batting helmet. Moreover, fans everywhere are connected to ballplayers in one way or another. They are either part of the crowd during a game, or they play some supportive role in the communities. They are part of The Buzz that they make.

John Sexton teaches a class at his New York University that is titled the same as his book: *Baseball as a Road to God, Seeing Beyond the Game*. It's about parallels and connections between baseball and religion. Between baseball and the ineffable. We learn here that Sandy Koufax's curveball was ineffable. So were the curveballs from our two great local lefthanders, Lefty Weckman and Johnny Garbett. That connects Weckman and Garbett with Koufax, as well as with each other. These lefthanders looked *really* good on the mound. They looked alike on the mound. They had the same stuff.

Baseball had its codes. "Nobody throws Clemente a curveball on a 3-2 count in spring training," Jim Stoll learned in 1960. In other words, don't mess with the stars. Young warriors defer to the older tribal elders who have already paid their dues and who respect those that came before them. "Don't walk the leadoff batter," pitchers learn. "Throw strikes," they are told. "You've got to hit the cutoff man," on balls hit deep to the outfield. "Get a good lead," base runners learn. "Break up two," also. "Back each other up." "Don't let the ball play you," every infielder everywhere learns. Baseball was a microcosm of American life, and even beer-drinking ballplayers learned, "If you want to dance, you've got to pay The Fiddler."

Leo Durocher probably knew baseball as well or better than any man who ever lived. He played at the Major League level for 19 years, and he managed four different teams over 24 years, including long stints in New York with both the Dodgers and the Giants and at least five seasons as player-manager. Controversial and candid, Durocher said, "Baseball is like church. Many attend, few understand."

You can't really understand baseball or church without trying them, learning first their history and their required skills and then exercising their values and basic tenets of faith. Then it's a matter of all the little things–making the plays and playing with heart. It's not enough to just watch baseball, especially on television, in order to understand baseball. Nor is it enough just to go to church on Sundays to really know church, or religion. While the baseball bench or a seat in the stands and the church pew give one a bird's eye view of some things, sooner or later you've got to get off the bench, out of the pew, and into The Game if you really want to know what's going on, what's needed, what your skills are, where you fit in, and what you can contribute.

Coming up with a list or a book of "the best" of anything is a risky business unless some common measure, a scale of performance, is used to weigh the subjects. Then the objective measure takes care of everything for you. Take baseball hitters, for example. If you believe that "best" is defined by batting average; i.e., number of hits out of number of official at bats, then the best hitters are those with the highest batting averages. Sounds simple, but the red flags are waving vigorously. That changed, or at least was challenged, with the advent of the long ball in 1920. Best hitters might be better defined by some amalgamation of average, power, and productivity. On-base percentage, which would include walks, intentional and due to careful pitching, should probably factor in as well, just not as much as game-breaking, fence-busting doubles. Then which factors are most important? How do you weight the factors? The point is that you end up getting to a subjective factor sooner or later. While managers and coaches cringe over walks, some pitchers dismiss them. It's the booted double-play groundball and shots off the scoreboard or over the wall that rip the guts out of the men on the mound.

Baseball has long been said to be a metaphor for life, American life. Baseball reflects the life and times, which, in turn, mirror baseball. They borrow and adopt from each other, sometimes indiscriminately. A thief in baseball is a hero for getting closer to home, even taking home itself, without getting caught and giving up an out, while a thief in life is a scoundrel at best, or a rogue hero like Robin Hood. Beginning in the post-war 1940s through the 1950s and into the early to mid-1960s, leaking at best into the late 60s and initial 70s, baseball was the altar of idolatry. It was The Golden Calf of the Old Testament. It was The Golden Age of Baseball, and notwithstanding the 2003 book by that title, *The Golden Age of Baseball*, whose authors are more inclusive in their defining years, from the 1920s through the 1970s, we think they are stretching things on both ends in order to appease or accommodate. Moreover, they're kind of late to the dance.

The 1950s were arguably the peak years of the Golden Age of Baseball. The reasons for this may be best summed up by the names of The Great Ones who played at least a portion of their careers then at the Major League level: DiMaggio, Williams, Mays, Mantle, Musial, McCovey, Matthews, Spahn, Feller, Kaline, Gibson, Koufax, Aaron, Snider, Banks, Clemente, Ford, and three Robinsons. They all played in at least a part of the decade. That's not to say there weren't good, even great, ballplayers before, or after, this decade. It means these ballplayers were the best or, at least among the best, professional ballplayers of all time. They set the standards in all areas of the game that kids everywhere tried to meet and the styles they tried to emulate. They were heroes, and American boys of all ages need heroes.

Bill Starr, former minor and Major League catcher, then later a team owner of the independent Pacific Coast League San Diego Padres during the 1940s and 50s, was "a baseball man" for over 60 years. He was considered an astute judge of talent, and some thought him the best executive in the game. In Starr's *Clearing the Bases*, published in 1989, he reasons that the 1920s and 1930s were the most prominent decades of baseball because, among other reasons, 68 future Hall of Famers were playing in those 20 years–more than *four times as many as any other 20-year span*.

We couldn't argue with those kinds of numbers. But for us, the icons of the game were worshipped during the 50s in the baseball cathedrals of our big cities, including Yankee Stadium, Ebbett's Field, and the Polo Grounds in New York, Wrigley Field and Comiskey Park in Chicago, and Fenway Park in Boston. They were worshipped, too, in the little German, Irish, and Scandinavian chapels all along the Minnesota River and its tributaries. Indeed, the game of baseball through the 1950s and into the 60s, and maybe beyond a bit in some areas and at some levels, was as close to being a religion in the Minnesota River Valley and the nation as any secular activity could ever be.

Starr makes a compelling case for the greatest era of the game in terms of quality of talent and play being the 1920s and 1930s. But he doesn't weigh heavily enough two important factors. First, the "Black Sox Scandal" in which eight Chicago White Sox regulars threw the 1919 World Series put a stink and a stain on the game that took a long time to eradicate. Second, segregation meant that some of the best baseball players in the country were being denied the right to play Major League Baseball because of the color of their skin. But with Jackie Robinson's integration of baseball in 1947 and a generation's passing since "Shoeless" Joe Jackson, Ed Cicotte, "Buck" Weaver and five other Sox players went into the tank against Cincinnati in the 1919 World Series, the game began to glitter like gold.

Baseball was life, and life was baseball. Like life, baseball was different during the Golden Age than it would become beginning in the mid-to late-1960s or the early 1970s, and into the 21st Century. Both were better all-around in many respects–baseball and life–each reflecting the other in terms of values, standards, and performance qualities.

Life was better for the individuals who plied their trades and worked their jobs; better for the mothers and the families they managed at home; better for the children with loving, caring moms around rather than the cafeteria care of the communal day care; better for sure with dads busy but around and in the lives of their children; better for the communities that thrived with the hustle of small businesses, schools, and ball clubs comprising boys full of aspirations and young men just wanting to play ball. Life was better in the Minnesota River Valley because people were better then, and if that sounds like judging, we readily admit to it. Moreover, it's judging what we are told to judge by Martin Luther King Jr. in his famous speech, imploring Americans to judge his sons by the content of their character rather than the color of their skin. Character counts in all things, including baseball.

It's popular today to condemn people for judging. Fact is, you can't avoid it. You must not avoid it. As M. Scott Peck, M.D., the psychiatrist whose books gained popularity in the 1980s pointed out in the beginning of *People of the Lie*, Christ is *not* telling us not to judge. Instead, He is telling us *to judge carefully* and to begin that judgment with self-examination. Baseball is predicated on the judgment calls of an umpire on every single pitch. The Game comes to an unacceptable halt without the call. One need only look at *The Gospel of John* for certainty on this subject: "Do not judge according to appearance, but judge with righteous judgment." In coming up with our list, then, we couldn't help comparing and judging.

A couple of comparisons and examples solidify our point: First, It's worthwhile comparing two "Kings of Golf" from two eras–Ben Hogan from the late 1940s to the early 50s and Tiger Woods from 50 years later, the late 1990s to early 2000s. Hogan actually fares better than one would have expected, better than what has been handed down to us, winning 30 PGA tournaments in his best-performing three-year period, 1946-1948, while Tiger won 22 PGA tournaments in his best three-year performance period, 1999-2001. But if we judge by what we are told to judge–by character–it's no contest. Ben Hogan brought his wife, Valerie, along with him on the PGA Tour.

Second, we can make a very limited comparison of local baseball hitters. Jim Pollard's career batting average over six years with the Jordan Brewers was .371, according to Tom Melchior's *Scott County Baseball*. Even without the massive number of mitigating factors, which we address throughout the book, Pollard's hitting of Class-A pitching compares quite favorably with the career marks of "Larca's legends": Jon Beckman (.400); Dave Hentges (.380); Ron Beckman (.363); and Paul Buss (.337), who may have been Class-A hitters feasting on Class-B and Class-C pitching. Unlike the Larca legends, Jim Pollard missed most of his best baseball-playing years, as he turned 27 his first summer in a Brewer uniform. He also did a lot of his hitting while concentrating on pitching ballgames, while we note that none of the Larca legends toed the mound seriously. Most significantly, Jim Pollard hit with wood bats, and the ferocity of the competition he faced just in league games wasn't typically approached until the semifinals of state tournaments by the Larca legends.

Jim Pollard was like his contemporary, Ben Hogan, in golf, who wouldn't think of doing things like replacing his ball two to four inches ahead of where he had marked it on the green with a coin; nor would he think of rolling his golf ball with the head of a club to improve his lie, or grounding his club in a hazard. If it happened inadvertently, he wouldn't wait for a playing partner or an official to call the penalty. He'd have called it on himself. Jim Pollard would argue with an umpire over a called ball or strike, but he would never have bullied an official scorer to change an error to a hit after a game in order to bolster his batting average and look better statistically. That's the sort of thing that was unheard of during the Golden Age of Baseball.

People of the Golden Age of Baseball were, for the most, people of what Tom Brokaw titled his popular book of 1998–*The Greatest Generation.* Indeed, as Brokaw wrote, "It is, I believe, the greatest generation any society has ever produced." He argued that these men and women fought not for fame and recognition, but because it was "the right thing to do." When they came back they built America into a superpower. They had what another writer, Tom Wolfe, chronicled in his book–*The Right Stuff.* This great generation of soldiers and test pilots and ballplayers, as well as the farmers, steelworkers, longshoremen, carpenters, and small business owners, the bakers, the bankers, the butchers, and the bartenders, were all made of pretty much the same mettle. They were born in the first half of the 20th Century. Most of them grew up in and lived through The Great Depression, or its lingering effects. Their characters forged of steel, they sacrificed selves to save this world from the evil of Hitler and the worldwide designs of his national socialism. Simply put, this generation and a half or so knew and did the right thing. It is certain that they danced the dance of youth and merriment, for Nature and Natural Law are never stymied. But it is just as certain that they paid The Fiddler His due, because that was part of the Social Contract. It's how it was done. It is why the value of gold endures. It is what gives the precious metal its glow and its glitter. It is what distinguished baseball during The Golden Age of the Game from all other periods.

There was a Golden Age of Baseball. As we've indicated, were it not for the Black Sox Scandal and the segregation in baseball, those who argue with Bill Starr that the Golden Age of Baseball began as long ago as 1918 and the end of World War I would have far more acceptance and support. Similarly, others argue that it began in 1920 with the end of the Dead Ball Era and the move of Babe Ruth from pitcher to full-time outfielder after the Red Sox sold him to the Yankees, and lasting through the 1960s. From all accounts, it is impossible to overestimate the impact that Babe Ruth had on the game. Not because of the impressive numbers he put up, a system of evaluation that Bill Starr totally debunks, but because of the *gestalt*. Babe Ruth transformed the game and transcended the day. He built the original Yankee Stadium that opened in 1923 and served baseball for 85 years. He re-built the game of baseball.

Others such as Hall-of-Fame slugger and long-time NY Mets broadcaster Ralph Kiner in the Foreword to Starr's book insist that the Golden Age of Baseball didn't begin until 1947 and that it ended in 1957 with the Dodgers and Giants abandoning New York. Still others claim that it lasted until 1964 with the end of a Yankee dynasty, or the very early 1970s. Danny Peary makes the case for the years 1947 through 1964 as being The Golden Age of Baseball. He gets a second from the author of *The Glory of Their Times*, Lawrence Ritter, who wrote in the Introduction for Peary's book, "'The best thing about baseball,' someone said, 'is its yesterdays.' Danny Peary's *We Played the Game* tells you why."

Charles Einstein defines Baseball's Golden Age as *Willie's Time*, precisely "beginning with the coming of Willie Mays to the major league in 1951 and ending with the addition of more teams, complete with divisional playoffs, in 1969." We think that such precision as to the exact years of Baseball's Golden Age is next to impossible to nail down, so we can defer to the experts who want to argue the point. It's also as unnecessary to be so specific as it is self-indicting to cynically dismiss it because you missed it. But we'll use Einstein's time period here and kindly extend it a bit on both ends, beginning then in 1947 after World War II and the return home of America's fighting men, as well as the inaugural season of Jackie Robinson with the Brooklyn Dodgers, and ending, more or less, with the 1973 season. Mickey Mantle would retire after the 1968 season. Mays would finish his career with the New York Mets and the 1973 season. While his performance definitely suffered his last few years, as it does with all old ball players, attendance records were set in appreciation at every park in which he played.

Like Camelot, this Golden Age of Baseball is about local and national heroes and heroism, character and goodness. It is about quality of ballplayer and the baseball they played. Make no mistake, we are well aware of the indiscretions of local baseball heroes as well as those of baseball's Great Ones. But the recent biographies of Cobb, Ruth, DiMaggio, and Mantle, for example, provide compelling psychological reasons why they were perhaps less noble, but more human, than the images that were projected of them years ago.

Baseball was like religion. It had strong connections to all aspects of life, including its past. It is sacrilegious to disparage the local and national Great Ones and to denigrate the saints and the sacred relics. You don't do that. You canonize them. You respect them. You retire the numbers of the legitimately great ballplayers. You showcase them by putting statues, paintings, and pictures on display at ballparks, in churches, in the Vatican, and at Cooperstown. When you disparage the old, you break the sacred connections that are woven into the very fabric of the present and that preserve the day for tomorrow. You destroy the game. You bury your own faith. Historian Doris Kearns Goodwin, an avid Boston Red Sox fan, writes in the Foreword to NYU president John Sexton's book, *Baseball as a Road to God*, "As Sexton rightly argues, the 'intertwining of past and present' is at the heart of baseball's appeal."

Others have called attention to the parallels between baseball and religion. The first sentence in the book, *GOD and Baseball*, by J.H. Sauls, reads: "Simply put . . . Baseball is the Game of Life," and the first sentence in *Crossing Home–The Spiritual Lessons of Baseball* by James Penrice, is, "Baseball is a lot like religion." Indeed, Sexton writes of baseball and religion sharing common attributes, with their *ineffable* nature a significant one. "That which we know through experience rather than through study," he writes, "that which ultimately is indescribable in words yet which is palpable and real. The word signifies the truths known in the soul."

If you play more games, bring the fences in, get more at bats, are juiced on steroids and human growth hormone, or are assisted with the trampoline technology and infinite sweet spot of metal bats, you are *supposed* to be more productive: You will hit more homeruns, have more hits, more RBIs, more *ad nauseum*. But it is questionable, at best, whether it is still baseball. It's like purchasing canonization in the Catholic Church with a huge contribution and then attaching *St.* to your name as though it were a designation like *Dr.* It's like creating a third place, or state, in the afterlife–Limbo–to increase revenues via the route of plenary indulgence in order to pay for massive reconstruction of deteriorating facilities in Rome. Deep down you know it's not real. You have a sense of being conned. It's artificial and doesn't count. Which is more suspect? Which is potentially more harmful in this country? The small religious shop owner in Rome selling warehouses full of "remnants of the *True Cross*"? Or the pretender with a metal bat or some injectable drug who has the temerity to post or just be pompous about, a .400 batting average or 75 homeruns?

Baseball and religion share some imperatives, too. You didn't bring a crossword puzzle to work at a ballgame during the 1950s any sooner than you brought the Sunday newspaper's comics section to read during a Sunday morning high mass celebrated by Father Sam at St. John's Catholic Church in Jordan. Just as the ritual of the mass was a communal worshipping of God, league baseball games were too exciting, too important, to miss a pitch unless you were working the creek on the ball-shagging crew. Defying the universal norms of church or baseball was sacrilegious and anathema.

Those Old Guys–We have been inspired to respond to the discounting and denigration of "those old guys" of the Golden Age by a more contemporary local cohort of ballplayers who came along after the Golden Age of Baseball and by others who never played the game. We honor and celebrate those whom they can't seem to respect.

Those who played did so at a time when the unmistakable *crack* of the bat had been replaced in amateur ball by the noisome *ping* or *clang* of the metal bat. Theirs was an era of bloated ERAs matched by bloated batting averages. Homeruns, RBIs, and runs scored went up in amateur baseball everywhere–a gift of new technology designed to inject excitement into the game artificially by taking from softball, which had a surging popularity in the 1970s, what had filled the void created by the end of the Golden Age of Baseball.

America's Gold Standard–We think there is more than coincidence to the curious fact that America's gold standard–the backing of the buck with real gold– came to end about the same time that baseball's Golden Age flickered out. "In February 1968," according to Bill Bonner in his July 25, 2014, online column– "Diary of a Rogue Economist"–"President Johnson asked Congress to end the requirement that dollars be backed by gold. A month later, Congress complied." "Then in August 1971," Bonner continues, "President Nixon cancelled the direct convitibility of the dollar to gold."

The result of these two actions meant the dollar would be allowed to "float" in value, relative to a basket of other nations' currencies, and the window at which you could ostensibly exchange paper money for gold was no longer open for business. The paper buck was now backed by the "good faith and trust of the U.S. Government," which is run by politicians and bureaucrats, rather than by time-honored gold.

Conservative economists, no less than baseball purists, wrung their hands and furled their brows. The most dreadful comment heard often was that "a buck wasn't worth the paper it was printed on" because it was no longer supported by gold. Loose parallels could be drawn with the nation's new morality, for where once we tried at least to live by and perpetuate the "faith of our fathers," we threw off those restraints and embraced moral relativism. What did that mean if not something like it was okay for me to cheat on my wife, but it was not okay for you to cheat on yours? It was okay to steal from my employer, but it was not okay to drag my neighbor's lawn ornaments over to my yard, because the theft would be obvious. Where once we aimed for the bull's eye on the target, now we had no clear, objective target. Clear distinctions between right and wrong grew subtle shades amounting to "I wanna," Nuance replaced "missing the mark" as the explanation for error of mind or bad behavior. *More* became the unrestrained, unchecked law of the existential self.

Red Smith, the dean of baseball writers, even warned Bowie Kuhn, the commissioner of baseball, in a 1971 column about the dangers of over-exposing baseball to the adulating public with "free" television. He reminded the commissioner of what had happened to professional boxing with the new media when highly touted prize fights were broadcast, first on the occasion of a championship bout, then weekly on "Gillette's Friday Night Fights," and then three times a week. There were simply too many "catchers" in the fight game and too many on the take. There weren't enough Sugar Ray Robinson's, Emile Griffith's, and Rocky Marciano's to keep The Buzz going among fight fans. It wasn't the death of Benny Kid Paret in the ring or the message we got from Anthony Quinn's character, Louis "Mountain" Rivera, in the 1962 movie, *Requiem for a Heavyweight*, that killed boxing. It was television's over-exposure of the sport. What would Red Smith have to say about cable television and the "double broadcasting" today of every single Major League game played–one by the home team and one by the visiting team?

Economists of the Austrian School worried about and warned us of dangerous consequences of meddlesome central banks like the U.S. Federal Reserve. The economy, they said, had natural ebbs and flows to it–like a ball game–cycles of prosperity followed by slowed retrenchment. No party can sustain itself continually. Winning streaks and hitting streaks inevitably come to an end. Mess with that natural energy and dangerous bubbles could result, which can really disrupt a nation's economy and a family's savings when they burst–and burst they must. Weaknesses in a hitter, for example, tend to become strengths. A pitcher's strengths, when that well is tapped too often, tend to become his downfall, for hitters catch up with piped fastballs when thrown too often. Runaway inflation and other disasters resulted from simply printing too much money. Keeping interest rates too low for too long and the savings of people–the lifeblood of a nation–dry up.

Print too much money and you dilute the value of the dollar, they said, with a photograph accompanying the article of a wheelbarrow full of German paper marks being pushed in Weimar Germany to a bakery to pay for a loaf of bread. As Major League Baseball began to expand in the 1960s from a long-standing 16-team constituency in two leagues (since 1901) to 30 teams of two leagues and multiple divisions requiring divisional playoffs at the end of the season, the fever of a

PART I • THE GAME

pennant race was destroyed. Somehow the World Series seemed to get cheapened a bit, too.

Baseball was life, and life was baseball during the game's greatest era, and ". . . what made it so appealing was the amazing bond between the underpaid players and their fans," writes Danny Peary in the Preface to his *We Played the Game*, "a connection that was heightened by the advent of television, the influence of newspapers and radio, and the popularity of the new lines of baseball cards." That bond existed between and among players everywhere.

Multiple levels of connections existed, because it was the same game, former MLB Manager Sparky Anderson tells us, at every level, and in the Minnesota River Valley's lower basin, from approximately New Ulm to St. Paul, the game flourished in its amateur, semi-pro, and professional play. Danny Peary's interviews with 65 former professional baseball players confirm the greatness of the era, for he writes in his Preface to *We Played the Game*:

> As do most of the players who played between 1947 and 1964, I believe that this was baseball's greatest era. It was an improvement over the past simply because the best black and white players now shared the field and because there was so much competition for so few jobs. I think there were an extraordinary number of great and colorful players, men who not only had talent but–in contrast to today's players–also knew how to play the game down to its most subtle aspects.

The 400 major leaguers and all other ballplayers played essentially for sheer love of the game. They played with passion, not for profit. Dick Siebert, University of Minnesota Gopher Baseball Coach, a former ballplayer himself with 17 years of *professional* play, 11 of which were at the Major League level, gave much in the way of support and promotion of baseball in Minnesota. In turn, he benefitted from the passion he helped to nurture, as native Minnesota ballplayers played well enough for him to win three NCAA National Championships–in 1956, 1960, and 1964. How many have been won since then? This was no small accomplishment given the handicap of the northern climate. But notice the dates. They are all presidential election years, and all are within our local Golden Age of Baseball. Fans filled little ballparks everywhere. It is as though it were playoff baseball, or state tournament baseball, every single mid-week *league* game. Until the regional playoffs, non-league games were merely *exhibition* games. They really didn't count. Key players often took the night off or just played a relaxed game. Managers let catchers pitch; they started young pitchers and dipped deep into their benches for these *practice* games. League seasons, on the other hand, were tenacious dogfights. Playoff games and a three-or five-game series between winning teams of different divisions or leagues were magnificent competitions. Why, even tiny St. Benedict in Scott County, consisting of a church, a school building, and a tavern in the center of an agricultural parish of family farmers, as well as a pasture ball field owned to this day by the Archdiocese of St. Paul, with bench seating for maybe 50, home of the DRS League Saints, drew nearly 1,000 people to a Labor Day regional playoff game with the Shakopee Indians in 1957.

It's been true for a long time–maybe since 1964–that, as Lawrence S. Ritter wrote for his 1994 publishing date, baseball had seen its best days. Ritter writes that

"... it was no wonder just about all the sports idols of kids growing up were baseball players" during this era. "Most definitely, these men were of a different, much harder breed than the athletes who followed," Peary adds.

Ball players are as susceptible to narcissism as performers of any other stripe. It seems that anyone who performs in front of, and receives attention, applause, and adulation from, an audience or congregation of people is likely to "fall in love with himself"–the classical definition of narcissism from Greek mythology. Politicians, pole dancers, priests, preachers, actors, teachers, models, and singers all seem to have the same occupational hazard–narcissism. Beautiful women who "do" fashion and makeup on a daily basis, drawing attention whether willfully or not, seem susceptible as well, as do the Adonis wannabes at the gymnasiums who flex their pectoral muscles and tout their ability to bench press a Buick. Their day isn't about living. It's about performing and feeding the narcissism. It's not about being and becoming. It's about looking like . . . something.

We feed the narcissism at the church services, the shows, the performances, and the ballgames. We ask for their autographs, which is still further confirmation for them of the specialness they harbor in their minds. Realities get distorted then, and the individuals turbo-charge their defense mechanisms to maintain their larger-than-life inflated selves. An idealized self-image takes over the living out of one's life. But super-sized salaries made for super-sized egos. They also served to disconnect the stars from the more common man. This disconnection, we submit, is part of the end of the Golden Age of Baseball. It may have caused the end of the age. The symbiotic relationships that existed between little leaguers, high school and college players, amateur and semi-pro players, and professionals disappeared.

It is impossible to overestimate the significance of Jim Pollard playing baseball in Jordan, Minnesota, during the summers of his great basketball career with the Minneapolis Lakers. He was the Michael Jordan of the NBA during his day. He was also an outstanding baseball player. Lefty Weckman said, "Pollard was a AAA-quality ballplayer," in his late 20s and early 30s, without the benefit of having played much baseball in his earlier years, which would only have further developed his skills to the level of a Major League ballplayer.

Willie Mays had played stickball in the streets of Harlem in 1951 after playing a "real" game earlier in the day for the New York Giants at the Polo Grounds. Babe Ruth, according to a recent biographer, Leigh Montville, in *The Big Bam*, would return to play another ballgame in the summer of 1914 with his St. Mary's Industrial School for Boys after playing earlier that day with the team that first signed him to a professional contract–the minor league Baltimore Orioles of the International League.

Ruth would go 26-8 pitching that year, according to Montville, then be sold for $25,000 by the cash-strapped owner, Jack Dunn, of the Orioles to the Boston Red Sox where he won two more games and lost one near the end of the 1914 season. Then, Ruth won 18 games against 8 losses, with a 2.44 ERA, in his first full season with the Red Sox the following year. He also hit four homeruns and batted .315 against other American League pitchers. On May 6, 1915, four games into the season, Babe Ruth led off the third inning in a game against the New York Yankees and starting pitcher Jack Warhop. Babe Ruth hit homerun No.1 of his storied career.

PART I • THE GAME   33

He hit a "dead ball" with a wood bat. But there wasn't anything dead about the last one he hit–No. 714–at a lifestyle-worn-out 40 years of age in May of 1935 that, in retrospect, was a kind of curtain call on his career. It was his third homerun of the day and the first ball to ever clear the roof and structure of old Forbes Field in Pittsburgh. Homeruns were an oddity during the Dead Ball Era. Nobody really thought about trying to hit them. Frank "Homerun" Baker had led the American League for the fourth consecutive year in 1914 with eight, according to Montville, nine according to online sources. Ballparks simply were not homerun friendly. Neither were the balls or bats. They were not made for homeruns. Hitters learned to hit line drives. The fly ball was a result of dipping the rear shoulder or some other faulty execution with the bat. The bunting game and a stolen base were supreme strategic baseball. The best hitters were those with the highest batting averages.

Baker was asked years later how many homeruns he thought he would have hit had he been playing with the conditions that evolved later with balls, bats, and ballparks. His nickname, "Home Run," had been given to him as a result of two big homeruns he had hit in the 1911 World Series. His most prolific home run season was 12 in 1913, but his response to the question, according to Montville, was profound: "'I'd say 50,' he said. 'The year I hit 12, I also hit the right-field fence at Shibe Park 39 times.'"

Home Run Baker was being modest about the number of homeruns he would have hit under conditions that the more modern ballplayers experienced. Then as now, half of the season's games were played as visitors at the spacious ballparks of other teams where Baker also had to have taken outfielders deep or slammed shots off of right-field walls for doubles. These balls, too, would have carried over the fences with the conditions the modern ballplayer takes for granted.

Shibe Park was home to the Philadelphia Athletics and the Philadelphia Phillies. It had a life span of 61 years (1909 to 1970). Original dimensions were 378 feet to left, 515 feet to center, and 340 feet to right field. Power alley figures could be found for the re-modeled park in 1950: Left-center was 420 feet; right-center was 405 feet for a left-handed hitter like Baker. Replace Baker's 52-ounce "two-by-four" with a modern, whip-handled bat in his hands, pitch baseballs to him that haven't been put through a wringer wash machine and kept in the game for all nine innings, or put him on steroids, or give him a metal bat and let him hit in a modern ballpark, and just imagine how many home runs he would have hit.

Babe Ruth had hit a ball in 1915 that resembled a beanbag as much as it did a baseball by the third inning. Baseballs were dead and soft. The Dead Ball Era prevailed until 1920, when Ray Chapman died 12 hours later in the hospital after being hit in the head by Yankee pitcher Carl Mays. Until then, the same ball was kept in play throughout a ballgame. With the death of Chapman, umpires were instructed to replace dirty, scuffed balls with new, clean, more visible balls.

Maybe the loss of the golden glitter of baseball wasn't organic at all. Maybe, because "Baseball was life, and life was baseball," the game suffered from what was going on in society. After all, Greenwich Village in New York and Haight-Ashbury in San Francisco, and the West Bank on the University of Minnesota campus, were not good baseball venues in the late 1960s. They were havens of The Left. There was no baseball vibe in these places, and The Buzz had nothing to do with the game. The changes promised by the experiments in "consciousness raising" taking place did not bode well for baseball.

Young people weren't playing ball anymore. They weren't going to the ballpark to take in a game either. They were smoking marijuana and hashish, sometimes laced with mescaline, dropping acid, or LSD, and taking speed–all for the rush of the moment or to help grasp the effects of a strobe light or the test patterns on broadcast television after stations went off the air. Instant gratification. Baseball was boring. Things were different when you were high. Boring sameness could be left behind in a trip that didn't require change of place. Some claimed that music could be *tasted*; food could be *felt* and *heard*. On some hallucinogenic drugs, it was reported that you could see the fourth and fifth dimensions of things that had only two or three dimensions to them. Then it was all so "groovy," just like everything would become "awesome" or "sweet" a few decades later.

Conscription–the military draft–ended in early 1973, possibly to the detriment of that generation of youth and the country, and even to baseball. Young men had been required since 1940 to give two years of their lives to military service. Boys, punks, thugs, farmers, and hotshots would undergo the metamorphosis into mature manhood that only a drill sergeant could ignite in America's young men. They would come home, if they made it home and in one piece, with a sense of responsibility to them that they had no clue about two years earlier. It's as though they had been to finishing school out East, but in a sense that helped to make them conscious of team being above self. They learned respect for others instead of demanding it of others without earning it. But the national ethic of God-country-team would soon be replaced by one of me-me-me. Service to others . . . would be supplanted by serving self. "What can I do for you?" would be replaced by, "What's in it for me?"

Very few people expected something for nothing. Rather, they valued and sought everywhere the opportunity to earn a living. Baseball was better during the game's Golden Age, because the ballplayers were better. While they may not, in general, have been as big or strong or as fast as they would get, they played better baseball. After all, it was the height of The Golden Age of Baseball. And it happened at all levels–from the Major Leagues down into the Minnesota River Valley towns of amateur and semi-pro baseball. One Larca legend intimated that the period was merely a "so-called" golden age. He can't know it, because neither Manager Larca nor any of his charges were around the Minnesota River Valley or old enough to have known the Golden Age of Baseball locally. Perhaps many players from the modern era have trouble accepting the fact that a golden age could possibly be defined without them. Narcissism will do that to good men. Just as it is impossible to measure that which you prevent, it is impossible to know what you have missed.

Jim Stoll put it most succinctly: "I was afraid that if I didn't produce at Arlington, I'd lose my job." He recognized the superior playing conditions, the equipment, and the size of some ballplayers today. "But we were hungrier," Stoll said. "I had a wife and five kids at home." That was in Arlington, Minnesota, playing so-called amateur ball. So-called in this case, because if he pitched well enough in a big-game win, Jim Stoll couldn't make it to the dugout after getting the last batter out in a 1963 game without getting mobbed and having his pockets jammed with $500 to $600 of pre-inflation money, which means that it was about $5,000 or more in today's money. The younger crowd, the legions of Charlie ball players who are too young to have appreciated Jim Stoll, tout the likes of Barry Wohler and his tenure of outstanding pitching for Belle Plaine in the 1990s. But Dave Hartmann caught Stoll at Arlington and he played against Wohler when he pitched for Belle Plaine in the 1990s and led them to the Class-C Minnesota State Championship in 1994. Wohler had been drafted and signed by the Los Angeles Dodgers in 1983 from the University of Minnesota. He pitched two years of Class-A and three years of Class-AA ball in the Dodger organization, compiling a 33-41 W-L record and a 4.34 ERA. "I know he signed and everything," Hartmann said of Wohler, "but you can't even mention his name in the same breath as Jim Stoll. It's not even close." It's not that there was anything inferior about Barry Wohler. It's that Jim Stoll was that good.

A clear distinction between The Golden Age of Baseball and other eras of life can be seen in the ethic of baseball's starting pitchers. Going back to the beginnings of baseball, with Christy Matthewson, Cy Young, Walter Johnson and through the careers of Koufax, Gibson, Carleton, and others, it was part of a pitcher's work ethic and his character to finish what he started. Complete games were an important part of one's resume. Getting knocked out of a game was more often as not taken as a character defect. So, you worked and tried harder the next outing. Getting lifted for a pinch hitter in any inning other than the ninth was regrettable. It was a matter of pride.

Basically, more people would say what they meant and mean what they said during The Golden Age. They would do what they said they would do, whether that meant a bit of inconvenience or not. This might be a good definition of integrity, and it was a crucial defining quality of character. It was also an aspect of the unwritten Social Contract. Those who violated it in any number of ways were ostracized, shunned from or within the community. This self-regulating mechanism has always been natural to men in groups of any kind, including ball clubs. External regulating mechanisms tended to be unnecessary and even counterproductive. You took care of your own. Outside "help" was seen as either oppression or meddling. Marriage, for example, meant the fulfilling of the vows–"until death do us part . . ."–and, indeed, divorce was quite rare in the small towns in the Minnesota River Valley. Nationwide, 25 percent of marriages would end in divorce in the 1950s, a rate that would double by the 1980s.

Divorce had negative effects on individuals, families, and especially children. A comparative study cited by a Baptist minister in a Sunday morning sermon at New Heights Christian Fellowship Church in Burnsville, MN, in the early 2000s was telling. The pastor said a study in 1968 of children showed the single greatest fear of children of approximately 6 to 12 years of age was nuclear annihilation. In retrospect, it's easy to see why: The Cold War with the Soviet Union was at its peak; news reports chronicled daily the chess game moves of the U.S. and the Soviets around the world; President Kennedy had averted what easily could have been nuclear holocaust earlier in the decade in what became known as "the Cuban Missile Crisis"; the Vietnam War was raging; sub-cultures and counter cultures were growing like mushrooms everywhere. Chicago nearly blew up or burned down during the 1968 Democratic National Convention. The country was coming apart at the seams. Kids were afraid.

In 1998, according to the pastor, the same polling organization studied the same demographic cohort, asking the same question of children of the same age: What do you fear most in your life? The Berlin Wall had come tumbling down, and another American president, Ronald Reagan, had successfully executed his policy of "Peace through strength," effectively ending the Cold War as the Soviet Union disbanded and the iron fist loosened its grip on its world. But kids were still afraid, and what they feared most in their lives was the loss of family, security, and love. They were most afraid of mommy and daddy getting divorced. Divorce had replaced nuclear annihilation as the single most feared event in the lives of most American children. It was that prevalent and had that much effect on the most vulnerable involved.

Commitment was a part of life in the 50s. Marriage was ordained by God. It had a Scriptural basis to it that was lacking in the government's counterpart secular contract: You still had to prove adultery or abuse to win a divorce in the 50s. By the 1970s, you could get divorced because of a *feeling*, or as one counseling psychologist told us at a social affair why she divorced her husband after 20 years and three children: "I wanted to talk about feelings," she said, "and he was an engineer." Never mind that she got the house and got to keep the advanced degrees that had cost her working husband a small fortune. Never mind that this psychologist would be hired to provide lessons in spirituality and moral guidance to troubled pastors. It's not that the pastors didn't need help if the reports from a young, ball-playing pastor we came to know were true: He stopped going to a Monday morning mutual support gathering of Twin City suburban pastors because, he said, he got fed up with hearing confessions week after week of his peers "borrowing" from the collection baskets and their admitting to sexual dalliances with distraught women during pastoral counseling sessions. These men of the cloth in whom the moral compass was held needed some help, but could it come from a woman whose counseling calendar and waiting room were always filled with post-abortion women who weren't there to celebrate choice.

These female counselors weren't Gypsies or Native Americans; they were white women who had graduated from suburban high schools. They wanted to be shamans and purveyors of guided meditation when those New Age modalities gained popularity. They were psychics and healers of all sorts and stripes. They were said to use crystals, stones, and colors in creative healing ways. They told others that God didn't write *The Bible* even as they claimed to channel Him in $200 per hour telephone therapy sessions. They were high priestesses of The New Age.

Perhaps the swapping of wives by New York Yankee pitchers Fritz Peterson and Mike Kekich in 1972, made public in 1973, epitomizes best our point here: The Golden Age of Baseball had come to an end. It was both an outcome of the proverbial slippery slope that The Old Guard always warns against at the outset of something new and, on the surface, exciting and good, the latest progressive thing from which The Fiddler hides His face, and a catalyst for still more. This slippery slope had been greased years earlier, and it eased the slide of still more in kind throughout the decade and the remaining years of the century. If everybody was "okay," and moral relativism the new index of right and wrong, then "anything goes," and it did.

You could raise a family in a small town along the Minnesota River Valley in the 1950s without having to worry about a child being abducted, without your son being molested by a teacher, the scoutmaster, or a priest, and without a minister seducing your wife. While those crises of character, those crimes, must have been occurring in places then, too, they couldn't have been occurring as often. There simply was no moral pandemic, as seems to have been the case since the end of what Jerry Stahl called "the golden age of everything." At any rate, they were off the radar screen. Those kinds of things didn't even cross your mind then. Young boys, but not girls it was true, could deliver the daily newspapers then and stash away enough money to pay for most of a private college education. Girls, on the other hand, could always waitress at restaurants. Both learned some basic business tenets: service, for one; the difference between gross revenue and net profit for another, which would later help them understand the difference between price and value. They also learned who the deadbeats at their tables and on their paper routes were and usually why.

There was no "daycare" outside of an occasional helping hand from neighbors, friends, or an aunt. You paid for this service, not with cash, but with a return of the favor, thereby strengthening community and family connections. There were no microwave ovens, remote car starters, or garage door openers. Pasta and popcorn were the closest things to instant food. No cell phones and texting, no electronic games, no computers or television remote controls existed to "make life easier." Electric refrigerators had replaced the old iceboxes to make life easier, as had automatic washers and dryers and sliced bread. But there was no epidemic of obesity either. For sure, the Fat Lady's closing hymn ended Sunday service, but she wasn't as fat, nor was she everywhere like she would become in a few decades. Families had one car. In fact, it was called "the family car" They had one television, many of which were still black and white. They had a ringer washing machine in their basement, and they dried their clothes on an outside clothesline, which gave rise to a common expression in sport: You didn't want to get "clothes lined," a reference to the dangers kids faced in chasing each other at night through backyards everywhere. There was one phone in the house, and families ate their meals together, particularly the evening meal, which was called "supper," before which you asked God, not government, to bless the food and your family and anybody who was sick in the community. Sick people with the help of God usually got well. Sick people with the help of government could be seen decades later in droves at Indian gaming casinos, propped up with prescription drugs and the illusion of health, wealth, and happiness, sucking heavily on cigarettes as they played their favorite games of chance. Bells and whistles, flashing lights, and sirens would tell them when to rejoice, would tell them they had hit the jackpot. A completely superficial reality would tell them they were "winners."

As a kid, you played with your friends, outside mostly. You played like puppies play, with lots of running, romping, and rambling all year long. But in the spring and until late fall, you played ball. Lots of ball. Every backyard, driveway, and street could easily be turned into a "ballpark" built with shared imaginations and minimal resources.

Playing outside, playing ball, especially by boys but not always exclusively, was how high-energy kids with trouble minding parents or teachers, trouble paying attention, were "managed" in the 1950s. Fifty years' later, these qualities became "symptoms" of disease conditions that required prescriptions for amphetamines first developed to "treat" depression. Attention Deficit Disorder (ADD) and Attention Deficit Hyperactivity Disorder (ADHD) would be diagnosed in something like 15 percent of boys and 6 percent of girls in the 2000s. Ritalin would make a comeback on the pharmaceutical scene after being vanquished to street drug status and use by over-the-road truck drivers and college students cramming for finals despite the widely known admonition: "Speed kills."

Character was still paramount as the measure you took of a man. It would be decades before the psychologists and psychiatrists of modern America would replace character with personality as the therapeutic focus of change and growth. One of the mantras of the late 1960s was, "If it feels good, do it." By the 1990s, high school girls in posh suburban communities had designed a color code for their fingernails that would signal to boys, or other girls, their sexual availability and the degree of their promiscuity. Worse yet, high school-age girls were reported to be knocking on winter ice-fishing shacks on lakes, offering to perform $20 "Lewinski's" for fishermen. Few had likely even heard of Mother Teresa, much less tried to emulate her. Rather instead, schoolgirls looked like they were auditioning to be porn stars or strippers. Many would adorn faces with hardware in a way that reminded The Old Indian Guide of the white city man getting his face caught in the fishing tackle box. Terminal tackle clung to ears, eyelids, and even nostrils as an everyday statement of contemporary fashion.

One supposes that the jewelry of tattoos and metal rings was a means of youth expressing their individuality. But to The Old Indian and to old pitchers like John Freund and Jim Kubes it was hideous. Better to have looked for a ballpark and a position that suited you.

In the 1950s, girls wore bobby sox, and they giggled a lot in gaggles of three, four, and more girls. You didn't worry so much about *looking* good or *feeling* good. You worried about *being* good, and you worked at it. It is what was parented at home, taught in schools, and preached at church. It was Old School morality. Nobody ever hit the bull's eye all the time, but at least a target was there to aim at. Eventually, most, if not all, hit the target; they "got it." Right and wrong. It's not that anybody was so angelic that there was no wrong then, but, Truth be told, "If you wanted to dance, you paid The Fiddler." It was part of the Social Contract. Consequently, the social pathologies that are undermining society today were minimal at most.

Catholics and people of other affiliations went to church on Sundays in the 1950s, and they dressed for it, with men wearing suits and ties, women wearing their best dresses. Black shoes were polished on Saturday night before popcorn and cokes. Church was both obligatory in the Catholic Church and an accepted part of life. Today, something like 24 percent of Catholics admit to going to church, and a Catholic priest in the Winona Diocese said in the early 2000s already that only 50 percent of the babies being baptized in the Church then were children of married parents. Such children were once widely known as "out-of-wedlock," and "illegitimate." They were bastards. Most children grew up in two-parent homes in the 1950s, but by the 2000s, 25 percent of white children and 75 percent of Black children would be living in fatherless homes. That existential reality–fatherless homes–correlated with crime to a greater extent than what had been presumed had been the strongest case–poverty. Imagine playing a baseball game without an umpire.

Service men incurring real disabilities during The Big One–World War II–were known to be sent home–honorably discharged–on 100-percent disability from the government only to spurn the monthly stipend because, "It wasn't right." They considered service to country a duty; they helped out their neighbors; they cared for parents and other family members needing a home; and they preferred to earn their way in life as part of the personal responsibility that was in the code of manhood. The public trough was pretty much a last resort. The line between opportunity and outcome wasn't blurred then with government handouts and the value system they created. They were connected by effort. Qualifying for "free" money didn't mean to these members of "*The Greatest Generation*" what it would mean to millions in the 2000s–entitlement. No, they knew the difference between earning their way and getting something for nothing. The difference was a matter of conscience and character. After a big payday fight in the 1930s, James J. Braddock, heavyweight champion of the world, would repay the government the relief money he had needed to feed his family during The Great Depression. By the end of 2013, nearly 11 million Americans had *qualified* for disability via the Social Security Administration. Conditions that used to warrant the paid time off to visit a doctor for some periodic treatment were now rewarded with a lifetime annuity. They would receive an average of $13,000 a year for any number of diagnosed conditions, most of which were self-induced at the super-sized takeout fast-food restaurants and buffets with the knife and fork. Or they were the consequences of lifestyle choices that fried brains with the likes of meth-amphetamine, crack cocaine, and crack heroin on top of speedballs, cheap whiskey, and magnum volumes of beer.

Some men and women gave up lucrative business and employment opportunities to fulfill caregiving responsibilities for aging parents and spouses. But later especially, others found ways to offload family responsibilities to the county and to game the system in any way they could to make sure their wheels were greased by one form of government handout or another. Double, triple, and even quadruple dipping at the public trough became common. Much of what had once been considered immoral became common and acceptable. People repeatedly pointed accusatory fingers at others. They found horrible fault in their brothers while unable to find the existential mirror and heed the call to examine their own conscience without the defensive mechanisms of The Lie.

The Ku Klux Klan, America's homegrown terrorist organization, still had a presence in the country with its third version. It would die out, or at least diminish in influence, soon enough with the same legal bear trap that had caught and shut down Al Capone's Chicago mob business–income tax evasion. The Jim Crow laws of The South, which gave the KKK some vigilante cover, would slowly evaporate with the national Civil Rights Laws of 1965. But Planned Parenthood, even more clandestine in a different sense, was beginning to get traction, its founder, Margaret Sanger, and her early work as a eugenicist forgotten or denied by the same people who would deny life to unborn children. Roe v. Wade would give the nation's number one provider of abortion the legal and financial support it needed to thrive. In 2015 a series of undercover videos by the Center for Medical Progress would have on tape the discussions by Planned Parenthood's MDs the harvesting for sale of baby parts. That slope, a descent into Hitler's Nazi hell, was greased in the late 1960s.

In the 1950s, you worried about making a ball club and breaking into the lineup someplace. You worried about getting permission from a landowner to hunt a field or wetland in the fall. You thought about your team and its chances in the pennant race or the series. You thought about classes, a girl who'd smiled at you, college, marriage, a family or your job. You talked about everything in the community living rooms that the bars were then. Renaissance Man–"The Man for all Seasons"–was *the* role model. You didn't concentrate then on one sport in order for your parents to manage their drive toward some vicarious victory, an idealized image perhaps, the college scholarship they envisioned for you, or the life they'd missed out on. You did it all–or tried to, playing and doing whatever was in season. Some recent thinking is calling for a return to this model of participation, because single-sport concentration is being called out as a cause of injuries and burnout in young athletes.

You didn't go to expensive, two-week summer camps that were marketed with the names of, and sometimes even run by, well-known sports figures. Kids didn't have personal trainers, coaches, and memberships in winter training "clubs." Children weren't managed in order to "build good resumes." They were parented and helped to grow up. You learned the game in the yard from playing it against older, better players. You played the sport that was in season. That meant you played basketball on the hard courts in the winter and on the churchyard in sloppy springs. You hunted and played football in the fall. In the summer, you might swim a little, fish a little, but mostly you played ball.

Unemployment and inflation weren't worth a news note in the post-war years marked by Ike's return to the national spotlight as the nation's president. He had led the Allied forces in Europe against Hitler and the Nazi's. He would lead the country's return to normalcy with an interstate highway system that was ostensibly for defense purposes modeled on German autobahns, and to full employment across the land. Interestingly, neither Dwight Eisenhower nor his supporters were quite sure of his party affiliation prior to his nomination at the Republican Convention in 1952.

The Gold Standard was solidly in place. Every U.S. dollar was backed by gold, and Fort Knox was full of it. When it was said of something or someone, "It's as good as gold," or "He's as good as gold," what was meant was that the value was authentic and enduring. It wasn't plastic or paper. He wasn't a phony. She was real. The Gold Standard had a way of keeping the partisan agendas of politicians in check. It kept them from spending too much money they didn't have on things that weren't needed. So rather than let an open, free market of buyers and sellers determine the price of gold, an official price of the metal was set by the government:

That figure was about $22 an ounce for a long time; in 1934, after confiscating the nation's gold, President Roosevelt reset the official value of gold to $35 an ounce. It was upped to $38 in 1972, the year after President Nixon closed the gold window, meaning the U.S. would no longer honor anybody's request for gold in exchange for IOUs being held. In 1973, the official price of gold was bumped again, to $42.22, where it has remained. In March of 2013, the market value of gold would soar past $1,600 an ounce again, two years after reaching an all-time high of $1,913.50 in 2011. In late 2015, the price of gold was in a slide below $1,100 an ounce, but in early 2016 it was rebounding. What's to be made of the huge discrepancy between what's official and what's real?

Gold experts insist that the metal's value has remained constant while the value of everything else has diminished when true reckoning is done. Standards don't change. A foot is a foot, and a yard is three feet; an ounce is an ounce, and a pound is 16 ounces. That which is measured against the standards does change. As evidence, they cite facts like the same number in ounces of gold are needed to buy the median-priced house today that were needed to buy the median-priced house in the 1970s.

As for baseball, just three men–Willie Mays, Roberto Clemente, and Brooks Robinson –would earn 40 Gold Gloves between them, an award first initiated in 1957 to highlight the standard of defensive excellence. Just ahead of these three, Ted Williams and Joe DiMaggio had done their stints in the service and had been leading their teams in search of pennants while stacking up individual records that will probably never be broken: Joe DiMaggio hit in 56 consecutive professional games in 1941 with the Yankees; he had hit in 61 straight games in 1933 as a 19-year-old kid with the San Francisco Seals of the old independent Pacific Coast League.

Williams would go six for eight at the plate in a doubleheader on the last day of the 1941 season and finish with a .406 average. Nobody has hit .400 since. Of perhaps greater note on the man and men of those times, his manager had asked him if he wanted to sit out the last day of the season in order to ensure the .400 average. Characteristically, Williams turned down the offer to manage his performance feat and actually raised his average that final day by doing it the old-fashioned way–earning it at the plate. As competitive, hot tempered, and bull headed as he was said to be, Ted Williams would have argued with an umpire over a called strike of a pitch off the plate, but he would never have tried to intimidate an official scorer into changing an error into a hit–just to help out his batting average. The Kid's goal from the outset of his career was to be the best hitter in baseball. He had a jump start on that achievement in our Minnesota River Valley's lower basin. Williams won the Triple Crown in what was in 1938 the Double-A American Association, playing for the Minneapolis Millers. At 19 years old, the native Californian hit .366, slammed 43 homeruns and another 30 doubles and 9 triples while compiling 142 RBIs. A ripping pull hitter, the 279-foot right field fence at old Nicollet Park beckoned the young left-handed hitter. But he and the fans got their money's worth. His homeruns often cleared Nicollet Avenue and the buildings on the far side of the street.

Williams learned at Minneapolis from Rogers Hornsby, a three-time .400 hitter in the National League, to hit his pitch. Consequently, he learned the strike zone well and carries to this day the highest career percentage of walks per at bat (20.64 percent) by any Major League ballplayer of 1,000 games or more.

The year, 1941, was memorable for two other reasons: The country entered World War II after being attacked by Japan at Pearl Harbor; and it was the year of the birth of Frank Hilgers, Jr., in Jordan, Minnesota. Eight days would separate the two events.

There were exceptions, of course, as there are with anything. But image wasn't as strongly managed in the 1950s as it would be later in the century. It was reflected by character and by performance-based reputation rather than being produced in a PR department or advertising agency in advance of any enduring quality of performance. Gold endures in value. But "All that glitters is not gold."

DiMaggio, to Yankee lovers at least, was arguably the best baseball player of all time; he would retire at a relatively young 36 years of age following the 1951 season, his body already creaking and aching with arthritis and heal spurs hobbling him. Williams, who would lead many lists as the greatest hitter who ever played the game, would continue hitting line drives through the decade and finish his career with the 1960 season. Mays's stats at the plate were also admirable, but he would roam with delight the deepest of centerfields–505 feet straightaway with power alleys of 450 feet at the Polo Grounds.

These greats of the Golden Age of Baseball were fueled and fired, not by the promise of megabuck salaries and endorsements, but by the want and will to compete and excel. The highest-paid baseball player earned $100,000 a year. That was the threshold that few attained: Mays and Mantle, DiMaggio and Williams earned what only The Great One–Babe Ruth–had come close to earning at the top of his game in the Roaring Twenties.

There were heroes and heroism evident outside of baseball, too. They helped to inspire kids playing ball everywhere. Bobby Jones would win 13 major golf titles to vie with Cobb and Ruth for status as the country's first superstar in the first decades of the 20th Century. He would remain an amateur while beating the best professionals in the world, winning The Grand Slam in 1930, which included The U.S. Open at Interlachen Country Club in Minneapolis. The format then called for 36 holes of match play in torrid heat on what was called "Open Saturday," the final day.

Gene Sarazen, Byron Nelson, Ben Hogan, then Arnold Palmer and Jack Nicklaus would, in turn, replace Jones as golf's best. But every spring at Augusta, Georgia, they all gathered by invitation, all the great ones, to compete and to pay homage to Bobby Jones, at The Masters. Hogan would go winless for most of the first 10 years of his professional career, then after two years of military service, finally break through and peak in terms of winning with 37 tour wins between just 1946 and 1949 when he met a Greyhound bus head on in the fog. He survived only because he threw himself over his wife in the passenger seat to protect her, the steering wheel getting driven through the back of the driver's seat.

Doctors said he would never walk again, and blood clots nearly took him a week or two after he had been admitted to the hospital. He would undergo a dangerous, clot-blocking surgery to the main vein returning blood to his heart and lungs. He would need to undergo four surgeries to his left shoulder the rest of his life, and suffer intermittent blindness to his left, dominant, eye, which translated to what looked like "the yips" on the putting green. Before he was 50 years old, Ben Hogan was stabbing at the ball on the green, because he had trouble seeing the ball and trouble taking the putter back. But Ben Hogan wasn't afraid of the work it took to be able to not only walk again, but to win again. He defied doctors and competitors and the sports writers who misunderstood the introspective, shy man who admitted he loved the game but not the limelight. He liked to practice. Alone. It was said of him that he would practice "until his hands were bleeding." He was a perfectionist, and tee to green, likely the best golfer the game has ever known, certainly among golfers using persimmon drivers and fairway woods. Before his accident, he was known as a good putter as well as a long hitter despite being just 5-9 and playing much of his golf at 140 pounds. His power was derived from the perfection in his swing–perfection honed in his countless hours of practice. He would play in 30 tournaments a year before his accident but just five or six a year afterwards. Sometimes, he would disappear for a year or more entirely, all of which fueled "The Hogan Mystique," which biographers would reveal only much later was based on his having witnessed his father taking his own life with a pistol when he was just nine years old.

His U.S. Open win at Merion in 1950, just 16 months after the accident, is probably one of the greatest achievements in all of sport. Then in 1951–DiMaggio's last year and Mantle's first with the Yankees–Ben won the Masters and $3,000. In comparison, Phil Mickelson, a gun on the PGA Tour 60 years later, would pocket $1,330,000 for his Masters win in 2010. In 1953, Hogan would enter six tournaments and win five of them, including The Masters, The U.S. Open, and The British Open. His shot at "The Grand Slam" was precluded by the overlapping schedule of the PGA Championship with that of the British Open at Carnoustie. His last win on tour was in 1959 at his beloved Hogan's Alley–Riviera Country Club and the L.A. Open. Had his left eye been fully operative, he'd have run away from Nicklaus and Palmer with the 1960 U.S Open and undoubtedly numerous other majors as well when long past his prime.

Sugar Ray Robinson owned the welterweight boxing title through the 1940s, and he would win the middleweight championship five times in the 1950s, earning him the oft-spoken accolade of "pound-for-pound, the greatest boxer of all time." The boxing classes each had a champion. There was *The* Heavyweight Champion of the World. Not five. And everybody knew who the current champion was. After Joe Louis's reign as heavyweight champion from 1937 to 1949 ended, several fighters would wear the crown in the 1950s. Most notably, Rocky Marciano would retire as World Heavyweight Champion in 1956 after defending the title six times and with a perfect, undefeated, untied 49-0 record.

The broadcast of a heavyweight championship fight was a major event–on the radio! Ten minutes ahead of the scheduled Round 1 bell, you dialed the knob on the radio to tune in to Howard Cosell's observations and reporting. A Canadian professor, Marshall McCluhan, would later explain the magical phenomenon of "warm" radio versus the "cold" television, an intrinsic effect lost on the consciousness of the masses. *The medium is the message*, McCluhan posited, with radio inviting and engaging The Whole Being of its listeners, while television made zombies of viewers.

Bill Russell would, in the single 1956-'57 basketball year, win an NCAA National Championship with the University of San Francisco, a Gold Medal with the U.S. Olympic Team, and his first of 11 NBA championships with the Boston Celtics, including 8 straight. Today's "experts" would say that Russell and the Celtics had no competition then. True, the Minneapolis Laker dynasty had come to an end, but Wilt Chamberlain of Philadelphia would score 100 points in a single game and average over 50 points a game in the 1962-63 season. Nonetheless, Russell and the Celtics would prevail in the championship, helping to give credence to the time-honored truism, "Defense wins championships."

Johnny Unitas would lead the Baltimore Colts to an NFL Championship in an overtime victory over the New York Giants in 1958. His career would be marked with many more wins and a penchant for late-game heroics with his "golden arm." When the inevitable arguments of "greatest quarterbacks" arise, he still leads many of the lists. Johnny Unitas not only had *the* arm at a time when the running game was still the foundation of football offenses, but he called his own game, because he was *the* quarterback.

Just as Unitas was the consummate quarterback, Chuck Bednarik of the Philadelphia Eagles would earn in his career through the 1950s the title of "The Sixty-Minute Man," because he went both ways. He played the whole game, center on offense and middle linebacker on defense. He played football. Today, everybody is a specialist at a "skill position."

John Wooden began the base of his great basketball coaching career in 1948 at UCLA, where he would win 620 games in 27 seasons and 10 NCAA titles during his last 12 seasons, including seven in a row from 1967 to 1973.

The greatness of communities was that they were self-sustaining through the 1950s and into the 60s. Just about every town had a movie theatre, where for two-bits a kid could watch the latest serial episode of *The Lone Ranger*, and get a good-sized bag of popcorn and a soda to take to his seat. A night in 2015 at the Southdale Theatres in Edina, Minnesota, would lighten the pocketbook as follows: admission–$10.50; large popcorn–$8.00; and a Dasani bottle of water–$4.50.

The towns along the Minnesota River all had their own restaurants, grocery stores, dry cleaners, jewelers, tailors, lumber yards, hardware stores, creameries, car dealerships, doctors, dentists, welders, carpenters, electricians, television repair shops, full-service gas stations, drug stores with soda fountains, schools, barber shops, bowling alleys, bakeries, beauty shops, independent banks, bars, breweries or soft drink bottling companies, butcher shops, and . . . ballparks.

Residents shared a love for baseball and beer. Nearly every town of any size had at one time a baseball team and a brewery. Both baseball and the brewing industry suffered pretty much the same fate: consolidation and the depreciation of quality. Chuck Warner at Brownton says that the arrival of the Twins in 1961 signaled the end of Minnesota's outstanding baseball. "Until then," Warner said of Brownton's baseball operations, "we were self-sustaining from the gate alone." Others say it was television. Why bother to go to a small, local ballpark to watch construction workers, schoolteachers, and farmers play ball and where you have to pay a buck to get in the gate, when you can watch Major League Baseball for free on television? Still others claim that the gradual exodus of young people from rural communities, including small family farms, to large metropolitan areas all over the country sapped the supply of ballplayers that small towns had relied on. We don't argue with any of these reasons by the sociological experts. But we know that the Golden Age of Baseball came to an end sometime in the 1960s or early 70s. Maybe it ended sooner in some places than it did in others, or at some levels while hanging on a while at others. We know that the baseball was better baseball during The Golden Age or nobody would have ever thought to call it golden. We think that it was better baseball, all around, because the ballplayers, in general, were better at all levels. In fact, it's not even close, when all of the mitigating factors are considered. Moreover, life was better, too, because the people, in general, were better people, judging how we are told to judge in the New Testament and by Dr. Martin Luther King, Jr., in his famous speech from the Birmingham jail.

Doctors still made house calls as late as 1967. Each community was distinct; each had its own character, its own sinners and saints. Sameness was anathema. You might buy hamburger and bologna at Pekarna's Meat Market in Jordan, a town with a population of fewer than 1,500 people, but you might have preferred the hot dogs and the summer sausage you could get from Langer's Meat Market a block away. Neither of these family-run businesses compromised its meat products with any sawdust, cereal or scrap, or more than a miniscule amount of fat for flavor. Neither would endanger the health of its customers by adding MSG, HFCS, or food coloring to the products, and government regulators looking over their shoulders at taxpayer expense weren't needed. They both thrived on Old School German quality and service, with Pekarna's still going strong in a fourth generation of family ownership in the 21st Century, a fifth waiting in the wings, working weekend and summer apprenticeships behind the counter and in the back room on the butcher blocks where the best bologna to ever fill up the space between two slices of bread is fashioned every week. Pekarna's signature bologna has defined "sandwich" for over a century. Like gold, quality endures.

Franchises and the sameness of one community to another that they brought to American life were just in their infancy. While Shakopee on the Minnesota River had a Dairy Queen that we liked to stop at on our way out of town after a Little League or Babe Ruth baseball game, we don't remember a McDonald's or any of the other franchises that would be born in the decade. Like its grocery stores, a town's restaurants were independently owned and operated. But gasoline stations had dealer relationships with the Big Oil companies through a distributor. Standard Oil, Mobil, Texaco, and others were big and everywhere. Yet, you wouldn't think of going to the gas station of your choice to buy glazed donuts or sliced bread. Two bucks could get you as many as 10 gallons of gas from the pump that the proprietor, not you, the customer, operated. While the gas was being dispensed, he'd clean your windshield and headlights and ask if you wanted the oil checked. You might buy a pack of cigarettes for two bits at the gas station, but you got a "baker's dozen" of your favorite pastry at the bakery. Schools were an integral, transparent part of their communities in the 1950s rather than the separate, quasi-government agencies they would become with the largest operating budgets and the highest-paid cohort of employees of any entity in town. Today, few teachers would live in and support the communities that employed them. A part of the old Social Contract–the quid pro quo–was torn up. The worst thing to happen in a school in the 1950s was a rowdy classroom on the last day before Christmas vacation or the discovery of chewing gum under the seats and desks. No kid got by with even thinking of taking a gun out of the house with him to school.

Jordan High School's Edna ("Ma") Beckman still made sure in the mid-1960s that by the time you passed through her sophomore English class you knew the difference between a noun and verb and could diagram a sentence. She had forearms that would rival Popeye's–from lifting–thugs and punks onto the coat hooks in the cloakroom of *her* classroom.

Edwin ("Shit mouth") Sanders would take a barrage of blows to his head and chest one day from an overgrown freshman in his industrial arts class, disappearing to the wide-eyed amazement of the rest of the all-boys' class into the back room. A moment of silence that must have been a mere awakening, like a horse twitching off a gnat or a fly, and the barrage resumed, banging and busting back into the classroom area. Then it was finished with a huge right-handed haymaker that laid the young bully out on a wood-block drafting table. That ended the bullying. It earned the respect and deference anew of the entire school for a teacher who was due both because of his age and position. The nickname he had been given would rarely be uttered again, despite his continued snuff-chewing habit. He would be *Mister* Sanders, and he would not have *his* shop class disrupted again.

High school basketball games were more exciting than Christmas to a kid. Every home game, especially on a Friday night, was so exciting you'd have thought the old gym in the school that is now special housing for seniors was Madison Square Garden. The gym would be packed as tight as a can of sardines, with young, small girls sitting two to a seat, the crowd spilling over into the aisles, and standing against back walls, while the bleachers on the stage were overloaded, too. If you wanted a good seat, you had to be in the gym before the start of the B-squad game at 6:30 p.m. Everybody in school and town went to that varsity game that was replayed over and over again at Geno's Tap Room until closing time or later, then replayed again the next morning at the coffee shops. It was that exciting, because the basketball was that good and that competitive.

This kind of competitive fire existed then because you were playing your neighbors, towns down the road 7 to 30 miles away, towns you had both competed against and cooperated with for years in many ways. Television wasn't that inviting or addictive then, and there was only one school activity going on that night. It was Game Night.

From time to time, there would be talk of making *the* state tournament, which was played at "the barn"–Williams Arena on the campus of the University of Minnesota. It was really big stuff, again because *one* state championship would be earned–not the four or five of the 2000s. With five "champions," you would really have no champion. But when you beat neighboring New Prague, Le Sueur, or Belle Plaine, it was a big deal, and when you ran a string of 10 or more wins against all your neighbors, the town couldn't help talking about a run into Williams Arena. The problem then was the competition: Larger and larger schools blocked your way in, first, district, then, regional tournaments. "One and done" was the rule. "Going all the way" was next-to impossible but an important part of the dream of youth. This was true for even the best of the teams, and Ken Hanson had several very good basketball teams in his tenure as coach at Jordan High School.

If you wanted to buy a new car in the 1950s, you went to the dealer, looked over *the* showroom vehicle and ordered what you wanted, using the showcased car and the color brochures as a guide. If you wanted to be loyal to your hometown, as most people were, you weren't locked into one make of automobile. In Jordan, you ordered a Ford from, first, Loren Haebegger, then, later, Werner Wolf, a Dodge from the Stang's, or a Chevrolet or Oldsmobile from Ben Engfer, where Tex Erickson, the great Jordan Brewer shortstop, worked. You could also buy a new DeSoto, Pontiac, Nash or Rambler from hometown dealers, too, for a number of years.

Everybody had a garden, a holdover from the "Victory Gardens" of the WWII years and the self-reliance ethic that persisted. You raised vegetables that you took for granted on the dinner table; extras were canned and stored for later consumption. You could never beat "Mom's home cooking."

Two-lane highways connected one community with another, while gravel roads connected farmers with their kinfolk in town. They brought commerce and trade to help fuel the life of small communities. Highway 169, like many other highways in other states, ran through the Minnesota River Valley towns, not around them. That meant business for the town's three hardware stores, and for restaurants like The Dutch Room Café, The Palace Café, The Broadway, and The Hamburger Home, as well as the bars.

Every fall, on Opening Day of the waterfowl season, then again on the pheasant opener, mothers forbade their kids to leave the yard. You might as well have been chained to the damned push lawn mower. The matter was not negotiable, even though the rest of the year all kids had the run of the town on foot or in and as far out of town as their little legs could pedal a bicycle. Traffic was bumper-to-bumper gridlock pretty much all day on The Opener, with city hunters taking to the country wetlands and fields with their bird dogs and shotguns. The skies in the early morning were filled with flock after flock of migrating waterfowl–mallards, pintails, gadwalls, teal mostly early in the fall, and then later the divers–the bluebills and the big canvasbacks incited the imagination and anticipation of bird hunting. It wasn't reality television that you watched. It was reality that you lived.

Arguably both every man's man for his outdoor pursuits and America's greatest writer of the 20th Century, Earnest Hemingway would reach the pinnacle of his acclaim, if not his talent, in the 1950s with a Pulitzer Prize in 1953 for his *The Old Man and the Sea*. The work about an old fisherman battling a big fish and Nature would help garner a Nobel Prize the following year, 1954, and Spencer Tracy would be nominated for Best Actor in the film adaptation in 1958. Naturalism and realism were hallmarks of his writing, in which the writer claimed to be trying to do what the Impressionist painter, Cezanne, did with his painting.

Hemingway, it was said, hung around with American baseball heroes. He liked to share a table and a cocktail with DiMaggio at Toots Shor's in Manhattan. He hunted with Cobb. The "Hemingway hero" had a code–*grace under pressure*–that we think he saw in the play of Joe DiMaggio.

We liked the bird hunting and wing shooting, too, with Frank relishing the same shotguns that had served his father so well–a Winchester Model 97 and a Winchester Model 12. He appreciated their solid hardware, their balance, the results they produced, and the mixture of memory and loss they could only hold for a son who had lost his father far too early, a boy who had lost his big brother even earlier. Shooting the guns that your father had shot was like a living, ongoing memorial to him and to wing shooting. We liked to shoot and to hunt with some of the same guys with whom we played ball. We liked to jump shoot mallards from the many and varied wetlands, potholes, sloughs, bogs, and swamps; from the creeks that emptied into the Minnesota River, and sometimes along or on the river itself.

You learned in the 1950s from your father, who had learned from his father; you hunted and fished for the pan. In the same way that a young pitcher learns how to pitch from a wizened old catcher, a boy learned to hunt and fish from his father and older brothers. There was a Scriptural basis to it in that you kept the bigger fish and threw back the smaller fish, unless you'd inadvertently hooked them deeply and hurt the fish while removing the hook. Similarly, you shot drake mallards and passed on the hens. You looked for a buck each whitetail deer season, passing on the does. Wasting fish and game was as much of a sacrilege in a beer-drinking baseball town as spilling a beer or a pitcher walking a batter with the bases loaded.

The ideal of individual stewardship seems today to have been far superior, at least more cost effective than modern government agency fish and game management. As a steward, you managed yourself. It was like golf in that there was no umpire or referee. Game wardens were scarce. Integrity and character were both built and revealed.

The Golden Age of Cinema coincided with that of baseball, ending in the early 1960s with the breaking down of the studio contract system. Much like the end to baseball's reserve clause, this gave stars the right to stroke their own egos while making themselves larger than the producers and directors, who gave them their opportunities to shine on camera. Willie Mays and Carl Yastrzemski were among baseball's stars who campaigned against Curt Flood's legal challenge of the reserve clause in baseball, according to Robert Weintraub in his notes to *The Victory Season*, and Hank Aaron, the author writes, said in 1971 that baseball would be destroyed by free agency.

Hollywood presented us with a showcase of great stars in the 1950s: Humphrey Bogart, Gary Cooper, Clark Gable and others would fade away as stars in this decade, while Frank Sinatra, Paul Newman, Marlon Brando, Grace Kelly, Elizabeth Taylor, Marilyn Monroe, and others would light their stars, becoming bigger than life. Humphrey Bogart, not Brad Pitt, Sean Penn, Johnny Depp, or any other more contemporary screen actor, would be named in 1999 as the greatest male star in the history of American cinema for his performances in films such as *Treasure of Sierra Madre*, *Casablanca*, *To Have and Have Not*, *The African Queen*, and *The Caine Mutiny*.

Our world of music would be rocked and rolled with the beginnings of the reign of The King. Elvis Presley's "Blue Suede Shoes," "Heartbreak Hotel," and "Jail-

House Rock" launched his career and introduced an entirely new genre of popular music. Sam Cooke, Little Richard, Jerry Lee Lewis, The Everly Brothers, and groups such as Buddy Holly and The Crickets followed closely with hit after hit of songs which played on vinyl discs that rotated on record players at 45 revolutions per minute.

The rpms of V-8 engines in cars that kept getting bigger fueled America's blooming love affair with the automobile in the 1950s. The muscle cars that came on in the early 1960s were the result of the marriage of horsepower to transmissions rather than noisy exhaust pipes and sound system subwoofers. The classic Ford Thunderbird was launched in 1955; the '57 Chevy would remain a collector's favorite forever.

Hugh Hefner's *Playboy* magazine, which all men claimed to subscribe to for its articles, would see its first issue in 1953. Airbrushing and less-than-the "full female Monty" poses left to the imagination what would be starkly revealed in coming years. It would be another decade before Gloria Steinem would launch *Ms. Magazine* and lead the Feminist Movement. Vatican II and The Ecumenical Movement in the Catholic Church were a decade away, too. Roe v. Wade, which made abortion-on-demand the law of the land, was handed down by the U.S. Supreme Court, with Minnesota's own Harry Blackmun, a Nixon appointee, writing the majority opinion in 1973. Homosexuality would be removed from the *DSM IV*, the standard-bearing psychiatric manual of disorders and treatments, in 1973. The next 40 years would reveal a closet more crowded than one would have thought possible. As even same-sex marriage gained legal status later, fewer and fewer people talked about what Scripture had to say on the matter, how the Author calls homosexuality "an abomination," not a sin, in several places. Nobody dared mention the science explained in "The Cat Study" at the Price-Pottinger Institute in the early 1960s, and the film that recorded the consequences of unnatural diets in three generations of alley cats seems to have been pulled from viewership. Even fewer people were aware of the entrance of excessive estrogen in the food chain and ecosystem since the advent of The Pill, first noticed in river fish downstream from large metropolitan areas where the hormones had been flushed. The fish couldn't reproduce. They had characteristics of both male and female fish.

Russia's Sputnik brought home the reality of a need to compete in space, and nuclear tests punctuated Cold War realities. School children would practice the government's survival plan by hunkering down under their wooden desks in classrooms everywhere. The Cuban Missile Crisis would test our young president's mettle and remind all that the Cold War could get terribly hot very quickly.

Fidel Castro would lead a revolution in Cuba and align his island nation, our neighbor just 90 miles away, with the old Soviet Union. That told us we weren't winning the battle against the Evil of Communism everywhere, which, we were told, was why we were stationing troops all over the world after the end of World War II. Somebody had to defend freedom in Asia and South America, we were constantly informed.

The New York Yankees defined the baseball era between 1947 and 1964 because they dominated the game, winning 15 pennants and 10 World Series Championships in the 18 years. Mickey Mantle would win baseball's Triple Crown in 1956, and Ted Williams, at age 38, would make a run at another .400 season in 1957; he'd finish at .388.

Baseball was king. The game has been called the metaphor of life and "a peacetime sport," and, indeed, it flourished at all levels after World War II like never before. In the small towns along the Minnesota River Valley, you followed your team, the Brooklyn, then Los Angeles, Dodgers via its AAA farm team, the St. Paul Saints, who played at Lexington Park until they moved into Midway Stadium, and you read the *St. Paul Pioneer Press's* sports pages every day. If you were a Giants' fan, you went to, first, Nicollet Park in South Minneapolis, then the original Metropolitan Stadium in Bloomington to watch the Minneapolis Millers. You followed the ballplayers you saw make it to the big club in New York, then San Francisco, or Boston, in the *Minneapolis Morning Tribune* and the afternoon *Star*. Among the most notable ballplayers to ever wear Miller uniforms were Ted Williams, Willie Mays, and Carl Yastrzemski. Most people, however, rode the big bandwagon; they were Yankee fans, and the broadcast of their games could be found on the radio.

Every chance you could, you played the game that you watched and learned to love. You played catch with yourself by throwing balls against steps, working the bounce to give you a chance to catch as well as throw. You threw balls against painted or chalked sides of barns and sheds and garages, or you found a brother or a buddy with whom to play your own game of "Giants vs. Dodgers" in the backyard.

You would learn more about yourself and your fellow man at the ballpark than any other venue in life. You learned whom you could count on in tough situations. You learned whom you wanted to bat with men on base, whom you wanted the inning-ending ground ball to go to, and whom you couldn't even trust to lay a sacrifice bunt down to move a runner into scoring position. You knew who the ace of your pitching staff was, who came up big in big games, and you wanted him on the mound in The Big Game.

You would learn later that many who never found their way to the diamond in a pair of spikes could talk the game with the beer they drank, but their bombast never jived with the reality you knew from the field of actual experience. They "talked the talk," but they didn't *know*. They were just blowhards. You learned the game, like everything else, by learning to "walk the walk."

The "It Girl," Clara Bow, would give way to, first, Garbo and Harlow, then Grable and Hayworth. Marilyn Monroe took that whole thing to new levels in the 1950s, and only long after her death and that of President Kennedy did we learn of just how high in the nation's hierarchy, with national security and all, she did take it in the early 60s. Joe DiMaggio would place a dozen roses on his ex-wife's grave every week. But he would refuse to speak to, or even acknowledge, the Kennedy's after Marilyn's death in 1962 from a reported overdose of sleeping pills.

Jordan, like all the Minnesota River Valley towns in the 1950s, and, indeed, like all towns across America, began to change. Many self-sustaining communities like Jordan would turn into bedroom communities. People resided in the little towns, but they worked in the larger cities. That put an even greater premium on the automobile. The expansion of debt that occurred after World War II in the country fueled consolidation of businesses and industries. Whether intentional or not, a consequence was increased government regulation and ever-increasing bureaucracies to administer the regulations. These were instilled to ostensibly protect the people from rapacious businessmen, landlords, and the captains of industry who had built the country, with politicians and "the government" coming along for the ride, then assuming control and "leadership" once the pioneering and heavy lifting work had been done.

The Jordan Brewery, whose "Old Style" tap beer was, according to one late, long-time Jordan resident, "the best beer I've ever had in my life," would close for good after a series of different owners in the late 1940s. "They just couldn't get it going again after The War," he said. Despite the lifting of the government's rationing of the grains essential to brewing beer, the small-town brewery, like many others of the same size (capacity–40,000 barrels a year) and outstanding quality, couldn't compete with the large brewing houses in Minneapolis, St. Paul, Milwaukee, and St. Louis. Mass marketing with virtually unlimited advertising budgets and better trucks and highways spurred the growth of large brewers. The three catwalks across Sand Creek and the highway from the brewery were gone. They had allowed brewery workers to wheel kegs of beer across the creek to serve to county fair goers, dance pavilion patrons, and fans at the ballpark. "I have never seen a beer with as creamy a head that would hold as that one," the old timer said.

After the bottling house "was built in 1935 or '36" we remember the old timer, a former employee himself, saying that the brewery would employ 25 to 30 workers. Men lined up for jobs, because the perks were so good. In a beer-drinking town, free beer could cause a riot, and you could drink all the beer you wanted as long as you kept up on the job. This was long before the behavioral health profession identified "functional alcoholism" for what it is. Al Woerdehoff's alleged record consumption of 72 longneck bottles of beer on a 12-hour shift would never be challenged, and the ball club, spawned and at one time sponsored by the business with a quality product across Sand Creek, would keep its name, "The Brewers."

The brewery would close, but the creamery that produced a good quality of butter and milk would stay open a few more years, employing about 20 workers in the small-town cooperative enterprise. The meat markets continued to do good business. Frank Pekarna would take over his family business from his father, Joe. But Ronnie Langer would fold up his family's tent and sell the family recipes to one of the large meatpacking houses in South St. Paul.

Before Jack Buss ruled the barber business in the town, parents had choices where to get their kids' heads buzzed: Rose Bush, mother of four ball-playing sons, two of whom, Rotz and Jim, were standouts for Jordan and Marystown, would cut your hair for two-bits in her kitchen. Jack Bauer, an old ballplayer and father of the great, one-eyed fast pitch softball pitcher and the quarterback on the undefeated 1936 Jordan Hubmen football team, Bud Bauer, had a real barber pole and a real barber's chair in a real barber shop attached to his house. He'd buzz you for a half a buck.

The Jordan Theatre was showing first-run movies, and Levi Morlock, who must have had either an eating disorder or a problem with his thyroid gland, would have the only reserved seat in the house. It was rumored that he was pushing 500 pounds, and the owners of the theater removed a n armrest in a seat to accommodate him with a double seater. Nobody complained of the special treatment. Room was made for the big guy.

The Gold Spot Dairy, run by Matt Bush and his sons, Bill and Bob, then Mike, too, included a milk route in which glass bottles of milk and cream were delivered each morning to the doorsteps of its customers. The convenience store had candy, pop, and various ice cream treats. A nickel got you a large, single-scoop ice cream cone. A dime got you two scoops. In contrast, a visit to an ice cream shop in Bloomington, "Scoops," in the spring of 2015 lightened the billfold by $5.25 for a double dip waffle cone. But the bonanza in the 1950s, for two bits, was a monster malted milk at the Gold Spot. It was the place, as a kid, to hang out before and after baseball in the summer, and you would buy and trade baseball cards there, too.

Lee Radermacher would begin his grocery store empire working for his father, Roman, at the old Red Owl grocery store on Water Street just down from Ruppert's Bar in the 1950s. Three other grocery stores and Sunder's General, where you could get just about anything, competed for the business of the town. You bought Lee jeans for $3.99 and Levi's for $4.99 at Sunder's then, and Paul Sunder would special order Converse sneakers for you for about $5.00 a pair, and Converse hip boots for around $20.00. At least three of the five grocery stores delivered their goods to customers at no extra charge.

Without ever using the term, Jordan, like every other river town, supported early versions of "sports bars." Counting Wagner's Supper Club, a private affair that is now a mortuary outside of the north end of town, and the J&W Tavern to the south on Hwy 169, which is now the site of the Jordan Supper Club, you could get at least a beer, if not hard liquor, at 10 establishments. The speakeasies of the Prohibition Era, which served "near beer" legally for its patrons to spike with the illegal Canadian contraband or local moonshine, had long ago shut down with the end of Prohibition. But The Tap Room from the Jordan Brewery, where Upshe Libra honored the second of two beer tickets in a bottomless 16-ounce copper stein of "Old Style" beer after work every day, survived in name on main street in what was "Mertz Tap Room," "Geno's & Gibby's," then "Geno's Tap Room."

Sports thrived in Geno's. Referees and umpires, for example, would cash their checks here after the games they officiated in the various neighboring towns. Fans would gather to re-play and argue the games they had just viewed. Patrons on the nights of Scott County's annual fair, maybe after the professional wrestling card in front of the grandstand, or after the local tug-of-war contests, would crowd three- and four-deep at the bar to get an order in for a beer or a cocktail. Patrons in the back room might visit in quieter booths or dance if music were provided. On Saturday mornings and most afternoons and early evenings, before the state government made gambling legal and got into it in a big way with its lotteries and pull tabs, and especially with its special exemption to the Indian community, you could find illegal gaming action of all kinds: "six-five-four" and "horses" with dice; euchre, cribbage, and poker with cards were all played for serious stakes. One, two, and ten-dollar "boards" were common games of chance for important sporting events like the Rose Bowl. Patrons didn't look at it as gambling. It was more like participation in the sporting event. Somehow the gambling helped to morph them from spectators into players. Nor did the house take off the top what is known as a vigorish, or "vig," as is the practice to this day with sports bookmakers and the state. Sports bars then ran a cleaner game with 100 percent payout. Their "take" was the business that the action brought to the house.

The bars would sponsor softball teams, first fast-pitch, then, later, slow-pitch, a game that provided wide participation, until rapidly advancing bat technology and administrative excess were rumored to have killed it. They'd pay the entry fees for bowling leagues and buy the bowling team members special shirts that identified them as the sponsor. A couple of the bars encouraged their patrons to have fish fries and frog leg feeds in their back rooms. These would usually be spontaneous social affairs, as you could never guarantee the fish. You had to catch and clean them, then prepare them.

Weymie Kerkow, a block layer by trade, handled 12-inch concrete blocks, two at a time like dominoes all day. He built basements for a living; in fact, he and his crew put up many of the original foundations for the homes in Apple Valley, MN, working for Orin Thompson. His union had negotiated, and his employer then required, all block-laying crews to lay a specific number of concrete blocks, maybe 300, each five-day workweek. Weymie would laugh years later when he told how he and each of his crew, having reached the union quota of 1,500 blocks laid for the week, would wrap up their lines and clean their mud boards, mixers, and trawls at noon–on Thursdays, then drink beer for the next day and a half onsite in a basement hole whose last five courses would be laid the next Monday when the block count began anew. If the employers were cheated out of a fair day's work for a fair day's pay, thanks to the labor union, that same union would be cheated out of the control of its members working scab jobs on summer nights and weekends for cash.

The absurdity of the union rule is matched by the 100-pitch practice in baseball today and the managing of a starting pitcher's length of service. The thinking is that it saves pitchers' arms. Maybe it does, and maybe it doesn't. Especially when you remember Warren Spahn at age 42 throwing over 200 pitches in a 1963 game against the San Francisco Giants before Willie Mays beat him in the bottom of the 16th inning with a solo homerun. You can read about Walter ("Big Train") Johnson pitching both games of a doubleheader in the 1920s for the Washington Senators. You can check the records of the other great pitchers' complete games as well: Robin Roberts, Bob Gibson, Sandy Koufax, Steve Carlton, Bob Feller and others at the Major League level. Part of the ethic of pitching, whether national or local, professional or amateur ball, was that you finished what you started. At least, you wanted to, and you tried to finish. The game was never played as if there were a tomorrow. The point is that Thoroughbreds are made to run, and you don't hobble a good horse when he's running well. You give him more rein and more oats.

"It was the Golden Age of Everything," Jerry Stahl, retired Minneapolis advertising executive, said of the 1950s and 60s over a beer in Zeke's Grill & Tap across Old Shakopee Road from Bloomington's Dred Scott Fields. Stahl was a member of the 1960 Minneapolis Washburn High School state championship baseball team and the starting shortstop on the school's state runner-up team in 1961. He had moved from Huron, S.D., where he grew up and lived baseball, to Minneapolis in 1957–in time to experience the beginnings of the distractions that diverted attention from the game.

Like baseball, "Business was fun in the old days," Stahl reminisced. He spent over 40 years serving the advertising needs of major clients such as Harley Davidson, 3-M, Polaris, and National Car, but fun was being 23 or 24 years old, selling advertising for *LIFE Magazine*, who gave Stahl memberships in the Edina Country Club and the Minneapolis Athletic Club downtown in order to schmooze with business executives and initiate the sale of advertising. He said he was given tickets with which to entertain clients for Super Bowl III in the Orange Bowl in Miami, Florida–the January 12, 1969, game Joe Namath "guaranteed" his AFL New York Jets would win despite being heavy underdogs to the powerful Baltimore Colts of the National Football League. Stahl took clients to Cape Canaveral to view rocket launches of the Apollo Program, which took America to the moon. He said he hosted clients at America's Cup–yachting off the coasts of New York and Rhode Island, too. It was all done with company expense accounts, and it was all tax deductible, which made it easier for companies to justify while it helped to spur business growth and overall economic strength in the country.

"There were many Fortune-500 businesses headquartered in Minneapolis back then," Stahl said. "Probably twice as many as there are today," he said. Major national magazines like *Readers' Digest*, *Look Magazine*, as well as *LIFE*, had offices here in order to be close to those potential clients.

"Business was just done on a whole different level," Stahl said. With all the decision makers in town at their corporate headquarters, a young salesman needed a big expense account just to be able to get close to executives. "The economy was just so different then," he said, adding, "In the 50s, if you represented a quality publication like *LIFE*, all you had to do was show up."

"The 1950s to early 60s," Stahl said, "was the last great era of patriotism, morality, law-and-order, and respect for family." By the late 1960s, he thought, nearing the end of The Golden Age of Baseball, these were all in the process of being lost with the upending of society that occurred with the Women's Movement, the Anti-War Movement, and other strong sociological forces. With the continued consolidation of business and industry, Minneapolis lost some corporations, and some businesses that weren't doing so well replaced their "players" with more serious people. "They wanted results," Stahl admitted. Some of the fun went out of the business game with that. With the decision makers of major client businesses out of town, you had to deal with "the committee," too, Stahl said, in reference to the frustrating need of dealing with a handful of managers and directors rather than the company president, as he had done in the past. "They weren't empowered to make the decisions that needed to be made," Stahl said, "and you dealt with an endless series of meetings rather than a definitive, 'Okay, let's do it.'"

The Bosses of Jordan baseball in the 1950s were Sid Nolden, a mortician by trade; Frank Hilgers Sr., who had resumed a teaching and coaching career after the close of the brewery; Ben Engfer, the Oldsmobile-Chevrolet dealer; Bill Breimhorst, who worked for the state highway department; and Max Casey, the venerable "Voice of the Brewer's" and the postmaster after a long apprenticeship working for his father, John E. Casey, editor and publisher of the *Jordan Independent*. They were old ballplayers, with the exception of maybe Ben Engfer and Max, who was the veritable wizard behind the baseball curtain. They knew people. They were connected. They were the movers and shakers. They were the Baseball Bosses. One of them, Bill Breimhorst, according to Tom Melchior in *Scott County Baseball*, was responsible for signing Jim Pollard, star forward on the Minneapolis Laker basketball team, who wanted to play baseball during the summers while working on his college degree at the University of Minnesota. He was the main attraction on the Brewer team for six years. When he didn't pitch, he usually played first or third base, occasionally shortstop when Tex Erickson was hurt, as well as second base and the outfield. He usually batted cleanup, and he hit a ton. His homeruns were towering blasts. Most significantly, there was no throttling back in Pollard's competitiveness between his play for the NBA Minneapolis Lakers and the Jordan Brewers.

Pitching was 80 percent of the game before the Metal Bat Era that invaded baseball in the 1970s. The springboard, or "trampoline," effect created in the metal bats, and proven in actual comparative studies, would turn routine groundballs into base hits and what would normally have been equally routine fly balls into doubles off the wall and homeruns over it. It was the same technology that made "big hitters" out of mediocre drivers of the golf ball, adding 50 to 100 yards or more to tee shots with a driver.

A major factor when comparing and ranking hitters in or between any periods of time is the metal bat. According to Arlington's Dave Hartmann, longtime catcher and umpire in amateur baseball, the metal bats came into use about 1973 and were allowed until 2001 in state amateur baseball. A baseball purist, Jim Stoll said he didn't like the metal bats that were just beginning to invade baseball about the time he was winding down his playing days in the early to mid-1970s. "I hated the noise they made," Stoll said, "and I couldn't *feel* the ball with 'em. I went back to wood. With wood, you know what you've got when you hit the ball, because you can feel it."

"When the metal bats first came out in the early 70s, they weren't very good," Hartmann said. "But they were *really* something later. The ball just jumped off those Easton bats."

"The metal bats meant a difference of 100 points in my batting average," Hartmann said. "I hit over .400, maybe .450, with that Easton metal bat, when the best I hit with wood was maybe .320."

"One year in the playoffs against Sleepy Eye, there were four or five of us using the same bat," Hartmann said, "and the bat boy broke it hitting rocks." We all switched to another bat that was a little bigger, longer, and heavier, with a bigger barrel. We choked up a little on it, and we hit nine homeruns with it. I hit three myself," Hartmann said, in the game he remembered winning something like 18-4. "It was the bat," he said, "an Easton 35-33."

"Let's just look at some numbers," Hartmann said. "The total batting average for the 2013 Minnesota State Tournament, Class B, was .242. For Class C, it was .235." By comparison, the continuously improving technology during the "Metal Bat Era" produced state tournament batting averages that were "routinely over .300," according to Hartmann. The metal bat made the same joke of America's pastime at the amateur level that steroids and human growth hormone made of

Major League Baseball. Scores in town team and collegiate level baseball resembled the scores of slow-pitch softball.

Imagine the batting averages and homeruns that technology produced during the regular seasons when good hitters faced patty-cake pitchers serving up lollipops. Turbo Tee-Ball might have described it. We can only imagine what hitters like Jim Pollard, John Freund, Jake Harsh, Jim Kubes, Pat Devitt, and Jim Stoll would have done had they been swinging that Easton metal bat against practice game pitching.

"The best hitter I ever played *against*," Hartmann said, "was Lew Olson at Dundas. I think he hit 38 homeruns in maybe 40 games one year, probably 1981, with the metal bat. He had really quick hands. His problem was his weight."

"Now, we're back to real baseball with the wood," Hartmann said, and the averages and homerun numbers reflect it.

Metal bats meant more balls getting through the infield for singles because of the greater velocity they generated. More balls were driven harder, because of the technology–the sweet spot on a metal bat could have been from the fists to the tip of the bat. The CM, or center of motion, of metal bats, was shown, independent of bat weight, to permit a hitter to swing the club faster. Greater bat speed, coupled with the springboard effect from compression and rebound that occurred with metal bats, some dramatically significant in comparison to wood, resulted in what looked to be better hitting, with more scoring and more excitement. Weak hitters were made to look good, good hitters great, particularly against the "batting practice pitchers" inevitably faced in tournaments and late-season makeup games. Moreover, there were no Pat Devitt's, John Freund's, Jim Stoll's, Lefty Weckman's, Johnny Garbett's, or Jim Pollard's pitching in the Minnesota River Valley towns anymore. No, pitchers of this quality were in at least the minor leagues, if not the bigs, by the time the 1980s rolled around, with torn rotator cuffs in shoulders and ligaments in elbows repaired with surgery. Baseball expansion meant more opportunities for more baseball players, even if it reduced quality at all levels. Blowhards of the day will argue one exception or another, but it's an economic Law of Nature that the more you create of something, the more you dilute the quality of the individual units. Quality of play, quality of the game, suffers. It's as true of baseball as it is of economics and the printing of money to "pay" for something. The naysayers are everywhere, but it's a good thing that the alchemists didn't succeed in turning bricks, stones, or doorknobs into gold. That's a sure way to destroy the value of real gold.

Ty Cobb stole home 54 times in his Major League career. By comparison, a generation later, Jackie Robinson stole home 19 times in a much shorter career it is true, but Paul Molitor, even later, managed just 10 successful steals of home in his 21-year, Hall-of-Fame career.

As for the exciting inside-the-park homerun, when Ty Cobb won the Triple Crown in 1909 with nine homeruns to go with his .377 average and 107 RBIs, all nine of the homeruns were inside-the-park jobs. The last leg of an inside-the-parker, third to home, would have every fan in the house on his feet as if home plate were the finish line at Kentucky's Churchill Downs on Derby Day. Likewise, triples are vanishing from the game. The all-time Major League leaders in triples played a century ago! Teammates Sam Crawford and Ty Cobb of the Detroit Tigers hit 309 and 297 triples, respectively, in their careers. By contrast, slugger-burner Willie Mays hit 140 in his career, and still later, Rod Carew hit 112. Baltimore's great modern day slugging shortstop, Cal Ripken, hit 44 triples in a 21-year career that ended after 2001. The career 100-triple Major League ballplayer is becoming rare.

Bringing the "Dead Ball Era" to a close by requiring the replacement of scuffed, doctored, and dirty balls after the beaning death of Ray Chapman changed the game immensely in 1920. So did the cork-centered ball and the tighter winding of better wool inside the red-stitched horsehide cover, and the protective batting helmet crusade after the career-ending fractured skull suffered by Mickey Cochrane from another bean ball in 1937.

We grew up without the requirement for a protective helmet, although it gradually made its way into the game, beginning with a simple plastic insert you put inside your cap that afforded about as much protection as the letter-logo on the crown of the baseball cap. The big push for real protection came from Little League Baseball, and it was well warranted, because pitchers were coached to pitch inside with tailing, skull-busting fastballs. The "brush-back" pitch helped to set up breaking balls, and they kept hitters from digging in as if they were on the tee box on the first hole of a golf course. The knockdown pitch was another matter altogether. It was a pitcher's signature on a contract that was negotiated with every hitter in the box. It was payback for a perceived slight by an opponent. Brush-back and knockdown pitches were part of the game. In fact, Weintraub notes that in the 1940s Cub pitchers once knocked down an amazing 15 consecutive Dodger hitters. The game was mostly pitching then–at least 80 percent, according to Connie Mack, baseball owner and icon of the 1900s, and, "Pitching is the art of instilling fear," according to Hall of Fame lefthander Sandy Koufax.

Slowly, the fear factor was diminished with, first, requiring umpires to keep new, white balls in play rather than the ball the game was started with regardless of its condition, then the protective helmet, and with restrictions on the high hard one. The pitching mound was lowered officially five inches, and the strike zone shrunk to the size of the batter's wheelhouse in 1969, neither one of which is common knowledge among today's fans and even modern players. Were it common knowledge, Mark Hess, who was as good and as knowledgeable a ballplayer as played the game since 1980, would have known. We asked him; he didn't know about either change. Both changes aided the batter immensely. The designated hitter (DH) rule got another real bat into the lineup and took what was usually an easy out for the pitcher away from him. It took some of the managing away from managers, too. It effectively changed a nine-man game into a ten-man game.

The end of the "Dead Ball Era" came just in time for Babe Ruth's transition from a pitcher to a full-time outfielder and, most importantly, to a slugger of authentic historic proportions. The baseballs in play were no longer dirtied, sullied beanbags by the third inning. Indeed, Ruth would hammer 54 homeruns in 1920 and follow that with 59 the next year in seasons of 154 games to usher in The Roaring Twenties on the diamond.

From 1903 on, the official baseball pitcher's mound could be no greater than 15 inches higher than home plate. That standard was lowered five inches to no greater than 10 inches higher than home plate in 1969. Hitters gained the advantage that pitchers lost. A lower mound meant less leg leverage and throwing thrust. Less leverage and thrust resulted in less velocity and torque on the pitches. Couple that with the metal bats and a significantly reduced strike zone, and you've got Homerun Derby for nine innings. It wasn't baseball.

Most, but not all, great pitching became merely good pitching; good pitching became mediocre pitching; and mediocre pitching became even a weak hitter's meat. Jim Pollard, at somewhere between 6-5 and 6-7 in height, must have looked like Goliath to Minnesota River Valley hitters in the 1950s from the mound that was then 15 to 20 inches higher than home plate. Yes, teams at all levels cheated. Especially if they were pitcher rich. At his height and with his skills, Jim Pollard was an imposing figure. He played large, and he had the "right stuff" to go with it, although intermittent arm problems kept him from reaching the consistency of greatness he was capable of achieving as a pitcher.

The strike zone was under almost constant attack, too, in still more effort to take away the domination of pitching and give more excitement to fans bored with "good baseball." What had once been an area bounded by the top of the shoulders and the bottom of the knees, or even lower to a good, "pitcher's umpire," the strike zone had shrunk to the point of the letters on the uniform to the top of the knees–the hitters' wheelhouse.

Metal bats, first all-aluminum, then alloys, then composites, were introduced into all levels other than professional baseball around the late 1960s to early 1970s. It was partly an effort to save money from the long-standing problem of costly cracked wooden bats, but it didn't take long for everybody stepping up to the plate to feel like a real slugger. And the technology just kept getting better. If baseball became a caricature of itself, softball got worse. They had to make up absurd rules to contain the game that the parks couldn't: Hitting a homerun became an automatic out.

Batting averages soared, homeruns increased dramatically, and the fun in the game of slow-pitch softball was stolen to revive the dying game of baseball in small towns. Indeed, for upwards of 20 years or more, small town amateur, high school, and college baseball scores resembled the typical scores being rung up in softball beer leagues. The metal bat brought the excitement back to the large diamond, but it wasn't the same game. Even Charlie Larca, who managed the Jordan Brewers for 24 years, winning over 600 games and three state championships in that span and who was a huge beneficiary of the metal bat because of the hitting strength of his teams, had this to say about it in *Scott County Baseball*:

> Aluminum bats suck. That's not baseball. Metal bats are the most detrimental thing to ever happen to baseball.

It was baseball but with another asterisk–just like the designated hitter, or DH, rule. They might as well have brought the fences in another 50 feet. Baseball, which had forever been known as a game of 80-percent pitching, would morph into a sort of parody of the much maligned and ridiculed slow-pitch softball. Double-digit run scoring became common, but the players and diehard fans were delighted with the action. After all, nothing was more boring in an age of buffet-style instant gratification than what had always defined "good baseball"–the pitchers' duel and a 2-1 ballgame. People wanted action, even if it meant a caricature of the game.

Maybe, along with easy, abundant money, and even easier credit, replacing good, boring games with the go-go version of ball were why shopping slowly replaced baseball as the nation's pastime.

Penn State Professor of Physics Daniel A. Russell, Ph.D., has analyzed and concluded what every ballplayer who has ever swung a bat at a baseball or softball knows: You get significantly more "pop" with a metal bat than you do with a wooden bat. While you must learn to drive a ball with a wooden bat, the balls "jump" off of metal and composite bats as a result of the springboard effect built into the bat. Moreover, there is a greater margin for the error of a mishit with metal. Citing a 2001 scientific study, Russell definitively concludes the following reasons why:

- Metal bats can be swung faster.
- Metal bats have the "trampoline" effect.
- Metal bats have larger sweet spots.
- Metal bats don't break.

Scientists, not beer-stand blowhards or old ballplayers, studied the physics involved with the different bats. Indeed, Russell writes the following:

> The most comprehensive study comparing metal and wood bats under realistic playing conditions that I have come across was published by Crisco and Greenwald. Their study involved actual players swinging bats at pitched balls in a batting cage. A total of 19 players (nine minor-leaguers, six NCAA college, four high school) participated in the study, swinging two wood bat models, and five different metal bat models (6 bats of each model). High-speed video was used to obtain a 3-D map of the bat swing, locating the trajectory of several points on the bat and ball before, during, and after impact. Video data was then analyzed to obtain batted ball speeds. The results, summarized in (a figure included in the online article) show conclusively that metal bats outperform wood bats.

Babe Ruth swung as heavy a wooden bat as has ever been used in Major League Baseball, with a 154-game season, and without performance-enhancing drugs. But maybe juiced balls should mark the genesis of asterisk baseball.

Roger Maris was given a 162-game season in 1961 to break Ruth's homerun record of 60 in a 154-game season in 1927. He deserves the double asterisk (more games, expansion team pitching) just as Bonds, Canseco, McQuire, Sosa, and others–pumped up biophysically on performance-enhancing steroids and human growth hormones–would be allowed to make a mockery of the standards of greatness. Asterisk baseball, like "reality television" and a nation's GDP ballooned by 70 percent consumer spending with credit, not cash, wasn't the same as the real thing. Saying that it is, or pretending that it is, because some aspirants want it to be so, just doesn't make it so.

Without the juicing of balls and hot bats or the availability of steroids, Babe Ruth in 1921, and Mickey Mantle in 1960, would retain the Guinness Book record for the longest homeruns ever hit. Both, free of steroids and HGH, launched balls out of Detroit Stadium with wooden bats, with the Baseball Hall of Fame settling on Ruth's shot at 575 feet as the longest after re-calculating Mantle's blast that had earlier been put at the record of 643 feet.

In the middle of the 1949 baseball season, the Baseball Bosses of Jordan brought a right-handed pitcher with a professional pedigree, "Bullet" Bob Shotliff, to town with the promise of a job that was eventually fulfilled at Continental Machines in Savage, Minnesota. How good was Shotty? He threw a 12-strikeout no-hitter to beat New Prague on June 25, 1952. In his very next start, July 7, he nearly repeated the masterpiece against the LeCenter Chiefs, who had won the Class-A State Championship in 1950 and finished second in 1951. Shotty lost his bid for two-in-a-row on a single in the ninth inning.

Some would say he just got lucky. But a financial statement of the Jordan Baseball Association, Inc., from 1950 indicates that Bob Shotliff was the highest-paid player on the roster. He was paid more money to play for the Brewers that summer than NBA superstar and Brewer legend Jim Pollard. The JBA Balance Sheet from the following year, 1951, indicates that player salaries were cut from $4,398 to $3,617, with Shotliff's pay reduced from $1,280 to $768, putting him behind Pollard that season. These figures represent above-the-table payments. There is good reason to suspect that some players were paid under-the-table as well. This stealth compensation could have come from individuals or a consortium of well-meaning baseball people. It could have come in the form of cash, a job, a car, a loan, or maybe a referral. It was done to lure and to keep specific ballplayers.

Some folks said that they got the sweetest little lefty you could ever imagine, Johnny Garbett, to come to Jordan for one-half ownership in The Corner Bar. Garbett became available after a couple others didn't work out, when Benson-DeGraf in the hot Class-AA West Central League folded half way into the 1953 season. Garbett was called a Boy Wonder in American Legion baseball as a 16-year-old kid. He would go 8-3 the first year, a half season at Jordan, then win 15 games with an ERA of 1.70 for the Brewers in the 1954 season, according to a synopsis in *Scott County Baseball*. Old timers talked about his curveball, until they talked about Weckman's curveball five years later. He could drop it off a table, or make it look like it was coming in from first base. When hitters were waiting for his curveball, he'd pop a tailing fastball that invariably caught them looking. And he could bring it. With his NBA pedigree, everybody always talked about Jim Pollard's pitching. But people who were closest to the scene, like Brewer second baseman Dick Nolden, readily admit that Johnny Garbett was the best pitcher on those early 1950s Brewer baseball teams. Playing together for two years, they brought Minnesota River League championships and trips to the Minnesota Class-A State Tournament in 1953 and again in 1954, despite the best efforts of the league to break them up by changing the residency rules at the winter meetings.

Granted, state tournament participation is a mark of distinction regardless of class or size of field. But let's be clear: (1) Comparisons between and among players and teams of the same and different eras are inevitable; (2) We're interested here in the reasons for calling baseball played between about 1947 and at least 1964, if not 1972, "The Golden Age of Baseball; (3) Qualifying for a state tournament berth between 1980 and 2015 wasn't anything like the dogfights they needed to win just to get in the tournament in the 1950s; (4) Class, or level, of divisional participation also means a lot; (5) Metal bat technology meant far more to performance than we could ever have imagined, as did pitching mound heights and strike zones. Quality of baseball can also be measured by its popularity, as measured by the number of fans reported in attendance. Ty Cobb, after all, said it: "The crowd makes the ballgame."

It's probably impossible to get a true apples-to-apples and oranges-to-oranges comparison for a number of reasons. But *Town Ball, The Glory Days of Minnesota Amateur Baseball*, by Armand Peterson and Tom Tomashek, is of considerable help. For example, they tell us that town ball in Minnesota peaked in the year 1950, with 799 teams playing amateur baseball in Minnesota. The website for the Minnesota Baseball Association, which is the governing body for amateur baseball in Minnesota, says that in 2012, there were "over 300 teams competing in three classes -Class A (44), Class B (32), and Class C (234)."

The state tournament pairings for 2013 included 4 teams for Class A in a double-elimination tournament; 8 teams for Class B; and 48 teams in a bloated Class C tournament. "What are they trying to do, destroy the game?" Jim Stoll would ask rhetorically of what he called, "My World Series."

The 1950 Minnesota State Amateur Baseball Tournament, held at St. Cloud's Municipal Stadium, according to *Town Ball*, also had three different classes of tournament play: 12 teams in Class AA; 8 teams in Class A; and 16 teams in Class B. Out of a total of 799 ball clubs, just 36 teams in three classes (4 percent) made it to the state tournament in 1950, whereas in 2014, 48 teams out of a total of 224 Class-C ball clubs (21 percent) made the state tournament, according to Dave Hartmann. That was just for one lowest class, Class C, which didn't even exist in the 1950s. Nobody then would have wanted to play down to that level. They even resisted going down to Class B, because they wanted to play and present a better brand of ball throughout the summer.

This "class and bracket creep" didn't happen overnight. In 1959, for example, consisting of two classes, the state tournament, again in St. Cloud, fielded 27 teams in total (7 in Class A; 20 in Class B) (5%), out of a total of about 520 teams in the state (about 60 Class A and 460 Class B Teams). According to the reporting in *Town Ball*, "Attendance at the 1959 state tournament in St. Cloud was 21,454, down almost 5,000 from the totals at the 1958 tournament held in New Ulm. It was to be the last time the state tournament exceeded 20,000 fans.

Why?

Peterson and Tomashek attempt to explain the reasons for the demise of state amateur baseball, which includes competition from other entertainment avenues, the mobility factor with the automobile and highways, expansion of Major League Baseball, including the presence of the Minnesota Twins in 1961, and television in particular. But they fail to even mention the strongest correlation of all, the most intrinsic factor itself; namely, the gradual degradation of the quality of baseball. The Golden Age of Baseball slowly ended. Bracket and class creep were happening, too. Teams were managing their way into the tournament rather than battling their way in.

Perhaps most significantly, at least during the early years of The Golden Age of Baseball, towns and teams and players seemed to want to "play up." Today and increasingly since the ending of this Golden Age, it looks like they want to "play down." In the old days, Jack hunted down the Giant; David sought Goliath and slew him. The tiny town of DeGraff, for example, with a population of fewer than 300 people earned berths in the Class A State Tournament four times from 1940 through 1945, according to *Town Ball*. In 1948, they played in the West Central League and played up to Class AA with the league in 1949. Atwater and Lake Lillian also had fewer than 1,000 people in their towns but played up in the Class-AA West Central League.

Delavan (population 302), Winsted (941), Watertown (837), and Kiester (541) played up. Delavan would beat Jordan (population about 1,400) and its great lefthander, Johnny Garbett, 1-0, in the first game of the eight-team, 1953 Class-A State Tournament. They would go on to win the championship.

Put simply, if you change the format of state tournaments, whether they be Minnesota high school basketball, or Minnesota amateur baseball, such that 36 teams out of 800 (4.5 percent) *earn* a seat at the table in one era, while 60 teams out of 300 (20%) are given admission in another era, you have a field of comparison that is one of apples to raisins. Conclusions about the "roll of the raisins," based solely on numbers, then, are a distortion of reality. They are a lie. Making it to the state tournament, or winning the state tournament, therefore, means one thing in one era and something else altogether in a later era of revisionism. The truth is that value, or quality, of baseball is diluted by such artificial means of propping things up. Teams making the state tournament are playing for the gold. But "all that glitters is not gold." With an arm and a bat of true gold, in spite of a torn rotator cuff in his right shoulder, Stoll played up in the 1969 Class B State Tournament at Jordan. He beat the highly favored "gods of Mount Olympus," the Prior Lake Jays, holding them to one unearned run and just five hits, three of which were infield bleeders, in the championship game and earning the MVP award for the second time in three years.

So why did The Golden Age of Baseball end? Maybe the ending had more to do with life than it did with baseball. For if, "Life was baseball, and baseball was life," then each influenced the other immensely. Baseball was the perfect microcosm of life, and life reflected all of baseball. After all, salesmen didn't give presentations to would-be customers; they *pitched* their products and services. When base runners occupied every base during a ball game, the sacks were *full*, *loaded*, and even *drunk*. Relief pitchers were *firemen*. Outfielders roamed *pastures*; infielders and outfielders with good throwing arms had *guns* or *rifles*. Pitchers threw *bullets* and *bb's*, *heat*, *gas*, and *flame*; managers were *pilots* or *skippers*. Misbehaving children weren't disciplined; they *caught* hell from teachers, coaches, and parents; estimates provided in any field on any subject are still today *ballpark* numbers. Maybe our most relevant example here with how our language became imbued with baseball vernacular is the expectation we have of ourselves and others when it's our turn, when it's time to *get off the bench*, when it's important that somebody do something, or at least try: We say that he needs to *step up to the plate*.

Maybe the things going on in society affected baseball to such an extent that the glitter wore off. Maybe it wasn't the long ball, the end of the dead ball, the shorter fences, the lower mound, or even the presence of Major League ball in Minnesota at Bloomington that would draw attention away from the rural communities and change the intensity of the attention paid the game everywhere.

Maybe it had to do with the matters of society and culture acting as a contagion. Former Constitutional law professor and U.S. Supreme Court nominee, Robert Bork, writes in his seminal work, *Slouching Toward Gomorrah*, that what roughly half the country considers the inevitable, indomitable march of Progressivism, the other half cites as nothing less than the spread of moral rot.

Bill Lee, a 14-year MLB pitcher, with three 17-win seasons with the Red Sox in the mid-1970s, would put the whole matter of baseball and its relationship to the life and times of American society succinctly: "I would change policy, bring back natural grass and nickel beer. Baseball is the belly button of our society. Straighten out baseball, and you straighten out the rest of the world."

There you have it. Could the connection really be that strong and direct? Nathan Lewis writes in *Gold, The Once and Future Money*:

> Despite unceasing attacks on the gold standard, it still worked to keep money relatively stable, and the inflationary trend of the 1950s and 1960s was modest compared to what followed. Business for the most part was good in the United States and around the world, and *the period would later be seen as a sort of golden age*, in which inflation and unemployment were both low, economic progress was impressive, particularly in Germany and Japan, and *the moral and civil foundations of society were sound*. (italics ours).

Can this just be merely coincidental? Or was all of life really "a sort of golden age" during the Golden Age of Baseball? Lewis, like Jerry Stahl, sure seems to think so, although he doesn't go as far as Bill Lee in connecting baseball to "the rest of the world." He connects things to the gold standard.

We didn't see every ballplayer play between 1950 and 2010. Some we only saw a few times. But that's all one needed to appreciate Jim Kubes at Lonsdale, and Jim Stoll at Arlington. These men had the same aura that emanated from Mickey Mantle in baseball or Ben Hogan in golf. We certainly didn't see them all in the same light and from the same perspective. But we saw a lot of them. Some we viewed through the wide-eyed wonder of boys in awe of heroes. How could you help but see Jim Pollard in any other way? He was a basketball All American at Stanford on an NCAA national champion, a superstar with the Lakers on an NBA dynasty. But when near universal consensus and a little analysis support your youthful observations, you hold even stronger to their legitimacy. Okay, we're biased. Our bias is informed by our experience. We would have welcomed the honest competition, but we are glad we didn't have to face Jim Kubes of Lonsdale, Jim Stoll of Arlington, or Terry Schmitz of New Market, for that matter, any more often than we did.

We viewed other ballplayers from the stands again after our own playing days had ended. We did see a lot of good ballplayers. Frank had a birds' eye view of the great John Freund, for example, from behind the plate and trying to hit him, as well as in the field on defense against him. We don't know why he left what became known as organized professional baseball with the Chicago Cubs organization after three seasons, then two in the army. Maybe it was simply because he could make more money at home and playing three days a week with the Rochester Royals in the Southern Minnesota League. Maybe it really was because the Cubs had traded him to their crosstown rivals, the White Sox, and he loved the Cubs. "He hit the shit out of the ball," Frank recalled with a misty glow in his eyes, "and he could play wherever you needed him to play."

Like Jim Pollard, he could play any position and did, except catcher–but only because he didn't like catching. Frank said that John Freund was the best pitcher he ever faced, and he was a great shortstop, too, with the Shakopee Indians. Cal Ripken, Jr., of the Baltimore Orioles would bring back memories of John Freund. Both were big men who moved like water in a brook–so smooth, so quiet, almost gentle, no wasted motions, and flawless execution of all the plays that shortstops must make.

Anytime anybody dares to make up a list of "the best" at anything, they open themselves to the gaggle of naysayers and contrarians with another view. The *Northwest Umpires Review*, at one time considered "the Bible" of local baseball, weighed in on the matter in its July 27, 1969, issue, specifically in regard to who was "the best major league baseball player of all time." Ty Cobb had worn that mantle from the onset of the first class of Baseball's Hall of Fame membership. Just five players were inducted, led by Cobb's garnering of the most votes from the Baseball Writers Association of America in 1936. The article notes that in 1961, after Cobb's death, *The St. Louis Sporting News*, no less, " . . . conducted a poll of all current and former major league players, managers, and umpires as to who was the greatest player of all time up to then."

"The result of the poll," the article continues, "was overwhelmingly won by Cobb with no close second." Yet, the baseball writers in 1969, some of whom might have seen Ruth, but not Cobb, et al, considered themselves more astute, more discerning, more intelligent baseball people than all the Major Leaguers in 1961, and all of their own predecessors in the writers' cohort who had set up and voted in the first members of the Hall of Fame in 1936.

But Babe Ruth was popular and likeable, and Ty Cobb was hated and despised as an irascible, nasty, venomous man–or at least that was the early image projected of him by the writers. "The Babe was a big, hulking, good-natured and generous man and his *popularity* far exceeded that of any player in baseball history. However, the vote for him was based on sentiment." The sentiment of the contemporary crowd . . . They were saying that they knew better than their own brethren who had actually been there and witnessed the action taking place. They were claiming to be even smarter than "real baseball people" involved in the game on the field. Whatever this phenomenon is called by psychologists, it's universal to human beings and more prevalent than ever today, since the end of the Golden Age of Baseball. To be kind, let's just call it The Bias of the Uninformed. Babe Ruth's popularity and mythologized, good-natured personality mis-informed the Baseball Writers Association to believe he was also the best ballplayer, according to *The Bible* of local baseball.

The Bible further notes, "Much is made of Babe's home run prowess, but at the time he played his best homerun records only exceeded those of Gehrig, Foxx, and others by one or two homeruns a season. That, of course, makes him the greatest player," the writer notes with irony, then adds: "Were it not for the Babe's tremendous ability as a pitcher it is doubtful that he would be included in the best five players of all time."

The article concludes with reference to two long-revered baseball people– Connie Mack and Dick Siebert. Siebert built the University of Minnesota Gophers into a national baseball power, winning three NCAA national championships in an outstanding coaching career. But, what few people remember, or know, is that he did this *after* a 17-year career in professional baseball, 11 years in the Major Leagues, most of which were played for Connie Mack and his Philadelphia Athletics. *The Bible* wraps up the article with the following:

> Connie told Dick that there were many arguments about who was the second best player in baseball history, but never any arguments about who was the best. That was reserved for Ty Cobb and he was considered all alone by himself as a great player with no other player in his class.

PART II
THE PLAYERS

The difference between the old ballplayer and the new ballplayer is the jersey. The old ballplayer cared about the name on the front. The new ballplayer cares about the name on the back.

— Steve Garvey, MLB Player, 1969-1987

Introduction

God, baseball was fun back then.
— Jim Stoll, Ballplayer

Three big men "juiced" on beefsteak, not steroids, hit three monster homeruns swinging wood *Louisville Slugger* bats at Fairgrounds Park in Jordan, Minnesota, during the Golden Age of Baseball. The bats were made by Hillerich & Bradsby of Louisville, Kentucky. They were made of ash, not the $400 metal or composite bats with the turbocharging trampoline technology that was fashioned in the laboratories and imported from softball and golf, beginning in the early 1970s.

These performance-enhancing bats gained widespread use throughout all levels of amateur baseball, including NCAA college ball. The technology just kept getting better, eventually destroying *real* softball and nearly destroying real amateur baseball. The technology got so as even the bottom of the order of every beer league softball team came to think of themselves as sluggers. Sweet spots were expanded; the trampoline effect was increased; hitters could swing these metal bats faster, even with bats heavier than wood, due to a better CM, or center of motion. The Ph.D.'s concluded all of the above from the studies that were finally performed in 2001. Baseball scores turned the game into a parody of itself and resembled that which was disparaged by the more pompous among the baseball elites–slow-pitch softball. But there was no doubt that the bat technology, combined with the lower pitching mound, the reduced strike zone, and the virtual doubling of the number of Major League Baseball teams, had immense impact on the game. Together, these and other changes to the game helped to make prolific hitters out of everybody who stepped up to the plate for 30 years. Simply enough, when awesome happens often; when awesome comes easy; when everything is awesome, nothing is awesome. To borrow with a twist a quote from Shakespeare: *There's something rotten in the state of baseball.*

When it is contrived and manipulated, manufactured, and medicated, awesome is tiresome and invites the scrutiny of historians, analysts, and professors of physics. Pete Incaviglia, for example, gained fame at Oklahoma State University in 1985 by hitting a record 48 homeruns in his college baseball season of 75 games, and 100 dingers in his collegiate career of 213 games between 1983 and 1985–but with a metal bat. It wasn't baseball. It was a caricature of the game, a mockery of baseball.

How could this superhuman miss in professional baseball? Hitting with a wood bat against admittedly what should have been better pitching in the American League, Incaviglia had one of his best years his rookie season with Texas, belting 30 homeruns, driving in 88 runs, and hitting .250, just above his 12-year career average of .246 during which he also slammed 206 homeruns. Considerably more was expected of him, but perhaps he was slowed by chronic injuries.

While baseball purists are still reluctant to acknowledge Roger Maris's 61-homerun season in 1961 as topping Babe Ruth's 60 in 1927, because of the longer season and the watered-down pitching staffs that expansion brought, Mark McGuire of the St. Louis Cardinals is credited with National League homerun titles, with 70 in 1998 and 65 in 1999. Sammy Sosa of the Cubs hit more than 60 homeruns in a season three different times. But Barry Bonds of the San Francisco Giants is acclaimed as the all-time single-season homerun king with 73 in 2001, and the all-time career leader with 762 homeruns in 22 seasons.

These magnificent numbers weren't put up with metal bats, because the external aids were never permitted in Major League Baseball. But internal aids delivered the same results as the metal bats. The performance-enhancing drugs slipped by any scrutiny of the teams and league enforcers; they slipped by any moral conscience of the users, either of which could have prevented the travesties, the tainting of the good game of baseball, and what had been hailed generations ago as our national pastime.

Asterisk baseball, in one form or another, had invaded the country like The Spanish Flu of 1918. It would wear the glitter off the gold everywhere, exposing many pretenders and wannabes for what they were–alchemists.

It makes you wonder how the newly minted, self-proclaimed Larca legends in Brewer Town would have fared playing real baseball during the game's Golden Age. It makes you wonder how much better John Freund's .525 league batting average in 1959 at Shakopee would have been with a metal bat, with a lower pitching mound, and a strike zone that was all in *his* wheelhouse. And without having to hit against the likes of Pat Devitt from Prior Lake and the kid, Weckman, from Jordan, neither of whom was afraid to bring it in high and tight.

"There's no question," Jim Stoll said, "today's players are, in general, bigger and faster. But we played hungry. If you didn't hit, you didn't eat–in professional ball." After a 60-year life's vocation in organized baseball as a player and club owner, Bill Starr makes the same observation in *Clearing The Bases–Baseball Then & Now*, published in 1989. Writing in the 1980s, Starr notes that the game just wasn't played as well as it had been in earlier times. He attributed the degradation of the game to the quality of ballplayer. While acknowledging the significant improvements in equipment, training, ballparks–all the trimmings–he said the modern day baseball players were lacking in important competitive fundamentals: intensity, mental toughness, and attitude toward the game.

"It must be the money," Stoll said of the post-Golden Age player, and as a consequence, "they don't have the heart or the stones."

"God, baseball was fun back then," Stoll exclaimed. Pausing then, he lamented, "But you can't do anything about it now." We think he's wrong, because you can remember and if you tell it right, tell it the way it was, then you can keep alive the reality and the Truth that are a part of you and a part of history. You can preserve and perpetuate something of value. You can keep alive something that is in you and of you, something that's important. Old ballplayers, even the heroes, will fade from memory, but the status of "legend" isn't a matter of a self-endorsement after five minutes in the microwave. Rather, legend is made like a good, stovetop stew, the long-simmering result of Time and the mixing of myth and magic in a cast-iron Dutch oven. The process of achieving legendary status isn't a mechanical or numerical thing. It's mystical. It's spiritual–one of the things that connected baseball with religion.

We enjoyed the yarns that the late, long-time Jordan Brewer Manager, Charlie Larca, told so emphatically with the New York accent, and we read in *Scott County Baseball* where he told author Tom Melchior that a part of his baseball pedigree was that he had "played some minor league ball." We checked on that in the same source we checked out everybody else in our research. The online resource, www.baseballreference.com, has no record of a Charles or Chuck or Charlie Larca playing professional baseball at any level. Conversely, it shows the records of most of the old ballplayers celebrated in these pages. Even more significantly, while most of these guys not only "played some minor league ball," few ever talked about it. Not even to family, according to John Garbett, Jr., or the sons, Jack and Jerry, of the late, great John Freund of Shakopee.

Bob Shotliff's brief sojourn with the White Sox organization and a 10-10 pitching record with a 3.64 ERA over at least portions of three minor league seasons (1947-1949) is captured in our online reference source. It's hard to believe, and the more contemporary crowd that only saw him and mocked him in his later years won't believe that Bob Shotliff at one time tipped the scales at an athletic 180 pounds on his six-foot frame, or that his nickname when he joined the Jordan Brewer pitching staff in 1949 was "Bullet" Bob because of the sizzling speed with which he threw baseballs. It was only in later years, well past a prime, that "Shotty" resorted to gimmicks and junk on the mound.

Long before any of them, Ollie Fuhrman, who was born in 1896 in Jordan and whose body rests in the town's Spirit Hill Cemetery, "played some minor league ball." In fact, the 5-11, 185-pound, switch-hitting catcher played seven years of minor league ball during The Roaring Twenties, compiling a career batting average of .292. He played his way up from Class-C ball to Class-AA Portland in the independent Pacific Coast League, and on Opening Day of the 1922 Major League Baseball season, Ollie Fuhrman was on the roster and in the dugout of the Philadelphia Athletics in the American League. But a month later, after a couple of token appearances in six games for the Athletics and two hits in six at bats and no catching errors, he was dropped from the roster. You have to wonder what happened, because he played no more baseball that year and he never played above Class-B again. We learn from a Max Casey news bit in the June 11, 1953, *Jordan Independent* that Ollie Fuhrman kept his game going after hanging up his professional spikes by "catching in a Sunday morning league for Cohens (*sic*), (where) his 1933 batting record of .522 still stands."

Charlie Larca had a habit of hyperbole–of exaggerating and blowing his horn and the horns of his "favorite sons" on his Brewer teams, while disparaging and discounting those who came before him. "They had never won anything," Larca told Tom Melchior of the ballplayers and the teams that came before him and his modern-day Jordan Brewers. The perception and habit wore off on his charges, on young men who should have known better, given their Minnesota River Valley roots. We have no problems with Larca's choices as his favorites from the teams he managed. They were the best of the bunch.

Our issue is with the comparative assumptions and fallacies spouted as gospel truth in his interview and assumed by his former dugout charges. Our issue is with their complaints of other teams loading up unfairly, while Larca & Co. loaded up, too, while continuing to deny the breaking and stretching of "rubber rules," of minimizing the contributions of imported players and denying the non-residential status of players living in communities outside the limits of an allowed radius. Our issue is with the criticizing of other Class-B teams, such as Hamel, Cold Spring, Miesville, and Dundas in the 1980s and 90s for their lineups of current and former college ball players, while fielding teams themselves of outstanding Minnesota Gophers and other college ballplayers.

These issues are why teams used to be restricted to both a radius-defined limit of non-resident players and just two college ballplayers as well. It's also why Dick Siebert of the University of Minnesota established a collegiate summer league for college ballplayers.

We take umbrage with much of what Charlie Larca says and what has been directly expressed and implied in innuendo about "those old guys like Tex Erickson," or "that fat old piece of shit," a reference to the late Gordy Gelhaye made by one of the more contemporary crowd upon meeting Jailor Gelhaye when he spent a night in the Scott County Jail. Larca and his cohort weren't here. They simply cannot know how good the best really were.

Nobody is around anymore who saw Ollie Fuhrman play ball. Neither Charlie Larca nor any of his ballplayers were around in the 1950s when the Jordan Brewers played *Class-A* baseball and twice made a tough eight-team state tournament after an absence of 15 years from the dance–the multi-faceted point being that it is extremely difficult to make an eight-team tournament from a field of 300 or more. The odds from just the numbers speak volumes. But there is far more to consider, for the point is that the military draft took young men of ball-playing age away to wars in Europe, the Pacific, Korea, and Vietnam. War and killing change young men. Some don't make it home. Some come home but are mere shells of men and can never play anything ever again. They are a mess of mind or mangled limb. The point is that it was extremely difficult to win the dogfight that characterized the Minnesota River League and its Class-A competition. Larca makes our point for us in *Scott County Baseball*: "I never played in a place where everybody makes the playoffs. It doesn't make a difference if you lose games during the season."

That's not the way things used to be and may explain why the game lost its ineffable appeal. Every single game meant a lot in the old days. Not everybody made the playoffs every year during the Golden Age. Teams *earned* the right to positions in the playoffs, the regions, and state tournaments. League seasons were The War. Each game was a major battle. It's why an honest count of up to 2,000 fans jammed tiny Tiger Stadium in Belle Plaine or Fairgrounds Park in Jordan to

PART II • THE PLAYERS • INTRODUCTION   73

watch a mid-week league baseball game between the two neighboring small towns. The competition in just a regular season game was ferocious.

Unlike "Charlie ball" time, losing a game during the season could make a huge difference–in how a player felt about himself or how the fans felt about their town and their team. Getting singled out as responsible for a loss could mean a demotion to the bench or getting dropped from the roster. Players were paid to perform. League standings alone meant a lot in terms of both pride and playoff position. Betting on games meant that sometimes-significant money was won or lost on the outcome of a baseball game. Fortunately, in the event of a disappointing loss of a game, redemption was possible in less than a week, with energy levels amped up by an entire octave. League games weren't passive cakewalks in the old days. They were major battles in The War that was a league pennant race. Multiple-game playoffs were even more exciting, as arm-weary pitchers reached back for still more heart and savvy and the bruised and beat-up catchers bit the bullet to catch another ballgame.

The point is that no matter how much it is wished or wanted by the more contemporary crowd, Class-C and Class-B baseball of any era can never measure up to Golden Age Class-A and Class-AA ball. So how good was the Class-A Minnesota River League in the early 1950s? It was far superior to anything that Charlie Larca saw in his 24 years of managing Class-C and Class-B baseball teams.

Peterson and Tomashek write in their *Town Ball* that George Thompson, who was secretary of the Northwest Umpires Association in 1950, claimed that the Class-A Minnesota River League teams were as good as the Class-AA Western Minny League teams and any other Class-AA league with the exception of the Southern Minny. In general, the ballplayers were simply better. There were solid professionals on nearly every roster. Some of the pitching, in particular, was outstanding. They played better baseball. Minnesota River League teams had payrolls of $4,000 to $5,000 a year. Southern Minny League teams like Rochester had payrolls of $20,000 on top of the jobs given to lure players to town. Payrolls were met with revenues from the gate and from concessions. Most teams were backstopped by major businesses such as Green Giant in LeSueur or individuals with a healthy savings account and a passion for the game. They put their money where their hearts and mouths were.

The state tournament wasn't set up for one in four or more teams playing baseball. It was rare and special. It was closer to the World Series of Major League Baseball than that of an open weekend softball tournament. It is far easier to make a tournament of 48 or 32 teams from a field of just 200 to 250 teams than it is to make an 8-or 16-team field out of 300 to 400 teams. The MO had changed between the 1950s and the 1980s from one of a summer of heat–immensely competitive, inter-town Class-A league baseball–to one of state tournament only, even if you had to sandbag your way into Class-C to qualify. League play became virtually meaningless, with some leagues even mixing somehow Class-C teams with Class-B teams. Today, there is even talk of adding still another class–Class D–to the state amateur baseball format, so that even more teams can "make" the state tournament. Therein lies a major distinction of the Golden Age of Baseball. More people then seemingly understood and lived in accordance with the time-honored axiom that *the ends do not justify the means*. Because they knew that the means must always justify themselves, the golden agers repeatedly opted to play Class-A baseball despite pressure every winter at league meetings from teams having trouble meeting higher and higher player payrolls. They wanted to make sure they were playing and presenting to fans the best quality of baseball possible in their little river towns.

In the 1950s, everybody went to the ballgame on Sunday nights. You strained on the edge of your seat with every pitch from or to Jim Pollard. In contrast, in the 1980s and beyond, a small contingent of ballplayers' wives and girlfriends got caught up with each other, chatting in the stands, and a few diehard fans got excited at the state tournaments. They read books and did crossword puzzles at the league games, and then in the 2000s they were running their "Apps" on smart phones while waiting for games to end so they could drive their sons and husbands home.

Just winning a league playoff after the exhausting grind of a regular season pennant race, to say nothing of the subsequent regional tournament, was an ordeal in the 1950s. This was made easy in the 1980s, in order to manage, we believe, a more financially successful state tournament. Moreover, the state's baseball bosses seemed to implement a version of what the public education system would do with a policy in the 2000s: "No child left behind." In Minnesota amateur baseball, it became, "No team left behind." In the classrooms, if you attended, you got a "C" on your report card. In baseball, if you fielded a team, won half your games, and turned in a roster to the state headquarters by June 1, you "qualified" for a Class-C state tournament. Pardon the exaggeration, but the point must be made.

It's even easier when you play down to Class C rather than up to Class A, a point also lost or ignored by the historical revisionists. Moreover, 1953 and '54 were the years during the state tournament to rob the bank in Jordan, not 1982, about which we believe Larca grossly exaggerates in an interview moment of euphoric recall. In 1954, they expected businesses in Jordan to close at noon on Saturday of the state tournament. The mayor actually issued a formal proclamation that all businesses close by 4 pm so fans could travel to St. Cloud for the state tournament. They expected 500 fans from the town of fewer than 1,500 residents to attend the state tournament at St. Cloud, and then counted up to 700 at the game, which meant that nearly half the town was there! Those left in town were the aged, the infirm, the feeble-minded, and the weak, as well as the women with young children.

Contrary to what Manager Larca claimed, Frank thought that 100 to 200 fans out of the town's growing population of 2,500 to 3,000 people went to the Minnesota Class-C State Tournament in 1982. Most of those were wives and girlfriends, or parents, of ballplayers. Girlfriends brought friends, so they would have someone to talk to during the games. Businesses did not close for baseball after the Golden Age had ended. They stayed open, baseball or not. In the 1950s, they shut down the town for the state baseball tournament. In the 1980s, it was "business as usual" even during a state tournament. Not so during the Golden Age, although it's probably not an indictment of the more contemporary crowd for not knowing this. After all, they weren't around to experience it. But *wannabe like . . .* is never the same as historical fact and personal experience no matter how badly we want it to be.

When we mentioned Johnny Garbett with the respect he actually earned from the time he was old enough to throw that deuce of his in the Minneapolis parochial school league, we were amazed at the universal deer-in-the-headlights look to a gaggle of the contemporary crowd. They'd never heard of "the crafty little lefty" with the wicked curveball who'd won 15 Brewer games in 1954 with the team playing in the competitive Class-A Minnesota River League. "Nope, never heard of him," Mark Beckman, a 1975 graduate of Jordan High School and a shortstop to boot, said of Johnny Garbett when we asked him in 2014. He and others had not heard of John Freund or Jake Harsh either. The Buzz had stopped or changed. The disconnect from baseball's reverential past had occurred with the end of The Golden Age of Baseball. Or maybe the disconnect was deliberate and is what brought the Golden Age to its end. The new crop of ball players thought history began with the "*pinggggg*" of the bats they brought to the game in the 1980s. Maybe they just didn't know any better and couldn't own what they didn't know firsthand.

As for the quality of those ball clubs, had Manager Leon Hennes or Manager Baldy Hartkopf and the Jordan Baseball Association's Board of Directors, which ran a *self-sustaining* entity in the late 1940s to mid-1950s, subscribed to the Larca School of Management, they'd have opted to play Class-B baseball–the lowest and weakest class in existence then. They'd have taken down to an area Class-B league their competitive Class-A team that was knocking on the doors of Class-AA ball before the middle of the decade in order to dominate weaker teams and ease the route to the state tournament and maybe go even further with the help of draft choices, too. Qualifying for and winning playoffs and associated region tournaments in the 50s, and thus gaining berths in a Class-B state tournament, would have been the same cakewalk with the Class-A players they had as it would become 30 years later. Just as with the drafted pitchers and catchers, on top of the players residing within the 494/694 corridor, and the "grandfather clause" that permits non-residents to play as residents, all of which made the Jordan Brewers and a handful of other dominating Class-B teams likely state tournament entries in the last two decades of the 20th century, the extra help of draftees in even Class-B baseball in the middle decades would have proven invaluable had the team chosen to play down then, too. But men of "the greatest generation" were made of a different mettle than they were just a generation or two later.

State tournaments were more difficult to attain in the 1950s because of the smaller tournament fields and the fierce competition that existed in, first, league and league playoffs, then, regionals. Every team had at least one good pitcher–a professional. Teams were paying good money to pitchers from professional and semi-professional ball. They hid aces on their rosters that were picked up from the neighboring Class-AA Southern and Western Minny leagues, both of which were well manned with professional baseball players. You had to beat in league and region play the teams that Manager Larca's Brewers faced in state tournaments. League and regional playoffs required the penetration of a virtual phalanx of good baseball teams. LeCenter, with its mob of mercenaries from Minneapolis and St. Paul, bought a state championship in 1950 and took runner up the following year. They were lucky to get out of the league playoffs. That's how strong the league was. Le Sueur, New Ulm, Waseca, Belle Plaine, and St. Peter, as well as Jordan, all had strong, winning *Class-A* Minnesota River League baseball in this part of the valley. Then, when Class-A baseball began going the way of the dodo bird, as Class-AA had done earlier, Shakopee had a dominating baseball team from the mid-to late-1950s through 1966 in the Class-B River Valley League. The Prior Lake Jays then dominated from 1968 through 1976, as well they should have with the Class-A ball club they assembled from Bloomington to play at the Class-B level, although they had trouble finding a league to call home after awhile. Both teams would typically win 18 of 20 to 25 of 30 games every summer, with one or two of the losses coming at the ends of their runs in state tournaments.

The two teams at their best–the Shakopee Indians and the Prior Lake Jays– make for an interesting mythical matchup. But while the Jays had a dugout full of ex-Gophers, none compared with John Freund.

Gerrymandering is the re-aligning of congressional districts in states to stack the deck of voters in favor of one political party, or candidate, over another.

Similar modifications were done with state baseball regions. Why would you have "good baseball towns" knocking each other off in league playoffs or regional play when, with a little management creativity you could get more of these better-drawing towns qualified for the state tournament and thereby improve gate admissions and concession revenues? Why not have Jordan, Shakopee, Chaska, Belle Plaine, Miesville, Dundas, and Lonsdale or New Market and St. Benedict ALL making the state tournament rather than having just one or two surviving? Just goose the qualifying field from 8 or 16 teams to 32 or 48! Instead of requiring all state tournament entrees to be winners of eight state regions, allow two of three, maybe even three of four, regional competitors to "qualify" for state tournament play, with losing teams just sent to a different bracket rather than home for the winter. It's not rocket science.

Miesville and Dundas had good baseball in the 1950s and '60s, too. Usually, Shakopee had better baseball. Lonsdale had great small town baseball, all local talent, but Prior Lake had better baseball talent, none of it local, in the late 1960s, as they violated the unwritten rule of crossing the river to fill their roster with former Lake Conference standouts, ex-Minnesota Gophers, and even professional ballplayers.

Values, focus, and perspective all changed. "Strategic management" compromised the game and the competition. It made for relatively easy entry into the state tournament, the failure to do so an obvious criticism by the Larca crowd of older teams and players. They don't know what they are talking about. They think they know the book, long at rest on the shelf, from glancing at the dusty cover. One of the Larca charges even asked the question, "Why, if Ken Hansen was a good basketball coach," he asked of the former Jordan High School coach and long-time athletic director, "did he never win a state tournament?" We actually had to explain how the road to *the* Minnesota State High School Basketball tournament got increasingly competitive in, first, District 13 play, then Region IV competition with St. Paul schools. Post-season play was never meant to be a cakewalk. "Best" was a competitive achievement, not a qualifying garland.

But when you ignore all the little things that matter in the reckoning of baseball statistics and comparative analyses, it's easy, in the words of an old marine who did two tours of duty in Vietnam in the mid-1960s, to "let your alligator overload your hummingbird." It's easy for narcissism to take hold. Then, when the lies and exaggerations reach print, you have the historical revisionism documented as "fact." But everybody knows, deep down, that regardless of how you turn the crank, baloney still comes out baloney.

"Well, I destroyed this league and I was on the worst team in the league," Larca told Tom Melchior for *Scott County Baseball*, and ". . . everyone knew who I was because I hit the shit out of the ball." Moreover, Larca said, "They brought in their best pitchers; they'd do anything and I'd hammer it." He said he played so well, hit so well, that he became Chaska's "worst nightmare." We honestly don't know about this. Maybe it's all true. But it sounds more like he was a legend in his own mind. He said he played for Victoria in a game against Carver at Jordan in front of 2,000 people, which, proportionally, is the equivalent of 75,000 in Yankee Stadium as a neutral site for an exhibition game between Chicago and Atlanta, and that he "could see thousands of bucks bet on that game" in a Carver bar before the game. It's doubtful that 2,000 people showed up at the ballpark in Jordan for a game since the night Jim Stoll and the Arlington A's beat the Prior Lake Jays in the 1969 Class-B State Championship in front of a reported 2,600 paid admissions, but which was probably closer to a crowd of 3,000 fans with all the waived-in walk-on patrons. We can believe "thousands of bucks" changing hands in a Carver bar in the 1970s, but not on a wager over a Carver-Victoria town team ball game then.

"The Devil's in the details," and if you are going to compare, you must be fair. First things first: Class-C and Class-B baseball since the 1980s isn't even close to the quality of Class-A and Class-AA baseball during the game's Golden Age. Not since Bobby Jones in golf has an amateur in any sport been better than the professionals of his or any other day. The Jordan Brewers, operating from the business entity of the Jordan Baseball Association, had a payroll to meet–as did every other Class-A and AA team in Minnesota. The baseball was better then, because the ballplayers were better. As athletic as the legion of Larca players were in the 1980s and 90s, they don't come close to, say, Jim Pollard, who was a three-time All-American in basketball and who is in professional basketball's Naismith Hall of Fame. Pollard could flat out play any position because of his athleticism. He turned down overtures from professional baseball teams in the late 1940s so he could work on his college degree during the summers while choosing to play baseball for the Jordan Brewers. His life's ambition was to be a teacher and coach, not a bloated-ego celebrity. He simply had too much character to want it any other way.

The outstanding numbers put up during Larca's reign are as tainted as the numbers put up by Bonds, McGuire, Canseco, Rodriquez, and Sosa at the Major League level. Moreover, we question Larca's instant self-proclamation of a handful of his favorites to the ethereal status of "legends." Manager Larca's favorites were good hitters in an era tainted by the sound of tin. But that's not how legends are made. They're not the result of a noisy clamor of the bat or the mouth. Legends are not an instant cup of soup from the microwave. That's faux food. Legends are made like good stew is made, with real meat, vegetables, and a favorite stock or sauce. Good stew is not the result of good packaging or the management of shelf location.

Good stew is about the contents, the sustaining nutritive value, and the taste bud-exploding flavor and aroma enhanced with the right tinctures of seasoning, all of which define "comfort food" on a cold winter day. Legends need long, slow simmering on the back burner or in a slow cooker to reach a state of refined, comingled oneness. Legends don't come out of the laboratory. They are not pre-packaged manipulations or the product of a manufacturing process.

Ty Cobb, Babe Ruth, Joe DiMaggio, Mickey Mantle, and Ted Williams are legends. So are Satchel Paige, Walter ("Big Train") Johnson, and Eddie Feigner. Bronko Nagurski, Bruce Smith, and Bud Grant are legends who gave the glitter to the gold in Golden Gophers. Gopher coach, Bernie Bierman, a native of Springfield, Minnesota, remains as golden as the players. As Gopher football coach between 1932 and 1941, and 1945 through 1950, he won five national championships and seven Big Ten Conference titles while going undefeated five seasons. How many of either have been won since?

Johnny Garbett and Jim Pollard were well on their way to becoming legends long before they came to Jordan, where Tex Erickson grew locally. Similarly, Jim Kubes, John Freund, Pat Devitt, Jake Harsh, and Jim Stoll from neighboring towns in this lower basin of the Minnesota River Valley are legends. But with the end of the Golden Age of Baseball, the heat was removed from the stew-making process. The Buzz stopped. The past was cut off and denigrated. Legend was flushed down the toilet. Greatness was forgotten if it were ever known. Or it was denied, if not defamed, by the ignorant and the narcissistic. Truth and sainthood were sullied by the irreverent contemporary crowd who, like the foodstuff folk, put more into packaging and brand management than they do into product integrity.

What would Manager Larca's legends, advertised in Tom Melchior's *Scott County Baseball* with the glowing offensive numbers, have done at the plate during the Golden Age of Baseball? Their metal bat is just one factor that prompts the question. The knockdown pitch is another. Would Ron Beckman have dug in on the likes of Giant Jim Pollard, Pat Devitt, or Big John Freund, all of whom were known to "be a little wild"? We didn't witness the 15-minute "nap" that former Notre Dame pitching staff ace, Jim Dalton, playing for St. Peter in the summer of 1954, took at home plate after taking a Garbett pitch in the head. We don't know if he ever played again. But we were in the on-deck circle at Fairgrounds Park in Jordan when, in what was likely 1968, Brewer Denny Peters tried to outwait a curveball from Lonsdale's Jim Daleidon that didn't break. The sound of that collision of baseball and human head was unnerving, to say the least. Denny went down, moaning in pain. He was a .400 hitter from Little League and Babe Ruth through high school and Brewer baseball. He would carry a pair of pliers around the rest of that summer in the event he swallowed his tongue and, to keep from choking to death, had to cut quickly the wires that held his healing jaw together. The pitch had broken his jaw, and he would take the sustenance of milkshakes and soup through a straw all summer long. He would never play baseball again.

Bean balls did that to good hitters. Tony Conigliaro was the slugging heir to Ted Williams in the Boston Red Sox lineup in the 1960s. Tony "C" holds the MLB record for the most homeruns hit by a teenager (24), which he accomplished in his rookie season of 1964. He led the American League with 36 homeruns in 1965, and he also remains the youngest American League ballplayer to reach 100 homeruns. But in 1967 he took a pitch in the face from Jack Hamilton that broke his cheekbone, damaged the retina of his eye, and dislocated his jaw. He hung around for a few seasons but was never the same again and his career was severely short-circuited. That's not all. In 1982 he suffered a heart attack, then a stroke that put him into a coma and a vegetative state for the next eight years, dying in 1990 at age 45.

Would the Larca legends, their heads protected only by a wool baseball cap, have teed off on fastballs coming from the Mt. Olympus of a mound they never knew when the pitch, strategically called by the catcher, was likely to be coming at their head? One of the pitching tenets of that day was, "Dig in, and you go down." If you gloated, taunted, trash-talked, or in any way tried to show up another team's player, it was a guarantee that the next time you came to the plate, you'd be going down.

The reality of the knockdown pitch at the level of Major League Baseball is captured by Roger Kahn in his *The Era* with a coaching lesson by 1952 Brooklyn Dodger manager Charlie Dressen for his rookie pitcher, Joe Black:

> 'You throw great Joe. Just throw where I tell ya. When we want it high throw it high–and tight. When we want that hard curve low, throw it down–and away. When I want you to brush a hitter, I want you to go right at his head. I want to see his bat go one way, his cap go another and his ass go somewhere else. Do what I tell ya, Joe, and you're gonna be a big leaguer, and the hitter will be whoops, 'Good-bye Dolly Gray!' . . . By June of his rookie season, Black was the best relief pitcher in baseball.

The same coaching instruction came from the Minnesota River Valley baseball dugouts in the 1950s and '60s: "Bring it up under his chin," chimed bench jockeys to young pitchers on the mound. "Let him see it!" Then, "Again!" and with more emphasis, "Stick it in his ear!" As barbaric as it sounds today, it was an accepted part of the game.

How would the Larca legends have fared against the Big-League curveballs of a healthy Weckman, Stoll, and Garbett? Curveballs set up with high, tight fastballs. Curveballs that just kissed the strike zone and then cut down into the dirt. The strike zone then was a full strike zone, too. It extended to below the knees, and if you had a "good, pitcher's umpire" calling balls and strikes, went down to the ankles. Just imagine . . . if Johnny Garbett could strike out 24 batters in a Class-AA West Central League game in 1950, how many of the Class-C and Class-B players of the 1980s and 90s would have managed to scratch a pitch of his? If Garbett as a 20-year-old boy wonder on the mound could handle in Class-AA the likes of former and future Major League sluggers–Rudy York, Howie Schultz, and Moose Skowron, to name but three–what would college boys with a Class-C pedigree have done against him? If Lefty Weckman, as a freshman on the University of Minnesota Gopher baseball team, could make a three-time All-Big Ten and All-American on an NCAA national champion look like a fool and lose his temper in the batting cage when he knew the kid's curveball was coming, what could one expect of the likes of Manager Larca's best players against him?

Jake Harsh of the Belle Plaine Tigers hit .500 with 15 homeruns in a 16-game season in 1970–with a wood bat. How much better would he have done just a few short years later with metal? Moreover, unlike "Homerun" Baker's home field, Shibe Park in Philadelphia in 1913, Harsh's Tiger Stadium in Belle Plaine was a friendly yard for Big Jake. How many would he have hit in a 35-or 40-game season, which would be a season's norm just 10 years later? How many would he have hit with a metal bat?

Chuck Warner, Brownton's "emeritus of baseball," said Jim Stoll "was at or near the top of the list of best ballplayers to ever play baseball in Minnesota." Warner is a past president of the Minnesota Amateur Baseball Hall of Fame, serving on the executive committee since 1990.

Jim Stoll was dangerous with a wood bat in his hands playing for Arlington. He'd have been lethal with the good metal bat that Easton came out with after Stoll's day in the sun. Dave Hartmann admitted that it would have been really something extraordinary to see Jim Stoll hitting with the good metal bats. "He was really something in the '60s and early '70s when he hit with wood," Hartmann said.

"Without question," Hartmann said, "Jim Stoll was a couple notches above guys like Joe Driscoll, and the guys like Ron Beckman, Dave Hentges, and Jon Beckman at Jordan. And they were good hitters." Jon Beckman may have had Stoll in terms of speed, according to Hartmann, "but Jim was really a smart base runner," he said, and he admitted he was comparing Jim Stoll in his 30s when he carried extra "winter weight" into the summer season to a younger, leaner Jon Beckman in his mid-20s. Moreover, Stoll made these impressions as a hitter and base runner on teammates, other players, and fans while working the mound. Most pitchers relax other aspects of the game while they concentrate on their pitching roles.

"I could run," Stoll said. "They timed me in the 100 at 10.2 seconds with full football gear on," he said, of his high school football days in Rio Vista, California, where he earned 13 varsity athletic letters–four each in football, basketball, and baseball, and one in track. Football cleats and the rest of the gear were considerably heavier and more cumbersome and restrictive in the 1950s on top of it. "Elder White was supposedly the fastest player in the Pirate organization in 1960," Stoll recalled. "He beat me by half a step" in a couple of sprints during the Pirate spring training.

Jim Kubes of Lonsdale was "in the zone," in a playoff series against Marystown and its two pitching aces, Donny Hennen and Dave Bakken, in the summer of 1965. He went five for five, then four for four at the plate in the first two games–four years before they lowered the mound at least five inches, shrunk the strike zone, and eight years before they permitted metal bats to be used in a baseball game. Seven of the nine hits were homeruns hit deep into the power alleys of the two ballparks. The eighth went off the fence at Lonsdale for just a single, as base runners ahead of Jim held up to make sure the converging outfielders didn't make the catch. It needed a foot more carry to clear the fence. There is no doubt that it, too, would have left the ballpark had it been hit with a metal bat, according to the studies done later by the Ph.D.'s in physics. The only question is whether he would have had another one or two at bats in each game, with still more homeruns, as a result of teammates hitting better, too. Metal bats turned high diamond drama into the "theater of the absurd."

The best ballplayers on anybody's list are complete ballplayers. In the Golden Age of Baseball, you could compensate a bit for lightweight hitting by playing great defensive baseball. Shortstops were usually a team's best athlete and best defensive ballplayer. Our list is no exception. We're loaded with shortstops.

Bobby Kelly at Prior Lake and John Freund with Shakopee were great shortstops. So was Jordan's Woody Peters, who had the quickness to give him the range, and he had a gun for an arm. Like Tex Erickson, he never failed to put the ball on the money. That was always the thing about the great shortstops. They had golden arms. While good shortstops had range and usually fielded cleanly the balls hit to them, the great ones had guns and always put the ball on the money: on the start of the double play; on completing the relay from a deep outfield throw; and on all the plays to their right, deep into the hole, and to their left behind second base. The great shortstops didn't pull the first baseman off the bag on the putout. They would have stopped his heart with the chest-high throw had he failed to catch the ball. Mark Hess, who played shortstop at Jordan into the 2000s, was a throwback to The Golden Age of Baseball. He was technically and fundamentally flawless; like most hockey players, he was tough as nails and a superior defensive ballplayer who probably booted a ball once or twice. We doubt he ever made a mental error after his sophomore year in high school.

They are the best shortstops we ever saw, and between Frank and I we saw them all over 50 years or more. John Freund's pedigree is stamped with the imprimatur of the Chicago Cubs' organization. You had to be something just to get a look then, because of the more limited roster spots available. It was extremely rare for a boy who could play the game of baseball well enough to be offered a contract by a Major League Baseball organization. You had to be special. Really special, because, first of all, until 1961 there were only 16 major league teams, eight in the National League and eight in the American League. That's 400 opportunities based on the 25-man rosters. Two teams were added to the American League in 1961, and two were added to the National League in 1962. Therefore, opportunities were more limited than they would become with further expansion to eventually 30 Major League teams and their 750 available spots on rosters.

Many high school boys who were special and did sign contracts to play professional baseball in the 1950s and early 1960s had their eyes of realism opened in a season or two, often before a season ended. They came home disillusioned, the dream vanquished by the long bus rides, cheap hotels, and cheaper food, or with sore arms that wouldn't heal and for which no orthopedic surgical solutions existed then. In the case of some standout ballplayers, it was the realization that they represented an investment and chattel property to the owners. Major League teams would favor the young prospects in whom they had the greatest investments, passing over others who might be performing better but in whom less money was at risk. It wasn't fair. It just was.

St. Cloud's Tom Hamm would skip a minor league all-star game, walk away from the Detroit Tiger organization, and show up in 1968 on the campus of St. John's University, where he helped an aging priest and Dante scholar, Dunstan Tucker, OSB, coach the Johnnies to a conference championship in 1969 as he finished the college education he'd suspended at Georgetown University to join the Tigers. Fr. Dunstan had coached Johnnie baseball in the 1930s and 40s, winning MIAC championships and proud of an unbeaten record one year with the likes of former U.S. Senator Eugene McCarthy, Bruce Frank of Le Sueur, and one of the O'Brien's from Belle Plaine playing for him.

Hamm would sign with the Minnesota Twins and be assigned to their farm team at Wisconsin Rapids those next two summers, then choose not to report to a Triple-A team the summer after graduating from St. John's. At 6 ft. –4 in. and 210 lbs., with good speed and a strong arm, the Twins still saw left-handed hitting talent worth nurturing. They saw Ted Williams in his size and his swing. But Tom wanted to ride the great rivers of Africa, and he would have more fun a couple years later, he said, playing softball with what he called "better, quicker heads" on Toby and Rollie's softball team. Steve Schneider of the Prior Lake Jays had even gotten wind of Hamm living in Prior Lake in the early 1970s and called weekly one winter to try to recruit the powerful left-handed hitter to join the already powerful Jays. But baseball had lost its ineffable appeal.

Jim Kubes of Lonsdale, Minnesota, and a 1961 graduate of New Prague High School, was really special, too. He signed a professional contract with the Minnesota Twins in the fall of the year he graduated from high school after pitching three no-hitters that spring and summer. Three or four months after reporting to the Twins minor league team at Ft. Walton Beach, FL, Kubes would be released because his sore elbow, which had already taken three shots of cortisone, couldn't stand up to the rigorous demands of a professional baseball pitcher. He would return home to Lonsdale and dominate the Dakota-Rice-Scott (DRS) League in amateur baseball for 10 years, pitching, catching, and hitting.

Jim Stoll would sign a professional baseball contract with the San Francisco Seals upon graduating from high school in 1955 at the age of 17. After the Boston Red Sox bought him and his team, they cut his salary in half without negotiation, prompting him to walk away from the diamond and into the office of an air force recruiter, which brought him to northern Minnesota, where things got interesting.

John Freund from Shakopee was good enough to play three seasons, 1948, '49, and '50, in the Chicago Cubs organization. He would play a good brand of baseball in the army with other professionals, some of whom were Major League ballplayers, turn down another shot in Chicago upon being discharged, opting to play for better money in the vaunted Class-AA Southern Minny before playing Class-A ball for still good money at Le Sueur and Glencoe. He would settle finally in Shakopee and help lead the Indians to a Class-B State Championship in 1959.

Donald "Tex" Erickson

He's the best shortstop I ever saw play the game.

— Frank Hilgers

We would play cork ball when we were kids in Jordan against Otto Kerkow's garage, which was next to craftsman Louie Stifter's welding shop and across from Ben Engfer's Chevrolet Dealership on Water Street. Louie's welding shop is today a house of the Lord in the name of Tree of Life Church, and Engfer's is most recently "Packrat Garage." In the 1950s, Otto's long driveway forced you to hit back up the middle. His house narrowed the "right-field line," and a row of cedar trees knocked everything down on the left side. Our "homeruns" and "doubles" would roll into the Engfer garage across the street when the big door was open. Usually, the ball would roll back onto the street, nudged by some invisible hand within, and we would resume our game. But every so often Tex Erickson would appear with the two-bit rubber ball tucked under an elbow, a wry smile on his face, wiping oil off his hands with a rag and challenging us to a bet for an ice cream treat on a hot summer afternoon. "Hold up your hand," he'd say, from the middle of the street. "Don't move it. If I hit it, you owe me. If I miss, I'll buy you both a treat." He never missed.

Nearly 20 years earlier, a brief report in the May 11, 1939, *Jordan Independent* on the Jordan High School baseball team, which played a five-game season, noted that normally solid mound ace Frank Betchwars was pounded off the hill in the first inning of a game against Lakeville. "Tex Erickson, who seems to do everything well on the baseball field then took over the mound duties and accredited himself very well. Tex pitched four innings and then gave over to Betchwars again."

Tex Erickson did everything well on the football field, too. He was a game-breaking, triple-threat halfback on the undefeated 1936 Jordan Hubmen high school football team. He drove defenses crazy with his elusive style of scat-back running. Tacklers had trouble bringing him down, because they couldn't get a hold of him, much less put a hit on him. As often as not, would-be tacklers got only air when they thought for sure they had him. Like Harry Houdini, he was an escape artist, and the best way to defend against him was to surround him and force him to the sidelines–your best tackler. *Jordan Independent* articles from the fall of 1936 note that Tex was "a marked man" in every game because of the frustration and humiliation he was causing defenses. He could turn on a dime, spin out of impossible situations on the field, and if he got behind defenders, he was gone for six. He could throw the football on halfback options, and he dropkicked extra points after touchdowns. It is likely as well that Tex did some "quick kicking," too, a third-down punting ploy that has virtually disappeared from football at all levels along with the drop kick.

We can picture Tex at right halfback in the old standard, tight "T" formation getting a pitchout from his one-eyed quarterback, Bud Bauer, who would later make a name for himself in Minneapolis, on the Iron Range, and throughout the state of Minnesota as a pitcher in fast-pitch softball. Tex would take the pitch and after feigning an end run with a step or two, time the footwork necessary to punt the ball on the run on third down, hoping to surprise the defense and pin the opponents deep inside their own territory with the benefit of a good roll. It was sound strategic football, because with a good defense a team could pick up 30 to 50 yards on the exchanges without risking a punt return by the other team or a fumble or interception with a third-down offensive play. The Hubmen of 1936 had a good defense, too. They shut out four of the six teams they faced, including the vaunted New Prague Trojans, 46-0, a game in which Tex scored three touchdowns. But here is presumably Max Casey in his report on the game filed under the headline, "Jordan Gridders Drub New Prague," and a subhead of "Erickson Was Star" in the October 8, 1936, *Jordan Independent*:

> Donald 'Tex' Erickson, Jordan's diminutive right halfback, was the sensation of the day. On numerous occasions, Tex would get loose for nice gains and his sidestepping and shaking of tacklers was outstanding.

In the final game of the 1936 Hubmen football season, a 40-6 blowout of archrival Belle Plaine, "Little Texas," as Max had labeled him a year earlier as a freshman, lit up the scoreboard again with four touchdowns and three drop-kicked extra points.

Physically, Tex Erickson peaked as a mature adult at 5-6 and, at most, 150 pounds, according to his son, Dwight Erickson. But in the October 22, 1936, report of the 21-0 win over Arlington, the *Jordan Independent* provided a little more descriptive color about Tex Erickson:

> In the backfield the laurels go to Erickson, who weighs slightly over a hundred pounds and who is so twisty and squirmy when carrying the ball, that a snake would have a hard time following in his tracks.

Tex Erickson's high school football seasons consisted of just six games three of his four years, seven games one year. Yet, in a November 16, 1989, *Jordan Independent* sports special publication of "Jordan Hubmen Football Records," Tex was *still* fifth all-time in scoring, with 101 points on 15 touchdowns and 11 extra points. While he played a little as a 107-pound freshman in 1935, it was merely as a substitute to give a breather to regulars like Captain Joe Bruenig. Given that high school seasons have expanded significantly since the 1930s, totals of any factor in a measurement table of this sort are not fair, while measures such as points *per* game, yards *per* carry, etc. are fair.

It's the single-season homerun record argument all over again: Roger Maris had 162 games in which he hit 61 homeruns, while the Babe had but 154 games in his season to hit his 60 homeruns. Expansion, and the dilution of pitching quality, which Ted Williams spoke to, is another factor in that argument. We think Tex

Erickson would move up a number of slots and maybe even be the all-time Jordan High School leader in key rushing statistics if the records that are presented to the public were reckoned with in a fair manner. We can only wonder if he would have bettered Ardie Hamer's eight to nine yards-per-carry in the 1966 season of nine games. As big, strong, and fast as Hamer was, he wasn't a one-pony circus.

This kept the 6-foot, 190-pound, 10-flat left halfback from going over the top in yardage and touchdowns. Wingback Paul Kragthorpe is remembered for his eight to nine yards per carry, too, with just a handful of selective rushes a game.

Bruising fullback Jim Yarusso looked for linebackers and defensive backs to hurt when they tried to tackle him head on. The 5-10, 205-pounder carried the mail on tough, short-yardage situations out of the same backfield, scoring a dozen TDs himself while averaging five yards per carry that year.

They didn't keep individual statistics like that in Tex's day, but we know that he, too, like Hamer, played in a backfield of talented running backs that complemented each other effectively and spread the mail-carrying duties around.

His 15 career touchdowns weren't on two-yard plunges up the middle. We can read between the lines of Max Casey's colorful reporting. Tex's TDs were homerun balls. They were open-field-running bombs, and we know that he had at least one–a 90-yard punt return–called back.

The presentation of "Jordan Hubmen Football Records" shows rushing records for single season and career. That's fair enough to measure and compare the performance of running backs. Greg Pekarna, 1978-1980; John McFarland, 1981-1983; and Mike Allar, 1982-1984 held the single-season and career rushing records as of 1989 and probably still hold them. They played 9-game seasons, as did Hamer in 1966. But in 1981, the Class-B Minnesota State Champion Hubmen were 12-1 on the season–13 games. If you're going to compare, you must be fair. By their very nature, lists of record holders present a comparison. The "order of merit" is presented for acclamation.

The rushing *averages per carry* of these obviously great running backs lag those of Hamer and Kragthorpe, and it is more than likely that the rushing averages of all these big backs would lag Tex's average gain per rushing attempt. The number of games he played limited Tex's single-season and career marks in simple yardage and scoring totals–just as Babe Ruth, who averaged a homerun for every 9 at bats in 1927, actually played in 10 fewer games than Maris did in 1961 (151 vs. 161). That's roughly 40 at bats, or four to five homeruns for The Babe on a statistical basis. What if he had gotten hot with his bat down the stretch run of chasing a pennant?

Had Tex played three or four more games per year, had individual rushing statistics been kept then, had his football seasons consisted of as many games as the leaders enjoyed, one can easily see how his numbers would have been better in a table of these statistics. It's easy to see how Tex Erickson, Class of 1939, could have put rushing numbers in the Jordan High School books that would have never been touched.

The Hubmen opened their 1937 football season, where they had left off in the record-setting previous fall, by blasting Shakopee, 44-0. Tex had a touchdown and several extra points, but without any statistics compiled, archived, and available from 1937 from what was just a high school football game, let your imagination fill in from Max Casey's reporting from the scene at the time whatever statistical blanks are needed in order to know the little running back's game. Or just visualize the excellence:

> Donald 'Tex' Erickson played a brilliant offensive game, carrying the ball a good share of the time and eluding tacklers by his twisting and squirming through the line and around the ends.

The team had 20 first downs in the game, 15 of them rushing. Odds are high that Tex, a veritable "buzz bomb," had a field day running the football. He was ejected in the season's second game, a shutout of Montgomery, "for slugging," Max reported, which would have been really out of character. But as a marked man on the football field who continued to frustrate and humiliate defenses, when they did get him down, they piled on. In the mess and mayhem of the pile, oblivious to officials whose whistles remained silent, Tex was attacked repeatedly on the bottom of those piles by the same humiliated defenders who couldn't touch him in the open field. Punches were thrown. Eyes were gouged. There were no facemasks on the helmets, which were little more than leather beanies in those days. You could get hurt in those piles. Teams wanted to take the little firebrand out any way they could. He retaliated finally in front of an official.

According to Max Casey's report on the Le Center game, a 7-7 tie, "Little Tex Erickson again *played brilliantly*, taking the ball on numerous occasions and *gaining many yards* for his team." The italicized emphasis is ours, not Max's, in lieu of the lack of statistics from the period. The following week, at Le Sueur, in the first night game under the lights in the history of the school, Tex Erickson intercepted a pass on the 12-yard line and took it 88 yards for a 6-0 Hubmen win, with no defender within 20 yards of him when he crossed the goal line, according to the report from the day. The Hubmen smashed New Prague, 21-0, and Belle Plaine, 54-0, with players deep into the bench seeing action early. Moreover, Tex "got away with one of his specialty runs *as per usual* . . .," according to the November 4, 1937, *Jordan Independent*. It was the school's 12th consecutive game over two seasons without a loss, and Arlington came next for a rare seventh game in the season. A fourth quarter field goal after a recovered fumble gave Arlington a 9-7 win. Tex Erickson had an electrifying 90-yard punt return called back in the first half by an official who claimed Tex had stepped out of bounds. Jordan partisans lining the sidelines and with a better, unobstructed view than the official had, according to Max's report, claimed that Tex never got within a yard of the sidelines. Their objections and castigation of officials were to no avail. Home cookin' prevailed at Arlington.

Max Casey was promoted from cub reporter and "printer's devil" on his father's newspaper, *The Jordan Independent*, on appropriately enough for this Irish family, March 17–St. Patrick's Day–in 1938. Max made the weekly publication's masthead as "Associate Editor" under his father's name–John E. Casey–and title as "Editor and Publisher." That year, 1938, Grover Cleveland Alexander was inducted into baseball's Hall of Fame . . . Hitler seized control of the German army and soon invaded and annexed Austria . . . Sandoz Laboratories manufactured LSD, illegal use of which would be chronicled in Tom Wolf's 1968-published *The Electric*

Kool-Aid Acid Test . . . Howard Hughes flew around the world in 91 hours . . . Cleveland Indian power-pitching ace Bob Feller struck out a record 18 Detroit Tigers . . . The Yankees swept the Cubs in four straight to win their third consecutive World Series in October . . . Four months earlier, in June, Johnny Vander Meer of the Cincinnati Reds pitched back-to-back no hitters.

With Marty O'Neil at shortstop and Al Litfin at second base for the 1938 edition of the Jordan Brewers, Tex played a couple of games with the newly formed Jordan "Cubs" in the Le Sueur County League before heading to northern Minnesota–Remer, his sister Madeline (Erickson) Gardner, who graduated from Jordan High School in 1947, thought–and a CCC camp to work for the rest of the summer. O'Neil would not look like a ballplayer years later when he worked the microphone in the professional wrestling ring as the public address announcer in Minneapolis. Short, bald, bespectacled, and pudgy looking in his tuxedo for the wrestling show, Marty O'Neil was ridiculed by many in the 1960s who couldn't have seen him playing ball. But in 1938 he was good enough to be picked up by J.J. Kohn of St. Paul for the *national* amateur baseball tournament in Battle Creek, Michigan, which the St. Paul team had won the year before.

Jordan qualified for the Class-A state tournament at Shakopee by winning the Minnesota Valley League playoffs against Shakopee, then beating Fairfax for the Region 6 crown. But for the second time in three years, Owatonna, gearing up for their run in the Class-AA Southern Minny, edged the Brewers, 1-0, in the big dance. Max's report of the loss in the semi-finals cast aspersions:

> The fact that the winners used a big league pitcher and also won the state title puts Jordan in as good a light, if not better, than the 1938 state champs.

The Class-A champion Owatonna nine then defeated a Class-AA team from St. Paul for the mythical state championship.

It was Tex's senior year of high school, and Geno Taddei of Hibbing, Minnesota, and St. Thomas College note, joined the school's staff as a teacher and the athletic director, with head coaching duties for football and basketball. The 1938 Jordan High School football season started with a bang again under Coach Taddei. The Hubmen defense shut out Shakopee for the second year in a row, and Tex Erickson, as usual, provided the offensive fireworks, scoring two touchdowns and drop kicking two extra points in a 20-0 win. But here's Max again with some color commentary on Tex Erickson's opening-game performance in 80-degree afternoon heat:

> Diminutive Donald "Tex" Erickson, as last year, again showed fans and opponents that he could carry that pigskin just about anywhere he wanted to.

Let's savor the situation: First, with a population of about 2,400 and Prior Lake sending its high school kids to Shakopee because they had no high school yet, Shakopee in 1938 was a "Goliath" in the valley, along with St. Peter (population 5,800) and Bloomington (population 3,600). Jordan, Max revealed, was the smallest school in the district with football. Instead of avoiding the big schools, Jordan sought out Goliath. The athletic directors scheduled Shakopee to open their seasons.

They didn't run to a soft schedule in order to pad their record. They didn't schedule Faribault School of the Blind, Randolph, Blakely, or Henderson in order to manage a desired statistical magnificence. They weren't thinking then of goosing the numbers in order to help market a kid to a college recruiter and an athletic scholarship. The competition with next-door neighbors, regardless of relative size differences, was important and valued. No school district or conference championships were awarded in football, but everybody recognized a mythical county championship, and, it's worth repeating, "[Tex Erickson] could carry that pigskin just about anywhere he wanted to" against anybody.

Tex's 15-yard TD pass and successful drop kick were all of the scoring in the team's second-game win, 7-0, over Montgomery. He was held scoreless in the 27-7 loss to Le Center, although it was reported that he "did get away for several nice runs, one nearly for a touchdown in the opening minutes of the game." Le Sueur held Tex in check and beat the Hubmen, too, 27-6. Then Tex re-discovered his groove for the last two games. He broke a 60-yard touchdown run in the 7-6 win over New Prague, and his touchdown and extra-point kick put a 12-7 lead over Belle Plaine on ice in the last few minutes of the game, with the final score 19-7.

As great of a running back as Tex Erickson was in the last three years of the 1930s, his best sport was baseball. But high school baseball in Minnesota has always been problematic because winter can linger long into spring. In the 1930s they might have scheduled just five games. It wasn't covered like football, and who knows whether they even got their games in. They certainly didn't go to Florida or Texas for a spring trip. They waited for school to end. They played baseball in the summer, the season in which the game was made to be played.

A good athlete in his own right and a good enough baseball player to be pursued by Coach Dick Siebert in the early 1950s for his Gopher team, Dick Nolden was the other half of what many locals who saw them and later duos called "the best double-play combination ever seen in Jordan baseball." Paul Sunder, a member of the Golden Age Brewer ball clubs, said of Dick Nolden, "He and Tex had that 'connection' with each other" that is as important with double-play combinations as it is with marriages. "They flew Nolden back for a game from up North one time, too," Sunder said, "and picked him up at Flying Cloud Airport."

Nolden said he went to a few Gopher baseball practices and participated in the workouts, but the baseball demands, especially the out-of-state travel, would have compromised the demanding course load and work he had signed up for in veterinary medical school. He was in school to become a veterinarian, not to play baseball. Very few young men would major in baseball in the 1950s. Nolden moved to Detroit Lakes, Minnesota, with his DVM (Doctor of Veterinary Medicine) from the University of Minnesota in 1957. He said, in what we came to appreciate as typical Nolden understatement, that Tex Erickson, who was about 10 years older, was "a good athlete." He was better than good, according to what Tom Betchwars said his father, Frank, always said of his classmate and earlier teammate. "'Tex Erickson was an amazing athlete,'" Frank Betchwars told his son. He was smart. He was quick. He had a great arm, and he was tough as a railroad spike. Outdoor physical work in the CCC camp had honed his small body into lean muscle, gristle, and grit.

Tex Erickson's game was one of speed, quickness, and smarts. His typical MO was likely a walk or a bunt for a base hit, a steal of second base and on to third with a late, muffed throw from the catcher dribbling away from an infielder relaxing on the play. You couldn't relax with Tex Erickson on the base paths. He liked to steal home, too. Tex "bothered" pitchers while he was hitting because of his small strike zone and his ability to get on base. He bothered them on base because of his ability to steal second at will, and then take third, sometimes on the very next pitch. He bothered infielders with his ability to bunt and beat out groundballs they thought were sure outs. They couldn't afford to misstep or miss their grip on the ball in the glove or take an extra step to get more leverage on their throws to first on his ground balls. If they did, he was likely to beat the throw. So they knew they had to hurry, and in their haste infielders bobbled balls that were ruled errors. Nonetheless, the on-base percentage statistic would have highlighted Tex's contributions at the plate much better than his career .261 batting average. The point is that Tex Erickson would beat you with his bat, his legs, his arm, and his head. He was never out of position, and he was never out of a game.

His son, Dwight, said he'll never forget how his uncle, Bill Erickson, used to tell the story of Tex getting to first on a bunt single, then stealing second, stealing third, and after stealing home the catcher disgustedly threw the baseball into the creek. They all laughed every time Bill told that story.

"Tex was just good all around," Sunder said. "He could do everything." Tex made all the plays at shortstop, including the ground balls into the hole between short and third. Probably the toughest play for a shortstop of any day to make, "He had no problem making that play," Sunder said. "He had a great arm and was really accurate with his throws." Tex strengthened his arm and worked on throwing accuracy by pitching a lot of batting practice. "He liked to throw batting practice," Sunder said.

The slow roller that dribbles between the pitcher's mound and the third-base line might be second in difficulty for a shortstop to make, according to several good shortstops we talked to, including Mark Hess, the 1986 All-Big Ten Minnesota Gopher shortstop. "You've got to make that play with your bare hand," Hess admitted, and Tex's hands were huge and strong. Because of his height, his center of gravity was low to the ground and he was never off-balance, even when running full-tilt to make a play like that. If the play could be made, Tex would nail it.

Former Brewer infielder Ed Breimhorst said that Tex made a lot of plays with his bare hand. He'd take the throw from Nolden coming across the bag on a double play with his bare hand, his throwing hand–the quicker to relay the ball to first base to complete the double play. We saw him catch a scorching line drive in the hole with that bare right hand. It was all instant, intuitive, athletic reaction–the ball hit beyond the reach across his body with his gloved hand. Most shortstops would have merely waved at the liner and awaited the cutoff throw from the left fielder. These are the things that don't show up in box scores or statistics. They are the defensive gems of pure baseball IQ and athleticism that are etched in the memories of those privileged enough to have witnessed them. They are of the same golden glove mettle as that shown at the Major League Baseball level by the likes of Brooks Robinson, Willie Mays, Ozzie Smith, and Roberto Clemente.

Then there's the "Texas Leaguer" and the infield popups. "Tex called for everything right away," Paul Sunder said. "And you've got to remember the gloves." Baseball gloves were mere dishrags or furniture doilies in comparison to the modern bushel basket-sized leather system introduced in 1957 by Wilson with its game-changing Model A2000 and in widespread use since about the mid-1960s. It's why infielders and outfielders were coached to use both hands in fielding ground or fly balls. Backhanding a hot grounder or catching a lazy fly ball with just the glove hand was verboten. You got in front of balls to knock them down at least– to prevent the potential extra base. One-handed catches were considered to be hot-dogging, or showboating, and unnecessarily risky. They could get a player booed and benched whether it was in Baltimore or Belle Plaine, Minnesota.

"Tex had really good eyesight," Sunder said, "and quick hands–he was really quick with the release of the ball." He didn't boot many balls and never made a bad throw. He got to balls that others couldn't have touched. But the errors he was charged with were just as likely to have been balls he got a glove on because of his quickness. Scorers tended to charge an error if ground balls touched the gloves of infielders. It's how the term, "clean single" was born. Bad hops over an infielder's shoulder would be scored a hit, but ground balls that nicked the glove of an infielder or went through his legs were likely to be errors in the official scorebook.

"Remember, too, the fields," Sunder said. They weren't anything like the manicured smoothness of a golf course green that they've been playing on for the last 40 years. "But we had that black sand at Jordan," he said, that they got along the creek out near Brentwood. "It made for a really good infield."

Tex Erickson was a fiery competitor. He exuded intensity on the field. There was no other way to play the game. "But he seldom even argued with an umpire," Sunder said, adding that off field, "he was a happy-go-lucky guy."

Naturally, he was ridiculed for his size from the time he started playing ball in the back yards. His response was always to play harder and smarter, burning opponents with his hustle and speed. Like Phil Rizzuto, the similarly diminutive Hall of Fame New York Yankee shortstop from the same period, Tex Erickson defined for decades the position and play of shortstop locally. It was as true more than a half century later as it was in the 1950s, despite what his detractors said of him–people who never saw him play, people who seemed to need to be in tune with the noise they could make with their own horns. People who thought history began in 1980.

"Scooter" Rizzuto, as he was known, was told in 1935 at a Brooklyn Dodger tryout by Casey Stengel, who was managing the Dodgers then, that he should "go get a shoeshine box," according to Wikipedia. But when Stengel joined the Yankees as manager in 1949, Rizzuto had a secure lock on the shortstop position. Casey reportedly said later of Phil Rizzuto, "He is the greatest shortstop I have ever seen in my entire baseball career, and I have watched some beauties." Having managed for 25 years, until 1965, after playing in the Major Leagues from 1912 to 1925, Stengel had to have seen the best play. But his change of mind on Rizzuto was quite a turnabout from the manager named in 1997 as the All-Time Best Manager in Major League Baseball history by a panel of 36 members of Baseball Writers Association of America in connection with the All Star Game that year.

Tex Erickson was one of 13 boys in a high school class of 34 that graduated in the spring of 1939. He was 19 years old–a year older than the oldest of usual high school seniors. He wasn't a slow learner, nor was he held back for any other reason. Tex Erickson took a year off from high school, his son Dwight thought, and went to work at a Depression-era CCC (Civilian Conservation Corps) camp to help put food on his family's table. Tex's teenage years coincided with the Great Depression. Nobody had any money. Jobs were scarce. High school, you could say, was a luxury in some homes.

He got his nickname from his father, Augustus, or "Augie," Erickson, who was called, "Texas." "The way I heard it," Madeline said of her brother, "is that they started calling Don "Texas," too, and that didn't work, so they shortened it to "Tex." According to Madeline, their father picked up the name from his travels around the country, hopping freight trains. "He rode the rails," Madeline said of her father, "and must have gotten to the state of Texas looking for work or adventure."

History was unfolding with events of long-lasting impact throughout 1939: Adolph Hitler threatened the Jews in his speech to the German Reichstag . . . The comic strip, "Superman," debuted in daily newspapers . . . Nazi Germany dissolved the Republic of Czechoslovakia and occupied the country . . . Italy invaded Albania . . . Ted Williams got his first hit in MLB–a double . . . *Batman* comic books were introduced . . . Lou Gehrig ended his streak of 2,130 consecutive games . . . The first night baseball game in the American League was played at Philadelphia's Shibe Park. . . Germany and Italy announced their pact as allies . . . Food stamps were first issued . . . Hitler announced his designs on Poland . . . Churchill signed a pact with Russia . . . Baseball's Hall of Fame opened in Cooperstown, NY . . . The Yankees announced Lou Gehrig's retirement after he was diagnosed with ALS . . . The German Nazis closed the last Jewish business enterprises . . . *The Wizard of Oz* premiered in Hollywood . . . Germany and Russia signed a 10-year non-aggression pact . . . The first Major League Baseball telecast saw the Reds beat the Dodgers . . . New York Yankee pitcher Atley Donald was clocked at 94.7 mph with his fastball . . . Hitler ordered the extermination of mentally ill . . . Poland mobilized and Switzerland proclaimed its neutrality . . . World War II began with Germany's invasion of Poland . . . FDR declared U.S. neutrality . . . Russia invaded eastern Poland . . . Hitler denied he planned to go to war against France and Britain . . . The Yankees swept the Reds for their fourth straight World Series win . . . Albert Einstein informed FDR of the potential of the atomic bomb . . . Joe DiMaggio won the AL MVP award . . . The first air-conditioned automobile, a Packard, was exhibited in Chicago . . . The Nazis began their "Final Solution"–the mass murder of Polish Jews . . . The Soviets invaded Finland . . . *Gone With the Wind* premiered in Atlanta, Georgia.

Before the gates of hell were opened in Europe for the second time in just the first half of the 20th Century in September of 1939, Tex Erickson and two local clubs had some baseball to play. As good as he was, Tex Erickson had no illusions about replacing veteran Jordan Brewer shortstop Happy Boll, who had replaced Marty O'Neil in the lineup. He would play with his high school classmate, Frank Betchwars, and the town's other young players for the Jordan Cubs in the Le Sueur County League. The May 18, 1939, *Jordan Independent* reported on the early season action of both teams. While the Brewers went to 2-0 in the Crow River League with a convincing 10-2 win over St. Boni on the strength of Bobby Vestal's two-hitter, the Cubs lost to Montgomery, 13 to 4, despite a home run by Tex Erickson. Both the Cubs and the Brewers had respectable seasons, but both lost in early rounds of their respective league playoffs.

Tex moved up to the Jordan Brewers in 1940. After one season in the Crow River League, the Brewers returned to the Minnesota Valley League with its more familiar neighboring towns, which promised more admissions and revenue. Happy Boll was still a fixture at shortstop, and, indeed, from the cleanup position he would hit well over .400 on the season in Class-A ball. But Tex moved into the lineup at second base. He pushed Al Litfin into the outfield. Litfin had played for Chaska's 1937 state tournament team and had been a member of the professional barnstorming House of David team. Tex started the season batting seventh in the order. By the end of the first month of play, he was batting second. Tex helped the Brewers to finish the regular season tied with Chaska in second place with 10-4 records, while Shakopee led the league at 12-1. His bases-loaded, game-tying triple in the bottom of the ninth gave the locals second wind and a tie ballgame, before falling in playoff action to Lakeville, 7-4, in 10 innings and ending their season. In fact, Tex led the Brewer attack that game with four hits in five at bats, raising his average to around .260 for his first year of play with the big club.

The drums of war began to beat even louder. On September 16, 1940, the military draft was re-initiated with the Selective Training and Service Act. While technically it established the first peacetime conscription in the country's history, the times were hardly peaceful. Males between the ages of 18 and 65 were required to register.

Young men–men of baseball-playing age–were getting drafted into compulsory military service at an ever-increasing rate, and there was talk about suspending baseball in the coming summer. Tex and the Brewers lost two starters to Uncle Sam. Then the talk of going with younger players, all from town, rather than better but paid players from out of town, cost a couple more starters, including Happy Boll, who while continuing to live in Jordan, jumped over to play with Shakopee in 1941–probably because the Indians made him an offer he couldn't turn down. The Shakopee Indians had drafted him for the playoffs at the end of the previous summer, and he'd helped them win the state tournament with what was hailed as "near-perfect play" at third base while wielding a hot bat at a .533 clip for the Class-A tourney. Minnesota Governor Harold Stassen awarded Boll "The Governor's Trophy" as the tournament's Most Valuable Player.

Happy Boll's departure opened up the shortstop position for Tex Erickson and, except for the four war years, 1942 through 1945, when Tex served his country in the U.S. Navy, he anchored the Jordan Brewer infield there for most of the following 15 years. But Dwight Erickson said that his father always said that he had lost a lot of his game in the service. Not that anybody else noticed, but Tex lost the best four years of his baseball-playing young manhood, and much more with it, we would learn, to military service. That wasn't uncommon. The great DiMaggio was said to have lost a step and a little bat speed during his service break. Ted Williams undoubtedly lost a legitimate shot at Babe Ruth's career homerun record with most of five years of military service–as a fighter pilot in both World War II and the Korean conflict. Phil Rizzuto–Tex's New York Yankee mirror image–missed three years, 1943 through 1945, due to military service. He'd batted .307 and .284 his first two years, 1941 and 1942, as a Yankee, but couldn't hit .260 his first year back from the war.

J.J. Krautkremer advertised new 1940 eight-cylinder Buicks for $895 in Jordan, and John Stang countered with 1941 Dodges starting at $825. Lenten specials advertised by Jordan's restaurants seem equally unbelievable today: The Hamburger Home Café, for example, got 10 cents–one thin dime–for a diner's choice of walleye pike or bullheads, salad, and French fries on Saturday nights. Meanwhile, the Café Minnesota next door offered its rich turtle soup for a dime as well. The turtle meat and fish didn't come from a Twin Cities restaurant supply firm in 1940. They most likely came from other local entrepreneurs working the Minnesota River, Sand Creek, and the many lakes and sloughs in the area. The Jordan Brewery announced its "New Carry Home Carton" of twelve 12 oz. "Steinie Bottles" of "Old Style Brew" for 95 cents plus 15 cents deposit on the bottles, "Available at any Jordan Retail Dealer."

Tex Erickson found a job after graduating from high school with the Schutz and Hilgers Jordan Brewery, his son thinks today, on the strength of his baseball skills and promise. It only makes sense: Tex was a local star already, having excelled in football and baseball throughout his high school years; the Brewery was the largest employer in town; and its owners were huge supporters of everything Jordan and everything baseball. They didn't want to lose a ballplayer of Tex's caliber to a neighboring town. They would give the likable kid a job and find something for him to do after bringing him in. Still, it's mostly conjecture, as Dwight Erickson wasn't even born until 1957, he said, and by then much had already passed and he doesn't remember his father talking about it much.

Tex got a little ink early from Max Casey's coverage of the Jordan Brewers in 1941: "There was no doubt," Max wrote after a couple of games, that Tex Erickson was ". . . an outstanding player for the locals." But the team was decimated by the local pride factor and by the selective service draft. Each week, more names of local county men called to serve were published. The Brewers would finish a disappointing 6-8–fifth place in the league dominated by teams less reluctant that year to procure the pitching or other outside talent they needed to compete, they said, but which meant, as it always has, the talent to win. Excelsior at 12-2, followed by Chaska and Shakopee at 11-3, set the pace. Shakopee took the Brewers out in the playoffs, 12-1, sending the baseball folks home to await the winter–and war.

It came soon enough–on December 7, 1941, with the Japanese surprise attack on Pearl Harbor, Hawaii. Seven men from Scott County were known to have been on duty in Hawaii when the attack occurred. All survived. Then the U.S. got off the fence post of neutrality and declared war on Japan. Germany declared war on the U.S., and the U.S. declared war on Germany. The country now was in it to win it, and Prime Minister Churchill of Great Britain was pleased. He had been seeking this country's help against Germany for several years, and now he had it. At war's end in 1945, with over 12 million American military personnel, a buildup for the war effort from 334,473 in 1939, Weintraub writes in *The Victory Season*, "Nearly a million and a half men were discharged each month starting at the end of 1945 and continuing throughout 1946." They would return home to fuel and lead the unprecedented economic recovery of the nation and to restore baseball to its place as America's pastime.

Baseball and the beer industry had suffered in America without them. Our service men were primarily 18 to 35 years of age–prime ball-playing and beer-drinking age. From the economics of universal supply and demand, they provided the supply in baseball at all levels and the demand in the beer industry.

War meant killing and suffering on the battle fronts, and sacrifice everywhere: Automobile production had ceased, with plants re-tooling to produce military vehicles–tanks and jeeps; rationing went into effect of common foodstuffs and other consumer items that everyone had taken for granted, including coffee, sugar, meat, butter, gasoline and tires. Dated, color-coded coupon books were issued to manage the rationing, but an underground black market developed that allowed consumers to buy things if they wanted them bad enough. A call went out for scrap metal to make bombs, and a concerted campaign resulted in the collection of tons of scrap metal at the county level. Even Hillerich & Bradsby, maker of Louisville Slugger baseball bats in use throughout the country, re-tooled to fashion the M1 carbine rifle. War bonds were issued time and again to borrow the savings of Americans in order to augment the taxes they paid that were increased to marginal rates as high as 90 percent in order to finance America's war effort.

Cargill stretched beyond its core business grain trade at Savage, Minnesota, to build a shipyard that promised 1,000 jobs and the production of six fuel tankers at a cost of $10 million to the U.S. Navy. By the end of the war the contract had grown to over 20 ships for $30 million while providing jobs for as many as 2,500 employees. The private, family-held company based in Minnetonka dredged the main channel of the Minnesota River to a depth of nine feet in order to tow the tanker hulls from Savage 14 miles down river to the Mississippi. From there the ships were towed to New Orleans for final fitting and then put into salt-water service to the navy.

Tex Erickson enlisted in the U.S. Navy on April 6, 1942. After boot training in San Diego, California, he attended Navy Aviation Machinist schools in Jacksonville, Florida, and Chicago, Illinois, according to the February 21, 1946, *Jordan Independent*. Upon completion of his training, Tex was assigned to Naval Air Stations in Alabama and Pensacola, Florida. He became a specialist on aircraft engine carburetors, which ought to terminate a 60-year suspicion voiced by many that Tex Erickson's job at Engfer Motors in Jordan, Minnesota, was to play shortstop for the Jordan Brewers.

Dwight Erickson said his father held the position of "Parts Man" with Engfer, but there's no way that an aircraft engine carburetor specialist wouldn't be doing some tune ups and tinkering on the carburetors of cars and trucks of all models and makes at the Engfer Garage in the 1940s and 1950s. Maybe Tex moved to the head of the line of applicants at Engfer's because of his baseball skills. Maybe his availability and need of a job upon his discharge from the navy in 1946 were enough to put Ben Engfer over the top on a decision to add another employee to his payroll. But Ben Engfer, "a Baseball Boss," was no business fool. Carburetors were always a problem with cars, especially in the Minnesota winters, until fuel injection came along decades later. Engfer Motors could use a good man like Tex Erickson. Employing the popular athlete had to have helped sales, too. You can't buy that kind of advertising in a small town.

There was no baseball in Jordan in 1942, and the ball club they fielded the next couple of years was a collection of kids, retreads, and the 4F military deferred. In 1945, however, they were at least competitive, with the mammoth Gordy Gelhaye catching and Roger McDonald on the mound. Both, as draftees, helped lead Excelsior to the Class-A state championship that year. Gelhaye pounded the ball at the plate in the tournament, and McDonald chalked up the first no-hitter in the history of the state championship game and the first no-hit game in the tournament since 1932. Al Litfin, the former Jordan Brewer second baseman kicked into the outfield by Tex Erickson, won tournament MVP honors while playing errorless first base for Excelsior and swinging a hot bat–8 for 19 with three homeruns. Armand Peterson and Tom Tomashek write of Litfin in their *Town Ball*:

> St. Louis Cardinal scout Jack Ryan said that Litfin, although 29 years old, might be offered a professional contract. Ryan thought that Litfin was good enough to hold his own immediately in the American Association.

Meanwhile, Gelhaye had actually hit better than Litfin in the tournament, going 7 for 11 with two homeruns. But the authors of *Town Ball* suggest that Gelhaye was passed over for MVP honors because of the image of his body. Without the war, this 1945 state championship could easily have been a Jordan Brewer celebration, and Tex Erickson would have been playing shortstop to support the pitching of McDonald and Vestal and the hitting of Litfin and Gelhaye.

"War is hell," and it was hell on baseball at all levels. Major League Baseball was big league in name only. "Some five hundred major leaguers traded in baseball uniforms for service uniforms, and their absence was keenly felt," Weintraub writes in *The Winning Season*, while estimating that over 4,000 minor league baseball players fought for God and country in The Big One. Local amateur ball all but dried up along with beer sales.

Italy surrendered unconditionally in September 1943, and a series of surrenders by German forces brought World War II to an end in Europe in late April and early May of 1945. Then Japan's unconditional surrender on Friday, August 10, was caught in the full spirit of banner type in the August 16, 1945, *Jordan Independent*:

"The War Is Over."

A week earlier, the same weekly publication in the same top right-hand corner above the fold had headlined "The Week's Biggest News–World-Shaking New Bomb." Second-tier headlines read: "One Has Been Used Against Japan With Awesome Results"; and more: "Called 'Atomic Bomb' Its Supersmash is *U-235* From Uranium."

The article relates how 60 percent of the city of Hiroshima had been destroyed by one 400-pound bomb. The explosive element may have been no larger than a golf ball and the U-235 in it the size of a pea. President Truman was quoted: "U-235 may be God's instrument for a quick peace now and a preserver of peace in the future."

Prime Minister Churchill of Great Britain said that the entire world was amazed, adding, "God gave the Allies this bomb. The heart-shaking risk and secrecy for over three years stands to the everlasting honor of President Roosevelt and his advisers." Japan was told that if they did not quit, more atomic bombs would be used to annihilate them.

The end of the war and two deaths marked the year, 1945. Franklin Delano Roosevelt, just recently having inaugurated his fourth term as president, died in office on April 12. Vice-President Harry Truman took over the presidency. Locally, E. H. Seeman, owner since 1916 of the Mudbaden Sulphur Springs health resort just north of Jordan, died at his home in Chicago on the same day.

Then the troops began to trickle home–about 200 to the Jordan area alone after the trickle swelled to the discharge of nearly a million and a half men per month, according to Weintraub, beginning in late 1945 and continuing through 1946. The country wasn't ready for their return. There was a shortage of everything, because everything had gone into the war effort. This unmet demand spurred the black market in consumer goods once again. Lifting of price restraints resulted in a skyrocketing increase in the cost of living in just one year. Labor unrest made for powder kegs of violence everywhere, as everybody seemed to feel that they had sacrificed much–always more than their neighbor–and now it was time they had a piece of the action and some cake, too.

The men came home from the two battlefronts and from the pockets of espionage and communications activities in diplomatic zones, and from established combat bases, as well as maintenance depots, designed to keep men and equipment battle ready. The February 21, 1946, *Jordan Independent* carried a front-page item in a column entitled, "Home Again For Our Boys":

> Receiving his Honorable Discharge from the Naval Separation Center at Wold Chamberlain Field in Minneapolis on Jan. 23rd, Donald Erickson, Aviation Machinist Mate Gird Class arrived at the home of his folks, Mr. and Mrs. August Erickson that same day.

Tex was back!

He was bigger, thicker all around. He had filled out from the rigors of boot camp, then regular exercise and three square meals a day at the naval base mess hall. He had reached his full maturity–about the same size as Phil Rizzuto at 5-6, maybe 150 pounds at the most in the winter months. More than likely though, both men played at around 135 to 140 pounds, and even the 5-6 height might have been stretching things. Rizzuto was two years older than Tex Erickson and hailed from New York, baseball mecca of the world with three Major League teams in the city alone, and others nearby at Boston, Philadelphia, and Washington, D.C. If you had anything going for you on the diamond, they heard about you, and you got a look. But Tex was in the wilderness of the Midwest. Farm clubs. Good baseball, it was true. But it was still minor league and so-called semi-pro ball. Scouts were active, following their minor league affiliates, and bird dogs would report regularly on prospects in high schools, colleges, and on amateur teams. But with only 16 MLB shortstop positions available, the chances for a kid to even get a look were rare.

Unknown to most people, Tex had a tryout, his son and sister said, with the Baltimore Orioles, she thought. "He was really excited about it," Madeline said of her older brother. "He was talking to them and talking about it at home," she said. The talk was about playing shortstop for the AA-Baltimore Orioles in 1942, something he couldn't share with friends uptown for several reasons. First, he'd likely lose his "friends"; second, he didn't want others thinking he was blowing his own horn, and he didn't want others to blow his horn either. "Beer is a mocker and wine a fool," or something close to that can be read in *The Book of Proverbs* or learned growing up in a small, German beer-drinking town. After a couple of beers, he knew, some men couldn't help talking, especially about others. Cutting others down was a habit too many learned in order to falsely prop themselves up. They were likely to feel abandoned or belittled, he thought, and there was no need for that. They would resent him for his success, or his opportunity. He would be seeking *his* own level, reaching for his star, his potential–something, he noticed, was difficult for some to understand. But the war intervened in the Big League potential for Tex Erickson. "He didn't sign because he knew he was going to be drafted," Madeline said, and he decided to enlist in the U.S. Navy.

Since the Baltimore Orioles in 1942 were a Class-AA affiliate of the Cleveland Indians of the American League, more than likely Tex's tryout had been with the Indians in the fall of 1941, maybe early spring of 1942, and they had him talking to their people at Baltimore, where he was likely told he would be assigned. Nonetheless, the Tex Erickson Story is another tale of unrealized potential, cut short not by injury but by World War II and duty to country, which was so typical of his generation. Country, community, and team came first for this generation. They didn't insist on getting their wheels greased first before putting anything on the line. They put it all out there; moreover, they didn't ask, "What's in it for me?"

Was Tex as good as "Scooter" Rizzuto, the Hall of Fame Yankee shortstop of the Golden Age of Baseball? We don't know. But he was an outstanding athlete and a great baseball player. "He was the best shortstop I ever saw play the game," Brewer infielder Ed Breimhorst of Jordan echoed what Frank had said independent of each other. He was such a far cry from the "scrawny, little, old man," that one from the contemporary crowd so unfairly called him, and others who saw him only during his 60s and 70s implied with their hurtful innuendo while they talked and danced with the insolence and arrogance of youth. But then again, they never had the privilege of seeing him play, and many of them are number geeks. They need to consult 60-year baseball man Bill Starr for a lesson on what transcends numbers. They weren't around for the Golden Age of Baseball. How could they possibly know how good of an athlete, how great of a baseball player, Tex Erickson was?

Tex made it home with some money in the bank he'd saved while in the navy. But he needed a job and didn't want to wait long to get it. Problem was his old job with the Jordan Brewery wasn't there anymore. The brewery was having trouble keeping things going. The government's rationing program had cut deeply into the ability of the brewery to stay in business. Barley malt and hops were severely restricted. Even tires for the beer delivery trucks were difficult, if not impossible, to get. They had been laying off workers and consolidating their distribution network. Baseball Boss Ben Engfer, owner-manager of Engfer Garage, heard soon enough about Tex looking for work. He hired him and then made available to Tex, who needed some wheels, a brand new 1947 Chevrolet Fleetline Aerosedan. New car buyers had to put their name on a list after the war to purchase a vehicle. Manufacturers and dealers couldn't keep up with demand. Ahead of Tex on the list was a family man with a need for a family car–a four-door sedan. The 1947 Chevy Aerosedan was a fastback-style two-door. It was sporty. It was the most popular, and the most expensive, model in the Chevy fleet of cars. Tex got first dibs on the green coupe after a neighbor declined the car. Ben Engfer probably gave Tex an "employee discount" to boot. After all, Tex Erickson was the best shortstop around.

Two other veterans who made it home announced in the April 4, 1946, *Jordan Independent* their acquisition of the Mertz Tap Room and Beer Garden. Geno Taddei and Gibby Mickus began the evolution of the local American sports bar and invited the patronage of one and all. A month later, the Brewers, with Tex and mostly other returned servicemen in the lineup, opened the 1946 Minnesota Valley League season in front of over 400 fans by hammering St. Peter, 11-0, at Fairgrounds Park. Bobby Vestall, another service veteran, fired the five-hit shutout, and the Brewer defense supported him with errorless ball. Tex must have looked good in early Brewer batting practices; he was batting cleanup in a powerful order while anchoring the infield at shortstop. His two long triples, including a first-inning shot that scored two runs against Chaska in a 7-5 win at Fairgrounds, made Manager Bill Breimhorst look like a genius. After splitting the next two games, two losses in a row put the Brewers at 3-3, as Jordan pitchers had trouble finding the strike zone and were giving up too many walks.

A front-page story in the June 13, 1946, *Jordan Independent* announced the sale of the 40,000 barrel-per-year Schutz and Hilgers Jordan Brewery to J.F. Lanser, a successful brewer in Phoenix, Arizona. The brewery had been experiencing problems throughout the war due to two things: government rationing of grains needed in the brewing process; and the dent the war had put in the demand for beer by depleting the industry's primary market of 18-to 35-year-old men in the local market area. Lanser admitted that he had bought the Jordan operation for the grain allotment alone, so when the government lifted the quotas shortly after buying it, the Arizona brewer sold the Jordan Brewery to the Mankato Brewing Company of Mankato, Minnesota, for $125,000 after just buying it for $450,000.

The numbers alone still say it was a good buy. The numbers would have told Dan Bruzek of the Mankato Brewery that it was a steal. The proximity of the new owner should have made for a better transition and consolidation. But the Mankato Brewery manager was the former Jordan Brewery head bookkeeper. He was a bean counter. He needed someone to help him read the tea leaves. Marketing, vision, and strategic planning are less tangible and defy a place on the Balance Sheet. They have never been strong suits of bean counters. Hunch and "gut" are too often ignored by managers of this mettle. Mr. Bruzek added 20,000 barrels-a-year in production volume for his Mankato Brewery with the Jordan operation, half its capacity, and he must have thought he could simply leverage the quality reputation of Jordan's Old Style Beer, as well as the small brewer's distribution network under the Kato Beer label in a competitive market against the heavyweights from Minneapolis and St. Paul–Gluek's, Hamm's, Schmidt, and Grain Belt. He must have tried to manage by the numbers–a hazard of his accounting discipline.

It didn't work. After Gluek's, Hamm's, and Grain Belt each seemed to take a turn as the most popular beer, the area would become known as "Schmidt Country" soon enough.

On Sunday, June 30, the local contingent of what Tom Brokaw hails in his book of the name as "*The Greatest Generation*"–Jordan area's World War II veterans– were given a homecoming celebration that included a parade, entertainment, free beer and other refreshments, free food, and a dance at the Fairgrounds pavilion at night. Tex Erickson is conspicuously missing from the group photograph taken on the hill above the left-field corner of Fairgrounds Park and published in the August 15, 1946, *Jordan Independent*. The veterans could order a print of the photograph taken by a professional photographer, and over time it became a kind of relic and an heirloom. Frank Betchwars, Frankie Hennes, and Al Woerdehoff, to name but a few, made it home with Purple Hearts for their heroic action in the line of duty, a fact with little recognition and even less promotion. The war heroes certainly didn't talk about it.

Al Woerdehoff drank but not so as anybody paid any attention in the town of about 1,400 people with 10 bars and every restaurant serving as a distribution network for its own brewery. He was ridiculed somewhat for his habits and a rather disheveled appearance, as were others of the town for theirs. But in retrospect, this amounted to self-medication for what was probably military shell shock, known today as PTSD, or post-traumatic stress disorder. None of the younger people knew he was a war hero. Those guys of that era didn't talk about themselves much or about their experiences in the war. Staff Sergeant Al Woerdehoff, "a member of the famous 34th "Red Bull" Division of the American Fifth Army, saw action in campaigns in Africa and took part in the bitter fighting at the Volturno River crossings, Cassino and the Anzio beachhead in Italy," according to the July 27, 1944, *Jordan Independent*. His job in the army? Machine gunner.

If the *Jordan Independent's* February 8, 1945, front-page report on Frank Betchwars is accurate, that he served in a combat unit–Company E, the Fortieth U.S. Army Engineers–that chased Nazis out of North Africa, Sicily, and Italy, then he served under General George Patton at least part of the time. In North Africa, the German enemy forces were likely to have been led by Erwin Rommel–the "Desert Fox." The news report indicates that Frank suffered the wound for which he was given the Purple Heart in the invasion of Sicily, a wound that required a period of hospitalization in North Africa. Frank returned home after the war to marry and raise a family, while running a succession of small businesses with extraordinary success, and to play a little ball.

A power pitcher who often took the mound without a baseball cap, Frank worked fast and threw hard. He played with Tex, usually pitching for the same high school nine, as well as at various times the town's A-team Brewers and B-team Cubs and Rockets. In the early 1950s, when Class-A baseball was wide open and Jordan, like other river towns, had a revolving door that saw a succession of paid pitchers, catchers, and infielders like Roger Brown, who we think is the same Roger Brown who anchored the infield of Minnesota's first *national* American Legion baseball champion, Richfield Post 435, in 1943. The same Roger Brown who represented the state of Minnesota in the first national boys' All-American All-Star game sponsored by *Esquire Magazine* in 1944. The east team, managed by Connie Mack, defeated Mel Ott's west team, 6-0, on August 7, 1944, at the Polo Grounds in New York in front of 17,803 fans. Brown missed the first game of a three-game playoff with Minneapolis rival Chamber of Commerce, won by Richfield without him. Then little Johnny Garbett rang up the defending state and national champion Richfield nine, 3-2, both runs unearned, to force a rubber game won by Richfield. Brown then led the Richfield post to a second consecutive state championship.

Broadcast on a national radio network by the dean of baseball's broadcasters, none other than "the Voice of the Brooklyn Dodgers," Red Barber, the *Esquire* All-American Boys Baseball Game featured 29 boys from as many states, including Roger Brown of Minneapolis. Nineteen of the 29 boys eventually signed professional baseball contracts. At least four played some Major League baseball, and two, Richie Ashburn and Billy Pierce, had more than token Major League careers, with Ashburn a Hall of Fame centerfielder with the Philadelphia Phillies.

We don't know what happened to Roger Brown between 1944 and 1951. War probably took him out of Minnesota and baseball. A shortstop named Roger Brown joined the Jordan Brewers after mid-season in 1951, but he wasn't good enough to move Tex Erickson off the key infield position. Instead, he moved third-baseman Clark Rice, another mercenary from Minneapolis, into left field.

But Frank Betchwars had played third base and left field when he wasn't on the mound, and with highly paid Bob Shotliff and Jim Pollard sharing most of the pitching duty beginning in 1949, he took his arm and his game elsewhere. Neither he nor any other local position player was paid the kind of money that Brown and Rice were paid. After a couple of games in 1951, rumor had it that they wanted more money. Neither Frank nor any other local pitcher was paid the kind of money that Shotliff and Pollard got. Understandably, Frank felt he wasn't wanted. Importing outside ballplayers has never been accepted with some local baseball people, regardless of how much quality they added to the team. While Rice was paid $300 and Brown $135 for less than half the season, Frank Betchwars " . . . played against Willie Mays," his son Tom said, for what was likely a team of league all-stars against the 1951 AAA Minneapolis Millers when Mays was burning up the American Association at a .477 clip and the Giants brought him up to New York. "He later regretted it," Tom Betchwars said of his father's leaving town to play– maybe at Carver or Chaska, possibly even Cologne, because Tom said he still has a photo of his father in a baseball uniform that has a big "C" on the chest, which also could have represented the "Cubs" of Jordan. "My mom told me that he got $50 or $75 a game," Tom said.

Tex and Frank hunted squirrels together, too, preferring the wooded ravines near the river town of Henderson, where they designed a two-man stealth hunt of the bushy-tailed small game. They took turns walking through a wood with one man leading, the other following about 30 yards behind. Wary of the hunters, the squirrels would scamper around the trunk of a tree as the lead man walked by. But that made the critter an easy shot for the follower with a .22 caliber rifle. You made sure you shot the game in the head so you wouldn't waste any meat. "We never ate chicken for Sunday dinner," Tom Betchwars said.

As a Rocket, Frank fired a no-hitter against Excelsior in 1947, and he once struck out 22 batters in a seven-inning game, a feat possible only because of a passed ball by his catcher on a third strike. Tom said that his father watched him throw a no-hitter at Belle Plaine in a high school game. "After the game," Tom said, "the umpire told me I'd thrown a helluva ballgame and showed some good stuff, but that I needed to keep that curveball down on the hitters."

"Later, my dad asked me, 'Do you know who that was?'"

"Yeah, the umpire, I said."

"'That was John Freund. Whatever he told you, do it.'"

Now 60, Tom Betchwars said his dad turned the small town's Jordan Beverage into the second-largest Schmidt Beer distributorship in the state of Minnesota in less than 10 years, after running what was the most successful of restaurant enterprises at the Hamburger Home since Herb Wagner ran a common café upstairs and a posh speakeasy club downstairs during Prohibition. But The Fiddler brought Frank's dance of life and that of Dorothy, his wife, to an end at about 5:30 p.m. on Monday, August 7, 1972, in a head-on collision with another vehicle on what was described in the front-page headline story in the August 10, 1972, *Jordan Independent* as "rain-slicked County Road 12 along the north shore of Spring Lake and about one-quarter mile east of County Road 17." Frank was 51, Dorothy 44. It was one of the most tragic accidents in the history of the community. It left four children, ages 12 to 16, alone in the world.

Tom, the oldest of the kids, said that his parents had become very close friends with Dick and Jan Ballard. "They stepped up in a big way," Tom said, taking in Tom and his siblings and integrating them with the Ballard family. "They doubled the size of their house with an addition, and they bought a second refrigerator, a second washer and dryer, second stove and so on." Tom said the Ballard's then had eight teenagers under one roof at the same time, three boys and one girl from each family.

Moreover, the Ballard's did it all with their own nickel. As far as Tom knew, there was no government program involved in the family foster care provided by the Ballard's. No church either, for that matter. That meant no administration, no paperwork, and no bureaucracy. No social workers checking and filing reports. Just caring and compassion by people, which began in the alley between the café and Ballard's furniture store and the sharing of an early morning smoke by two small town businessmen. The difference speaks volumes about one's thinking, philosophy, and practical living. The Ballard's weren't even family, and they were relatively new to the community. The Ballard's were simply good people, stepping up to help four kids in need by doing the best they could do for them.

You also get the sense that had the opportunity and roles been reversed, Frank and Dorothy Betchwars would have stepped up in the same way for the Ballard bunch that Dick and Jan Ballard did for the Betchwars family. Frank and Dorothy opened up the back room, the banquet room, of the Hamburger Home Café as a *non-union* gospel mission every major holiday. "We had our Thanksgiving and Christmas dinners with 30 or 40 people from around town who were alone for the holidays," Tom said. No government agency or church subsidized the good will, and Frank didn't pass the hat. Frank Betchwars didn't blow his own horn about the holiday feasts or the fish fries he and Dorothy put on in the back room of their restaurant business. Frank would speak high praise in an understated way of the likes of John Freund and his own teammate, Tex Erickson. But he just walked the walk about his own game and about that Purple Heart.

Among those who didn't make it back from the war was Jerome Beckius, son of Mr. and Mrs. P.J. Beckius and brother of Al, Norm, and Gene. Reported as missing in action as of July 13, 1943, James Forrestal, Secretary of the Navy, informed the parents of Jerome Beckius, in a letter dated August 24, 1945, and published in the September 6 *Jordan Independent*, that their son, who had turned 23 years of age just 10 days before his ship went down, was now considered deceased. In it, everybody learned, "He was serving on board the *USS Gwin* when that vessel was torpedoed and subsequently sunk, while operating as a unit of a group whose mission was to intercept an enemy fleet off the Kula Gulf in the Pacific."

No reports were ever received as to the survival of any personnel aboard the ship. Killed in action, World War II, Pacific Theater.

Then there was Ossie Hannigan. He inherited the mantle of Jordan High School's "little big man" from Tex Erickson. Like Tex, he was small of stature and maybe went 130 pounds. But also like Tex, he was quick and tough. Tough enough to make the fight card in the 11th District Golden Glove Boxing Tournament held at the Jordan High School Gym in January of 1942. He was smart enough, too, to make the A-Honor Roll on occasion. He was described in the *JI*'s reports of the day as a popular student and a good athlete. He made the list of single-season scoring leaders published in the 1989 *Jordan Independent* with eight TDs and six extra points in the six-game 1943 football season. In fact, in the last two games of his senior season, Captain Ossie Hannigan put on a Tex Erickson clinic of open-field running and dropkicking. He scored three TDs, one a 50-yard run, and kicked two extra points in the 20-14 win over New Prague. With Max home on leave, here's his observation of the 33-14 loss to Belle Plaine: "Hannigan was superb in his final game. He scored all of the JHS points for the second consecutive game."

Ossie's five rushing touchdowns in the last two games vaulted him into an elite set of premier running backs at the school. He's in the box scores of Hubmen basketball games, usually scoring in single digits, as did most high school basketball players then, and he played baseball as well, starting in centerfield and batting leadoff for the Jordan Brewers after his junior year in high school, with Rollie Sunder, the all-time great Brewer centerfielder, bumped into playing third base.

He enlisted in the U.S. Army Air Corps in the fall of his senior year of high school while still a teenager after the football season was over. He was inducted after the turn of the calendar year, and after appropriate training, was assigned to the B-29 Superfortress–as a tail gunner.

They gave him his high school diploma *in absentia*, after he was reported missing in action in the Pacific Theater. This Jordan boy was on a B-29 bomber on a mission over Kobe, Japan on June 5, 1945, just two months before the Japanese surrender, when his plane was seen to be spiraling down after being hit by enemy fighter aircraft. Eight parachutes were seen unfolding as the plane sank beneath them, smoke trailing from the wounded bird. Each B-29 carried a crew of 11.

Nobody knew who the eight men were. Ossie would not make it home. Some reports, maybe based on hope, had him surviving as a POW in a Japanese prison camp. Then young Ossie Hannigan was reported by the War Department in a letter home to his mother, Mrs. Mike O'Day, dated June 6, 1946, to have been reclassified by government regulation from MIA to presumed deceased. Two years later, an October 7, 1948, *Jordan Independent* headline read, "Was O. Hannigan Warcrime Victim?" Ossie's older brother, Norris, now living in Brentwood of Jordan, had received a letter from Major General Edw. F. Witsell, Adjutant General, U.S. Army, indicating that Ossie Hannigan may have been among a group of American prisoners held by the Japanese that were executed by their captors. People talk. The letter had them buzzing that the newspapers never print the whole truth and that "war crime" and "execution" were code words. "The word then," Paul Sunder said, without any official substantiation, "was that he had been beheaded."

We can't help contrasting Ossie Hannigan, Class of 1944, with another Jordan youth 70 years later in the spring of 2014. It was a nice, warm day that invited a walk in the Lagoon Park and another visit to the ballpark and the ghosts of the Great Ones there that will talk to you if you will listen. School was out. We met three teenage boys who looked to be about 16 or 17 years old–high school teenagers like Ossie Hannigan when he enlisted in Uncle Sam's Army Air Corps. The three boys were wearing t-shirts, and something prompted a look back at them after meeting on the road along the left-field fence. One boy's black t-shirt in white letters read: "This isn't love. This is getting fucked."

Odds are the kid never heard of Ossie Hannigan.

Hannigan, Beckius, Ira Beckman, and John Casey, Max's brother and the son of John E. Casey, editor and publisher of the *Jordan Independent*, were just four of the local area boys who didn't make it home from the war. They were among the 407,316 Americans killed in World War II and another 671,278 wounded in the war.

Gordy Gelhaye, the hitting star, as a drafted catcher from Jordan, for Excelsior in their 1945 state championship run, went home in 1946 to Shakopee to manage the Indians who had not fielded a team the year before. But McDonald, the draftee-pitching star with the no-hit gem in the championship game for Excelsior, would pitch at Jordan again. Bob Vestal made it home from the war, and he would pitch well again that summer. With two strong pitchers, the season bode well for the Brewers. Jordan finished the regular season in a three-way tie for second place with Bloomington and St. Peter with a 6-4 record. Tex had had a good year at the plate, batting .371 for the regular season, trailing two teammates by just a few points.

Jordan beat Bloomington two out of three games in the first round of the league playoffs, then dropped the three-game series to Shakopee for the championship. Jordan had agreed to play the entire playoff series at Shakopee, because even during the workweek day games, the Jordan ballpark couldn't handle the crowd.

Shakopee's Riverside Park handled the three afternoon games of more than 1,000 fans each, and Vestal's two-hit shutout in the second game kept Brewer hopes alive. But six runs in the fourth inning rallied Shakopee from a 3-1 deficit in the rubber game on the way to a 10-4 win and the championship. Led by player-manager Gordy Gelhaye and his .465 batting average, Shakopee won the regional playoff and entered the 1946 14-team Class-A state tournament. Despite the big guy going three for three in each tourney game, Shakopee fell to Detroit Lakes in the second round, 8-7.

The biggest event of the year in the county, the Scott County Fair, scheduled for the middle of September, was cancelled ". . . because of poliomyelitis in the county." Dr. Havel concurred with the fair board's decision, saying, "It should not be held this year as a help in the fight against infantile paralysis." In October, natural gas was piped into the city of Jordan, and Ben Engfer's garage was the first commercial user. December brought news of the purchase of the Jordan Brewery by Mankato Brewing Company from the Lanser Brewing Company of Phoenix, Arizona, which had purchased the business from the Jordan principals in May. A crew of seven regular employees was preparing the plant for brewing, with the promise of bottling operations resuming after the first of the year. A week later, the Mudbaden Sulphur Springs health spa and resort was reported to have been purchased from the heirs of the late E.H. Seeman of Chicago by "a man from St. Paul." One of the two properties was to be presented to a group of nursing nuns and used as a hospital.

Minneapolis Mayor Hubert H. Humphrey addressed the November-December meeting of the Jordan Commercial Club, and "In holding the audience spellbound for more than an hour," according to the December 12, 1946, *Jordan Independent*, "Mayor Humphrey delivered one of the finest addresses the club has been privileged to hear." He spoke well of small towns and small business being the lifeblood of the nation. He would achieve political success as a U.S. Senator, Vice-President to Lyndon Johnson, then make a run at the presidency himself after a turbulent Democratic primary season, only to lose in 1968 to Richard Nixon, who promised a secret plan to end the war in Vietnam.

Weather conditions kept area teams from working out before the scheduled April 27, 1947, Minnesota Valley League baseball opener. Jordan and Chaska agreed to postpone their season-opening game. The decision would add to the drama at season's end.

Tex Erickson's four hits in five at bats led the Brewers attack in their win over St. Louis Park, 8-4, to even their record at 2-2 at the end of the first month of play. His grand slam home run was the margin of victory. Gordy Gelhaye was back in a Brewer uniform at first base, and his bat promised some big-time power down the stretch. At the halfway mark of the season, Tex was hitting .303, but nobody else was hitting his weight. Bobby Vestal had pitched well at times, but he was starting to show some age on his long-reliable arm. A 4-3 win over neighbor Belle Plaine of the Scott-Carver-Sibley League in a Memorial Day classic in front of 1,000 people fanned some flames of optimism. Then for the second Sunday in a row, Shakopee beat Jordan soundly to put them at 2-5 in league play. Gelhaye hadn't played in the two games against his hometown of Shakopee. He asked for his release, and St. Peter put the Brewers at 2-6 in the league, prompting Max Casey to write the following in his June 19, 1947, report of the second loss to Shakopee:

> Although Jordan did get one run in the contest, like the Sunday before it was scored by Don Erickson only because of his exceptional speed as a base runner. Don is really one of the redeeming factors in what is

considered a poor Jordan club this season. His baserunning has been a pleasure to withhold and when Tex gets on base he invariably steals second and many times third base. He is one of the fastest ballplayers ever to don a Jordan uniform and we proudly believe the fastest and smartest baserunner in the league.

Frank Betchwars fired his no-hit shutout against Excelsior for the Rockets, and Bobby Vestal hurled a superb, four-hit, 3-0 shutout of St. Louis Park with eight strikeouts for the Brewers. Three more consecutive wins in the league, and the Brewers had pulled to .500 at 6-6. The capper was Vestal's six-hitter to beat league-leading Bloomington and Gene Cooney, 4-2, just their second loss of the season. The big win set the Brewers up for a chance at the league playoffs, as the top four teams out of the eight-team league made the post-season show. The Chaska Cubs stood in their way, but with the makeup game to play from the season's opening game postponement, it meant the two remaining games, both against the Cubs, would decide the fourth and final participating team in the playoffs. Tex had three hits in the first game, including two doubles, but Chaska prevailed, 9-8, in what was reported to have been "a slugfest," with the lead changing five times in the game. The postponed game was played because it meant positioning to Chaska, which overcame a 4-1 deficit to win again, 6-4, with some hotly disputed umpiring the deciding factor in the game.

Chaska, which had struggled to make the MVL playoffs and which was taken to the edge of summer's abyss by the fifth-place Brewers, won the league playoffs, the region, and the Minnesota Class-A state tournament at Mankato. Anderson and Cooney combined for a no-hitter to beat Maple Lake and the magnificent Johnny Garbett, 1-0, in the opening game on an unearned run in the ninth. Then they beat New Ulm and Olivia before smoking Rochester, 10-6, in the championship game. Were they lucky? Did they just get hot at the right time of the year? Or did Chaska come out of a really competitive Class-A Minnesota Valley League?

Baseball in 1947 was dominated, however, by the introduction of Jackie Robinson to the lineup of the Brooklyn Dodgers. He was the first African-American to play U.S. Major League Baseball in the 20th Century. He stole home at least once during the season, which he would do 19 times in his 10-year career, and he was named National League Rookie of the Year. The Dodgers won the pennant without Manager Leo Durocher, who had been suspended by Happy Chandler, the Commissioner of Baseball, for "association with known gamblers." Joe DiMaggio won his third MVP award by one vote over Ted Williams . . . The Yankees had a remarkable run of 19 wins without a loss in June-July . . . The first Little League World Series was won by the Maynard Midgets of Williamsport, PA . . . Outside of baseball, President Harry Truman introduced the "Truman Doctrine" to fight Communism . . . The U.S. Department of Defense was formed . . . Chuck Yeager made the first supersonic flight . . . India and Pakistan gained their independence from Great Britain.

Jordan and St. Peter bolted from the Minnesota Valley League during the winter meetings after a vote, dominated by the four Minneapolis suburban teams, opened wide the eligibility of experienced, high-quality Twin City ballplayers to them. The Brewers and the Saints would then become charter members of a newly created eight-member league of "rural communities," with more equitable distribution and availability of quality ballplayers, and as was correctly anticipated, better attendance because of the competition between neighbors. The Minnesota River League would be home to Tex Erickson and the Jordan Brewers for most of the next decade. It provided highly competitive Class-A baseball, invited community involvement, and oversaw the gradual transition to night baseball, with lighted ballparks doing the same thing for the game as Edison's invention had done for productive shift work and nightlife in general.

All around, 1948 was a seminal year: Israel gained its statehood, but was soon attacked by five of its Arab neighbors . . . Mahatma Gandhi won independence for India with fasting, prayer, and peaceful demonstrations, but he was assassinated . . . . Russia-backed Communists seized Czechoslovakia . . . The U.S. Supreme Court ruled that religion instruction in public schools is unconstitutional . . . President Truman signed the Marshall Plan, which provided $5 Billion in aid to 16 European countries . . . The UN formed the World Health Organization . . . California's Supreme Court ruled that the state's ban on inter-racial marriage is unconstitutional . . . "Hopalong Cassidy" premiered on TV . . . The Honda Motor Company was founded and opened in America . . . Ben Hogan won the U.S. Open and the PGA . . . Citation won horse racing's Triple Crown . . . The Cleveland Indians signed 42-year-old Satchel Paige . . . The Indians, not the Yankees, won the AL pennant and beat the Boston Braves in the World Series, 4 games to 2 . . . Casey Stengel took over as manager of the Yankees . . . Three MLB teams were fined for signing high school baseball players . . . Babe Ruth bid final farewell at Yankee Stadium and died two months later.

A special committee from the Jordan Commercial Club was formed to take the next steps necessary " . . . to make plans for what may develop into one of the most ambitious baseball programs ever undertaken in Jordan," according to the January 29, 1948, *Jordan Independent*. While continuing to work both inside the Commercial Club and outside it in the community at large from at least a dual, if not triple, post, Max Casey lobbied, promoted, reported on, and led baseball development in Jordan. The 36-year-old, 1930 graduate of Jordan High School also tested for, and received the appointment of, postmaster of the city, effective April 30. The brewery shut down due, it was reported, to government grain allotments again. The move left just one employee, Henry Mayer, to burn a light bulb in the plant.

New Brewer Manager Russ Stark was optimistic about the coming baseball season, which was scheduled to open Sunday, May 2. Max's April 22 *JI* coverage reported, "Manager Stark and Field Captain Bill Kaczrowski are whipping their team into shape for the season opener at Fairgrounds Park on that day."

A rain-soaked, five-inning practice game against Bloomington didn't tell Manager Stark much. But Max's headline to the game story in the May 6 *JI* spoke volumes the next week: "Jordan Romped Over St. Peter 11-1 In River League Opener." Tex opened the game at his usual shortstop position, but to the surprise of many, Manager Stark had him batting cleanup. The unusual move paid off, for Tex cranked a three-run homer in the bottom of the fifth inning to put the game out of reach. We can only wonder today whether that was the ball Tex gave his little sister,

Madeline, who has kept an autographed homerun ball Tex gave her nearly 70 years ago.

The Brewers smashed Prior Lake, 14-4, but lost two games to Belle Plaine Memorial Day week, including the inaugural game under the lights at Tiger Stadium, 2-1, in front of more than a reported 1,500 fans on a Thursday night. The Brewers stood at 2-3, and then won two in a row to go above .500. At the half-way mark of the league season, Tex was hitting a respectable .321, but his younger brother, Bill, "a lanky first baseman," was hitting a torrid .438, second on the team to the .474 of LeRoy ("Boom-Boom") Voigt, who had, according to a news note in the March 22, 1945, *Jordan Independent*, run with General George Patton's Third Army in Germany near the end of the war.

A month later, at Fairgrounds Park, Tex hit for the cycle in a 10-inning win over Le Sueur. He was five for six–a homerun, triple, double, and two singles. The Brewers closed with strong wins over Prior Lake and New Prague, finishing the regular season with a 7-7 record, good for fourth place, with Belle Plaine setting the pace at 10-4.

Montgomery ousted Jordan from the playoffs in the opening round. Meanwhile, Belle Plaine rode its Irish luck and the big broad back and hot bat of Gene O'Brien through the league playoffs, the regional, and all the way to the 1948 Class-A state championship game against Winsted, losing, 6-4, in front of over 7,500 fans at Shakopee's Riverside Park.

The bosses of baseball everywhere got serious about business in 1949. David Halberstam, in *Summer of '49*, provides some important national baseball background to his chronicle of the season's classic rivalry between the Red Sox and Yankees: Halberstam notes that crowds doubled in the National League between the last year prior to the war, 1941, and 1947, with the intensity amping up considerably as well. In terms of attention, the writer says that baseball was rivaled in those days only by the occasional heavyweight championship fight and college football. Baseball, according to Halberstam, was rooted in the traditions of the country's past and in the current culture. "It was not so much the national sport as the binding national myth," Halberstam writes.

The same thing existed at every level. Proportionally, things were the same up and down the Minnesota River Valley. Baseball was life, and life was baseball. Locally, the Baseball Bosses were organizing. They formed the Jordan Baseball Association, elected officers, and then incorporated their business entity. They promoted and solicited membership in the association, and they sold stock in the corporation. They asked for donation pledges, and they assigned members to committees. They planned and they budgeted. Baseball was like a beehive, with everybody pitching in. Their due diligence and a committee concluded that the existing site–Fairgrounds Park–with modifications, was the most suitable site for a new ballpark with lights for night games. That required more cooperation with the fair board and with each other. But the necessary forces and elements were coming together.

The bosses and the community at large drew inspiration and confidence from the successful run that Belle Plaine had made the summer before in the state tournament and from the huge crowds that witnessed not only the state championship but the games with Belle Plaine that summer, including the inaugural game under the lights. After all, they were neighbors, and the Brewers felt they could play with the Tigers and the other teams in the Minnesota River League.

Then the "tall drink of water" showed up after helping to lead the Minneapolis Lakers to a championship of the Basketball Association of America (BAA), one of the two organizational forerunners to the NBA. An All-American on NCAA national basketball champion Stanford in 1942, then AAU All-American the next two years, Jim Pollard was arguably the best athlete in the country. If he wasn't the best it could only have been because of Jackie Robinson, of whom it was said that baseball was his worst sport after playing football, basketball, and competing in track at UCLA. Jim Pollard could run like a greyhound; he could throw and play any position on the diamond, and, Lord, could he hit a baseball. Most significantly, although a giant of his sports day, he was genuinely humble and likeable.

"Don really liked that Laker basketball player," Madeline Gardner said of Jim Pollard. The feeling was mutual, according to Paul Sunder, who said, "They really appreciated each other. Jim thought a lot of Tex." Both were exceptionally talented athletes despite the contrasts in physical size. Both were leaders. Both men were capable of carrying a ball club and winning a game in many ways. Both ignited efforts of teammates and infuriated opponents. In today's vernacular, both were gamers.

Despite Jim Pollard's arrival in Jordan, the Brewers had a disappointing season again. They finished the season with a MRL record of just 9-12, putting them in sixth place in the eight-team league. Too many changes in personnel may have been to blame. They changed managers in mid-season; they changed pitchers and catchers and infielders as well. They never got settled. While Pollard hit well, .426, with seven homeruns, his pitching was inconsistent. He won six and lost seven on the mound. Tex did not have a good year at the plate, with just one or two multi-hit games. Still, his walk-off, two-run homerun to beat Le Center, 11-10, in late June showed his ability to win a ballgame with his bat as well as his legs and his glove.

Tex's next five Brewer years, true golden years of Jordan's Class-A baseball, are inextricably woven with the stories of Jim Pollard and Johnny Garbett, each man supported on the mound by the stellar defensive play of Tex at shortstop and Dick Nolden at second base, and each pitcher fortunate at times to have Tex stealing a game for him with his speed and smarts on the base paths. Tex Erickson was the epitome of river-town small-ball.

Tex Erickson retired as a player after the 1955 season, after Garbett hurt his arm in the season that Pollard's Laker retirement created such a huge hole in Jordan Brewer baseball. He left the employment of the Engfer Garage in 1957, the year his only child, Dwight, was born to Tex and his wife, Delores, three years after their marriage in 1954. Tex went to Dunwoody Institute in Minneapolis, according to Dwight, where he learned the plumbing trade. He took that trade school accreditation to full-time employment with the plumbing and heating division of the Simones Hardware/Plumbing & Heating business run by Roy Simones on Broadway in downtown Jordan. After about 10 years of turning pipe wrenches while on his back on cold concrete, Tex began to experience some physical issues.

He left the plumbing trade and picked up a custodial job at Jordan High School, Dwight thought, for the 1965-66 school year. Pushing a broom in the hallways, cleaning bathrooms and scrubbing scuffmarks off painted walls didn't work for him, and he finished his working career at Thermo-King from which he retired in 1981 at age 62. He'd moved from Jordan to his wife's hometown of Montgomery in 1976. "He liked to go back to Jordan," Dwight said, "and he would visit with his best friend–Henry ("Luke") Betchwars." After his best friend died in 1997, Tex quit going back to Jordan.

He didn't go to doctors either and when he started having some problems, Delores finally made him go. "But it was too late," Dwight said. "He had cancer all over, and they put him on oxygen the last month or so." Tex was a two-pack-a-day man, "Bel Aires," his entire adult life. "He tried to quit a couple times, but just couldn't do it," Dwight said of his father, who died in 2001 at the age of 81.

Jim Pollard

And those who knew him off the court were always struck by his special grace.

— Dolph Grundman in *Jim Pollard, The Kangaroo Kid*

He was an anomaly in so many ways. Not only was Jim Pollard tall, for example, he was athletic. It was rare for a man over six-feet tall in his day to be able to walk and chew gum at the same time, or to navigate a dance floor with anything other than a shuffle. Not only was he a white man, he could jump and run, dribble and shoot the ball. He is likely to have been the first basketball player to take the game off the floor and play it above the rim. It was said of him that he could dunk, going airborne from the free-throw line in warm ups, but not games, because the shot was banned. Some have compared his game to that of Dr. J (Julius Erving) and Michael Jordan. He was graceful. He had hang time, and he used his great leaping ability, which earned him the nickname, "The Kangaroo Kid," to rebound and to block shots.

Grundman writes in the closing pages of his book that in a poll taken of Jim Pollard's professional basketball peers, he was named as *the best player* in the game's early history. Moreover, Grundman writes, " . . . in 1963 the Academy of Sports Editors named him one of ten members of the *All Time NBA Team*. Others on the list included Bob Cousy, Bill Russell, George Mikan, Elgin Baylor, Wilt Chamberlain, Oscar Robertson, Bob Pettit, Dolph Shayes, and Paul Arizin." Just as his teammate, George Mikan, is said to have been the cause of the institution of the three-second lane rule and the widening of the lane from 6 feet–a veritable campground for the massive Mikan–to 12 feet, some sources cite Pollard's blocking of shots as the inspiration for the change in the rules of goal tending, or blocking the basketball on its descent into the hoop. Pollard swatted away everything above the rim. Mikan and Pollard were game changers as members of the first NBA dynasty–the Minneapolis Lakers.

Not only was Pollard a native of the Bay Area of California, he chose to sign with the Minneapolis Lakers at a time when numerous teams from different leagues were vying for his services in an open bidding war, as the National Basketball Association was in its pre-embryonic stages and would only be formed from a merger of the old NBL (National Basketball League) and the BAA (Basketball Athletic Association) in 1949.

Jim Pollard was an All-American at Stanford University as a sophomore in 1942 and a star on the team's NCAA national championship team. He was the leading scorer in the tournament despite missing the championship game with the flu. He was also a two-time AAU (Amateur Athletic Union) All-American, playing for the San Diego Dons, then the Oakland Bittners, in the American Basketball League, each year finishing second in the national tournament to the Phillips 66 team, which was the dominant amateur team in the country during the 1940s.

Pollard was the ultimate athlete and the consummate professional. He was a superstar with a "West Coast offense" built into his legs and his greyhound-lean body. He was a slasher, who liked to take the ball to the hoop, twisting, turning, leaping for two and drawing the foul for a third point at the line. But the Laker game was a Midwestern workhorse's dream. Coach John Kundla's game plan was to get the ball into Mikan, the first real big man in basketball, for the high-percentage close-range shot. At 6-10, George Mikan ruled basketball from the inside, *averaging* as many as 28 points a game during a season in his prime years and dumping in a career-high 61 points in a double-overtime victory over the Rochester Royals on January 20, 1952, "this unusual feat being made largely possible," according to the likely eyewitness report by Max Casey in the January 24, 1952, *Jordan Independent*, "by the fine feeding play of Jim Pollard, who is having the best season of his professional basketball career." The feat was all the more remarkable for the fact that the NBA was slowly adopting a foul-plagued, slow-down style of play, a virtual stall at times, until the 24-second shot clock was instituted in 1954. That opened the game up and would have demanded a style of play more conducive to Pollard's athleticism and run-and-gun game. Alas, the 1954-'55 season was his last as a professional basketball player.

Jim Pollard, superstar, could do it all. Initially, his style clashed with that of Mikan's, for George clogged up the middle–Jim's driving lanes–with his own body and the defenders sagging around him. But Pollard was also a team player. He fed and supported Mikan. When needed, due to an injury to Mikan or maybe foul trouble, however, Jim Pollard could take over the game and light up the scoreboard. He could dominate on both ends of the court, taking defensive rebounds off the boards and leading fast breaks with the ball or dishing off to a teammate breaking for the basket. Teammates and opponents were in awe of his athleticism. The back cover of Grundman's book highlights a quote from Hall of Fame Philadelphia 76-er coach Alex Hannum: "To describe Jim as a player, just combine Julius Irving and Michael Jordan and imagine the best in basketball before it was popular to dunk. The game has never known a finer gentleman and player."

Grundman continues: "Pollard's graceful, acrobatic style has inspired comparisons with more modern players Clyde Drexler, Scotty Pippin, and even Michael Jordan. In an era when dunking was forbidden, he played above the rim." These modern-day NBA pros could dribble, run the court, rebound, shoot, and play "Doberman defense" when called upon. These guys were smooth, explosive, and exciting to watch. So was Jim Pollard.

Jim Pollard was instrumental in bringing six world championships to the Minneapolis Lakers before he retired after the 1954-'55 season. Even though he was one of the highest-paid superstars in the NBA during that run, he played baseball summers in Jordan, Minnesota, while at the same time working on the completion of his bachelor's degree in physical education at the University of

Minnesota. He had always wanted to teach and coach, which necessitated the degree. Professional ballplayers were not paid anything like the astronomical figures of more contemporary players, even on a relative basis with the inflation factor stripped away. When you "follow the money," that trail leads to ticket prices of just $2.40 a seat for "Jim Pollard Appreciation Night" at the Minneapolis Auditorium. "For 1951-'52, the average price of a ticket was $1.25," Grundman writes in his Pollard biography. "The Laker payroll, according to Winter, was $100,000. Salaries ranged from $4,000 for rookies to $25,000 for Mikan. Promotions cost $40,000, equipment $7,500, and the rental of the auditorium ranged from $20,000 to $28,000. Over four years, Winter claimed the Lakers earned a profit of $25,000." Careers were shorter; many were ended by injuries that today can be repaired with surgery and therapy. They worked off-season jobs. Brewer teammate Paul Sunder said that Pollard played all those years for $45 a game and could have gotten $100 to $125 a game had he chosen to play with Southern Minny teams like Faribault or Owatonna. The Buzz for all these years since then, however, was that Jim got $100 for a game that he pitched, $50 when he played an infield position. Some said that he tore up his check if he got beat. Everybody seems to agree that if Pollard played a bad game, he would tear up his paycheck.

In any event, Bill Breimhorst, former Brewer player and, once again, the manager, signed Jim Pollard to play baseball in Jordan in 1949. We thought there must have been some intriguing connections and introductions to pull off such a coup then. After all, nobody in Jordan, Minnesota, during the 1990s would have had the cash, the cachet, or the *cojones* to call up Michael Jordan and ask him to come to play Class-C town ball.

Bill is gone now, too, so we couldn't talk to him or any of the others. But Bill's son, Bill, Jr., is a pastor in Waconia, Minnesota, and he told us that Pollard worked for his father one summer on the state highway department in which the senior Breimhorst had a supervisory position. Jim Pollard told Bill Breimhorst that he was looking for something to do to stay in shape through the summer months between basketball seasons, and Breimhorst simply asked him if he might want to play baseball out in Jordan. No intrigue. No extortion. No money under the table. No ruse or undue influence anywhere. Just The Fiddler at work.

Jim Pollard is in professional basketball's Hall of Fame, its highest honor. But he was a great baseball player, too, and Grundman quotes him in his book that if he were to do things over he'd have chosen to pursue professional baseball. He had played high school baseball and earned a letter in baseball from San Francisco State College while playing AAU basketball for the Oakland Bittners. He was a power pitcher, but prone to wildness, and a good third baseman and first baseman for the Brewers for six years. Actually, because of his athleticism, he could play any position on the diamond and did, with the exception of catcher. "He was really athletic," Dick Nolden said of his Brewer teammate, "and a team player." Jim Pollard was the real deal, a thoroughbred. Nolden called him "a svelte greyhound." On and off the hard court and the baseball diamond, Jim Pollard moved with natural grace. But his forte in baseball was hitting. He crushed baseballs, launching towering blasts that cleared the fences at Fairgrounds Park with a wide margin. His shots cleared the railroad tracks with ease, and one that is memorialized forever took out a window on first bounce in Al Beckius's rambler on the left-field horizon, well over 500 feet from home plate. This was the homerun that everyone talked about for decades, the souvenir ball that Al Beckius turned into a public relations gem at his Jordan Feed Mill, which guarded the entrance to Fairgrounds Park on Sand Creek.

Disagreement exists about just how tall Jim Pollard was. Grundman says Jim was 6-4, 171 pounds as a senior in high school, and a half-inch taller as a sophomore at Stanford. He refers to Pollard as being 6-5 a number of times in his biography, and that is what the *New York Times* listed Jim Pollard as in his obituary. Former Brewer manager Earl Dean claimed in Tom Melchior's book, *Scott County Baseball*, that he was 6-7. Brewer teammate Dick Nolden thought Pollard was probably 6-5 or 6-6 and between 190 and 200 pounds of lean-muscled thoroughbred legs and heart. "He was 6-7," Paul Sunder said. He looked even taller on the pitching mound that was officially five inches higher and probably even more than that in many cases. He looked taller at third base, too, leaping to snare line drives and high hoppers that mere mortals would have only been able to wave at.

Jim Pollard played large. The bigger the game, the better he usually played, whether it was NBA basketball or Class-A Minnesota River League baseball. "He was really something," Fred Keup of Belle Plaine said of Jim Pollard in a casual conversation.

Even though Jim Pollard was a national celebrity, a basketball icon already with two world championships and four more on the way before he packed it in to take a head coaching job at La Salle College in Philadelphia, he was known for his genuine modesty and humility. LaSalle was a school with an enrollment that would give it Division III status today; however, the Explorers had won the NCAA national championship in 1954 over Bradley and finished runner up to San Francisco and Bill Russell in 1955. But Jim Pollard remained immune to the narcissism that seems to afflict performing stars at levels far beneath the level at which he excelled. "He was just really down-to-earth," Paul Sunder said. He was a nice guy who cared beyond the immediate gratification of his own needs and desires. Moreover, he went out of his way to meet and greet people, exchange pleasantries, and extend well wishes without any condescension. He had no need to blow himself up. He didn't need to try to be somebody he wasn't, to be somebody other than himself. He was authentic.

In 1949 the Chairman Mao-led Communists drove the Chinese Nationalist forces led by the U.S.-backed Chiang Kai-Schek off the mainland of China and onto the island of Formosa . . . The Soviets under Stalin had seized Eastern Europe and half of Germany after World War II . . . The Cold War was simmering, and now another large segment of the world had gone Red–fallen to Communism, the ideological antithesis of both Christianity and capitalism . . . Meanwhile, on the domestic front, President Harry Truman nearly doubled the minimum wage from 40 cents an hour to 75 cents an hour . . . The 45-rpm vinyl disc record was introduced, and the parade of popular music hits took off in a new way . . . George Orwell's *Ninety Eighty-Four* was also published.

The New York Giants followed the Brooklyn Dodgers in integrating their baseball club with the signing of Monte Irvin and Hank Thompson in 1949 . . . Joe

Louis retired as heavyweight champion of the world . . . The USSR performed its first nuclear test . . . "Hopalong Cassidy" and "Roy Rodgers" premiered on nationwide television . . . Fourteen U.S. Communist Party leaders were convicted of sedition . . . WCCO, Channel 4, in Minneapolis (a CBS affiliate) began broadcasting . . . Baseball owners agreed to add warning tracks in front of outfield fences . . . Jackie Robinson was awarded the National League's MVP honor after hitting .342 . . . Ted Williams won the AL MVP award after belting 43 home runs and 39 doubles, amassing 159 RBIs, 150 runs scored, an on-base percentage of .490, and a slugging percentage of .650 . . . He would lose the batting title to George Kell of Detroit by the slimmest of hairs: .3429 to .3428, and the Red Sox would lose the American League pennant on the last day of the season.

The Yankees won the 1949 American League pennant, and then they beat the Dodgers in the World Series in five games, after the two league champions exchanged 1-0 victories in the first two games. But the Yankees blew it when General Manager George Weiss sent a scout with racially clouded vision to Alabama to watch an 18-year-old phenom with the Birmingham Black Barons of the Negro League. Willie Mays was tearing it up. But the scout reported that while Mays had a decent arm and "could run a little," he couldn't hit the curve ball. The Yankees missed what everyone knew even then, that nobody at 18 years of age hits good curveballs. They passed and remained an all-white ball club in the city in which the Dodgers and Giants had integrated already. Speculators would wonder for years what a Yankee outfield of Joe DiMaggio, Mickey Mantle, and Willie Mays would have been like in 1951, had the Yankees been open to integration when they had the opportunity to land Willie Mays. "The Yankees could have signed Willie Mays in 1949 for a bonus of $5,000," writes Roger Kahn in *The Era*. "They made no offer . . . One has to conclude that bigotry is not simply wicked. It is also pretty damn dumb."

Roger Kahn added, "Sometimes Leo Durocher," the controversial, but successful, big league manager whose playing career began in 1925 and lasted for about 20 years, whose managing career then began and ended in the 1970s, and whose watching of baseball did not end until the early 1990s, "used to say that Willie Mays was the best baseball player he ever saw. Then if he were feeling even a little contemplative, Durocher added, 'Willie was, but Pete Reiser coulda been.'"

"In his first full season at Brooklyn, 1941, Reiser led the National League in doubles, triples, runs scored, slugging percentage, and batting average (.343)," But with the performances of Ted Williams and Joe DiMaggio in 1941, Pete Reiser and his great year would easily be forgotten. Kahn writes, "He could bat right handed or left-handed and he could *throw* right-handed or left-handed. In full baseball uniform, wearing spikes, Reiser sprinted 100 yards in 9.8 seconds. Although he didn't compete at track, Reiser was probably the fastest man on earth. He had it all, everything, and he was tough."

W.C. Heinz, perhaps most recognizable today for his book, *Run To Daylight*, in 1963 with Vince Lombardi, and his collaboration on the writing of *MASH* under the pseudonym, "Richard Hooker," with Dr. Richard Hornberger, was more graphic and expansive in his portrayal of Pete Reiser in "The Man They Padded the Walls for" from the collection, *Once They Heard The Cheers*. Pete Reiser was signed as a 15-year-old teenager, played over 15 seasons, 10 in the big leagues. Nine of the 11 times he was knocked unconscious from either a bean ball or from running into or through an outfield wall, he came to in either the clubhouse or in a hospital. He broke both ankles, broke his collarbone, fractured his arm throwing a ball, tore a cartilage in his knee and ripped muscles in his leg sliding.

Seven times he stole home in 1946 with the Dodgers, a number that was actually eight and a Major League record tied by Rod Carew in 1969 with the tutelage of Manager Billy Martin of the Minnesota Twins. But the home-plate umpire admitted later that he'd blown the call, having raised his thumb above his head in anticipation only of the catcher making the tag. Reiser, like many professional baseball players, lost three years to military service during World War II. But even in the army, playing ball for base commanders wanting some bragging rights, Pete played all out. His style cut his career short, and he would suffer dizzy spells for the rest of his life, because he played the game so damned hard.

On Feb. 28, 1949, on their way to a second consecutive professional basketball championship, the Minneapolis Lakers, with George Mikan and Jim Pollard, played a rematch of their 1948 game with the Harlem Globetrotters. The Trotters, with Marques Haynes, Sweetwater Clifton, and Goose Tatum, claimed a 113-game winning streak, and they had beaten the Lakers, 61 to 59, on February 19, 1948, at Chicago Stadium in front of 17,853 fans. The Lakers had led at halftime, 32-23, with Mikan and Pollard already in double figures. But the Trotters came back in the second half, and Ermer Robinson's 30-foot buzzer beater, just beyond the fingertips of a leaping Jim Pollard at the net, was the difference. In front of 20,046 fans, again at Chicago Stadium, the Trotters claimed to be the best basketball team in the world in 1949 after beating the Lakers, 49 to 45. But sports fans argued that the first game was a fluke, and the second was done with two Laker starters, Jim Pollard and Swede Carlson, out with injuries. On March 19, 1949, a third game was played at the Minneapolis Auditorium in front of a full house of 10,122 fans. The Lakers took their inside power game to a decisive 68 to 53 win, with Mikan pouring in 36 points.

Greatness inspired sports fans, especially kids, wherever it was found. It wasn't limited to baseball and basketball. Sometimes, it couldn't be recognized or appreciated without tragedy, however. On February 2, 1949, Ground Hog Day in fact, Ben Hogan and his wife, Valerie, were heading home to Fort Worth, Texas, on a foggy morning after Ben had finished second to Jimmy Demaret in a playoff for the Phoenix Open. He was creeping along at maybe 25 mph in his $2,800 Cadillac, heading east on two-lane Highway 80. He was on a roll on tour, too, having won two of the four tournaments he had entered that year, 37 golf tournaments in all since his discharge from the Army Air Corps in 1946. It had taken him a long time to succeed on tour, not winning through most of the first 10 years of play until he was almost 30 years old, about the age at which the immortal Bobby Jones, still an amateur, had retired from tournament golf. But after he put all the pieces together, including dealing with the vestiges of emotional and psychological trauma of witnessing at age nine his father, Chester Hogan, shoot himself with a revolver, he owned golf. "It took a 10-ton bus to stop him," Curt Sampson writes in *Hogan*.

Ben Hogan met head-on Greyhound Bus 548, a General Motors Super Coach, on a bridge on Highway 80 in dense fog. The only reason he survived the collision is that, at the last moment, Hogan cranked the steering wheel to the right so his side of the caddy would take the brunt of the hit. He let go of the wheel and threw himself over Valerie to save her, just in time to avert the steering column being driven into the driver's seat, but catching enough of the 200-pound missile to fracture his left collarbone. The Cadillac's 500-pound engine followed the steering column, crushing bones and mangling Hogan's left leg.

Hogan made it to the hospital finally after gawkers at the scene of the accident realized that nobody had called for an ambulance. In an amazingly short time he showed signs of recovering, his status upgraded almost daily. Then two weeks later the blood clots began to break loose in the veins in his left leg. They'd no doubt formed from both the severe bruising in the car and from what doctors refer to as "stasis"–being immobile in the hospital bed. They started in his leg and moved upward to his heart and on to the lungs where the coagulated blood mass is called a pulmonary embolism, treated today with anticoagulants, Heparin and Warfarin Coumadin, and implanted mesh screens to catch them before they enter the heart or lungs and kill, but treated in Hogan's day with mostly hope and prayer. What affects the lungs affects the heart and vice versa. Ben Hogan, mangled and broken, was a heart attack or stroke waiting to happen. A specialist, Dr. Alton S. Ochsner–"the Ben Hogan of vascular surgery," according to Sampson, was flown in from New Orleans on a U.S. Army Air Corps B-29 bomber out of El Paso, Texas. The clots had to be blocked. Ochsner tied a knot around Ben Hogan's inferior vena cava–the main vein for returning blood from the legs to the heart and on to the lungs for re-uptake of oxygen. Collateral veins would hopefully compensate and Ben Hogan would live, although there were doubts by doctors about his ability to ever walk again, much less play golf.

But Ben Hogan was Old School. What had gotten him to the top of the golf world would get him back to the game he loved. He was determined, dedicated, and diligent. He began with painful walks in the house, then outside the house, and around the block. It began with putting in his living room and just handling a golf club–working his grip and waggle. Then he was back doing what he thoroughly enjoyed–hitting golf balls alone–and soon he was playing a couple holes at a time. Ben Hogan would not only walk and play golf again–he would win again. Sixteen months later, he won the U.S. Open at Merion, where his one-iron to the Par-4, eighteenth green, the 72nd hole of the tournament, is captured in Hy Peskin's black-and-white photograph that is a classic to this day. Hogan's two-putt par forced a playoff that he won handily. Hogan would finish his career with 64 tour wins, but before the accident he had been playing 25 to 30 tournaments a year. After the accident, he would manage just five or six a year.

In 1953, he would enter six tournaments and win five of them, including the Triple Crown–the Masters, the U.S. Open, and the British Open. The fourth leg of what golf publicists and writers would later claim as the Grand Slam, wasn't possible in 1953, as the schedule of the PGA Open overlapped the British Open.

Hogan would need four surgeries on his left shoulder before he retired, and he would have a three-hour ordeal of soaking in hot Epsom salt baths and wrapping his legs to control the swelling before every round of golf or practice session. He would have to be careful for the rest of his days in how long he simply sat or stood in one place. Walking was his circulatory friend, but he limped with pain from the fractures and damage to soft tissue. He would need to elevate his legs when he sat or lay in bed to keep the legs from swelling as a result of the compromised vascular system and to keep blood from pooling in his lower limbs. Tiny valves in the veins, which function as a conveyor belt to move blood up the legs, once hyper-extended from clotting, would never work again. The body, however, with the infinite wisdom of the Creator, would build new but less-efficient vascular routes to return blood to the heart and lungs. Although it may not have been known in medicine then, the aspirin he took for pain would also make his blood platelets less sticky, lessening the chance of more clots and a stroke or heart attack.

How good was Ben Hogan? Had he and Valerie, who accompanied him on the tour, left their motel just five minutes earlier, or later, he would have met the bus on Highway 80 someplace other than on the bridge. Had he not had the crippling accident, would he have won 100 tournaments and 20 majors? Would he have set an impossible target for subsequent golf kings to shoot at? He certainly had the swing, the game, and the mental discipline. As Sampson writes,

> Hogan left no doubt as to his place. He became an idea quite apart from golf. His name alone defined concentration, determination, even perfection. The Little Man had no yardage book, no golf glove, no self congratulation, no logo, no bullshit, and no pretense.

Only Ben Hogan could respond with an authenticity that defied doubt in anyone when asked about the sensation of hitting the perfect golf shot. In an unscripted commercial interview, Sampson writes, "Hogan talked about the feeling that goes 'up the shaft, right into your hands–and into your heart.'" That feeling was not unlike the homeruns hit by Jim Pollard with a wood bat at Fairgrounds Park. You know the ball is out of the park as soon as your bat meets the ball, because you can feel it.

Jack Nicklaus or Tiger Woods is usually selected as the best golfer of all time when the question is asked or polls taken today. But they are more current in terms of our conscious awareness, and they got the benefit of extensive exposure of television as well as print media the entire length of their careers to promote their significant abilities and performances. Both were charismatic and, especially Nicklaus, open to inquiry and dialogue with reporters. Hogan was an enigma, usually appearing blunt and brusque with people asking him questions. Even other golfers referred to him in terms of "the Hogan Mystique." He merely went his own way. There wasn't anything casual about him, not since that day when he was nine years old and he watched his father take his own life.

He was simply being honest. He liked to practice alone, and he didn't give away to anyone what he had learned by "digging it out of the dirt." When others asked him for tips, he invariably told them they would learn better what they needed to know by learning for themselves. They wanted a shortcut, and Ben Hogan didn't believe in the easy way.

When Jack Nicklaus was still reigning atop the golf world, it was said that former professional Tommy Bolt was asked by a reporter to compare Ben Hogan to

Jack. Bolt reportedly observed that while he had seen Nicklaus watching Ben Hogan hit golf balls, he had never seen Hogan watch Jack Nicklaus hit golf balls.

It was Hogan, not Nicklaus, who first came up with the concept and practice of "course management" in his golf game. Moreover, it was Hogan, not Nicklaus, Woods, or any other more modern-day golfer, who first practiced "until his hands bled." And it was Hogan, Nicklaus observed, who hit every single fairway and every single green on Open Saturday's 36 holes in 1960 at Cherry Hills.

Nobody has ever hit fairways and greens the way Hogan hit them, especially under pressure. Moreover, he did it with a persimmon-headed driver and fairway woods; he did it with one and two irons made of forged steel, attached to steel shafts, not the remarkable "rescue" clubs that a contemporary has called "almost like cheating." He did it with laser-like precision with his short irons and wedges. Contrary to commonly held belief, he was also a good putter–until the accident's long-term effects set in. He didn't get the yips as most presumed, costing him precious major tournament wins even in his sunset years. He couldn't bring the putter back! He was losing his sight in his dominant eye, his putting eye–another long-term result of the accident in 1949.

Ben Hogan was an introvert. Despite being a national celebrity, he was modest and shy, shunning the limelight. Sampson quotes him in a chapter lead in his book, *Hogan*, "I don't like the glamor. I just like the game." This was always misunderstood. Golfers, like ballplayers, as well as the writers who cover them, tend to be enamored of themselves, legends in their own minds, and desirous of the intoxicating glamor and attention. As a result, the public didn't appreciate Ben Hogan until after the accident and the revelation of his true character and courage.

There were only a few golf courses in the Lower Basin of the Minnesota River Valley during baseball's Golden Age. There were country clubs, to be sure, in the larger cities or in towns with a significant corporate presence, such as Le Sueur with Green Giant, but few public courses, because "golf was a rich man's game," we were told. Ben Hogan had become one of the wealthiest men in Fort Worth, Texas, after he sold his company, The Ben Hogan Company, for a reported $3 million in 1960. He built his company the same way he had built his golf swing–from the ground up. He "dug it out of the dirt." Hogan had started dirt poor, and he had dropped out of high school without graduating, which would embarrass him in later years. In Minnesota, like everywhere else in the country, rich and poor alike revered Hogan after the accident for his brilliant golf game and the comeback he made against all odds. But baseball was king, and the drama unfolding on the diamond with the integration of great Black baseball players transcended the game itself. It changed life, culture, and country.

Jim Pollard brought the same kind of brilliance and character to professional basketball and the diamonds in the Minnesota River League that Hogan brought to golf during these years. There were many parallels between the two superstars despite the nature of their sports being worlds apart. Both men grew up in fatherless homes, Hogan from the age of nine on, Pollard from birth. Both were men of humility and modesty. But both were highly competitive superstars. While Hogan preferred to let his golf game do his talking, Pollard made the case for himself on the basketball floor, inviting comparisons to inevitably be made between George

Mikan and himself, just as they were made between Hogan and Snead, Hogan and Nelson, Hogan and Nicklaus. But Max Winter, owner of the Lakers, borrowed from baseball in his comparisons of George Mikan and Jim Pollard, likening Mikan to Babe Ruth and Pollard to Ty Cobb. "Mikan beat you with power, Pollard hurt you in any number of ways."

The post-war boom in baseball was evident in the winter of 1948-'49. Everything else was booming, too: The war was over; the boys were home; they were marrying, settling into jobs and families; they were building homes and furnishing them with appliances and the latest furniture. They were buying new cars and building businesses of all levels. While Ben Hogan was knocking on heaven's door in a Texas hospital, Pollard and the Lakers were in the process of taking their second consecutive world basketball championship, this one under the aegis of the BAA, beating the Washington Capitols 4 games to 2. Meanwhile, the Baseball Bosses in Jordan were busy organizing.

The Jordan Brewers had finished the 1948 Minnesota River League (MRL) season in the middle of the pack with a .500 season at 7-7. But in front of what was reported as "a record crowd" at Fairgrounds Park on Sunday, July 25, they got beat by the league-leading Belle Plaine Tigers, 8-2, despite outhitting them. Led by ex-professional Gene O'Brien and his .420 season batting average, the Tigers bunched their hits and the Brewers handed the visitors too many opportunities with walks and errors. Then in the last game of the regular season, the Brewers blasted New Prague, 13-0, to raise some hopes of a run in the playoffs before bowing out early. Belle Plaine went on to the state tournament, losing the Class-A championship game to Winsted, 6-4, in front of a crowd of 7,513 fans at Riverside Park in Shakopee that re-defined "capacity" and "standing-room only."

Ten men "interested in the promotion of good baseball in Jordan" met on Friday, February 6, 1949. They talked and blew the smoke of seasons past. Of what might have been and what could be. If only. They set out to do it right and to do it well. According to Max Casey in his July 13, 1950, review of the ballpark renovation project, "During last season, main objective of the infant organization was to put baseball on a business proposition by having a definite organization to back up the team, both financially and morally."

Most of the original 10 key individuals were businessmen. The exceptions were a professional or two, and one government man. But they agreed on the business model for their development and operation of a baseball organization to promote baseball. Wisely, they broadened the base of participation and responsible management to avert the "Boss Hog Syndrome"–power vested in one man whose MO is always, "My way or the highway." They set goals and budgets. They formed the Jordan Baseball Association and elected temporary officers. Then they signed up over 150 Jordan residents the next day, Saturday, in a membership drive. For a dollar, "Anyone interested in good baseball in the community is welcome to join the association," read the front-page story in the February 10, 1949, *Jordan Independent*.

They opened their single set of financial books to scrutiny and oversight by publishing the actual numbers, because transparency is so important when a special-interest group takes on a project with community funds–the people's money. They publicized the first annual meeting of the association, which was to be held a week later in the Jordan High School auditorium. A board of directors was elected, and Judge Connolly of Shakopee, who was a member of the State Amateur Baseball Association Board of Directors, addressed the group on matters of night baseball, financial expectations, indebtedness, and other problems that other communities with a similar commitment were having. The board elected its officers, with Max Casey as president, Frank Hilgers Sr. as vice-president, and Ben Engfer as secretary-treasurer. They set up two-and three-man committees to get things done that included a team advisory committee, and others for concessions, gates-admissions, grounds, membership, and transportation.

The advisory committee procured the services of William Breimhorst to manage the team at no cost, and a special committee had been formed to draw up a set of by-laws by which the board of directors and the Jordan Baseball Association were to operate. The Brewers would again play in the Minnesota River League, the composition of which would remain the same as it was for the 1948 season. Eight teams. No surprises. Belle Plaine was the early favorite based on their great run the previous year in '48. Baseball fever was running high and rising. Momentum was increasing. The March 17 *Jordan Independent* carried the headline, "Cage Star Pollard Signed By Jordan." Membership in the association had grown to nearly 250 townsmen who had given up a buck apiece to be a part of something they loved–baseball.

Jim Pollard joined the Brewers for their non-league opener on Sunday afternoon, April 24, against Hopkins from the neighboring Minnesota Valley League. Pollard did not take the mound in the 5-1 loss at Fairgrounds Park, but did play the entire game at first base. The Brewers then opened the regular league season the following Sunday, May 1, at St. Peter. They scored three times in the top of the sixth to take a 3-1 lead, but five runs by St. Peter in the bottom of the seventh iced it. Pollard saw his first duty on the mound as a Jordan Brewer, striking out four in his two-inning relief stint. Then they opened at home the next Sunday, May 8, with Jim Pollard on the hill against LeCenter. His performance at Fairgrounds Park, both on the mound and at bat, put the Brewer's 11-2 win on the front page of the May 12 *Jordan Independent*. More importantly, in the words of Max Casey at the time and on the scene, the game brought a realization to local fans that "Jim Pollard will hold his own on the mound against any team in the league." Max elaborated:

> Big Jim, in his first pitching start of the season, hung up an impressive record during the seven innings he pitched in Sunday's contest. He struck out seven LeCenter batsmen and allowed the visitors but two hits. . . Pollard also showed unusual hitting prowess by banging out a long homerun in the second inning to spark Jordan's 8-run rally in that frame, also a stinging single in three official trips at bat.

Pollard had two hits in the 13-3 mid-week loss to Dick Siebert's University of Minnesota Gophers in a night game at Belle Plaine's Tiger Stadium. Whitey Skoog, who would join Jim on the Laker basketball team following his All-American senior year at Minnesota in 1951, was too much on the mound this early in the season, and the collegiate team, which was well into its season, hammered Jordan's pitching. Jim then shut out Montgomery the next Sunday, May 15, on seven hits and four walks. But his 15 strikeouts took the wind out of the sails of any home team rallies all afternoon. Moreover, Jim's two-run homerun in the third inning and a double in three official at bats powered the win, putting the Brewers in a three-way tie for second place in the MRL at 2-1, a game behind the undefeated Belle Plaine Tigers.

Pitchers lose concentration and determination when their infielders boot ground balls, especially two-hoppers with "double play" written on them, and make errant throws. Too many errors in too many games dropped Jordan to just one slot ahead of bottom-dwelling, winless New Prague in the June 16, 1949, *Jordan Independent*. Things didn't look good. The infield was leaking like a sieve, and a distraught Jim Pollard was giving up hits and walks as a result. Then Dick Nolden was brought up from the "Rockets," the Jordan "B" team, if you will, to plug the dam. Although just 16 years old, Nolden took over second base and seemed to be the catalyst of confidence for the whole team.

Over 60 years later, Nolden admitted that making the big club at 16 was a really big deal–with his father, Sid Nolden, who was a local baseball icon and one of its bosses, and with the younger kids in town, who elevated Dick Nolden to the top tier of heroes. After all, Dick Nolden had made the starting lineup that included Tex Erickson and Jim Pollard. In his first game with the big club, he even had two hits in his two official trips to the plate. Pollard hit a home run and a double to lead the Brewer attack, and he pitched a three-hit, 9-0 shutout, with five strikeouts in the six-inning game shortened by rain to earn the win. But the errors had been cut down to just one, and Pollard cut his walks down to one as well. Then the Brewers finished the month of June with a pair of wins to put them at 5-6 but still mired in second-last place. Jim took a rest from the mound with a sore arm, but he had started to hit. His three hits in the 11-10 win over LeCenter at Fairgrounds Park in Jordan included two triples, a difficult feat in the small yard on the banks of Sand Creek.

A week of torrid heat, with temperatures in the high 90s and 100 on the Fourth of July, brought concern for crops and gardens, feed stock, and even people. Attendance went down at ballparks, but beer sales were up. Mankato Brewery was advertising "Jordan Beer" with a slogan, "Just Like Old Times," but the slogan didn't ring true. Beer drinkers are a discerning lot. You just can't replace the real thing with the brand management of good advertising. Calling it so doesn't make it so. Putting a "Jordan Beer" label on a Mankato product just didn't make it. Gluek's and Schmidt, out of Minneapolis and St. Paul, respectively, and Schell's from New Ulm were advertising in the local weekly as well, each trying to gain the foothold to fill the void left by the local brewery having gone out of business. Just in time for the heat wave, the Gold Spot Dairy advertised "Curb Service" of its "Ice Cold Root Beer" for only a nickel in the June 23 *Jordan Independent*.

Two more losses at the hands of "Dame Fortune," the Bitch of Baseball, if reports of the day by correspondent Max Casey have any credibility, put the Brewers at 5-8 on the season. But they had Belle Plaine on the ropes, 3-1, in the bottom of the eighth inning on the strength of a good pitching performance by Jim Pollard. Then the defending league champions scored three runs to win 4-3. Pollard then beat Prior Lake, 6-5, at Shakopee under the rented lights at Riverside Park, despite giving up nine hits and eight walks. Jordan was on its third catcher of the season and a new manager, Leon Hennes. Bobby Shotliff made his debut on the mound for the Jordan Brewers and shut out Montgomery, 4-0, on five hits with 12 strikeouts. The Brewers were inching toward .500 at 7-8, with the playoffs coming up after just six more league games.

Batting in his usual cleanup position, Pollard had four hits, including two doubles, at Belle Plaine on Sunday, July 24, as the Brewers beat Belle Plaine for the first time in two years, in front of more than 1,400 fans at Tiger Stadium. Jim's three hits against Prior Lake then helped in the win that moved the Brewers into a virtual four-team tie for third place with 10 losses. Pollard was lifted in the third inning against New Prague; control problems had beset him again. But he was hitting. "Jim Pollard boosted his season hitting average with the Brewers to .480 on Sunday," Max Casey reported in the August 4 *Jordan Independent*, "when he again came through with three for four," including a homerun and a double in the game that was reported to have been completed in one hour and 35 minutes.

The front page of the August 18, 1949, *Jordan Independent* carried the stories of two linemen for the Minnesota Valley Electric Cooperative, or MVEC, taking huge doses of electrical voltage while on the job. One lived, and one died after taking as much as 7,200 volts of electricity.

Former professional Bud Kleidon and Prior Lake shut out the Brewers, 6-0, to end Jim Pollard's rookie season with the Jordan Brewers. Then Max Casey received his commission as permanent postmaster in Jordan, and with government-paid time on his hands, the push began in earnest for a new, lighted baseball park in Brewer Town. Good teams have good, lighted ballparks, and they play in the state's top leagues, the sales pitch began.

Mudbaden, the nationally renowned sulphur mud bath spa just outside of Jordan, shared a page of advertisements with the Hotel Jordan's Coffee Shop. Each establishment welcomed Scott County Fair Visitors, the hotel featuring turtle soup and Mudbaden requiring reservations in its dining room for its "Tasty Dinners" at $1.50 per plate.

The front-page headline of the November 17, 1949, *Jordan Independent* tells of "Ground Broken In Scott Fairgrounds For Enlarged Baseball Field With Lights." A 10-member special committee of the Jordan Baseball Association had reported its findings to the board after reviewing at least six potential sites for a new ballpark with lights. With some cooperation from the Scott County Good Seed Association, which owned the property at the time, and the moving of some buildings and dirt, as well as a new infield, backstop, and the lights, Fairgrounds Park was the committee's recommended site for a new ballpark. Principals from the fair board, the seed association, and the baseball association agreed unanimously to the renovations and responsibilities, and they signed a 25-year lease that allowed baseball to be played on the best diamond that men could dream up in the last months of the first half of the 20th Century. Ground would be broken before the onset of winter, the Jordan Baseball Association would be incorporated, and a major fund-raising effort was initiated to pay for the new, lighted Fairgrounds Park.

The work was more than just a minor facelift with some selective injections. It was a major makeover–a conversion experience. Trees were removed. Nine thousand yards of dirt were moved, and Haferman and Stark Construction Co. hauled away from Al Breimhorst's hillside, by one account, 70 truckloads of black dirt for the new diamond. At least three buildings were re-located to new sites with concrete footings laid, a new 4H building built, and the circular wooden dance pavilion that had been built in 1903 was dismantled. Large fair-and-fun-going crowds from as far away as the Twin Cities, traveled then by train to the country for its music and its beer, which was carted from the Brewery to the pavilion over the three catwalks that spanned the creek in the early 1900s, connecting thirsty fairgoers and dancers with "the best beer I ever drank," according to one now-deceased old timer who said he had worked for the Brewery in 1936. "The head on a glass of that Jordan Beer would hold like it was a scoop of ice cream," he said.

The Baseball Bosses also promoted a "Jim Pollard Appreciation Night" at a Minneapolis Laker basketball game in the Minneapolis Auditorium under sponsorship of the Jordan Commercial Club. Over 200 Jordan fans were reported to have taken the opportunity at $2.40 a ticket and another buck for bus transportation to see *their* baseball player on the hard court of the Minneapolis Auditorium. "Jim and his teammate, George Mikan, are to basketball what Babe Ruth and Lou Gehrig have been to baseball," Max Casey wrote in the final promotion of the game three days before the tipoff. The Lakers ran through the NBA's playoffs later that season and then beat the Syracuse Nationals, four games to two, in the finals, with Mikan scoring 40 points in the championship game on assists from Pollard, Mikkelson, and Slater Martin, and Jim adding 16 points of his own in the 110-95 win.

The bosses also promoted the public's purchase of stock in the Jordan Baseball Association, Inc. at $10 a share to help come up with the $20,000 that was estimated to be needed for the ballpark's renovation and the construction and installation of the light towers that would illuminate the night to bring more baseball to town. The MRL was a night baseball league, and Chaska and Shakopee would make it a 10-team league in 1950, with a 27-game schedule. Final reckoning in the fall would show that a bank loan, proceeds from sale of stock, and donations from individuals and businesses paid for the work and materials that couldn't be procured through the loving labor of volunteers. The year's gate admissions and a healthy profit off the revenues from the beer stand and all concessions were used to repay the loan that had paid for the work on the baseball organization's leased ballpark. While tax money was not used, both the City of Jordan and its school district paid leases to use the park. Everything was above board; there was no slight of hand, no "borrowed funds" from the public trough, no lingering questions, and it could have been done easily, one would think, with Mayor Peter Schmidt also President of the Jordan Baseball Association that year.

People were *asked* for contributions, and many gladly handed over $10 to $500. They were urged to buy stock, but *the decision* to contribute *their* money was done individually and of their own volition. Baseball would thrive with the bosses championing due diligence, transparency, clarity, accountability, and the sovereignty of the individual and his preferences for supporting the causes that he deems worthy of his support. They did it right, with the exception of the lease that was for only 25 years. It should have been a 99-year lease with a rent-to-own contingency if the Scott County Fair ever moved or shut down, and with a sweetheart purchase deal with the seed association in the event of their demise.

Jim Pollard would miss the first two weeks of the 1950 season, because the Lakers, after winning their third straight world championship, took their show on tour of the northwest part of the country and a series of promotional exhibition games. Scores of volunteers, over 100 on several occasions, spread, leveled, and raked fill over the entire field, then spread the 70 truck loads of rich, black loam hauled by Haferman and Stark Co. from the hillside behind Al Breimhorst's farm house north of Jordan on Hwy 169. They laid the sod that promised a playable field in a month or two. As luck would have it, the rains that the newly laid sod needed desperately came on the weekends. MRL baseball was rained out the first two weeks, and Jim Pollard did not miss a game. Then they finally opened the 1950 MRL season, with a reported "several hundred fans making the trip to Montgomery on Sunday," May 14. Bob Shotliff scattered seven hits and struck out 14 in the Brewer's 8 to 4 win. Jim played third base and went hitless in three at bats. He went hitless in the next Brewer win and in the Chaska game as well that was called because of fog with the score tied 2-2. But the team stood at 3-0 on top of the MRL on June 1, 1950, and Pollard broke out of his hitting slump with a searing triple to the deepest pocket of Tiger Stadium's center field. Moreover, according to the Max Casey report in the June 8 *Jordan Independent*, "Nearly 1,500 people saw Jordan get revenge for defeats of the past several seasons, as they bowled over the Belle Plaine Tigers in a decisive 7 to 4 victory."

Jim's double and triple in three at bats powered the Brewers to a 5-0 win over Le Sueur to put them at 4-0. But LeCenter, with what Max Casey noted "was rumored to be the most expensive ball club in the league," was closing at 5-1. They would square off in a week. Jim Pollard took the mound for his first start of the season at LeCenter and was said to have looked much better than the 10-3 loss would indicate. Opposite-field base hits by LeCenter's newly recruited ex-professionals, swinging late on Jim's heat, fell just inside the lines and led to the locals' undoing. Jim then went three for four in the 6-3 win over New Prague, and with another win over Shakopee, who had beaten LeCenter, the Brewers were back on top of the MRL with a 6-1 record, two games ahead of LeCenter in the loss column.

Then, in the first night game ever played under the lights at Fairgrounds Park, in front of over 1,300 fans, reported by Max to be "the largest crowd to ever see a baseball game in Jordan," the Brewers beat arch-rival Belle Plaine for the second time in as many meetings, 5-3. Pollard had two hits in the game, as newly acquired Glen Johnson went seven solid innings on the mound before giving way to Shotliff in the eighth to preserve the win. But here's Max Casey in the June 29, 1950, *Jordan Independent* on the front page:

> So near perfection were preparations for the 'air launching,' so correct the measurements, that the eight 80-ft. steel light towers with scores of fixtures were aloft within eight hours, Tuesday. Electrical service connections then followed quickly. They say that more than 100 men and boys of the community helped during those days and a 'near miracle' of accomplishment occurred.

Thanks to Louie Stifter's handiwork with a welding torch at a cost of $3,461.85 to the JBA, Jordan was done with the leasing of a lighted ballpark from a neighbor for a night game. They were through with their tenant status. They were now full-time landlords of Fairgrounds Park. From now on, other teams in other leagues and school clubs would increasingly want to rent their home field. Just as Jim Pollard was gaining his batting eye and his stroke, the team went into a nosedive. They lost three of four league games in the week of coverage by the June 29, 1950, *Jordan Independent*, knocking them out of first place in the MRL. Jim's three-run homer in the top of the ninth beat Chaska 8 to 7, then three straight losses to Prior Lake, Montgomery, and St. Peter toppled them to 7-4 on the season, behind LeCenter with its 10-4 record.

Two wins the next week, including a 21-hit barrage to beat Prior Lake, 23-6, and the 5-3 win over Belle Plaine, put the Brewers back in the league lead at 9-4, a game ahead of LeCenter in the loss column. The lead actually lasted a day, as the Brewers got beat at home by the resurgent Shakopee Indians, 9-7, in front of over 1,000 fans on a Monday night. But the pennant race, as usual, was turning into a real donnybrook, as five teams were vying for top honors, led by LeCenter and Belle Plaine. Mandatory makeup games were stretching pitching staffs thin, but the lighted ballparks were paying off all over the league. Jim's pitching arm was sore, but his bat was hot, as the July heat turned on in the Minnesota River League. In addition to his two hits in the win over Belle Plaine, he was three for four in the pounding of Prior Lake, then two for five with a triple with over 750 fans on hand, mostly Jordan residents, as LeCenter did not draw well in support of its hired guns from Minneapolis and St. Paul. It was a big win over Bob Dill and the LeCenter Chiefs, who would win the Class-A Minnesota State Championship in two months. He had three of the team's six hits in the 4-1 loss to Le Sueur, then went two for four in the 5-3 win over Shakopee at home, with a two-run, 500-foot, monster homerun for the ages the difference in the game. Here's Max Casey with the view from the press box at Fairgrounds Park, as reported in the July 20, 1950, *Jordan Independent*:

> Jim Pollard's homer, by far the longest seen in Fairgrounds Park this season, came in the bottom of the fifth and came at a time when there was a man on base, Bud Schwingler. He scored ahead of big Jim. Pollard's homerun ball which wasn't found until the next morning, it being discovered then in the Phillips garden about 500 feet from home plate. The ball went over the left field fence at the height of the lower row of lights on the left-field tower, about 60 feet over the board fence.

Front-page banner headlines in the July 27, 1950, *Jordan Independent* proudly announced, "Dedication of New Lighted Baseball Grounds, Jordan, July 28." A special dedication committee consisting of L.C. ("Fats") Herder, Ben Mertz, and Ben Engfer of the Jordan Baseball Association put together a program that they bundled with a replaying of the game with Chaska that was tied 2-2 in the ninth inning earlier in the season and called due to fog. A buck got fans a commemorative button and admission to the program, which featured a dedication address by the Honorable Joseph J. Moriarty, District Judge, of Shakopee, and the ballgame under the lights on Friday night.

The ballgame was a disappointment to the Jordan fans, as Chaska won 8-1, a Jim Pollard dinger the Brewer's sole run in front of a reported record crowd of over

1,300 paying customers. Max Casey noted in his review of the program in the August 3, 1950, *Jordan Independent*, "Some thought Judge Joe went off the deep end; but all admired his good form, enjoyed his candor and his courage." The speech came on the heels of "The Star Spangled Banner" by "Miss Luverne Beckius, sweet singer of Jordan, with accompaniment by Jordan Municipal band, while the national colors were raised at the ball field." The judge's speech, replete with baseball metaphor and comment on the Cold War with Soviet Russia, stirred the locals and the visiting fans with a shot at President Harry Truman's Secretary of State, Dean Acheson, and a call for his removal from office.

"Baseball was life, and life was baseball." The connections between baseball and God and between baseball and geo-politics, during the game's Golden Age were never more evident than here in Judge Joe's dedication of Fairgrounds Park in 1950.

Jim had two hits in the 8-3 loss to Le Sueur, then went one for four in the 5-2 win over Prior Lake and Bud Kleidon, whose baseball talents were obvious but who had reportedly been kicked out of the Northern League as a result of an altercation with an umpire. He had one hit in the last game of the regular season, a 6-5 loss to LeCenter, which left the Brewers in third place with a 16-11 record. Playoffs began immediately, with all 10 teams in it. The Brewers squeaked by Montgomery, 4-3, with Jim going two for four, including a triple at Fairgrounds Park. Then the Brewers edged Chaska, 5-4, in the second sudden death round of league playoffs, with Pollard again legging out a triple in two official at-bats.

With Jim's arm sore for most of the last half of the season, outsiders Glen Johnson, Earl Daniels, and Frank Pugsley came through "the pipeline" and were given shots to join "Bullet" Bob Shotliff with turns on the Brewer mound. After Belle Plaine won the first game of the three-game series, 7-1, in front of over 2,000 fans at Belle Plaine on Sunday evening, Pugsley got the nod from Manager Leon Hennes in the second game, Tuesday night at Jordan. In front of more than 1,700 fans packed into the grandstands, along the right-field fence line, on the hillside down the left-field line, and taking up whatever elbowroom was left around the beer stand, Frank Pugsley scattered seven Belle Plaine Tiger hits and got beat 7-4. Jim had just one hit in the game, but the Brewers had pounded Tiger pitching for 16 hits. They stranded 13 runners on base and as a result watched Belle Plaine and LeCenter fight it out for the championship in a series that took all five games to decide the winner–LeCenter, which then defeated Excelsior of the Twin Cities Suburban League in the best-of-three series to earn its trip to the state tournament.

LeCenter squeaked by Granite Falls, 4-3, in the first round of the Class-A State Tournament at St. Cloud. Then they pasted Cold Spring, 12-2, and beat Winsted 4-3 in the championship game. A record 35,318 fans attended the state tournament games at St. Cloud that year. There were 799 teams in 106 statewide leagues of three different classes (AA, A, and B) playing so-called amateur baseball in 1950. "So-called" because being paid to play a game has always been what has distinguished the professional from the amateur. Fact is, Class-AA ballplayers were paid to play baseball, as were many, if not most, of the Class-A ballplayers. Teams had payrolls to meet. The good players were paid. The better the ballplayer, the more he got paid. Full-time and part-time jobs were also offered as inducements to ball players.

After batting .426 in 1949, according to "Jim Pollard's Statistics" in Tom Melchior's *Scott County Baseball*, he hit .444 in 1950 for the 18-13 Jordan Brewers, according to the same source, with a slight drop off in home runs from 7 to 5, but a jump in triples from 2 to 7. "He could run," Ed Breimhorst recalled. "He had a lot of extra-base hits because of his speed."

"Hub Baseball Finances Good," heralded the front-page headline in the November 16, 1950, *Jordan Independent*. "New Plant Built in '50 Pleases. Gate Receipts of Season $8648," the subhead explained. The "Open Door" and "Open Book" MO had proven itself once again in a community baseball operation in the Minnesota River Valley. Two teams, Shakopee and Chaska, were voted permanent membership in the Minnesota River League in November. Applications by Excelsior and Bloomington were rejected by a vote of 6-3 at a league meeting in January.

The banner headline across the top of the front page of the February 1, 1951, *Jordan Independent*: "Was 38 Degrees Below Zero In Hub Tuesday." The subhead added, "Broke All Previous Cold Records in Jordan. So Did Sunday With 35 Below." But Max Casey warmed all over with his persistent promotion of "Jim Pollard Night" at the Minneapolis Auditorium, Sunday evening, February 11. As many as 200 Jordan fans took in the special night at the Minneapolis Auditorium, and Max's first-hand report in the February 15 issue of the Jordan weekly noted, "Pollard Hit Peak For Jordan Fans." Pollard had broken a cheekbone in mid-December and been out of the Laker lineup for three weeks. Here's a portion of Max's report:

> Reversing the order of the evening, big Jim Pollard showed his own appreciation to the nearly two hundred Jordanites who went to Minneapolis Sunday evening to see the Lakers play Indianapolis and pay tribute to Jordan's summertime baseball star. He turned in his best cage performance of the year. Jim connected for 26 points, being outdone only by his great teammate, George Mikan, who hit 27 for the evening. Jordan fans were right proud to see Jim also come through with one of his best defensive games, stealing the ball from the visiting Olympians time after time and controlling nearly all evening. The World Champion Lakers won the contest 91 to 78 from the always tough Olympians of the Hoosier state, to increase their hold on first place in the NBA Western Division by 5-1/2 games.
>
> Following the game, Jim and his lovely wife Arilee, were hosts to members of the Jordan baseball team, members of the Laker basketball team and a group of friends at their home in south Minneapolis, where a delicious luncheon was served. Much baseball and basketball chatter took place in the spacious Pollard basement, Jim and his baseball teammates talking over plans for the coming campaign in the Minnesota River League.
>
> At the basketball game in the auditorium, the Pollards were presented with two pieces of fitted luggage by Ray Joachim, chairman of the Pollard Nite Committee. Several pounds of good Jordan manufactured

creamery butter were also presented to each and every member of the Laker squad and coaching staff as a gesture of good will from their many fans in and around Jordan.

Luggage and freshly churned butter aside, Jim Pollard liked Jordan and the friendly gestures he had come to know from its people. It was better baseball there, too, than he had expected, and the investment the town had made in the last year showed him that they were serious about the game. On the other hand, the Baseball Bosses of Jordan, who were the town fathers, would have given Jim Pollard the keys to the city, had they ever bothered to ask craftsman Louie Stifter to put forging fire to forming raw steel or brass. They would have given Jim Pollard and the entire Minneapolis Laker organization an appreciation night to remember in the town's original taproom within the stone walls of the Jordan Brewery, too, drawing thick-foaming lager into naturally insulating copper mugs from a mother load of kegs stored in naturally cooling and aging caves.

But the beer business was changing, just as most businesses and industries were changing. What had once been a thriving business in a small German town, providing employment for local residents while netting a fair profit for the brewery's owners and delivering a quality product for the beverage-consuming public in a reasonable distribution radius, had become an absentee owner's white elephant. Mankato Brewing Company had bought out the Jordan Brewery, and now, according to the February 15, 1951, *Jordan Independent*, a twice-removed absentee owner, the Cold Spring Brewing Company of Cold Spring, Minnesota, would hold title to the Jordan Brewery by way of its purchase of the Mankato business. The Jordan Brewery was dying. The "Hospitality Room" had become a thing of the past. An appreciation night hosted in the style of once-large local ownership and the quality of their German brew master's lager would never be known again.

The Minneapolis Laker dynasty was interrupted as well. With George Mikan suffering a hairline fracture to a bone in his ankle, Jim Pollard had been forced to pick up the pace and the slack for the Lakers. He couldn't do it alone. The Lakers lost in the semi-finals of the 1951 NBA playoffs to Rochester, three games to one, ending the three-year run of world basketball championships.

The rest of the world wasn't standing still either. Chinese forces on the Korean peninsula first captured Seoul, South Korea, then were driven back by the U.S./ UN forces, which would reach 2.9 million U.S. military troop numbers alone . . . President Truman fired the narcissistic General Douglas McArthur . . . The first commercial computer, UNIVAC 1, entered service at the Census Bureau . . . Both the U.S. and U.S.S.R. were performing nuclear tests underground and in the atmosphere, and Winston Churchill was re-elected prime minister of Great Britain.

In golf, Ben Hogan won his first green jacket at Augusta, in 1951, and his third U.S. Open . . . In baseball, Mel Ott and Jimmie Foxx were elected to the Hall of Fame . . . The St. Louis Browns signed 45-year-old Satchel Paige . . . Mickey Mantle and Willie Mays played their first games with the New York Yankees and New York Giants, respectively . . . Mantle went 1-4 in his first game . . . Mays was 0-12 before getting his first hit, a shot over the roof and out of the Polo Grounds off Boston Braves pitcher Warren Spahn, who would win 363 games in his long and splendid career–the most of any lefthander in the history of the game.

Bill Veeck sent 26-year-old Eddie Gaedel, a 3 ft. 7 in. midget, with number "1/8" on the back of his uniform, to pinch hit for the Cleveland Indians in the first inning of the second game of a double header against the Detroit Tigers on August 19, 1951. Veeck reportedly coached Gaedel to take a stance at the plate in a slight crouch to shrink his strike zone a little and to keep the bat on his shoulders. Under no circumstances was he to swing at a pitch. Veeck told Eddie that he had taken out a $1 million insurance policy on his life and that he would be stationed on top of the roof of the stadium with a high-powered rifle to make sure. He promised Eddie that he would kill him if he tried to swing at a pitch. Eddie ignored the coaching instructions when he stepped up to the plate. He took the classic, upright stance of Joe DiMaggio, legs spread wide, bat held high, and waiting for a pitch he could turn on in his wheelhouse. Bill Veeck was mortified by the thought that Eddie was going to try to swing at a pitch. Bob Cain, on the mound for the Tigers, couldn't keep from laughing. He couldn't hit the one-and-a-half-inch strike zone presented to him either. Eddie, who had signed for $100, walked on four pitches. The crowd of more than 18,000 fans gave Eddie a standing ovation as he paraded his way to first base, tipped his cap in appreciation, and then was lifted for a pinch runner. His Major League contract was voided the next day by the president of the American League, and because of Eddie Gaedel, every Major League contract has had to be approved by the Commissioner of Baseball since 1951.

National League umpire Frank Dascoli cleared the Dodger bench, ejecting 15 Brooklyn players during a game . . . The Giants beat the Dodgers in a three-game playoff to win the National League pennant after trailing by 13-1/2 games in August . . . Joe DiMaggio announced his retirement from baseball in December, after playing his last game in the World Series win over the Giants in October.

Despite the sudden rise in the Minnesota River, described as a "wall of water" in news reports of the day, the Minnesota River League opened its 1951 season on Sunday, May 6, with all but a full slate of games played. Eight of the 10 teams played, including the Jordan Brewers with Jim Pollard at first base. Shakopee's Riverside Park was reported to be under water, but Fairgrounds Park was high and dry. Despite giving up nine walks, Bob Shotliff struck out 11 Robins and allowed four hits in the game that the Brewers won with just one hit and seven walks, and aided by four New Prague errors. It wasn't the cleanest of ballgames. Meanwhile, David E. Braun of Chicago informed the *Jordan Independent* that he had completed his purchase of the Mudbaden Sulphur Springs Health Resort north of the city of Jordan. "'My program for the immediate future,'" Braun announced, "'calls for the complete modernization of Mudbaden Sanitarium as a mud bath resort' . . . the only curative institution of its kind in Minnesota."

Jim Pollard took the mound for the first time in the new season against Shakopee under the lights on a Wednesday night. Max Casey reported in the May 31, 1951, *Jordan Independent*:

> Jordan fans were well-satisfied with what they saw over at Shakopee, a return to pitching duty of Jim Pollard. He not only went the entire route, but pitched one of the real good games of his career. Jim's fastball was working to perfection. He had the hard-hitting Shakopee sluggers swinging regularly as he racked up an even dozen strikeouts for the

evening while allowing but five hits, one a circuit clout by Kelly Roth with two men on for Shakopee's only tallies of the night.

The 4-3 win was followed by a 9-5 loss to Chaska to drop the team to an even 2-2 record after the first month of the season. After losing to St. Peter, Jordan won two in a row, including a Pollard win over Belle Plaine in which he also hit a home run. Then they lost two in a row, the first a 7-6 affair in 11 innings to Le Sueur, which supposedly had paid handsomely for a fine ball club they thought could compete with the state champion LeCenter Chiefs–Jordan's next opponent. Jim took a shutout into the ninth inning, but a grand slam beat him, 5-3, in the ninth. Max Casey, doubling his duty as the "Voice of the Brewers" from the press box, had the best view of anybody in the ballpark of the ball clearing the left field fence. The press box window on the top floor of the county fair's sandstone poultry building below and education exhibit above was the perfect spotting perch for balls hit down the left-field line: "The four bagger. . . was foul by at least four feet," reported Max in the *JI* on Thursday, June 21. "Calling the game a heartbreaker for the team and fans is putting it mildly," wrote Max. Pollard had pitched well, only to get beat by one of the vagaries of sport–an official's call. The Brewers closed out the month of June in fifth place in the MRL with a 5-6 record. LeCenter was running away with the pennant at 9-1.

Jordan split its first two games in July, and then shut out second-place St. Peter 7-0 at Fairgrounds Park to set up a big showdown at Belle Plaine. They took a 3-1 lead into the ninth that evaporated on another umpire's decision, according to Max Casey's report in the July 19, 1951, *Jordan Independent*, and ended up losing 4-3. Despite Jim's two homeruns, the Brewers lost to Prior Lake, 7-5, to put their record at 7-9, five games off the league-leading LeCenter Chiefs. They then lost to Le Sueur, 9-7, before committing nine errors and getting smoked by the defending state champion LeCenter Chiefs, 20-3. Jim relieved Shotliff in the third with eight runs in already. After a settling down period, he struck out the side and gave up but three hits and one run the rest of the game.

Jordan pitched lefty Bob Wildes at Belle Plaine on the night they picked him up from the Austin Packers of the Southern Minny. He fired a six-hit shutout to beat the Tigers, 4-0, stopping a four-game Brewer losing streak, and he followed it up with a 2-1 gem over Chaska four nights later. Jim's game-tying home run against Prior Lake put them in position to win that game, 6-5. Then Shotliff repeated what Wildes had done the week before. He came back on Sunday night and won again, 5-1, over Shakopee, with Pollard and Hartkopf pacing the Brewer attack with two hits apiece. The Brewers finished at a disappointing 11-11, good for fifth place and two games behind the tied, fourth-place finishers, Le Sueur and St. Peter.

Jim took the mound in the first game of the best of three game playoff series against Le Sueur and got beat 7-1. Seven Jordan errors gave Le Sueur nine unearned runs and the second game, 9-3. Another disappointing Brewer season was closed out. Still, many one-run games decided by questionable umpire calls hurt. Pollard's arm, too, was questionable all year, and maybe he was still a little gun shy after the injury to his eye socket and cheekbone in the winter. His offensive Laker game certainly suffered, as the 1950-'51 NBA season was his poorest, averaging just over 11 points a game that season while scoring at a 15-point clip the years before and after. The season split two Laker three-peats of the world basketball championship. Similarly, Jim's batting average in the summer dipped below .400 for the first time, with just four homeruns, six doubles, and a solitary triple, according to *Scott County Baseball*. Likewise, his pitching wasn't up to par, as he recorded two wins against three losses, and just 19 strikeouts in 46 innings pitched. Jim Pollard was a Thoroughbred, but it was like the horse just wasn't running well.

"One of the gratifying aspects disclosed by the records," Max Casey reported in his 'Baseball Roundup' column at the end of the season in the August 23, 1951, *Jordan Independent*, "is that the Brewers for the third straight season have not been shut out."

"LeCenter bought a league title, it is generally agreed," Max explained, adding that other teams had followed suit but failed to mention what the locals had done to field the team and find the pitchers they put on the mound. Five of the seven Brewer catchers over the past three years were "outsiders." Pugsley, De La Hunt, and other pitchers were "recruited" from Class-AA teams to the south and west. Nobody in town knew the two new infielders, Clark Rice and Roger Brown, both carrying pedigrees and some history with them. These guys were guns for hire. Indeed, outside mercenaries received two-thirds of the JBA's player salaries in 1951. The Class-A MRL was slowly pushing toward Class-AA status. Paul Sunder thought that umpire Lou Cardinal, a former catcher and a resident of St. Paul, who called a lot of balls and strikes at Jordan and who liked to stop at Geno's after the games, could possibly have been an informal recruiter for the Jordan Brewers. He certainly had the contacts from playing and umpiring for years throughout the lower end of the Minnesota River Valley, as well as umpiring in the Southern Minny. But outside players, who were paid more money than locals received, fanned the flames of resentment and an argument that would never be settled.

On top of the disappointment on the field, the finances had suffered. The Balance Sheet for the 1951 Jordan Baseball Association showed an operating deficit of $1,753.67. Fence advertising revenue of $620 over the winter would cut the debt going into the new 1952 season. Bad weather, it was thought, had hurt attendance. With smaller crowds, of course, the concessions had suffered, showing a profit that was down to $1,279.21. The federal government was still collecting an amusement tax, which meant $653 off the gate admissions in Jordan, Minnesota, had to be sent to Washington, D.C. Meanwhile, player salaries had gone up. Max noted that there were rumblings at the winter meetings of secession, too, because the smaller towns, as usual, felt they were at such a disadvantage that they couldn't compete with the larger towns. Number of outside players was going to be cut to two, possibly three, players, and "home" players would be strictly limited to year-round residents. Still, there was pride throughout the league for LeCenter's strong showing in the Class-A state tournament at Faribault, where they finished second after having won the championship the previous year.

Jordan fans again bought a section of seats at the Minneapolis Auditorium in appreciation of Jim Pollard, Laker/Brewer great. The Lakers took on their archrival Rochester Royals on Sunday, February 3, 1952. But this year, fans were also treated to their Jordan Wheels basketball team taking on the Rush City five in the preliminary game, which the locals won handily, 32 to 24. In the main event, fans saw their own Jim Pollard set up big George Mikan for the game-winning basket with three seconds to play, good for a 77-75 win, "in a game," Max reported, "that had everyone in the auditorium standing on their ears during the last three minutes of play."

At winter baseball league meetings, Shakopee and Chaska dropped out of the Minnesota River League, opting, perhaps wisely, to play down to the Class-B levels in other area leagues. The MRL of now eight teams again adopted the stricter residency rules, along with a limitation of just two "outside" players. The residency radius defining a "home" ballplayer was changed from 15 miles to 8 miles. Moreover, you had to be living in the town in which you were to play by January 1. Payroll costs, not pure principle, were behind the rule changes for the 1952 season. The league also adopted as its official baseball the Lowe and Campbell No 1021.00. This "cushion cork center ball," Max reported in the February 14, 1952, *Jordan Independent*, would save each team $6 a dozen through the season.

Ben Engfer was advertising the 160 horsepower "Rocket Engine" in the new 1952 Oldsmobile 88's that came with "Hydra-Matic Super Drive."

The Lakers began their second of two three-peats with the 1951-'52 NBA season. They finished the regular season, 40-26, a game behind the Rochester Royals. Highlights of the season included Jim's back-to-back 25-point games against the much-heralded Boston Celtics. His play drew rave reviews in the *Minneapolis Star* and *The Christian Science Monitor*. Dick Cullum of the *Minneapolis Tribune*, according to Grundman in his biography, said of Jim Pollard: "'Against the best players, when it counted the most, Pollard was in a class by himself,' and that 'Pollard had been playing at this exalted level for five years.'"

The Laker highlights also included their defeat of the Harlem Globetrotters. In front of 20,084 fans at Chicago Stadium, the Lakers demolished the Trotters 84-60 for their fifth straight victory over the court jesters, who had won the first two games. The frontline of Pollard, Mikan, and Mikkelson was just too much to handle. Abe Saperstein, owner of the Globetrotters, was so annoyed with the margin of defeat that he terminated the rivalry.

After defeating Rochester three games to one in the semifinals of the 1952 NBA playoffs, the Lakers met the New York Knicks for the championship series. Jim Pollard led the Lakers in the opening game with a career-high 34 points in the 83-79 overtime win at the St. Paul Auditorium. The two teams then alternated wins until, with the series tied at three games each, the seventh game would decide the championship.

With a strained back, Jim saw limited action in Games 5 and 6, but he came off the bench, heavily wrapped, in Game 7, scoring 10 points in the fourth quarter to boost the Lakers to an 82-65 win and the fourth championship in five years. It was an especially gratifying year for Pollard, Grundman noted. "He played 65 games, scored 1,005 points for a 15.5 average, pulled down 593 rebounds, and dished out 234 assists."

Max Casey noted in his "Sports Chatterbox" of May 15, 1952, that the Minnesota River League would be opening its new season the coming Sunday. He also mentioned that the Lakers and Jim Pollard were touring the Hawaiian Islands after their successful NBA Championship, that they won 12 consecutive exhibition games on the islands, and that Jim Pollard was expected to be back in time to join the Brewers for another summer baseball season by June 1 and possibly a week earlier.

David E. Braun of Chicago sold the Mudbaden Sulphur Mud Baths Sanitarium after one year of ownership to the Sacred Heart Novitiate, Holy Cross Fathers of South Bend, Indiana, an affiliate of the University of Notre Dame. Possession was to take place July 1, 1952. Its current facilities built in 1915, the health resort and spa had treated thousands of patients from around the country for rheumatoid arthritis and related pain and ailments over the previous 50 years. Warm baths of high content sulphur mud of the kind found in the bogs and sloughs in the vicinity of Mudbaden were said to pull toxins from overloaded bodies. Duck and pheasant hunters who ventured into the sloughs wearing hip boots and waders knew that the mud smelled awful. They didn't understand anyone wanting to take a bath in it, something they tried to avoid while hunting. Some called Mudbaden a "jag farm," because more than a few patients were said to be famous celebrities who checked in to get off the booze and to dry out. Rumors persisted, too, that the resort's clientele often catered parties, with the locals providing some entertainment and some participation in the monkey business. That would come to an end quickly, one presumed for years, and Mudbaden would become known simply as "The Novitiate" where young men would complete their preparations to become Catholic priests.

The MRL split into two 4-team divisions, North and South, for 1952. Jim Pollard's athleticism allowed him to play any position on the diamond. He would play wherever he was needed. In 1952, he was needed all over. Injuries to three starters resulted in Jim playing some at each infield position. Jordan started 0-3, then went to 1-5 in mid-June when rookie Paul Sunder beat Prior Lake, 5-2, on a three-hitter and beat them again two weeks later, 2-1, with a neat five-hitter. Jim gave up six hits, but seven walks, in a loss to Montgomery, before Bob Shotliff no hit New Prague, 1-0, with 12 strikeouts. After losing to Le Sueur, 8-1, the Brewers ignited and won three straight to go to 6-9 on the season, including another gem by Bob Shotliff who lost his bid for a second-consecutive no-hit shutout in the ninth inning against LeCenter. Pollard's two home runs paced the Brewer's 17-hit attack. His two-run blast in the first inning was all Shotliff needed in a 7-1 win. Jim then went nine innings on the mound and beat the Southern Division-leading St. Peter Saints, 8-4, on five hits with 11 strikeouts. A good sign, he got stronger as the game got into the late innings, and he struck out the side in the ninth on 10 pitches. The Northern Division-leading Belle Plaine Tigers then took the wind out of the Brewer sails with a convincing 10-3 drubbing at Belle Plaine.

Jim won his second game in a row, beating New Prague, 3-2, in a tough pitchers' duel with Jim Geske to put the Brewers at 7-10 on the season after the horrendous start that had them mired in the bottom of the division. He made it three straight in the 5-2 win over Le Sueur at Fairgrounds Park, scattering eight hits and striking out 10 Green Sox batters. He also had three hits in the game, including a triple and a double. Pollard was running on all eight cylinders as the playoffs approached. The Brewers then split their last two games of the regular season. Max's page-2 sub-headline in the August 7, 1952, *Jordan Independent* told the story: "Jim Pollard Threw Five Hitter Against St. Peter Last Thursday Evening To Spark Jordan to 3-1 Win For Brewers First Victory At St. Peter Park In Five Years."

MRL pennant-winning Belle Plaine crushed Jordan, 8-1, at Fairgrounds Park in the regular season finale in front of what was reported as "the biggest crowd of the year." But the big loss was Bud Schwingler, Northern States Power lineman and a regular in the Jordan lineup. The outfielder had fallen from a highline pole in the last week of July and suffered a compound fracture of his arm and a dislocated vertebra in his back. The third Brewer regular to suffer a fractured bone, he would spend the next two weeks in the hospital and miss the rest of the season.

Jordan beat Prior Lake two straight in the elimination round of the MRL playoffs. The first game shutout, 2-0, was followed by a 16-2 drubbing that could have been billed as "Jim Pollard Night." Indeed, Big Jim mowed down Prior Lake, firing a six hitter with 15 strikeouts. He played the other half of the game as well, with five hits in five at bats, including two doubles.

That set up Jordan and Belle Plaine for the championship round. It's never gotten any better than this. Belle Plaine ran away with the Northern Division of the Minnesota River League with a 16-5 record, good enough to beat St. Peter by one game for the regular season league-best honors. Six Brewer errors cost Bobby Shotliff, no doubt, a four-hit shutout win in the all-important first game of the best-of-three series at Belle Plaine on Wednesday night, August 13. Two nights later, at Fairgrounds Park in Jordan, in front of over 900 fans again, the Brewers exploded for six runs in the sixth inning to break a 2-2 tie. Jim Pollard scattered eight hits in the game to win it, 8-4. Knotted up at a game apiece, the two teams took it back to Belle Plaine on Sunday night for the rubber game. Belle Plaine took an early 1-0 lead off Shotliff. The Brewers loaded the bases in the fourth, their only chance to break the game open. Despite several hard-hit line drives, they managed just one run in their only real opportunity in the ballgame. Final score: Belle Plaine 4, Jordan 1.

Belle Plaine went on to beat Southern Division winner St. Peter for the MRL championship and the right to advance to the Region 1-A tournament. Belle Plaine had seen enough to draft the Jordan battery of Jim Pollard and Baldy Hartkopf, along with New Prague pitcher Jim Geske. Bad weather and the state tourney schedule forced a double header for the regional opener. *The Belle Plaine Herald's* September 4, 1952, two sub-headlines tell the tale: "Geske's 3-Hitter Stops Bloomington," and "Pollard Strikes Out 18; Gives Up 2 Hits." Jim helped himself with two hits and an RBI in the game against a Minneapolis team as well. He was back in form. Back to his old self: "Doing it all."

After beating Fulda, 4-2, in the opening game of the 1952 Class-A State Tournament at Austin, Jim started and pitched seven solid innings with 11 strikeouts in the Tiger 10-6 semi-final win over Glenwood, which had just dropped down from Class-AA play in the West Central League. He also had two doubles in the game. Belle Plaine then lost the state championship to Cannon Falls, 5-4, in 10 innings. Jim had come on strong the last half the year, both on the mound and at the plate. According to *Scott County Baseball*, he was 6-1 pitching, with 67 strikeouts in 66 innings of work. It's hard to tell whether the 18-K performance for Belle Plaine in the regionals against a Minneapolis nine, and the 11 strikeouts against Glenwood in the state tournament are included in the final season accounting. On a team that averaged less than .200 at the plate, Jim's .344 batting average was outstanding. He couldn't have gotten many good pitches to hit with that kind of hitting around him. Pitchers get wise in a hurry.

"He was a good all-around guy," Dick Nolden said of Jim Pollard. "He was always behind you and helpful in all ways." A retired veterinarian who moved in 1957 to Detroit Lakes, Minnesota, where he practiced his profession until he retired, Nolden found it easy to compare Pollard with the more modern-day ball players. "Pollard was very humble," Nolden said, "and a team player. Today's athletes," he noted of the more modern era, as he hesitated, "are full of themselves." Public reporting showed the major tenants of Fairgrounds Park to be doing fine. The Scott County Fair made headlines in the area weeklies with its profit of $1,202. The Jordan Baseball Association remained in the black as well. An epidemic of polio was surging through Minnesota that would hit over 4,000, killing nearly 300 people, and the Jordan Creamery's head butter maker, Edmund Haferman, scored an outstanding 99.44, the highest, in the District 15 competition among creameries. The 1952 Presidential Election went Ike's way in what was headlined a "Tidal Wave Victory" on the front page of the November 6 *Jordan Independent*. A week earlier, a Republican Election Committee advertisement quoted six prominent Democrats, including his challenger, Governor Adlai Stevenson, on the virtues and merits of Dwight D. Eisenhower. The vote disparity suggested a large crossover segment of voters for the popular World War II general. Conscience and sensibility trumped party favoritism, but, then, until the Republican convention neared, people really weren't sure of Ike's party affiliation.

The November meeting of the Minnesota River League found the member teams wanting a reversal in 1953 of the tightening of rules they'd opted for the previous year. They wanted the residency radius expanded from the eight-mile limit they had imposed for 1952, and they felt the residency time limit also needed to be relaxed. At the next month's meeting, the league directors voted to change the residency time limit from four months to 30 days. They also voted to permit towns of fewer than 1,000 residents to consider players residing up to 15 miles from the city as "home" players. But both changes were controversial because of the inherent lack of fairness. The change in residency date favored towns with seasonal employment opportunities such as the vegetable canning operations in Le Sueur and Montgomery, as well as the light industrial character of St. Peter. They could bring transient ball players into town in April, give them jobs in the factories and warehouses for the summer, while Belle Plaine, Jordan, and Prior Lake, without industrial bases, couldn't play that game. Votes went along the lines of unilateral interests and deadlocked at a 4-4 roll call vote. That called for a compromise on the radius rule: Towns under 1,000 in population (i.e., Prior Lake) were allowed to draw two additional players residing between 8 and 15 miles from town. Towns with a population of between 1,000 and 2,000 were allowed to draw one additional player from the expanded radius area, with no more than two players being battery men. Towns of more than 2,000 people, which included Le Sueur and St. Peter, had to abide by the old rules of a two-player draw from outside the 8-mile radius.

It was an old story—one that would be repeated time and again for decades. Nobody wanted to give any other town a perceived advantage in the setup, the structural arrangement, and rules by which the league operated. They wanted to keep such advantage in their own quarters, while denying the advantageous nature of a particular consideration to others. Yet they wanted to play within, and in fact needed, a league in which to compete. So team representatives would sandbag, so to speak, like golfers, their true handicap, in order to win, not on the field of competition, but in the boardroom, in the meeting hall, and at the tavern. And they would cheat, or at least stretch rules to their own advantage while scrutinizing with hair-splitting margins the efforts of other teams. Playing fields would become so tilted, realities so lopsided, in some years that outcomes of ball games and seasons were a forgone conclusion. Any alternate outcome was an upset of such magnitude as to defy possibility. In stark contrast, aging warrior Ben Hogan, tied for the lead after 15 holes of play on the last day, drew back with too much backspin his approach shot to the severely sloping 17th green at Cherry Hills in the 1960 U.S. Open, the ball finding the water, and took a bogey, followed by a triple bogey on the long par-four eighteenth that cost him his fifth Open title. A rules official told him afterwards that had Hogan touched the water on his backswing when he blasted out on No. 17 and been guilty of grounding his club he would have had trouble calling the penalty on him. Hogan's response, characteristically, was, "You wouldn't have had to. I'd have called it on myself."

Like Ben Hogan, Jim Pollard was a purist and an honorable man. Neither man was boastful or arrogant. Somehow, they had remained immune to the narcissism that accompanied celebrity. They certainly could have been—and probably would have been had they been born a generation or two later. Sphinx-like, the Hogan Mystique included his virtual ignoring of playing partners during entire rounds of golf as he concentrated on managing *his* game and hitting *his* shot. He rarely granted interviews and usually went his own way—back to the hole farthest from the clubhouse with a bag of balls and a couple of irons to work on his approach shots while the clamor of the cocktailing crowd ensued in the clubhouse. He didn't understand being casual—at golf or anything else. Pollard, meanwhile, was called "the quiet man" by Jim Kaplan of the *Minneapolis Star* in a review of the Pollard-coached Minnesota Muskies' 50-28 record in the inaugural season, 1967-'68, of the American Basketball Association.

The Minneapolis Lakers continued their dominance of the NBA, with a fifth world championship in the spring of 1953 after finishing a league-best 48-22. According to Dolph Grundman in his biography of Jim Pollard:

> On December 16, 1952, The Sporting News carried an article by Jack Barry called, 'The Ballplayer's Ballplayer.' It presented the results of a survey taken among active players who had spent at least 6 years in professional basketball. They were asked to name the most outstanding ballplayer they had played against. Jim was voted #1 with 33 votes, followed by George Mikan and Ed McCauley with 27 votes apiece.

Pollard's Brewer teammates and fans made a night of it again at the Minneapolis Auditorium on Sunday night, March 8, 1953, in a regularly scheduled game against the Milwaukee Hawks. The Jordan people presented Jim with a barbecue set at the auditorium, and Max published his thank-you letter in the March 26 *Jordan Independent* in which he also said he was looking forward to the coming Brewer baseball season.

In winning the 1953 championship, the Lakers took two straight games from Indianapolis in the first round of the playoffs. Then, they beat the Fort Wayne (later, Detroit) Pistons 3-2 in games to advance to the finals for a rematch of the 1952 championship finals against the New York Knicks. The Lakers lost the initial game, 96-88, at the Minneapolis Armory, won the next three straight, two of them by just two points, and then won game 5 in New York, 91-84, with six Lakers in double figures, led by Pollard's 17 points to give them their fifth world championship in six years. Grundman notes that "Lou Miller of the *New York World and Telegram* summed up the season best: 'The Lakers proved themselves the Yankees of the basketball world.' " Jim Pollard truly was the 'straw that stirs the drink,'" to quote subsequent Yankee generation great Regi Jackson in assessing himself. But Jim Pollard would never make such a remark about himself. It just wasn't part of his character.

"He was a great team player," fellow Brewer Dick Nolden said of Jim Pollard.

His Laker teammates said the same thing about him.

The Pollard's family grew with the birth of a boy, Jay Clifford, on March 17, but six weeks later, the baby died of suffocation in the crib, according to a report in the May 7, 1953, *Jordan Independent*. Known years later as "sudden infant death syndrome," or SIDS, the baby had died of what was called "crib death" at the time, and nobody ever knew for sure or explained how that happens. The Pollard's, of course, were devastated, as any parents would be when a child is lost. Regardless of the circumstances, or the age of the child, it's not the Natural Order of Things. Children are supposed to be born to grow to bury their parents.

Max reported that Baldy Hartkopf had taken over the managerial reins of the Jordan Brewers from Leon Hennes and that the fans could expect a better brand of baseball this summer due to the league's retrenchment of some of the rules regarding residency. He also expected player salaries to increase without a concurrent increase in attendance. Schmidt Brewery of St. Paul was taking out huge display advertising space to help sell its "City Club" beer with, "Real Draft Beer Flavor" now in bottles and cans as well as from the tapped barrel at your favorite pub. A St. Peter newspaper columnist predicted the Brewers would be the team to beat in 1953, because Jim Pollard, he noticed, had found the control he had needed near the end of the last season.

Pollard opened the season on the mound with a five-hitter in a rain-shortened, seven-inning win over New Prague, 7-2. Playing third base the next week, with John Hovanec, who had been picked up from Shakopee, on first, he homered in the second game of the season, a 9-6 win over Prior Lake, after smacking a triple in his only official at bat in the first game. Jim had another home run the next Sunday at Belle Plaine, as did teammates Hovanec and Hartkopf, but the Tigers got to him early and knocked him out, then continued to beat up Brodahl in relief for an 11-5 win. Then, Jim came back strong against LeCenter, firing a four-hit, 7-0 shutout with 12 strikeouts. He also had two hits in the game, including a double to go with another crank by Big John Hovanec. The Jim Pollard-led Brewers were 3-1 and leading the Northern Division of the Minnesota River League going into the second week of June. Pollard then beat St Peter, 4-1, on Sunday, June 14, at Fairgrounds Park. He struck out 11 Saints and held them to six hits in another complete game on the mound, while again collecting two hits himself. It was a classic Pollard performance: both ends of the basketball court; both ends of the baseball diamond. He swung a 35-inch Louisville Slugger at the plate, and he brought the heat on the mound. He brought it the way fullback Bronko Nagurski had carried the football as a Gopher and a Chicago Bear. He brought it the way fullback Jim Brown was used by Paul Brown at Cleveland, and the way Bum Phillips used to bring fullback Earl Campbell with the Houston Oilers in NFL football. Again and again. . . and again. "He threw mostly fastballs," Paul Sunder said, "and he had a good one." Power pitching, like power running in football or a strong wind in a round of golf, wears you down. There's not much finesse in it. It's not the teasing cat-and-mouse game that crafty left-handers like Johnny Podres or Whitey Ford played with hitters. It's a battle of wills like Cardinal Bob Gibson engaged in with the hitters he faced with so much success throughout the later years of the Golden Age of Baseball.

The headline in the June 25 sports page of the Jordan weekly read, "Brewers Retain M.R.L. Lead As Half-Way Point Nears." Paul Sunder pitched a four-hitter to beat Prior Lake, 4-1, but then the Brewers lost two straight, shut out 4-0 by New Prague, and 9-0 by Belle Plaine. Max noted that the shutout losses were the first by Brewer teams in five years. Worse, they were knocked out of first place, as the dogfight for MRL supremacy began in earnest. Max wrote that Belle Plaine's shortstop, Pete Johnson, was getting a serious look from the New York Giants, and he thought Jordan's Dick Nolden was worth a look as well by area professional scouts, as he was hitting over .400 and his work at the keystone sack was flawless and second to none.

The Brewers slipped to 7-5, according to the July 9, 1953, *Jordan Independent*, tied with New Prague, fully three games behind Belle Plaine in the loss column. Pollard looked to be recovering from a sore arm, as he relieved in the 10-7 win over Prior Lake, his first work on the mound in a couple of weeks. If Saturday were "moving day" on the PGA Tour, as it would come to be known in golf, then July was "moving month" in MRL baseball. If you were going to make a run at a league pennant, you needed to do it now, and pitching was always at a premium, because rainouts bunched up makeup games on teams already scheduled with two and three games a week. The good thing was that the July heat was always therapeutic for arms. They didn't get as sore in a game in July as they did in April or May. Arms tired, but they didn't tear, and they came back much quicker, making two-game outings a week possible for a pitcher then.

Included among the news notes in Max's "Sports Flashes" in the July 16, 1953, *Jordan Independent* was the announcement by Manager Baldy Hartkopf that Brewer pitcher Don Brodahl had been released. Lefthander Johnny Garbett, who was 6-3 on the season with Benson-DeGraff in the very strong Class-AA West Central League, had signed with the Jordan Brewers after Benson-DeGraff folded. Pollard was 5-2 but had taken most of the previous two weeks off to heal. Now he would get the help the Brewers needed so they wouldn't have to over-pitch Jim.

The little lefthander could bring the heat, too, and he mixed it well with a sharp curveball.

Jim beat Belle Plaine, 10-4, despite Gene O'Brien's perfect night at the plate, five for five, against him. More importantly, his arm appeared sound again, as he struck out seven Tigers in going the distance at Fairgrounds Park. Garbett lost his debut Wednesday night with the Brewers, 4-2, in 10 innings against the Le Sueur Green Sox, despite rousing his new hometown fans with 14 strikeouts. Then Jim beat the powerful St. Peter Saints, 5-4, in their ballpark for the fourth consecutive time on Sunday night. The two hurlers had also taken turns helping each other out at the plate. Pollard had staked Garbett to a 2-0 lead with what Max described in the July 23 Jordan weekly as, "a terrific slam high over the left field wall for one of the longest hit balls in Fairgrounds Park this season." Garbett returned the favor for Pollard at St. Peter, going three for four, including an RBI double and two runs scored.

Pollard then provided the final punctuation to Garbett's one-hit shutout of LeCenter–an emphatic exclamation, with his two-run blast in the seventh that Max described as his "longest home run of the year when he drove a high line drive a hundred feet or so over dead centerfield fence to score Tex ahead of himself to bring Jordan's total to eight runs." He followed up two nights later at Fairgrounds Park in Jordan with his seventh win of the year, 8-5, over Montgomery, and he hit yet another monster home run to help his own cause.

Garbett's turn at Prior Lake on Sunday made it four in a row for the Brewers. Jim Pollard was putting on a power-hitting clinic, as he crushed his seventh home run of the season, as captured in Max Casey's "Sports Chatterbox" column:

> When Jim Pollard belted out that long four-bagger at Prior Lake last Sunday afternoon, it was Jim's seventh circuit clout of the season. According to the records, Jim is well out in front of the field of homerun kings in the league, his closest rival being Gene O'Brien of Belle Plaine, who has four round-trippers to his credit. Jim has collected five of his blasts in the last six games.

O'Brien, one of three ball-playing brothers from Belle Plaine, had played professionally as high as AAA in the Yankee organization before the war. Then what did that make Jim Pollard, fans asked rhetorically? It was the end of July, and the Brewers had made their move back into first place in the hotly contested Minnesota River League. It wouldn't last, however, as the dogfight would resume through the close of the regular season. Garbett's 1-0 loss of the game and a no-hitter at Belle Plaine was the deciding contest. Three Northern Division teams (Belle Plaine, Jordan, and New Prague) and Le Sueur from the Southern Division all finished the season with identical 12-8 records. Nonetheless, pennant races are about a distinct winner taking honors. League rules stipulated that in the event of a tie at the end of a season, the team that went furthest in the playoffs would be declared the winner.

Jordan opened with New Prague in a best-of-three game series. After Garbett beat the Robins, 2-1, in the first game with a five-hitter, Pollard followed up with a win at Jordan, 4-2, to put the Brewers in the Division finals against Belle Plaine. The Tigers were defending MRL champions and runners-up in the 1952 Class-A

State Tournament. Like old warhorses, led by Gene O'Brien and Warren Stemmer, they'd smelled the oats in the barn again as July turned into August and the campaign engaged the best in men of the day. They had beaten Garbett, 1-0, a week ago, then won two straight from Prior Lake in the first round of the playoffs, 2-0 and 5-4. Prior Lake had given them trouble all year until the playoffs, too. They had won the MRL pennant three of the five years of the league's existence, going back to 1948. Now they had Jordan's number, they felt, and this thing was theirs to be had again.

In front of more than 1,500 fans on Sunday night at Belle Plaine, Johnny Garbett on the mound again for the Brewers, Pollard at third, Jordan played errorless ball and won 6-5 in 10 innings. Max called it "poetic justice" after the heartbreaking 1-0 loss suffered by Jordan a week earlier in as fine a baseball game as he'd ever seen, a great pitchers' duel if ever there were one. Garbett rang up 14 Tigers again and scattered eight hits, including two round-trippers to the old pros, Stemmer and O'Brien, who had five of the eight hits off him. It was an old-fashioned barnburner. "Jordan started the scoring in Sunday evening's thriller," according to Max Casey in the August 20, 1953, *Jordan Independent*, "when Jim Pollard singled after two were out in the first inning, stole second, and scored on Hartkopf's little single into right-center." Belle Plaine tied it up in the bottom of the first on a Warren Stemmer solo shot over the right-field wall. Belle Plaine broke the tie in the bottom of the fifth with a double following a walk. The Brewers knotted the game up in the top of the sixth.

"In the seventh," Max reported, "things were nip and tuck for both sides, and the deadlock wasn't again broken until the eighth, when the Brewers bunched four hits to score three runs and leave the bases choked as they went ahead 5-2." With one run in and a man on in the bottom of the eighth, Gene O'Brien tied it up again with a long homerun off Garbett. The score remained tied through the ninth, and the Brewers won it in the tenth on a triple by Tex Erickson, which was followed by Shrake's hitting Garbett. Two on, one out, top of the 10th inning . . . 1,500 fans "gasping for air," as Max described it, and Jim Pollard at the plate. They had to pitch to him, because Hartkopf, Hovanec, and Nolden would follow, and they were all hitting the ball on the button that night. Pollard took Schrake deep. The ball stayed in the park to dampen the heroics, but Tex Erickson scored from third on the catch, and the Brewers took the 6-5 lead into the Belle Plaine bottom of the 10th. Garbett held. Game on! Tuesday night. Fairgrounds Park. Jordan.

Tuesday night . . . a work night. The house was full, and it was rockin' with the same level of excitement that marked the game two nights earlier at Tiger Stadium. Jim Pollard scattered seven hits and beat Belle Plaine, 3-2. In what Max headlined in the *Jordan Independent* of Thursday, August 20, 1953, as a "Story Book Finish," Belle Plaine led the whole game. They scored a run in the top of the second to take an early lead, which held up until Jordan tied it in the bottom of the seventh. Back-to-back Tiger doubles gave them the lead again in their half of the eighth. Jordan failed to score in the bottom of the eighth, as did Belle Plaine in the top of the ninth. Then, with two on and two out in the bottom of the ninth, Jim Pollard lined a single to left to tie the game. John Hovanec's hard grounder to short went through Pete

Johnson, who had signed a Major League contract with the St. Louis Cardinals a month earlier. It meant the ball game and the Northern Division crown.

Jim Pollard had won his ninth game of the year and had a big RBI in the win at home. Jim was jubilant in victory, and he celebrated with his Jordan teammates and the Jordan fans. That was four straight playoff wins, two sweeps, over good, competitive baseball teams. But Jim Pollard was used to winning, and he knew there was more heated competition ahead. They still had to finish off matters with the champs from the Southern Division.

To everyone's surprise, Montgomery tipped over Le Sueur in the playoffs for the Southern Division crown. Then a little scrutiny of the latest Monty roster explained their surge. To the surprise of nobody by now, 23-year-old Johnny Garbett pitched a masterful two-hit, 2-0 shutout with 18 strikeouts in the opening game of the best of five series with Montgomery at Fairgrounds Park on Sunday night, August 23. He had a perfect game going for six and one-third innings, before walking a man. Then he struck out the next two batters to get out of that inning. He did give up two hits finally in the eighth; however, he broke the scoreless tie with a sacrifice fly that scored Tex Erickson. Jim Pollard gave him an insurance run that Max Casey described this way: "Jim Pollard, next up, then drove one of Jan's (Janikowski's) offerings into the stratosphere high over the left centerfield wall to give the Brewers their second tally of the inning and their final run of the game."

Jim went the distance on Tuesday night at Montgomery in a sloppily played game of four errors apiece. He scattered 10 hits, half of them to two batters, and he walked five. But he also had 10 strikeouts. Jordan pounded Monty pitching for 20 hits, three of them by Pollard, including a homerun. Garbett then slammed the door, 9-1, on Montgomery Thursday night with a four-hitter and eight strikeouts to make it a three-game sweep of the championship series. Jim lashed out three hits in the game, including yet another monster homerun. Max's headline in the September 3, 1953 *Jordan Independent* celebrated, "Brewers First Team in MRL History To Sweep Series in Seven Straight." With 35 hits in the last two games, the Brewer team batting average had risen to a respectable .269. The team was clicking on all eight cylinders, and they picked up two pitchers and a catcher for the Region 1-A playoff with Dundas, winners of the Cannon Valley League.

Johnny Garbett was white hot. He fired another gem, a three-hit, 7-0 shutout with 19 strikeouts at Fairgrounds Park on Tuesday night. Jim staked "Li'l Johnny" to all the runs he needed in the bottom of the first inning with a two-run double, then scored himself on a pair of ground ball fielder's choices. Manager Baldy Hartkopf started his lefthander again, five days later, Sunday afternoon, at Dundas. But he pulled himself from behind the plate to treat drafted catcher Gene Parrish of New Prague to the best seat in the house. Garbett gave up three hits in the four innings he worked, but he rang up another nine Dundas batters before being lifted with a 10-1 lead to give drafted pitchers a little work. Filling in at second base for the honeymooning Dick Nolden, Pollard led the power surge with a homerun and a triple, as the Brewers ripped 19 hits in the game that ended 16-2. Max's September 10 headline: "Brewers Win Region Title, Enter State Tournament."

The Brewers hadn't made the state tournament since 1938. It was a long time coming, 15 years to be sure, and there were many reasons for the long intermission, including the leasing of ballplayers to Uncle Sam to take care of business in Europe and the Pacific. Some of the boys were gone for two years, others for four. Some never came back. Then, too, baseball was a peacetime game, and the country, the world, was at war. Once you had the bodies who wanted to play and could play, you needed the right chemistry. You always needed the pitching, too, and, my God, wasn't that little lefthander something? Isn't that Jim Pollard a nice guy? How'd you like to have to face Garbett and Pollard back to back? The boys are really hitting the ball lately. So went The Buzz the next week. Jim Pollard had been to The Dance the year before as a drafted pitcher for Belle Plaine. It was big stuff, but it paled in comparison to the NBA finals, a full house in New York or Boston, or 20,000 fans at Chicago Stadium for the so-called "exhibition" games with the Harlem Globetrotters. He would have been a natural with his heat and his big game experience to start the first game of the 1953 Class-A Minnesota State Baseball Tournament at New Ulm. But Garbett had been to The Dance before, too. Nobody knew that much about him, and he was quiet. But they sure liked what he had shown down the stretch of playoff wins. He'd been around and had pitched some big games. Manager Hartkopf stayed with his hot pitcher against Delavan, a town of just 300 people from the northern part of Faribault County, south of the Twin Cities but warily close to the Southern Minny teams of Class-AA ball. Nolden was back from his honeymoon and resumed his spot at second base. Pollard played third base and batted third in the order, getting one hit in four at bats. Garbett pitched a wonderful seven-hitter, with 14 strikeouts. But Rich Weigel silenced the big booming Brewer bats with a four-hitter. Well-hit Jordan line drives that had found holes the last two weeks found leather at New Ulm. Delavan 1, Jordan 0. Weigel went on to win the MVP award with two wins and the save in the final game, while giving up just two earned runs and 10 hits in 20 innings of work, leading Delavan to the Class-A State Championship.

Everybody said it was only a game and didn't matter anyway, but nobody believed it. Really important things were going on that dwarfed the loss of a ballgame. But this was baseball, and "Baseball was life, and life was baseball." The boys were coming home from Korea, with the truce signed back on July 27. Still, 36,914 American GIs had died in another country, on another continent, on the other side of the world. For what? To stem the tide of the growing menace of worldwide communism, we were told. "Baseball, apple pie, and Chevrolet . . . " became an American jingle, with a lot of simplistic truth in it.

In seizing the league pennant and playoff championship, the 1953 Jordan Brewers had beaten three highly competitive teams, winning seven consecutive playoff games, "the least number possible to cop the league bunting," Max wrote, then two more regional games to make it nine in a row. Jim Pollard had batted .315 on the season in the league, with 10 homeruns. The Brewers had slugged 19 total home runs in the 21-game regular league season and 7 league playoff games. Max suggested that both figures were thought to be league MRL records. Jim Pollard had also led the league in pitching with 10 wins in 13 decisions.

"Life goes on."

While Jim Pollard was exchanging his baseball cleats for his Laker sneakers once again in the fall of 1953, Chevrolet introduced the first American sports car–

the Corvette. It would become extremely popular with test pilots, ball players, and playboys. The year, 1953, was busy all over: The Philadelphia Athletics changed the name of Shibe Park to Connie Mack Stadium . . . August A. Busch purchased the St. Louis Cardinals for $3.75 million . . ."Uncle" Joe Stalin of the Soviet Union died after a stroke . . . The Boston Braves moved to Milwaukee, Wisconsin . . . Albert Einstein revised his unified field theory . . . Mickey Mantle hit what has been recorded as a 565-foot homerun at Griffith Stadium in Washington, D.C. Edmund Hilary became the first man to reach the summit of Mt. Everest . . .The U.S. Congress officially credited Alexander Cartright as being the founder of baseball . . .The New York Yankees won 18 straight games, and later won their fifth consecutive World Series in October. . . Fidel Castro began his rebellion against Batista in Cuba . . .Dizzy Dean, Chief Bender, and Al Simmons were among eight inductees into baseball's Hall of Fame . . . Ernie Banks became the first Cub black player . . .The U.S. Supreme Court ruled that baseball is a sport, not a business . . . Walter Alston was named Manager of the Dodgers, and they signed Sandy Koufax . . . Junior Gilliam of the Dodgers was named NL "Rookie of the Year . . ." Jockey Willie Shoemaker shattered the record by riding 485 winners in the year . . .Test pilot Chuck Yeager reached Mach 2.43 in the Bell X-1A rocket plane.

The City of Jordan got a traffic control light at the intersection of Trunk Highway 169 and Hwy 282, where St. John the Baptist Catholic Church and its parochial elementary school occupied two of the four corners. With all the young kids on foot and on bicycles in the area, and daily mass-goers of all ages in those days, it just made sense to slow down and regulate auto traffic at this main intersection. Over 50 years later, the intersection and the lights would make for a rhubarb between the Catholics wanting to protect the foundations of their church building, now about 150 years old, and the city council, dominated by Lutherans who wanted another lane at the intersection to help manage traffic flow during rush hour.

But in October of 1953, baseball helped the faithful adherents of the two major local denominations to suspend the four centuries-old schism that had begun in Wittenberg, Germany, with the nailing of 95 theses to the heavy oak church door by a German monk and scholar who heartily disapproved of the Church of Rome selling indulgences to finance temporal projects. Baseball helped the local faithful to transcend their differences. Lutherans crossed the Catholic threshold for the banquet in the basement dining hall of the St. John's Catholic Church to honor the 1953 Jordan Brewers.

Winter baseball meetings of the MRL followed soon enough. There was a consensus decision made to remain a Class-A ball operation for its better quality of baseball, despite the objections of a couple of towns wanting to drop down to Class-B ball because, they said, they couldn't compete with the towns with larger populations and payrolls for good ballplayers were straining budgets. The Minnesota-Wisconsin Umpires Association, represented by Shorty Mathes, was favored by the league to officiate again. The same baseball used the previous season would be played again, and a group of three was formed to devise the playing schedule.

Residency rules would be adjusted again in an effort to "level the playing field," but this was seen in Jordan as a legislating ruse to strip away its newly found thunder. Number of outside players would be limited to two, and it meant home players had to be bonafide residents on December 1. Despite four teams having finished the regular season tied for the league pennant with identical 12-8 records, something just had to be done about Pollard and Garbett being on the same team at Jordan. A long story shortened here, but covered in more detail in the profile on Johnny Garbett, Jordan solved its league-imposed problem of one too many outside players by player-manager Baldy Hartkopf leaving the team. Pollard and Garbett would come back for the 1954 Jordan Brewer season as its two allowed outside players, even though Garbett would take his wife that year and make an effort to settle down and jump into business in Jordan as an owner and operator of The Corner Bar at Broadway and Water Streets, making him a resident "home" player if ever there were one.

The Jordan Baseball Association again sponsored a "Jordan Night" at the Minneapolis Auditorium on March 7, 1954, when the Lakers played the Milwaukee Hawks. This year they got the block of 140 tickets for $2.00 apiece, 40 cents off the regular price. The Jordan Wheels again played the preliminary game, this year against a Brainerd five. Pollard helped the Lakers take care of business that year again in the NBA, bringing the sixth and final basketball championship to Minneapolis. They finished the season with a Western Division-leading 46-26 record. Jim finished second to Mikan in scoring, led the team in minutes played, and was second in assists to Slater Martin. He made the fourth of four NBA All-Star teams and led all scorers in the All Star Game with 23 points in front of 16,487 fans at Madison Square Garden in New York. Despite a confusing round-robin playoff structure, the Lakers prevailed in their preliminary rounds and met the Syracuse Nationals in a best-of-seven series for the NBA championship. The two teams alternated wins to reach a seventh and deciding game. Jim Pollard led all scorers with 21 points in the 87-80 Laker win. It was their third straight NBA championship, their sixth championship in seven years. "Each of the players and coach Kundla got $1,590.91 as their share of the playoff pot," according to Dolph Grundman.

Val Ruediger dropped Pontiac and picked up Nash automobiles for sale at his dealership on Broadway in Jordan. John Stang offered "Elegance in Action" with the 1954 Dodge, and Ben Engfer advertised the new Chevrolet as "Powered for Performance and Engineered for Economy." A new Chevy convertible debuted that year, too. Loren Habegger offered Fords with 115-horse power inline, six cylinder engines or 130-horse power V-8s. Effertz and Roster invaded Jordan's auto territory with the posting of their price, $2,293, for a 1954 Buick Special 2-door, 6-passenger sedan in neighboring Shakopee.

Jim Pollard continued to be mentioned through the winter of 1953-'54 as a candidate for the vacant head basketball coaching position at his alma mater, Stanford University. Without any coaching experience, it was quite an honor to even be considered. Eventually, the job went to Jim's old Stanford teammate, Howie Dallmar, who had not only played professionally with the Philadelphia Warriors in the BAA, but had been highly successful as the head coach at

Pennsylvania, where he had compiled a 105-51 record. Baseball Bosses and teammates in Jordan breathed a sigh of relief, for if Pollard had gotten the Stanford job, it would have meant an end to his baseball in Jordan. Jim Pollard was 31 years old that spring, and he was thinking about his future. The 1954-'55 Laker basketball season would be his last. The 1954 Jordan Brewer baseball season was his sixth and last. It was a good one.

With Garbett getting more and more starts, Jim's pitching record slipped to 6-4. He batted a solid .356 and slammed eight homeruns, according to Tom Melchior's *Scott County Baseball*, batting third and fourth in an order that gave him some slugging support. He powered the Brewers to a second straight first-place Northern Division finish at 12-8, one game ahead of Belle Plaine at 11-9, but four games behind 16-4 St Peter in the Southern Division.

With player-manager Baldy Hartkopf falling on his sword after the Minnesota River League invoked "the Garbett Rule" regarding player residency restrictions, Leon Hennes resumed the helm of the Jordan Brewers for the 1954 campaign. They had their pitching tandem intact, but they needed to find a catcher who could hold Pollard's heat and Garbett's deuce.

Jordan split its first two games of the new season, losing the opener to New Prague, 5-1, but bouncing back against Prior Lake in the second game, 10-8. Jim started with some heat on the mound and some fireworks at the plate in the very first inning in the Sunday afternoon game at Prior Lake. We like Max's report of the game in the May 20, 1954, *Jordan Independent*:

> Jim Pollard, who was on the mound for the Brewers in his first such appearance of the season was also the big lumber toter as he poled out two long four-baggers to help win his own ballgame, one with Tex Erickson on the paths in the opening stanza and his second being of the grand slam variety in the eighth when he connected with the bases clogged.

The Brewers survived a shaky start in their home opener against Belle Plaine. They recovered from a 4-0 deficit to chase Tiger starter Paul Keup from the mound in the fourth inning, thanks in part to a bases-loaded double down the line by Jim Pollard, who had three hits in the 8-4 win. Most importantly, the club looked to have found a young catcher who could handle Johnny Garbett. Bob Radde, a student at Gustavus College from Shakopee took over for the newly released Baldy Hartkopf. Jim's bases-loaded double at LeCenter, which observers claimed had been blown at least 40-feet back into the field by a strong wind, helped Garbett post another win, 6-1, firing a four-hitter while striking out 19 LeCenter Chiefs.

Next up, the Le Sueur Green Sox at Fairgrounds Park in Jordan on Sunday afternoon, June 6. In the bottom of the first inning, Jim Pollard followed two singles with a towering shot off former Brewer teammate Jim Kieger to left-centerfield that cleared the railroad tracks. As Max Casey noted in the report he filed on the game, it gave John Garbett all the cushion he needed in the 7-1 win that put the Brewers at 4-1 and atop the division. Manager Leon Hennes liked the looks of the 1954 pennant race by the middle of June.

Nobody likes to see a relic and an institution gutted without deserving the fate. The June 17 Jordan weekly's front-page headline had the "Former Schutz & Hilgers

Brewery Gutted By Fire Tuesday Afternoon." Shakopee and Belle Plaine Fire Departments were called to assist the Jordan Fire Department in putting out the blaze. Recently purchased by Green Industries, Inc., 800 Mississippi St. in St Paul, the building, which had been unoccupied for several years, was undergoing salvage operations by a Shakopee contractor, who had been busy with a cutting torch, dismantling interior piping, equipment, and fixtures for the cash they could bring the salvage company. "Among the spectators," the *Jordan Independent* reported, "was Lanny Schutz of Hopkins":

> 'I was on my way home from New Prague and here I see the old brewery on fire. Many a barrel of beer I handled in that place,' Lanny reminisced. His father, Peter Schutz, was partner with Peter Hilgers in Schutz & Hilgers Brewery before the days of prohibition.

Garbett had gone into the eighth inning deadlocked at 0-0 in a duel with Notre Dame's pitching ace, Jim Dalton, now firing for the Saints. With Dalton at the plate and a 1-2 count on him, Garbett planted a baseball in Dalton's ear. He went down and was out at the plate for 15 minutes, according to reports at the time, before he stirred and the crowd sighed a collective relief that the young pitcher hadn't been killed. Shaken by the accident, Garbett had lost his effectiveness and walked the next man he faced, putting men on first and second with nobody out. Garbett struck out the next two batters, then walked the third to load the sacks. Quite uncharacteristically, Garbett then did the unthinkable. He walked the next batter to force in a run. Jim Pollard replaced Garbett and a second St. Peter run scored on a passed ball, and the 2-0 score held up.

Pollard then beat Montgomery, 6-3, on a seven hitter that was no-contest at 6-1 in the ninth. Coupled with Garbett's 4-1 defeat of Prior Lake, the Brewer record of 6-2 gave them a solid hold on first place in the Northern Division. Then they split the next two games, which included a 15-2 drubbing at the hands of Belle Plaine, a game in which the defense sprung a leak and committed 10 errors with Jim on the mound on Sunday night for part of the beating. But they had shut out New Prague at Fairgrounds Park two nights earlier, 3-0, with Jim's three-run blast off the light tower in the first inning all Johnny Garbett needed to cruise home a winner. Garbett beat New Prague a second time, 3-1, in less than a week with another strong four-hitter and 15 strikeouts. Jim scored what Max described as the "game clincher" in the eighth, when he singled, stole second, and scored on a single by Rollie Sunder through the box.

Jim got knocked around a bit by Prior Lake in a 9-8 loss at Fairgrounds Park on a Monday night in front of over 700 people. Four Brewer errors didn't help. The Brewers blew a 5-0 lead, gained on the strength of two base-clearing doubles by Jim Pollard. Prior Lake, helped by four Brewer errors, pecked away until they held an 8-5 lead going into the bottom of the ninth. Jordan rallied to tie the game and send it into extra innings. Jim had struck out 10 Lakers but yielded nine hits. Garbett came on in relief after the ninth, and the Lakers nicked him for a run in the top of the 11th frame. Then Johnny was called out in a close play at the plate, "by inches," Max reported, in the bottom of the inning to prevent another tie and still more extra innings. It was Prior Lake's third straight win, and they had done it with high drama. They beat Belle Plaine, 4-3, during the week at Shakopee with a steal of home in the eighth inning, a loss that dropped the Tigers to 6-5 on the season. The Brewers were 8-4, still on top of the division, but still trailing powerful St. Peter from the Southern Division by two games. Belle Plaine and Jordan would tee it up next.

That contest went well for Belle Plaine, as old-pro Gene O'Brien took Lefty Johnny Garbett deep in the sixth inning with one man on to beat Jordan 2-1. The MRL was tightening again in the Northern Division. Jim Pollard scored Jordan's only run in the game after hitting a triple to deep center field in the eighth inning. Pollard's home run against LeCenter helped win the next ball game 5-4. Four Brewer starters were hobbled by injuries, and lights dimmed on the Brewer season. They went to 9-7, caught by Belle Plaine for the division lead going into the last week of July.

Both teams won their next two games, and the July 29, 1954, *Jordan Independent* sports page headline said it all: "Brewers and Tigers Enter Last Games All Tied." The Brewers' two wins were both blowouts, 13-3 at Montgomery, and then 15-2 over Prior Lake at Fairgrounds Park when they pounded four Laker pitchers for 13 hits, including one of Jim's two hits ". . . a tremendous round tripper with the ball landing well on the roof of the cattle barn in deep centerfield," Max reported. Four hurting Brewer regulars were healing, and one of them, Jim Pollard, was looking good again on the mound with a couple innings of relief work in both wins, as Manager Hennes fine-tuned his team at the right time. Saving Garbett for the grand finale against Belle Plaine on Sunday, Hennes gave the starting nod to Jim against New Prague on Thursday night. He fired a five-hitter, and Max reported that the game was his finest performance on the mound that season. But New Prague won, 4-2, and the Tigers came to town on Sunday evening. Here's Max's lead to the story he headlined as follows: "Brewers In First As Garbett Aces Tigers In Finale"

> Fairgrounds Park, packed with more than a thousand baseball fans last Sunday evening, witnessed one of the finest baseball games and best pitchers duels ever witnessed in this section of the state barring none.

Jim filled in without an error for the absent Dick Nolden at second base and had one of the team's three hits, a double. This ball game was "One For The Ages," and it was won by Johnny Garbett, who fired a two-hitter and struck out a dozen Tigers to beat their tough little lefty, Joe Shrake. Garbett faced just 29 Belle Plaine batters. Nobody reached first base on him after the third inning when a Tex Erickson defensive gem brought the crowd to its feet. Johnny Garbett's solo shot in the fourth inning was the only run of the ball game. Jim's double was hit hard to right center immediately after the Garbett home run, but the ball bounced hard, over the fence for a ground-rule double, and he was stranded at second.

Garbett took a hot hand into the playoffs on Friday evening, August 12, at Fairgrounds Park. He shut out Prior Lake, 11-0, on four hits, while slamming two home runs and a double himself. Pollard joined the hit parade, going four for five, including a home run, while playing errorless ball at third base. Then Jim took a page out of Garbett's book on Sunday afternoon at Prior Lake. He fired his own four-hit, 6-0 shutout, while striking out 10 Lakers and going three for four at the plate to lead the Brewer attack as well. With errorless ball supporting him, Pollard slammed the door shut on Prior Lake and the first round of the playoffs.

After a 10-day wait for New Prague to wrestle away its two-of-three game playoff win over Belle Plaine, Jordan hosted the Robins at Fairgrounds Park on Tuesday night, August 17, for the divisional playoff crown. More than a thousand people reportedly jammed the stands and the hillside on a work night to watch the opening game of what was expected to be a war. Nursing a 2-0 lead in the third, Garbett was cruising along in his typical fashion. Jim caught New Prague pitcher Wroge's offering on the meat of his Louisville Slugger and lifted it high and deep over the left-center field wall to make it 3-0, Jordan. Garbett continued to cruise until the seventh when the roof fell in on him and New Prague, Max reported, "gave him the worst time he has had on the mound all season."

Pollard came in to relieve Garbett with the score 5-3, New Prague, still in the seventh inning. The score held through the eighth inning and in New Prague's at bat in the top of the ninth. Then lightning struck again. Johnny Garbett must have been pissed at himself for opening the door in the seventh inning. He drove a long home run over the left-field fence to cut New Prague's lead to one. Jim followed with a triple and still nobody out! The house of mostly partisan Jordan fans smelled the blood. A pitch then got away from catcher Parrish, and, ever-alert, Pollard sprinted home with the tying run. A force at home, then a strikeout took some of the wind out of the Jordan fans and the ballplayers as well. But with the bases still jammed, two out, a 2-2 count on him, Joe Pekarna drilled a Geske pitch against the boards in left field for a walk-off, 6-5 Brewer win.

Jim Pollard started Game 2 two nights later at New Prague. He pitched well enough to win, scattering seven hits over the full nine innings. But Jim Geske must have felt he'd given away the farm with that wild pitch two nights earlier at Jordan. He pitched a perfect no-hit game against the Brewer team that had been pounding the ball the last month. Even Garbett and Pollard had been collared in the 4-0 loss that evened the series at a game apiece.

The two teams took it back to Fairgrounds Park the next night, Friday night, and in a near repeat of the Tuesday night thriller, Jordan beat New Prague in the bottom of the 12th inning on John Hovanec's walk-off liner to right field that scored catcher Radde from second. Garbett gave up six hits and struck out 13 in going the distance, and Jim was held to a single in two official at bats.

Rain postponed the Sunday night's first game of the MRL finals with Le Sueur to Monday night. Despite giving up 11 hits, Jim came up with a gutsy 5-4 win at Le Sueur. It was his third win on the mound since the playoffs began. But then Le Sueur beat both Johnny Garbett and Jim Pollard to take a 2-1 lead in the playoffs. The two teams were playing every other night, alternating fields. Arms were tired. Bodies were sore. Radde finally caved in to his doctor's orders to stay off his feet. The Brewers got a special dispensation that brought Class-B Shakopee catcher Butch Kreuser to substitute for Radde. Ten walks by Le Sueur's Wick and three errors behind him on top of seven Brewer hits gave Garbett an 8-5 win in the fourth game on Sunday night at Fairgrounds Park to tie the series at two games apiece.

Jim Pollard shut out Le Sueur, 3-0, at Le Sueur to win the Minnesota River League Championship for the second consecutive year. He scattered 11 hits over the nine innings in the game that was described as brilliant defensive play behind him, which means that Tex Erickson put on his usual clinic at shortstop. He also had an RBI double in the first, and then scored himself on a double by Hovanec. Jordan's final run was scored in the sixth when Dick Nolden singled and went to second on a passed ball. He then stole third and home in what was described by Max as a "brilliant display of base running."

Jim had one of a handful of Brewer hits in each of the two consecutive Region 1-A wins over Winnebago of the Le Sueur County League. Both games were well-pitched affairs, with Belle Plaine draftee Joe Shrake beating the much-heralded Minnesota Gopher ace, Ron Craven, 4-1, in the first game at Fairgrounds Park Thursday night, September 2, and Johnny Garbett taking care of business at Winnebago on Sunday night, winning 6-2 while scattering eight hits and striking out the side in the ninth to bring his total to 15 for the game. Big John Hovanec's three-run blast in the top of the sixth put the Brewers on top, 3-1. He also doubled home Pollard, who had singled ahead of him in the eighth for the sixth and final Brewer run.

For the second year in a row, the Jordan Brewers lost their opening game in the Class-A Minnesota Baseball Tournament to the eventual winner of the tournament, giving the champion the best game they faced. It was Delavan and the 1-0 loss in 1953 at New Ulm. This time Benson, which had risen from the ashes of its failed experiment in 1953 with DeGraff as a combined Class-AA team in the hot West Central League, beat the Brewers, 4-2 in the opening game. But Max Casey's first-hand report from the scene at the home of The Rox, St. Cloud's New York Giant's affiliate in the Northern League, suggests heavy rains and poor officiating by umpires under the thumbs of the state board wanting to "get games in" and keep the tournament moving, cost Jordan that first ball game.

In what headlines called the "Biggest Rhubarb in State Tourney History. . ." Johnny Garbett was locked in a pitchers' duel with Benson's Ronnie Tucker. Jordan's ace lefthander took a no-hitter into the sixth inning, and he had the only Brewer hit in the game, a double in the third. A couple of bad calls, according to Max, gave one Benson batter a free pass to first and another Benson hitter enough life to reach first on a water-logged ball that couldn't be fielded, the first hit off Johnny Garbett. The gates were opened, and a double and a single netted Benson three runs. But, "It was in the bottom of the sixth when the real rhubarb developed," according to Max Casey on the scene at the time. "By this time the rains were coming down heavily. Jordan had two men on base with two away and Dickie Nolden batting when the umpires stopped the game because of the heavy rain."

Forty-five minutes later, the game still not called, Umpire Berg, under pressure from the state board to "get it in," and Jordan's Dick Nolden doing everything he could to delay stepping back into the batter's box with the two strikes on him, the umpire, according to Nolden from his home in Detroit Lakes 60 years later, "called a third strike without a pitch even being thrown." Had the game been called, as Max claimed it should have been, the score, which was then 3-0 Benson, would have reverted to a 0-0 tie, because the sixth inning had not been completed. When the third strike was called on Nolden, the rhubarb turned into a donnybrook on the water-soaked diamond. Led by future NBA Hall of Fame forward Jim Pollard, the Brewers emptied the bench. "Pollard was the first man out of the dugout," Nolden said, "and those long legs of his were pumping up to his chest, as we charged Umpire Berg."

The man in blue held his ground and the third strike with an empty box ended the inning. The game was completed finally around 1 a.m., with the Brewers scoring a couple of runs in the bottom of the seventh to make the final, 4-2. Changed to a double-elimination format for 1954, Jordan then hammered Pipestone, 11-4, "as they pounded three Pipestone hurlers for twelve hits," Max reported in the September 16 *Jordan Independent*. "Jim Pollard led the parade with two doubles and a single and Dick Nolden collected a double and single." Manager Hennes then went with drafted pitchers Shrake and Geske against Spring Grove out of the Fillmore County League. Described as a "submarine ball artist," Spring Grove's drafted pitcher, Hugh Orphan, a former Class-AA player-manager at Winona in the Southern Minny, stymied the Brewers on two hits, one by Jim Pollard, and sent the Brewers home with their second loss in the tournament, 1-0.

You can't make a prologue out of a season-ending, heartbreaking loss. There's only next year.

Jim Pollard joined his Laker teammates for the beginning of training camp a week later on the campus of Hamline University in St. Paul, Minnesota. It would be his last NBA season as a player. George Mikan retired. Coach John Kundla hoped Clyde Lovellette could fill the big man's shoes. Pollard's playing time was down and so were his points. But the Lakers made the playoffs and lost to Fort Wayne in the Western Division finals, 3-1, with Pollard scoring 19 points in his last professional basketball game. In April of 1955, Jim Pollard replaced Ken Loeffler as head coach at La Salle College in Philadelphia. With six returning regulars, new Coach Pollard was hopeful of continuing a strong program. They went 15-10 on the season, which was respectable. In Jim's second year of coaching, La Salle went 17-8. After going 15-9 in his third year at La Salle, a disappointed Jim Pollard resigned his coaching position.

The Pollards returned to Minneapolis, and Jim sold automobiles for his friend, Oscar Borton of Borton Volvo in South Minneapolis. The Jordan Brewers had begun to slip without, first, Pollard, then without Garbett. The Minneapolis Lakers slipped rapidly without Mikan and then Pollard. The team, without solid stars and a permanent place to play, had trouble winning and keeping their fan base. Pollard was brought in to coach during a brief part of the 1959-'60 Laker season. The Lakers moved to Los Angeles, took Jerry West as their first pick in the NBA draft on the advice of Pollard, and replaced Jim with West's coach at West Virginia, Fred Schaus.

With Max Winter, the original Laker general manager involved with the ownership group in Chicago, Jim signed to coach the NBA expansion Chicago Packers in 1961. But despite the 31.6 points a game by 6-11 center, Walt Bellamy, whom Jim had drafted as one of his first actions in Chicago, the Packers finished 18-62 and fired Pollard at the end of the season. Jim was essentially out of basketball for the next five years, with the exception of doing some color commentary for Chicago Loyola University games. Then, in February of 1967, Pollard was named coach of the Minnesota Muskies, one of 11 teams in the newly formed American Basketball Association. The Muskies finished with the second-best record in the league at 50-28. After beating the Kentucky Colonels in the first round of the playoffs, the Pittsburgh Pipers took the semi-finals 4 games to 1. Grundman describes the season as being extremely satisfying for Pollard. He had brushed off the monkey that had found his back in Chicago with the Packers.

A business flop in Minnesota, the Muskies and Pollard moved to Miami and became the Floridians. Pollard guided the team to a 43-35 record after a poor start. Then they won their first playoff round before losing the second round to the Indianapolis Pacers, 4-1. The Floridians started slowly again in the 1969-'70 season. At 5-15 in the Eastern Division cellar, the management fired Jim in November. In 1971, Jim was hired by Fort Lauderdale University as its director of athletics, basketball coach, and fundraiser. Two years later, the university dropped its basketball program and Jim resigned. For the next five years, Jim taught social studies at a Fort Lauderdale High School while earning his master's degree at Florida Atlantic University. He continued to support community programs, and in 1978 the Pollards went home to California.

Jim failed to land what he was looking for–a position as an athletic director for a small college–but he settled finally as physical education teacher for the next eight years at Lodi Middle School and Delta Sierra Middle School. Always active in church and family, Jim increased his involvement with St. Paul's Lutheran Church in Lodi where he served as a deacon.

In 1978, Jim was inducted into professional basketball's Naismith Basketball Hall of Fame in Springfield, Massachusetts. In 1989 the Bay Area Hall of Fame and Stanford University Hall of Fame honored Jim Pollard with inductions. Jim retired from teaching in 1990, and by 1992 he was fighting a life-threatening disease–Waldenstrom macroglobulinemia, which is related to leukemia, according to Dolph Grundman, and suffering the debilitating effects of chemotherapy. In the summer of 1992, Jim and his wife Arilee, travelled the country to see old friends and likely to say good-bye, for not long after, in January of 1993, Jim Pollard died. One of his high school baseball teammates and a lifelong friend, Frank Isola, said of Jim Pollard that he was always the same with you. Always loyal, Jim Pollard had "the ability to 'make you feel so important'," Grundman notes.

Whether playing any game, at any level, coaching and teaching, or just being, Jim Pollard pushed himself, his teammates, his players, his students, and anybody around him to strive for excellence. Most importantly, he did it with an exceptional grace.

Johnny Garbett

He is one of the smartest young pitchers I have ever seen.

— Rosy Ryan, General Manager, Minneapolis Millers

"He was a really good pitcher," Dick Nolden said of Johnny Garbett. Nolden had the best seat in the house–second base–from which to watch the left-hander work his craft. "Sometimes I just marveled at him," Nolden, a retired veterinarian, said. "He could really get them to nibble," he said of hitters chasing pitches off the corners and into the dirt. Then he'd ring 'em up.

One of the rumors that persisted for years was that the Baseball Bosses of Jordan persuaded lefty Johnny Garbett to join the Brewers Class-A baseball team in 1953 with half ownership in The Corner Bar. The public house, now an antique and memorabilia store, "Water Street Antiques," at the corner of Broadway and Water Streets, was popular with the sporting crowd of young men. They served 3.2 Gluek's Beer in the 1950s for a dime a glass to anybody who looked like he might have started using a razor blade. It was a raucous crowd that tested the theory that this beer of low-percentage alcohol made intoxication impossible. That gave the bar and its various owners through the 1950s a good volume of business. In turn, that made it a good account for the Gluek's wholesale distributor from Shakopee who devoted a day each week solely to "marketing" to The Corner Bar. That meant free Gluek's to anyone in the bar, and it didn't take long for the local beer-drinking crowd to get wise to that. Everyone became a regular on Gluek's Day at The Corner Bar.

The establishment was known in the 1950s for its spontaneous celebrations over events as great as opening day of the squirrel hunting season, and a patron's good luck fishing on a nearby lake. Situated above and across the right-field elbow turn of the creek that runs around the ballpark and through the town, The Corner Bar and Ruppert's Bar, located half a block down Water Street, were classic versions of the 1950s "sports bar." They put on fish fries, frog-leg fries, and booya feeds, which were long-simmered stews of various wild game and fowl organs–hearts and livers, gizzards and such. One favorite story of a fish fry at The Corner Bar has George Vohnoutka returning from his service to the country in the Korean conflict with hand grenades stuffed into his duffel bag. In the right time of the year, spring, the backyard of The Corner Bar–Sand Creek–was teeming with walleye, northern pike, and various rough fish, all having traveled upstream from where the creek empties into the Minnesota River in what is now labeled "Louisville Swamp."

With a little diversion, Police Chief Matt Theis would be called to the other end of town, out of earshot and none the wiser. Without the need to buy bait and find the fish in a lake, Friday Fish Fries were made easy at The Corner Bar. George pulled the pins on a couple of his grenades and tossed them into a favorite pool of water at the bend in the creek. After the water-muffled explosion, his bar buddies scampered to the nearby bank with nets to scoop out everything that was belly up from the concussion.

Rich Hartman said he borrowed the money from the Prior Lake bank to get into the bar business with Frank Betchwars. Then they sold The Corner Bar and bought The Hamburger Home Café in partnership. Wasn't long, according to Hartman, that he sold his half in the café to Frank Betchwars and got back into the bar business with, first, Johnny Johnson, then Butch Oldenberg. He's not sure when all of this happened, but we know it all happened in the 1950s. We also know that Garbett pitched for Jordan between 1953 and 1955. It's not clear how Garbett, a young man then in his early- to mid-20's, could have pulled off ownership of a business. But when you realize that one of the Baseball Bosses and a manager of the Brewers for several seasons, Leon Hennes, was vice-president of the Northwestern State Bank of Jordan, one way of connecting those dots is clear. It was possible for a left-handed pitcher with a Major League curveball to get a business loan during the Golden Age of Baseball. One of the Baseball Bosses could also have co-signed the loan application. What is fairly certain is that Johnny Garbett got paid. First of all, he had been getting paid to play baseball since he was at least a 17-year-old high school graduate. Secondly, he was that good. He would have been paid to come to Jordan. But how? It is possible that he, like Jim Pollard, was paid with a check after each game, or with cash from the gate receipts. The Balance Sheet for the 1953 JBA is conspicuously missing from the archives, and the salaries of individual players for 1954, unlike other years, are not itemized. Total salaries of ball players paid amounted to $4,232 in 1954.

"My mom told me that they (the Jordan Baseball Bosses) wanted to give them a house and the business (The Corner Bar) outright," John Garbett said of his mother and father. "Dad really liked Jordan and wanted to settle down there."

Dale Oldenburg, who sells insurance in Jordan, said the average price of a house in Jordan today is $220,000, and that in 1954 the average house in Jordan would likely have been $8,000. The Corner Bar changed hands at least twice in the 1950s at a price each time of $6,000 to $8,000. So how good was Johnny Garbett? It looks like he could have been offered at least $14,000 worth of house and business, and maybe a new car worth about $2,500 to boot. Add some profit from the bar business, and Johnny Garbett's "pay" to play baseball looks pretty good. Just for some perspective on baseball during its Golden Age, Whitey Ford, the preeminent left-handed American League pitcher in the 1950s and 1960s, made about $9,000 in 1953 and about $16,000 in 1954 pitching for the New York Yankees.

"I wish I had grown up in Jordan rather than Robbinsdale," John Garbett said. Then the veteran of the Gulf War who spent 10 years in the U.S. Navy aboard nuclear-powered submarines said, "But Mom wanted to go home to Robbinsdale."

Some people remember Johnny Garbett driving an Oldsmobile during his years in Jordan. The Rocket V8 engine powered the Super 88 Oldsmobile in the 1954 model year, and it would have appealed to a young sporting man. One of Jordan's Baseball Bosses, Ben Engfer, sold Oldsmobiles as well as Chevrolets, and it's conceivable that Boss Ben put Johnny Garbett behind the wheel of a new 1954 Super 88 Olds in the late summer of 1953 when the new cars were launched. With a sticker price of around $2,500, Boss Ben's cost with his normal 20 percent profit would have been around $2,000. Maybe several other bosses helped out with a couple hundred bucks apiece.

If Jim Pollard was paid the $100 he was always rumored to have been paid when he pitched, and if Garbett was the real ace of this Class-A pitching staff, then he must have been paid as much or more than Pollard. How did he get paid and by whom?

There are no notes, memos, or contracts among the interesting artifacts in the Johnny Garbett scrapbook that was kept by his mother, then his wife and the mother of John Garbett, from whom we got the Garbett archives. John said his father passed away in 2011, and he'd only recently had the emotional strength to look through it in 2014. "He never talked about any of this stuff," John said as he handed over the two-inch thick bound leather volume of his father's athletic career. "I think he was so disappointed in himself that he just couldn't talk about it."

"And he wouldn't let us pitch when we were growing up," John Garbett said of his father, "I was a catcher."

Paul Sunder, another of the last five living members of that great Class-A Jordan Brewer baseball team of the 1950s, said Garbett lived in town for a while before buying into the bar business. "He lived above the store," Sunder said, in one of the two apartments that were always occupied atop Sunder's General, the mercantile store next to the town's log cabin, where Joe Sunder taught his two sons, Paul and Rollie, the business of retail trade.

Jim Pollard got all the acclaim with the Brewers of those years because he was a star forward with the Minneapolis Lakers of the National Basketball Association and because he was a really good baseball player. But, according to Nolden, Pollard wasn't near the pitcher that Johnny Garbett was.

Left-handed hitters didn't stand a chance against him, and right-handed batters had trouble, too, because he broke his good curve ball sharply down and into the dirt. Butch Kreuser of Shakopee said he caught Garbett once on a special exemption from the league when the regular Brewer catcher was injured, and he said, "I had to use a shovel to catch him. Everything was in the dirt…"–where it is damned near impossible to hit.

Johnny Garbett didn't fool around with any junk. He threw the fastball, curve, and change up, according to Nolden, from a three-quarter overhand delivery. "His fastball really tailed up and away from right-handed hitters," Nolden said. "It was almost a screwball."

According to Armand Peterson and Tom Tomashek in *Town Ball*, Johnny Garbett began the 1953 Minnesota baseball season with a combined Benson-DeGraff team in the Class-AA West Central League. Johnny must have liked his turn with Benson as a drafted pitcher in the 1949 season when Clara City paid him

$550 a month. But Benson-DeGraff folded half way through the season, and somehow Garbett caught on with Jordan.

But how did this little lefthander with the big-time curveball ever find Jordan? How did he get to the Class-A beer town in the Minnesota River Valley? Who knew him? Whom did he know? The young man from the city of Minneapolis with the blue-ribbon pitching pedigree was 23 years old, a veteran of the Korean War conflict, and single. Whom did he hang around with? Where did he hang out? Where did he work and live?

Did he just show up by coincidence and play for nothing? The blue-ribbon hogs at the Scott County Fair in Jordan that year must have distinguished themselves by flying, too.

More than likely, Baldy Hartkopf, 1953 Brewer player-manager, a member of the Jordan Baseball Association Board of Directors, or one of the Brewer Baseball Bosses behind the curtain had his ear to the rails or the ground and learned of the little lefthander's availability. Networking wasn't a technique born in the 1980s. It's only conjecture now, but the bosses, maybe Sid Nolden or Max Casey, knew Dick Siebert, who would have been keeping an eye on his former Gopher pitcher in western Minnesota. Siebert had eyes everywhere in the state, and Johnny Garbett, when he was healthy, had a habit of filling scoreboards with goose eggs and scorebooks with K's. Once you knew the name, you couldn't miss him in the sports sections of the Minneapolis and St. Paul daily newspapers. Somebody had to have brought him in.

It was a win-win situation: Jordan needed a left-handed pitcher to bolster a pitching staff of all right handers who often had trouble finding the strike zone; Johnny Garbett was eager to get back on the mound in a baseball uniform after spending most of the last two years in a U.S. Army uniform. He'd only pitched a few brief stints of service ball exhibitions and while on military leaves home in 1951 and '52. His last regular ball, we learn in *Town Ball*, was the 1950 summer season with Morris (population 3,811) in the Class-AA West Central League where, pitching for $100 a game, he won 13 games, according to Peterson and Tomashek.

They write in *Town Ball* that Garbett was "... discharged in 1952 (from the Army) and signed a minor-league contract with the Chicago Cubs, but he injured an elbow and was released." We know he had elbow problems and who wouldn't with the torque he was putting on tendons and ligaments with that deuce he threw? He's shown in a scrapbook news photograph the night before a big game his senior year at Minneapolis Edison High School in 1947 with a heat lamp on his elbow. While pitching for Dick Siebert at the University of Minnesota between 1948 and 1950, the Gopher baseball coach is quoted in one article as lamenting the "chronic elbow problems" of his left-hander. But what is amiss is the 1952 signing with the Cubs. We think he signed earlier than that, as early as 1950, because a letter in the Garbett archives, dated February 13, 1951, from Harold George, Vice President and Assistant Farm Director of the Chicago Cubs, is addressed to John Garbett:

> Dear John:
>
> Please advise the latest on your military status and if you have been inducted, I would appreciate your service address by return mail. Also the date of your induction. This is very important to both the player and

the club and after receiving the information, your club will request that your name be placed on the National Defense Service List of professional baseball, which will entitle you to certain benefits after your discharge from service and reinstatement to the Active List. The envelope is being marked "Parents May Open" so that they may reply for you if you have been called.

An earlier letter from Harold George of the Cubs, dated December 29, 1950, thanking John for informing him of his anticipated call to military service, ends with "Please let us hear from you by Wednesday so that we can announce your signing Sunday, January 7th."

Mel Jones, General Manager of the AAA-St. Paul Saints, the top Brooklyn Dodger farm club, had written an interesting letter to Johnny Garbett in Morris, Minnesota, where he was pitching Class-AA in the West Central League. Dated August 5, 1950, the letter reads in part as follows:

> Dear Johnny:
>
> Tried to reach you by phone today but understand you are out of town for several days.
>
> I see by the schedule that your season up there is scheduled to end on August 13. No doubt your Club is going to be in the play-offs which will mean that you will continue to play in that area for perhaps another two weeks.
>
> I want to talk to you and was wondering if it would be agreeable with you to contact me immediately upon your return home to the Twin Cities so that we can get together. If this is agreeable with you I would appreciate your dropping me a note or a penny postcard advising me that you will contact me as soon as you return home toward the end of the month. May I hear from you by return mail on this?

Was Mel Jones looking to sign Johnny Garbett for some help down the stretch run of an American Association pennant race in 1950? The Saints had won the pennant the year before by just a half game over Indianapolis, with a 93-60 record. They would finish the 1950 season in fourth place, six games back of the crosstown rival Minneapolis Millers. But in August, he might have been looking for some insurance help. The American Association was hot Triple-A baseball at the time, and the Saints were one step away from the Brooklyn Dodgers and the National League. Mel Jones was a little too passive. He should have pursued Johnny Garbett more aggressively.

Johnny Garbett was getting noticed. Because of his dominance for Morris in 1950, Litchfield, winner of the Class-AA West Central League playoffs, drafted him. Then they pitched him in the second round of the state tournament against defending state champion Austin, a power in the vaunted Southern Minny. Ted Peterson of the *Minneapolis Tribune* lauded Garbett in Litchfield's 3-2 win.

Bill ("Moose") Skowron, who would join the New York Yankees in 1954 and be a fixture at first base for the next nine years, played third base for Austin. He doubled off Garbett in the second inning when the Packers did their only scoring on two hits, an outfield fly ball, and an infield out.

Then there is the interview with Johnny Garbett in a feature article in the July 17, 1974, *Midweek Sun* by Dick Bonneville, which pretty much settles it:

> 'I gave up my amateur eligibility in 1950,' said Garbett, 'when I signed with the Cubs. I was assigned to Des Moines of the Class A Western League. I always relied heavily upon a fast ball and curve, seldom using a change-up. At Des Moines I threw my arm out, losing the effective curve.'

It wasn't the first time, and it wouldn't be the last. While at the University of Minnesota, a May 3, 1950, *Minnesota Daily* article reviewed Coach Siebert's pitching plans and options for the day's game against Macalester College. Johnny Garbett was included in a list of five Gopher pitchers who were likely to see some action in the non-conference game. In Garbett's third Gopher season, "Siebert is especially anxious to learn whether Garbett has completely recovered from his chronic elbow trouble." He had pitched an inning of successful relief a week earlier against the University of Illinois.

In a badly weathered scrapbook clipping from what is likely a *Minneapolis Tribune* review of the 1949 Gopher spring trip to Texas in which they went 1-7, the headline reads, "Pitching Sours; Siebert Optimistic," with a sub-headline of more interest: "Gophers' Garbett May Be Lost For Season." Johnny Garbett had a bad elbow. But warmth from a heating lamp or an early spring must have helped him recover, because Stu Baird wrote in the May 18, 1949 *Minnesota Daily* about the Gopher baseball prospects that day:

> Siebert is expected to call upon Whitey Skoog to do the pitching against Carleton and John (Lefty) Garbett will face Owatonna. Skoog authored a win against Jordan last week but Garbett has been the victim of three tough luck losses against Notre Dame, Michigan, and Carleton.

Sid Hartman of the *Minneapolis Tribune* reported on Garbett in an article headlined, "Gophers Trip Macs 10-2; Garbett Ace":

> But even more impressive than the victory was the pitching performance of Johnny Garbett, who cut loose for the first time this season. He limited the Macs to one hit in three frames.

Garbett wasn't having trouble with college hitters. He was having trouble with his back and his elbow. But Sid Hartman reported that he looked so good in "opening up for the first time" against Macalester that Coach Siebert announced he would start against their upcoming Big Ten opponent, Northwestern, that Saturday.

While still in high school, Garbett is shown in what is likely a May-June, 1947 clipping from the *Minneapolis Daily Times* above Sid Hartman's column, "The Roundup," which first appeared in the September 11, 1945, edition of the *Times*. He has a heat lamp on his pitching arm, prior to the Minneapolis City high school baseball championship, which drew 2,500 fans at Nicollet Park. Glen Gaff reported on the game for the *Minneapolis Tribune* under the headline, "Washburn Edges Edison in Ninth." With the score tied, 3-3, Washburn squeezed home two runs in the ninth inning. Edison scored a run in the bottom of the ninth to make the final score 5-4, and Gaff wrote, "Garbett was brilliant even in defeat. He yielded only three hits and struck out 16 Washburnites along the way."

Little Johnny Garbett was a baseball Boy Wonder. He started early, playing for St. Hedwig in the St. Boniface Parochial League of some 20 teams. This was grade school age baseball, but Johnny Garbett set a pattern of dominance as a left-handed shortstop in sixth grade already that would be repeated for more than 10 years at every level he played. He moved to the mound because first basemen had trouble handling his throws from shortstop. Like most lefties, his ball moved a lot. He struck out 18 of 21 batters as his team beat St. Lawrence, 5-1. A brief clip from an unnamed publication in the Garbett family scrapbook notes, "Good pitching featured the day, John Garbett of St. Hedwig giving St. Anthony one hit and fanning 19," in another 7-1 win. Johnny led St. Hedwig to a National Division lead after beating St. Lawrence, 5-1, then striking out 14 in a 2-1 win over St. Cyril. As a 13-and 14-year-old in the Midget League of Northeast Minneapolis, young Johnny Garbett lost one game. According to a dog-eared, fading scrapbook clipping, he "... racked up seven victories against that one loss which came in the city semifinals of the midget tournament. He wound up the season with two 2-hitters against Columbia Heights and the runner-up, Logan Park. But the crowning effort was the no-hit, no-run contest he served up to St. Charles." It was all promising prelude with the same storyline to an outstanding high school and American Legion baseball career and more.

Between 1944 and 1947, Johnny Garbett won 27 games and lost 3, pitching for his high school, Minneapolis Edison, and the two Minneapolis legion posts for whom he toiled: Chamber of Commerce his first year; and Fire and Police American Legion the next two. In this span, he fired four no-hitters and seven one-hitters, four in a row his junior year. He led teams to three consecutive Northern Division titles at Edison, the state American Legion title in 1945, and the city championship in 1946.

Just how good was this little lefthander who lived in apartments above Sunder's General Store in 1953 and above the Corner Bar in 1954 while pitching for the Class-A Jordan Brewers?

He was good enough to make All-City three years in a row at Minneapolis Edison at a time when the metro area dominated all state high school sports. He was good enough as a 125-pound, 15-year-old, pitching for the Chamber of Commerce American Legion team, to beat the defending *national* American Legion Champion Richfield nine, 3-2 (neither run earned), to even up the 1944 playoff series before Richfield won the rubber game in front of 2,500 fans at Parade Stadium, then went on to win the state championship for the second year in a row. Then, Johnny beat the powerhouse from Richfield the next year, 1945, by the score of 5-2, helping to put his Fire and Police Legion Post into the state tournament, which they won, with the little lefthander shutting out Stillwater 12-0 on three hits in the opening game. Fire and Police beat Winona in the championship game 3-2 in front of 6,894 fans at Lexington Park, which, according to Don Riley's feature article in the August 9, 1945, *St. Paul Dispatch*, "brought the official five-day total attendance to 20,633." The headline reads, "Legion Meet Sets National Crowd Record."

That put Johnny Garbett and his Fire and Police American Legion team in the double-elimination national regionals in Mason City, Iowa, where state champions from Wisconsin, Iowa, Nebraska, and Minnesota met to determine an entry in the national section playoffs in Oklahoma City. They beat Omaha, Nebraska, 4-1, in the regional opener, and then Johnny got the call against the team from Bancroft, Iowa, that was favored to win it. He pitched a sparkling, three-hit, 11-inning gem, winning 1-0 while striking out 16. The win put the undefeated Minnesota boys in the driver's seat, but Bancroft came back and won three straight, the last two over Fire and Police, 3-0 in the first game, and 6-5 in 13 innings to win the regional championship. Johnny made the *Minneapolis Daily Times* American Legion All-State baseball team, but it was small consolation to the fiery competitor, "with the cute curve and the sneaky fast one," as described by *Times* writer Tom Briere. The curveball this writer called "cute" would soon be called "nasty" and "wicked."

Johnny Garbett won Minneapolis All-City honors his junior year at Edison, too. His record of 4-0 included three 1-hitters and a 3-hitter. In the city championship game, which Edison lost to Minneapolis West and Lloyd Lundeen, 3-2, at Northrup Field before 2,500 fans, Garbett came on in the third inning, down 2-1. Glen Gaff reported in the *Minneapolis Tribune*, "Southpaw Johnny Garbett replaced Hollom in the third and was the most masterful of the three (pitchers). The dropball specialist gave up only one hit and one (unearned) run while whiffing 11 and walking four the rest of the way."

Johnny Garbett had to be doing one of two things for his breaking pitch to be called a "dropball." Thrown right, the spitball drops off the table at the plate. Almost impossible to hit, the pitch had been declared illegal with the end of the Dead Ball Era in 1920, with but a few "registered" spit ballers being allowed to continue to throw the devastating pitch, Burleigh Grimes being the last of them.

Johnny Garbett was never rumored to throw the illegal pitch. If he wasn't throwing the spitball, then he was really imparting an almost inhuman amount of twisting torque as he released the ball. If the wrist breaks about 90 degrees throwing a slider, as was taught in the late 1960s, and something short of 180 degrees for a curveball, "Little Johnny" had to have been snapping, not just turning, his wrist a full 180 degrees. That's hard on the elbow, to say the least, especially a 16-year-old elbow working in the northern climate of Minnesota.

In winning his four games for Edison, Johnny Garbett did not give up an earned run, and he struck out 65 batters. That's better than two strikeouts an inning on average. It also means he averaged more than 16 strikeouts per game! Sportswriter Jim Bryrne wrote of Garbett's win over Minneapolis Vocational, 4-1:

> Left-handed Johnny was in his best form of the season under the warm Tuesday sun as he fanned 20 Vocational batters, and gave up only one hit. It was his third one-hit game of the season and he has allowed only six in winning his four games.

Earlier, Garbett pitched a one-hitter, giving up a double in the first inning, with 18 strikeouts in a 4-1 win over Marshall High. In his one-hit shutout, 8-0, of Minneapolis Henry, he struck out 12 batters. Johnny Garbett also proved he wasn't just a one-hit pitching wonder, as he batted .437 on the season as well.

Summer brought another Minneapolis Fire and Police American Legion season. The boys won 20 straight ballgames, and Johnny Garbett remained undefeated on the year, counting high school and legion ball. "He won five games over the season as against no defeats, allowing only seven runs and eight hits in 35 innings of pitching," according to a feature article by Tom Briere in what was likely the *Minneapolis Times* with 48 point headline type: "Garbett Carries F-P Hopes."

Johnny Garbett had beaten Montana's defending American Legion State Champion, Miles City, 6-0, at Nicollet Park before 1,600 fans. He started the game and was credited with the win, striking out nine and giving up just one hit. Two other pitchers got work on the night in a game both teams needed to stay sharp for their respective tournaments. Then Garbett shut out Richfield, 1-0, on another one-hitter that helped put his Fire and Police legion team in the 1946 state tournament at Duluth. Fire and Police blasted Moorhead, 24-0, in the state tournament-opening round, and then Garbett shut out Winona, 4-0, in the second round.

Fireman-coach Rudy Tersch was confident of his team going all the way to the national title, according to the report in Joe Hendrickson's "Sports Opinions" column of the *Minneapolis Tribune*. Maybe too confident. He compared his 1946 Fire and Police team favorably with the 1943 national American Legion Champion Richfield nine:

> 'I think Fire-Police is faster than the 1943 Richfield boys and a better fielding club. Even though they had Bob Danielson, our pitching is as good as theirs.'

Everybody was thinking state championship repeat and a shot at the national championship. Don Riley, whose daily column, "The Eye Opener," beginning in 1956 and continuing for 31 years, both delighted and infuriated readers of the *St. Paul Pioneer Press*, wrote of Garbett and his pitching peers in the Sunday, July 28, 1946, edition under the banner headline, "Mill City Nine Favored":

> The terrific trio has been going along at an almost unbelievable mound pace this year as Fire and Police rolled up 18 straight victories. They have given up only 20 runs and 34 safeties in 84 innings. Garbett's victory bag includes a no-hitter, a pair of one-hitters, and a two-hit performance.

But the Minneapolis Fire and Police team ran into a superhuman effort by Stillwater's pitching ace, Frank Stewart. Here's the lead by Ted Peterson, datelined Duluth, in the *Minneapolis Sunday Tribune* the day after the heartbreaking loss:

> Stillwater's man of iron, stout-hearted Frank Stewart, jolted Minneapolis' Fire and Police from its state American Legion baseball championship when he blanked the defending titlists 2-0 in the semifinals of the tournament here Saturday.

At 6-4, 200 pounds, the big kid could bring it. It was his third straight day of shutout pitching, according to Peterson, who reported that Stewart gave up just 13 hits in 23 innings and three games while recording 32 strikeouts.

Johnny Garbett was in the lineup, batting third in the order against Stewart, but he wasn't on the mound. He was in left field, and he went hitless in the game.

After Stewart and Stillwater got beat in the championship game by Christie DeParcq, 2-1, Tom Briere in the *Daily Times* reviewed the tournament and anticipated format and venue changes for the following year.

> Duluth did a grand job, Briere wrote, and the total attendance for the five-day extravaganza was estimated around 14,000, second highest

attendance in state Legion history and not far back of the national mark of 20,633 in St. Paul last season.

Johnny Garbett joined three pitchers from the two teams in the championship game on the 1946 *Times* All-State Legion Team.

Half way through the 1947 Minneapolis prep baseball season, with Edison and Washburn leading their respective divisions, Jim Byrne reviewed the city baseball situation for the *Minneapolis Star* under the banner headline, "Prep Talk Begins, Ends With Garbett." Byrne called Johnny the "mighty mite of a pitching gem" and summarized his season, which included his third no-hit, no-run game, a 4-0 shutout of Minneapolis Marshall and his third league win without a loss on the season while giving up a total of just four hits on the year. With 14 strikeouts in the seven-inning win over Marshall, Johnny brought his strikeout total to 41 for the season, just one under an average of two per inning.

It was one of the biggest high school baseball games of all time–Washburn vs. Edison at Nicollet Park. A reported 2,500 fans watched Johnny Garbett cut down 16 Washburn hitters while giving up just three hits. But three errors led to his undoing. Washburn prevailed for the Minneapolis title, 5-4, scoring two runs in the ninth on suicide squeeze bunts to break a 3-3 deadlock.

A brief scrapbook blurb in what looks like it might have been a clipping from the *Minneapolis Tribune* in the spring of 1947 announced, "John Garbett, Star Edison pitcher, is going to be a priest. So he will enroll at St. Thomas instead of Minnesota as previously reported here." Then, in what might have been a tease to influence the young left hander, the article refers to AAA Minneapolis Miller General Manager Rosy Ryan having seen Garbett pitch and that he "thinks he has a chance to make it in pro baseball, although his size is against him."

How good was Johnny Garbett? Rosy Ryan said of him, "He is one of the smartest young pitchers I have ever seen."

Regardless of the seriousness of the young man's interests in becoming a priest, there is no doubt that every fiber and sinew in Johnny Garbett, every aspect of his being, wanted to be a Major League pitcher. Garbett changed his mind about St. Thomas and the priesthood, and enrolled at the University of Minnesota, along with teammate Bill Hollom, Lloyd Lundeen of Minneapolis West, and Frank Stewart, the big horse from Stillwater. Sid Hartman reported in "The Roundup":

> Left-handers have never had any trouble winning in the Big Nine and it's a cinch that Garbett, who despite his lack of size, is one of the best southpaws ever developed in local prep circles, will also be successful.

The University of Chicago formally withdrew from the Big 10 Conference in 1946, making it the Big 9, until three years later when Michigan State College (now Michigan State University) joined the conference to once again make it the Big 10.

We don't know how much pitching Johnny did for Triangle Sales of the Minneapolis National Park League in the summer of 1947. He also pitched for Elk River in the Class-A Wright County League that first summer out of high school. An undated clipping from an unnamed publication indicates Johnny had a typical season. The clip reads, "Garbett has given up an average of three hits per game while striking out about 14 or 15 batters–yet his team has lost four out of 10 games."

Post-season brought out Garbett's best. A headline from what is likely the *Elk River News* tells the story of Johnny's big win over Maple Lake, perennial Wright County League power in the first game of the three-game championship series: "Elks Defeat Maple Lake In First Of Championship Series," with a subhead of more interest here: "Johnny Garbett, Sensational Rookie Pitcher, Wins Own Game by Doubling in Second." He scattered four hits and struck out eight in front of 1,200 fans, losing his shutout in the seventh on a walk, an infield out, and a single along the third-base line.

Maple Lake came back and won two straight to take the league playoffs. They drafted the young left-hander and "after helping to get Maple Lake through the regionals," according to *Town Ball*, Johnny started the first game of the Class-A State Tournament at Mankato. Using a questionable, late-season acquisition, Don Anderson, from Excelsior, and three draft choices, including Bloomington pitcher Gene Cooney, Chaska, out of the Minnesota Valley League, won the 1947 Class-A championship. Anderson and Cooney combined for a 1-0 no-hit game against Maple Lake in the first game. But little Johnny Garbett had them to the edge of the abyss, firing a five hitter with 14 strikeouts, including three K's in the ninth. A passed ball on the third strikeout of the inning put a base runner on who eventually scored on an infield out with a throw wide of first base.

Maple Lake bought Johnny Garbett's services for the 1948 summer season for $75 a game, according to *Town Ball*, after the left-hander's freshman spring with the Gophers. By all accounts, Johnny Garbett had a great summer pitching for Maple Lake in the Class-A Wright County League. In a tiny, timeworn, weathered newspaper clipping on a scrapbook page filled with Johnny Garbett gems, we read the following:

> Maple Lake failed to gain a state tournament berth, but that community figures its pitching ace, Johnny Garbett, is worthy of a 'pitcher of the year' award. In 19 games that youngster allowed an average of only nine-tenths of a run per game, an average of 2.48 hits while fanning an average of 13.3. It is claimed not another pitcher in the state can better those marks . . ..

Highlights of games were reported in Minneapolis daily newspapers, with headlines praising Johnny's pitching: "Garbett Hurls One-Hitter As Maple Lake Wins 13-1," with Johnny beating Annandale in a playoff game on 14 strikeouts. Earlier in the season he struck out 17 Monticello batters in a 1-0 shutout. The newspaper articles never reported how Johnny Garbett got to his Maple Lake games from his home in Northeast Minneapolis that summer. "He hopped freight trains," John Garbett, said of his father. "They went right into downtown Maple Lake out west of the cities."

"Garbett Again in One-Hit Win" headlined the next Sunday's game, with the lead telling the story, "Maple Lake marched into the finals of the Wright County baseball league playoffs Sunday when it blanked Monticello 3 to 0 on a second straight one-hit pitching performance by little Johnny Garbett," who struck out 12 in the playoff game.

He still wasn't finished, as "Garbett Pitches 1-Hitter Again," headlined a "Special to the *Minneapolis Tribune*," report with Maple Lake beating the league's top finisher, Buffalo, 2-0, on Johnny Garbett's third consecutive playoff game one hitter. He fanned nine in the game that was completed in the time of one hour and 40 minutes in front of 2,500 fans at Buffalo.

Maybe it's a good thing that Maple Lake didn't make the state tournament at Shakopee in 1948. Johnny Garbett's Gopher coach, Dick Siebert, stepped back into the role of ballplayer for the summer with the Shakopee Indians under Manager Gordy Gelhaye, batting .434 with seven homeruns on the year and winning nine games on the mound for the Indians, according to Tom Melchior in *Scott County Baseball*. Shakopee did make the state tournament and was favored to win it all. It would have been an interesting matchup, lefty on lefty, with the young Garbett facing his coach, the former St. Louis Cardinal and Philadelphia Athletic first baseman with an 11-year, career *Major League* batting average pushing .300. At 36 years of age, Dick Siebert still had his Big League eye and a good swing. But he was a left-handed hitter. Garbett made fools out of most left-handed hitters, even the good ones.

Making a fool out of his college coach would not have helped Johnny Garbett in his sophomore year, 1949, as a Minnesota Gopher. It was bad enough that he had arm trouble that spring, pitching in Minnesota's cold spring weather. Baseball has always been a summer game, and warmer bodies tend to perform better athletically than cold ones. According to *Town Ball*, Clara City signed Johnny Garbett to a baseball contract in 1949 that paid the young man $550 a month to pitch for them in the first year of the West Central League operating in Class AA. Benson drafted him and pitched him in the semi-finals of the state tournament against Fergus Falls, who beat him, 6-1, before losing to the powerful Packers from Austin in the championship game.

Johnny Garbett, like golfer Ben Hogan, was a small man, maybe 5-8 or 5-9 and 150 pounds finally in 1950. He got everything possible out of his delivery motion, just as Hogan got everything out of his golf swing. As soon as he was finished with his spring quarter that year at the University of Minnesota, he headed three hours west of Minneapolis to Morris, where his old friend from the streets of Northeast Minneapolis, Paul Scanlon, was catching and managing the Morris Eagles in their first year in the Class-AA West Central League. *Town Ball* authors Peterson and Tomashek write that Garbett signed with Morris for $100 a game.

It was an eight-team league with a 35-game season and a four-team playoff to send the winner to St. Cloud for the Class-AA state tournament. Regular league games were played Sundays, Wednesdays, and Fridays. Players were put up at motels and private homes. A community effort had resulted in the installation of lights the year before, with a Class-A team playing the first night game. Vern Ploof pitched for Morris that night against Chokio's Joe Kelly, father of the future Minnesota Twins Manager Tom Kelly, according to the July 6, 1995 *Morris Tribune's* nostalgic feature story, "Semi-pro baseball team provided thrills in the '50s."

Each league game was thrilling, but 1950 was another step up in both quality of play and intensity of competition. Morris baseball men were interviewed for the *Tribune's* piece, including one John Bauman, who remembered Johnny Garbett: "He tossed his cookies before every game because he was so nervous. That little left-hander was a good pitcher though. He pitched 16 innings in one game once." You wouldn't have known Johnny Garbett had a problem with nerves or his stomach, with the composure he showed so consistently on the mound. Two days after pitching his first game of the 1950 season for the Morris Eagles, Johnny made the sub-headline in the May 30 *Morris Sun*: "Garbett Throttles Litchfield In Initial Appearance For Morris." He missed a shutout with one pitch that went out of the park for a three-run homerun by the Optimist cleanup hitter, Jack Verby. But he gave up a total of just four hits while striking out 13 and winning the game going away, 15-3.

Garbett pitched seven shutout innings in his next outing, against the Benson Vets, before getting knocked out in the eighth inning in a game won by Morris in the tenth. DeGraff beat Garbett on the mound, 4-3, and then the Eagles bombed Alexandria, 17-6, with Johnny banging two triples, a double, and a single while playing left field. That got him bumped up in the batting order to second, and he got two more hits in a loss to Glenwood, 5-4, before he took the mound again with a three-hitter and nine strikeouts to beat Atwater, 5-3. The Eagles had recovered from a slow start. They were now 6-6, in the middle of the eight-team pack, according to the June 20, 1950, *Morris Sun*.

The next week's *Sun* reported a rare Garbett relief stint and an 8-7 win in 10 innings over Benson. It also included a note of interest on Johnny by Phil V. Ploof in his column, "Diamond Dust":

> As a pitcher Johnny Garbett is tops but he ranks even higher as a hitter. Right now the little portside pitcher is hitting well over .470, all sure enough safe hits.

Morris was 8-6, tied with DeGraff, and climbing in the standings. Two weeks later, Gorman beat Glenwood, 7-3, on a three-hitter on Sunday. Johnny's Thursday night performance was captured in the headlines of the Tuesday, July 11 edition of the *Morris Sun*: "Garbett Fanned 23 For New League Record In Eagles' Win Over Atwater." Peterson and Tomashek count 24 strikeouts in that ball game.

Atwater scored an unearned run in the eighth inning or his three-hit gem would have been a shutout. Here's the report from the scene at the time:

> Garbett hasn't had more speed or flashed more stuff than he showed Thursday. He struck out three men in each of five innings and two in each of the other four. He granted only three bases on balls –all three coming in the eighth inning to help Atwater count its lone run. The little portsider was in complete control all the way.

Sixteen-year-old Ronnie Fredrickson had the best seat in the house, catching seven innings of the game after Manager-catcher Paul Scanlon was ejected from the game in the third inning. A subsequent win over Glenwood, 7-3, put Morris in sole possession of third place at 12-8, just one loss behind second-place DeGraff and two behind league-leading Willmar.

Johnny Garbett came on like a heat wave in July. A week later, he made the headlines again in a huge win over league-leading Willmar: "Garbett Hurls 4-0 Victory Over Willmar." The lead to the Tuesday, July 18, 1950 *Morris Sun* continued the tribute:

Sunday night was Johnny Garbett's night. The little lefthander of the Eagles, touched with a bit of stardust this night, wove his magic around Willmar for nine full innings to turn the heavy-hitting Rails with 4 hits, striking out 10, as Morris blanked the Rails, 4-0.

Garbett's mound magic put his Morris Eagles in second place, just a game behind Willmar. The *Sun* reported ". . . a crowd of approximately 2,000 fans– probably the largest crowd ever to watch a baseball game in Morris." In allowing only four hits on the night, he collared power-hitting Howie Schultz, just a year out of his six-year career in professional baseball in the National League. The Brooklyn Dodgers had found Schultz, a St. Paul native, expendable with Jackie Robinson in the system and slotted to play first base in 1947 and Gil Hodges on the way as well.

Johnny rang up DeGraff, 7-1, on a five-hitter, then Atwater, 7-0, on a four-hitter, in the next week to make it three wins in eight days. A small sidebar to the report of the two games highlighted Johnny Garbett as "The Mighty Mite":

> The diminutive southpaw of the Morris Eagles has been awfully tough to opposition batters in his recent mound appearances. In his last four West Central League games Garbett has given up just one earned run and a grand total of 15 hits. When he defeated Atwater Sunday it was his third victory in eight days.

The season closed rapidly, with Morris tied for second place with DeGraff at 22-13, three games behind Willmar. Litchfield, another game back, rounded out the playoff field. Willmar eliminated Morris in three straight in their best-of-five series, and Litchfield prevailed over DeGraff. Litchfield then upset Willmar to advance to the state tournament, with Johnny Garbett their ace-in-the-hole as a draft choice. Well-rested, because he wasn't used in the playoffs, Johnny was given the starting assignment in the second round of the tournament against the defending Class-AA state champion Austin Packers. He went the distance for a 3-2 win, but Litchfield then lost twice in the double elimination tournament.

How good was Johnny Garbett? Sid Hartman in his column, The Roundup, wrote: "Dick Siebert thinks Johnny Garbett, freshman Minnesota left-hander and former Edison and Fire and Police ace, has more ability than Marvin Rotblatt, star Illinois southpaw, who has been beat but three times in 28 college starts." Then Sid quoted the Gopher coach who was a veteran of 17 professional baseball seasons:

> "'Garbett has more stuff than Rotblatt right now,' Dick says."

Marv Rotblatt, a 5-7, 160-pound left-hander was the dominant pitcher in the Big Ten in the late 1940s. He signed with the Chicago White Sox after the 1948 collegiate season, pitched brief parts of three seasons with the big club, but spent most of eight years playing AA and AAA baseball in the Sox organization. He was 4-3 at the Major League level, pitching 74 innings. In minor league ball, Rotblatt was 78-48 with a 3.54 ERA. He had a banner year in 1950 when he won 22 games against 10 losses for AA-Memphis.

The year, 1953, brought Dwight D. Eisenhower into the White House as the nation's 34th president and the first Republican since Herbert Hoover left office 20 years earlier at the start of The Great Depression . . . The first nuclear bomb was tested in Nevada . . . The Academy Awards were televised for the first time, with

The Greatest Show on Earth being awarded Best Picture . . . Jonas Salk's creation of the polio vaccine was announced . . . Julius and Ethel Rosenberg were found guilty of espionage and executed . . . The U.S. involvement in the Korean War ended . . . With the bad legs and a bad eye to boot as a result of the car accident, Ben Hogan won the Masters, his fourth and last U.S. Open, and then won the British Open at Carnoustie in the first and only time he participated in it. His shot at The Grand Slam was made impossible by the fact that the fourth and last leg of the slam, The PGA Championship, overlapped in schedule with The Open in Scotland . . . *Gentlemen Prefer Blondes*, starring Marilyn Monroe and Jane Russell, was released . . . The year also brought publication of the first issue of Hugh Hefner's *Playboy Magazine.*

It also brought Johnny Garbett to Jordan, Minnesota, in the middle of the Class-A Minnesota River League's baseball season.

Johnny Garbett must have found his curve ball again, because, in 1953, after his two-year hitch with the U.S. Army at Ft. Rucker in Alabama was up and after being released by the Chicago Cubs with his old elbow and back problems, he started the 1953 baseball season with the newly combined Benson-DeGraff in the Class-AA West Central League. But the wheels were beginning to come off the well-paid Class-AA baseball already because of the growing difficulty in meeting payrolls. The ball club folded in mid-season, and somehow Johnny Garbett became a Jordan Brewer and was healthy enough to put enough mustard on his breaking ball to go 8-3 through the remainder of the summer. Some who saw him pitch at Jordan said he threw "a big roundhouse curve," and maybe he did by then for some variety. It was also easier on his arm than the pitch with the vertical break down and into the dirt that he had been throwing for almost 10 years. He saved that good one for when he needed a strikeout or a ground ball double play against a good hitter. Coupled with Jim Pollard's 10-3 season record on the mound, the Brewers were tasting post-season tournament by late summer.

Max Casey, the "Voice of the Brewers," also had baseball as his beat for the *Jordan Independent*, which was edited and published by his father, John E. Casey. Max supplemented solid partisan reporting of games with his column, "Sports Chatterbox," in which he provided insightful analysis of what was going on off the field, around the league, and behind the curtain. He noted, for example, in his June 18, 1953, column that the Jordan Brewer Baseball Association was a self-sustaining business enterprise and that a good reason for day games on Sundays rather than night games was that, "a night game costs the association anywhere from 8 to 18 lost balls and at about $2.75 apiece." In contrast, he noted that no lost balls had occurred during a recent Sunday afternoon game. The ball-shagging crew of scrambling, pre-teen boys in their blue jeans and PF Flyer sneakers needed the light of day to do their job. It was a job done for a bag of popcorn and a soda or two during games in the front half of the 1950s, but itemized on the JBA's Balance Sheet at $26.00 in 1955, $22.25 in 1956 and an even $22.00 in 1957.

Nearing the halfway point of the 1953 season, the Brewers held a half-game lead over the Belle Plaine Tigers. But a showdown was looming. Jordan lost three straight games, including a 9-0 whitewashing to Belle Plaine. In the July 9 issue of the *Jordan Independent*, Max dutifully covered the local's losing streak and the "torrid pace" set by Belle Plaine who had overtaken Jordan. He also ran a short sidebar on the game to have been played between Jordan and Belle Plaine the night before the Thursday publication of the paper. Without time to report on the actual game, Max, nonetheless noted a change had been made:

> Manager Baldy Hartkopf was expected to have a new pitcher on hand for this Belle Plaine tussle, replacing Don Brodahl who has been released from active duty with the Jordan Brewers.

The game on Wednesday night, July 8, 1953, was played by the Jordan Brewers and with their new pitcher on the mound. But it was against the Le Sueur Green Sox, who were running second to St. Peter in the Southern Division of the Minnesota River League at the time. Here's the report from Max Casey a week later under the headlines, "Brewers Lost In 10 Innings 4-2–Pitchers Duel In Game With Le Sueur In Fairgrounds Park Last Wednesday Night."

> To the more than 400 baseball fans who attended the Le Sueur Green Sox –Jordan Brewer game in Fairgrounds Park last Wednesday evening, it was a game long to be remembered as one of the greatest pitching exhibitions to be seen in MRL circles this season. Jordan's manager Baldy Hartkopf sent Johnny Garbett, recently acquired from the Benson-DeGraff team of the strong West Central League, to the mound to oppose Jim Bickhaus, star hurler for the Green Sox and a member of the University of Illinois pitching staff this spring. Both boys were in top form. . . Garbett was making his first appearance in a Brewer uniform . . . and struck out fourteen men, gave up eight hits, five of them coming in the ninth and tenth innings . . .. In addition, the left hander is reported to have hurled a full game only three nights previous in AA competition.

Manager Baldy Hartkopf, according to Max in the July 3 *Jordan Independent*, had discussed the need, given the coming schedule, for some pitching help with several board members after a Sunday game during the Brewer three-game skid. According to Max, " . . . they gave him the green light to look around for a new hurler."

He found him.

Johnny Garbett had lost his first Brewer game on the mound while pitching a gem. But over 400 people watched this game, this pitchers' duel, at Fairgrounds Park on a Wednesday night. Little Johnny Garbett stopped the Brewer bleeding, despite the loss, and turned around the season for his new team. Pollard had been pitching well, too, for Jordan, and now the two of them fed off each other as only two outstanding pitchers can do for a team: Spahn and Sain; Spahn and Burdette; Koufax and Drysdale; McLain and Lolich. It was classic stuff.

Max Casey's July 23 "Chatterbox" column addressed the regular monthly meeting of the Minnesota River League with an opener titled "Flaunting The Rules":

> With the MRL teams getting set for the final stretch in regular season play, several of the clubs are openly and definitely breaking the league rules so far as outside players are concerned It was a four hour stormy session with all teams throwing verbal charges at the others in regards

ineligible players No players were disqualified, consequently it can truly be said that the Minnesota River is now a wide open League.

Trouble was brewing in river city, but two nights later, Johnny Garbett did what he had been doing since his schoolboy playing days at St. Hedwig and Minneapolis Edison. One headline on page two in the July 30 *Jordan Independent*: "Garbett Hurls One Hitter At LeCenter":

> Jordan Brewers, behind the near perfect hurling of Johnny Garbett, broke the LeCenter Park jinx last Wednesday evening when they defeated the Chiefs by a score of 9-0 to stay in the running for first place honors in both the division and overall standings of the Minnesota River League . . . Garbett's one-hit performance in this game last Wednesday was truly a masterpiece to behold, for only twenty-nine LeCenter batsmen faced the Jordan left hander during the entire nine innings of play . . . In addition to facing but 29 men, thirteen of the twenty-nine were retired via the strikeout route.

Jim Pollard beat Montgomery, 8-5, on Friday night, and then Garbett came back on Sunday to defeat Prior Lake, 4-3, giving up seven hits while striking out 10 Lakers. The win put the Brewers on top of the division with a 12-6 record, a game ahead of New Prague and Belle Plaine, who were next up on the schedule to close out the regular season and decide the pennant.

The impossible happened. First, New Prague beat Jim Pollard, 7-4. Then, Max Casey reports in the August 13, 1953, *Jordan Independent*:

> Johnny Garbett was given the pitching assignment for the Brewers by Manager Baldy Hartkopf and came through with one of the finest hurling exhibitions seen this season in MRL ball yards.

Johnny fired a one-hitter with 11 strikeouts against Belle Plaine and got beat, 1-0, in front of more than 1,200 fans at Tiger Stadium. The lone hit, according to Max Casey's report on the game, was a result of a misjudged fly ball that had to be scored a hit. It spoiled a possible no-hit, no-run game for the Jordan left-hander. Moreover, the run scored by Belle Plaine was the direct result of that lone hit and a dropped ball at home on the outfield throw to the plate.

The last two games of the regular season threw the final standings into a tie-breaking point system to determine playoff pairings. Four teams, three from the Northern Division and Le Sueur from the Southern Division, finished with identical 12-8 records. The point system in effect in the event of ties resulted in a fourth-place seeding for the Brewers, who then drew New Prague in the first round of the playoffs, a best of three-game series, which opened three nights after the heartbreaking loss at Belle Plaine.

Johnny Garbett again, on three days' rest, came up with still another pitching gem. He managed the 2-1 win on a five hitter, three of them to the Robin cleanup hitter, while striking out eight and walking two. Pollard then closed the door on New Prague, 4-2, two nights later at Jordan to sweep the series.

Belle Plaine had dispatched Prior Lake in a sweep of their series, and that brought Jordan and Belle Plaine together for the divisional playoff. Here's Max

Casey reporting in print with the "voice" you can almost hear across the public address system at a jammed Fairgrounds Park:

> After losing a one-hit heartbreaker to the Belle Plaine Tigers in their last meeting, Johnny Garbett and the Jordan Brewers evened the score in the Belle Plaine park last Sunday evening, when they emerged victorious 6-5 in a ten inning ballgame which left the more than 1500 fans gasping for air before the final out was made in the bottom of the tenth.

Johnny struck out 14 while scattering seven hits, including a long, two-run homerun to Tiger legend Gene O'Brien in the bottom of the eighth. All the stars were out this night, for in addition to Garbett and O'Brien, Belle Plaine centerfielder Warren Stemmer of mostly Shakopee fame had two big hits; Tex Erickson, Jordan's mighty mite shortstop had a big triple in the top of the 10th inning, and Jim Pollard brought him home with a shot deep into the cavernous centerfield of Tiger Stadium.

With Pollard's 3-2 win in the second game, Jordan's sweep of the divisional playoff series put them in the MRL finals against Montgomery.

The Montgomery Commanders had shocked the world by winning the Southern Division playoffs, beating in succession St. Peter and Le Sueur. After a mediocre 8-12 regular season mark, it didn't make sense. But Montgomery had raided Class-AA Mankato of two ballplayers for the playoffs and played them under assumed names. Suspicions ran high, but Jordan remained mum and opened the best-of-five series with Johnny Garbett at Fairgrounds Park on Sunday night, August 23, in front of more than 1,300 fans.

They weren't disappointed, as they saw their great 23-year-old southpaw fashion a two-hit, 2-0 shutout with 18 strikeouts. It was his best performance of the year, as he hurled perfect ball for six and one-third innings, a spell broken in the top of the seventh when he walked Harry Pan. He gave up the two hits in the top of the eighth, but struck out two batters and got the third on a popup to get out of the inning without giving up a run.

Jordan followed up with Jim Pollard in the second game of the series at Montgomery on Tuesday night. He responded by winning his 10th game of the season, 9-7. He and Tex Erickson and Johnny Garbett all hit homeruns in the game, with Pollard's blast his eighth of the season. That brought the series back to Jordan on Thursday night where Johnny Garbett did it again, this time, 9-1, on four hits, with eight strikeouts. The Jordan Brewers were the 1953 Minnesota River League champions, and the headline that Max Casey ran on page two read as follows: "Brewers First Team In MRL History to Sweep Series in Seven Straight." Jim Pollard had won three of the playoff games, and Johnny Garbett had won four. Quite simply, he was magnificent.

Jordan continued to roll, taking two straight from Dundas in Region 1A, 7-0 and 16-2. Garbett started and won the second game but was lifted in the fifth with the score 10-1 at the time. He had nine strikeouts in the short stint on the mound. He also hit a homerun and had two other hits in the game.

That meant nine straight playoff wins, with the next stop The Big Dance in New Ulm. Jordan hadn't been in *the* state tournament since 1938 when they lost the championship game to Owatonna. These were A-ball days, playing just a notch below the class of the state's AA leagues with payrolls that paid everybody, such as the Southern Minny. They were on a roll. The big guns were booming. The stars were shining.

Jordan drew Delavan in the first round of the 1953 Class-A State Tournament. Then, as now, nobody even knew where Delavan was. It was a town of about 302 people, according to *Town Ball*, in northern Faribault County, seven miles east of Winnebago, playing in the Faribault County League that was formed in 1949 with Blue Earth, Kiester, and Winnebago. But their proximity to the very hot Class-AA Southern Minny towns such as Faribault and Owatonna is what made them sleepers and should have been a concern to the Baseball Bosses in Jordan who had pulled off the coups that landed Jim Pollard and Johnny Garbett. Personality clashes with managers or team members, lack of playing time, or maybe just the need for a bigger pay day, made disgruntled, good ballplayers available to teams like Delavan. Just one wealthy farmer, we would learn 10 years later with Arlington and Jim Stoll, could transform a mediocre ball club into a great one. Although a team game of nine men, baseball could be dominated by one great ballplayer. Nor should Delavan's Weigel have been a surprise to the Jordan Brewers, as he had pitched for Excelsior's 1949 Class-A state champions. Moreover, Delavan had gone 11-1 on the season in the league that had been dominated by Winnebago for several years. Size shouldn't have been a factor either, as the era's characteristic ethic was to play up, not down.

Johnny Garbett had led the Brewers in hitting with a .321 average in his half season of play in the MRL. Jim Pollard was right behind with his .315 average, but his 10 homeruns had led the league, a circuit that included sluggers Marty Lee and John Mauer at Le Sueur and Gene O'Brien at Belle Plaine. Garbett liked to hit and, like many pitchers, he liked to talk about his hitting. But his game was on the mound, where he was all business. Johnny pitched another great game in the opening round of the 1953 Class-A Minnesota State Baseball Tournament at New Ulm. He scattered seven hits, with one walk while ringing up 14 strikeouts. That kind of performance should be good enough to win most ballgames, but Rich Weigel, a high school teacher at Delavan that belied his baseball pedigree, fired a four-hitter to beat Johnny Garbett, in what was considered "the best game of the tournament." Tiny Delavan went on to win the Class-A State Championship, with Weigel winning MVP honors after a second four-hitter to beat Minneapolis DeVac's, 5-2, in the semi-final game, then throwing 2-1/3 innings of relief in the 5-3 championship game win over Little Falls.

Here's Max Casey's front-page report of the game in the September 17, 1953, *Jordan Independent*:

> Jordan's 1953 Brewers baseball team wound up their playing season in a blaze of glory on Sunday evening in the state baseball tournament at New Ulm. . . Press and radio men watching the Jordan-Delavan game that evening were loud in their praises of both teams and stated the contest would perhaps be the best game of the meet . . . Defensively, both teams played errorless ball . . . The Panthers' lone tally came in the second frame when with one away Weigel singled into centerfield and scored all the way from first on a triple by J. Murry. From this point on, Johnny Garbett . . . was in no serious trouble and as the game wore on the lone tally loomed bigger and bigger for the opponents, as Weigel was cutting

the Jordan hitters down with air-tight support behind him . . . (He) had the kind of support behind him which one would expect to find only in major league ball. Jordan was hitting Weigel's offerings hard and often enough to win most ball games, but always right at one of the Panther defensemen.

It was classic Class-A baseball during the Golden Age of the game, and Delavan was a worthy champion, with Rich Weigel a great ballplayer worthy of his state tournament honor. Max Casey captured the tone and the talent of the day near the closing of his report: "Jordan ballplayers and fans wish the Panthers the best of luck in their remaining tourney games, having nothing but the highest respect for this so-called underdog nine in their march to the state title in Class A ball."

The English poet, Alexander Pope, penned the classic line, "Hope springs eternal in the human breast: Man never is but to be blest," in the 18th Century. The Brewers had hopes of keeping their team intact for the 1954 season. Pollard was a question over the winter, as rumors were floating around that he was being considered for the head coaching position at Stanford University, his alma mater in California. His 10-3 record on the mound was tops in the league. Pitching just the last half of the season, Johnny had gone 8-3, all close, tough-luck losses. According to Tom Melchior in *Scott County Baseball*, Johnny had 138 strikeouts and a chintzy ERA of 1.71. The team had jelled and hung together during a mid-season slump, then toughened down the stretch and in the playoffs, winning the must-win games with dominating pitching and stout defense, the hallmarks of good baseball anywhere. They had learned how to win in a tough Class-A league of baseball.

The problem then, in the Golden Age of Baseball locally, was that everybody else had top professional talent, too, especially the teams to the south and west of the Twin Cities, where Class-A baseball teams in the Minnesota River League raided the Class-AA Southern Minny and Western Minny towns when they could get by with it. Everybody was always looking for an edge. The rules of Class-A baseball in Minnesota, as they slowly evolved, stipulated that teams could have two "outside" players. The rest had to be what were called "home" players, who usually resided within the limits of the town in which they were playing, but who had to live within a radius of 15 miles of that town. Typically, teams kept an eagle's eye watch on the rosters and lineups of other teams, while stretching rules or seeking exceptions to the rules in their own cases.

The Minnesota state baseball board required established residencies of players as of March 1 in 1954, for example, but the Minnesota River League's residency deadline was a stricter December 1. The three-month period was a limbo that nearly turned into a living hell of dashed hopes for the Jordan Brewers. Protests and a league ruling held that Jordan, in 1954, was one player over the two-player limit of outside players allowed: Jim Pollard, a five-year Jordan veteran; player-manager Baldy Hartkopf in his third season; and Johnny Garbett, who had also been a home player in 1953. What had changed? In short, Jordan had won the league title in 1953, with Johnny Garbett and Jim Pollard too tough to beat down the playoff stretch. Moreover, St. Peter wanted Johnny Garbett pitching for the Saints, and according to sports scribe Max Casey's account in the *Jordan Independent*, controversial, off-field politicking began at the monthly meetings of the Minnesota River League's directors. He reported, for example, on the front page of the January 21, 1954, *JI* under the headline, "Tightened River League Rules May Force Some Withdrawals," that the league had adopted a completely new set of rules and bylaws, raising the bar so high as to force some teams to withdraw from the league:

> It was pointed out at the meeting that the rules by which the league is governed have been too lax in years past and that a general tightening was needed. Some of the directors felt however that the new regulations as proposed and adopted went too far in the other direction and would lower the standard of play to such an extent that the MRL would lose its reputation as being one of the better "A" leagues in the state.

With President Paul Erhard of Montgomery presiding over the meeting and Secretary Paul Boys of St. Peter recording the decisions, votes went in favor, 5-3, of the more stringent rules. It was an early warning, a harbinger, of more to come. Max Casey smelled the proverbial rat in his February 11 column, "Sports Chatterbox":

> Talk about your sportsmanship. We have always been told that the team in the MRL that wins the league title can be expected to be legislated against the following season. After winning our first league pennant last year, we are beginning to realize there is more truth than fiction in the statement. After listening to the league director from St. Peter tell at the last meeting of the need for retrenchment by all the towns in the MRL (his town of course having a natural population advantage of 5-1 over Jordan and more than 15-1 over Prior Lake), he convinced enough of the other directors to vote down a proposition to let Jordan and Prior Lake have the same outside help they had last season and which those towns felt they needed to field a representative team in the MRL this year Jordan was told they have to get rid of Hartkopf, Pollard, or Garbett, despite the fact that Jim has been with the Brewers for five seasons, Baldy for three seasons, and John a member of last year's team.

> Payoff came the day after the meeting when Johnny Garbett was contacted by the St. Peter representative at the former's home in Minneapolis, who told John of the league action the night before and tried to sign Garbett to a St. Peter contract for 1954. Tsk, tsk, knock 'em down and then rob 'em.

Tommy Lane, sports columnist for the *Le Sueur News-Herald* the past year, after covering MRL sports for the *LeCenter Leader* the previous four years, had been critical of Jordan's argument in the league controversy. The scribes were in a war of words. Max took Lane to task for hypocrisy:

> What we find hard to comprehend, Tom, is your veddy, veddy (sic) deep concern over Jordan's having one too many ballplayers, when a few short years ago you were heralding the great LeCenter team composed of Bob Dill & Co. which was manned if memory serves us right, by something like eight or nine ballplayers who never even heard of LeCenter until they found themselves in Chief uniforms.

LeCenter loaded up in 1950 with the signing of an entire team of "outside" players, including Bob Dill, who was then playing hockey for the St. Paul Saints of the U.S. Hockey League and who also owned a career .308 batting average over nine years of minor league baseball, mostly in the Red Sox organization. LeCenter finished the MRL regular season with a record of 18-9, second to Belle Plaine, and then beat the Tigers in the playoffs. That gave them Belle Plaine's slugging catcher Gene O'Brien and pitcher JeRoy Carlson as draftees. Both were instrumental in the regional and state tournaments. LeCenter won it all in Class A in 1950, 4-3 over Winsted in the championship game, then finished second in 1951 to Watertown, 9-4 for the title.

Peterson and Tomasheck in *Town Ball* call the Minnesota River League "The Class of A." Indeed, from 1948 to 1954, the Minnesota River League was the best Class-A league in the state of Minnesota.

Belle Plaine took second in the state tournament twice during this period, while Waseca, St. Peter, and LeCenter all won state championships. In addition, Jordan's 1953 and 1954 teams were outstanding, as was the 1959 St. Peter nine, which finished third behind Shakopee and Springfield.

Johnny Garbett was 24 years old in the winter of 1954, and he must have been thinking about putting down some roots. He liked the level of baseball in the Minnesota River League, and he liked the beer and the baseball in Jordan. "He was just a little guy, and he had a little potbelly," according to his teammate, Dick Nolden, who added, "He liked his beer." It was another perfect marriage of beer and baseball consummated in an old German river town.

Johnny made the business news section of the February 18, 1954, *Jordan Independent* with a thumbnail note that he and George Johnson, official scorekeeper for the Jordan Brewers, had formed a business partnership that had purchased The Corner Bar from Mr. and Mrs. Joseph Fischer, effective Monday morning, February 15. In addition, Max wrote in his "Sports Chatterbox" that Johnny was living with his business partner in Jordan ". . . until his marriage this spring to Miss Ruth Maebele" of Robbinsdale, scheduled for May 1.

It was all good news as far as Jordan baseball was concerned, made better even by news in the "Chatterbox" on April 15 that Jim Pollard had lost his bid for the head coaching position at Stanford to Howie Dallmar of Pennsylvania. Fans could look forward to another year of Garbett and Pollard. To top it all off, the April 29 *JI* carried news of the reduction in baseball ticket prices throughout the MRL from 60 cents to 50 cents, children remaining the same at two bits. "Tony Anthony of St. Peter," Max wrote, "expressed the opinion that now, with the elimination of the federal tax, the benefit should be passed on to the customers. It was so decided by a vote of 7 to 1."

Johnny Garbett missed the May 9th opening night pitching start against the New Prague Robins due to unplayable weather conditions. But, nonetheless, he was the center of attention at a mid-week league meeting. Max on the matter in the May 13, 1954, *Jordan Independent*:

> At a special meeting of the MRL directors requested by Jordan to clarify the home player status of John Garbett, ace Brewer hurler, the directors by a 6-2 vote upheld their controversial December 1 deadline date for residence, which is in great variance with the March 1 deadline date of the state amateur baseball association rule and ruled that Garbett would not be permitted to play with Jordan as a home player. The directors also

failed to act on a compromise solution by refusing to consider an amendment to the by-laws which would permit any player in the league who purchased a business and becomes a bona-fide resident of that community to be considered a home player. Most leagues in the state have such a rule, but evidently the directors were bent on one thing only and that being to break up by league legislation the Brewer triumvirate of Garbett, Pollard and Hartkopf.

The Jordan Brewers appealed the league's ruling to the Minnesota State Amateur Baseball Board of Directors. Max reported on the appeal in a sidebar story in the May 20, 1954, *Jordan Independent*:

> At their regular monthly meeting held in St. Paul on Monday evening of this week, the State Board in a closed session of nearly an hour voted to uphold the MRL rules in regard to residence which in effect denies the Brewers the right to use Garbett as a home player.

The Brewers had split two games in the week between the Thursday publications. Johnny pitched the opener against New Prague, and despite 14 strikeouts, he got beat, 5-1. Three errors didn't help him, nor did the replacement catcher for Baldy Hartkopf, who would be the self-sacrificing lamb in the matter of residency ruled on by the league and the state board. Jordan had no backup catcher. Pat Moriarty tried, but Garbett had too much stuff for him, and Pat's catching hand got bruised. Joe Pekarna replaced him in the fifth inning. Pollard beat Prior Lake on Sunday, hitting two homeruns, one a grand slam in the eighth inning, to win his own game, 10-8.

But the Brewers had a tough decision to make: One of their three outside players had to go. We believe Baldy Hartkopf fell on his sword, giving up his player-manager role in order for Jordan to keep intact the irreplaceable Garbett-Pollard pitching duo. With Hartkopf released and going to Prior Lake for the remainder of the season, the Brewers needed a bona-fide catcher–somebody who could hold Johnny Garbett and Jim Pollard. They got lucky in picking up Bob Radde, a student at Gustavus Adolphus College in St. Peter and a resident of Shakopee, which was within the required residency radius of Jordan.

Johnny started Jordan's home opener against Belle Plaine. He gave up three hits in the first two innings, but four errors cost four runs. Garbett tightened things up, allowing just three more hits in the game, and the Brewers fought back to win, 8-4.

Jordan was rolling again. Headlines of the lead story on the sports page of the June 3, 1954, *Jordan Independent* tell our story: "Garbett Whiffs 19 As Brewers Win From LeCenter 6-1 Sunday." The win put them at 3-1 on the season, a half-game behind the unbeaten New Prague Robins.

Max couldn't leave the matter of the league's residency ruling die. He brought it up again in his column, "Sports Chatterbox":

> This column thought at the outset and still thinks that the Garbett case had plenty of merit for favorable consideration by the league directors, but when it became plainly evident that a campaign against John and Jordan was being waged within the league and that good common sense

thinking was being shunted aside for technicalities, we realized that Jordan could expect no consideration in this matter.

The columnist then reviewed teams around the league and concluded that Le Sueur and St. Peter, both in the Southern Division, were the strongest teams in the league, giving a nod to St. Peter with its addition of two pitchers of questionable residency. But then with the patience and precision sighting of a German sniper, he put the crosshairs on his target and squeezed off a round:

> Incidentally, we were wondering how many native St. Peterites were on their team when we were watching them one evening last week and could only find one or two who we believe fall in that category. And they are by far the biggest city in the league.

The Brewers, behind Johnny Garbett's 12 strikeouts and second consecutive four-hitter, beat Le Sueur on Sunday at Fairgrounds Park, 7-1. He got all the cushion he needed in the bottom of the first, as Jim Pollard slammed a three-run homerun off former Brewer teammate, Jim Kieger, with the towering blast clearing the railroad tracks over the left-center field fence.

Two days later, on Tuesday at approximately 5 pm, according to the front-page, headline story in the June 17, 1954, *Jordan Independent*, "Former Schutz & Hilgers Brewery Gutted By Fire." The stone structure was an artifact from a bygone era of small breweries operating successfully all along the Minnesota River Valley. The business had supported and given the name, "Brewers," to the town baseball team. First Prohibition, then World War II and rationing of the grains needed to brew beer, then finally business consolidation forces had brought the local brewery, like so many others up and down the Minnesota River, to a close. Mass-market advertising and modern production and distribution trumped quality and customer loyalty. It was an old tune that would be replayed over and over again.

At 4-1 on the season, the Brewers sat atop the Northern Division of the MRL, while St. Peter, undefeated at 5-0, led the Southern Division. A "Shootout at OK Corral" was coming up. Johnny Garbett got the call and was cruising along on a four-hitter with 16 strikeouts in the bottom of the eighth, with the scoreboard full of goose eggs, when the lights went out. Literally. Garbett beaned Jim Dalton, pitching ace of the University of Notre Dame, now with St. Peter. Dalton went down and was out for about 15 minutes, according to the *JI*'s report of the game. Dalton regained consciousness and play resumed, but Garbett was upset, "unnerved" the report called it. He walked two to load the bases, and then appeared to get out of the jam by getting two hitters out, only to walk another batter, his third of the inning, and the ice-breaking, go-ahead run for St. Peter. Pollard finished up for Garbett, and Straka replaced Dalton, with St. Peter winning by a final score of 2-0.

Jim Pollard beat Montgomery, and then Manager Leon Hennes called on Johnny against the Prior Lake Lakers. He gave up five hits, three of them to Bud Kleidon, including a homerun that he matched himself, and he struck out 13 Lakers in a 4-1 win at Prior Lake. That kept the Brewers on top of the Northern Division at 6-2. Meanwhile, St. Peter had finally lost a game but remained atop the Southern Division at 5-1.

Max picked up the issue of the day in his "Sports Chatterbox" column again:

> We were more than mildly surprised at the St. Peter-New Prague ball game last Thursday evening when we saw "Ditch" Boys in uniform as a home player for the Saints. Asking one of the league officers, "How come?" we were given the answer that the St. Peter moguls had called the Directors around the league and received an OK via telephone to use him . . .This to this writer is a direct violation of the league rules and coming from the town that is leading the league makes it appear at this stage that after forcing Jordan to follow the rules and regulations of the league to the letter by not giving consideration to the Garbett case that the by-laws might just as well be thrown out the window. Now, Ditch Boys is no ordinary ball player. He is perhaps one of the best in this section, having an extensive background in pro ball and playing for several seasons in the fast Double-A ball of this state. We've been told time and again at league meetings by the St. Peter representatives that they would not try to "load up" by taking advantage of the use of Gustavus players in addition to having a population advantage of 5 or 6 to 1 over, let's say, Jordan. Their team now is manned by GA stars Kent Musser, Glen Mattke, and Cliff Straka and former Double-A players Boys and Berguson. How, by any stretch of the imagination, can small towns like Prior Lake, Jordan, LeCenter, and any of the others for that matter, hope to compete with a star studded lineup like the Saints present and then have the Directors of the league nod a telephone OK (in violation of the league rules) to give them additional home players. What proof did the Directors have when they gave the OK that Ditch Boys was even a bonafide resident of St. Peter? We can only think back to the treatment these same Directors gave to Jordan's request of John Garbett as a home player and wonder how they can justify action such as this which makes the strongest team in the league even stronger.
>
> We predicted a breakdown of the league rules would be coming before the season was over, but we sure missed the boat when we figured St Peter would be the last to violate a rule which their own representatives injected into the by-laws. We can now look forward to almost anything to the much heralded tightened MRL rules and by-laws this summer.

Johnny Garbett glittered like pure gold again on Friday night in a 3-0, three-hit shutout with 13 strikeouts against New Prague. Then on Sunday night at Belle Plaine, 10 Brewer errors and 15 Tiger hits led to an embarrassing 15-2 loss, putting the Brewers at 7-3, but still leading the division at the half-way point of the season. Max reported diligently on the two games in the July 1, 1954, *Jordan Independent*, but he devoted most of his "Chatterbox" column to the re-publishing of much of the sports feature, a tribute to Johnny Garbett, by Ted Peterson in the *Minneapolis Tribune* of the previous Sunday. How good was Johnny Garbett? Here's just some of what Peterson wrote about Jordan's ace southpaw:

> The biggest breaking curve ever to hit state baseball is gone, but the fellow who used to bend 'em, Johnny Garbett, still is very much in evidence. Even though that curve 'sort of disappeared,' Garbett still is sporting an earned run average of around 1.000 a game as the ace of the Jordan mound staff in the Minnesota River League.

Once considered as one of the best lefthanders ever to come out of Minneapolis sandlot baseball, Garbett's sizzling curve attracted attention of major league scouts and he was signed to a Chicago Cubs contract by Joe Kernan in 1950. Two years in the armed service followed, however, and when Garbett returned he went to Des Moines, only to be pestered by a sore elbow and ailing back–which meant ruination of his number one ambition–to be a major league baseball player.

Meanwhile, when Garbett every once in a while risks an elbow pain to toss a bender, that old complaint of batters facing him pops up again, "You think he's throwing that ball in from first base."

"He had really good stuff," Dick Nolden said from Detroit Lakes, Minnesota, as he reflected back 60 years to when he watched, from his catbird seat at second base, the left-handed craftsman make fools of Class-A hitters in the Minnesota River League.

Johnny beat New Prague again, 3-1, the second time in less than a week. This time, he gave up four hits while striking out 15 on Thursday night. The win was followed by a 9-8 loss to Prior Lake in 11 innings on Monday night at Fairgrounds Park before the largest home crowd of the season, more than 700 fans.

Belle Plaine's Gene O'Brien beat Johnny at Belle Plaine on the following Thursday night with a homerun in the sixth inning with one runner on second base after a double. They were the only two hits he gave up, but they were enough for a 2-1 Tiger win. The Brewers then beat LeCenter on Sunday at Fairgrounds Park, 5-4, with Johnny coming on in a two-inning relief stint in the eighth inning and registering five strikeouts to preserve the win. But the next week, the Brewers lost twice, with John dropping a 3-1 game to Le Sueur despite a three hitter, and then giving up five hits and two runs in relief of Pollard in the Thursday night loss to St. Peter. The losses dropped Jordan into a 9-7 tie with Belle Plaine for the division lead. Moreover, they were limping, with three starters nursing injuries.

Max focused on St. Peter having picked up another Class-AA pitcher (Smullen) from Shanty Dolan at neighboring Class-AA Mankato, bringing their number of former AA players to "four or five," Max guessed, while lauding them with the capability of "fielding a team that could compete with many of the AA teams around the state."

Radde, the young replacement catcher for Baldy Hartkopf, ignored his doctor's orders to call it a season and sucked it up. Tex Erickson got his doctor's okay to return to the lineup, and Dick Nolden was back in town from his outstate summer job related to his degree work in veterinary medicine. And the bats came alive!

Led by Johnny Garbett's perfect night at the plate and another fine performance on the mound, the Brewers clobbered Montgomery, 13-3. Johnny went five for five, and he gave up but six hits in six innings of pitching, striking out nine. The Brewers then beat Prior Lake, 15-2, with Garbett taking a no-hitter into the seventh inning with 12 strikeouts. They had kept pace with Belle Plaine, the teams deadlocked for the division lead with identical 11-7 records. Both lost their next game, setting up a finale to the dogfight that had gone down to the wire again. It was billed as the "Battle of Southpaws"–Shrake vs. Garbett, with Belle Plaine at Jordan on Sunday night. Here's the report from Max Casey in the August 5, 1954, *Jordan Independent* under the headline, "Brewers In First As Garbett Aces Tigers in Finale":

> Fairgrounds Park, packed with more than a thousand baseball fans last Sunday evening, witnessed one of the finest baseball games and best pitchers duels ever witnessed in this section of the state, barring none . . . Both of the ace southpaws worked effectively with Garbett having the edge in all departments including slamming out a four-bagger for Jordan's lone winning tally.

The Jordan Brewers played errorless ball to back up Johnny Garbett's two-hit, 12-strikeout win. He faced just 29 batters and, after giving up a double in the second inning, retired 24 straight Belle Plaine Tigers. The 1-0 win gave Jordan the undisputed first-place position in the final MRL standings. Position was important for town bragging rights and for pairings in the playoffs.

The August 12, 1954, *Jordan Independent* announced the centennial celebration of the founding of the city on its front page. It reported a two-game, shutout sweep of the Prior Lake Lakers in the first round of the league playoffs on the sports page. Johnny Garbett gave up four hits, two in the ninth with the game well decided at that point, and he struck out 16 Lakers as he shut out Prior Lake, 11-0. Pollard then equaled the effort with a 6-0, four-hit shutout to put the Brewers into the semifinals of the MRL playoffs against the winner of the Belle Plaine-New Prague quarterfinals.

A sidebar story paid tribute to "a number of Jordan's Baseball Greats who had burned up the diamond. They played ball in the 1890s and early twentieth century when Jordan's field was near Brentwood and later on Small Field, present site of what was the new St. Paul's Lutheran church." That's just 30 to 40 years after the Dakota (Sioux) Indian Uprising in the Minnesota River Valley. Max, from memory, listed 29 old-time baseball players who laid the foundation for the game in this part of the river valley. Men like Carl Herder and Cap Richter, Jack Bauer and Pops Mertens, Ollie Fuhrman and William Speck. Max ran photo's, one of an early Jordan "White Caps" team, and individual shots of Felix ("Jinxeye") Schneiderhan, who, we learn, once had 21 strikeouts, and George ("Hawger") Herder, an early slugger. The scribe was paying homage at an appropriate time, invoking Spirit, as the Dakota had done before their battles on the plains and along the same Minnesota River Valley. No, you don't denigrate or disparage the Great Ones who came before you. They are all saints whose help you can use. Baseball was life, and life was baseball. The Great Ones are part of The Invisible Hand from the other side of the veil that help to sustain you. They serve at the pleasure of The Fiddler–His minions at work and play.

Jordan faced New Prague for the division title as a result of the Robins taking out Belle Plaine, 3-2, in 11 innings of their rubber game. More than 1,000 fans were reported on hand at Jordan for the first game of the best-of-three division title series on Tuesday night. Johnny Garbett started and cruised along for six innings in his typical four-hit, shutout fashion. But New Prague got to him in the seventh for five runs on six hits, his worst outing of the season, which gave New Prague a 5-3 lead after seven. Pollard had come in to put out the fire, but they'd lost the lead and it looked like the game as well. Neither team scored in the eighth. New Prague was blanked in the top of the ninth. It was late. Late at night under the lights that had been put up just four years earlier to bring night baseball to Jordan, the towers welded and assembled on the street between the Engfer Garage and Louie Stifter's welding shop on the other side of Water Street. It was a workday tomorrow, and the farmers in the crowd on hand had their dairy herds to tend to early in the morning. The cows had to be milked.

But nobody was leaving the ballpark or their seats. They sensed something was up. Indeed, "How many angels can dance on the head of a pin?" The Fiddler was tapping his foot and striking his tune. The pinhead was jammed. All the angels and all the saints were out dancing tonight. People were at the edge of their seats for every pitch....

Max Casey's first-hand account of the game's high-drama finish began with a subheading, "Exploded In Ninth," with the meat of the Brewer batting order coming up. We pick up Max's report of the action at Fairgrounds Park directly from the August 19, 1954, *Jordan Independent*:

> In the bottom of the ninth, however, it was Jordan's turn to shine. Johnny Garbett drove a long homerun over (the left-field fence). Next up was Jim Pollard who slammed out a terrific in the park triple. Geske took over the mound work. With one run in, Pollard on third and nobody out, Jordan's chances rose rapidly when Geske threw a wide pitch to Dick Nolden which got away from catcher Parrish enabling Pollard to dash for home with the tying run. Geske then walked Dick, John Hovanek, and Bob Radde in order to fill the bases with still nobody out. Jordan fans went wild as they smelled victory....

Cigar and cigarette smoke rose from the stands as one large cloud of high-mass incense at the altar. Beer vendors carrying the metal pails of iced-down, longneck bottles were selling out fast. Popcorn vendors seemed to be spilling more corn than usual as they handed the bags to paying customers. They couldn't keep up with demand either, and the crowd didn't like them getting in the way of their view of the diamond and the drama unfolding in front of them. They wanted it both ways. They wanted their refreshments and they couldn't miss a pitch. Too much was at stake–all the proverbial marbles, and all the tea in China. Max weighed in on the moment:

> ... Manager Jimmy Anderson of the Robins set up a unique defensive maneuver, bringing Rathmanner (the shortstop) in beside the pitcher, Mickus in from centerfield to cover short and Tupy from rightfield to cover center, leaving the rightfield unguarded. Rollie Sunder slammed a hard one to Rathmanner who forced Dick Nolden at home for the first out, leaving the sacks still jammed. Truman Carlson attempted the suicide squeeze, but Geske bore down and struck him out for the second out.
>
> Big thrill of the game came at this point, when Joey Pekarna with a 2-2 count on him slammed a long line drive out against the tower boards in left field to score Hovanec from third and win the game for Jordan by a score of 6-5.

The crowd exploded in exuberance and ecstasy. Most of them failed to see the New Prague left fielder, Walt Kranke, lying on the field after crashing into the fence while giving chase to the walk-off shot hit by the young man who would retire from his dental practice in Jordan exactly 60 years later.

The Brewers were one up in the three-game series. All systems were go. The Buzz was turned up full blast. All the lights were on in the house, the sails were full of fair wind, and The Dance was in full swing. Then Jim Geske took the wind out of the Brewer sails, dimmed the lights, and dampened the music. He shut out the Brewers two nights later, 4-0, with a no-hitter. Game on! That set up the series finale and the division crown for the next night at Fairgrounds Park in Jordan, the third game of the week.

New Prague had taken what looked again like a game-winning lead, 5-2, in the seventh inning on a bad-hop single that scored two runs. But Jordan pulled out another dramatic finish at Fairgrounds Park in front of too many patrons to count, the excitement too great to recall in detail. They tied the game in the bottom of the ninth on Garbett's "stinging double through Geske at third to score Carlson and Erickson with the tying runs," and went on to win, 6-5, in 12 innings. Johnny Garbett went the distance for the Brewers with a six-hitter and 13 strikeouts.

First, the house rocked. Fairgrounds Park stayed lit, with the beer-stand cooler running dangerously low, and the vendors' arms dragging from lugging pails of beer and ice around for a long, extra-inning game. Then, the hottest corner on the hottest street in downtown Jordan rocked some more. Beer flowed all night, nearly till dawn, and whiskey, too, as fans left the ballpark and swarmed into The Tap Room, the Hotel Jordan a block down Broadway, and at Ruppert's Bar a few doors away on Water Street, and especially at The Corner Bar with its new proprietors, Johnny Johnson and Johnny Garbett, serving it up on a Friday night MRL Northern Division championship. You'd have thought that Broadway and Water Streets in Brewer Town were paved with gold and someone had struck another new vein. The vein of gold in the left arm of 24-year-old Johnny Garbett.

Saints be blest, and angels rest, even The Fiddler finally put down the bow and shut out the lights on a long, late Friday night.

Jordan had a day off, Saturday, before they were to open the five-game series against the Le Sueur Green Sox for the MRL championship on Sunday. Their front-line pitching was worn out, too, from taking the best team in the MRL, the Double-A-rich St. Peter Saints down in their three-game series in the Southern Division. They'd finished on Thursday night, however, giving them an extra day of rest, and then both teams got a reprieve with a rainout on Sunday's scheduled game. They opened instead on Monday night at Le Sueur.

Johnny's two-run triple to deep right-centerfield in the first inning staked Jim Pollard to a lead he would never relinquish, as the Brewers won 5-4 to take the all-important opening game in the series on the road. Le Sueur then pounded an arm-weary Garbett for 13 hits in the second game at Jordan, but four walks and four errors didn't help Johnny in the 9-4 loss that evened the series at a game apiece. After Le Sueur shut out the Brewers 6-0 in the third game, the Brewers evened up the series at home with an 8-5 win, the margin of victory a long, three-run blast by Johnny Garbett over the left centerfield fence at Fairgrounds Park in the bottom of the seventh. Hard-hitting Marty Lee and John Mauer had four of the eight hits off Garbett, who struck out just six Green Sox in this game, which sent the series back to Le Sueur for the fifth and final game on Tuesday night. Lou Cardenal and Shorty Mathes worked the game in blue.

Jim Pollard shut out Le Sueur, 3-0, to win the MRL title for the second year in a row. But here's Max Casey's account of what he dubbed, "Tuesday's Thriller" in the September 2 *Jordan Independent*:

> Jordan's win on Tuesday evening over at Le Sueur was truly a thriller, with the Brewers turning in one of their top performances of the season . . . Time after time, brilliant defensive play nipped potential Le Sueur rallies in the bud. Johnny Garbett scored the first and winning run on what Max described as a "lofty double" by Pollard to right-center. Pollard went the distance on the mound to put the Brewers in the regional playoffs against Winnebago, winners of the Faribault County League.

The baseball team got the prime newspaper real estate for the September 9, 1954, *Jordan Independent*: "'On To St. Cloud' As Brewers Cop Regional in Two Straight" spread across all six columns on the top of the front page. Lefty Joe Schrake, draftee from Belle Plaine, beat the much-heralded University of Minnesota Gopher ace, Ron Craven, 4-1, with a four-hitter at Fairgrounds Park in the first game. Johnny Garbett iced it in the second at Winnebago, 6-2, scattering eight hits and striking out 15, including an emphatic three straight hitters with two runners on base in the last of the ninth to clinch the region title and qualify for the Class-A State Tournament at St. Cloud's Municipal Stadium.

The records show that Johnny Garbett and the Jordan Brewers were defeated for the second year in a row in the first round of the Class-A State Tournament by the eventual champion. In 1953 it was Delavan. In 1954, Benson turned the trick on them. But "The Devil's in the details," and as Paul Harvey's signature line on his radio program of over 50 years, after you get beyond what's in the book as "official," "Then you know. . . the rest . . . of the story."

First of all, this was the same Benson team that had competed at the Class-AA level until midway through the previous 1953 season, when, combined with DeGraff, the team folded. They had been more than competitive in the West Central League, and the best of their ball club formed the nucleus of the team that faced the Brewers. The 1954 Minnesota State Amateur Baseball Tournament reverted to a two-class event, with Double A dropping out. As a consequence, the state board changed the Class-A tournament to a double-elimination format for the eight teams that had made it to St. Cloud. That gave the Brewers a chance at redemption after the opening loss to Benson. But weather and officiating ruled the tournament.

The front page of the September 16, 1954, *Jordan Independent* tells a lot. Max's three-column headline reads: "Jordan Lost To Benson in First State Tourney Game Saturday, Won From Pipestone Sunday." A subhead gets into the heated details: "Poor Officiating And Rain Ganged Up On Brewers in Benson Game Creating Biggest Rhubarb in State Tourney History As Jordan Was Victimized 4-2, State Board Disallowed Protest Of Game."

"Biggest Rhubarb in State Tourney History. . ." Johnny Garbett was locked in a pitchers' duel with Benson's Ronnie Tucker. He took a no-hitter into the sixth inning, and he had the only Brewer hit in the game, a double in the third. Max Casey covered the game from the press box of "The Home of the Rox," St. Cloud's entry in the Northern League and a minor league affiliate of the New York Giants. His report continues with some of the important details on the rhubarb:

> In the top of the sixth, however, the game opened up as a result of two bad calls by Umpire Berg on balls and strikes, unfortunately both against the Brewers and in favor of Benson. With two away, nobody on base for Benson and a full count on the hitter, the ump called what appeared to be a strike a ball, putting a man on base. Garbett had two strikes on the next hitter, Bonsacker, when the ump made his second poor call in a row, calling what likewise appeared to be a perfect strike, a ball. The batter as a result of the life dribbled a ground ball to third, which was impossible to field because it had been intermittently raining for several innings and the ground was heavy, and which went for the first hit of the game off Garbett. A double and single in order for Benson netted them three runs and put them ahead 3-0.
>
> It was in the bottom of the sixth when the real rhubarb developed. By this time the rains were coming down heavily. Jordan had two men on base with two away and Dickie Nolden batting when the umpires stopped the game because of the heavy rain. Ironically, the Benson players were in full accord with the decision to halt the game at this point, evidently thinking they had the game sewed up and not realizing that unless the bottom of the sixth was completed the game would revert to end of the fifth when the score stood at 0-0. After comprehending the situation, the Benson players and manager began putting pressure on the umpires to resume play, knowing that if the rains continued they were only one strike away from victory.
>
> After about a forty-five minute stoppage of play, the plate umpire ordered resumption of play despite the fact it was still raining hard. Although the Jordan manager and players protested it was raining too hard to resume, Umpire Berg said he was having play resume on orders from a member or members of the state board of directors. Under playing rules, the umpire is sole judge in such cases. The umpire repeated his order to resume play right in the middle of another heavy downpour from the heavens and Dick Nolden was ordered back to the plate. With the field in muddy condition and while Dick had stepped out of the batter's box to clean the mud from his cleats, Tucker threw the ball across the plate and the umpire called it the third strike. When this happened the Jordan players rushed out to protest the call and a real rhubarb developed, causing another delay in the game, the ump's decision standing, however.
>
> The game was completed around 1 am under soggy conditions; the Brewers scored their two runs in the bottom of the seventh but lost, 4-2.

The closest man to the action in 1954 was Dick Nolden. He was holding the bat with the two strikes on him and the hard rain coming down. He said in a telephone interview from his home in Detroit Lakes, MN, that he kept doing everything he could think of to avoid going back into the batter's box, trying to bide time, precious seconds even, in hopes of the umpire calling the game unplayable on account of the rain.

"The umpire called the third strike without a pitch even being thrown," Nolden said.

"Pollard led the charge out of the dugout," Nolden said, "and those long legs of his were pumping up to his chest," as he rushed the umpire. But it didn't do any good. Nothing could. Umpire Berg was under orders from the state board to get the game in under any circumstances. The Fiddler had changed His tune. In the loser's bracket, Jordan crushed Pipestone, 11-4, with two draft choices doing a credible job on the mound for the Brewers and Johnny holding down an outfield position. Continued rains forced the tournament to be moved back, and the originally scheduled Jordan game with Spring Grove was moved from Thursday to Saturday night. Between 600 and 700 Jordan fans had made the first weekend's games. That was nearly half the town's population in 1954. The weekly newspaper published on its front page the mayor's formal request for businesses to close at 4 o'clock on Saturday and remain open Friday night instead to give Jordan fans opportunity to accompany the team to St. Cloud for the game against Spring Grove.

But Spring Grove had a trick up its sleeve, too, in the name of submarine pitcher Hugh Orphan, a draft choice from Lanesboro. Max Casey searched for the scoop on Orphan and learned that, of course, he'd been around. He had joined Lanesboro late in the season after having served for several years as player-manager of the Winona Chiefs in the hot Class-AA Southern Minny. "Orphan had the Brewers completely fooled with his unorthodox delivery," Max wrote. "Result was that he was nicked for only two hits during the nine innings, one by Jim Pollard and the other by Gene O'Brien."

Max's last headline of the 1954 Jordan Brewer baseball season hurt: "Brewers Ousted From State Meet By Spring Grove 1-0, On Sunday." According to Tom Melchior in *Scott County Baseball*, Johnny Garbett won 15 games on the mound for Jordan in 1954, one win less than Whitey Ford's 16-win season with the New York Yankees.

Neither Garbett's business partnership nor his marriage on May 1, 1954, was specious whim or residency ruse. He moved to Jordan because it was where he wanted to play ball. His wife and the eventual mother of their five children set about making a home for her husband–above The Corner Bar. But while these intentions could have been mitigating factors in declassifying the ace lefthander from ringer to regular, things couldn't have been too sweet for the new Mrs. Garbett, a native of Robbinsdale, MN, trying to make a home out of the apartment above the tavern at the hottest intersection on the hottest corner and street in downtown Jordan in 1954.

Gone With The Wind, the 1939 film rendition of Margaret Mitchell's 1936 novel nearly swept the 1940 Academy Awards, winning 10 of 13 honors. It played Wednesday through Saturday, December 18, one 7 pm showing nightly at the newly renovated wide-screen Jordan Theatre. It may have been prophetic in more ways than one, as the 1954 calendar year came to a close.

The 1954-55 NBA basketball season was Jim Pollard's last year in a Minneapolis Laker uniform. That meant he was finished as a Jordan Brewer, too, and the May 12, 1955 *Jordan Independent* reported that Pollard was at LaSalle College in Philadelphia, where he had accepted a position as head basketball coach.

Tex Erickson and Rollie Sunder, both defensive standouts, announced at least "semi-retirement." The problem behind the plate would be solved with Butch Kreuser from Shakopee for $170. But Johnny Garbett, ace of the staff, was back for 1955, and Bobby Shotliff had decided to come back home from his two-year stint at New Prague. Bud Kleidon, for $177, decided to come over from Prior Lake. Kleidon, who had played some professional ball in the 1940s, hit well and wanted to continue to play Class-A baseball. Moreover, he could play just about any position, including pitcher. He was a welcome addition, as were the Gittens brothers, Ed and Tommy, from Shakopee. Ed Gittens was paid $360 to play baseball in the 1955 season with the Jordan Brewers. He'd had a six-year career of minor league baseball that was interrupted for four years of military service during World War II. He's the same Ed Gittens, who had played in the hot Southern Minny at both Mankato and Winona. Ed Gittens had some game left in the summer of 1955, but mostly he was in a Brewer uniform to help out his 18-year-old brother, Tommy. He'd had a career batting average of .301 in professional baseball, including several seasons in the Northern League. Tommy, would die of Bright's Disease, according to a brief note in a 1956 *Jordan Independent*, after having been invited to spring training with the Milwaukee Braves that year. But in 1955 the Gittens brothers played wherever Manager Leon Hennes needed help, and they usually batted in the power slots. Interestingly, the MRL directors in their winter meetings rescinded "The Garbett Rule" by moving their residency deadline from December 1 to coincide with the state rule of March 1.

Garbett sat out a pre-season exhibition game with New Prague, according to the May 19 *Jordan Independent*. He reportedly had suffered a sprained ankle in an early workout and was resting and rehabilitating the injured ankle. A week later, he gave up the three runs in three innings of work in a 3-1 loss to New Prague in another pre-season warm-up game.

Bloomington, Shakopee, Chaska, and New Ulm all made overtures of interest in joining the Class-A Minnesota River League for the 1955 season. League directors wanted at least a sixth team, but it didn't happen for some reason. There was talk during the winter meetings of the league directors of giving up on Class-A baseball and dropping down to Class B. Three teams dropped out of the league: Prior Lake, Montgomery, and LeCenter–probably because they realized that they couldn't compete at the Class-A level with payroll or player quality. Whatever the reason, the March 24, 1955, *Jordan Independent* reported on the most recent of league meetings and the resolve of the five remaining teams to remain Class A. Directors cited a "lack of incentive" to play at the lower level and that Class-A competition "assures fans good baseball throughout the season."

The round-robin season schedule of a five-team league meant a bye for somebody each week. Jordan sat out the league opener of May 29. But the Brewers played an exhibition game on Memorial Day against Chaska in which Johnny Garbett pitched five solid innings in a 6-5 Brewer win in front of more than 250 avid baseball fans at Fairgrounds Park in Jordan.

Jordan finally opened the regular 1955 MRL season on Sunday, June 5, with a 4-1 win over the team Max Casey labeled the "Giants of the MRL," the St. Peter Saints. Johnny Garbett scattered seven hits in going the distance. Then something happened: "Army Worms Invade Scott County" was the front-page headline in the June 15, 1955, *Jordan Independent*. Meanwhile, on the sports pages of this and succeeding issues, one thing was becoming evident: Johnny Garbett had a sore arm. He was in the lineup in the top of the batting order, but he was usually playing centerfield. When he started on the mound, he needed relief, something new to him and baseball fans. He wasn't recording the strikeouts everyone had become accustomed to either. They weren't even being reported. Moreover, he was getting hit. Although he pitched well in a 10-5 mid-season win against the tough Le Sueur Green Sox, a report from the July 14 *JI* hinted at problems: "Garbett threw against Le Sueur Sunday, and he might not be ready to work that often this year." He asked for relief in the eighth inning after a couple of walks and a run-scoring single by none other than left-handed slugger John Freund. Johnny Garbett had never asked for relief help in his life. He always sucked it up and pitched out of jams, which usually resulted from his own easing up mentally, losing his concentration, or throwing lollipops to number eight and nine hitters. But his tailing fastball had lost its pop, and he couldn't throw his good curveball anymore. He could no longer reach back for more when he needed it. It was no longer there. Now there was pain.

Max Casey gave away a little of the story in the July 28 *Jordan Independent*'s review of the Brewer season to date, which included a surge from a slow 1-5 start to an 8-7 record in league play and an important win over a tough Excelsior ball club riding a 15-game winning streak. Excelsior featured Johnny's old teammate, also a pitcher, at the University of Minnesota–Whitey Skoog, the 5-11 shooting guard who averaged just under 10 points a game in his six-year career with the NBA Minneapolis Lakers before coaching basketball for years at Gustavus Adolphus College in St. Peter. But here's what Max reported about Johnny Garbett:

> Johnny Garbett has a slightly sore arm, and it would be wise to give him a little additional rest for the playoffs which will start in two weeks. John is a pretty valuable piece of equipment to have patrolling centerfield and his hitting is always potent.

Maybe the handwriting was on the wall or, rather instead, on page 3 in the July 7, 1955, *Jordan Independent* three-column, six-inch display advertisement for a grand opening of the Corner Bar by its new owners, Frank Betchwars and Rich Hartman. The bar and liquor business has always been tough: tough to manage; tough to operate; tough to lay off the sauce if you are behind the bar or working the door as a front man. It is tough on partnerships and on marriages. Maybe the partnership unwound. Garbett had no business experience before getting into the bar business a year earlier, and Johnson, according to Rich Hartman, "was always on the move," looking for the next opportunity. Maybe Mrs. Garbett, from the cities like her husband, didn't take to the life in the small town. Maybe the town didn't take to them.

More telling perhaps was the fact that the Jordan Brewers picked up another left-handed pitcher, Ken Reitmeier, of Eau Claire, Wisconsin, and nearby Shakopee. Johnny Garbett was 25 years old in 1955. Had he been healthy, he'd have been pitching important games. Moreover, the Baseball Bosses at Jordan would not have had to go after another pedigreed lefty. Kenny Reitmeier, who had pitched 135 innings and gone 8-7 with the same Eau Claire nine that nurtured Hammerin' Hank

Aaron in 1952, started the first playoff game against Le Sueur and chalked up 17 strikeouts in the 12-inning, 7-6 win over former Boston Red Sox and Minneapolis Miller pitcher Otey Clark and Le Sueur.

The next morning, the league gave the ballgame to Le Sueur as a result of their protest of Reitmeier, who, after two years of military service, had pitched again that summer for Eau Claire in the Northern League and for Boise in the Pioneer League, both Milwaukee Brave affiliates. Jordan appealed the protest ruling to the state board, which reversed the league's ruling and gave the win, once again, to Jordan. But the Brewers then lost to St. Peter in the next playoff game, 5-4, with Johnny Garbett again in centerfield, not on the mound. Jordan and Le Sueur, each with a loss, faced playoff elimination, Jordan losing to New Prague and Le Sueur to St. Peter, who ended up winning the league playoffs, then the Region 4A tournament, and then the Class-A state tournament at Chaska, with their drafted battery of Clark and Lee from LeSueur the heroes. Baseball Boss Max Casey really liked Johnny Garbett, but he knew the lefthander was damaged goods. He also knew that the veteran Otey Clark was not going back to Le Sueur for the 1956 season. A decade earlier and pitching for the Louisville Colonels, champions of the AAA American Association, Otey Clark had lost a shutout and then the lead, and finally the ballgame in the tenth inning to Jackie Robinson and the Montreal Royals, champions of the International League, in the Little World Series. Max went after Clark, and the 41-year-old pitcher who had gone 4-4 with a 3.07 ERA for the Boston Red Sox for $5,000 in 1945 responded to the overtures in a return letter to Max:

> Dear Mr. Casey:
>
> I will endeavor to give you the answers to some of the questions you asked in your recent letter.
>
> I would have to have $50 per game to pitch for your club plus $5 expense money for driving. On the nights that I wouldn't pitch would be in the bull pen or in relief (sic) I would have to have $20 and $5 expense money. As for exhibition games, I think $15 per game is fair to cover expense of driving etc.
>
> The catcher I mentioned is a good catcher, he caught in the Southern Minny league in 1954 and caught and managed in the Western Minny last year . . .
>
> This is the situation to date but however, we both have been contacted by other clubs and if and when we get together we will sign up. May I suggest you answer as soon as possible so I will know how you feel about us getting together.
>
> Very truly yours,
>
> Otey Clark

A P.S. followed:

> I don't know how you are fixed for other ball players, such as, infeilders (sic) and outfeilders (sic) but if you need any let me know as I know a couple good boys that aren't signed yet.

Either Max Casey didn't get back to Otey Clark in time, or he couldn't get the support from other Baseball Bosses to pay Clark what he wanted. It's also possible that St. Peter, which acquired the services of Clark for the 1956 season, simply outbid Jordan and other potential suitors. Our point is what the Otey Clark pedigree brought to river-town small-ball during the Golden Age of Baseball.

We think Johnny Garbett moved back home to Minneapolis after the 1955 baseball season ended, maybe even before it ended. But the next season, 1956, he drew the starting assignment of the opening game in the Minnesota River League– for Montgomery, which had rejoined the MRL, *against* Jordan! Here's the eyewitness report in the May 31, 1956, *Jordan Independent* under the sad headline, "Jordan Took Game From Montgomery–First Game of League Competition. Johnny Garbett Quits Baseball":

> Big offensive gun in the Jordan victory was Dick Naylor, who homered with Dick Nolden aboard in the fifth. Exit John Garbett. That blow had somewhat of a tragic significance. It brought relief to the mound for Montgomery's starting hurler, Johnny Garbett, who moved to right field. Johnny has pitched a lot of very fine baseball around the state and has done so for Jordan in the past. He formerly lived in The Hub. At the end of the game, this same likeable Mr. Garbett calmly announced his retirement from baseball, at least as a pitcher. Stating his shoulder, which troubled him throughout most of 1955 when at Jordan, again bothered him Sunday. He believes he can no longer hurl effective ball.

Johnny Garbett finally had enough. He had long nursed chronic elbow and back problems. The elbow had forced him to ease up on his curveball. Instead of dropping it off the table right at the plate, which he had been doing since he was 13 years old, he usually threw a flatter, wider breaking pitch that was easier on the elbow. The roundhouse that wouldn't work in Major League Baseball worked well enough in amateur A-Ball. Besides, when he needed it, he always had the good one in reserve. The back and elbow problems had cost him while at the University of Minnesota, and they cost him the shot he had with the Chicago Cubs after he got out of the service. Now the shoulder, and rest didn't seem to help. He'd rested it all winter. Garbett probably had a torn rotator cuff in his pitching shoulder. They don't heal completely without surgery and extensive rehabilitation. Getting a forkful of food to your mouth at the dinner table can be an ordeal, drinking a cup of coffee next to impossible. Orthopedic doctors didn't even diagnose the problem specifically in the 1950s much less repair it surgically. At 26 years of age, Johnny Garbett was on the shelf–an old pitcher with a sore arm.

Later that summer, in July and in time to get in the required number of games ahead of playoff roster jockeying, Johnny played an encore. He answered the curtain call at Orchard Lake, playing in the Class-B DRS League. The lake is located south of where the Burnsville Center shopping center sits today, near the Chart House restaurant off of County Rd. 5. Orchard Lake in 1956 was a good place for a family picnic on a Sunday afternoon. There were shade trees, a beach for swimming, and the lake offered good fishing. Moreover, the community had an ill-kept ballpark, where we're not sure. Possibly, it was the field used for softball that existed in the 1970s behind "Jack's," a bar and restaurant that was the only business in the area then on the northwest quadrant of the intersection of 35W and County Rd. 42.

Orchard Lake surprised everyone by opening the 1956 season with a 3-0 record. By the middle of July, they were 10-1, one game up on perennial powers Lonsdale and St. Benedict. Somebody was thinking that if they were going to make a run at a pennant and playoff title, they could use some help. Johnny Garbett might be just the help they needed. Max Casey's coverage of local baseball on his *Jordan Independent* "Sport Page" of July 19, 1956, included an eye-opening headline: "Garbett Signed At Orchard Lake–He Will Strengthen Club In Race For The Pennant In D.R.S.":

> News of the first order broke in this league this week when Orchard Lake signed former star Jordan hurler, Johnny Garbett. Adding that name to the roster easily makes Orchard Lake the strongest team in this circuit. As a pitcher, Garbett at this writing is unpredictable, although it is possible he can work in this league. Starting this season with Montgomery, his old shoulder injury returned in a game against Jordan on May 27th, and he stated at that time he was retiring from baseball. It is reported he will be used as an outfielder by Orchard Lake and will be available for relief duty on the mound.

Orchard Lake won the DRS League pennant and drew St. Benedict in the first round of the playoffs, a best-of-three series. Garbett won the first game for Orchard Lake, 3-2, with a long sacrifice fly in the 13th inning, St. Benedict took the second, and they won the rubber game, 9-4, in a game, appropriately enough, at Fairgrounds Park in Jordan, as Johnny Garbett threw one and two-thirds innings of relief in the losing cause, probably his last stint ever on a pitching mound.

He's off the radar screen for 1957, and not surprisingly, he shows up, "back home," in the Minneapolis Kozy's Bar team picture after a 1958 state tournament appearance by the Class-A team. But he's identified in the photo as "co-manager."

Johnny Garbett loved baseball, as did most of the young men who had the game's gold bug in their system. He couldn't stay away from it. Dick Bonneville, in the July 17, 1974, Midweek Sun wrote under the headline, "Garbett led '45 legion nine":

> Garbett besides playing excellent golf, coaches a Babe Ruth team in the Robbinsdale area. "I can't get away from baseball," admits John, "because it's been a part of my (life) since I was 13 over (in) Northeast."

An August 4, 1977 article in a northern suburban *Post* weekly mentioned John Garbett as an assistant coach on the 1975 and 1977 Robbinsdale Mickey Mantle state championship teams. Moreover, his daughter, Nancy, at age 12, wrote Bonneville in 1974, "was one of the first girls in the nation to play on a Major League Little League baseball team."

Johnny Garbett turned up at the ballpark in Jordan for an old-timer's game in July of 1979. It was just an informal gathering of old Jordan Brewers, but regardless of how much he got paid to play baseball at Jordan in the Minnesota River Valley, his participation in the reunion speaks volumes about his three-year visit in the mid-1950s when he made fools of batters chasing his deuce into the dirt.

John Freund

He was the best ballplayer I ever saw around here.

— Earl Dean, Mgr., Jordan Brewers

Anybody who ever saw Mickey Mantle play baseball was treated to an unforgettable gift from the gods of Mt. Olympus. Anybody who ever had the privilege of stepping onto a baseball diamond at the same time as Mickey Mantle, whether on the same team or with the opposition, had to have experienced a kiss from the immortal Aphrodite herself. Mickey Mantle, more than any other ballplayer during the Golden Age of Baseball, personified on the field what the greatness of the gilded age was all about.

The demons resulting from child abuse and the consequences of lifestyle choices aside, Mickey Mantle was truly blessed: He hit for average and he hit with power from both sides of the plate; he could drag bunt or beat out infield dribblers for base hits, and his speed on the base paths was electrifying; he had a rifle arm; and it was all packaged in an All-American boyish grin and an Oklahoma angel's charm. At least some of that ethereal stuff couldn't help but rub off on anyone else on the field. John Freund, playing for Class-C Springfield, Missouri, in the Western Association, played against Mantle, a switch-hitting shortstop then with the Joplin Miners in 1950. While John Freund truly appreciated anybody of any age anywhere who put on a baseball or softball uniform, Mickey Mantle was his favorite ballplayer.

Freund saw the 18-year-old Mantle hit .383, with 26 homeruns, and, according to Wikipedia, 136 RBIs for Joplin, which was in his Oklahoma home backyard. The hitting clinic he put on as a kid foreshadowed a similar kind of year he would have as a young man in 1956 with the Yankees, when he would hit .353, with 52 homeruns and 130 RBIs. Not even the presence in Boston of The Great One–Ted Williams–could prevent Mantle from winning the coveted Triple Crown and MVP award.

Meanwhile, in 1950 in his third year of professional baseball and 20 years old at the end of the season, John Freund hit .253 in 110 games, according to online sources. Mickey Mantle would play about 40 games of the 1951 season with AAA-Kansas City and finish with the New York Yankees. While The Mick got the call from the Yankees, John Freund got the call from Uncle Sam. After basic training, then more advanced training in radio communications at a number of different bases, John was shipped west to Camp San Luis Obispo in California, about half way between Los Angeles and San Francisco. He made a good army ball club in a league of all-service military teams made up of many professional ballplayers, the most prominent in name being Del Crandall, who had already caught two years in the National League with the Boston Braves and who would return to anchor the Braves in Milwaukee, catching the likes of Lew Burdette and Warren Spahn through the 1950s.

Crandall played for Fort Ord, which was loaded with professional baseball players, including five other major leaguers besides Crandall. Another eight players on the roster were the property of major league teams, playing at levels as high as AAA. The point is that this West Coast military service league in 1952 was no bush league, schoolyard, or beer league brand of baseball. Players were motivated just to play baseball, to play hard, to win. Being on the baseball team allowed them to escape ordinary soldier time such as KP duty and the cleaning of latrines with toothbrushes. Ballplayers ate better than ordinary servicemen, too. Army ball was all about company morale, esprit de corps, and the bragging rights for the generals and other COs at officers' clubs.

John played more than 60 games during the warm months, playing shortstop and doing some pitching as well. Selected Freund family scrapbook issues of the *Camp San Luis Obispo Transmitter* from 1952 report John hitting and pitching well on a good ball club, the Signalmen, which finished the season with a record of 46-15 after starting red hot with 19 consecutive wins. Half way through the season, John pitched a no-hitter with 18 strikeouts. His best day hitting was a Freund slugfest of 5 for 6, with two homeruns and three doubles.

None of this went unnoticed to John's baseball owners. Indeed, the Cubs and other major league organizations watched closely their properties on loan to Uncle Sam during the Korean War period.

Upon his discharge, service to country fulfilled, John Freund had the opportunity to return to professional baseball, according to his brother and sons. He turned it down, according to Bob Freund, John's younger brother. He'd had five years of bus rides, cheap hotels, restaurant food, barracks, and mess halls. It was time for some home cookin'. Besides, had John Freund chosen to stay in professional baseball, and had that big league team remained the Chicago Cubs, he would have run into a major obstacle at his favorite position: "Mr. Cub." Ernie Banks broke in with the Cubs in 1953 and would be a fixture at shortstop for approximately half of his 19-year career, which included 512 homeruns and entry into Cooperstown in 1977. Money was a factor, too. As good of a shortstop as Ernie Banks was, he earned all of $2,000 in 1953 and $6,000 in his first full season, 1954, as the Chicago Cub shortstop, according to on-line sources. John Freund probably made $150 a month as a corporal in the army in 1952, according to the best guess of a retired navy captain and student of military history. But with clothing, room and board, some entertainment, transportation, and health insurance paid for, the money was all "discretionary allowance."

Dick Erickson, long-time Freund friend, co-worker at Rahr, and golfing partner, teammate and officiating partner, said John told him that he had been sold to the Chicago White Sox while in the army. Indeed, an "Official Notice of Disposition of Player's Contract and Services," dated December 27, 1950, shows John being assigned to the Topeka Owls in the Western Association. A follow-up letter from the Topeka Baseball Club, Inc., signed by E. L. "Butch" Nieman, Mgr., acknowledges a letter from John and his returned contract. Butch wrote, "Hope you can get into something that will enable you to play some baseball while in the service." He asked for John's date of induction and serial number, "so that we can place you on our National Defense Service List."

The letter closes with, "You will be given every opportunity upon your discharge." The Topeka Owls were affiliated with the Chicago White Sox. That meant the White Sox, not the Cubs, owned John Freund as of the winter of 1950-'51.

"He didn't care for that," Erickson said, being a lifelong Cubs fan, and he couldn't have cared for another assignment in the Western Association where, during the baseball months of July, August, and September, temperatures average in the mid- to high-90s, with humidity levels at 75 percent and higher. Moreover, the bus rides would be even longer from Topeka than they had been from Springfield in 1950. And he knew that if he didn't hit like he should, he'd never see Wrigley Field or Comiskey Park. But John had two years to think about it. Meanwhile, Uncle Sam owned him.

While John couldn't have known it in 1953 when he made his decision, he would have faced huge obstacles with either Chicago baseball organization eventually: Ernie Banks with the Cubs; Luis Aparicio, nine-time Gold Glove winner and another Hall of Famer, who would debut in 1956 with the White Sox. The handwriting was on the wall in the invisible ink of time. Looking back 60 years later as a special guest of MSNBC's broadcast of *Morning Joe* from Wrigley Field in Chicago on the 100th anniversary of the iconic baseball park on April 23, 2014, television hosts asked Ernie Banks, "What does all this mean to you –the Cubs, Wrigley Field, and baseball?"

"It's my life. It's my Bible," Ernie Banks replied, and then repeated, "It's my life."

He couldn't have given any more telling testimony to the difference between the span of time that marked his 19-year career and the post-Golden Age of baseball since, when baseball morphed into a major business enterprise at one level, and "a hobby," a pastime, recreation, and "just a game" at other levels.

"He told me one time," Erickson said of John Freund, "that because he filled out, got bigger in the army, that he should have been an outfielder, that he'd have had his best chance of making the Big Leagues as an outfielder." But John was a shortstop, even though the prototypical Big League shortstop was 160 pounds and usually the quickest man on the team. John was quick for a big man, and he could run with anybody, he knew, but he was pushing 200 pounds when he got out of the army. Once made up, baseball minds tend to stay set, as if in concrete. Shortstops were not John Freund-sized men in the 1950s.

Because of Major League Baseball's reserve clause in the standard baseball player's contract, which effectively shackled a player like chattel property to his owner, John Freund would likely have remained mired in the minor leagues. Not until Curt Flood's challenge of the reserve clause in 1969, although unsuccessful, would players make headway in their drive for free agency. That would come in 1975 with the removal of the clause from the standard contract. This gave the players' union some teeth at the negotiating table, and, together with the diluting value of the dollar due to continuous inflation, and huge television contracts, led to the obscene salaries of the modern ballplayer–and equally obscene prices for tickets, beer, and hot dogs paid by fans at the ballpark.

John Freund knew years later that a buck went quite a bit further in 1954 than it did 10, 20, and more years later. But he also knew that the buck was a lot more elusive in 1954. You had to work for it. Baseball just didn't pay that well. "He told me one time," his son Jack said, "that he couldn't raise a family on what he was making playing professional ball."

John Freund returned home in 1953 to South Minneapolis where he worked for his father at Cepro, a Rahr-owned grain elevator in South Minneapolis. He worked for maybe $1.50 an hour, his brother, Bob, thought. He worked 40-hour weeks and during the summer got in an additional 10 hours of overtime each week at time-and-a half. He played baseball for Rochester, too, and a "1954 Southern Minnesota Baseball League Official Contract" with the Rochester Royals shows John making an additional $400 a month during the summer to play typically three baseball games a week. Some admittedly rough mathematical calculations show that John Freund made about $300 more in 1954 working for Rahr-Cepro and playing baseball for the Rochester Royals than the great Ernie Banks made playing shortstop for the Chicago Cubs.

John, and later Bob, too, worked unloading barley from railroad cars that came in from all over, especially Canada and North Dakota. The barley is teased and cultured into the malt product that Rahr produced and sold, and continues to sell to brewers all over the country. But three days a week in the summer of 1953, John Freund drove to Rochester for a home game with the Rochester Royals of the class of Minnesota "amateur" baseball–the Southern Minnesota League, or to any one of seven other cities for an away game. He drove to Austin, Albert Lea, Owatonna, Faribault, Winona, Waseca, and Mankato. He batted .265 while playing as many as five different positions, including some relief pitching, according to scrapbook clippings from the 1954 *Rochester Post-Bulletin*. "I'd go along sometimes," Bob Freund said, "and I would drive home, so John and this other guy who lived near us in Minneapolis–Platzer, a catcher–could get an hour or two of sleep. Highway 52 was mostly just two lanes then," he said, "and John would tell me, 'Now take it easy. Don't speed.'"

Some of those games that were played under the lights might end late into the night and it would be midnight before the boys got on the highway heading home. It could be after 2 am when John got to bed, and he started shoveling barley at 7 am, under the strict direction of a tough, old German boss–his father.

John Freund would make the long drives in 1954, too, and he began the season on fire at the plate. Then he slumped, due in part to an injury to his hand when hit by a pickoff throw to first base. But John also got married that summer. This great transition, which marks the end of youth and one gateway to manhood, weighed on him. John Freund had trouble concentrating on baseball in 1954. His mind was on more important things. He was listening to The Fiddler, dancing the Dance of Life, and his batting average fell to under .250 while, again, playing wherever the manager asked him to play. He played a lot of first base after the injury to his hand,

and he liked the infield best, especially shortstop, which he loved playing, according to Bob Freund. But he would be asked to play centerfield more and more through the year, because of his range and his arm, and the needs of the team.

The Chicago Cubs had liked his range and arm enough to sign John Freund to a professional baseball contract right out of high school. In fact, two days after graduating from Roosevelt High School in South Minneapolis in 1948, he left for a tryout with the Cubs at their farm school at Janesville, Wisconsin, which had a team that played in the Wisconsin League. He played in 59 games of what remained of that summer, then 111 games the following year, 1949, with the Sioux Falls Canaries in the Northern League. Sounds like a storybook beginning to a megamillion dollar super athlete's life. But that's not how it was then. Top salary in the 1950s and '60s was $100,000, and that kind of money was paid to an exclusive cohort of major leaguers: first, Hank Greenberg; then, DiMaggio, Williams, Mantle, and Mays. Minor leaguers barely earned enough to afford to buy a round of beer in a local tavern. John Freund's 1949 Chicago Cub contract to play with Sioux Falls paid him $200 a month.

A note in the Freund papers, presumably written in the hand of John Freund on his first summer, 1948, with the Janesville ball club reads, "Got a $300 bonus after I was with them a month." Still, it was not expected, and in 1948, $300 wasn't chump change. Like most ballplayers in those days, John worked in the off-season. He worked at the Sears store in south Minneapolis in the off-seasons of his three professional baseball years. Minor leaguers were playing on hope and a dream. But even that nearly failed to materialize for John Freund. He suffered from a heart murmur as a fifth-grader, but grew out of it over the course of five years. In 1945, when he was 15 years old, John was accidentally shot with a .22 rifle by a friend, the bullet piercing a kidney and shattering his spleen. Hospitalized for nearly a month, according to family records, he required 110 shots of penicillin, and the spleen was surgically removed. Then he developed peritonitis, which required another surgical procedure.

While some wonder at the young man's luck, others marvel at the Great Design–The Fiddler's choreography of this Dance. John Freund lived to look for a ballgame everyday after school just as he had before the accident. He'd ride his bike for a mile and more, past South Minneapolis city parks, looking for the unmistakable sights and sounds of a ball game. Everyday, John Freund looked for a game.

Years later, nearing the end of his Dance, while going for drives with one or both of his sons, Jack and Jerry, he would lament the absence of kids and ballgames in the Shakopee parks, according to Jerry. He'd wonder what the kids were doing. It bothered him. The fields were so nice these days, and they weren't being used. According to Jerry, the kids, John Freund's own grandchildren and their friends, were home in bedrooms after school or during summer days and even on vacations, texting on their smart phones and playing games on their computers. Texting . . . tweeting . . . and posting or "friending" on Facebook or another "social networking" computer website, and shopping had replaced ball playing as favorite activities among young people.

All of this and the empty parks bothered John Freund. But he grew up and learned to play ball long before we were told by a prominent politician that "it takes a village" to raise a child rather than the presence of a mother and a father in the lives of their children. He grew up long before the gay community bullied the American psychological and psychiatric associations to remove homosexuality from the DSM IV–the diagnostic manual of disorders. And he grew up long before the feminists lobbied the National Weather Service into alternating male names in 1979 with the names that were exclusively female in gender since the practice of naming storms began in 1950. Boys didn't play with dolls during John Freund's adolescence. Few boys braved the ridicule of even taking music lessons unfortunately. They didn't even play board games, unless it was raining outside or a snowstorm was raging and their shoebox of baseball cards was complete and in order. Boys played ball. Some girls did, too.

John Freund lived to grow up into a great athlete and a fine young man at Roosevelt High School, playing baseball and hockey. That he played basketball on a church team and in the service speaks again to his remarkable athleticism. Hockey and hoops usually don't mix in the same jock. Years later, Rochester columnist Dave Pennington quoted John's high school baseball coach, Wayne Courtney, on John: "He was one of the nicest boys I ever had." That's what everyone who knew him still says about John Freund: "He was such a nice guy." That's as remarkable as his athleticism, for in most of the great ones at any level, narcissism usually bloats the waistline or the ego and they end up blowing gas out of one end or the other.

John Freund did neither. Perhaps the bullet's near-miss was part of The Fiddler's Grand Design, helping to forge the mettle in a young man that would, like the value of the Midas metal, gold, endure for all time. Character counts. "He never bragged about things," Butch Kreuser said. "He was always the perfect gentleman."

As for his waistline, John Freund liked his beer–as did most baseball players and employees of Rahr, where it was very nearly an understandable requirement of the job. At a minimum, you didn't want to be seen ordering or drinking a mixed drink in public. Beer at Rahr Malting remained part of the German tradition in which it is considered "liquid bread." The malt company couldn't have had a better ambassador. But after his ball-playing days were over, and he played softball until he was 55 years old, John played golf four or five times a week, walking with a pull-cart for his clubs well into his retirement years, playing, his son said, to a seven handicap, which Dick Erickson, his playing partner said was a 10, at local public courses. That means, more times than not, he was shooting in the high 70s to low 80s. "He was just a natural," his brother Bob said, and although he batted left handed in baseball, he played golf right handed. "He could really hit a golf ball," Erickson said.

John played touch football, basketball, and volleyball, as well as softball and baseball as long as he could play without embarrassing himself or his team. But he tore an Achilles tendon in 1972, according to the family's biographical notes, which required surgery. That slowed him down as far as playing sports was concerned, so he took up officiating. He refereed high school basketball and umpired baseball, beginning in the late 1960s. He took a whistle to high school football games, too, beginning in 1968, and he began officiating MIAC (Minnesota Intercollegiate

Athletic Conference) games in 1975, which Dick Erickson thought might have been even earlier.

Erickson said that he and John Freund officiated a lot of games over 20-plus years, and that John's officiating partners for MIAC games included his old catcher from Rochester and Glencoe baseball days–Don Wheeler. More surprising yet, Erickson said that he and John umpired, for the few years of its existence, the American Softball Association's professional slow-pitch games, which were played in the Twin Cities at the old Midway Stadium in St. Paul. He said the big names like Joe Pepitone, the former New York Yankee first baseman; Norm Cash from the Detroit Tigers; and Billy "White Shoes" Johnson, who provided electrifying punt and kickoff returns for the Houston Oilers of the NFL, played for teams from Louisville, Milwaukee, Chicago, Detroit, Philadelphia, and New Jersey, as well as the Minnesota team. Erickson said that a snow fence had been installed inside the confines of the park, but that "they were putting the balls over the regular baseball fences." Old Midway Stadium, remember, was built for the St. Paul Saints in the late 1950s, a AAA baseball team in the American Association. Fences were 321 feet down the lines and 420 feet to straight away centerfield. That would make for power alleys of approximately 375 feet. But the technology built into the Easton metal bat in use by then made fences virtually irrelevant and the frequency of homeruns absurd in softball as well as in baseball.

The 1950s are usually characterized as serene, peaceful times. The Yankees were dominating baseball, and their dominance of The City motivated the Giants and the Dodgers to finally move west in 1958. Don Larsen pitched the only perfect game in the history of the World Series in 1956, the same year that Mickey Mantle won the Triple Crown.

Inflation and unemployment were at record lows, reflecting healthy growth and perpetuating it. Ike was shown each October in newspaper photographs holding a double-barrel shotgun and a brace of mallards after the morning shoot on the Duck Hunting Opener. He golfed regularly at Augusta National, home of Bobby Jones and The Masters' Golf Tournament each spring. The tree named after him that came into play on the No. 17 tee shot went down finally in a storm in 2014. He took enough time off from his recreational pursuits to promote, then sign, the Federal-Aid Highway Act of 1956, which created and funded a 41,000 mile "National System of Interstate and Defense Highways." Germany's autobahn had impressed President Eisenhower while he was leading the Allies' efforts in Germany during World War II.

Hawaii and Alaska were moving toward statehood in the 1950s, a status they realized in 1959. Dr. Jonas Salk's vaccine would be declared "safe and effective" in 1955 and begin being used to knock out the dreaded disease of polio, which would cripple and kill thousands in the wake of its periodic viral epidemics.

Cigarette advertisements inundated television and magazines. "Buy 'em by the carton," became Arthur Godfrey's trademark plug for Chesterfields. "Lucky Strike means fine tobacco," was heard over and over, as was "Winston tastes good–like a cigarette should." People in the advertising scenes were always attractive and upbeat. The message was clear and consistent: It was cool, hip, exciting to smoke cigarettes. Studies were cited even then, but with "More doctors recommend Camel cigarettes than any other," and "More doctors smoke Chesterfield cigarettes than any other." Kent cigarettes were special because of their micronite filters. They were made of asbestos, we would learn years later.

Paul Hornung, "The Golden Boy," who has the distinction of being the only winner of the Heisman Trophy from a team, Notre Dame, with a losing record, smoked a Marlboro in a tan overcoat from the stands while overlooking Lambeau Field in Green Bay. The Marlboro Man, handsome, rugged, and weathered in leather vest, cowboy boots, blue jeans, and chaps atop a horse, looped rope in hand, working cattle on a ranch, appealed to another part of men. Real men were the strong, silent type that smoked Marlboro. The concept and advertising campaign were successful in reversing a common perception that Marlboro cigarettes, like all filtered cigarettes, were for women. Until The Marlboro Man, real men smoked unfiltered Lucky Strike, Camel, Chesterfield, or Pall Mall cigarettes. Ballplayers in dugouts throughout the land began switching to Marlboro and other filtered brands of cigarettes.

Bill "Hopalong" Cassidy didn't smoke or drink. William Boyd played the squeaky-clean cowboy version of the fictional character created in 1904 by the author, Clarence E. Mulford. "Hoppy" wore black well, including a black hat, but he rode a big white horse named "Topper" while taking on evil and injustice in the 66 films produced. The character and films were popular serials, then even more popular as adapted for television and radio in the early 1950s. The primary television advertiser we remember was the dairy industry or perhaps a specific dairy producer. "Hoppy" would be seen in a studio after an episode of rounding up cattle rustlers, drinking a large glass of milk. The theme: "If you want to be like Hoppy, you've got to drink like Hoppy."

But the most significant advertising from our perspective was for another beverage–beer. Moreover, it was local, but probably repeated throughout the nation, for it spoke to a national trend. Two weekly newspaper display ads tell the story of baseball's brother–the brewing industry. The August 23, 1951, *Shakopee Argus-Tribune* carried a six-inch, three-column ad with a heading, "**The American Way**" in large, bold type over a baseball scene of a base runner sliding safely into second or third base just ahead of the ball:

"He's safe!'" the copy reads. . .

"That's the umpire's exciting cry in America's greatest sport–Baseball.

And it's the American Way, after watching nine innings of baseball to relax and enjoy a sandwich and a cool, refreshing glass of Minnesota-brewed beer, for in this friendly, freedom-loving land of ours–

Beer belongs . . . enjoy it

Published on behalf of the following Minnesota Breweries:

Bub's Winona

Gluek Minneapolis

Hauenstein New Ulm

Royal Bohemian Duluth
Fitger Duluth
Grain Belt Minneapolis
Kiewel Little Falls
Fleckenstein Faribault
Hamm St. Paul
Schell New Ulm
Schmidt St Paul

Beer–America's beverage of moderation

It was a nice, tasteful advertisement. It aimed its product at baseball fans. But in 1945, just six short years earlier, and with over eight million of the nation's largest beer-drinking age group busy taking care of business with the nation's enemies in Europe and the Pacific, one brewer out of the 11 above advertised by itself in the July 26, 1945, *Jordan Independent*. This was more typical of competitive industry.

The Schutz and Hilgers Brewery in Jordan had closed with Prohibition in 1918, but it re-opened and was thriving until the World War II rationing quotas of grain hobbled the small brewery with its 30,000 barrels of production a year then and a distribution radius of perhaps 30 miles. Gluek Brewing Company of Minneapolis, 200,000 barrels-a-year strong, sensed weaknesses in local competition and saw the opportunity to expand its market.

The Gluek ad was four columns wide and 10 or 12 inches in depth. That's a large display ad in any day, and it was tasteful. It pictured a gentleman in a suit lifting a glass of beer to his mouth. The ad copy is mature and low-keyed. It merely suggests, "A lot of people seem to like Gluek's Beer best of all. Maybe you will, too."

"Better try it anyway. Put a few bottles of Gluek's in the icebox where it will be handy. Have some tonight –tomorrow –the day after . . .."

**"Gluek's
The beer for the man who knows."**

Schutz and Hilgers tried to restart their brewery in Jordan after the war. They failed. They sold out to an Arizona brewer, who almost immediately sold it to the Mankato Brewing Company who, in turn, tried running Jordan's brewery as a branch. They closed their Jordan operations in 1948 and their Mankato operations in 1967. Gluek Brewing Co. was finished in 1964. In fact, only one brewery out of the 11 who jointly participated in the 1951 ad in the Shakopee weekly has survived to this day–the August Schell Brewing Company of New Ulm.

Every other brewery was out of business by 1976–all part of the massive consolidation that occurred nationwide in the brewing industry and resulted in two survivors–Budweiser and Miller. The years are significant for their approximate coincidence with The Golden Age of Baseball. What happened to beer and the brewing industry happened to ballplayers and baseball. What engineers in an engineering firm call "the fluff "–the packaging, the distribution, the advertising and promotion, the availability–have all gotten better in both baseball and beer. But the quality of play and the quality of brew aren't even close to what they were during The Golden Age, at least not in the Minnesota River Valley.

Norm Growe pumped in 70 points for Foley High School in a basketball game in 1958 without the benefit of a three-point shooting line. That would remain a single-game Minnesota high school scoring record until the three-point line was painted on basketball floors and charter schools would beat up one another with 100-point performances that were allowed as new records.

The Cold War was on during the 1950s, and "flash points" would flare up around the world from time to time, reminding everyone again how dangerous the world really was. The United States and Great Britain were continually testing nuclear weapons. Soviet spies who had infiltrated American agencies during World War II got our classified documents into the hands of the Soviet Union, who then built their own nuclear bombs and began testing them, too. The Rosenberg's, Julius and Ethel, were tried and convicted of conspiracy to commit espionage in 1951. Two years later, they were put to death in an electric chair. Soon, Wisconsin Senator Joseph McCarthy began finding Communists in every corner of the government and throughout the country. He was soon proven to be both a blowhard and a bigot. Nonetheless, a common refrain was heard: "Better to be dead than Red." The Korean War, which occurred during the first three years of the 1950s, was another flashpoint with the potential for wider involvement, as the Soviets backed North Korea, and the U.S. supported South Korea. To this day, it's a stalemate, with 30,000 to 40,000 U.S. troops stationed in South Korea and Aegis-based cruisers patrolling the peninsula to protect the South Koreans.

Citizens in Hungary and Czechoslovakia protested Soviet oppression, which prompted mobilization of The Red Army. Front-page news photos showed Soviet tanks bearing down on peasants in Budapest and Prague who were barricaded behind upturned wheelbarrows, tables, chairs, planks, and sticks, and "armed" with glass bottles filled with gasoline and a rag stuffed into them for a fuse–the Molotov cocktail. While the Soviet Union had been our ally during World War II, stories were slowly leaking out about "Uncle" Joe Stalin having purged his nation of as many as 50 million of his own citizens. The Russians always meant business. Their ideology was based on the tenet that the ends justify the means.

Indeed, Nikita Khrushchev, who succeeded Stalin, reportedly told a group of Western ambassadors in the Polish embassy in Moscow in 1956: "We will bury you." What he actually meant has been debated, but he said it, and there was no doubt we were in a lasting struggle that would remain ideological and more. In 1957, the USSR launched the world's first intercontinental ballistic missile, with the first man-made satellite, *Sputnik*, aboard. Game on! And we were behind, because the technical and military implications of the space race had profound influence throughout the world.

Egypt's President Nasser nationalized in 1956 the Suez Canal, which connects the Eastern end of the Mediterranean with the Red Sea–an important shipping route. While Ike played it cool, Britain and France supported Israel and efforts to take back control of the Suez. This nearly brought in the Soviets on the side of Egypt to give them a foothold they had been seeking in the Middle East. Tensions never subsided completely, and 10 years later, in what has been called "The Six-Day War," Israel took out air defense and strike capabilities of the Arab nations–all of them.

Culturally, Rock and Roll was born as a distinct musical genre from the amalgamation of rhythm and blues, gospel, and a hint of country. Elvis became "the king," but hits also came from Little Richard, Jerry Lee Lewis, Buddy Holly, Bobby Darin, and others. The Everly Brothers followed up their No. 1 hit of 1956, "Bye-Bye Love," with another No.1 in 1957–"Wake Up Little Susie." It stirred the moral foundations of the country, because somebody read into the song's lyrics that a teenage boy and girl had fallen asleep after having had sex in a car at a drive-in movie theatre. Indeed, radio stations in Boston were banned from playing the song. School Sisters of Notre Dame nuns at St. John the Baptist Catholic School in Jordan, Minnesota, strictly forbade their seventh and eighth-grade charges from listening to the song.

The students rushed home after school to tune radios into WDGY, a Twin Cities AM station that specialized in popular music, waiting to hear "Wake Up Little Susie." What was so bad, these kids everywhere wanted to know. What did they need protection from? Somebody bought the 45 rpm record so they could play the song over and over again. Nobody could figure out what the flap was about. Two kids had fallen asleep at a boring movie and woke up six hours after they were supposed to be home.

The Everly Brothers were in good artistic company in Boston, which had also banned Walt Whitman's *Leaves of Grass*, Earnest Hemingway's *The Sun Also Rises* and *A Farewell to Arms*, among numerous other literary works.

Marlon Brando and James Dean burst onto the scene in Hollywood with *On the Waterfront* and *Rebel Without a Cause*. The Beat Generation had little toehold in the Midwest, but as the progenitor of the Hippie Movement of the 1960s, it had gurus in writers like Jack Kerouac and Alan Ginsberg. These new anti-heroes didn't go with the flow. They didn't belong. They were anti-establishment before the phrase and concept were used. They had attitude and charisma.

Marilyn Monroe had sex appeal. At age 27, she owned the silver screen and the desires of every man in the world in the 1950s. Joe DiMaggio, 39 and three years retired from his ownership of Yankee centerfield, was still worshipped in New York, a post-playing day reverence that included booing of his successor, Mickey Mantle. The two stars, Joe and Marilyn, met in 1952; they married in January of 1954. The marriage would not last the year. Joe was a recluse who loved privacy. Marilyn came alive in front of the camera or a crowd, especially a crowd of men. She claimed "mental cruelty" in their divorce. He claimed she was the only woman he ever loved, and he was heartbroken in 1962 upon hearing of her death, in what was officially called a suicide from an overdose of sleeping pills. Joe DiMaggio sent roses to her gravesite every week for the rest of his life. Dramatic stuff–as though it were all an extra-inning game that couldn't end. Baseball and life.

The most important development at home in the 1950s had roots in, and help from, baseball. Jackie Robinson had broken the so-called color barrier in Major League Baseball with the Brooklyn Dodgers in 1947. His competitive play led the

Dodgers to six National League pennants and finally a World Series championship in 1955 over the Yankees. But it was his character and temperament in defiance of racial abuse and constant on field racial slurs from opposing players and fans that define his contribution to the game and the country. In fact, his response of "turning the other cheek," ignoring insults, and transcending the abuse with superior play on the field served as models for Dr. Martin Luther King, Jr., and the Civil Rights Movement, which gained traction throughout the 1950s.

John Freund met his wife and the mother of their four children after a ball game in Rochester. He and Patricia Ann Ryan were married in July of 1954. In 1955, the 40 to 50 games with their 150-mile round-trip drive three times a week were too much.

Freund was far from finished as a ballplayer, however. He and Otey Clark, the 40-year-old, much-traveled former Boston Red Sox, Minneapolis Miller, and Toledo Mud Hen pitcher, who had managed briefly and pitched relief for Rochester in 1954, joined the Le Sueur Green Sox of the Class A Minnesota River League as its two allowed "outside" players. The league was down to just five teams and would play a 16-game schedule, which, with all games much closer to the Freund home in South Minneapolis, was much more family friendly. But Le Sueur and Class-A baseball everywhere were in trouble.

A July 20, 1955, *Le Sueur News Herald* explained the dilemma in terms of simple economics: The Green Sox needed to average 1,000 paid admissions at home games in order to break even; they were running just 300 per game with a good ball club. Lifetime Le Sueur resident and a batboy for the Green Sox when his father, Joe, played third base for the Green Sox in the mid-50s, Dan Driscoll said he had tried for years to learn just how much players like Freund and Clark were paid. He admitted that he never did find out, but he did learn that the town's sugar daddy, Green Giant, which was headquartered in Le Sueur for years, had been the source of the cash needed to pay the players and keep the team operating.

Freund and Clark lived up to their billing, and each earned his pay. Both started the season hot. Clark gave up just seven hits in a 5-4 Le Sueur win over New Prague in the opening game of Minnesota River League play. Freund was three for four, with a two-run homerun. But here's how the June 1, 1955 *Le Sueur News Herald* reported it:

> John Freund, veteran shortstop beginning his first season with the Green Sox, proved to be a valuable asset to Sox slugging power as he pounded out one round trip, a three bagger and drove in three of the five Sox tallies.

Clark was 3-0 after the first three games, with an ERA of 1.24; Freund was batting an even .500, with two homeruns, including what was described as "a 400-footer" at Jordan's Fairgrounds Park in a Le Sueur win. If onlookers could call the Freund blast "a 400-footer," then it cleared the county fair's horse barn that butted up against the fence in right to right-centerfield, for John was a pull hitter. If the ball cleared the barn, then the gawkers never saw it land, and if they didn't see it land, chances are the ball got wet. Sand Creek winds down the first base line, then around behind the outfield fence, turning west and through town until it turns north and heads toward the Minnesota River. We think the creek and the fence are pretty much where they were 50 to 60 years ago, but the scoreboard isn't. The old scoreboard was to the foul-line side of the light tower. The existing scoreboard is the right-field power alley aiming point. It's 342 feet from home plate. Another 81 feet gets you to the bank of the creek, and another 66 feet gets you to the retaining wall and creek-side foundation of the old Ruppert's Bar building at 224 Water Street. If John Freund's ball got wet, it went 420 to 490 feet, and it's possible he banked it off the brick and concrete wall on the far side of Sand Creek.

It was quite a poke, but Gordy Gelhaye hit the longest ball ever hit to the right side at Fairgrounds Park. Mark Beckman, 1975 graduate of Jordan High School, hails Brad Gulden of Carver and Chaska High School as having hit a ball that stopped up against the curb at Geno's Tap Room on Broadway and Water Streets. Gulden is listed in online sources at 5-10, 175 lbs. He was a catcher and a left-handed hitter who signed with the Los Angeles Dodgers in the post-expansion years of Major League Baseball. Still, he played 11 seasons of professional baseball, most of it at the AAA level. He caught 40 games for the New York Yankees in 1979 but batted just .163. In 1984, he caught 107 games for the Cincinnati Reds of the National League, batting .226. His lifetime minor league batting average of .271 is respectable. We saw him, but he was pretty young then, playing Babe Ruth baseball. The ball Gulden hit at Jordan's ballpark and which elicits the awe from Beckman was a foul ball, a mere strike. That's like hitting the longest drive in golf . . . out of bounds.

Gordy Gelhaye's historic 500-foot smash was a homerun. "He was really something," Butch Kreuser said of the 300-pound Gelhaye in his prime. He played for both Jordan and Shakopee and managed at Prior Lake as well. "I didn't see it," Fred Kerber said of Gelhaye's Sand Creek-clearing shot, "but I heard about it." Kerber said it happened before he began playing for Shakopee in 1952.

"I saw it," Lefty Weckman said. "It was in the early 1950s. I was a Jordan ball shagger, and we were stationed behind the screen at home plate" when the very large and imposing slugger caught a pitch in a wheelhouse that pitchers feared and crushed it far over the right-field fence. Gordy Gelhaye was no ordinary baseball player. Contrary to the impressions he made on youth incarcerated in the Scott County facility where Gelhaye served as The Jailer in his 60s, he was huge hell-on-wheels, rolling thunder, in his 20s and 30s. If he appeared less than handsome and less than fine of feature, maybe it's because the facemask was yet to be implemented in football anywhere when Gelhaye played college and professional football. Maybe professional football was more vicious, if less technically refined, in the 30s and 40's. Huge fists and forearm flippers knocked out teeth, bloodied and rearranged noses, and blackened eyes on what was called with real meaning then– the line of scrimmage. Punches were thrown in the piles of bodies that literally fought for turf with every snap of the football. Nearly everybody who graduated or retired from the game did so then with blown-out knees, because crack-back blocking and clipping were common. The same crowd that thinks history began in 1980, the cohort that never even heard of John Freund, could only ridicule and disparage the venerable, but aging, giant of another era.

Gordy Gelhaye was a 1932 graduate of Shakopee High School, according to his August 1, 1991 obituary in the *Shakopee Valley News*, and a 1938 graduate of the College of St. Thomas, where he starred in baseball and football, earning all-conference honors as a bone-crushing tackle. And, yes, they played both ways in college then. They also played beyond today's limit of four years of eligibility when they could get by with it, and Gelhaye may have been a six-year tackle at St. Thomas. Or he may have squeezed in his two years of military service sometime between 1932 and 1938.

We know that Gordy Gelhaye made an All-Star team in 1939 while playing with the Edmonton Eskimos in the league, which was a forerunner to the current Canadian Football League that was founded in 1958. That means he was All-Pro as a rookie in Canada. He played a total of five years with Calgary and Regina along with Edmonton. Shakopee's great Warren Stemmer, "one of the two best baseball players to come through Shakopee," according to Butch Kreuser, and a pallbearer for the funeral of his former teammate, Gordy Gelhaye, is interviewed in Melchior's *Scott County Baseball* on Gelhaye:

> 'He was unbelievable. Gordy was maybe five-eleven or six feet. He played in pretty good shape at just under 300 pounds. It sounded like a thundering heard of buffalo when Gordy ran from second to third base. Gordy was very fast for his size. He was an excellent athlete. He was all-pro Canadian in football. He was a legend up there, too. Never was another one like him.'

"He pulled it," Weck said of the ball Gelhaye hit, "and hooked it high and deep down the line. It cleared the creek and came down in the pumps at the gas station just around the corner from the Corner Bar. I think it was a Cities Service with green and white paint."

Was it possible? Or was Weckman engaging in the euphoric recall of a nostalgic moment? We wanted to know 60 years later in May of 2014. We checked the possible angles of flight from the corner of the building on the lot now housing "Hennen Electric." Looking back at the foul pole, it didn't look as far as we had pictured the distance in our mind from memory. It had seemed an impossibility there–more myth than reality. The angle of flight of a high hook was also possible, we concluded.

We crossed the creek and entered the hallowed grounds of Fairgrounds Park, now named "The Mini-Met," where the presence of the Old Great Ones can still be felt. We smelled tobacco on the breath of a few grizzled veterans looking over our shoulder as we started shooting distances with our Bushnell rangefinder and discovered that the 315 sign on the right-field fence is off more than the marker on the left-field fence. It's 306 feet from home plate to the right-field fence at the line on our rangefinder, 315 feet to the fence at the light tower in right center, and 342 feet to the scoreboard in the power alley. We don't think the fence has been moved much, if at all, since the park was rebuilt in 1949-50 after having been built in 1938, according to an August 21, 2014, *Jordan Independent* editorial, which stated the ballpark was built by the WPA, President Roosevelt's Work Progress Administration. It's had at least a couple of major facelifts, and the barns that butted up on the backside of the fence for showing livestock during the Scott County Fair each summer are gone now. But there was a day when left-handed hitters targeted the roof of the old horse barn in right field, and any ball hitting the top tier of the roof bounced over and clear of the barn.

We shot another 66 feet from the backside of the fence at the line in right field to a heavy tree on the same line at the creek bank. We found a clear view through trees to a concrete wall on the far side of Sand Creek and noted another 81 feet. That's 453 feet from home plate at Fairgrounds Park to the far side of the creek as straight down the line as we could get, then "hooking" a little with the flight line we imagined Gelhaye's ball had taken. We eyeballed a guess that another 60 to 80 feet *but up* the far bank would find our spot where Gordy Gelhaye's monstrous homerun rattled the gas pumps at the Cities Service station on what was Jordan's main street and Hwy 169 running through town. That's a shot of 513 to 533 feet by a man ridiculed for his body type and his age 30 years later by youth without a clue as to The Jailer's resume.

That resume includes a .348 lifetime batting average with the Shakopee Indians, according to *Scott County Baseball*. A cursory look at the box scores with his name in them at Jordan in 1945 and, again, in 1947, suggests a batting average of over .400 in the town with the beer advertised to have been "Aged in Caves." We noticed that he put on a hitting clinic over the course of five games near the end of the 1945 season when he went 15 for 19 at the plate, batting fifth in the order. It was good enough to be drafted by Excelsior, which went on to win the Class-A Minnesota State Championship on the arm of Jordan's Roger McDonald, who pitched the first no-hitter in the championship game of the tournament's history, and Gelhaye's hot bat. The hitting clinic continued, according to Peterson and Tomashek in *Town Ball*, as the drafted Jordan catcher sat out the first game, then went 7 for 11 with two homeruns in the next three games.

The behemoth Gelhaye, who played right field as well as first base and occasionally still pulled a game behind the plate, had pulled a pitch down the right-field line, the ball hooking high and deep around the foul pole for a homerun. "It must have hit something," Weckman said, 'cause it came down in the gas pumps at the old Cities Service station next to the Corner Bar, a building now housing at least one antique store. It's possible that the ball could have hit and caromed off and up out of the far bank of the creek. No man alive could have put one into the pumps of that gas station. No normal man swinging a wood bat. But Gordy Gelhaye wasn't normal.

Paul Sunder, former Jordan pitcher during the Golden Age of Baseball and former editor of the *Jordan Independent*, said the ball was picked up in front of the old Hamburger Home Cafe, another 366 feet down Broadway, not at the gas pumps. That means that Gelhaye's baseball traveled 900 feet in all from home plate at Fairgrounds Park before coming to rest. It happened long before ballplayers were supposed to be that big and that strong. Gordy Gelhaye was playing Class-A baseball in the Minnesota River Valley. It was long before such big men were supposed to be capable of the legs or the lungs to get a triple, regardless of where they hit a ball. Gordy Gelhaye, we noticed, in *Scott County Baseball*, had four triples in his Shakopee Indian career. We noticed in the box scores and articles we reviewed in the weekly *Jordan Independent* quite a few doubles and two grand slam homeruns while playing for Jordan.

"*Never was another one like him*," Stemmer's words reverberate in juxtaposition to the more contemporary man's claim that "Today's ballplayers are bigger, better, and faster." That doesn't play. The greatness of gold is its endurance and the fact that it can't be manufactured. The greatness of the old heroes was in their heroics that happened *naturally*, while the greatness of the newer ballplayers is that it was manufactured and needed an asterisk.

Most left-handed hitters enjoyed hitting balls off the roof of the old horse barn at Jordan's Fairgrounds Park. When they got in a groove while taking batting practice, you couldn't get them out of the batting cage. You'd think they were hitting balls into the upper deck at Yankee Stadium or something. Hitters like Jake Harsh and Dave Wagner from Belle Plaine; John Dill and Fred DeGreggoire at Prior Lake; the Seiferts, Bill Buesgens, and Jim Taddei at Jordan. We thought John Seifert had more potential as a hitter than a pitcher because of the towering blasts he hit high off the roof of the old horse barn. Had he been able to change his swing slightly in order to get rid of the severe over spin that resulted in "sinking" balls, Big John's towering shots would have assaulted the foundation of Ruppert's Bar on the far side of Sand Creek, 490 feet from home plate on our rangefinder. Instead, both he and the Los Angeles Dodgers thought his pitching was worth a good look. Jim Taddei, of course, won the River Valley League batting title in 1971, he said, with a .402 batting average. The league was without Shakopee, Prior Lake, and Savage then, but, still, hitting .400 with a wood bat was quite an accomplishment.

John Freund and his Green Sox teammates were looking for a close game in 1955 with the Brewers, who had made the eight-team Class-A state tournament the previous two years. But Brewer pitching and hitting star, Jim Pollard, had hung up his Brewer baseball spikes along with his Laker basketball sneakers after six years, and it would be three decades before a Jordan Brewer team returned to a Minnesota state tournament, albeit at Class-C level. Le Sueur pounded Jordan 15-4.

John Freund missed a couple of games in mid-season, and Le Sueur dropped three straight. An arm injury caused by a play at the plate hobbled his throwing and swinging of the bat. He got the collar two consecutive games after returning to the lineup, dropping his average to under .400. Worse, the team was floundering with a 6-5 record. But here's what Jim Kruse wrote in his June 29, 1955 column, "Kruse's Kolumn," which he titled "Freund returns to action Sunday":

> In 1948, John signed a pro contract with a Chicago farm club at Janesville, Wisc.
>
> He advanced to Sioux Falls in the Northern League the following year where he hit .249. During the 1950 season, he played with Springfield, Wisc. (sic) and upped his average to .260.
>
> While at Rochester he was a utility man... That's right, he played every position in the ballpark but water boy.
>
> Freund also has, in the opinion of this writer, the best arm in the MRL.

Otey Clark, was beginning to tire in the late innings of games and get hit by Minnesota River League teams. At 40 years of age, it was questionable whether the Old Pro still had the stamina and the stuff that had taken him to Fenway Park with the Red Sox or even what he'd had with the Minneapolis Millers and other AAA teams, including Louisville, Columbus, and Toledo of the old American Association. Indeed, Otey Clark had won 112 games, with a compiled ERA of just over 4.00 in 11 seasons of high-level minor league baseball, approximately half of which he played at AAA. Still, here he was–in the Minnesota River League trying to pitch twice a week for the Le Sueur Green Sox. But games were bunching up, with playoffs looming. John Freund was pressed into action on the mound. He responded like the gamer he always was. Freund beat Belle Plaine, 5-3, on Sunday, August 7, with a 7 hitter and 11 strikeouts, after Otey Clark had beaten Jordan, 10-3, on Wednesday night.

John had two hits in each of the first two playoff games, the first a win over New Prague, the second a game that turned into a political rhubarb, as Jordan first won the game 7-6 in 12 innings, then forfeited to Le Sueur 9-0 on a league protest ruling that was subsequently overturned by the state board under heavy pressure from Jordan's Baseball Bosses. At issue was Jordan's signing of pitcher Ken Reitmeir from a higher level of baseball after the July 15 deadline. Jordan's political power prevailed. The wind taken out of their sails, Le Sueur would lose the second game in the double-elimination playoff format, 3-0, to St. Peter, with John Freund taking the loss on the mound. St. Peter, with Clark and Marty Lee, a catcher, drafted from Le Sueur, then went on to win the 1955 Class-A State Championship.

Lee's game-winning double in the 15th inning of the semi-final game against Little Falls gave Clark the win for his 8-2/3 innings of relief pitching; moreover, it put St. Peter in the championship game against Hutchinson. Clark's door-slamming relief stint helped preserve a 7-2 win for the championship.

But that's what teams and towns expected and got from the great baseball players during the game's Golden Age. Fast-forward three decades and players like Otey Clark and John Freund would likely be on Major League rosters for serious money, because they were that good and expansion meant that many more opportunities. Instead, they played semi-pro baseball in the Class-AA Southern Minny and for Class-A town teams and blue-collar pay. But with only 16 teams in the Major Leagues throughout the 1950s, opportunities were severely limited. The demand for pitching, in particular, was always great, and it was never fully met with a supply of pitchers in the pipeline. Otey Clark, with 11 years of professional mound service, could be on a professional American League roster just after the league's first round of expansion in 1961. The two additional teams meant 22 more pitchers on American League payrolls–an increase of 25 percent who "couldn't make it" the year before but did make it with the addition of teams in Minnesota and Los Angeles.

No less an authority on the subject than Ted Williams had weighed in with this mathematical logic, according to Red Smith in a *New York Times* column on January 11, 1962, and included in a delightful collection of Smith's columns republished in 2000 under the title, *Red Smith On Baseball–The Game's Greatest Writer On the Game's Greatest Years*, to explain how Roger Maris had been able in the new, 162-game 1961 season to beat Babe Ruth's single-season homerun record of 60, set in 1927 in a 154-game season. Simply put, expansion diluted the quality of baseball being played everywhere–from Major Leagues down to semi-pro town team levels. Pitching, according to Ted Williams, had been watered down with expansion.

But in the 1950s, these pitchers, on the face of simple analysis, probably could have made it in the future years when opportunities were nearly doubled from expansion. Instead, they lit up the scoreboards of semi-pro and amateur leagues like the Minnesota River League with goose eggs and filled scorebooks with K's. Pitchers like Otey Clark and John Freund.

Had it not been for the mid-season injury, Freund's batting average would likely have remained over .400. His pitching late in the season gave the Sox a much-needed boost when the overworked, 40-year-old Otey Clark needed some rest. Dan Driscoll remembers being the batboy for the Le Sueur Green Sox in the mid-1950s when his father, Joe, Sr., was playing third base for the Sox. A 1965 graduate of Le Sueur High School and the older brother of the 2013 Minnesota State Baseball Hall of Fame inductee, Joe Driscoll, Dan said his father told him that "John Freund was one of the best ballplayers he ever saw anywhere." That qualification, "one of," leaves only enough understandable slack not to slight two good, ball-playing sons by their father. We liked both on the diamond. While Joe set longevity records starring for Le Sueur, Arlington, and Prior Lake, Danny–a better pitcher with more promise at the same age in our view–flamed out in Vietnam by picking up some shrapnel in his pitching elbow. It took the pop off his fastball and the mustard off a sharply breaking curveball that had elicited comparisons to Lefty Weckman of Jordan.

"He was a hell of a hitter," Driscoll said of John Freund, "and he was just smooth as silk at shortstop." Ten years later, in 1966 and an outstanding left-handed pitcher with what had become the Le Sueur Giants in a new league called the River Valley League, Dan Driscoll would be drafted by the habitually state tournament-bound Shakopee Indians. The informal "captain" of the team to whom everyone deferred, according to Driscoll, was none other than John Freund. "He was still 'the stud' of the team," Driscoll said.

Here's how Jim Kruse wrote about John Freund in his *Le Sueur News Herald* column of August 31, 1955:

> John was a real help to the Sox this season as he was the leading hitter on the ball club with a .339 average and 13 RBIs. Freund also was a fine defensive man as he made many unbelievable stops from his shortstop position. He was a frequent base runner as he reached first safely 33 times. Freund also showed some fine pitching form when he got his chance to throw later in the season.
>
> His fastball was tops in the league.

St. Peter liked Otey Clark and his contributions to their '55 state championship, and the feeling was mutual. He would play for St. Peter in 1956, probably for more money than Le Sueur or Jordan was willing to pay him, and John Freund jumped to Glencoe in the Class-A Twin Trails League. "It was all about the driving," Bob Freund said. "It was always about the driving," and the 60-mile drive to Glencoe on Hwy 212 promised to be quicker than the 50 miles to Le Sueur on Hwy 169, which was undergoing construction.

Delays and detours could turn an hour's drive from Minneapolis into a heated, two-hour adventure and missed infield practice at the ballpark if not an inning or two of the game. John didn't like being late. Highway 169 was being re-routed around the towns it had taken traffic through for decades. John Freund would join Don Wheeler, another teammate with the Rochester Royals in 1954, at Glencoe. A catcher, Wheeler's resume included nine years of professional baseball with a cumulative batting average of .301 at the AA and AAA level. He played part of one season with the Chicago White Sox, but a .240 batting average wasn't enough for the Sox to retain him at that level. He and John Freund were presumably the two outside players Glencoe was allowed under the rules of Class-A baseball in 1956.

Without Otey Clark and John Freund in 1956, the Le Sueur Green Sox finished last with a record of 4 wins and 12 losses in what had become a six-team league. St. Peter would win the league again, with Clark helping them to a 16-2 record.

Meanwhile, John Freund and Don Wheeler led Glencoe to a 17-5 regular season record and the championship of the Twin Trails League. They beat Brownton soundly 16-6 in the last game of the regular season and drew them for the first round of the playoffs, a five-game series. Brownton had escaped the cellar in the regular-season league play, but they brought a 7-15 record into the playoffs.

The August 11, 1956, *Glencoe Enterprise* reported a split between Glencoe and Brownton in the first two playoff games. Glencoe beat Brownton, 3-2, in the first game, then Brownton, with Gerald Hochsprung, a big lefthander and a 1976 inductee into the Minnesota Amateur Baseball Hall of Fame, beat Glencoe and John Freund, 4-1. Then, Brownton and Hochsprung made it three straight over Glencoe, 9-3 and 10-2, to advance in the playoffs, which they won over Bird Island, again with three straight wins after dropping the first two games. They lost their magic in Region 3 action against Little Falls, which went on to finish second to the Minneapolis Teamsters in the Class-A State Championship.

John pitched and hit well for Glencoe in 1956. He batted .359, with four homeruns and 20 RBIs, behind Wheeler who hit nearly .500. One Freund highlight was "a long homer off the lights in right field" in the All-Star Game against Hutchinson. Another highlight was also captured in the reporting of the June 14, 1956, *Glencoe Enterprise*:

> Johnny Freund won his own ball game over Fairfax in the 10th inning when he hit the scoreboard for a homer. Wheeler crossed home plate ahead of him, making the final score 5-3 Glencoe.

He gave up only five hits in recording this second win of the season as a pitcher. But after the successful regular season, Glencoe found the playoffs disappointing. Nobody was to blame other than the hard-throwing southpaw from Brownton.

John Freund returned to Le Sueur for the 1957 season. The highway construction was likely to have been completed, with expressway bypasses of all the little towns that had impeded a quick trip for him from South Minneapolis. Perhaps he felt he owed the team something after jumping ship like he did with Otey Clark after just the one season. After the Western Minny folded, Waseca and New Ulm joined the MRL, making it a tougher Class-A league with an 18-game schedule.

With John Freund playing and in a tougher league in 1957, the Le Sueur Green Sox would finish in the middle of the league standings with a 9-9 record, far behind New Ulm at 16-2, and Waseca at 12-6. The June 19, 1957 *Le Sueur News Herald* published batting averages, and John Freund was hitting what for him was a less-than-respectable .286. But John was pitching more. He'd beaten Waseca with a fine performance in which he scattered seven hits while giving up no earned runs in the 7-2 win. Then, the next week John went head to head with Ol' Pro Otey Clark and St. Peter. Clark beat him, and Le Sueur hit the skids. Le Sueur and John lost a couple of low-scoring one-run games down the stretch. Then, they were blown out by Waseca, 10-0, in the rubber game of the first round of the playoffs.

John Freund didn't have the best year of his baseball life in 1957, but "the rest of the story," in the words of Paul Harvey, long-time radio commentator, tells us that he was a father for the third time that year in April, one child with special needs at a time when there wasn't a lot of help available for people with special needs. Pat Freund had to have been nearly overwhelmed at home. The Rockefellers and Kennedys had nannies. The Freunds didn't. Nor was daycare available. It wasn't even acceptable. Mothers raised children, took care of the home and their husbands, who were charged in the Social Contract to bring home the bread and the bacon. Mothers got help from family and close friends, giving in kind when asked. But Pat's family was in Rochester, not Minneapolis.

Moreover, half way through the baseball season, the Freunds were expecting again. Pat was pregnant with their fourth child. The next spring, Jack would be born, and the Freund family would number six, with four toddlers under four years of age. Their house on 16th Avenue in South Minneapolis was getting crowded, and John, ever attuned to the rhythm and beat of The Fiddler, was feeling underwhelmed at work. He was 28 years old, married and the father of four in a job in which he had already plateaued in 1958. The Fiddler's timing was impeccable, as an opening came up for a supervisor in the Rahr plant in Shakopee. He applied for the position and did well on the aptitude test he had to take.

John got the job and presumably a nice pay raise. The Freunds moved into a house on the Rahr property that they rented from the employer in July of 1958, marking this, July of 1958, the actual genesis of Shakopee's run for the 1959 Minnesota State Baseball Championship. Rahr Malting Company didn't pay John Freund cash above or beneath the table to play baseball. Rahr paid John Freund in terms of decent pay, self-respect, responsibility, stability, and job security. This, too, can be seen as The Fiddler at work if one is but tuned into, present with, and sensitive to . . . the Dance of Life.

"Rahr is one of the few companies in the country," Dick Erickson said, "that truly cares about its employees." He said that he, like John Freund, and the Rahr Malting Company, was born in Manitowoc, Wisconsin. "Longevity is an important part of the company," according to Erickson, because it helps to promote the stability and continuity that are desirable to both employer and employee. It's win-win in a world rapidly becoming a repeat of the lose-lose of a century ago when envy and jealousy roared behind the mask of social justice then. Like John Freund, Erickson retired from the company after 39 years.

John played closer to the Freund's Minneapolis home in 1958. Then, despite the move to Shakopee, the fourth child in as many years, and a new job with responsibilities and a new boss, he played well enough and had to have pitched well for Class-A DeVac's to get drafted by Minneapolis Cozy's Bar. While details are sparse, he played in the state tournament at New Ulm in 1958, but Cozy's lost its second game in the double-elimination tournament to the Austin Packers, a long-time powerhouse in the Southern Minny.

Meanwhile, the Shakopee Indians, after starting slowly, won the league title, the league playoffs, and entered Region 6B play on the strength of Fred Kerber's arm and bat. Shakopee then went with the 17-year-old high school junior from Jordan–Fulton Weckman. The draftee beat Lonsdale, the perennial power from the DRS League, on a five-hitter and 19 strikeouts. That meant 11 straight wins. But Lonsdale rocked Kerber and draftee Pat Devitt in the second game. That meant a rubber game was necessary to crown a Region 6B champion. Weckman nearly repeated his first-game performance against Lonsdale, with another five-hitter and 13 strikeouts while losing 4-3. Lonsdale advanced to the state tournament at New Ulm, where they took powerful Springfield to the edge of the abyss in the opening round before losing 10-9. It was all a prelude in a way, because Springfield and Shakopee would provide the cast of characters in the state tournament the next year, 1959, at St. Cloud. John Freund and Lefty Weckman would play huge roles in the drama on the diamond.

The Freunds settled into Shakopee through the winter of 1958-'59 and were already talking about building a new house. The new job at Rahr was working out better than they expected, and the job was made to order for John Freund. He had responsibility as the supervisor of the barley elevator, and he had men reporting to him, both of which meant a bigger paycheck. Now, John could enjoy a lot more of what had been his second job for years, but his first love–baseball.

Baseball and beer have been supporting each other in this country since the first Sunday picnics in the 1800s included a pickup game of ball. As the game grew up, with rules and organizations creating structure, the relationship to the brewing industry strengthened. Breweries lent their name to ball clubs at all levels, and both baseball players and fans swilled the brown brew that youth of every generation seem to think is "nectar of the gods." Milwaukee, Jordan, and New Ulm are not the only towns in the country with baseball teams named "Brewers."

Breweries built ballparks and bought uniforms as a part of their sponsorship of baseball teams. They helped pay ballplayer salaries, whether underneath or above the table, in cash and trade or with a job. They gave players jobs to entice them to play in their town. Their product helped to fuel the passions of competitive fire and to provide the word-of-mouth advertising that fanned the interests of followers. They were early advertisers on radio and television broadcasts of ballgames as well as on the outfield fences. Chances are pretty good that if you've ever watched a game of baseball in the United States, you've enjoyed a beer or two while doing so.

Chances are even better that if you've enjoyed a beer, you've ingested one of the brew's primary ingredients, malt, made by Rahr Malting Company of Shakopee, Minnesota, and you didn't even know it. The privately owned company is the largest single-site malting company in the world. Employing about 110 people, according to Dick Erickson, who said he retired from Rahr in 1992, they provide malt to virtually every brewery, large and small, in the country. The Rahr family dates its beginnings in the brewing business to 1847 in Wisconsin. Its first malt house in Shakopee was built in 1935, and today, its Shakopee footprint includes five separate malting houses covering seven city blocks.

It's been assumed for decades that through its connections with Rahr, the Shakopee Indians hired John Freund in 1959 with a job there to play baseball. He was that good, and Rahr was always community minded. But John's connections with Rahr were much stronger and older than baseball. He had strong family connections. John Freund's father had worked for Rahr in Manitowoc, Wisconsin, before moving his family to South Minneapolis and transferring to a Rahr facility there. An uncle or two, according to Erickson, had also worked for Rahr. John Freund's father got him the job with Rahr, not the Shakopee baseball powers of the day–a baseball board that included Howard Heller, who was in a management position at Rahr-Shakopee and the father of Howie, Indian third-baseman.

The late Earl Dean of Jordan, Minnesota, was considered an astute baseball man. He played for and managed area baseball teams as far back as the 1930s, according to Tom Melchior's interview with him for *Scott County Baseball*, and he saw everybody who was anybody play the game as the loving fan of baseball he was well into the 2000s. His son, Joe, a 1980 Jordan High School graduate, said that he and his dad enjoyed talking baseball in Earl's golden years. Like most guys his age, Joe Dean had never even heard of John Freund. He never saw him play ball. Like Jim Pollard and Tex Erickson before him, John Freund's time was a bygone era and the years that Joe grew up defined for him what good athletes and ballplayers were.

Just as it seems as though the history taught in the public schools had been revised to fit a new agenda sometime in the 1970s, the teachers of local culture and history disappeared with the closing of the public houses. Restrictive dram shop laws and increasing issuance of DUIs saw to the demise of the original "sports bars. First, the local "color" disappears. Then, forgetting some facts and distorting Truth to fit a new agenda, a new crowd wanting legendary status in its own time, at least in their own minds, revises the history. But something about John Freund piqued Joe Dean's curiosity and, upon visiting his father again soon after meeting Freund, Joe asked, "Dad, how good of a ballplayer was John Freund?" Joe said that his father, without hesitation, responded:

"'He was the best ballplayer I ever saw around here.'"

Earl Dean saw everybody who ever played baseball in the Minnesota River Valley. He saw everybody before, during, and after the Golden Age of Baseball. He saw Jim Pollard and Johnny Garbett and Tex Erickson from Jordan in the 1950s. He saw the O'Brien's at Belle Plaine. He saw a myriad of ballplayers from several leagues and decades of play, and that includes a fine new crop of ballplayers in the 1980s and 90s just in Jordan. What's remarkable is how little anybody knew about John Freund, not just Joe Dean and his peer group. John had played a lot of baseball before even showing up in Shakopee in 1958 and playing his first season with Shakopee in 1959. His teammates didn't even know his past. "He just didn't talk about himself," teammate and manager Butch Kreuser said of John Freund. "He wasn't like that."

"That was John," his brother, Bob Freund, said. "Even at his funeral (in 2010) there were guys he played ball with at Shakopee who came up to me and said, 'Geeze, I didn't know that he had played against Mickey Mantle, or I didn't know he played in the Southern Minny for two years.'"

Bob Freund said that his brother John was paid to play baseball at Rochester, Le Sueur, and Glencoe. "John never said how much. He just didn't talk about stuff like that." We mention it to help prove a point about quality of ballplayers during the game's Golden Age and those who came after. Playing for pay during the Golden Age of Baseball, before expansion and other changes, remains a stamp of excellence, an imprimatur, which just can't be matched since then. It certainly separates the men from the boys who played for varsity jackets and sweaters with their high school and college logo-letters sewn on the chest.

But Shakopee baseball had nothing to do with John's employment at Rahr Malting, or his transfer from Minneapolis to Shakopee and the supervisor's job. "He had to take an aptitude test and everything," according to Bob Freund. "I took the same test and applied for it," he said, "because I was working at the time for our Dad at the elevator, too."

What was good for Rahr was good for John Freund and the Shakopee Indians. They got lucky with John Freund, just as they did with the pitcher from Jordan, Weckman. Without MVP Weckman, Shakopee doesn't win the 1959 state championship, but without John Freund, the Shakopee Indians don't even make it to The Dance.

He was a good fit immediately and long term for Shakopee and baseball, and for Rahr. He made a 39-year career out of the job, and he raised a family of four children in the small city on the Minnesota River he called home.

While Rahr Malting Company has succeeded for five generations by focusing on essentially one product, malt for the brewing industry, John Freund succeeded in baseball by doing it all. "He's one of the best ballplayers I've ever seen that played in Shakopee," his former teammate and manager, Butch Kreuser, said. "Maybe *the* best, because he could pitch, too."

Indeed, John Freund took the mound for Shakopee in the first game he played for the Indians. It was opening day of the 1959 River Valley League season, Sunday, May 24, at Riverside Park in Shakopee. Belle Plaine had gone 6-7 in 1958 and would go 2-9 in 1959. Belle Plaine wasn't expected to give Shakopee much trouble. But Fred Kerber was Shakopee's pitching ace. He'd won 13 games each of the previous two seasons under the helm of Manager Lefty Odenwald. The May 7, 1959, edition of the *Shakopee Valley News* reported that Butch Kreuser, Shakopee's catcher, would be player-manager of the Indians that year. Baseball tradition called for Kerber to be the starting pitcher as part of the opening game ritual.

"We knew what Fritz could do," Kreuser said, "but we didn't know much about John, and we had to find out." Kreuser went against "the book," because he was thinking strategically. He knew his team needed two reliable pitchers to repeat as league champions and to have a chance at getting back to the state tournament.

Besides, he also knew that Kerber wouldn't mind as long as he was in the lineup. He and Freund both loved to hit, too.

"I didn't' like catching him," Kreuser said of John Freund. "He threw a heavy ball, and my hand would hurt. It was like catching a shot or a maul." Howie Heller, third baseman, said the same thing. "I hated to even play catch with him," Heller said, "because my hand would hurt when we got done."

Freund needed to show his new manager and new team what he could do. He shut out Belle Plaine 5-0 with a no-hitter and 15 strikeouts.

Just a week after the no-hitter, John Freund pitched a four-hitter against Savage, losing his shutout in the ninth inning, but winning the game 12-2. He led the Indians' hitting barrage as well, slamming two homeruns in a solid three-hit day at the plate. The following week, the *Shakopee Valley News* reported Freund's 7-4 victory over New Prague with, "Big John Freund hurled his third straight victory " and noting that the big right-hander had struck out 9 of the first 12 batters he faced while finishing with 12 strikeouts for the game.

The next Sunday, June 14, 1959, John made it four in a row, with a big 4-3 win over Jordan and the 17-year-old Weckman on a wild pitch in the 13th inning. The young lefthander was brilliant, with 11 strikeouts over the nine innings he worked. But Big John Freund had Jordan shut out on three hits until the seventh inning, when he was nicked for three hits and the three Jordan runs. He went all 13 innings and struck out 13 Brewers.

Next, John was beaten by Prior Lake, despite hitting a homerun among the three hits he had at the plate. The loss dropped Shakopee out of first place, but the following week he rebounded with a four-hitter and 11 strikeouts, losing a shutout in the ninth inning in the 5-1 win over Savage.

The July 16, 1959, *Valley News* reported that John suffered his first loss of the season on the mound in a 5-4 loss to New Prague. Only two of the runs he gave up were earned, and a throwing error beat him. But the Indians were 6-2, two games behind Prior Lake, and John was 6-1 as Shakopee's new power pitcher, which provided a nice mix to go with Kerber's curveball. Moreover, the weekly newspaper reported that he was also hitting at a .485 clip (16 hits in 33 at bats), just behind Chuck Kreuser's team-leading .500 average.

Prior Lake lost two games in a row, and everybody was looking for The Game of the Year in the River Valley League on July 19, 1959: Shakopee at Jordan; under the lights; John Freund versus Lefty Weckman. A left-handed hitter, John went three for four at the plate against the best lefthander in the league that year and maybe the best pitcher in the state. That bumped his batting average to .514. As for the expectations of the two pitchers, Freund and Weckman, it might as well have been one of the heavyweight fights between Frazier and Ali. There shouldn't have been a loser. Freund matched Weck's 10 strikeouts, and he bettered him in hits allowed, giving up four to the young Jordan ace's six. More importantly, the win brought Shakopee back into a tie for first place with Prior Lake at 7-2. They would play for the league title the following Sunday.

The Shakopee weekly's sports headline read: "Indians Edge Lakers 5-4 For RVL Crown." John had pitched again, giving up nine hits, three earned runs, while striking out eight. Always tough in the clutch, both on the mound and at bat, a sidebar headline read: "Freund Tops RVL Hitters, Hurlers." He was acknowledged in the article as " the loop's top pitcher and hitter," with a .525 batting average on 21 hits in 40 at bats, including 5 doubles, 2 triples, and 4 home runs. He had 15 RBIs in the 10 games.

While four homeruns in a season pales in comparison to homerun totals by hitters in the league a generation later, his ratio of one homerun in every 10 at bats is Ruthian. Moreover, there was no "trampoline effect" in the wood bats, and the sweet spot in wood was miniscule in comparison to the Easton rocket launchers which were used later and that made big hitters out of everybody in a lineup. You couldn't just meet the ball with wood to get an extra-base hit. You had to meet it well, and you had to drive the ball. John Freund was a great hitter with a beautiful swing. He had the great vision that all good hitters have, and he met the ball well, driving it down the line, into the alley, and off or over the wall. Freund's pitching record of eight wins against one loss was also tops in the six-team league.

Lefty Weckman of Jordan said of John Freund, "He was such a good ballplayer that he could play any position he wanted to play." Like Weckman, Kreuser maintains that John Freund could play any position because of his athletic skills and knowledge of the game. Freund moved like water flows in a brook. He moved like a top-end Porsche at LeMans–smooth, natural, effortless–making others look like tractors and trucks on the track at the same time. Kreuser admitted, "If I had to pick one position, I would say that shortstop was his best position."

John Freund was a big shortstop for his day–the day of shortstops like Phil Rizzuto, Pee Wee Reese, and Tex Erickson. At 6-1 and maybe 170 pounds when he graduated from Minneapolis Roosevelt High School in 1948, John Freund would fill out to an athletic 6-2 and 200 pounds by the time he was playing with the Rochester Royals in 1954, according to a profile of him in the *Rochester Post-Dispatch*. "I think he carried 215 to 220 later," Erickson said.

His size belied his speed. He could run. He hit a lot of doubles and triples in every level of baseball he played for two reasons: (1) He was a line-drive hitter; and (2) he had the wheels to take the extra base along with being a smart base runner. John Freund made very few mistakes playing baseball. Not at bat; not in the field at any position; nor on the mound pitching.

"He knew and worked the whole strike zone," Weckman said of a fellow pitcher in admiration of a ballplayer he recognized for his professional skills. "He didn't have a great curveball," Kreuser, a catcher, said, "but he could bring it and put it where he wanted to put it."

John Freund continued to hit and pitch the Shakopee Indians through the league playoffs, including a 5-3 loss he suffered at the hands of Savage in a game in which he took a one-hitter and the lead into the eighth inning. He relaxed and gave up four runs and five more hits, while striking out 11 in the losing effort. It would be Shakopee's fourth, and last, loss of the 1959 season. Shakopee put Savage away in the rubber game of the three-game series, and then put away Prior Lake to advance to the Region 6B tournament.

Freund and Fred Kerber led Shakopee to the league and playoff titles. Then, both relinquished pitching duties for outfield positions and a concentration on hitting, as Indian player-manager Butch Kreuser went confidently with drafted pitchers, Lefty Weckman of Jordan and Jerry Meyer of Savage. "We knew what they could do," Kreuser admitted, "because we had played them quite a few times."

The August 27, 1959, *Shakopee Valley News* announced in a headline: "Indians Play Lakeville in First Game of Region 6B" after Kerber's big-game pitching and hitting eliminated Prior Lake. Manager Butch Kreuser started Weckman, who threw a dazzling three-hitter with 12 strikeouts in the 6-2 win over Lakeville. John played first base and went three for five at the plate. He played centerfield in the second game and went two for four in the 9-2 win over Lakeville in front of 1,302 paid admissions.

The scenario was much the same in the regional finals the next week against Northfield. Home of Malt-o-Meal, a cereal company, and two posh private liberal arts colleges, Carleton College and St. Olaf College, Northfield had promised to provide stiff competition. But Weckman threw a six-hitter with 17 strikeouts, and John gave him all the support he needed. He drove in six runs with a homerun, a double, and a single in four at bats. Then his two hits helped Shakopee win the second game, 14-6, over Northfield and advance to the state tournament at St. Cloud.

Butch Kreuser knew that when you've got a good horse, you ride him. He stuck with his game plan of starting draftee pitchers Weckman and Meyer in the state tournament. Freund played centerfield and batted cleanup behind Kerber, who started in left field. John was two for three, with a triple and an RBI in the spacious Municipal Stadium that few people knew he was familiar with from his year in the Northern League while playing with Sioux Falls.

John Freund and Fred Kerber were Shakopee's bangers. They batted in the middle of the order, usually third and fourth, or fourth and fifth, and they produced, leading the team in RBIs throughout the season. Weckman's two-hit pitching with 14 strikeouts in the 4-1 win over Lake Henry was just what Shakopee needed to get past the first-game tournament jitters.

After going two for five in Game 2 against Pipestone in a 5-2 win, then being held hitless in their third-game win over Virginia, 4-3, John was three for five, with a two-run triple, a shot off the right-field wall, in Shakopee's 7-0 whitewashing of St. Bonifacious.

The heroics in the championship game against Springfield went to Weckman for his third straight dazzling performance on the mound, and to Fred Kerber for his two-out, two-run homerun in the bottom of the ninth to tie the game 2-2. Howie Heller's walk, steal of second, then scoring the winning run on a throwing error gave Shakopee the 1959 State Championship. It also gave Vic Haas a huge payoff on his bets, which he was still taking in the ninth inning down 2-0. "I wonder how much money he made," Heller said, over 50 years later, and Fred Kerber said that he never heard either.

But John Freund made Kerber's dramatic homerun possible. With two out, Freund beat out an infield hit that Butch Kreuser remembered as being hit up the middle, over second base. "John could run for a big man," Kreuser recalled. Fred Kerber was on deck, of course, and he said that the ball was hit to the second baseman in his normal position, deep between first and second. "I'm still amazed by it," Kerber said in his kitchen on the morning of Holy Thursday in 2014. "He took off like a streak of shit," Kerber replayed for us. "Somebody upstairs helped us."

He simply beat it out for a scratch single, and Vic Haas, owner of "Vic's Place," had the first hint of being a winner that day. All season long, like every year in Shakopee, the team drank the first pitchers of beer on Vic after their games. "We'd go to either Vic's Place or to Johnny Abeln's," Heller said. "When we would get there, they'd have the tables set up with pitchers of beer waiting for us." Players who hit a homerun in the game got a steak dinner on Vic–"and a steak dinner for the wife, too," Kerber smiled, as he said it.

Vic Haas collected a fistful of cash in the seats of St. Cloud's Municipal Stadium after the dramatic win over Springfield. For all anybody knew, Fred Kerber never had to pay for a beer or a steak in Vic's Place again. That's not all either. Ed Hennen, a Shakopee homebuilder in the 1950s and 60s, according to Fred Kerber, and a member of the Shakopee baseball board, thought Kerber should be a homeowner. In 1960, Hennen gave Kerber a check for $3,000 to cover the down payment of 20 percent on a $15,000 home in Shakopee. There was no contract-for-deed, no paper work at all, according to Kerber. "He told me," Kerber said, "'just pay me back when you can.'"

Three years later, Kerber said he thought he'd better repay that loan. When he asked Hennen how much interest he owed on the $3,000, the homebuilder and baseball man just shook his head. The numbers mean more when you factor inflation into a comparison of today's average home price of, say, $200,000, which would mean an equivalent gift of an interest-free, no-document loan of $40,000, and "just pay me back when you can." The gift, the character, and the trust, too, were all hallmarks of the Golden Age of Baseball in the Minnesota River Valley.

We didn't audit the box scores or scorebooks, but Melchior writes in *Scott County Baseball* of the 1959 Shakopee Indian season: "John Freund led the Indians at the plate with 49 hits in 106 at bats for an average of .462." He also had a team-high 27 RBIs, or nearly one a game. Other than Kerber, he didn't get a lot of help at the plate, and he usually batted after Kerber, so opposing pitchers could afford to be careful with him. "We won with pitching and defense," Heller said. We think they hit well in the Golden Age of Baseball, however, when pitching and defense continued to define baseball. A quick check of *The Bible* of the area and era, the *Northwest Umpires Review*, shows Shakopee team batting averages running between about .270 and .340 and usually leading the league during the 1958 to 1968 seasons.

Once settled into the rhythm and the beat of The Fiddler's tune in Shakopee with Rahr and family, John Freund played ball the way he was made to play ball. He did it all–at shortstop, pitching, first base, and centerfield. And he hit. The line drives screamed off his wood bat. He was a pull hitter, and teams would sometimes employ "the Williams shift" on him, moving their second baseman over toward the right field line and deep into shallow right field, the shortstop over to the right side of the bag, and the third baseman into the vacated shortstop position. But John wasn't as stiff-necked and bull-headed as Ted Williams. He would simply stroke the ball to the left side of the field or lay down a perfect bunt that he would beat out for a hit. But he loved to drive the ball with the smoothest swing you'd ever seen.

John Freund was no mere schoolyard ballplayer. This year, 1959, marked the 12th year of playing baseball since he had been a school boy–and the first year, counting his military service, since then that he hadn't been paid to play ball.

The year, 1959, also marked the last year in which the Minnesota State Baseball Tournament drew more than 20,000 paid admissions.

The same September 24, 1959, issue of the *Shakopee Valley News* that bannered the Indians as "First State Champions Since 1940" on its front page ran a Red Owl grocery ad on an inside page that offered fresh fryers for 27 cents a pound, beef short ribs for 29 cents a pound, and smoked Armour Star picnic hams for 37 cents a pound. Bread was on special for 21 cents a loaf, two loaves for two bits, and whole bean coffee could be had for 59 cents a pound.

All was right with the world. At least the world bounded by the Minnesota River and its valley of little towns and baseball teams. The Freunds were building a new home and would move into it in January of 1960.

With another new manager at the helm, John Schaefer, the Indians started the 1960 season the way they had finished 1959. Opening against Savage on Sunday, May 29, Fred Kerber fired a six hitter, and John Freund, playing shortstop and batting cleanup, went three for four with two doubles and an RBI to lead Shakopee to a 4-2 win, according to the *Shakopee Valley News*. The next week at New Prague, Kerber took a no-hitter into the seventh, then gave up a couple walks and the lone hit he yielded in the game, good enough to win 6-1.

In a makeup game, under the lights at Belle Plaine, John Freund took what seemed like a safe 7-1 lead into the bottom of the ninth inning on the strength of a three-hitter, two of which were base-hit bunts, and 10 strikeouts. But he had control problems, which nearly cost him dearly in the last inning. A triple with bases loaded was the big blow that closed the game to 7-5.

Kerber then beat Jordan, 9-5, with "a neat five-hitter while fanning 13," and Freund's "long homerun to deep right centerfield" with a man on in the fifth inning was a huge blow. They won two more, 7-6 over New Prague, then 22-4 over Prior Lake in which John Freund had two doubles and a homerun with two walks. He not only scored five times, he batted in five runs to lead the onslaught and give Shakopee a perfect 10-0 record in the River Valley League. It also gave them a bye in the first round of the playoffs. They wouldn't just sit idle.

In a non-league tune-up for the playoff run, John pitched a four-hitter to beat Norwood 8-2, and he had a homerun and two singles in four at bats. The Indians drew Prior Lake in a two-out-of-three game series and swept them 12-2 and 7-5, with John pitching the second game. He was cruising into the sixth inning with a no-hitter, when Prior Lake erupted and tagged him for five runs. But relief came in time to put out the fire and preserve the win.

The August 18, 1960 *Shakopee Valley News* reports Shakopee and Freund taking down the Jordan Brewers two straight in playoff action, 11-3 and 5-2. Freund pitched the clincher and had 10 strikeouts while yielding seven hits, three to one hitter. The fourth straight playoff win put Shakopee in the Region 6B playoffs for the sixth consecutive year.

Shakopee took out New Market in two straight, the first game 5-1 at Shakopee in front of a crowd of 1,000 fans. In the second game, John Freund beat the DRS champions, 3-1, in a brilliant pitchers' duel. Shakopee repeated the scenario against Miesville, with Freund pitching the second and decisive game, striking out 13 in a 7-1 rout and putting the state champions back in the tournament to defend their crown at Springfield.

Shakopee lost its opening game, 2-1, to Grand Rapids in 14 innings, then their protest was upheld and they were given the win, 9-0. The Indians then beat Warroad, 4-2, with Freund scattering eight hits and fanning nine, to qualify for double elimination, but they lost two straight games: 4-0 to Fergus Falls, then 6-3 to Norwood. Melchior notes in *Scott County Baseball*: "The Indians had only 20 hits in 140 at bats for a state tournament average of .143." John Freund's bat was uncharacteristically quiet in the tournament.

But overall, he had a good year again. The *Northwest Umpires Review* of July 24, 1960, has him in second place in the league in hitting behind Walerius of Belle Plaine with a game to go. John had three hits and two walks in five at bats in his last regular season game to push his average to an even .500. The team record was nearly identical to the championship season the year before at 24 wins against just 5 losses, according to Melchior's *Scott County Baseball*. Kerber did the yeoman's share of the pitching, according to Melchior, and was 12-2 on the mound. Meyer took a loss in the state tournament, as did Kerber. That leaves two losses on the season that John Freund *may* have suffered. But it also leaves open the possibility that he won at least 10 games, as he did win one game in the state tournament, two in the Region tournament, and two more in league playoffs.

In his final address to the nation as president, Ike warned of the dangers of concentrated and unmitigated power in "the military-industrial complex." John F. Kennedy was inaugurated as the 35th President of the United States on January 20, 1961. Millions of viewers had watched the first televised debates between the charismatic standard bearer for the Democratic Party and what would become known as "Camelot," and his opponent, Richard Nixon, who appeared on camera without makeup, looking surly with a five-o'clock shadow and the beady, darting eyes of a convict.

Fidel Castro had overthrown Cuban President Batista in 1959 and was busy installing his Marxist-Leninist-Socialist-Communist revolution into political policy just 90 miles off the coast of Miami, Florida. Cuba was friendly with the Soviet Union, with whom we continued to wage the Cold War. President Kennedy would admit to complete responsibility for what became known as "The Bay of Pigs" invasion of Cuba by Cuban American refugees.

It was the year that Major League Baseball would begin to expand, and it was the year in which Roger Maris would break Babe Ruth's homerun record in the American League. Willie Mays hit four homeruns in one game at Milwaukee's County Stadium, and Warren Spahn, age 41, threw his second no-hitter, beating the Giants 1-0. He would also win his 300th game in 1961.

In a two-column, three-inch display advertisement in the April 6, 1961 *Shakopee Valley News*, Vic Haas was giving away fish during Lent: "All You Can Eat $1.25." Fifty years later, even the churches were getting as much as $12.00 for the same deal.

John Freund was rewarded for his tournament-hitting slump by being named manager of the Shakopee Indians for 1961. "Nobody wanted it," Butch Kreuser said, explaining why the Indians had a different manager every year for several years in a row. But player-manager John Freund's Shakopee Indians would perform much like the previous teams. They lost the league opener to Jordan, and then put together a run that left them atop the league at season's end with a 9-1 record. Kerber resumed his dominance of River Valley League teams, and John would spell him now and then when games bunched up from making up rainouts or just the vagaries of scheduling. Kerber's 11 wins against just 2 losses led the Indians to their overall season record of 17-4. But John was 5-0, pitching well when he answered his own call, such as the second game of the season, when he fired a three-hitter to beat Prior Lake, 4-3.

The headline on the sports page of the June 22, 1961 *Shakopee Valley News* was a familiar testimony: "Kerber, Freund Power Indians to 4-0 Win at Savage Sunday." Leading 1-0 in the eighth inning on Kerber's four-hit pitching and solo shot early in the game, John Freund sealed the deal with a three-run blast in the eighth inning. The win brought Shakopee to a 4-1 record and second place. Jordan was leading the league at 5-0 and coming to town for a Sunday night showdown at Riverside Park. Shakopee won a tight game, 3-2, with Kerber pitching a five-hit gem and Freund getting an RBI with one of the three hits the Indians managed against Jordan's Dick Hellmer. Kerber's string of 36 consecutive innings without giving up an earned run ended, and John Freund, playing right field, was noted in the newspaper's account of the game as having made "a fine, running catch in deep right center to take an extra-base hit away" from a Jordan hitter in the ninth inning to help Kerber retire the side and put the game on ice.

"He was just a super guy," Fred Kerber said of John Freund. "If you were down, he would pick you up. He loved ball, and he was fun to be with." Then Kerber, recalling the hundreds of baseballs that he had hit in batting practice and games, compared his hitting with that of John Freund and Joe Schleper, another Shakopee great. With his finger in the air, Kerber traced trajectories of typical balls he would hit, and you could follow a long, lazy fly ball in your mind's eye at the tip of Kerber's finger until it fell gently to the ground on the other side of the fence. "And Schleper's would go like this," Kerber said, as he again traced in the air with his finger the trajectory of a batted baseball that was a little longer and a little deeper than his own before it looped down.

"The balls that John hit would come off his bat like this," Kerber said, his hand darting across his chest and finger pointing up rather than looping down, "and then they seemed to just take off," like a turbo-charged engine giving boost to a sports car accelerating on the straightaway. "The difference in the way the balls were hit was unbelievable," Kerber said.

"There was only one stud on our team," Kerber said.

Shakopee won its fourth straight River Valley League title with a 9-1 record for Manager John Freund, who admittedly didn't hit well again while worrying about egos and lineups, arms, and opponents. They drew Belle Plaine in the first round of the league playoffs and won the first game handily, 8-3. Then, in a near-replica of his opening game performance in 1959 and headlined on the sports page of the August 10, 1961, *Shakopee Valley News*: "Indians Advance On Freund's No-Hitter." He shut out Belle Plaine, 6-0, while striking out 13.

In the league playoff finals, a two-out-of-three affair, Jordan won the first game 5-4, then Shakopee took the next two games, with Freund and Kerber each winning a game on the mound. John took another no-hitter into the sixth inning in his 12-5 win. Kerber pitched a two-hit, 5-0 shutout in the rubber game at Shakopee in front of a crowd of 1,000 baseball fans.

Tuned up and running on all eight cylinders again, Shakopee blew away Farmington 8-4 and 15-2 in the first round of Region 6B play. John led off the first game with what was described as "a towering homerun." Then, the Indians defeated Waseca two straight to gain another state tournament berth. They drew the same Springfield nine at the same venue, St. Cloud's Municipal Stadium, they had won the state championship from just two years earlier. Manager Freund went with the same strategy that had worked then. He pitched the draftees, but Weckman wasn't among them in 1961. John, himself, took the mound in the fifth inning after Springfield had scored all of its nine runs in the game. But it was too late. Springfield 9, Shakopee 4.

John Freund didn't play much baseball the next three years. He couldn't. He didn't play at all in 1962 or 1964. He played only about half time in 1963. He hurt his hand opening his garage door at home sometime during this period. Somehow, he got his hand caught in the bi-fold door sections as they roll up and down on the track. "He really ripped his hand bad," his brother Bob said. "He tore tendons and couldn't grip a bat or throw a ball for a long time."

Shakopee won the River Valley League again in 1962 with a record of 8-2 without John, but they lost the league playoffs to Jordan.

The next year, 1963, would be the last for Fred Kerber as a Shakopee Indian and the first year for a new slugger, Joe Schleper. Despite the conspicuous absence of John Freund from the lineup and Howie Heller's claim that the Indians really didn't hit that well, that "we won with pitching and defense," everybody hit through the first half of the 1963 season. The headline in the June 27 issue of the *Shakopee Valley News* sports page would tell the story: "Indians Blast LeCenter 11-4 As Team Batting Average Hits .372." They'd come back from a 3-2 deficit at Belle Plaine in the seventh on Jake Harsh's three-run blast, winning 7-3. Then, two wins against New Prague, including a 4-0, three-hit shutout by Ozbun on Sunday, June 30, put Shakopee back in their accustomed lead of the River Valley League with a 7-1 record.

Then John Ozbun threw a four-hit, 16-strikeout shutout to beat Jordan, 6-0, and give Shakopee a commanding two-game league lead at 9-1 with playoffs looming. Just in time to tune up for the playoffs, John Freund re-joined the Indians from what the July 18 *news* account of the game referred to as "a two-year retirement" and helped Shakopee win its 10th game of the season. His old teammate was apparently glad to see John return, as the July 18 weekly headline read: "Fred Kerber Homers, Strikes out 16 As Indians Edge Le Sueur 7-6." Freund played both second base and third base in the game and went two for four at the plate.

It's not clear from records and memories of teammates whether John Freund had ever retired. We know he hurt a hand severely one year, and we know he also played some fast-pitch softball that summer and was reported to have hit three homeruns in two games in the Shakopee Fast-Pitch League. He may have just been enjoying the ball, or he may have been trying to get a feel for his hand and arm after a year of rehabilitation.

Regardless, the Indians finished atop the league again at 12-2. John pitched credibly in an exhibition game against Chaska, scattering nine hits while striking out 10 in an 8-3 win over the neighbors and a tune up for league playoffs. They swept LeCenter and Jordan each two straight, then lost the first game of the Region 6B tournament, 5-1, with John playing shortstop. He went two for three in the 6-1 win over St. Benedict, then two for two in the 12-0 shutout over Canon Falls on the combined two-hitter by Ozbun and Kerber. That set up the deciding game with Canon Falls and the state tournament entry for the winner. John Freund had a habit of playing big in big games, and he would take Shakopee to the state tournament for the fifth time in seven years. He took a shutout into the eighth inning in the 4-1 win, and here's the report from the September 5, 1963 *Shakopee Valley News*:

> John Freund pitched a magnificent two-hitter and struck out 10 Comets.
> He won his own game in the seventh inning with a two-run homer over
> the right-field fence.

Biwabik sent Shakopee into the loser's bracket, 9-6, in the second round, after Shakopee had shut out Nisswa, 4-0, on Ozbun's four hitter in the first game. John Freund then took the mound for Shakopee against Battle Lake and fired a three hitter, taking a shutout into the eighth inning, when two costly errors lost the game, 1-0. The game was even closer than the score, as Shakopee cleanup hitter Joe Schleper twice took Battle Lake outfielders to the wall with long fly-ball outs. Tom Melchior, who played left field for the Indians, compiled team batting averages in his *Scott County Baseball* and shows Freund's average at .375 for the 1963 season, behind Schleper at .385 and Larson at .381. The team's won-loss record, according to Melchior, was 21-5, excluding "exhibition" games.

John Freund either retired again in 1964 or did have the mishap that injured his hand and the tendons up into his arm. At any rate, he didn't play baseball for the Shakopee Indians in 1964. Neither did Howie Heller. That meant the left side of Shakopee's reliable defensive unit would be re-tooled. It also meant a 10-4 league record and a tie for the title with Belle Plaine. But Jordan took out Belle Plaine in the playoffs, and Shakopee cruised past LeCenter, then Jordan, winning two straight games against each of them. They then beat Northfield and Lonsdale in the Region 6B tournament to once again gain entry to the state tournament, held in 1964 at Brownton. They won three straight close games, then lost a nail biter, 3-2, to St. Bonifacius, which went on to win the state championship.

Like Houdini, disappearing then reappearing, John Freund returned for the 1965 Shakopee Indian baseball season, and he brought Heller back with him. Oh, was he back. Freund combined with Mike Nevin on a five-hitter to beat Jordan in the flood-delayed league opener, 16-2. He pitched seven strong innings and went three for four at the plate, with a homerun and five RBIs. He had a triple in the 8-1 win over Le Sueur, went three for five with three RBIs in a 13-3 rout of Prior Lake, a single hit against Savage, then three for seven with four more RBIs in the 35-run outburst at LeCenter. Shakopee and John Freund were hitting on all eight cylinders again. The team batting average of .340 was led by Schleper's .500 and Freund's .462. Not far behind were Larson at .426 and Stemmer at .393.

John continued to lead Shakopee's mopping up of the rest of the league with his solid hitting. He went three for four, with "a long homerun and six RBIs," according to the *Shakopee Valley News* on July 21 against Prior Lake, then two for two with another homerun and two RBIs in a shutout of Savage on July 25. The team batting average was a torrid .366. Schleper was batting over .500, and Freund was just under .500. With the 12-1 win over New Prague and John going three for five at the plate, Shakopee closed out the regular league season with an unblemished 14-0 record.

The Shakopee Valley News of August 5, 1965, notes that Joe Schleper, the club's top hitter at .528, sat out the final game. Meanwhile, John inched up to .458.

Shakopee swept two games from LeCenter, with John hitting a homerun and knocking in four runs in the 8-3 elimination game win. They repeated the sweep of Le Sueur in the finals of the league playoffs. They beat Northfield and Lonsdale in a repeat of the previous year's Region 6B tournament. John had two of the team's three hits in the 6-4 win over Northfield–a double in the first inning and an RBI-triple "off the wall" in the third. Then, Shakopee cooled off the torrid Jim Kubes of Lonsdale in a 5-1 win, followed up by a 4-3 win over Lonsdale again and their New Market draftee, Terry Schmitz. They'd beaten the best pitchers from the DRS League, Kubes and Schmitz, and would take their 21-0 league-playoffs-regional record (23-3 overall) into the state tournament against Pipestone at a favorite venue, St Cloud. In a warm-up game against Arlington, John stole home in the bottom of the eighth to give Shakopee the 5-4 win. Jim Stoll hit a long homerun in the game, "into the trees," according to the *Valley News* account of the game. The two teams would see each other again soon enough.

Shakopee won its first two state tournament games at St. Cloud, 8-1 over Pipestone and 4-1 over Halstad. Then St. Boni, eventual state champion, shut them out, 3-0, despite John's two doubles. With one loss, Shakopee went up against Jim Stoll and Arlington. Stoll collared both Freund and Schleper in pitching a five-hitter and striking out 15 Indians in Arlington's 2-1 win. The two losses in the state tournament meant a season record of 25 wins against 5 losses for Shakopee.

The 1965-'66 Indians were arguably the best baseball team in the history of Shakopee. Their string of 29 straight wins in the River Valley League ended on July 28, 1966, at Riverside Park in Shakopee. They had gone undefeated in the league with 14 wins in 1965 and were in the process of going undefeated again, when, with the league title wrapped up and nothing really to prove or to show anyone, lowly New Prague beat them, 3-1. But 13 straight league wins and 18 straight overall in 1966 made them a strong contender in the state tournament again.

According to the inaugural issue of the 1967 *Northwest Umpires Review*, Shakopee's team batting average for the 1966 regular season was a blistering .312, with Roger Lambrecht leading the league with his .500 average. Schleper and Freund had batted just north and south, respectively, of .500 in 1965. Schleper nearly duplicated the feat in 1966, batting .417 while O'Brien, Heller, and John Freund hit over .300 in regular league play. Moreover, John had nine wins against the sole loss to New Prague at the end of the regular season to go with Mike Nevin's

16-1 pitching record for the season. Both were impressive, but John's power pitching had a way of demolishing teams as it disheartened them. He beat Savage 6-3, for example, early in the season on a five-hitter with 12 strikeouts. He went seven innings and got the win with another 12 strikeouts against a St. Paul Class-A team that managed only three hits off John and Mike Nevin in relief.

The Shakopee Valley News of June 30, 1966, reported on the team's 9-1 win over New Prague: "The strong, seven-hit pitching of Righthander John Freund gave the Indians their 10th victory overall this season against no losses." He had 10 strikeouts in the game.

Freund and Nevin combined to shut out Prior Lake on one hit July 21, 1966. He gave up just four hits in an 8-inning stint against the league all-stars in which Shakopee won 2-1, and he fired a six hitter to beat Le Sueur, 8-2. "Freund Blanks Savage 8-0 in R-V Play-Off Semi-Finals" headlined the sports page of the August 18 *Shakopee Valley News*. He scattered six hits and struck out 11 in the playoff win. Shakopee earned a berth in the state tournament again by beating Lonsdale, 7-6, in the Region 6B finals. Lonsdale had knocked out Nevin with three runs in the third inning. Le Sueur draftee Ron Anderson gave Manager Joe Schleper five good innings of relief, but Schleper wanted his big warhorse throwing his heavy ball against the likes of Smisek and Kubes in the last inning. In the final battle of the game, power-pitching John Freund fanned power-hitting Jim Kubes for the final out of the game with the tying run on third base.

John hit a homerun in the 11-1 pasting of LeCenter, and under the sports page headline, "Down Savage with 4 Homers–Seek 30th Straight League Win," Rick Luis of the *Shakopee Valley News* reported in the July 28th issue on the 8-3 win over Savage that could have been much worse:

> Savage's Warren Butler Memorial Field was its usual hot and steamy self this July 24, but nothing could stop the Shakopee bats. John Freund belted two homers far over the right-field wall.

"When he hit the ball," Danny Driscoll said of John Freund's hitting, "it made the same sound that major leaguers make when they hit the ball." Weckman affirmed Driscoll's assessment of John Freund's attack of the baseball. "He hit the ball just like Dick Siebert did in batting practice," Weck said. "Every ball was hit on the button," and Siebert had 11 years of Major League Baseball play on his resume, with a lifetime batting average of over .280.

Shakopee's fourth straight Region 6B championship put them into the Minnesota State Tournament in their own backyard: Belle Plaine. Tiger Stadium's short right-field fence is marked at 300 feet from home plate, but every hitter who gazes down that line wishes he were a left-handed pull hitter. And every left-handed hitter with any pop at all drools and lusts for pitches in his wheelhouse. The distance down the line is closer to 275 feet than it is to 300 feet. Freund and Schleper knew that they only needed to get the bat on the ball with their normal swings at Belle Plaine. They were probably the best left-handed hitters in the tournament.

Shakopee beat Ely, 6-4, in 10 innings in the second round of play and beat Springfield, 7-3, in the quarterfinals. Springfield chased Shakopee draftee starter Ron Anderson off the mound with three runs in the first inning. Enter John Freund.

While Joe Schleper led the attack at bat, John Freund pitched one-hit ball for eight innings to win the game and put Shakopee in the semi-finals against Perham.

Here's the report from Rick Luis in the September 15, 1966, *Shakopee Valley News* under the headline, "'Battle of Homers' in State Semi Finale For Indians' 1966 Season":

> The Shakopee Indians came to the end of a brilliant season on a muggy Sunday afternoon, September 11, when they dropped a 9 to 4 decision to Perham's Pirates, the eventual Class B State champions . . .
>
> Shakopee and Perham staged a 'wild and wooly' struggle, before 1,839 paid fans. The game saw eight homeruns, seven by left-handers, for what is believed to be a State tournament record.
>
> All Shakopee's runs were scored on homers, all coming with no one aboard. All four came shockingly close together, cutting the Indians from a 5 to 0 deficit to one of 5 to 4 and electrifying the large spectator throng.

John Freund started the homerun parade with what was called a "routine fly ball" over the short, right-field fence, one of three hits on the day for him. Schleper, Kuehl, and Larson also homered for Shakopee. But Perham had brought their own big guns to town:

> The Perham Pirates supplied plenty of power to match that of the Indians with four homers of their own, three off starter-loser Mike Nevin, who dropped his first of 17 decisions this year.

It would be 13 years before another Shakopee baseball team made it to the Minnesota State Amateur Baseball Tournament. In 1979, three familiar names, but a generation removed, would help the Shakopee Cubs return to the state tournament: Joe Schleper, Jr., Jack Freund, and Dan Heller.

Perham would win the 1966 state championship, beating Brownton, which had beaten Arlington in the other semi-final game, 4-3, on three unearned runs and the left arm of 38-year-old Gerald Hochsprung. It was the rubber game in five meetings between the two towns in 1966, and it would tee matters up for 1967 between Arlington and Perham.

John Freund would play his last season of serious baseball in 1967–20 years after graduating from Minneapolis Roosevelt High School and signing a contract to play professionally in the Chicago Cub organization at Janesville, Wisconsin.

John's baseball skills had shown some wear and tear the previous season. Now, he was another year older, a little thicker in the waist, a little heavier in the legs. Young men had replaced him as the hitting stars on the team. In fact, Dale Hauger of Shakopee would lead the league in batting with a .431 average that year in comparison to John's .316 and Joe Schleper's .250, according to the July 30 *Northwest Umpire's Review*. The world was turning. The fat lady was singing, and The Fiddler was playing. But John Freund was still dangerous at the plate and on the mound. He helped lead Shakopee to another 13-1 record and another River Valley League title.

Nevin had taken over the yeoman's share of the pitching duties, much as Fred Kerber had done for 10 years up until he retired in 1963. But an August 3 issue of the *Shakopee Valley News* summarized Indian pitching: John Freund had pitched 15 innings for a 2-0 record. He had given up a measly 9 hits and struck out 17 opposing batters. His ERA? Zip, as in 0.00.

The sports page of the July 20 News had headlined John's gem against Savage: "Freund's 2-Hitter Brings 5-0 Win Over Savage," and the article notes that he went two for four at the plate to raise his batting average to .355. Then, he seems to have vanished for several weeks by his conspicuous absence from game accounts, probably nursing an injury to make sure he would be healthy for another playoff run. Indeed, John was ready and would pitch the elimination game of league playoffs against New Prague and a couple of newbies in the league. He went seven innings against Gary Connolly and Vic Moore, giving up just four hits, three of which were infield scratches. Meanwhile, Shakopee knocked out Connolly early with five runs and beat up Moore for 15 more runs on 12 hits the rest of the way. John had an RBI-triple off the centerfield wall to show he had some power and some leg left to go with a strong right arm. But Shakopee's reign of Region 6B ended, and the doorway to the state tournament at Alexandria was blocked with losses to Lonsdale and Miesville, 17-2 and 4-3, respectively.

Shakopee was 20-6 on the season overall, a good record again. But it wasn't good enough. "The handwriting was on the wall."

"The fat lady had sung–Church was out." Shakopee's phenomenal run of Minnesota River Valley baseball dominance was over. Table 1 below spells out that "Yankee dominance" of Shakopee's reign during the Golden Age of Baseball in the Minnesota River Valley. It also punctuates what the presence of John Freund meant. In short, the best years that Shakopee had were with John Freund in the lineup. The worst years, while still not bad, were without him. With John Freund, the Shakopee Indians get to the Big Dance. Without him, they bog down in RVL playoffs or region play. In sum, it looks like this great team that rules baseball on the river for a decade or more needs the great lefthander, Weckman, to win the state tournament. But they need John Freund to get there. What these statistics and all other statistics fail to show is how many ways John Freund could beat you. He beat you with his arm pitching and in the field. He beat you with his legs on the base paths or in getting to balls in the field that most players couldn't get to. He beat you with his glove at any position he played. He beat you with his head-from knowing how to play the game regardless of the position he was playing. He beat you with his mere presence in a thousand ways that can't be counted. These are the intangibles that fell under his role as "The Captain," and the immeasurable qualities of his character that so pleased The Fiddler.

Table 1. The John Freund Years At Shakopee–*A good ball club without him, Shakopee was a great ball club with John Freund.*

Year	RVL Record	Overall Record	Culmination	Freund Play?
1958	7-3	14-7	RVL & Playoff Champs	No
1959	8-2	25-4	RVL, Playoff Region & State Champs	Yes
1960	10-0	24-5	RVL, Region Champs	Yes
1961	9-1	17-4	RVL, Playoff & Region Champs	Yes
1962	8-2	13-5	RVL Champs, Lost RVL Playoffs	No

1963	11-1	25-8	RVL, Playoff, & Region Champs	Yes
1964	10-4	21-8	Tied League, Region Champs	No
1965	14-0	25-5	RVL, Playoff, & Region Champs	Yes

"That was it for most of us then," Howie Heller said. Without the horses, especially their big warhorse, in 1968, the team would go 6-11, Shakopee's first losing season since 1953–nearly a generation. The John Freund generation. His was a bridge between "the Greatest Generation" and The Boomers and Generation X-ers. His greatness was taken for granted in the Golden Age of Baseball, masked as it was in a lingering character asset of The Greatest that would sadly and slowly evaporate in the coming decades: humility. Again, "He just didn't talk about himself," his manager of the 1959 state champion Indians, Butch Kreuser, said. He wasn't like that."

"Nobody ever quit on him at Rahr," his son Jack said, "because he was so fair with everybody." He could be tough as a supervisor in management, and even Fred Kerber admitted that John "chewed my butt out one time. But I knew he had to do it. I was wrong."

He was really something," Weckman said. "I just liked watching him. He could do everything so well."

He like the officiating that he took up after 1967, according to Jack Freund, who said he worked high school games with his father for a few years. "He liked umpiring the girls' softball, because there was no wasted time," Jack said. "We'd be done in 45 minutes or an hour."

"He told me that he liked working the girls' games," Ken Hanson, Jordan athletic director, who wrote out the checks to Freund and other officials working Jordan High School games, "because he wouldn't get 'F-bombed' during the games and the pay was the same."

"He worked a lot of MIAC football games," Dick Erickson said, "but he didn't really care for the highly successful coach at St. John's–John Gagliardi." John Freund was always a gentleman, on and off the field, and "Gagliardi was pretty hard on officials."

John Freund made a comeback of sorts on the diamond in 1976, according to his son Jack. He wanted to play a baseball game with Jack and his other son, Jerry, both of whom played for Marystown that year in the DRS League. "He pitched seven innings and did well," Jack said, "and he went two for four at the plate with a pair of singles," Jack recalled. Undoubtedly, one of the only sporting achievements John Freund ever boasted about was the inning in his game with his sons when Marystown loaded the bases with Freund's": John on third; Jerry on second; and Jack on first. It was "one of the biggest thrills," according to the brief memoirs included in the Freund estate papers.

The same papers, written by his wife, Pat Freund, indicate that John was in the coronary care unit of St. Francis Hospital in January of 1979 with an irregular heartbeat. But the boys maintain that their father's cardiovascular issues didn't show up until much later, maybe three years or so before he died. He did, however, have atrial fibrillation, which is a specific type of arrhythmic heartbeat. Electric shock is one means of restoring the heart to what is called "normal sinus rhythm." John had the treatment twice, and he was put on the high-risk prescription drug

Coumadin-Warfarin, known generally, but erroneously, as "a blood thinner." The drug doesn't change the viscosity, or thickness, or the blood. It changes the time the blood takes to coagulate.

He'd had a stroke, and "we noticed that he started to drift to the right when out going for a walk," Jerry said. "Then he had a series of TIAs, or mini-strokes."

"One night, he got up from watching TV, went to bed, and a half hour later he was gone," Jerry said of his father. John Freund was 80 years old when he crossed Home Plate in the evening of October 7, 2010. No better ballplayer ever played the game in the Minnesota River Valley, and if a better man ever played baseball around here, we never knew him.

Jim Stoll

*He is at or near the top of the list of best
ballplayers to ever play baseball in Minnesota.*

— Chuck Warner, Past President, Minnesota Hall of Fame

"We were having a steak dinner–Arlington always took good care of us–in the back room of that bar on main street in downtown Jordan, waiting for the game that night," Jim Stoll said, as he recalled the 1969 Class-B Minnesota State Amateur Baseball Championship game. "I could hear a lot of talk coming from the bar up front," he said, "and this guy comes back to where we were eating, and says, 'Hey! Who's Arlington pitching tonight?'"

"And Eddie Mueller, our manager, says, 'Jim Stoll.'"

"He turned and walked back into the bar," Stoll said. "I got up and followed him in there, and I watched him count out eight fresh, crisp one-hundred-dollar bills on the bar." Stoll could do the inflation conversion as quickly as anyone: "That's like 10 grand in today's money," he said. The guy was betting $800 on Prior Lake.

It stung. The stranger in Geno's Tap Room with the mouth and the money was betting against Jim Stoll. But Jim didn't say a word. He didn't have the money in his billfold to back up his own mouth with what he wanted to do–bet the farm on his own arm and his own heart.

The sting didn't go away. It had become a deep burn a couple hours later when he began to put on his baseball uniform. "We dressed for the game up at the high school–both teams," Stoll said. "With just my sliding pad shorts on, I walked over to the Prior Lake locker room and said":

> Hey! I'm Jim Stoll. You college boys can't hit a curve ball. That's all
> you're gonna see tonight. And I turned and walked out.

Stoll said that he had met Dick Siebert, long-time baseball coach of the University of Minnesota Gophers, when he was in the air force in Grand Rapids, MN, and playing baseball for the Marble Mallards in the late-1950s. Siebert liked to come up to the Iron Range to scout the tough baseball players that were hockey players in the winter.

"Siebert had told me that the college kids hit fastballs well, but that they couldn't hit the curve ball. I remembered it."

With awe and respect usually reserved for the deity, Dave Hartmann said over lunch, "Jim Stoll had a Major League curveball–a Blyleven curveball." Hartmann would know. He was a high school, college, and amateur town team catcher for more than 25 years. He'd caught Stoll and probably another 100 pitchers in that span, and called balls and strikes behind the plate or just watched with a wizened eye another 100 or more pitchers.

A member of the Minnesota State Baseball Board since 2005, Hartmann recalled having to ride out the postseason games in the dugout while a drafted catcher, Gary Porter from Chaska, caught the two pitchers Arlington had also drafted. "I was on the bench for that championship game," Hartmann said. But it was a good seat in a full house for a magnificent performance by a great ballplayer, with an arm that one more time, despite the bad rotator cuff, glittered as though it were made of pure, 24-karat gold.

"Jim Stoll was the best amateur baseball player in the state of Minnesota between 1963 and about 1974," Hartmann said. "He might be the best baseball player in Minnesota I've ever seen."

Jim Stoll was at least among the best amateur baseball players in the state as early as 1957, when he played for the Marble Mallards. But what few people realize, and even fewer baseball people would want to acknowledge, is that Jim Stoll played softball for an air force base team in a Grand Rapids league before he played baseball in Minnesota. He was picked for an area all-star team that played Eddie Feigner–*The King and His Court*–that year. Feigner had been timed at 104 mph in one instance, and 114 mph in another, pitching from the softball mound that at 46 feet from home plate means significantly less time for a hitter to react and swing than in baseball with the mound at 60 feet, 6 inches and reaching the plate at slower speeds. But Stoll said he hit two line drives the first two times up "right at the lone fielder," he said, with Feigner on the mound. "But he struck my ass out from second base the third time," Stoll said of Feigner. "He threw a riser I swore was going to bounce in front of me. It broke up sharply and crossed the plate at my waist." Stoll was in good company, for Eddie Feigner struck out six Major League baseball players in succession at the 1967 Major League All Star Game: Willie Mays; Willie McCovey; Maury Wills; Roberto Clemente; Harmon Killebrew; and Brooks Robinson.

Yet, softball–both slow-pitch and fast-pitch–has always been considered a poor stepbrother to baseball–by baseball elitists. Eddie Feigner's career tells the story of a great athlete, a great pitcher, between 1946 and 2007: 9,743 wins; 141,517 strikeouts; 930 no-hitters; 238 perfect games.

Jim Stoll had a genuine ballplayer's respect for *The King and his Court*: "The three guys that played with Feigner could all have played Major League Baseball," Stoll said, "especially the catcher. He hit three homeruns in the game over the 360 foot fence in left-center field." Not even the poor, early version of the metal bats existed then. These balls were hit with a wood bat by a great hitter. Jim Stoll would know: "I pitched a little softball myself at Arlington," Stoll said. "But I'd get wild once in awhile and have to throw changeups."

Jim Stoll would meet another old-timer of national prominence in 1957 while stationed at Grand Rapids and playing baseball for Marble. He said the Mallards were playing a doubleheader in International Falls. In between games, he inquired as to the whereabouts of Bronko Nagurski, All-American fullback and tackle with the University of Minnesota, and charter member of the National Football League

Hall of Fame after a professional career with the Chicago Bears. He wanted to meet the Minnesota legend. "I went out to his gas station," Stoll said, and on his way into the station he asked an older guy sitting outside watching the traffic where he could find Bronko Nagurski. "He was a big guy, stout," Stoll said, "and he said to me, 'You found him. That's me.'"

"I shook his hand," Stoll said, "and what I noticed was how his hand just dwarfed mine. And I've got big hands." Huge for his day in the 1930s as a running back at a thick 235 pounds on a 6-2 frame, what Stoll noticed remains a Nagurski NFL record: Bronco Nagurski's ring size of 19-1/2 is reported to be the largest NFL Championship ring on record.

Stoll said he sat down and talked with the giant of Minnesota Gopher and Chicago Bear football for about 15 to 20 minutes. "We talked football," Stoll said, who then returned to the baseball park and the second game of the doubleheader.

Dave Hartmann has been around and seen a lot of good amateur baseball. He said he started playing amateur baseball in 1968 for Arlington and that he played on three state championship teams–two at Arlington (1969 and 1979) and one at Dundas. He played at St. John's University for four years, and he played for good town teams until 1993. Then he said he umpired and followed and supported baseball before he joined the Minnesota State Baseball Board in 2005.

As for pitching, catchers know even better than pitchers who can pitch. They know who's got some stuff on the ball and some smarts upstairs. Most importantly, they know who's got the heart to come up with big pitches in big situations. Hartmann, a long-time catcher, had this to say: "If I was going to pick one guy to pitch for me–in all my years of baseball–Jim Stoll is the guy."

Dave Hartmann ticked off a litany of pitchers he's seen as an umpire or a fan, caught, or batted against in his 25 years of playing amateur baseball, and another 20 years of umpiring and in various supporting roles.

"It's not even close," Hartmann said, "between Jim Stoll and the rest, and I've seen them all over a very long time."

Interestingly, Chuck Warner, the first Brownton baseball man inducted into the Minnesota Hall of Fame, in 1971, and who chaired the Hall's Selection Committee for eight years, mentioned Stoll's hitting with the same singular respect in an interview in August of 2013: "If there's anybody I'd want to hit with the game on the line, it's Jim Stoll."

Individual statistics weren't kept in the 1950s and 1960s for amateur ballplayers the way they have been kept since the 1980s. Official scorebooks of games, and won-lost records of teams and their place in league standings were meticulously tracked. But individual stories and statistics were kind of verboten in the community weeklies in an era when team play was more celebrated than individual statistics. That, too, may tell a major difference in ballplayers of the different eras. A scouring of newspaper clippings revealed the publication of just two years of Stoll batting averages: .403 in 1963; and "just under .500" in 1967.

"I don't think I ever hit under .400 in amateur ball," Stoll said, an assessment seconded by Brownton's Chuck Warner: "I think he hit over .400 every year he played." But Stoll admitted he was walked a lot, which helped his batting average, not so much intentionally by pitchers, but from just pitching carefully to him. "After awhile," Stoll said, "you don't get a lot of good pitches to hit." Invariably, two walks in a game that left him with two hits in three official times at bat helped his average. That pitchers grew increasingly wary of pitching to him speaks volumes about the respect and fear they had of Stoll at bat. Remember also that much of Stoll's great hitting was done while pitching a game.

Warner wrote of Stoll's pitching in an August, 1963, *Brownton Bulletin* column: "Miller (sic), a bachelor, says Stoll has been the standout in his team's drive this year. He won 11 of the team's league games and in 79 innings allowed just two earned runs and 25 hits. He walked but 10 and struck out 172, or better than two per frame." That means Stoll averaged, on a nine-inning-per-game basis, 18 to 20 strikeouts. Moreover, such high praise came from the weekly newspaper editor of a competitor.

Indeed, a review of the brief summaries of Arlington games in *The History of Arlington Baseball* reveals the dominating nature of Jim Stoll's pitching: Stoll pitched a no-hitter against Gaylord in his second start of the 1963 season, after shutting out Stewart and striking out 15 in the home opener. Then he shut out Brownton, 7-0, on a two-hitter with 16 strikeouts. This was followed by a relief stint against Gibbon, coming in to pitch in the first inning with only one out and finishing the game with 17 strikeouts while yielding two hits and no runs. These were *typical* Stoll ballgames and seasons, not cherry-picked exceptions. He routinely pitched one-, two-, and three-hitters while striking out 10 or more in the game. He just missed a no-hitter against league nemesis Chaska in 1967. With two outs and a two-strike count on the batter in the ninth, his centerfielder misplayed a fly ball into a double. His performance at the plate was equally impressive.

"Jim Stoll was the Mickey Mantle of amateur baseball back in the 1960s," according to Dave Hartmann. While he said that Stoll was "still a good hitter in his later years, he was nothing like he was when he first came to Arlington." And Mickey Mantle never pitched. When you're pitching a baseball game, you don't concentrate on the opposition pitcher. You concentrate on the hitters. Your own hitting can suffer.

Warner, the first Hall of Fame inductee from Brownton, in 1971, for his baseball organizing and promotion efforts, said of Stoll that his induction into the Hall of Fame was delayed because he was "just a ballplayer." The committee, according to Warner, was into selecting people for the Hall on the basis of their community services rather than their skills or performance on the field. Cutting the ballpark grass, chalking the lines, selling tickets and promoting the community in bars and at meetings had replaced excellence on the field in the game of baseball for admission into the Hall of Fame.

"Jim Stoll was first and always a ballplayer," Hartmann said.

"He'd have gone in right away," Warner said, had the committee been committed to ball playing. Instead, Stoll would not be inducted into the Hall of Fame until 2004 at age 67–nearly 30 years after he said he pitched his last game–for the Marble Mallards against one of Dick Siebert's summer collegiate league teams in 1976 and no-hit them for eight innings.

Stoll's forearms made Popeye's look like those of a stickman. His right arm reminds you in team pictures of the serving arm of Rod Laver in tennis, or the pitching arm of Eddie Feigner. He was *really* intense, and he expected of others what he demanded of himself–excellence. "He was the type of guy," according to Hartmann, "who would go out and give you everything he had–and then some." Moreover, according to Hartmann, "He's probably the toughest guy I've ever known. In a bar fight, he's the guy I wanted on my side." He was the type of man of whom it was said, "You gotta kill him to beat him."

"Hell," Stoll said, "I *had* to play well at Arlington–I had a wife and five kids. If I didn't produce, I was afraid I'd lose my job."

As good as Jim Stoll still was on the mound and at the plate in the late 1960s, the Prior Lake Jays had arguably the best amateur baseball team in the state of Minnesota between 1968 and 1976. Don Meyer, a Baseball Boss in Prior Lake, and Herb Isakson, assistant baseball coach at the University of Minnesota, had assembled a team of mostly former Gophers, most of whom had likely grown up in and were living in Bloomington–across the Minnesota River and into what everybody just referred to as "the cities." Bloomington was within the 15-mile radius of Prior Lake required by written league rules, but a violation of the unwritten rules in being across the river. Prior Lake was loaded.

It was said of Gordie Nevers that he had pitched AAA ball for five years. In fact, Gordie Nevers played four years of professional baseball, *as high as AAA for a part of one season*. His won-loss record had been 25-25, with an ERA of 5.14, according to the online source. He had also pitched in the Southern Minny.

Fred DeGregoire, at bat and in the outfield, was a clone of Fred Lynn, the great Boston Red Sox centerfielder. Although not a former Gopher, Bobby Kelly was simply an outstanding shortstop who would win the MVP award in the 1976 state tournament–"Only his size kept him out of the major leagues," scouts were heard to say. Gary Reieirson, the big first baseman, had played professionally in the Northern League after playing both football and baseball at the U of M. John Dill from St. Cloud State, Brian Love, Steve Schneider, and other Gophers would all play for Prior Lake during their great, if controversial, run.

Stoll admitted that he'd had arm trouble since making an off-balance throw to first after coming off the mound and picking up a dribbler down the third-base line while playing for the Pirates' Savannah farm team in a game at Asheville in 1960. "It was like somebody jammed an ice pick into my shoulder," Stoll said. He'd never known any arm trouble before. But it would never be the same again. If he pitched, it would be four or five days, sometimes a week or more, before he could lift a cup of coffee to his mouth or comb his hair. There was a numbness and dull searing pain he couldn't shake or stretch out.

He said he was 9-1 at the time he went on the disabled list, "actually 10-1," he said, with the game he pitched for the parent Pittsburgh Pirates against their AAA team from Salt Lake City in the middle of the summer. He hoped the time on the DL would give him the time he needed to heal. He would finish strong enough, at 16-7 on the season, he thought, but Jim Stoll knew he was in trouble. He couldn't throw between outings, and sometimes he felt the pain just warming up or after a couple of innings. He could no longer keep his arm in shape, or strengthen it, with regular throwing. He had to rest, hope the pain would go away, and take aspirin before he took the mound again in a game.

He hoped his arm would heal over the winter, so he could report with a healthy arm to the Pirates AAA affiliate, Columbus, the next spring. He reported and said he even threw a one-hitter in the last preseason game of the 1961 season for AAA Columbus. But his arm had not healed. He knew the routine well. He couldn't lift his arm for a week after that performance, and he hobbled through the year with ever-shorter stints and limited service and a burgeoning ERA. "I'd lost speed and control," he said. In the off-season, the Pirates sent him to Johns Hopkins in Baltimore for orthopedic diagnosis and surgery, if necessary.

He'd torn the rotator cuff, a kind of universal joint in the shoulder where four muscles and tendons come together to serve human needs for the strength and range of motion required in lifting, rowing, painting, swimming, brushing your teeth, and combing your hair–and throwing baseballs. Doctors told him that he could undergo surgery to repair the rotator, or he could go home and rest, hoping for healing. Stoll had seen a number of guys who'd had the surgery, and from the scars he saw, he thought that option was little more than a barbaric roll of the dice in the fall of 1961. "There was no way, I was gonna let them cut me," Stoll said. The Pirates released him. His professional baseball career was over.

In the winter of 1962, after the Pirates released him, Jim Stoll went "home" to the Iron Range of Northern Minnesota. After getting special permission from the state board to play amateur baseball, needed because he had signed a professional contract, Stoll would play baseball for the small town of Taconite, population about 200, that summer. He said they went to the state tournament that year and won their first three games before losing two games in a row in the double elimination format, 2-1 to, first, Gaylord, then Little Falls. "The only reason we lost," Stoll said, "is that all of our high school and college ballplayers were playing football and couldn't stay with us."

Augie and Eddie Mueller and Arlington were a season away, but they had seen Stoll pitch and they liked what they saw. The first state championship in 1967 at Alexandria was five years out.

"Arlington baseball was my major leagues," Stoll said, adding "But I had to take 12 aspirin before a game if I was pitching." Stoll and Arlington going against the Prior Lake Jays for the 1969 state championship in Jordan would attract the largest final day crowd for over 50 years. It was another chapter in *The David and Goliath Story*, too. "I think we were maybe 7-7 in league play that year," Stoll said. "Then we started playing good ball as we got into the playoffs."

Meanwhile, Prior Lake finished the 1969 season with a record of 20 wins and just four losses, according to Tom Melchior's *Scott County Baseball*, after having waltzed through the River Valley League again with a 12-1 record that followed on the heels of a 14-0 league record in 1968. After a relatively close game against Forest Lake in their opening round, winning 4-2, the Jays cruised past Cold Spring 5-1, Lake Henry 4-0, and Winona 13-1.

Jim Stoll liked the odds: big money against him; going against the best team in the state, but with a lineup of mostly college players–outstanding athletes, he knew, and good baseball players, but *school boys*. He liked the Jordan ballpark, too, he said. "It's tight and really contained and protected," he said. "You're there in a world all its own." You're insulated and isolated from the world–the way it should be for a ball game.

That world then included the continuing war in Vietnam in 1969. Indeed, 1500 miles west of the Minnesota River Valley, that world included Charles Manson, who had played out his "Helter Skelter" in California a month earlier. Then, between August 15 and 18, that world included "Woodstock," which happened on the pasture of a 600-acre dairy farm in upstate New York. A reported 500,000 people would fill the farm with the fumes of hashish and marijuana and human excrement.

Bob Dylan's "The Times They Are a-Changin'" had foretold of things "Blowin' in the Wind" five years earlier on all fronts. Astronaut Neil Armstrong would take "a giant leap for mankind" as he stepped from the lunar module to the moon. But Senator Ted Kennedy would walk away from the scene after swimming away from the vehicle he'd driven off a bridge on Chappaquiddick Island, Massachusetts, with Mary Jo Kopechne drowning in the car underwater. The book, *Honest to God*, by John Robinson, the popular and respected Anglican Bishop of Woolwich, England, published in 1963, would gain widespread awareness by 1969 in the U.S. Its message: "God is Dead."

Mickey Mantle would retire from baseball before the season began. Curt Flood would challenge baseball's reserve clause in December of that year, 1969, turning the entire structure of Major League Baseball on its ear. Indeed, the whole country had been turned inside out with the turbulence of the times. But you wouldn't know it at the Jordan ballpark.

The legal case involving Muhammed Ali's refusal of draft induction into the U.S. Army in 1967, for which he was stripped of his heavyweight title, was moving through the courts. Eventually, the U.S. Supreme Court would rule in his favor on the grounds he claimed–that the Vietnam War was against his Black Muslim religion.

The controversy would cost the boxer precious title-reigning years in the prime of his career, but it would help set up during the early 1970s some of the most memorable heavyweight bouts in the history of the sport. As a result, anticipation was at unprecedented levels by the time the first match between Ali and "Smokin'" Joe Frazier came off.

The first fight wasn't just a boxing match. It was "The Fight of the Century." Ali would taunt and insult Frazier publicly as an Uncle Tom. Frazier would let his vaunted left hook do his talking for him in the ring. He would knock Ali down with a crushing blow in the 15th round and win a decision between the two undefeated heavyweights to settle the dispute over who was the real heavyweight champion.

The second fight wasn't for the title, which Frazier had lost to George Foreman. It was for money and pride. Ali won a unanimous decision, which many said Frazier had actually won, setting up the rubber match, billed as "The Thrilla in Manilla." The fights were a clash of opposing styles and personalities, as well as the cultural distinctions each fighter symbolized. Ali talked trash and read the stuff of Elija Mohammed and Malcom X. Joe Frazier was quiet, brooding, and was said to read *The Bible*. Ali danced in the ring. Frazier stalked and churned relentlessly. A handsome man, Ali called Frazier "ugly," "a gorilla," in public. Frazier burned deep within, from where he stoked the fires that ignited his devastating left hook.

The fight lived up to its billing. Ali, as usual, dominated the first few rounds. By the start of the seventh, Frazier had found his rhythm. He looked to be coming on, while Ali looked to be tiring. Ali reportedly whispered in Frazier's ear, "Joe, they told me you was all washed up." Frazier replied, "They lied."

Eddie Futch, Frazier's trainer, refused to let his fighter return to the ring for the 15th round, because Frazier couldn't see. He had a cataract in his left eye, and his right eye was closed from the punishment Ali had given him. Joe Frazier had fought the 14th round virtually blind. Ali had won and after getting up off his stool to raise his hands in victory, he collapsed to the canvas, all in. He reportedly said of the fight, "That's the closest thing to dyin' I know of..." And *Sports Illustrated's* Mark Kram wrote of the fight, "Once more had Frazier taken the child of the gods to hell and back."

Jim Stoll, like millions across the country, liked Ali for his style and grace of movement as an athlete in the boxing ring. "But I liked Frazier after the fights," Stoll said. Ali was a showman and a media darling in the build up to the fights, but he crossed the line in his comments about Joe Frazier as a man. Frazier earned the respect of all for taking each fight to Ali with the enormous size of his heart and his left hook.

An old argument about the curveball being an optical illusion would re-surface about this time. Dizzy Dean's rebuttal over 30 years earlier had been to challenge the illusion theorists to stand behind a tree so he could show them firsthand what a curveball does. The freak show was well underway; all the crazies were coming out, not just the new breed.

It is doubtful that any fan at the ballpark or anybody in Jordan, Minnesota, that fall evening in 1969 knew who Charles Manson was. Some would have known Joan Baez, but they were not likely to have known other Woodstock performers such as Richie Havens, Sly and The Family Stone, The Jefferson Airplane, Jimi Hendrix, or Joe Cocker.

Most Jordan and other baseball people knew the living God from the Catholic, Lutheran, and Baptist or Methodist pulpits, and from their lives. They also knew that the curveball was real and that some pitchers, namely, lefthanders Johnny Garbett and Lefty Weckman, had thrown it better than others. They would see that night in their dandy little ballpark the best curveball they had ever seen from a righthander. "Mine went straight down," Stoll said.

River town baseball people knew at least the name, Jim Stoll. He had led Arlington to the state championship just two years earlier in 1967 at Alexandria. Arlington had ridden Stoll's arm and bat to six state tournaments, dating back to 1963, when, according to The August 22, 1963 *Brownton Minn. Bulletin*, "Arlington won the game without a hit in their big eighth inning." Stoll and teammate Larry Klunder executed a double steal to tie the game. Then, "Stoll made a theft of third and with two out..." stole home on the catcher's throw back to the mound, which won the playoffs for Arlington and got them into the state tournament for the first time in its history.

Big game heroics were not new to Jim Stoll, however. A newspaper clipping from a 1957 Iron Range paper noted that Jim Stoll "... pitched a perfect no-hit, no-run game [to give] Marble the championship of Region 15-B in the state amateur baseball program and moves the Mallards into the state tournament at New Ulm Sept. 5-7." He was 19 years old. Marble, a town of about 800, has, like Jim Stoll, always liked to play "up." They played in the Arrowhead Baseball League in the 1950s, which included teams from towns that dwarfed Marble in size: Hibbing; Coleraine; Eveleth; Virginia; International Falls; and Chisholm.

Stoll said he hit a two-run homerun and pitched a three-hitter with 18 strikeouts against Norwood in the first game of the 1957 state tournament at Cold Spring, but got beat, 4-3. "We played a drafted catcher and put our regular catcher in right field," Stoll said, "to keep his bat in the game." But the catcher dropped a couple of fly balls in the outfield that gave Norwood two unearned runs and the ball game. "A Red Sox scout, Denny Galehouse, tried to sign me to a professional contract after the game," Stoll said, "but I had to tell him that I had three more years of commitment to the U.S. Air Force."

In the 1958 state tournament at New Ulm, Stoll said he played third base for a Marble team that won its first two games and then got crushed by Pipestone, 16-5, in the semi-finals. "I was slotted to pitch the championship game," Stoll said, but Marble didn't make it that far. "A scout from the Giants wanted to sign me as a third baseman," he said, "because I'd had a good tournament at the plate, two or three hits a game and handled everything at third." Stoll said he hit a shot off the flagpole, "about half way up," which was inside the park in dead center, the outfield sloping up toward the fence at 425 feet from home plate. "They were waving me home," Stoll said, "but I stopped at third and told Anderson, who was coaching third base, that when a man hits a ball that far he shouldn't have to run."

As we saw through the 1960s and 70s with the great heavyweight fights, it's not the size of the man in the fight that ennobles and inspires. It's the size of the fight in the man: first, Ali as Cassius Clay against Sonny Liston; then, in turn, Smokin' Joe Frazier against Ali three times; then, in turn again, Ali against George Foreman. If the parallels seem a stretch, it's about playing up and playing large. Nobility isn't generated from playing down, playing beneath yourself. Nobility, like grace, is granted seemingly to those whose reach exceeds their grasp. To those who stretch and strive beyond what is normally expected of them. It's Bobby Jones in his Grand Slam performance in 1930. It's Babe Ruth in 1927 and Hogan in the 1950 U.S. Open after the car accident. It's Nicklaus in The Masters, and Williams hitting .400. The nobility of these heroes allowed them to transcend their individual sports and accomplishments to inspire professional athletes in all sports, as well as the rest of us at various levels of competition and walks of life. This transference is how the nobility of an athlete at one level could inspire an athlete, even a kid, at another level and in another sport. It is the stuff of heroes that may even border on idolatry. But it worked for generations to motivate people to be more than they inherited, more than what they were told to be, more than what they grew up in, and thought they could be. It helped to make them want to be the best that they could be. Baseball, more than any other activity, provided the medium for this becoming.

"A pride developed in communities and with teams," Chuck Warner noted, "and baseball was really fun then," he said of The Golden Age of Baseball. Warner says it ended with the Minnesota Twins' arrival, but we think that while that played a part no doubt, there were other, greater factors at work, too; namely, expansion of baseball in general, and the cultural and societal changes reflected in things like Woodstock, Charles Manson, Jim Jones, the assassinations of our political leaders, Lyndon Johnson and *his* war, Kent State, Nixon and Agnew. There was too much easy money around, too little restraint, too little respect, and a degradation of Old School values that had stood the test of time but had gotten rocked.

"There's no hero today in baseball like we used to have," Jim Stoll said. There is no Joe DiMaggio or Mickey Mantle. No Ted Williams or Babe Ruth. "The ones who would be heroes are all on drugs," he said. That's not the stuff of nobility and inspiration. Jim Stoll learned from his idols–Mickey Mantle and Ted Williams. "I tried to run like Mantle," Stoll said. "I wanted to *be* Mickey Mantle."

"That's how we learned," Dave Hartmann said of his early years of playing amateur baseball in Arlington. "We learned from Stoll and Klunder." Getting the opportunity to play with other good ballplayers whom you admire is a privilege. It's as close as any kid can get to a dance with the gods. Teaching and learning become a matter of osmosis, or the "brush border effect." It rubs off on you. Excellence and effort and the matter of the heart are melded into the inspiration that moves and molds the young. Heroes are brought back to earth. The young with feet of clay are elevated to the greatness of the gods at play.

"Jim Stoll exuded confidence, and he elevated the play of everybody around him," Gary Porter, another catcher, said of Stoll. Porter had played against Stoll and Arlington for a couple of years and at age 22 Arlington drafted him in 1969.

Although not a small man at 6 feet, one-half inch, and 185 pounds, Jim Stoll played up, and he played large. He was rewarded for it at Marble, he said, with his pockets getting stuffed with as much as $200 in cash between the mound and the dugout after more than one good pitching performance. "It was more than that at Arlington," Stoll said. In some of his big wins against Gaylord and Chaska, in particular, he said he would have as much as $500 or $600 handed him by Arlington fans who had to show their appreciation for him beating their neighbors, sometimes, it seemed, almost single handedly. "Arlington was still getting 800 to 1,000 people at the games during the 1960s," according to Dave Hartmann, a gate that Warner said was more than 1,000 when Brownton played Arlington.

Baseball teams weren't comprised of Catholics and Lutherans; conservatives and liberals; Republicans and Democrats. "Baseball transcended those things," Hartmann said, in the German agricultural communities like Arlington and Jordan, Shakopee and Belle Plaine, Chaska and LeSueur, where the differences could easily foment ill will toward one's neighbor. Baseball teams are made up of pitchers and catchers, infielders and outfielders, power hitters and singles hitters. Baseball brought a religion all its own to the players and the fans during The Golden Age.

"I think I'm the first one to bring the practice of situational fundamentals to Arlington baseball," Stoll said, who also suggested that the beer stand under the grandstand at the old fairgrounds ballpark be opened to help induce the Arlington ballplayers to come to practice. "We'd practice every day," he said, "and I usually threw batting practice." Stoll said they would alternate each day with two or three different players getting an extra 30 minutes of batting practice. "Then we'd hang around the beer stand and drink two or three beers."

Stoll was 20-2 as the pitcher of record in Arlington's '67 season of 28 wins against just 5 losses. He won the MVP award in the state tournament for his performance on the mound and at the plate. He won three games and pitched five innings of relief in the semi-finals before winning the championship game against Perham. At the plate, he batted a reported .588, with four homeruns.

For Jim Stoll, "The state tournament was my World Series."

"There was no way, sore arm or not, that anybody but Jim Stoll was going to pitch that '69 championship game," Dave Hartmann said.

Stoll said, "That curveball's gotta go into the dirt," and he threw it all night, just as he had promised the Prior Lake team in their locker room just before the game. Three walks and two errors, according to a game synopsis in *The History of Arlington Baseball*, gave Prior Lake a 1-0 lead in the third inning. But Stoll and his defense settled down the rest of the way, with the pitcher throwing a five-hitter, three of which were infield singles, striking out 11, and winning the game, 6-1, and the MVP award for the second time in three years.

Arlington would repeat what they had done in the 1967 tournament, according to Stoll. "We didn't have an error the whole tournament until the championship game," he said. "Then, our infielders couldn't pick up a ground ball." That made for an interesting finish, which Chuck Warner covered this way in his *Brownton Bulletin*:

> The game ended in sensational fashion. Two errors and a bunt single loaded the bases with one out. Then Stoll fanned cleanup hitter Fred DeGregoire on a high pitch. The last batter, Gary Reierson, pounded a Stoll change-up curve deep to left and it looked for a time like a grand slam homer coming up. But the leftfielder Dick Cahoon, his back to the wall, leaped high and snared the ball one-handed near the top of the wall.

"Reierson was the only guy we were worried about," Stoll said. "Kelly was a tough out because his strike zone was so small" and he was so quick, "but DeGregoire didn't bother us. He was opening up too quick. We knew we could get him on curve balls. I think I struck him out three times."

Stoll says he learned how to pitch while catching. "I studied hitters, and I learned how to set them up," he said. "You don't want to let what I call the piss hitters, the guys batting seventh, eighth, and ninth in the order, beat you," he said. "Don't pitch those guys outside. Pitch 'em inside, because they can't pull the ball."

"When there are runners on base," he said, "it's really important to keep the ball in play *ahead* of the runners. That cuts down the number of bases they can get when they do get the bat on the ball."

"I threw him the change curve," Stoll said of the game's final pitch to the big first baseman, the same pitch that had impressed Bill Virdon, Pittsburgh Pirate centerfielder, at their 1960 spring training after 30 minutes of batting practice to tell Stoll: "You throw that change curve up here and they won't touch you."

Reierson had more than touched it, "I knew he didn't hit it really well," though, Stoll said. "But that Jordan ballpark is a small yard, and the ball carries there." He'd learned that well the year before in a neutral site playoff game against archrival Chaska. "Jordan's where I got my worst whippin' in baseball," Stoll said. "I lasted two or three innings, and they got something like 11 runs off me. They kicked the shit out of me." The *History of Arlington Baseball* records Stoll pitching just the first inning against Chaska on August 15, 1968, with the final score, 15-3, Chaska.

Jim Stoll hadn't liked the taste of that, and when just the hint of it returned as he watched Reierson's ball drift farther and farther out to left field, he prayed the prayer that every pitcher who has ever thrown a slow curveball a little too high and a little too flat to a big hitter has prayed: "'Stay in here, you sonofabitch. Stay in here.'"

"He didn't get it all," Porter, the catcher, said of Reierson. "It went to the warning track, but it was hit sky high."

"I love baseball," Stoll said. "It's all I ever wanted to do." He grew up in Stockton, California, a Bay Area community, but "I consider myself a Minnesota boy," he said. Stoll played semi-pro baseball when he was as young as 15. He signed a professional baseball contract with the San Francisco Seals right out of high school in 1955 at age 17. This was the same San Francisco Seals that the great Joe DiMaggio had been playing for when the New York Yankees "discovered" him and bought him for $25,000 in 1934. The Seals played in the independent Pacific Coast League, which toyed with the idea for a while in the early 1950s, when St. Louis was still the western-most city in the Major Leagues, of becoming baseball's third Major League.

Now closing in on 80 years of age and living near Reno, Nevada, since 2005, Stoll said he hunted elk in Colorado every year until health problems forced him out of the saddle in the high country. The image is fitting: Jim Stoll as *The Marlboro Man*, an advertisement character who hawked the brand of cigarettes Stoll still smokes. "They keep telling me I need to quit," Stoll says.

He said he had surgery three to four years ago to relieve compressed spinal nerves in the neck and back, "from baseball," he said. While coming out of the anesthesia from that surgery, he said his heart went into an abnormal rhythm for which they jolted him with enough electricity to restore a normal sinus rhythm. But he said he noticed almost right away that he had trouble breathing. Blood clots had formed on the backs of both lungs. "Hell, I'd be out of breath after ten steps," he said. Then, while doing some yard work, he bumped his head, a serious risk while on Coumadin. He said he had terrible headaches and upon a scheduled visit to his doctor, they found the headaches were a result of still more clotting in his brain that required still more surgery in about 2010. "I'm alright now, though," he said.

"The guys who came after us have been playing on wall-to-wall carpeting, if you know what I mean. I know my baseball history," Stoll said. "They need to know how the rug got laid for them."

"I knew I was going to be a baseball player when I was eight years old," Stoll said, and 13-year-old Jimmy Stoll listened to what he remembered being "The Game of the Day" on the radio, "brought to you by Falstaff Beer." That would have made it 1952, with the Mutual Broadcasting System (MBS) broadcasting to non-Major League cities across the country. Two former Major League ballplayers, Buddy Blattner and Dizzy Dean, handled the broadcasting. He said that Buddy

Blattner did the play-by-play, and Dizzy Dean, the last National League pitcher to win 30 games, was the color commentator. "And he was colorful," Stoll said. "One game, a runner on first was stealing second, and he says, 'There the sonofabitch goes'!" Dizzy Dean would be reprimanded and suspended from the broadcast booth for his colorful commentary.

Radio engaged the listeners with baseball, in particular, in a sort of magical way. Jimmy Stoll would get out his box of 1952 Topps Baseball Cards, "and I had every Major League player's card," he said. As the starting lineups were announced, he put the home team "in position" in his "ballpark"–on the kitchen table or the living room floor while holding in his hands in their batting order the cards of the visiting team's starters. "I scored the games, too," Stoll said, having copied on note paper a scoring sheet from an official program he'd kept from a San Francisco Seals game.

Jim Stoll was hooked on baseball. Radio had done its magic on a young listener's imagination: "Ted Williams was my hero and the first time I saw him on television, I was disappointed," Stoll said. "He popped up and struck out, while everything on the radio was a shot," Stoll said.

Five years after leaving home and starting his own family, he said he asked his mother about the box of baseball cards. They suffered the same fate that has befallen many young boy's keepsake collection–his mother threw them out in a cleaning purge. What is it about mothers everywhere and their near universal need to throw out their sons' baseball card collections while holding on almost indefinitely to things like the first spoon they used to feed you as a tot?

Jim Stoll said he had four or five original Mickey Mantles and at least as many Ted Williams cards. But the original 1951 set of Topps major leaguers, too! It was small solace that he would sign his own contract with Topps at the 1960 Pittsburgh Pirate spring training camp for a new baseball glove and a set of baseball spikes. He said he had the option of a set of golf clubs but that he needed the glove and shoes then and didn't even know anything about the game of golf at the time.

"I'm the last guy to bat against Satchel Paige," Stoll said, evoking immediately both disbelief and amazement. "He was still barnstorming in the 1960s."

"I was playing at Arlington," he said, "and I got a call from Dale Serum up at Alexandria." Serum had been Stoll's catcher at Taconite the year before. "It was a Wednesday night," Stoll recalled, and "he said he'd give me a hundred bucks, my room, food, and whatever I wanted to drink if I'd come up to Alex to pitch against Paige and his barnstorming team of young, Black ballplayers. The game was on Friday night, so I drove up for it."

"He came out to pitch in the eighth inning," Stoll said. "He must have been 70 years old."

"He threw me that 'hesitation pitch,'" Stoll said, which was a pitch that Satchel Paige had patented in the old Negro Leagues. It had tied hitters up in knots for decades and extended the pitcher's career. "I hit it right back at him," Stoll said. "It took out his knee, and he went down."

"They'd probably figured," Stoll said, "that since I was the pitcher, I couldn't hit or something like that."

"I never left the plate area" Stoll said. "I just cried, because I knew his story."

"I beat 'em 4-2," Stoll said. "They had a good ball club, and after the game their centerfielder, a tall, lanky kid who got a double off me, came up and said, 'You've pitched before, someplace, haven't ya?'"

"Yeah," I said.

"I thought so."

Stoll said he was a huge fan of Ted Williams, the last man to hit .400 in Major League Baseball. "But Babe Ruth *has to be* the greatest hitter of all time," Stoll said. Ruth's achievements were legitimate and prolific. He was primarily a pitcher for the first five years of his career with the Boston Red Sox, winning more than 20 games in each of two different seasons and nearly 100 games in all on the mound, with a measly ERA of 2.28. His switch to full-time play in right field after being traded to the New York Yankees in 1920 signaled the beginning of the new era in baseball: The Long Ball.

"Hell...," Stoll mused, "Ruth had a lifetime batting average of .342!" That's on top of all the homeruns he hit and with the big swing he took on every pitch. "With a wooden bat of 52 or 54 ounces that nobody else could swing, because it was so heavy," Stoll said. "Somebody had broken one of his favorite lighter bats, and so he started swinging that big old heavy bat that nobody else would pick up." Ruth consciously tried to hit the ball out of the park, or at least to hit it as hard as he could every pitch, which means you're going to strike out far more than what we call the "good contact hitters" do.

Neither Babe Ruth nor Ted Williams ever stepped up to the plate to "just meet the ball," or to "just get good contact." They didn't choke up on the bat. They gripped it all the way down to the knob. It was the same with Mickey Mantle. He even wrapped his pinky around the bottom of the knob of the bat. "They swung as hard as they could on every pitch," Stoll said.

"When I first started playing at Marble," Stoll said of his introduction to Minnesota amateur ball while stationed at an air force base in nearby Grand Rapids, Minnesota, in 1957, "they told me Roger Maris had once been cut from the Marble Mallards."

"I wondered what kind of team and league they had," Stoll said. "I wondered what I was getting myself into." After all, Roger Maris would break into the big leagues with the Cleveland Indians in 1957. He would break Ruth's single-season homerun record in 1961 with the Yankees. He thought that Maris had come out of North Dakota. Fact is, he was born on the Iron Range in nearby Hibbing, Minnesota, same town in which Gopher baseball coach, John Anderson, was born, and the same town in which music legend Bob Dylan had been raised.

Before moving to Fargo, North Dakota, where he would graduate from Bishop Shanley H.S. in 1953, then promptly sign with the Indians and play for Fargo-Moorhead in the Class C Northern League, Maris had, indeed, tried out for, and been cut by, the Marble Mallards. "Then, they told me that he was 15 years old," Stoll said. Roger's grandmother was living in Calumet, another small town just down the road from Marble, "where my wife, Becky, is from." Roger Maris had simply lived with his grandmother one summer and tried out for the Mallards.

Then there was the whole thing with Black ballplayers. Sure, Jackie Robinson had broken the color barrier in 1947, but that didn't make things right overnight. The Civil Rights Act wouldn't become law until 1964. Jim Crow was still the common MO in the South.

It wasn't right that Donn Clendenon, who would be named MVP of the 1969 World Series for his clutch hitting for the New York Mets in their win over the highly favored Baltimore Orioles, couldn't eat with Jim Stoll and the other white Savannah ballplayers in 1960. Stoll couldn't do anything about the laws or the social norms, but he could make sure that a teammate didn't go hungry. He took sandwiches out to the bus for Clendenon.

It wasn't right that Willie Stargell couldn't eat with the rest of the ball club when Stoll and Stargell were teammates on the Asheville Tourists in the South Atlantic League in 1961. Jim Stoll would take chicken, burgers, or whatever he'd ordered for himself out to the bus to feed the big guy. Willie Stargell, for God's sake . . . He would hit 475 homeruns in his Major League career with the Pirates, hit 16 of the 32 balls ever hit out of Forbes Field, and be inducted into the Hall of Fame in 1988.

It wasn't right, Stoll mused, that after a long bus ride of 500 or 600 miles into, say, Knoxville, Tennessee, that he and the other white teammates would be left off at their hotel, and *then* the Black players would be taken to *their* hotel. In the morning, when it was time to pick the guys up, the bus driver would reverse the order: He'd stop at the "Colored" Hotel first and then pick up the white players. This standard MO meant more sleep and rest for the white players.

It wasn't right, Jim Stoll recalled, when in a 1960 spring training game against the San Francisco Giants, Smokey Burgess, his Pirate catcher, flipped his thumb– "like you flip a marble," Stoll said. That meant Stoll was to knock the hitter down. Deliberately. Not get close. Knock him down, even if it meant you hit him. The batter when Stoll got the call to throw the knockdown pitch? Willie McCovey. He was 6-4 and looked bigger than the 210 pounds they listed him. McCovey had been National League Rookie of the Year in 1959, batting .354 that first year before the Giants made him into a homerun hitter. He would hit 521 homeruns in his 22-year career and be inducted into the Baseball Hall of Fame in 1986.

"I wasn't afraid of him," Stoll said. "I thought he would charge the mound, but he got up, dusted himself off, and I could tell he was pissed. I could see the whites of his eyes, and then I looked at my catcher for the sign." Burgess flipped his thumb, calling for the knockdown pitch again. "I shook him off," Stoll said, "and then I heard somebody say, 'Timeout'."

"Danny Murtaugh, the Pirate manager, came out to the mound. He was just a little guy–maybe 5-8 or 5-9. He says, 'What's the problem out here'?"

Stoll said he looked at his manager, then at his catcher, and then back to Murtaugh, and said "'You want to call that knockdown pitch? Here you throw it." He tossed the ball to Manager Murtaugh, who, according to Stoll, turned away from the mound laughing. As he headed back to the dugout, Stoll said that Murtaugh muttered, "'Fuckin' rookies today.'" Stoll said that, after walking McCovey, he was taken out of the game. "They were just checking to see if I had any stones," Stoll said.

"I got to pitch against Clemente in an intra-squad game," Stoll said. "We got to a 3-2 count. I shook off the fastball twice and threw him a hard curveball right down the pipe," Stoll said. "It was my good one. He damned near fell on his back, and the umpire called ball four."

"They were tellin' me, 'Nobody throws Clemente a curveball with a 3-2 count in spring training.'"

Roberto Clemente won the National League batting title four times, and he had a lifetime Major League batting average of .317 over 18 seasons. "He could hit anything he could get his bat on," Stoll said, and was known as a "great bad-ball hitter." He had 3,000 hits, and he won 12 consecutive Gold Gloves for his defensive play as perhaps the premier right fielder of all time. "You do that once or twice, it's one thing," Stoll said. "But when you do it year after year, it's really something." He was inducted into the Hall of Fame in 1973 after dying in 1972 at sea in the Caribbean on a cargo flight out of San Juan, Puerto Rico, carrying relief supplies to the victims of an earthquake in Managua, Nicaragua.

Mickey Mantle was Jim Stoll's boyhood hero. Stoll, like millions of boys across America, wanted to be Mickey Mantle. Mantle was a thick 5-11, 198 pounds. He hit from both sides of the plate, and he hit with power. "And, God, could he run. I saw him steal third base one time, and this was after his knee had been blown out," Stoll said of the outfield accident Mantle had in 1951 against the New York Giants in the World Series. "It looked like he took two steps and, just like that, he was on third," Stoll said. "Nobody has ever been faster, home to first, than Mickey Mantle. Nobody."

So, when Mickey Mantle came to bat against Stoll in a spring training game, the young pitcher was awash in emotion. Mantle had won the Triple Crown in the American League in 1956. By 1960, he had made people begin to forget DiMaggio. He was a god.

"Smokey Burgess came out to the mound and told me not to pitch him low. "How the hell was I gonna pitch to him?" Stoll recalled the awe and the big question. "Yeah, I was scared."

"He was grinning and waiting for me," Stoll said. "I'm a curveball pitcher, and, of course, Mantle is batting left handed against me. Burgess had told me that he crushes everything low from the left side, like he's hitting a golf ball. When he's batting right, he hits the high pitches best."

"'So you pitch him low when he's batting right, and high when he's batting left,'" Burgess told Stoll.

"How the hell am I gonna throw a curveball high?" Stoll remembered wondering. "He popped it up," Stoll said, "but it was hit really high." Mantle had just missed the rookie's best pitch, and after the next batter got a hit off him, he was taken out of the game.

Jim Stoll said he was eager to learn as much as he could from the veteran players. He went to Harvey Haddix, who had pitched a perfect game for 12 innings in 1959 and lost in the 13th. He sought out Vernon Law, who'd been 18-9 in 1959 and would be a 20-game Pirate winner in 1960, and Elroy Face, one of the first dominant relief pitchers in baseball. Face actually won 18 games in 1959, solely in relief.

"You can't beat the wisdom of experience," Stoll said, "and we respected our elders in our youth. That hasn't been true for quite a few years in young people," he said.

And he listened. He said after taking batting practice one day, George Sissler, who was the Pirate hitting coach and who had a lifetime batting average of .340, twice hitting over .400, told him in a critical, but helpful, vein, 'Jim, you're hitting everything on the button. You've got to learn to hit half the ball.'

"I thought, what the hell is he talking about, hitting half the ball."

"'Yeah,' Sissler said. 'You've got to hit the bottom half of the ball.'"

Stoll said that he then read the Ted Williams book on hitting, and he saw it there, too. "Williams always tried to hit the top half the ball in the early parts of a game, and the bottom half in the later innings," Stoll said.

"I listened," Stoll said, "But here's the thing about the great hitters like Williams and Ruth. They had *really* good eyes."

"Ted Williams had 15-20 vision," Stoll said. "They said of him in the Marine Corps," for which he flew jet fighters for five years during the prime of his baseball career, "that he had the best eyesight of anybody they'd ever had as a pilot."

It was the same thing with Babe Ruth. While his training habits left something to be desired, especially by the standards of today's ballplayers, "he had great eyesight."

"They said Ruth could still read the numbers on a license plate," according to Stoll, "when nobody else could tell what color the plate was!"

Knowing baseball history and appreciating just how good those ballplayers were who made the game America's pastime is akin to the time-honored societal tenet of respecting tribal elders. Viewing old, black-and-white 8 mm film footage or meeting a former ballplayer in his 50s or 60s and just not seeing what was said of any of the Great Ones, said of them when they, too, ran with the wind and pounded baseballs into powder, isn't fair or honest.

"I don't know where or when it changed," Jim Stoll reflected, "but there's a big difference" in the values, the work ethic, and the character of people today and in the days of my youth. "I think our family lives have gone to hell in the last 20 to 30 years," Stoll said, "and there's no respect today for elders" or history. Or even life itself. You wonder what they're teaching in the schools and what's going on at home when you listen to what comes out of the mouths of most people today.

"Here's the way it was," Stoll said. "I learned to hit the low ball by hitting rocks. I was a freshman in high school, and we lived in a little shack about a mile from town. I'd get home and go over to this pile of rocks the city had heaped up there for road maintenance or whatever. They were perfect, about the size of a half dollar, and I'd throw them in the air and hit them with a bat, a broom handle, an axe handle–anything I could find that I could swing," he said. "I did that every day after school, all winter long in California, and that's where I learned that you couldn't hit a rock up high. But if you hit it low, you could really get into it."

"The city sent my dad a bill for $17 for those rocks," Stoll said, "because somebody had seen me hittin' these rocks out there, day after day, watching the pile gettin' down to nuthin'."

Jim Stoll had been living his life–in and out of baseball–according to the first principle and rule of golf, 13-1, which says simply, "Play the ball as it lies." In golf, it means you don't get to improve the lie or position of your ball in order to get a better, cleaner swing at it, in order to get the head of the club on the ball and have a better chance of advancing the ball toward or onto the green. That's called cheating, and cheaters are penalized. Stoll would learn in a new game, golf, what he had lived in an old game, baseball, and in his life. "I didn't cry or anything," he said when the Pirates released him after he'd torn the rotator cuff in his pitching shoulder. "'*This can't be over with*,'" he said he remembered thinking, and "I remember telling myself that I was going to be the best baseball player that I could be. I just didn't know what I was going to do. All I knew how to do was play baseball."

"I think it was just meant for me to play baseball in Minnesota," Stoll said.

"You get out of something what you put into it," Stoll added, which is an important tenet of The Old School in which "The Greatest Generation" and its progeny learned "The Right Stuff." That school taught you to give a day's work for a day's pay. It taught you the value of earning what you took home, whether on the job or at the ballpark. Simply put, you learned that you don't get something for nothing. You get what you deserve, sooner or later. The Fiddler is in charge of the music, and He's going to be paid.

"I played with a lot of pain," Stoll said. "I can remember biting my lip lots of times out there on the mound, saying to myself, 'one more pitch, just one more pitch.'"

Stoll said he watched his grandson take batting practice one day a couple years ago. "When he hit the ball, he hit it a long way, but he missed a lot of balls. So, I asked him how many pitches he was used to taking swings at, and he said 10 or 15. Hell, you can't learn to hit taking 10 or 15 swings a day. You've gotta swing until you're tired."

When you're young and all you can hear is the music, and all you want to do is dance, it seems you can never grow tired. "And here's how that went down for me back then," Jim Stoll said. "My first wife was Serbian. She had another kid, wasn't married, and I was 18 or 19 years old and we got to goin' out and whatever." Stoll said that Nellie's father was from the old country, and he had moved to the United States illegally in the 1920s. "His name was John, but we called him Janko. He was a short, stout man, maybe 5-7, but stronger than a horse."

"I went to talk to Janko," Stoll said. "He was a nice man. One of the best men I've ever met in my life. He got out the slivovich," a Serbian brandy made from plums. "It's strong. It takes your breath away," Stoll said. "I wasn't much of a drinker, but I drank slivovich with Janko and told him, 'I love your daughter; she's three months pregnant; and I want to marry her.'"

"He said, 'I think a lot of you. You have my approval.'"

Another young man with "The Right Stuff" had heard and danced to the music that makes for the generations. He would fulfill the ages-old Social Contract. Jim Stoll would pay The Fiddler.

"We drank the whole bottle," Stoll said, a male thing to do then and a sort of signature on The Covenant.

He didn't know then what he knows today, that things as fundamental as doing the right thing would change. In today's world, the world of the last 30 years or more, the young man informed by his girlfriend of being pregnant is just as likely to respond as follows: "Don't look at me, honey. You're on your own. We were just pokin' fun."

And worse, the young women are just as likely to visit Planned Parenthood to "get rid of it" on their own. Anything to keep from having to face Daddy or an aloof husband. Anything to keep career goals on track. Anything to show a man up on something. Anything just to be able to keep partying.

The young Stoll was married and moved with his pregnant wife and her son, whom he would adopt, to Coleraine, another small range town midway between Grand Rapids and Marble on Hwy 169. One night, about six months later and after the birth of their baby, Jim Stoll said he'd had a couple too many beers after a basketball game. When he got home, he and his wife got into an argument. "I slapped her," Stoll said, "and she ran home to Daddy."

Nellie's parents lived only four blocks away, and after his daughter burst into his home in tears and told him what had happened, Janko grabbed the bottle of slivovich and called on his son-in-law, Jim Stoll. "He came in the house," Stoll said, "and he slammed it down hard and said, 'We're gonna talk.'"

"That's why I admired him so much. I thought, oh-oh, I'm really gonna get the lecture now. But he gave me some of the best advice I've ever heard. He said, 'You get drunk, you don't come home and beat the women. You don't like what they're doin,' you go back downtown and get drunker. But you don't hit the women.'"

"That's all he said. Then he got up, took his bottle and left, and I admired him for it," Stoll said. "If I said something like that today to my grandson, who likes to drink and party, he'd probably never speak to me again."

"How often do you even hear, 'Yes, sir' or 'No, sir' anymore?" Stoll asked. "There's just no respect anymore," he said. "Don't get me wrong, there's some good kids out there yet, but it's not like it used to be."

Nor has Jim Stoll forgotten how he learned the lesson of respect from his own father as part of his growing up in Stockton, California. He remembers when he was about 10 years old and how his father used to come home from work, pitch batting practice to him, play catch, and whatever.

"We had boxing gloves," Stoll said, "and my father showed me how to box– lead with the left and I had a good jab," he said. "We'd box but only tap each other."

Then one night Stoll said that his father came home with some buddies and they were drinking in the house, and "we put on the boxing gloves."

"He wanted to show off to his drinking buddies, I think," Stoll said, and instead of just tapping me, "He hit me a couple of times, you know, in front of his buddies. When he hit me, I hit him back. I bloodied his nose."

"'We were just tappin' . . . You hit me,'" his Dad said.

"'Well, ya hit me'!"

"'I just tapped ya,'" Stoll's father said.

"'You're a liar,' I said."

"Next thing ya know, I'm against the wall on the floor, and he gave me a black eye. I mean he punched me."

"'Don't ever call me a liar again,'" the elder Stoll told his son.

"What he was tellin' me was you better respect your elders. That's how we were raised. We never talked back to people."

Jim Stoll began and ended his Minnesota baseball-playing days in Marble, a small Iron Range town of about 800 people in 1956, just 13 miles north of Grand Rapids. In between 1956 and 1976, he played four years of professional baseball, as high as AAA, and he played what he has often referred to as "my major leagues"– at Arlington, Minnesota, as well as a year at Taconite, several years at Marble, and a couple years at Gaylord.

Two encores mark the end of Stoll's baseball in Minnesota. They are most memorable and telling. After devoting himself to Arlington baseball from 1963 through the 1973 season, he left for Gaylord, he said, because they offered a much better high school athletic program than Arlington for his three sons, all of whom were outstanding athletes, too. "They had good coaches at Gaylord," said Stoll, who regretted not having the benefit of good coaching and guidance while young. He figured that there just had to be a better way to learn how to hit baseballs than the way he had–by hitting rocks with a broom handle for an hour or more each day. With all the equipment–bats, balls, hitting gloves, the batting cages and pitching machines–a good coach should be able to make hitters out of every kid on a team.

"I was a catcher," Stoll said, "and I loved hitting." He said he was batting over .400 in the Northern League for Grand Forks in 1959 while still in the air force. "Instead of shifting over to block an outside pitch," Stoll said, "I just reached out with my mitt for the ball. Nobody was on base, so a passed ball wouldn't have mattered. But the ball ripped a fingernail off, and after that I could barely hold onto the bat with that hand. I had to swing one handed, and so my batting average fell to about .200."

Then, he said that somebody saw him throwing batting practice, and, "all of a sudden, I was a pitcher." To his own surprise, he would go to the 1960 Pittsburgh Pirates' spring training as a pitcher. "But spring training is just batting practice," Stoll said. "Nobody's in shape," he said, "and you don't throw a ball unless a coach tells you to."

Stoll pitched a near-perfect game for Gaylord against Arlington in the summer of 1974. "I think I gave up a second-or third-inning walk," he said. It was a bittersweet homecoming for Jim Stoll, who said he spent the two years at Gaylord managing the team, catching once in a while, but rarely pitching.

Then, after two years with Gaylord, Jim Stoll returned to his Minnesota roots– the Iron Range, where he is likely the only non-Minnesota native and legend without a hockey pedigree in the area's Mythical Hall of Fame. He returned to Marble, where he had shown up as an 18-year-old air force recruit 20 years earlier, and where he'd hunted whitetail deer, and fished walleyes and shot bluebills on Lake Winnibigoshish–"Big Winnie"–in the years when The Bluebill Flight in November was an event as large as Thanksgiving and the Deer Season in Northern Minnesota.

"I was bartending nights and welding during the day," Stoll said. He hadn't really pitched much other than batting practice, but Dick Siebert had brought one of his better summer collegiate league teams to the North Country again and had scheduled the Marble Mallards for two games, Saturday and Sunday.

"I was bartending Saturday night," Stoll said, "so I didn't go to the Saturday game. I think they beat us something like 12-2, and they were all in the bar after the game having a good time."

"'You're in trouble,'" Stoll said he told Siebert after serving the legendary coach a couple of cocktails at "Harley's Hut" in Marble.

"'Why's that?'" Stoll said Siebert asked him, his young ballplayers swilling beer at the tables.

"'Well, first, I'm gonna get you all drunk tonight,'" Stoll said, "'and then I'm pitching tomorrow.'"

Stoll said the plan was for him to pitch three innings, then two other Marble pitchers would each work three innings. "I pitched three good innings," Stoll said. "The manager, Ralph Guenzel, whose son is now the assistant coach of the Gopher hockey team" according to Stoll, "kept saying, 'One more inning, one more inning,' and Siebert was sitting in the dugout, wearing dark glasses. He was hung over." Stoll said he stayed in the game through eight innings, but told his manager that was enough finally.

"I no-hit 'em for the eight innings," Stoll said.

"It's true," Guenzel said in a telephone interview from his home in Scottsdale, Arizona. "He threw knuckleballs and other junk and had them popping up and hitting weak dribblers to the infield." Coach Siebert didn't like what he had witnessed–a 40-year-old burned-out bartender making fools of some of the best college baseball players in Minnesota and, according to Guenzel, "He chewed their butts out for getting beat by a ragtag bunch of rangers."

"Bobby Bolf gave up four runs in the ninth inning, but we hung on to win something like 7-4." Stoll also said that Bolf had been "a big homerun hitter for the Gophers" a year or two earlier and that he and John Anderson, who would go on to coach the Minnesota Gophers, were Iron Rangers. "That's how we got on their schedule," Stoll said. "It's the last game I ever pitched."

It wasn't his last baseball episode with the Gopher baseball coach though. A couple of years later, "1979, '80, maybe 1981" Stoll tried to recall, "I was umpiring a game, and I kicked John Anderson out of the game." Anderson would create his own legend at the University of Minnesota but in the late 1970s, he was living in Pengelly, Minnesota, according to Stoll, and managing the Marble Mallards.

"I called a runner out at second," Stoll said, "and he protested the call, using language you don't use on an umpire." So, Stoll kicked the player out of the game, and that brought the future Gopher baseball coach, John Anderson, out of the dugout and into Jim Stoll's face. "I kicked him out, too," Stoll said.

Jim Stoll would leave Minnesota in 1982, because "there was just no work," he said. He'd return to northern California where he would work as a carpenter and welder, rising in the ranks to a superintendent responsible for as many as 150 carpenters for Billingham Construction Company on contract with Shell Oil. He would retire at age 62 and take up golf seriously, but only after finally having surgery on the torn rotator cuff in his right shoulder. The orthopedic surgeons had come as close to perfecting the shoulder surgery as they had with what they called "Tommy John Surgery" to repair pitchers' elbows.

With a year of rehab after the surgery at age 61, Stoll said he started hitting golf balls on the practice range–with the same dedicated fervor he had once hit rocks with a broom handle as a freshman in high school. "I'd hit 600 to 700 golf balls a day," Stoll said. "That's how I got to be a scratch golfer." At age 76, Stoll said he's shot his age twice, a 74 and a 75 in 2013. He still hits a bucket of balls most days, and he plays when he feels like it.

But The Jim Stoll Story could just as well begin and end with what he did in Arlington, Minnesota. "Arlington was my major leagues," Stoll said, "and the state tournament was my World Series." Reflecting on a number of "coincidences," beginning with his joining the air force and being assigned to Grand Rapids, tearing his rotator cuff and being released by the Pittsburgh Pirates, Stoll said: "Call it Fate or The Big Guy being in charge of the music box, I just think I was destined to play baseball in Minnesota."

In the winter of 1962-'63, Stoll was working in a gas station in Grand Rapids for, he said, $1.25 an hour, when, along with four of the five other employees, he was fired. "We went to "The Rainbow Lodge," Stoll said, "and Steve Atchhecovich, who was Secretary/Treasurer of the Marble Mallards, was in there drinking." Stoll said he and Donny Anderson, a second baseman for Taconite, joined Atchhecovich and told him what Paul Harvey called, "the rest of the story," and what the loss of the job meant. Jim Stoll had four kids at home and a fifth on the way. "He told us that we should go see Augie Mueller down at the Capitol in St. Paul."

Augie Mueller was a lifelong bachelor, who lived with his brothers, Eddie and Al, and their four sisters in a big farmhouse outside Arlington. They farmed over 600 acres, according to one newspaper account, and raised purebred Holsteins. Augie served Arlington and a constituency of Sibley and parts of two other neighboring counties in the Minnesota State Legislature as state representative for over three decades, 1941 to 1974–during The Golden Age of Baseball. Dave Hartmann called him "an ambassador of Arlington baseball." He served Arlington baseball his whole life. He was connected. He knew people, and he meant well. He would die at the age of 91 in 1996 in Arlington. They would name a portion of State Hwy 5 after him. And Steve Atchhecovich knew Augie Mueller from baseball and politics, according to Jim Stoll.

This was bigger than Taconite or Marble baseball. This was life and family for two good ballplayers needing work so they could support their families. Steve Atchhecovich would call Augie Mueller and tee it up for them.

"We drove down to St. Paul and met with Augie," Stoll said, and "after talking with him, he told us to come to Arlington the next week."

"So, Donny and I drove down to Arlington the next Friday–it was the middle of February and colder 'n' hell," Stoll said. "We got a motel room in Arlington and drove out to the Mueller's farm to meet Augie again and his brother, Eddie, the manager of the Arlington baseball team, at about 9 o'clock." The four of them visited for a short time, Stoll recalled, and "they told us to meet at the Municipal Liquor the next day, Saturday, at 1:00 o'clock."

"So, we met at the bar and had a few drinks with Arlington businessmen–Eddie and Augie Mueller, LeRoy and Les Pinske, Jim O'Brien, and I think Joe Thomes was there, too. Then, they showed us around and took us out to the old ballpark at the fairgrounds."

Stoll said the group then went to Les Pinske's office at the Arlington Cement Works, which Pinske owned and where O'Brien worked as his manager. "They asked me what I had to have to come to Arlington," Stoll said. "I told 'em I needed at least $400 a month and a place to live."

"'That's no problem. We can handle that,'" Stoll said Pinske told him.

"But wait a minute," Stoll said he remembers saying, "What am I gonna be doing?"

"They said, 'Don't worry about that, we'll find something for you to do.'"

"So, I always laughed," Stoll said. "Donny's wife was a teacher and they gave her a job in the bank, and they gave Donny a job in the hardware store selling shoes. Me, they gave a shovel and construction work."

"They didn't tell me that I'd be working 10-hour days, five and a half days a week, though," Stoll laughed. "I think we figured it out that I was getting $1.50 an hour."

Jim Stoll went to work for the Arlington Cement Works that winter, working with Les Pinske's oldest son, Harmon, in the shop. "Harmon was a big guy and real smart," Stoll said. "He knew welding, machine work, and stuff like that." Stoll was the apprentice, learning from the owner's son. But he said that he and Harmon ran around quite a bit together, too. When summer came, he went outside and worked as a tender for the block layers and bricklayers. "That's what I was doing when Kennedy got shot," Stoll said of the November 22, 1963, assassination of the nation's young president. Like every American of a certain age and older, Stoll remembers what he was doing when he heard the fateful news.

"Some of them got pissed," Stoll said of the bricklayers and truck drivers, "because they learned that I was getting $1.50 an hour and they were only getting $1.10 and that was after working there 10 years."

"I told them," Stoll said, "if you're dumb enough to work for that kind of money after 10 years, that's all you've got coming."

"They treated me real good," Stoll said of Les Pinske and Jim O'Brien. "Les would come around on Thursday and ask me how long it had been since I'd seen my wife. I'd tell him a week and a half or whatever it had been, 'cause she was still up north with the kids in school. He'd say, 'Why don't you take off. We'll see you Monday morning.' And I got paid for the time off."

He worked on the pitching mound at the old ballpark, too. "I re-built it," Stoll said, and "some of the guys would get off the mound after throwing batting practice and say things like, "Jeeze, you can get a nosebleed up there . . . "

"The higher mound helped pitchers," Stoll said. "Higher mounds helped curve balls. It was in the momentum they gave you. The higher the mound was, the lower you could pitch. That's why they lowered the mound (in 1969). It forced pitchers to pitch higher."

About the same time, they changed the strike zone, shrinking it to the area bound in the Major Leagues by "the bellybutton to the top of the kneecap," Stoll said. In amateur ball, Stoll agreed, the top of the strike zone would be closer to the shoulders–the letters. "But it was really up to the umpire," Stoll said, "and you never knew what you were going to get." Some umps just couldn't believe that a curveball that went into the dirt could possibly catch the strike zone. They couldn't believe their own eyes.

The Arlington Baseball Bosses and the ballplayers from up north had one glitch to overcome in 1963. The state baseball association at that time had a residency requirement that stipulated a ballplayer had to be living in the community or within the required radius by February 1 to be eligible to play in that community that season. It was already mid-February. Stoll was still living in Coleraine.

"I think I moved to Arlington around mid-March," Stoll said, "and my wife was still up in Coleraine because the kids were all in school yet."

"I was illegal as hell," Stoll said. He said Chuck Warner, long-time editor of the *Brownton Bulletin*, sent detectives to Arlington, nosing around trying to prove Stoll was ineligible for Arlington in that 1963 baseball season. Warner said they knew Stoll hadn't met the residency requirement, but he dismisses the claim about sending detectives to Arlington. He said that Ed Glavin, a Glencoe attorney, had looked into the matter, but they dropped it.

The Arlington Baseball Bosses won this game of cat-and-mouse, which remains a part of amateur baseball to this day. Rules are made. Rules are stretched if not broken. The breaking of rules is as much a part of the legend and the lore of state amateur baseball as getting paid to play as an amateur. Teams and towns are looking for an edge–or a ringer. "They backdated payroll checks in Arlington," Stoll said, to help substantiate the residency claim. Detectives or not, Stoll played, and he played well. He would steal home to win the rubber game of the league playoffs against Brownton, sending Arlington to the regional playoffs and eventually to its first state tournament his first year in town.

Mel Pederson's "The Wait at MUELLERville," published in the 1976 Arlington State Baseball Tournament Program Guide, *Spirit of '76*, captures the agony and the ecstasy of Arlington baseball fortunes. In 1963, with Larry Klunder and Jim Stoll in the lineup, Eddie Mueller would unseat Brownton in the playoffs. Jim Stoll would hit a homerun and hold Wadena to just 7 hits while striking out 12 in the 7-1 win in the first game of the state tournament. Arlington would win three straight games before losing two in a row in the double-elimination tournament, including a 9-1 shellacking in the semi-finals by Pipestone whom they had beaten earlier. But it was a taste of what Mueller and Stoll had been seeking. It was Mueller's first taste. Stoll had known it before–with Marble as a teenage airman and a year earlier with Taconite. But here's Pederson's much closer account:

> They would return home and Eddie and Augie would return to the farm for the long wait through the winter, never letting the conversation of baseball out of sight. The winter would go slow, and the summer of 1964 at Brownton; the summer of 1965 at St. Cloud; the summer of 1966 at Belle Plaine; the Mueller's would again be denied their prize. The wait would continue. 1966 would be an extra long winter. Brownton, a team Arlington had whipped twice during the season, would beat the A's 3-2 in the semi-finals, and Eddie's close baseball friend, Jerry Hochsprung

from Brownton, would be the pitcher that would send Eddie back to the farm for another year to wait.

But then it was opening day of the 1967 season, and, as Pederson continues, "Stoll would tell Eddie 'we'll be state champs this year.' Eddie knew that Jim was getting better and better with each season. Before the state tournament started, Stoll's prediction would prove out. Stoll would have a pitching record of 18 wins and 2 losses (going into the tournament). In between this, Klunder would throw a no-hitter in the tough Carver-Hennepin League. The A's would edge out Chaska and advance to Alexandria (and the state tournament). . . . They would have a nine-game winning streak.. . . This team would hit their peak at the tournament: they would then average eleven runs per game; they would hit eighteen home runs; they would advance to the finals against the '66 state champs–Perham–but this year the wait would not be denied. Eddie's nephew, Steve Cary would hit a two-run homerun in the top of the tenth for a 9-7 lead. Stoll would then shut the door and the A's would be champions.

Jim Stoll was all business in a ballgame, intensely competitive and focused, but he was a fun-loving trickster off the field. Getting into the state tournament in the 1966 season highlights another Jim Stoll classic. The night before Arlington was to play New Germany for the regional championship and the right to go on to the state tournament, Stoll and Klunder drove to New Germany and went into a bar for a drink. They started talking baseball with the bartender, who didn't recognize the two Arlington ballplayers. "He started telling me how much of a horse's ass I was, only he didn't know he was talking to me," Stoll said. "So we got to talking about the game the next day and ended up with a bet of $5 per strikeout over or under 15 strikeouts. I'd pay him $5 for every strikeout by "Jim Stoll" under 15, and he'd pay me $5 for every strikeout over 15."

"I ended up throwing a one-or two-hitter with 21 strikeouts," Stoll said, a number listed as 23 in Stoll's 6-0 shutout in the *History of Arlington Baseball*. "It was all for fun," Stoll said. "None of that was about making any money or anything, and the guy was standing there behind home plate the next day during the game while I was on the mound."

Eddie and Augie Mueller knew they had a gem of a ballplayer in Jim Stoll, and they liked him as a person. The feeling was mutual. "They were great people," Jim Stoll said of the Mueller's, who lived with a third brother, Al, who practiced law in New Ulm, and four sisters. "None of 'em ever married," Stoll said, except a fourth brother who lived in the cities. "You couldn't beat 'em." Stoll talked of Sunday dinners at the Muellers' farm in rural Arlington. "I was treated like a king out there," he said. "You couldn't get up to get a glass of water. They served you."

"When I was pitching, Eddie never took me out of a game," Stoll said. "And in that championship game against Perham, we were ahead 7-5 going into the ninth inning. I think we'd had about five errors. A guy hit a two-run homerun off me to tie the game, 7-7. Then the bases were loaded with nobody out, and Eddie comes out to the mound to talk to me. With as much calm and concern for me as you can imagine, he asked me, 'Jim, is everything alright?'"

"'Eddie,' I said... 'Other than the bases loaded, the last of the ninth, and the state championship with the game tied, everything's fine.'"

"Eddie turned around and walked away."

"I remember saying to myself," Stoll said, 'I've been waiting 10 years to win one of these son of a guns, and I'm letting it get away.'" Stoll toed some dirt around the mound. "Then Menzel," his shortstop, didn't help matters any. "He said, 'Get me outta here. I can't field a ball. Get me outta here.'"

Don Brand, Sports Editor of the *New Ulm, Minn., Journal*, reported in the September 11, 1967, edition:

> Stoll got a strikeout on a 3-2 pitch. Then Stoll fielded a squeeze bunt and tossed home for a close force play and two outs. Stoll then retired a pinch hitter on an easy grounder to the mound for a superb piece of clutch pressure pitching.
>
> Bruce Pinske led off Arlington's 10th with a single. He was forced on Mike Dooner's grounder before Cary blasted a pitch over the left-center fence.

Jim Stoll remembers the game well, especially the strikeout for the first out of the tenth inning. It had turned the momentum around for Arlington. He said that a couple of weeks after the game, at work for Steiner Brothers Lighting in nearby Winthrop where he was working as a welder, he went up to Kenny Norman, who was working the assembly line there. Norman had been behind the plate, with his sidekick, "Slip Mahoney," umpiring the bases at Alexandria in the championship game against Perham.

"I asked Kenny Norman what he thought of that curve ball I threw that Perham batter with the 3-2 count and the bases loaded." It was his "out" pitch, his good one, and Stoll said he threw it right down the pipe.

"'God, Jim,' Norman said, 'I thought it was low. If he hadn't swung at it, I'd have had to call it a ball.'"

Chaska beat Stoll three times in 1968, including the 15-3 pasting in the final playoff game at Jordan, ending the five-year string of Arlington appearances in the state tournament. They would draft Stoll and Klunder for the trip to Springfield, even though Stoll said he told them he had, at most, one five-inning stint in his arm. He was hurting. He'd been hurting all year. "They should have won it," Stoll said, "but they just pitched the wrong pitchers at the wrong time." Klunder would be named to the All-Tournament Team as a catcher; Stoll would not play at all.

"Klunder was driving," Stoll said, "and Dale Welter and I were in the car with him coming home from Springfield. Naturally, the three ballplayers reviewed the tournament and the loss. Then they dared tread on sacred, partisan ground. They got into "a discussion," comparing Chaska's team to Arlington's team. "We went right through the lineups, position by position," Stoll said. "When we got to comparing shortstops, our Bob Menzel with Welter, it got heated." Stoll said that Menzel was the better shortstop, Welter the better hitter, with an advantage because he batted left handed.

"Welter and his brother were both good, competitive ballplayers, don't get me wrong," Stoll said. "But they weren't as good as they thought they were, and he didn't like hearing that."

Klunder ended up stopping the car out in the boondocks somewhere and kicking Chaska's Welter out of the car. It was no longer any of Larry Klunder's business how the Chaska high school teacher got home that night. He had school to teach the next day, too. After driving away, Klunder turned back and picked up his passenger. But the tone of conversation was decidedly different the rest of the way home.

"When Chaska had their year-end dinner party," Stoll said, "we were invited. But Klunder said there was no way he was going to show up for that." So the two skipped the dinner and fanned the flames of the inter-city rivalry a little more. The 1969 season would right the ship in Arlington, although a slow start and mediocre league season didn't bode well as the summer wore on toward playoffs.

Jim Stoll remembers working for Les Pinske and Jim O'Brien at the Arlington Cement Works for about a year and a half. "Then," he said, "I went to work for Ray Odegaarde, a carpenter, for $2.00 an hour." After a couple years, he said he began working in Green Isle at the Farm Hand, an agricultural store owned by the father of John Wilkens. He would learn to weld there, and he began recruiting Big John Wilkens for the Arlington A's.

"That's how we got Wilkens to come and play with us," Stoll said, "giving us a pretty good nucleus for our ball club." He ticked off the names: "Wilkens catching; Sylvester on first; Klunder at second; Menzel at short; and I could play third or pitch."

Stoll had taken a welding job in the Twin Cities that required him to be at work in downtown Minneapolis at 6 am. That meant getting up at 3:30 to 4:00 am for the long commute. "I was used to getting up at 7," he said, scoffing with laughter, "to be at work in Arlington at 7:30."

The Arlington A's would have just four wins at the start of the 1969 season against six losses after getting beat by Chaska, 2-1, on July 20. It is the first game in which Stoll's name appears in any of the 1969 game summaries in *The History of Arlington Baseball*. He is mentioned as having gotten a hit in the loss to Chaska. He would be 32 years old that fall, and he said he had a habit of putting on weight in the Minnesota winters. "I'd get up to maybe 220 pounds," he said, "then play myself into shape at around 185."

On July 27, he pitched six innings and is credited with the 9-8 loss to Chanhassen. But he hit a homerun in the losing cause. He would pitch only three, then two innings in his next two starts.

The History of Arlington Baseball notes that on August 10, 1969, Arlington defeated archrival Chaska, 12–5, as "Jim Stoll went the distance for the first time this season scattering 10 hits to pick up the win." It was the first game of a best-of-three playoff series. Four days later, on August 14, Stoll shut out Chaska, 5–0, on a five hitter with seven strikeouts. He would not pitch again for three weeks, not until the state championship game against Prior Lake. Drafted pitchers would lead Arlington through the regional tournament and the first four games of the state tournament. While his arm was quiet, Stoll's bat roared. He would hit .500 for the tournament and lead the A's to a 14-1 win over Brainerd in the semi-finals with a 3 for 4 showing at the plate that included a grand slam homerun.

But as Dave Hartmann had said, "Sore arm or not, nobody but Jim Stoll was going to pitch that championship game." Stoll said that he never knew what he was going to have on the mound at any given time when just warming up, because, he said, "You need the adrenaline going through you to really have an idea." But over 2,600 fans jammed Jordan's ballpark with an idea that they were in for something special. People were ushered inside the fences, down both lines to give them a "seat" on the grass. It was the largest baseball crowd in the history of the ballpark. It remains the largest crowd to view a final game of the state tournament since 1959 at St. Cloud.

Gary Porter said he recalled playing for Chaska against Stoll and appreciating him for being a heady pitcher. "He would throw a strike here, throw a strike there, and you'd think his fastball's nothing special. He's not going to throw that by me. His curveball was okay, but it can be tracked. He doesn't have anything exceptional. And then as the game goes on and the importance of each pitch increases, suddenly the fastball gets faster, the curveball gets sharper. He was pacing himself early to save his arm for later."

"That's what he did in the championship game," Porter said. " He didn't start out a house on fire. He started slow. He just got people out, but as the game wore on, he just got better and better."

"He stuck it to us," Gary Reierson admitted, "and we weren't used to that, because we had a pretty good hitting team."

"I remember him sweating profusely," Porter said, "and I think it helped him, helped his arm. Then he took control and just dominated them. He dominated those guys."

"I still can't believe he threw me a change-up on a 3-2 count with the bases loaded," Reierson lamented over 40 years later.

"Jim Stoll had such a presence about himself," Porter said. "He was like a man amongst boys."

Pat Devitt

*There's no doubt that he was the best-
hitting pitcher I've ever seen.*

— Lowell Stark, Former Shakopee Indian and Prior Lake Jay

Everybody always said that Pat Devitt signed right out of high school. They said he reported to the minor league team he was assigned to by the Major League club with which he had signed, but that he got terribly homesick and missed his high school sweetheart and wife-to-be, Rosemary, of now over 50 years. They said he packed his bags and came home to marry Rosemary. The rumors persisted for over 50 years.

"No, I never signed," Pat Devitt said on a September morning in 2014. He said he wasn't offered a contract to sign either. But Jerry Flathman, a representative of the Chicago White Sox, who moonlighted as an umpire as well, talked to Devitt after calling one of his games. Nothing ever came of that, and Pat Devitt would wait until he completed his college education at St. Thomas College in St. Paul, Minnesota, and had secured full-time employment with Control Data in Bloomington before tying the matrimonial knot.

With what professional baseball was paying in the 1950s, Pat Devitt is probably fortunate that he wasn't teased with a typical offer of the day. He probably would have jumped at any offer, because it was every American kid's dream to play professional baseball. Instead, after 10 high school letters in three sports and a straight-A average in the classroom, Pat Devitt chose to continue his education. He was awarded a "full ride" from St. Thomas on a *grant-in-aid* of $500 a year. The same full ride today, for the school year 2016-17 at St. Thomas, carries a tab of nearly $50,000 for tuition and fees, room and board, according to the Minnesota Private College Council's website.

Private colleges and universities such as St. Thomas in the Minnesota Intercollegiate Athletic Conference, or MIAC, say that they don't give athletic scholarships. They say it in a way that tries to imply, at least, that they are above that. Instead, they claim to support the talented student-athlete whose family's financial resources are such that attendance at the private school would otherwise not be possible. But to the student-athlete and the parents, "a rose by any other name is still a rose."

Pat Devitt came from a family with eight children. There wasn't any extra money in those days. Not in the Devitt home. St. Thomas was close to home, and Pat didn't have a car. He would hitchhike everyday.

Prior Lake High School opened its first doors in 1952. The high school kids had gone to Shakopee until then, "and it was a big thing," Devitt said, because of the size of the community and what it meant to have your own high school. Pat got straight A's throughout high school, and that made him a good candidate for St. Thomas College. But it didn't hurt that he'd pitched the Lakers to Little Six Conference championships in both his junior and senior years, going 8-1 his junior year and 5-1 or 6-1, he guessed, his senior year. He capped off the season with a no-hitter against Randolph High School in which he struck out 19 of the 21 batters he faced. Two batters touched him–ticked balls for fouls, and he walked a man to mar a perfect game. Nor did it hurt his chances to become a Tommy when he batted .430, he thought, his senior year, following a .409 batting average his junior year, and .375 as a sophomore. He'd even hit .304 as a freshman, and just making the high school baseball team as an eighth grader speaks volumes of the talent he showed at a young age already.

Prior Lake is a growing suburb south of the Minnesota River and about 20 miles south of downtown Minneapolis. The 2010 census showed a population of 22,796 people, which would be close to 30,000 in 2020. But in 1950 the census showed the village to have but 536 people and 848 in 1960. Incorporated as a village in 1891, Devitt thought for sure that fewer than 1,000 people inhabited Prior Lake in the 1950s. It's hard to say, because some people stayed on the lake longer each summer season and neither Prior Lake nor adjacent Savage had annexed perimeter land or the entire lake area yet. It was rural and lake resort country. It's hard to tell boundaries today as well, because what one always considered Prior Lake is part of Savage now. In the 1950s, "Savage" was the On-and Off-Sale "Dan Patch" Municipal Liquor Store and adjacent commercial enterprises and residential area just off Highway 13. But they had a ball club, too, the Savage "Pacers," and "Earl & Dorothy's," a 3-2 bar and truck stop, was open on Sundays. It served as a watering hole for ballplayers and fans after ball games in Savage.

Pat Devitt played ball every day as a kid growing up in the Village of Prior Lake. His playground was rough gravel and located adjacent to the railroad tracks that ran through the middle of downtown Prior Lake. "Railroad cars would constantly be dropped off for removal of lumber and other material," Devitt writes in his informal, unpublished memoirs, which continue:

> These boxcars were about the length and width of today's outside batting cages. So an empty railroad car became my baseball Mecca. My brother and I would (grab) a bat and some tennis balls and take batting practice inside the railroad car. He would bat and I would pitch and then we would reverse roles. We did this numerous times until outside baseball games became more prevalent. We had no organized baseball programs offered by the community. So your participation, in the sport, was keeping your eyes and ears open for upcoming neighborhood games. The ground around the railroad tracks was packed gravel from trucks driving on it. Then when I wasn't playing somewhere in the area, I would bounce rubber balls off the side of the railroad cars to enhance my throwing and fielding skills. Today, when I look back on those days, these routines had a lot to do with making me a more competitive and capable ball player.

High school baseball was a huge step for Pat the spring after Prior Lake High School opened its doors for the first time in the fall of 1952. Kids had been going to Shakopee High School after their first eight grades of education in Prior Lake. The high school baseball team was an even bigger step for Pat because he was only an eighth grader. Here he was already, playing with the big kids. It was just the way he'd always liked it. "One of my earliest memories was as a 3rd grader (8-9 years old)," Devitt writes in his memoirs:

> Two eighth graders were working on their pitching and needed a batter to test their abilities. Most kids my age shied away but not me. So I grabbed the only bat available and stepped up to the makeshift plate–which was probably a folded over Gunny Sack. Even though I probably missed a pitch or two, I had some very good hits. I felt very good about myself. I'm not so sure how my older opposition felt.

Gene Olive had been hired to teach at Prior Lake High School and to coach its very first high school baseball team in 1953. In fact, he coached all three sports: baseball, football, and basketball. Devitt remembers Gene Olive as having played for and managed Waseca in the fast Southern Minny, a league with paid ballplayers, many of whom it was said, were as good as, or better than, most of the professionals playing in the minor leagues. Olive would move on to Richfield after two years at Prior Lake. He won 146 high school baseball games there between 1955 and 1965 and two Minnesota state championships, in 1962 and again in 1965. Gene Olive finished his career in education as a principal, but in the 1940s, he'd signed with the Chicago White Sox after playing some service ball in the Coast Guard.

Gene Olive hit .331 with the Class-C Henderson Oilers in the East Texas League in 1946. First the Philadelphia Phillies, then the Chicago White Sox, owned him in 1947 and '48, riding the bench for all but 25 games and batting under .200 for the Memphis Chickasaws of the AA-Southern Association. Then he came home to Minnesota and played in the vaunted Southern Minny, settling in at Waseca as its player-manager. In 1956 he had moved on to the LeSueur Green Sox as one of its two allowed outside paid players while beginning the coaching legacy he left at Richfield High School.

Devitt said that he doesn't remember playing much as an eighth or ninth grader, but he does remember being asked to hang around after practice one day:

> There was another good baseball player called Bud Kleidon who had played previously with a professional farm club. Apparently, they decided to have a home run contest and I was their pitcher of choice. I don't know who won the contest, but I can surely relate when I watch the annual home run contest at the Major League Baseball All Star Game–and I didn't have a cage in front of me for protection. They both batted left-handed and had no trouble pulling the ball at my delivery speed.

Bud Kleidon took a shot at professional baseball after The War in 1947. He's shown with a .233 average for Superior in the Class-C Northern League. But in 1954 he played first base, a little outfield, and did some pitching for Prior Lake in the Northern Division of the Class-A Minnesota River League. "He was one of the first switch hitters I saw around here," Devitt said. They would finish on the bottom of the division with a 6-12 record, while Jordan and Belle Plaine led with identical

11-7 records and St. Peter from the Southern Division would have the overall best league record at 14-4.

The professionals, Olive and Kleidon, looked different at the plate than high school, college, and most town team batters. They seemed more focused. They swung the bat with more discipline and authority. They hit line drives that seemed to jump off their bats. Every once in a while they'd get ahold of one and clear the fence with plenty of room to spare. They hit young Pat Devitt hard, and he wasn't lobbing the ball into them.

But, like most high school ballplayers, he started to see some action his sophomore year, and he recorded some early memories:

> As a 10th grader, I remember relieving in a game against Montgomery that was a lost cause. I think it was my first time on a mound in a real game. They had the All State Athlete of the Year, Bob Ilg, playing on their team. He zeroed in on my first pitch and drove a hard line drive right back at me. My follow through form was pretty good and the ball ended up in the webbing of my A2000 glove. I felt great but Bob must have felt robbed. He could not have hit my pitch any harder than he did.

"He was a high school phenom," Devitt said of Bob Ilg. So was Pat Devitt, and he was recognized for it as an inductee of the inaugural class of Prior Lake's Hall of Fame in 2002–fully 50 years after putting on his spikes as an eighth grader for the high school baseball team. Devitt was All-Conference in football his junior and senior years; All-Conference his senior year in basketball, leading his team to a 9-1 record and the Little Six Conference championship, 15-3 overall. He scored 18 points in one game, 19 in another when, outside of the fabled Ron Johnson of New Prague, that was rare. Many teams were still scoring only 30 to 40 points a game then.

Pat Devitt would, in all likelihood, have been All-Conference in his best sport, baseball, probably both his junior and senior years, except that the conference coaches did not recognize, nor award, the honor for baseball then. Devitt thought it was because the end of the high school baseball season coincided so closely with the end of the school year and the closing for summer that they just didn't get that on anyone's agenda.

The junior and senior years of Pat Devitt's high school baseball were virtual carbon copies of each other. The Lakers went undefeated each year in their Little Six Conference. Each year they got beat in their District 14 championship game by Twin Cities metro high schools of significantly larger enrollments. In 1956, it was Columbia Heights that beat Pat Devitt and his Lakers. In 1957, West St. Paul turned the trick, 3-1, despite Devitt's seven hitter and 11 strikeouts. Ironically, the game was scheduled for nine innings when the standard high school game had been seven innings. Prior Lake was ahead 1-0 on Devitt's arm after seven.

To get into the championship, Prior Lake had defeated North St. Paul, 8-3, with Devitt leading the attack with a perfect day at the plate, four for four, with four RBIs, and pitching a five hitter with 11 strikeouts. They then drubbed Red Wing, 9-2, before bowing out to West St. Paul.

Pat's 8-1 record on the year was highlighted by a 5-3, two-hit gem he threw to beat St. Paul Park, a game in which he also scored the winning run on battery mate

Art Snell's seventh-inning triple. He also fired a one hitter for six innings in the 17-3 win over Randolph, which would have been a shutout had it not been for three errors in the first inning.

The 1956-57 Prior Lake school year was a resounding Devitt success trail. While the football team lost his services for several games and rival St. Paul Park went undefeated to capture the Little Six Conference title, Devitt was a unanimous selection to the All-Conference team at end. Like most football players in the 1950s, Pat played both ways–safety on defense and end, halfback, and quarterback on offense. He had been voted the top athlete in the Prior Lake school his junior year, 1955-'56, and there was no reason why he couldn't repeat.

The *St. Paul Pioneer Press* sports section headline on Saturday, February 9, 1957, captured the tone and the talent of the Prior Lake basketball season: "Prior Lake Upsets Parkers, 52-34." Having won seven straight conference tilts, St. Paul Park was unbeaten and alone on top of the Little Six with a perfect 7-0 record. Prior Lake had lost to the metro school, 53-44, in a pre-holiday game in St. Paul. The return match promised a classic duel between the offense-minded Parkers, who were averaging 70 points per game, and the Lakers, who were playing defense to the tune of yielding just 32 points per game. Dick Edwards of St. Paul Park was averaging over 20 points per game, which was phenomenal for the times.

With the conference championship on the line, the Parkers scoring more than twice as many points a game as the Lakers, a pre-game scrapbook clipping noted, "The Lakers, the top defensive team in the conference, have the task of stopping the Parkers' Dick Edwards and Roger Pribnow, who have scorched the league with their scoring efforts." But it has been said of every sport forever, "Defense wins championships."

The Lakers had held St. Paul Park to one of its lowest-scoring efforts of the season in their first meeting. "Friday night," presumably the *St. Paul Pioneer Press* reporting on Saturday, February 9, 1957, "it was much the same story as the defensive minded Lakers were at their best with Pat Devitt breaking through enough times to score 19 points." Prior Lake put "The D" on St. Paul Park, 52-34. That put the conference into a deadlock at the top, with each team at 7-1 on the season. The deadlock would hold. The two teams would share the title with identical 9-1 records at the end of conference play. It was high school basketball at its best. Conference games and championships at stake filled the high school gymnasiums everywhere. Prior Lake had its first conference championship, and the town was filled with The Buzz of tournament fever.

District 14 was a huge step up for the Prior Lake Lakers in 1957. Devitt said that they didn't play well against West St. Paul and got blown out by 12 to 15 points.

Pat's no-hitter with the 19 strikeouts against Randolph was his personal highlight of the 1957 high school baseball season. It punctuated the team's second consecutive conference championship with an undefeated record. For Prior Lake's High School Class of 1957–20 students, 12 of whom were boys–it was a great year. Devitt's future was bright. He'd always dreamed of becoming a Major League pitcher. Many thought he was on track. He was so good that it had to be true. That began the rumors that persisted to this day of him walking away from it to get married.

"Pat Devitt was a great athlete," Lowell Stark exclaimed of the man he played with and against in amateur baseball. "He belongs on anybody's list of the all-time best ball players around here. There's no doubt," Stark continued, "that he was the best-hitting pitcher I've ever seen." Stark played well, too, and said that he went 8-0 as a pitcher for Shakopee's American Legion baseball team in 1955, the year Fred Kerber went 16-0 for the Shakopee Indians, pitching for Stark's father, Russ, who managed the team to an 18-1 record while playing in the Class-B Valley Six League. He later played for both the Shakopee Indians and the Prior Lake Jays in Minnesota River Valley amateur baseball.

A feature article by Hank Kehborn in the *St. Paul Pioneer Press* was headlined, "Pat Devitt, Prior Lake's Greatest Athlete, College Bound." Pat is shown in a picture accompanying the article stocking shelves at Monnen's and Hennen's Fairway Foods grocery store, which used to be on Main Street, where the bakery is today. Pat had worked there for three summers and weekends for three years. But in that first season of the first year of high school baseball in Prior Lake, everything was new–new coach, new school, and everybody sporting what looked like new baseball gloves, Devitt recalls, and "I only had one glove during my playing career and it was a Wilson A2000. I was going into the Eighth grade, at our newly opened Prior Lake High School in 1952," Devitt writes in his memoirs:

> The only glove I had was a hand me-down pancake one received from my uncles. When I saw what type of gloves that other players had, I didn't dare show up with it. So I talked to Coach Olive and he said he would get me a glove for $20. I was part of a family of eight children and there was no extra money available for this type of purchase. At the age of 14, I got a job working at Monnen's and Hennen's grocery store on Saturday's earning around 50 cents an hour. It took me about 5–6 weekends to make enough money to purchase this magnificent glove. It was a beauty as anything new is. It served me well for 5 years of high school baseball, 4 years at the University of St. Thomas, 9 years of summer town ball and another 10 years of slow pitch softball following my baseball career.

Coach Olive got the glove for him at Bill St. Manes Sporting Goods store in South Minneapolis, "where we (made) all our baseball equipment purchases," Devitt said.

Kehborn's article was written as if Pat were actually weighing his options between going to St. John's University at Collegeville, or St. Thomas College in St. Paul. He said there was never a doubt. He wanted to be a Tommy, because St. Thomas was close enough for him stay at home, keep his job at the store, and commute daily by hitchhiking.

The article notes that Prior Lake High School Athletic Director Joe Tousignant and Coach Byron Blake called Devitt "the greatest athlete in the history of the high school." Devitt said he never considered football or basketball at St. Thomas. But he still entertained thoughts of professional baseball. While getting his education from a good school, he could work toward his dream at the same time.

But before starting college, Pat Devitt played summer baseball after his junior and senior years of high school in 1956 and 1957 for his hometown Prior Lake Jays of the Class-B Valley Six League. In fact, he played a little after his sophomore year of high school, too, in 1955. A game of note near the end of that first season shows

Devitt pitching a few innings after the game was already out of hand against Shakopee in a losing cause, 14-7. But the 16-year-old had three hits in four at bats.

Devitt notes in his memoirs that the town team had a turnover of personnel in 1956 after his junior year in high school, and several of his teammates from the successful high school nine joined him in playing that summer for the Jays. Bloomington and Shakopee had good ball clubs. A triple-game headline from the May 24, 1956, *Shakopee Argus-Tribune* showed both winning their opening games of the season, with Prior Lake on the short end against Bloomington. After the games on Sunday, June 21, Bloomington was leading the league with a 5-1 record, while the Jays were knocking on the cellar doors at 2-4, one game ahead of Savage.

Seventeen-year old Pat Devitt served notice to the league leaders that Prior Lake's days as the doormat of the league were over. Just under another story of interest in the same July 12, 1956, *Jordan Independent* in which people read, "Twin Cities Will Have Major League Club–Ollie Fuhrman," they also read, "Prior Lake Played a 1-0 Ballgame":

> Prior Lake's Pat Devitt and Bloomington's Don Miller engaged in an old-fashioned pitching duel in a regularly scheduled Valley Six game played at Bloomington Sunday afternoon. Devitt yielded 7 hits and the one run, while Miller hurled a shutout on five-hit ball.

He lost by an eyelash again the following Sunday, 2-1, to Marystown and Jim Busch, despite giving up only four hits in the game. Three Jay errors were costly. Then, in the last game of the regular season, Devitt beat Chaska, 12-2. The August 2 *Jordan Independent* reports a six-hit, 9-0 shutout of Marystown and Jim Busch by Pat Devitt in the first round of the league playoffs. A week later, Devitt did it again–another six hitter in Prior Lake's 6-1 win over Marystown, which put the Jays up against Bloomington in the next round of the playoffs. Bad luck returned to cost Devitt two unearned runs on four errors late in the first game in which, again, he gave up just six hits in a 4-2 loss to Bloomington. Then Bloomington took the Jays out of the running by defeating them 5-2. Shakopee and Fred Kerber then beat Bloomington two straight to take the league playoffs before getting crushed in the sudden-death regionals by the heavy-hitting St. Benedict Saints of the DRS League.

Without its own community newspaper, coverage of Pat Devitt and Prior Lake's baseball was limited to sporadic, inconsistent reporting in the weeklies of neighboring towns–*The Jordan Independent* and *The Shakopee Valley News*. But Jordan included a small piece on Prior Lake's boys taking it to the Savage Pacers in the 1957 opener of the Valley Six League. Pat's high school catcher, Art Snell, was behind the plate for the Jays as well. He smashed a three-run homerun in the first inning.

The big change with the 1957 Prior Lake Jays over the previous summer was that Pat Devitt became the primary pitcher for the team after sharing mound duties with others in 1956. It made a big difference in the success of the team. A year older and stronger, and coming off another great high school baseball season, Pat Devitt started on the mound for Prior Lake in the league opener against Savage. He went five innings in the 6-2 win without giving up a hit. Then, he beat vaunted Shakopee, 6-1, with a sparkling three hitter while striking out 11. His two-run double in the eighth inning broke the game open and gave the Jays a perfect 5-0 record. He also beat Savage that week in a makeup game, 16-3, going four for five at the plate and earning the win on the mound as well. The July 18, 1957, *Jordan Independent* ran the story: "Lakers Twin Win Hikes Flag Stock." Pat Devitt was hot–on the mound and at the plate. He had 13 hits in his last 21 at bats.

Then the Shakopee Indians woke up and salvaged their season, pounding Devitt and the Jays, 10-1, and taking over first place with an 8-1 record to the Jays' 7-1 record. A makeup game with Bloomington at Jordan under the lights gave Prior Lake an opportunity to tie Shakopee for the lead. It wasn't to be. Bloomington used six doubles and a triple in the game to edge the Jays, 5-4. Shakopee would prevail for the league title, with playoffs looming.

Pat beat Bloomington in the first game of the best-of-three playoff series, 3-1, on a three hitter. He hit, going three for four in the second game, but Bloomington just had too much firepower and beat Prior Lake, 15-4. Devitt's arm was tired. He didn't pitch that game, but he started the third and rubber game. But he tried to catch with his bare hand a line drive back at him on the mound. The ball nearly tore off the tip of a finger. He gave way to a reliever and as a result Bloomington won, 6-2. But Shakopee would prevail again, beating Bloomington in the final round of the league playoffs. To Pat Devitt's delightful surprise, Indian manager Lefty Odenwald called and asked Pat if he were available to play as a draftee pitcher for the Shakopee Indians. "Ramblings from a Draftee" in Pat's memoirs:

> Being a draftee is like being a guest in someone else's house. It's like when a girl friend invites you to her home for a major gathering like Thanksgiving or Christmas dinner for the first time. You attend without really knowing anybody and you are the center of attention. You are meeting people face to face for the very first time. You are in foreign territory and don't know what is expected of you. You are an outsider. You show up for team practice. You shag balls in the outfield, take a little hitting (you are a pitcher and won't bat much), and throw some batting practice. At the end of practice, a team meeting is held and everyone goes their separate ways until next practice or game. Then game day comes. Manager has big decision to make–start your team's best pitcher or one you drafted? As a draftee the manager has you loosening up/throwing from the start of the game, so you are ready to save the day in case the roof falls in on the current pitcher. Then it happens, the opposition starts a rally and the call is made to bring you in–someone to shut down the rally. Many thoughts go through your mind. Can you put out the fire? What if you can't? What will the fan base think? If you can't, they say to themselves we drafted the wrong guy. You get through your warm up tosses and the pressure is on. Three things are for certain. One, you won't be facing the bottom of the opposition's batting order; two, there will be runners on base, so you need to throw from the stretch position (i.e., no wind-ups); three, you have been a starting pitcher and now you are thrown into a relief role. You just want to throw strikes and get out of the inning as quick as possible. If you get the job done, you are a hero (temporarily). If you don't, you are the goat because you let the team and the fan base down. As a draftee for the Shakopee Indians in 1957, we won a few games in the tournament but not the State Class-B Title. The town of Shakopee celebrated their successful season with an evening event at the St. Paul House–one of the premier dining places at that time.

> It was a very, very nice evening. Halsey Hall was guest speaker for the event. I would watch Halsey Hall deliver the sports news every evening on TV, but it was just great seeing and meeting him in person.

On the way to the ballgame, Pat Devitt admitted that he entertained no thoughts about pitching that day. "So at this point, I was just plain excited about being part of the team," he writes. He said that after being handed the ball, which meant he was starting, the adrenaline got going and so did the thoughts: *Will I be good enough*, he worried. *What if I stink up the place? What will the Shakopee fans think of me if I lose?* Lots of things like that were going through Devitt's mind.

> But the Good Lord was on my side that day, plus Shakopee was a really good ball club. When the game was over and everyone was happy that we were moving on, I think I was walking about six inches off the ground. What a great feeling knowing that you contributed and now you really are part of the team.

Lefty Odenwald gave Pat the new ball just ahead of Shakopee taking infield practice, signifying he was to start the championship game for Region 6B's qualifying entry into the 1957 Minnesota State Amateur Baseball Tournament. Region 6B then comprised four area Class-B leagues: the DRS, including St. Benedict, Lonsdale, and New Market, among others; the Valley Six, with powerful Bloomington and Shakopee, Chaska, Prior Lake, Marystown, and Savage; the Cannon Valley, which included teams from towns such as Dundas, Northfield, Rosemount, and Farmington; and the Dakota County League, which included Vermillion, Miesville, Hampton, Cannon Falls, and Hastings. This regional qualifying tournament was no cakewalk. Moreover, it was truly competitive in that only one team would advance. Ballplayers from the other teams would go home for the squirrel-hunting season and to wait out a long winter.

No team or league lasted forever. They were constantly getting reshuffled in name and composition and class. Jordan, for example, was playing Class-A baseball with the likes of former Class-AA Southern Minny Waseca, who would win the 1957 Class-A state championship, despite being what many claimed the third-or even fourth-best team in the Minnesota River League that year; Western Minny's New Ulm, as well as teams of longer standing in the Minnesota River League, such as St. Peter, which had won the state championship in 1955, were also strong.

LeCenter had won the Class-A state championship in 1950 and finished second in 1951. Belle Plaine had lost Class-A state championship games in 1948 and, again, in 1952. Powerful Shakopee, with Gordy Gelhaye at the helm and still pounding prodigious homeruns, as well as Dick Siebert, newly retired from 11 years of Major League Baseball with St. Louis and Philadelphia, Warren Stemmer, and Doug Shonka, was upset in the semifinals of the 1948 state tournament by Winsted, who then beat Belle Plaine in the championship game. Jordan had won the league dogfights in 1953 and 1954, but some say got jobbed in the tournament two years in a row in 1-0 losses. Some of the best baseball ever played in Minnesota was being played in the Class-A and B leagues of the lower basin of the Minnesota River Valley during the Golden Age of Baseball. There was no Class-C amateur baseball then outside of the schoolyards.

The September 5, 1957, edition of the *Shakopee Argus-Tribune* and the lead to its account of the Labor Day "Game of the Century," beginning with the headline: "Indians Win Spot in State Tourney," "Tip Canons 7-2, St. Benedict 14-4 For Region Crown" tell us much.

Fred Kerber had come up big in a big game win over Cannon Falls of the Dakota County League in the first round of region play, firing a five-hitter with nine strikeouts, while St. Benedict had clobbered the Cannon Valley League's champion, Northfield, 15-2. Then 18-year-old Pat Devitt got the nod in the Region 6B showdown:

> In the game that put Shakopee in the state tournament at Cold Spring, a crowd of over 1,000 was on hand at St. Benedict to watch the Indians avenge last year's 20-13 massacre on the same field. A courageous right hander, Pat Devitt, hurled beautiful ball in the clutch and overcame an injury that supposedly was going to keep him out of playoff competition. The speed merchant drafted from the Prior Lake Lakers suffered a dislocated finger on his pitching hand two weeks ago when reaching for a line drive. With no sign of irritation from the wound, Devitt kept the Benedict hitters off balance with a sweeping curve ball and a hopping fast one.

Shakopee's Fred Kerber hit a long homerun in the top of the third inning. Actually, according to the *Argus-Tribune*, he "lifted one into the stratosphere and out of the park for a homerun." The solo blast gave Shakopee what would hold up as the winning run, making the score 5-2 at the time. But with the wind blowing out on this Labor Day and the short right-field fence of just 250 feet–the same distance as the left-field fence at the LA Coliseum where the Dodgers would erect a 42-foot screen to cut down on homeruns in 1958–no pitcher felt he was at a holiday picnic. Devitt pitched out of trouble time and again in going the distance, giving up but six hits, three of them homeruns, and he helped his own cause with a homerun–one of a ballpark record eight hit that day.

The September 5, 1957, *Jordan Independent* reported an announced crowd of 896–"The largest crowd ever to witness a baseball game at St. Benedict." Where did they put the people, we wanted to know almost 60 years after the fact, for the ballpark then, as now, was a small, church yard, owned and maintained by the Catholic Church, for years thought to be the property of the Parish of St. Benedict, but which remains owned by the Archdiocese of St. Paul. It was small, but it worked. It's still working today, despite the Archdiocese having closed the doors of the church while retaining title to the ballpark for some reason.

"They put up temporary bleachers down the right-field line, and we packed 'em in from home plate to the fence," Lyle Lambrecht of St. Benedict said. They packed in the people, who came, according to the newspaper accounts of the game, from Shakopee, Jordan, Lonsdale, New Prague, and the local farming community to watch a big game in a small yard. It must have been at least some of what E.F. Schumacher had in mind while writing his 1973 classic work on economics, *Small is Beautiful*, at the close of the Golden Age of Baseball.

We don't know today what St. Benedict charged for admission in 1957. We can guess that it was six bits or a buck on Labor Day. But without a controlling turnstile gate or a pinch-point of picket fencing, they probably passed the hat, or maybe they doubled up the duty of the baskets they used at the church on Sundays. The year before, in the May 17, 1956, edition of *The Jordan Independent*, the neighboring Class-A Brewers advertised season tickets at $5.00 for their 10 home games–"a savings of $1.00" off the single-game ticket price of 60 cents. But this was the playoffs, and people would pay the buck for a big game like this with Shakopee–especially after what St. Benedict had done to Shakopee in the same playoff situation a year earlier.

"As a pitcher, each game is big," Pat Devitt writes in his memoirs. "But this one was the biggest so far." He went the full nine innings and checked a hard-hitting St. Benedict nine on the six hits. He gave up three home runs in the game, including a monster shot by Marv Hartman, but whom didn't "Mutz" hit in those years? "After the game," he writes, "my girlfriend and future wife (Rosemary Cates) and I celebrated with a burger and malt at the local diner"–the Town Treat Café–which Devitt said was owned by Gene & Dorie Didion and located in the heart of downtown Prior Lake next to Monnen's Lumber Company on main street. "We couldn't go too far without a car," Devitt added.

Pat Devitt felt good about having helped the team he considered, even before that year, the best in the area. He had pitched better ballgames, he knew, but never in a game as big as this one had been. He would savor the win for the rest of the day, but already he was beginning to feel the excitement of the state tournament at Cold Spring, his first state tournament, coming up in less than a week. He was also a freshman in college. He would need to register for classes, the letter from St. Thomas had said.

He didn't even know what that meant–registration. But he soon found out. It was overwhelming, as anyone who has ever been a college freshman anywhere in the days before online, stress-free registration. Devitt said that after getting about half way through the "Day from Hell" only to learn that some of his classes were already filled with the maximum number of students allowed, "I threw in the towel and returned to Prior Lake unregistered to attend," Devitt writes in response to our queries, and he continues:

> Giving up was very frustrating to me. It was not part of me to do this, but I was so overwhelmed by the process. I came home and relayed my experience to my best friend and store boss (Lambert Hennen). He listened and recommended we give it another try, which we did. I don't know how much time elapsed, maybe a week. Plus, he probably called the college to get some help with the procedures for late registration. This was such an unusual experience for me I didn't want anyone else to have to go through it. About four or five years later, a friend of mine was off to St. Thomas. I made sure he didn't experience the same thing that I did. So I shadowed him through registration so there would be no hitches. The registration went fine.

Pat Devitt had some unfinished business to attend to and a commitment to fulfill with the Shakopee Indians. The 1957 Minnesota Class-B State Amateur Baseball Tournament was held at Cold Spring in Stearns County, about 90 minutes mostly west of the Twin Cities and just 15 to 20 miles from St. Cloud where the team would stay overnight at Swiggum's Motel.

Baseball headlines made the front page of the September 12, 1957, *Shakopee Argus-Tribune*. The headlines tell us a great deal: "Rallying Indians Defeat Steves on Devitt's Brilliant Relief Job."

Shakopee blew a 2-0 lead and trailed St. Stephen, 5-2, before rallying to win the game on the strength of the young Prior Lake draftee's stunning relief pitching. Here's how the *Argus-Tribune* reported it then:

> Pat Devitt's relief hurling and a 'lucky' seventh inning rally spelled victory for the Shakopee Indians in their first game of the state tournament, Sept. 7. . . . The fifth inning proved to be the darkest of the game for Shakopee players and fans alike.

With two runs in, one out, and a runner on first base, Manager Lefty Odenwald replaced his starting pitcher, another draftee from Bloomington, with young Pat Devitt. The leased Laker got the batter to hit into a double play and got Shakopee off the hook of what could have been a game-busting inning, "and from that point on, St. Stephen's touted hitting strength was completely muffled."

Shakopee surged in the seventh, led by Butch Kreuser's two-run double deep to right field, pulling Shakopee ahead in the game. Then, "using his 7-5 cushion, Devitt really bore down and whiffed four men in the last innings. He ended the game by retiring the side in the ninth on strikeouts." Pat Devitt had a "W" in his first state tournament appearance. In 4-2/3 innings of relief, he did not allow a run, gave up one scratch single, and had five strikeouts.

Fred Kerber, whose 31-game winning streak had come to a halt a month earlier, smothered Big Fork, 11-2, on four hits in Shakopee's second round of tournament play. Then Manager Lefty Odenwald came back with Devitt against the defending champions from Bemidji. Pat responded with a 7-3 win that put Shakopee in the semifinals on Saturday night. Helped by four double plays, Pat scattered eight hits in the win and helped himself and his mates at the plate as well, going three for four, with a single, double, and triple, and three RBIs.

Kerber started on the mound against Norwood for Shakopee, which took an early 2-0 lead. But Norwood came back in the third to tie the score. Devitt came on in relief and pitched well again. But the last two innings were a proverbial comedy of errors. Norwood scored three runs in the eighth and three more in the ninth to win, 8-2. The wind had been taken out of their sails, too, and Braham beat Norwood in the title game, 3-1.

Pat Devitt had his game going at Cold Spring. He had every right to be a proud 18-year-old freshman on the campus of St. Thomas College in the fall of 1957. In the just-completed state tournament, he had won two games and lost one in relief. His complete game victory had come against the defending champions from Bemidji. His earned run average for the three games was a stingy .050. Moreover, Pat Devitt had led the Shakopee Indians in hitting for the tournament, batting .566 on five hits in nine at bats.

There was that "little matter" of registration at St. Thomas hanging over Pat Devitt though. "Lambert Hennen was a special friend," Devitt said. He was not only Pat's boss at the grocery store, but he had substituted for Pat's father at the spring father & son athletic banquet. Pat's father had to be on the road with his job, and Lambert Hennen stepped in for him on a special night. He had his own family, but he had taken young Pat Devitt under his wing, too. Hell, he'd given the young man the keys to his store! But when he saw how anxious Pat had come home from his experience of failing to complete his registration at St. Thomas, he thought they needed to "do lunch," as it would become known decades in the future.

Pat Devitt and his mentor, Lambert Hennen, took time off together from duty at the grocery store. That was unheard of then. "We went to Marv's Dairyland, a diner on the south end of downtown Prior Lake," Devitt said. They discussed Pat's issues with getting registered for classes at St. Thomas. One of Devitt's issues was ROTC. It was mandatory at St. Thomas for all freshmen in 1957, but Pat said that he just wasn't prepared to have to put on a uniform and practice soldiering every week. "I think we discussed for over an hour with a hamburger basket," Devitt recalled. "The point is it wasn't done in his office at the store."

Lambert Hennen recognized the situation for what it was, a defining moment in the young man's life. Nobody liked putting up with what seemed like a crazy-making runaround and endless lines at every stop, which was college registration in those days. He cared enough about the young man to want to give him his undivided attention on the matter and to make sure Pat knew he was getting it.

But college was another new experience for Pat Devitt that fall at St. Thomas. He commuted everyday between Prior Lake and St. Paul, using his wits, his thumb, and a smile. He hitchhiked. Pat said that a schoolteacher he knew from Prior Lake worked within a few blocks of St. Thomas and gave him a ride in the mornings. In the afternoons, he said, "If I could get across the Mendota Bridge to Hwy 13, I had a great chance of getting picked up."

While Pat had been a straight-A student in high school, he soon learned that he had to study in his college classes just to keep up. There was an old college course dictum that said that for every hour of class time, you needed to put in something like eight hours a week of study time. The Devitt home that Pat grew up in was not conducive to study. It was a small, basement home, and eight kids with Mom and Dad made it impossible to find a Quiet Zone with the space needed. Lambert Hennen gave Pat his own key to the store. Pat turned it into his "private study" after store hours and on Sundays. It was perfect. Today the Speiker office building stands where the grocery store once was and where Pat is currently employed, thus completing a circle of sorts spanning the better part of his life.

Still, college classes were anything but a breeze for Pat Devitt. At least two of his classes were required–ROTC and religion. While he had no problem with religion, having to put on a uniform and the marching and drill instruction in the military officer training class was one of the issues that had befuddled him when he first tried to register. Pat thought he pulled about a 2.5 GPA, or grade point average, his first semester. While he got an A, he said, in math/advanced algebra, the English professor gave him a C. He said the first paper she asked the class to write was to compare the differences between "high-brow" and "low-brow." Devitt had no idea what she meant. Had it not been for Lambert Hennen's mentoring after hours at the grocery store, he might have submitted a paper on eyebrows.

The academic world has always been insulated from the real world. Math and business professors and classes weren't as bad. At least, Pat could frame things in the context he knew from what could be called an apprenticeship at Monnen's and

Hennen's Fairway Foods. He had another part-time job, too, in the back of the building that housed the grocery store. Here, Walter Monnens had a meat-processing operation and locker plant where beef and pork were butchered, cut up, and packaged for the area farmers. Walt's son Howard helped his father in the locker plant, but he was drafted into military service. Walt needed some part time help. "On Tuesdays," Devitt said, "someone helped Walt kill and skin the animals and quarter them." After hanging in the cooler for two to three days, Devitt said that Walt would cut up the meat and package it for the owner. "My job was to cut up the meat that was designated to be hamburger or pork sausage," Devitt said, "and place the packaged meats in the freezer for future pickup by the customer."

Unlike most college professors and students, mostly big city people, who probably thought that hamburger came from the grocery store, Pat Devitt learned where meat really came from. He said that Walt was busy with his meat-processing business, and the extra work gave Pat some spending money he needed, although he still didn't have a car because he didn't need one to get to work.

College slowly got better for Pat Devitt, as he became familiar with professors and their expectations, and the larger college classrooms. He said that his early anxiety was just the freshman jitters and blues and getting to know the college life. "I did well in the business and economic courses and ended up with a 3.2 GPA," he said. That's better than we know today, because the same thing that has happened with the dollar has happened with high school and college grade point averages–inflationary creep. What used to be a C is now a B. What was a B yesterday has become an A today. After all, insurance rates, popularity, scholarships, Ivy League and graduate school admissions are at stake. More people than ever in all areas of American life have come to believe that the ends justify the means. Management of grades would replace earning them.

Winters have always been long for Minnesota baseball players. Seasons made short by school calendars are shortened further by weather. Southern trips for high school and college baseball teams, other than Dick Siebert's University of Minnesota Gophers, were unheard of because of the expense. Fourteen-game seasons and seven-inning doubleheader games were the rule in Pat Devitt's day at St. Thomas. Still, it was baseball in the Golden Age of the game when baseball was king. Spring and the 1958 college baseball season came soon enough. Pat tried out for and made the St. Thomas baseball team as a pitcher his freshman year.

Devitt remembers the baseball kickoff meeting. He said he was in a room with 25 to 30 other guys. He sensed quickly that he was the new kid on the block. He only knew one other guy in the room–Chuck Kreuser, the Shakopee Indian shortstop he had played against and with the past summer. Nobody knew him, he was sure. But Coach Ken Staples, a St. Paul native, knew baseball. He had played professionally for eight years, five of them at the AA level. He would manage Minnesota Twin farm clubs at St. Cloud and Wisconsin Rapids after leaving St. Thomas. Out of the blue, after welcoming everyone, he asked in the meeting if Pat Devitt were present. "I identified myself and that was it," Devitt said. "It just caught me totally by surprise and until this day I don't know why he asked."

Perhaps student-coach Ken Staples had seen Pat pitch in the state tournament at Cold Spring the previous fall. It's possible at age 32 that he even played in the tournament, likely a Class-A metro area team. Regardless, Devitt was a known commodity to the coach who would be making the decisions about the roster and starting lineups. Staples had effectively nullified the class caste system. The room was full of returning lettermen, and the only ballplayer recognized by the coach had been Pat. Ken Staples had inquired about Pat Devitt. He didn't ask about anybody else.

Pat remembers well his first pitching assignment with St. Thomas. He was scheduled to start the second game of the doubleheader with Gustavus in St. Peter. He was warming up on the sidelines for the second-game start when the Gusties loaded the bases in the bottom of the seventh inning with one out, threatening to steal a Tommy game.

> I was called in to put out the fire," Pat said. "I threw one pitch. The batter hit a one hopper back to me. I threw home for the force out, and the catcher then threw to first to complete the double play and the victory. I then went on to throw a complete second game for our second win of the afternoon. What a great day. What a great feeling.

Pat had a great start to his first college baseball season, giving up just four hits and one run. Later, he shut out perennial conference champion St. Mary's, 1-0, on four hits. The lone run came on his RBI-single in the second inning. In a May 4 game reported on by Mike Fridgen for the *St. Paul Pioneer Press*, Pat Devitt and senior ace, Jerry Friedmann, combined on the mound to match what was described as a "sparkling pitching performance" by Al Eisele of St John's, with each team managing just four hits in the game won by the Johnnies. Pat started and took a 2-1 lead into the sixth inning at St. John's, but, "An infield error opened the gates for the Johnnies who capitalized with the tying and, what proved to be, the winning run."

Devitt's most memorable game of the 1959 St. Thomas baseball season was another game at St. John's. His account from his memoirs:

> I was the starting pitcher. Early in the game, the Johnnies got one or two runners on. Their number 4 hitter was at bat. I was given the sign to knock him down. I have hit a few batters in my pitching career but never intentionally threw at anyone's head. So I ignored the sign and tried throwing it by the batter. Mistake, mistake, mistake. He timed the pitch and hit it well beyond our outfielders on this open field. It was a round tripper.

Pat's junior year brought a new baseball coach, Don Saatzer, and aspirations of a run at a conference championship again. But the year was highlighted, according to Devitt, by his being nominated for the prestigious "Mr. Tommy Award," which was won by another candidate but still quite a feather in a baseball cap at St. Thomas. An injury marred Pat's senior year at St. Thomas. He suffered a severely sprained ankle in a pickup basketball game after a baseball practice. Despite hours in the whirlpool and on the trainer's table and many visits to doctors, only time could heal the torn ligaments. Time that ate up the baseball season. But he said that his new coach, Tom Feely, gave him the ball on the last home game of the season. "I think he did this out of the kindness of his heart so I could go out a winner," Devitt writes in his memoirs. But his lack of mound work and favoring the ankle resulted in wildness. Pat had trouble finding the plate. "I was removed in the early part of the game, but I do appreciate the coach giving me a chance to go out a winner," he writes.

Pat Devitt continued to play baseball for his hometown of Prior Lake during the summer months of his college years at St. Thomas. But the Valley Six League in which he had competed the previous three years folded. Geographically, culturally, and demographically, Marystown did not belong in a league with Bloomington in the 1950s anymore than they do today. Moreover, while Bloomington's population of 3,647 in the 1940 Census "qualified" it for Minnesota River Valley town team baseball, the 1950 Census figures of 9,902 and the 1960 numbers of 50,495 put this "river town" in another league. With the same residency requirements of other teams in the river leagues, Bloomington had what was impossible for other town teams–access to every ballplayer in the metropolitan area.

Bloomington probably did not belong in the same league with the rest of the teams of the 1950s anymore than they did in the late 60s to mid-70's. So Marystown looks to have evaporated for a couple years before re-joining the Dakota-Rice-Scott (DRS) League; Chaska joined Waconia, St. Bonifacious, Victoria, Carver, Chanhassen, Watertown, and Cologne–all on "the other side of the river"–in the Carver-Hennepin League; Bloomington went with the 7-High League, which included appropriately four other suburban teams and, oddly enough, New Germany out west of the cities.

The big move was in the creation of a brand new league–the River Valley League–out of the remnants of the Class-B Valley Six League and the Class-A Minnesota River League. Shakopee, Savage, and Prior Lake joined with Jordan, Belle Plaine, and New Prague. The May 15, 1958, front page of *The Jordan Independent* heralded the debut of the new league and the new baseball season. An editorial reinforced the article with the following:

> Sunday is the day baseball fans in Jordan have been waiting for. It is opening day for the 1958 season This year sees Jordan playing class B baseball for the first time in many years. Despite the drop from A to B ball, the general opinion of league officials and many fans is that spectators will still witness some exciting and satisfying baseball.

The well-intentioned editorial concluded with, "Eventually, league officials hope to return to class A ball." That would never happen. That kind of hope and the accompanying will were just some of the micro and macro forces that were all heading in the other direction. First, Class-AA would disappear in Minnesota, as teams struggled to meet payrolls with dwindling revenues from waning admissions, and Major League Baseball's expansion and ever-increasing salaries cornered the market on good baseball and the best ballplayers. Then, Class A would slowly follow, as happened in the now-defunct Minnesota River League. Class-B ball by the 2013 state tournament for sure seemed to be going the way of the dinosaur and dodo bird, too. Teams were playing down. Class-C baseball, which didn't even exist during the Golden Age of Baseball, was popular, as 48 teams filled tournament brackets in 2013, 2014, and again in 2015, with some cries being heard for still more lower brackets to accommodate more teams wanting to win a state tournament, even if it were Class C, or lower. Then, in a slight-of-hand that few would notice, they would call it *the* state tournament.

But in 1958, with close coverage of the River Valley League on the front pages of at least two of the league's town weeklies, an old-fashioned pennant race ensued, with baseball fever rising with the mercury columns as the summer ensued. Pat Devitt was a major player in that race, which turned into a barnburner. With as much as six to eight weeks' head start in throwing the baseball, and at least a month of competing in 14 games, at least six of which he actually pitched and hit in, Pat Devitt had the distinct advantage of fitness to play that all high school and college baseball players brought to Minnesota amateur baseball every summer. Town team veterans would need two or three weeks to play themselves into some semblance of condition. Hitters' timing was off from the rust of winter. Pitchers' arms, likewise, needed work to find lost control, strength, and endurance.

The Jordan Brewers lost their opener to New Prague, 3-1. Coverage of Prior Lake lapses for a couple of weeks, then in the June 12, 1958, *Jordan Independent* it's noted that Prior Lake was tied for first place with Belle Plaine, with a 3-1 record. A week earlier, June 5, the weekly's front page story was headlined, "Lakers Nip Brewers, 5-4":

> For the Lakers, it was all Pat Devitt. Pat came into pitch in the fourth, closing the door on the Brewers; he also contributed three hits, driving in the tying and winning runs.

The Lakers went to 4-2 after beating still-sleeping Shakopee, 6-1, during the week of June 22. Devitt scattered seven hits and five walks while striking out eight Indians, and he hit a homerun in the eighth inning for the final run. They were tied for first place with New Prague at 4-2. Then, Devitt shut out Belle Plaine, 7-0, again scattering seven hits to take his team to 5-2, atop the league.

The teams then beat each other to tighten up the race even more. "Brewers Defeat Prior Lake Jays, 9-1, Here Sunday Night" headlined the July 10 *Jordan Independent*. The final score belies the pitchers' duel that had ensued for five innings. Floodgates opened on Devitt, as he left the mound after 6-1/3 innings, having been reached finally for five runs on seven hits. Weckman, the 17-year-old Jordan phenom, beat him, going the distance and giving up just four hits, one a Devitt triple, while striking out nine Lakers. Weckman was just warming up, as the Lakers went to 5-3 on the season, now tied with the Shakopee Indians for first place.

A week later the two teams were at 6-3, and the *Shakopee Argus-Tribune* of July 17, 1958, reported on another game:

> Shakopee's junior legion baseball team was knocked out of third district competition Monday, July 14 as Jordan's Fulton Weckman shut them out 1-0 on a sparkling no-hitter. The lanky lefthander struck out 17 swingers in the six-inning ballgame played at Chaska.

Weckman had struck out 17 of the 18 batters he faced. Lost in the brilliance of such a performance by the youngster was the fact that George Lill, Shakopee's losing pitcher, had struck out 13 while allowing just one hit.

The same July 17 *Argus-Tribune* reported an upcoming "Cardinal Tryout Session" at Shakopee's Riverside Park, with St. Louis Cardinal Farm Director,

Walter Shannon, hopeful of discovering local talent: "We regard the Shakopee area as fertile baseball territory and expect a good turnout."

Shakopee and Prior Lake had trouble getting their Game of the Year played. Rain had postponed it twice. Catch the pennant fever in the August 7 Argus-Tribune headline and lead: "Shakopee Takes Loop Flag In Photo Finish."

> Nearly 1500 fans watched Shakopee's 'come-back kids' cop their fifth straight league ball game, 7-3, with a booming five-run rally in the ninth inning and win the first River Valley League pennant.

Pat Devitt vs. Fred Kerber at Shakopee's Riverside Park. It was high drama in the Minnesota River Valley Lower Basin. Prior Lake took a 3-0 lead into the fourth and a 3-2 lead into the ninth. Both pitchers were on their respective games. Then Prior Lake walked Kerber intentionally, which was followed by an error, a hit batter, and a two-run single. Game–Shakopee. Playoff advantage–Shakopee.

Then the post-season playoffs ensued, with Devitt beating Weckman and Jordan two straight playoff games, 9-6 in the first with nine strikeouts, then again in the second game, which was headlined in *The Jordan Independent*, "Prior Lake Blasts Brewers 8-1 To Take Playoff Series." It was a tight game, another pitchers' duel between the league's two best young pitchers, Devitt and Weckman. Both pitchers were throwing lights-out BB's, with the game hitless and scoreless until the seventh, when Weckman was taken out by Devitt's two-run homerun to ignite Prior Lake. "Devitt pitched the full game for the Jays," the *JI* reported, "allowing three hits and a single run."

Shakopee and Prior Lake would once again battle each other in another best two-of-three playoff series. Devitt gave up eight hits and had 12 strikeouts in the 6-5 loss to Shakopee in the first game, despite taking a 5-3 lead into the bottom of the ninth, according to the report in *The Jordan Independent* of August 28, 1958. With the win in front of 1,174 hometown fans, Fred Kerber went to 10-2 on the season for Shakopee with a stingy ERA of just 1.65. Then he came up even bigger in the second game, winning 8-1 on a three hitter, running his season record to 11-2, despite Devitt's 16 strikeouts in front of a reported hometown Laker crowd of 864. But Devitt gave up 11 hits, including a homerun to Fred Kerber and another to Chuck Kreuser.

Shakopee drafted Devitt and Weckman with intentions of repeating their 1957 romp through the regions and into the state tournament. They drew Hampton, which had survived the likes of Northfield, Dundas, and Miesville in the Cannon Valley League. Lonsdale, loaded with local ballplayers, brought an end to the reign of St. Benedict in the DRS. The Indians hammered Hampton, 15-6, in sudden death, with Devitt getting some work in the middle innings. Weckman then beat Lonsdale, 4-3, on a five-hitter with 19 strikeouts in front of 1,450 fans at Riverside Park in the first game of the next round, a three-game series.

Devitt started the second game but got knocked out in the second inning when an error on a double-play ball cost a run and opened the floodgates for four more runs. Shakopee fought back to tie the game with Kerber in relief, but another five-run outburst in the eighth by the local Czech bangers tripped Shakopee, 10-5, ending their 11-game winning streak. Weckman came back with another fine performance for Shakopee in the rubber game, striking out 13 Lonsdale batters this time, but

Lonsdale prevailed, 4-3, and went on to New Ulm and the 1958 Class-B Minnesota State Tournament, where for the second straight year, Norwood would lose the championship game by two runs, this time to Pipestone, 5-3.

Throwing batting practice at Shakopee one night, Pat said he felt a "pop" in his shoulder. He didn't think much of it at the time. But he said what felt like a "knot" had formed the next morning. To this day, he said he sees a chiropractor about every three weeks for an "adjustment" that must untie the knot and lay out the tissues where they belong. In 1959, he would begin seeing Dr. Richter of New Prague every Saturday before a scheduled pitching assignment on Sunday. "It took care of my problem," Devitt said.

Pat Devitt looked forward each summer to town team baseball and another crack at the Shakopee Indians. But there was just too much talent and too much depth there. It seemed that every time Shakopee lost a ballplayer to retirement, a move, sickness or injury, or whatever, the guy who replaced him was even better. Moreover, they got better together, gelling as a team.

The inaugural season of the River Valley League, formed in the heart of the Minnesota River Valley's Lower Basin from three Class-B Valley Six League teams and three Class-A Minnesota River League teams had been a success in 1958, the centennial anniversary of statehood for the former territory that had taken its name from the Minnesota River. In and out of baseball everywhere, things were happening: Sir Edmund Hilary, the Brit who was the first man to scale Mt. Everest, reached the South Pole overland. The Soviet's Sputnik 1 burned up after re-entering the earth's atmosphere. Fidel Castro's Cuban revolutionaries overran Batista forces and took Havana. Oscar Robertson scored 56 points for the University of Cincinnati in a basketball game against Seton Hall, which only managed 54 points. Jerry Lee Lewis's "Great Balls of Fire" reached No. 1 on the UK's pop charts. Dodger catcher Roy Campanella was paralyzed in an auto accident. Ted Williams signed with the Boston Red Sox for $135,000, making him the highest paid baseball player in the world. American League hitters were required to wear protective batting helmets, a testament to the persistent influence of Little League of America on American baseball. The U.S. performed nuclear land tests in Nevada and atmospheric tests. The Soviets performed nuclear atmospheric tests. A National League single game record of 78,682 fans watched the San Francisco Giants lose, 6-5, to the Los Angeles Dodgers at the LA Coliseum where the Dodgers had erected a 42-foot screen to the 250-foot fence in order to cut down on cheap homeruns. Stan Musial became the eighth player in Major League Baseball history to get 3,000 hits in his career. Roberto Clemente tied a record with three triples in a game. Lefty Warren Spahn of the Milwaukee Braves became the first lefthander to win 20 or more games nine times. The Yankees won their 24th pennant, the ninth under Manager Casey Stengel, and the seventh out of the last nine World Series. Pope John XXIII was elected Pope. Young Johnny Unitas and the Baltimore Colts upset the New York Giants for the 1958 NFL Championship in sudden death overtime in what has been called "The Greatest Game Ever Played."

On the Sunday opener of the 1959 River Valley Season, "Timber" Jack Wagner shut out New Prague, 5-0, on five hits. Pat was in left field, and his two-run triple in the fourth inning was all Wagner needed. But Shakopee had a new pitcher, as if they needed any help for Kerber. John Freund had shown up out of nowhere, and there was some mystery about him and his past. Like Heller and Kerber, he was working at Rahr Malting in Shakopee. That raised eyebrows around the league, and he threw a no-hitter against Belle Plaine, 5-0, on that opening day, raising even more eyebrows around the league as well as hopes in the river town.

"Timber" Jack Wagner pitched his second shutout in a row, beating Belle Plaine, 8-0, with Pat going two for four at the plate, including a two-run blast over the left-center field fence in the sixth. Then, Prior Lake beat Jordan, 5-4, in an 11-inning thriller. Pat pitched 4-1/3 innings of relief, giving up one run on four hits and striking out nine Brewers in the short stint. That brought the first showdown of the new season: Both Prior Lake and Shakopee were 4-0. Headlines read, "Jays Hand Indians First Setback to Take Over First Place in RVL." Pat pitched 3-2/3 innings of relief and got the win. He also had two hits again at the plate.

The Shakopee Valley News of July 16, 1959, carried a report on league batting leaders to go with the most recent games played. Chuck Kreuser of Shakopee was leading the league at a .500 clip. Teammate John Freund was second at just a few points back, and Pat Devitt was right on their heels with a .412 average. But his Prior Lake Jays led the River Valley League with a perfect 5-0 record after tipping over the Shakopee Indians. Most poignantly, *Some Like It Hot*, with Marilyn Monroe and Jack Lemmon, was playing through the torrid July weekend at the Flying Cloud Theatre, an outdoor venue located on top of the hill overlooking the majestic bottoms of the Minnesota River Valley. Indeed, the River Valley League was heating up once again, just as it had a year earlier.

Devitt had two hits, including a leadoff seventh-inning homerun, to give "Timber" Jack Wagner all the support he needed in beating Belle Plaine again, 6-1. Then, Pat got the win against New Prague in two innings of relief work, as the Jays scored three runs in the ninth to beat the Robins.

"Prior Lake Win Streak Snapped At Seven By Jordan" headlined the July 16, 1959, *Shakopee Valley News* sports section. Pat Devitt pitched brilliantly in relief of Jack Wagner who got roughed up in the third inning. In six innings of scoreless pitching, Devitt gave up just two hits while striking out 14 Jordan Brewers. He also had two of the three hits the Lakers managed off Weckman, who went the distance in the 6-2 win.

In a repeat shootout of the 1958 game to decide the league crown, John Freund and the Shakopee Indians beat Wagner and Prior Lake, 5-4, giving them an 8-2 record to Prior Lake's 7-3. John Freund, it was noted in the Shakopee weekly, was both the league's top pitcher with an 8-1 record, and hitter with a .525 batting average. The Buzz surrounding the mystery of John Freund would mount, as league playoffs ensued. While Shakopee was disposing of Savage in its best-of-three series, the Jays of Prior Lake beat Jordan and Lefty Weckman two straight, 4-1 and 6-1. That set up another playoff series final between Prior Lake and Shakopee.

With both Wagner and Devitt experiencing control problems, John Freund and Shakopee handcuffed Prior Lake in the playoffs, winning the deciding game, 7-2. Then Pat's season was over again, as Shakopee drafted Weckman from Jordan and Meyer from Savage, along with catcher Tom Preston of New Prague. Pitching their draft choices throughout the region tournament, Shakopee rolled to St. Cloud and the Class-B Minnesota State Amateur Championship, winning it in dramatic fashion on the arm of Lefty Weckman and Fred Kerber's game-tying, two-run homerun in the bottom of the ninth inning against Springfield. The winning run was scored in anti-climatic fashion; nonetheless, Shakopee won the 1959 state championship, with Weckman the MVP of the tournament and Fred Kerber the toast of the town of Shakopee for the rest of his life.

The 1960 Shakopee Indians continued to do in the River Valley League what the Yankees were doing in the American League of Big League Baseball: They dominated. The Indians went 10-0, with Prior Lake giving up its second-place finish of each of the two previous years to Jordan and Savage. Shakopee's 10-year run, from 1958 through 1967, included a River Valley League won-loss record of 103 wins against just 15 losses. Seven of those losses came in just two years, 1958 and 1964, the first the year before John Freund showed up and the second a year he didn't play. They wrote their own script and played it out each year as well as the game can be played, adding talented depth with draft choices like Devitt and Weckman for their post-season playoff runs. Without Devitt appearing in the box score, Shakopee pounded Prior Lake, 22-4, in the last game of the regular season. John Freund had two doubles, a homerun, and two walks, good for five RBIs.

Pat Devitt, plagued with intermittent arm issues, too much healing time off and then wildness when he did pitch, gave way to Jack Wagner's pitching in 1960. But Devitt still hit. He finished the regular league season with a batting average of .400, second only to league-leading Bob Walerius of Belle Plaine, and just ahead of the great John Freund of Shakopee.

Shakopee swept Prior Lake in the first round of the playoffs, too, 7-5, with John Freund taking a no-hitter into the sixth inning of a solid pitching performance, while Pat Devitt's 10 walks and seven hits to a team like Shakopee gave him little chance of winning. The lack of work on the mound hurt Pat, and that put Prior Lake out of the playoffs again and once more ended Pat's season. He hadn't pitched enough to pitch well enough to be drafted. Shakopee rolled undefeated through league and regional playoffs, beating Miesville two straight in the region finals and finishing the season with an outstanding 1960 record of 24 wins and 4 losses. Two of those losses were in its last two games in the double-elimination state tournament, 4-0 to Fergus Falls and 6-3 to Norwood.

Prior Lake started the 1961 season 0-4, with Pat Devitt still nursing and rehabilitating the badly sprained ankle that had cost him his senior year of baseball at St. Thomas. Then the Jays won four of their next five games, with the July 13 sports headline in *The Jordan Independent* telling the story: "Jay Power Rips Brewers 11-4." With former professional Bud Kleidon going three for three while playing first base for the Jays, Pat pitched credibly well, scattering nine hits and walking four Brewers. The win put Prior Lake at 4-5 on the season, behind Shakopee and Jordan in the league standings.

After smashing Savage, 24-3 in the first round of the league playoffs, Prior Lake and Jordan went at a best-of-three series to see who would go at likely Shakopee again in the finals. In the first game, Devitt beat Dick Hellmer, 5-4, in 11 innings. He had two extra-base hits and three RBIs. It was all headlined in the August 10, 1961, sports page of *The Jordan Independent*: "DEVITT HURLS, HITS

AS JAYS TIP JORDAN 5-4 IN 11-INNING PLAYOFF." Pat Devitt was back. But the Brewers blew out Prior Lake in the second game, 15-5, and prevailed in the third game. Meanwhile, Shakopee took two straight from Belle Plaine, with player-manager John Freund throwing a no-hitter in the second win. Then Shakopee, after losing the first game to Jordan, 5-4, took two straight–12-5 in front of over a reported 1,000 people, and 5-0 on Fred Kerber's two-hitter.

Shakopee drafted Pat again in 1961, after passing him over the previous two years. He responded with a stellar performance against Farmington in the opening game of the Region 6B playoffs. The Cannon Valley champions had outlasted the likes of perennial powers Dundas, Miesville, and Northfield. Devitt started the first game and allowed just one hit over the first six innings. Farmington got to him in the seventh, but it was too late. He had given up four hits in seven innings and had eight strikeouts in a solid performance. His single and run-scoring triple were value-added benefits. Fred Kerber then stymied Farmington on four hits in a 15-2 rout in the second game to advance to the championship against Waseca, which had won the Class-A state championship just four years earlier.

Once again, player-manager John Freund called upon the right-handed power pitcher from Prior Lake. *The Shakopee Valley News* of September 7 headlined its report: "Indians Belt Waseca 12-1 On Devitt's Two Hitter." The game was called after seven innings on the 10-run rule in effect. But Pat Devitt had smothered the former Southern Minny nine, allowing just the two hits and a couple walks while striking out seven. More significantly perhaps, he beat Vern Edwards, the 1957 winner of the Governor's Award for the Most Valuable Player in the state tournament. Devitt was two for three at the plate. His bases-loaded triple in the seventh was the final blow.

Shakopee then drew Springfield in the first round of the 1961 Class-B State Tournament at St. Cloud, and John Freund stayed on point. He elected to go with Pat Devitt in the opening round again. "All I can say is that there are days that pitchers know they don't have their best stuff," Devitt wrote years later in his memoirs. "Well, this game was mine. I think I was replaced by the second or third inning. You don't wish for these days but they do happen. Tournament was single elimination and we were done." Springfield slammed Pat and another draftee for all nine of their runs in the first four innings. Four uncharacteristic Shakopee errors led to five unearned runs. Three walks and a bloop single led to two more. Freund shut the door on them in finishing the game, but Shakopee couldn't overcome the nine runs and lost the game, 9-4.

Pat was short a few credits of what was required to graduate from St. Thomas College in the spring of 1961. He returned to campus after the state tournament again, took a couple classes, and graduated in December. Then the real world called, and with the help of a friend from Prior Lake, Pat went to work for Barr Engineering in Edina. The summer found Shakopee playing out its script once again, winning the River Valley League's regular season pennant with an 8-2 won-lost mark. But Jordan tipped them over in the finals of the league playoffs, the first time in seven years that the Indians had failed to make it to the Region 6B tournament. "Jordan called to inquire about my availability as a draft choice," Devitt said. "But I was scheduled to work in Washington D.C. for three months beginning in August." His baseball was over for the year, and the Brewer season would end at Miesville.

Pat Devitt managed the Prior Lake Jays his last three years, 1962 through 1964. He limited his pitching more and more because of the chronic shoulder issues that power pitchers seem to develop. But he still hit. He batted a respectable .350 in 1962, and a solid .404 in 1963, which was third or fourth best behind the league leader by 50 points. But his big day in 1963 was his wedding. "The most important event of my life happened in June," he writes in his memoirs. "I married my long time baseball cheerleading sweetheart (Rosemary Cates)."

In June of the following year, his first child was born. The added responsibility, family life, managing the team, maintaining the field, playing the games, a change in jobs and increased work commitments, on top of the shoulder aches all told him that he'd had enough baseball.

But Pat made his last baseball year, 1964, a good one. He pitched in spots, mostly relief. But he hit. God, did he hit. Chased all summer long by a big horse from Belle Plaine that everybody was talking about, young Jake Harsh, Devitt ran away in the stretch. The June 14 issue of the *Northwest Umpire's Review* shows Pat actually chasing Harsh, who was leading the league with his .600 batting average to Devitt's .573. But Pat had five hits in the slugfest loss to Shakopee, 22-16, and the young Harsh slowed down his torrid pace. After two games in July, Devitt had passed Harsh and was leading, .576 to .528. Pat finished the regular season at .561 on 32 hits in 57 at bats, while Harsh slid to third at .458 on 27 hits in 59 at bats.

Pat wasn't quite finished. Apparently, he had still impressed his old nemesis, Shakopee, during another disappointing season at Prior Lake. Shakopee played out their usual script, winning the regular season and playoffs again, then drafted Pat for the post-season play. Devitt did not play through the regional tournament. But he had an important door-slamming relief stint in the ninth inning of the first game in the state tournament against Cold Spring to preserve the 8-6 win. Shakopee then won its next two games as well and squared off against undefeated St. Boni and Al Ebert, whom Devitt called, "The best pitcher I ever faced":

> He was a big tall right hander that threw bullets. I watched as he mowed down batter after batter. As a drafted pitcher, I was batting ninth in the order. My mind told me he was going to take me out with three hard fast balls because the weaker hitters are usually placed at the bottom of the order. So I got deep in the batter's box and started my swing early to meet up with his fastball. To my surprise I connected and the ball sailed to the right center field wall for a double.

Pat had a second RBI double in the ninth inning to cut the St. Boni lead to one run at 3-2, the final score. He out-pitched Al Ebert, allowing just three hits and no earned runs while striking out 10. Four Shakopee errors late in the game cost Shakopee and Devitt the win. But that's baseball, Pat Devitt's last baseball game. St. Boni went on to win the state championship, beating Caledonia, which had handed Shakopee its second loss in the double elimination tournament, and then won the mythical state championship as well.

Pat wasn't done playing ball though. The new job was with Control Data Corporation, or CDC, in Bloomington. They had a ball club that competed in an industrial slow-pitch softball league. Snell's Bar in Prior Lake had started a team in the new game, too, and they had asked him to play with them. "I took a liking to the game immediately," Devitt writes, "because the game time was shorter than baseball, there was always action, limited practice, and great competition." He said in the early years of the slow-pitch craze, the structure was wide open. Teams that would join in the top class in the state–The Classic League–would show up at tournaments with their great ballplayers. The teams included Duff's, Maplewood Plumbing, Faribault Eagles, Bunnies from St. Louis Park, just to name a few. These teams were loaded with great ballplayers–as was Snell's Bar in Prior Lake.

"The first tournament we won was in Austin in 1965," Devitt writes. "It was called 'The Marathon of Champions Tournament'." Obviously, the supercharged metal bats with their trampoline technology had yet to be developed. There was no metal of any kind yet. There were only wood bats, which limited distances that balls could be hit and obviously reduced dramatically the number of homeruns hit in games. "What a great feeling to come home victorious over so many great teams. You had to play about six games to win it all," he writes.

Pat Devitt was honored to be named to the 1970 Minnesota All State Softball Team for his play in the state tournament that year.

Slow pitch was a good game before it was ruined by the technology. It was fun and competitive. It allowed participation by everyone, and it promoted camaraderie throughout community leagues. Pat played left field initially in slow pitch because of his speed, his arm, and his overall skillset, all necessary in the hottest outfield position in that game. Gradually, over the 10 years that he played the new game, he moved over, first to left-centerfield, then to right center, and finally to right field, as younger legs showed up.

The $500-per-year grant from St. Thomas went a long way. Pat Devitt said that neither he nor his parents, as far as he knew, ever saw a bill. Again, in today's world whether we are focusing on inflation or the flipside to that–value–we're looking at $200,000 based on the 2016-17 school year costs of $50,000 per year at what is now The University of St. Thomas. But the $2,000 was a great investment in human potential. The education and the degree were probably more significant in real terms in the late 1950s and early 60s, when Pat graduated with a bachelor's degree for his major in business and a minor in economics. Pat, like most college graduates then, finished college without incurring any debt. Most significantly, the degree was a virtual guarantee of a challenging and rewarding job. Pat Devitt essentially invested his authentic self into academics and athletics, furthering a $500 grant into a 40-year career at Control Data, from which he said he retired in 2003. Today's college graduate is likely to have a school loan debt of $30,000 to $60,000, many with more than $100,000 of debt. Worse, many young people are having trouble finding other than menial jobs for minimum wage. The basic math just doesn't work today.

Fulton "Lefty" Weckman

All I ever wanted to do was play baseball.

Elmer Weckman was a baker. He owned and ran the bakery in Jordan "from 1930 until about 1946 or '47," according to his son, Lefty Weckman. "We lived above the bakery in a small apartment," and the day started early every day for the baker and his family. "It was a grind," according to Lefty, "and finally he just had enough of it." Then Lefty's father bought a mobile feed-grinding business and visited the area farmers with the same regularity and efficiency with which he'd mixed flour and sugar for bread loaves and sweet rolls for the previous 17 years. His mother taught elementary school after graduating from Mankato State Teachers' College, first in neighboring Belle Plaine, then, after the family was grown, in Jordan.

On Sunday nights, Elmer and Dorothy Weckman, like millions of other Catholics across America beginning in 1930, would tune into *The Catholic Hour* on the radio. It was an hour-long broadcast by Bishop, then later, Archbishop, Fulton Sheen, who is on a track today for beatification as a saint in the Catholic Church. The Weckmans would be encouraged and informed in matters of their Catholic faith and Christian living by the charismatic evangelist, who would win a couple of Emmys later in his broadcast work on television. An uncommon name of any baby name-picking era, the Weckmans thought "Fulton" an excellent choice to name their only son after his birth on June 28, 1941. So impressed were they with Bishop Sheen's words on the radio, it seemed only natural. Problem was, there weren't any Major League baseball players with the name, and Weckman denies it earned him any points with the School Sisters of Notre Dame who put him through the rigorous hoops and eight grades of a Catholic education at St. John's Parochial School. There would be no other Fultons in Jordan for this baker's son to commiserate with over names, wishing they were a "Joe," like DiMaggio, or "Ted," like Williams.

But, as good as Johnny Garbett was with the Jordan Brewers in 1953 and 1954, helping them to two consecutive eight-team, Class-A Minnesota State Tournaments, there would be no other left-handed pitchers in Jordan, maybe the entire Minnesota River Valley Lower Basin, before or after Weckman, who reminded you of Warren Spahn and Sandy Koufax. Spahn would pitch for the Braves for most of his professional career between the years 1942 and 1965, earning 363 wins and an ERA of 3.09. But while Spahn had the longevity, retiring at age 44, Koufax had perhaps the greatest, most dominant, five years of any pitcher ever. He struck out over 200 major league hitters six consecutive seasons, with nearly

400 K's in 1965. He retired at age 31 after the 1966 season with 165 wins and 2,396 strikeouts, but with a left elbow already crippled with arthritis.

Weckman had the longevity of Spahn, pitching in senior over-35 leagues until he turned 60 years of age. "That was enough," he said. And he had the trick elbow, having torn or ruptured a four-inch long ligament, he said, as he spread his thumb and forefinger apart. "It must have shrunk to two inches," he said, as he brought the digits together. "It was like I had my hand on an electric fence," he said, with pain shooting up into his shoulder and down into his hand. "I couldn't even hold a glass of milk," he said. "I went to the docs, and they just said I'd be fine. That rest would heal it."

"I hit a homerun off Weckman in high school," said Jim Kubes, who would sign a professional contract with the Minnesota Twins after graduating from New Prague High School in 1961. Kubes returned home to star for many years as a pitcher and heavy hitter for Lonsdale in the DRS League. "I told everybody for years that I got a homerun off a Major League pitcher." That's how good Weckman was.

"All I ever wanted to do was play baseball," Lefty said, "and pitching was there for me." But he said he wasn't any good as a player through all the years of the baseball program as it existed in Jordan–PeeWees, Midgets, etc. during the summer. He said he didn't necessarily want to be a pitcher. He just wanted to play ball. He wanted to be in the game. But he was on the bench all the time, right next to Tinker Elke. "He wasn't any good, and I wasn't any good," Lefty said. "So I decided to do something about it."

He said he told Elke to grab a catcher's mitt, and they would go out in front of the dugout to play catch while the others had their game going on. "I'd make him go down into the crouch, and I would throw to him, working on hitting the mitt."

"He would cuss me out," Weckman said of his practice catcher. "But I'd make him get back down there."

"Baseball was my life from the time I was five years old," Weckman said. "I'd go to the park everyday–after my bread route." He said that he had a little wagon with high sides on it that his father would load with loaves of fresh bread from the ovens. He would deliver to every store in town on the bakery side of the highway. "I wasn't allowed to cross the highway," he said. That meant the nuns at their house next to the parochial elementary school got bread from Li'l Fulty and his wagon, but Father Sam and his cohort of Franciscan priests would have to come to the bakery and pick up their loaves or wait for special delivery by Elmer himself. The church and rectory were on the other side of Highway 169, which ran right through town then.

"So I'd deliver to Sunder's General, Wally Huth's, the old Red Owl, and to Faye Leibrandt and her Red and White store that was perched in between the old Corner Bar and Ruppert's Bar on Water Street, but I didn't handle any of the money," he said. About the time he finished the bread route, the area farmers would be done with their morning chores and the first milking of the cows for the day. "I'd load up with the donuts, Long John's, bismarks, and sweet rolls and go over to the White Front Bar across the street," Weck said. "The farmers would be in there playing *shafskopf*," or sheepshead, a popular German card game played with 32 cards, reported to be at least 200 years old.

He said you could tell who was winning because those farmers would give him a dime for a nickel donut or jellyroll. "Then, I'd head for the park, because it's all I ever wanted to do." Weckman said he shagged balls as a kid to get in on the ballpark and more baseball action. "You got free admission to a Millers or Saints game at either Nicollet Park in Minneapolis or Lexington Park in St. Paul," he said, "if you could get a ride from somebody going to the game. They'd leave from Pauly's Pure Oil Station, but there was only room for so many in a car. Still they crowded us ball shaggers into the back seats."

"I wanted to play ball." Weck said, "but through maybe seventh grade, I just couldn't make the lineup."

Weckman threw the baseball to Tinker Elke every day at the park. He'd throw to his Dad at home, too, and he'd throw to any of the neighbor kids across the alley or the street from the home his family had moved into after his father got out of the bakery business. He was skinny, he knew, and needed to strengthen his arm. He figured that the best way to strengthen a pitching arm was to pitch. So he pitched every day. "Then, maybe in eighth or ninth grade, I forget which now, Jordan was playing Hutchinson. It might have been American Legion ball–I don't remember. The game was at Chaska, and I struck everybody out. All of 'em." Then the coaches and the other baseball people took notice.

The other kids stopped derisively calling him Fulton or Fulty then, or any of the other nicknames given to him like "Schultz." After filling up the Hutchinson side of the scorebook with "K's," he was "Lefty," or just "Weck." He liked that. There was a respect to it that was born on the baseball diamond and earned on the pitching mound. Even Billy Martin, the former Yankee player and manager, would call him Lefty in a Major League dugout one day.

You would think that Weckman would have learned a lot about pitching while playing for Coach Dick Siebert at the University of Minnesota. Seibert, after all, was a very successful college baseball coach, winning NCAA championships in 1956, 1960, and 1964 after a successful Major League career. "No," Weck said, "we didn't have a pitching coach with the Gophers, and other than Glenn Gostick giving us a physics lesson on the mechanics of delivering a pitch, I really didn't get much there."

"I learned how to pitch from throwing to Tinker Elke and from Bobby Shotliff in Jordan." He said that Shotliff ran a kind of baseball clinic one Saturday for Jordan kids, and "Shotty said that if you want to throw that fastball, fine, just keep it at the knees. Then, when you've got two strikes on the batter, bring it, high and tight–right under their chin."

"Shotty taught me everything I ever knew–in Jordan," Weckman said.

"And Shotty said that if that first one didn't take him out, bring it again, up where they can see it–eye level." Don't take anything off the pitch, and don't flinch. Just bring it. Hitters have trouble laying off the high hard one for some reason. As dangerous as the pitch can be–especially in the 1950s before the head-protecting batting helmets became mandatory–you can't be afraid to bring it high and tight.

Maybe Koufax said it best: "Show me a guy who can't pitch inside and I'll show you a loser."

"Arnie Giebel was a teacher and a coach at the high school freshman year," Weck said. "He taught me how to bring it. He had played some ball in the minor leagues, as a catcher, I think, and he worked with me on the mound. He taught me how to get a firm plant with my left foot on the edge of the rubber and how to push off and into the pitch. Get the long stride, and bend that front knee. I picked up velocity, and the fastball started to tail."

Weckman was a sophomore in 1957 when, somehow, they got on the schedule to play Cretin High School, now Cretin-Durham Hall, in St. Paul. "They were ranked Number One in the state," Weckman recalled, "after having won the state championship something like three years in a row."

"We rode down there in cars, maybe three or four players to a car driven by the coaches and another teacher or two," Weckman said, adding that he rode with Assistant Coach Don Wandra, who had a late model Pontiac convertible. "He was a nice guy who admitted that he didn't know a thing about baseball," but he got the baseball gig because every teacher had to have some extra-curricular activity in addition to his teaching. But Weckman said they got lost looking for Cretin High School.

"I started at second base, because they got lost," Ed Breimhorst said, "and the regular second baseman was in that car." The Hubmen took a lead in the game, and then their star shortstop, Warren Will, hit a homerun with one or two on base to extend the lead. "But he was called out at home," Weckman said. "The umpire said he missed home plate."

"That started it," Breimhorst said. "Warny protested the umpire's call, and he was hot."

"Yeah, the ump kicked him out of the game," Weckman said, "and that got Coach Jim Schoener into it. He got hot, and the ump threw him out of the game, too!" But Jordan had a good lead well into the middle of the game, maybe the fifth inning, when their starting pitcher, Bob Bush, got nicked for a couple of runs. The sophomore southpaw, Weckman, relieved Bush and held off the Cretin hitters for a win by the score of something like 13 to 5, according to Weckman.

"We beat 'em bad," Breimhorst said. "Number One in the state."

Finding their way out of St. Paul was no problem for Coach Wandra, but the boys persuaded him to put down the top of his convertible and to stop at a liquor store to buy some beer. "We went on a parade of Snelling and Grand Avenues," Weckman said, "drinking beer with the top down of a new convertible."

"I thought this Jordan baseball was really something," Weckman said, "and Coach Wandra was just a nice guy."

Before they changed the height of the mound, a pitcher could really get some leg thrust, and it helped with the breaking pitches, too, adding torque when you learned how to throw them. Weckman was a fast learner and more than willing to listen to anybody who knew what he was talking about.

The curveball would become his bread-and-butter trademark. Weckman learned that from another Jordan southpaw. He watched Johnny Garbett with the Jordan Brewers whenever he could. The little lefthander had "a helluva curveball,"

Weckman said. He admired him for it and for the way people talked about him and that wicked pitch. "I started to really turn it over–to snap my wrist down, not just over, just like pulling a window shade down by the ring," Lefty said. "It broke hard, into the dirt, where nobody could hit it."

"The curveball has got to go into the dirt," Weckman said, but he knew he had to throw it hard, too, with a sharp, cutting break just at the plate. Hitters would have trouble hitting the pitch, but catchers would have trouble catching it, too. "They had to dig it out of the dirt," Weck said.

Tom Preston, a New Prague teacher and baseball coach, was another pitching mentor for Lefty. A perennial draftee by Shakopee or any other team from the league winning the playoffs, "He was fundamental and strict about everything," Weckman said of his battery mate in the 1959 Minnesota State Amateur Baseball Tournament. "Preston was very sound, but unyielding. He was a fundamentalist."

"'Throw that curveball so it breaks into the dirt,'" Weckman said Preston told him. "'I can handle it, and I don't mind. Nobody can hit that pitch.'"

Preston handled Weckman and his wicked curveball through the regional playoffs and state tournament. Weckman was named MVP of the 1959 Minnesota State Tournament for the standout pitching he gave Shakopee: He started three games, completing the first two; he pitched 26 innings and gave up a meager four earned runs while notching 34 strikeouts. He was credited with two wins in the tournament and would have had a third if Fred Kerber had only come up to bat an inning earlier.

But the Shakopee Indians, as good a team as they were, had to beat Jordan and Weckman to get to the state tournament.

The late Wally Stang, a long-time Jordan resident and school bus operator, then Lake Inguadona Storyteller, had recalled during a visit in the 1970s a Sunday in the summer of 1959:

> *It was hot all week. Larry (Beckman) and I were drinking beer on Sunday morning in Vic Kaspar's joint, next to Geno's Tap Room. We'd both gone to 7:30 mass and about 10 o'clock we were in Vic's planning our Sunday. After a few games of cribbage, all the while drinking beer, we headed out to St. Benedict for an afternoon game. I forget who the Bennies were playing–It didn't matter–but it was hot and the beer and bullshit were really flowing. So we hung around after the game, drinking beer and planning the second game of <u>our</u> doubleheader–Jordan at Shakopee. It may have been the playoffs, I don't know, but it was a Big Game–and Weckman was going to pitch. We stopped someplace to eat, maybe the old Hollywood Inn on Spring Lake. Then we headed for Shakopee and Riverside Park. The stands and down both right and left field lines were jammed with people. There had to be over 1,500 people there, maybe 2,000. Half of Jordan seemed to be there, so you knew them and a lot of the Shakopee fans, too. Larry was really rolling by now, and he started betting. He liked Weckman on the mound. Everybody did. Larry always carried a lot of cash, because he played a lot of cards for money, and he didn't like keeping track of things in a checkbook. So he probably had $100, maybe as much as $500 bet with money he had covered in his billfold. That was a lot of money then. Then, he started to borrow money so he could bet even more. He borrowed money from everybody in the*

stands he knew, and there were a lot of people there who were willing to loan him the cash.

It was a good ballgame. Weckman threw a helluva game, but Jordan got beat 2-1. Larry was wild. And the end of the game wasn't the end of the day yet. On the way home to Jordan from Shakopee, Larry was hanging his head out the car, yelling at somebody as we passed them, and his false teeth popped out of his mouth! Yeah, and so we pulled over and with a flashlight we were walking up and down the shoulders of the highway, looking for his teeth. Never found 'em. It was an expensive day for Larry, and we didn't see much of him for a few weeks, as he was working hard and saving his earnings to make good on the game's losses and a new set of teeth.

But Shakopee had seen enough of Weckman over the past two seasons to know that he was a key to their tournament hopes. The Indians drafted the Jordan southpaw for the second straight year, along with Meyer from Savage. A year earlier, in 1958, Shakopee drafted Weck as a 17-year-old kid with a year left of high school. Player-manager Butch Kreuser copied Manager Odenwald's strategy of the previous summer and played his regular season pitching stars in the field, so they could concentrate on hitting while draftees, Weckman and Meyer, took care of business on the mound.

He started the first game of the playoffs for Shakopee in 1958, because, he said, "Everybody else had sore arms. Freund, Kerber, Devitt–everybody–had sore arms. You wonder why the hell they drafted anybody with a sore arm. But, anyway, I started and was doing okay against Lonsdale. I got into the eighth inning, walked two or three batters and knew I was done. I had nothing left," he said, "and when the manager, Lefty Odenwald, came out to talk to me, I told him I was done. He said nobody else could throw, that they all had sore arms. I had to stay in there. So I got rocked, and that ended that year with Shakopee."

"I got $65 for that game," Weck said in what was the end or near end at least, of the "play-for-pay" era of so-called amateur baseball in Jordan. "And, boy, I thought that was really something."

Weckman was really something, and the year 1959 was altogether different. A week after graduating from Jordan High School with what he said was a B average in school and a stack of wins for the baseball team, Weckman made the front pages of the sports sections of the *Minneapolis Tribune* and *St. Paul Pioneer Press* newspapers. The whole town was abuzz with rumors of him signing a professional baseball contract. Major League scouts were said to have watched him pitch high school games and came away impressed. Supposedly, he was getting calls every day at home from different teams.

Coach Dick Siebert of the University of Minnesota Gophers wanted him, too.

The photograph that made the newspapers showed Walter Alston, Manager of the Los Angeles Dodgers, on one arm, and Siebert on the other, each pulling the lefthander his way. It captured The Buzz: Which way would the great young lefthander go? With the Dodgers to join a pitching staff that included Sandy Koufax, Don Drysdale, and Johnny Podres? Or with the Gophers and a baseball program of Big-10 titles and NCAA championships being built by Dick Siebert?

Would it be professional baseball–the dream of every kid growing up in Jordan, Minnesota, and across the country–or a college education?

It was heady stuff for an 18-year-old kid.

The stuff was heady, too, for a small, beer-drinking town on the Minnesota River in need of a hero to replace the great Jim Pollard. Pollard's Jordan Brewer baseball career ended simultaneously with his retirement from NBA basketball after the 1954 season, and the end of that league's first dynasty.

"Siebert told me the facts of baseball life," Weckman said. The photo shot, according to Weck, was just a publicity thing that somebody put together. Dodger Manager Alston was in town overnight to check with the Saints management–to go over their roster of player personnel to see if anybody might be able to help the big club that year in the Los Angeles Coliseum, with its inviting leftfield fence. Duke Snider, the Dodger slugger batted left and pulled everything. He couldn't, or refused, to hit to the other side. His shots to the right side, homeruns at the old Ebbets Field in Brooklyn and most other ballparks, were just long outs in The Coliseum. The Dodgers were looking for a right-handed hitting slugger.

Everybody in Jordan thought Weckman turned down a big offer to pitch with the Dodgers. But professional sports retained a bit of a tainted image yet in the 1950s. The pros weren't "pure." Not like youth programs, school sports, college athletics, and especially The Olympics. Weckman, everybody thought, had made a mature, wise decision to get a college education.

"Siebert told me," Weck said, "'if they don't offer you really big money, you're better off going to college.' Big money then, in 1959, was $25,000. 'If they're offering you something less than $25,000 to $30,000 a year,' Siebert told me, 'you're better off playing college ball.' None of the scouts I was talking to mentioned much money at all."

Weck thought that Siebert should know, because he had spent 17 years as a player in professional baseball, including 11 seasons in the Major Leagues. Baseball, like all business, is about investment and return on investment. The bigger the investment, the more attention the player gets. That player gets the benefit of any doubts. "They'll stick with the high bonus players through slumps, bad breaks, and injuries," Weck said. "It's no different today. Only the numbers are much, much greater."

Weckman signed up for a college education. He said he got a Williams Scholarship and that to this day he doesn't regret the decision. He said that only six partial scholarships were given to baseball players in the fall of 1959. There were no full scholarships for baseball. The Williams Scholarship, on the other hand, was an academic scholarship, according to Weckman, that paid for the cost of his tuition, books, and fees. Moreover, it was guaranteed for four years. Even if he got cut from the baseball team, he would still get the scholarship. "It was the right move at that time," he said.

It wasn't the Dodgers and the Big Leagues, but the town buzz only abated a little. The Dodger loss, after all, meant a gain for the Gophers and the Jordan Brewers. Weckman would pitch that summer for the locals, they thought, and help unseat Shakopee from its high horse.

He pitched for the Jordan Brewers that summer, but Shakopee was just too strong. The Indians dominated again behind John Freund and Fred Kerber with a 25-4 overall record on the year.

Frank said that John Freund was *the best pitcher* he ever batted against and that Garbett and Weckman were the best pitchers he ever watched from the field, the dugout, or the stands as a fan. He said he never faced either one as a hitter. "Good thing, too," he added. "Freund was really tough," Frank said. "His professional experience really showed, because he had control of, and worked his pitches, through the entire strike zone. Plus, he could bring it. He had good stuff, and he was smart," the old catcher surmised.

Frank remembered that Freund threw a no-hitter against Belle Plaine in his first outing with Shakopee. "I had a lot of trouble with him," Frank recalled. "I couldn't lay off that high hard one, and he would set you up for it." Freund and Fred Kerber did most of the pitching through the season. They *won* the league and playoff games for the Indians. Then Shakopee had enough faith in their draftees, Weckman and Jerry Meyer of Savage, to "rest" their own stars in the field where they could concentrate on the pitchers they faced rather than the hitters they were trying to get out.

Weckman won his first game for Shakopee during that fabulous 1959 run with a three-hitter against Lakeville in the first game of the Region 6B playoffs. His second outing in the Regional Tournament came against Northfield. In that game, Weckman struck out 17 batters, according to the accounts in the Melchior book, *Scott County Baseball*. He gave up just five hits, three of them infield bleeders, but he walked seven, as the umpire behind the plate didn't like calling strikes of curveballs that cut into the dirt.

But Manager Butch Kreuser's strategy was working: pitch the draftees, Weckman and Meyer, and let Kerber and Freund do their banging. The pitchers pitched, and the bangers banged all the way into the state tournament, slumping a bit in St. Cloud's Municipal Stadium, but coming through big in the clutch.

Weckman opened the tournament for Shakopee with a two hitter and 14 strikeouts against Lake Henry in a 4-1 win. He took a no-hitter into the seventh inning before giving up a walk and a double for the sole run. Shakopee gave the lead back to their leased lefthander with three runs in the bottom of the seventh on the strength of a double and two triples by the bangers.

After Savage draftee, Jerry Meyer, held the 1958 Class B State Champions from Pipestone to just six hits in Shakopee's second tourney game on the way to a 5-2 win, Weckman came through with a 4-3 win over Virginia, scattering nine hits and striking out eight.

Shakopee and Meyer shut out St. Bonifacious, 7-0, in the semifinals of the tournament. Then, Weckman took the mound for the third time in the tournament against heavily favored Springfield. Meyer would get the win technically for Shakopee, but Weckman handcuffed the Great Western League champions for eight innings. He was lifted for a pinch hitter in the bottom of the eighth–because Shakopee was down, 2-0, on two unearned runs.

Meyer relieved in the top of the ninth for Shakopee. In the bottom of the final inning, according to Armand Peterson and Tom Tomashek in *Town Ball, The Glory*

Days of Minnesota Amateur Baseball, quoting King Grundman of the *St. Cloud Daily Times*, Springfield *lost* the game when a draftee pitcher hung a curveball. The sports editor more accurately reported the finish as "the most dramatic finish in state tournament history."

But winners get to write history and here's the real story: The Shakopee Indians won that 1959 state championship. Lefty Weckman *beat* Springfield by giving up only three hits and striking out 12 in eight innings. Fred Kerber *won* it for him, 3-2, with a two-run homerun over the left centerfield wall. Uncharacteristic of Shakopee, two errors gave Springfield their only runs. Kerber's shot "should have been" a walk-off homerun and a 2-0 complete-game shutout, with maybe a couple more strikeouts for Lefty Weckman. He earned the Most Valuable Player Trophy in that 1959 Minnesota State Tournament and with it a college education on a Williams Scholarship from Dick Siebert.

"He deserved it," Indian Manager Butch Kreuser said of Weckman over 50 years later.

Shakopee was ecstatic over their team and the young pitcher from Jordan. The hometown's buzz grew with *their* favorite son's performance on loan to its neighbor Shakopee. But Dick Seibert, who had played for the Shakopee Indians in 1948, was in the seats at St. Cloud's Municipal Stadium, watching and wondering. He had to have been entertaining thoughts of another run at the NCAA championship with *his* pitcher whom he would lock up for four years with a Williams Scholarship after the sterling performance he witnessed in St. Cloud.

Siebert had won Big-10 championships each of the previous two seasons, but he wanted another NCAA title after winning it all in 1956, having an off-year in '57, and bowing out early in the tournament the past two seasons. He liked what he saw in Weckman and was licking his chops in anticipation of the next four years. Good left-handed pitching went a long way in baseball at any level. People were comparing this kid, Weckman, to Warren Spahn of the Braves. Siebert saw some of Lefty Gomez, the Yankee great he'd seen too much of as a hitter while playing with the Philadelphia Athletics in the American League in the 1930s and '40s. Gomez was the starting, and winning, pitcher in the first Major League All-Star Game played in 1933 in Chicago. A lifetime left-handed .282 hitter in the Major Leagues, Siebert knew well how a good southpaw's curveball made a fool out of even good left-handed hitters. Yes, Siebert saw what few people in Minnesota could possibly have seen in the 1950s. He saw hints of Lefty Gomez in the lefthander from Jordan, and some of what the little lefthander with the bad elbow and the great curveball he'd had 10 years earlier–Garbett.

Weckman saw hints of fall in the early mornings–a few flocks of ducks over the Mississippi River, and leaves beginning to turn color on the University of Minnesota campus. He felt the season and the need to handle a football. He'd played three years at Jordan High, been All-Conference, had some speed, he thought, and could play end and do a little punting.

"So as a freshman, I thought I was gonna go out for football. I get down there in the locker room. I talk to Milt, the equipment manager, and I said, 'Milt, I wanna go out for football.'"

"'Really!' Milt said. 'Okay. I'll get your gear.'"

Milt put the gear in a big bag and handed it to Weckman. "I started marching to the locker room, and that's when I ran into Bill Munsey, Tom Brown, Julian Hook, Fran Brixius, Mike Wright, Bobby Bell, Sandy Stephens, and those guys. They were some pretty big guys. I thought I might be in a little bit over my head."

"I thought I could play a little football. But I got in there and saw the size of some of those guys. I put all my shit in my locker. I went back to Milt and I said, 'Milt, all my shit is in locker 173. You can give it to anybody you want.'"

The Gopher football team would return to national prominence with the likes of Greg Larson, All-America Tom Brown, Judge Dickson, and the others, losing the Rose Bowl to the Washington Huskies and one-eyed quarterback, Bob Schloredt, in 1959, but winning it the next year.

Weckman would concentrate on baseball.

Siebert would win another Big-10 title and another NCAA championship the following spring in 1960. But Weckman, as a freshman, was ineligible to compete. He would throw lots of batting practice to Gopher teammates. He got lots of special assignments, too, such as the day Coach Siebert had him throw curveballs to the big Gopher first baseman, Wayne Knapp. The three-time All-Big-Ten slugger would bat .358 on the season, with nine home runs and 27 RBIs. He would hit .367 in three NCAA District Playoff games, and .333 in four College World Series games to help Minnesota capture the national crown. But he had trouble with left-handed pitching, especially breaking balls.

"He couldn't hit a curve ball," Weckman said. "He was big, maybe 6-4 and 220 pounds. And he'd been in the service."

Walter ('The Big Train") Johnson said, "You can't hit what you can't see."

You can't hit a good curveball either–one that breaks so sharply that it has to be dug out of the dirt by the catcher after it just kisses the strike zone. Especially batting from the left side of the plate against a southpaw. You can't hit it even if you know it's coming.

"He had a hot temper," Weckman said of the big first baseman.

Teams and schoolyards have their own caste system. Freshmen are supposed to defer to seniors in all matters. Wayne Knapp had paid his dues, and he wanted the skinny freshman to serve him up lollipops–the stuff he could crush in front of Coach Siebert.

"He was an All-American on top of it," Weck said, "but The Chief said to keep throwing him the deuce. So that's what he got, and he couldn't touch it."

"He got pissed and was yelling at me," Weckman said.

Meanwhile, Coach Siebert and others were laughing. "Then he came after me with the bat. I ran like hell."

Sitting out of games that first year at Minnesota reminded him too much of the days of his youth with Tinker Elke in the Jordan dugouts. Still, thoughts of the next year, his sophomore breaking-out season, fueled the anticipation and competitive fires.

Gopher Coach Dick Siebert won his second of three NCAA Championships in the spring of 1960. Graduating seniors created holes in his lineup for next year. He saw Weckman filling one of the starting pitching slots as he dreamed of a repeat. But he knew the lefthander needed work at a higher level than his hometown could provide. He wanted him pitching in a more competitive environment than what had become Class-B baseball in the River Valley League. He wanted his pitcher throwing more than once every two weeks.

Weckman said he could have gone out to the reputable Basin League in South Dakota, or to Owatonna and the remnants of the once great Southern Minny League. The Basin League would launch Major-League pitching careers for the likes of Jim Palmer, Jim Lonborg, and the Twins' Tommy Hall. "I looked up Huron, South Dakota, on a map," he said, "and just thought that was the end of the earth. So I went to Owatonna to play for the "Aces" and a Siebert guy named Bob Anderson, who was a former catcher on the Gopher baseball team."

Weckman said that Anderson ran a school for special needs children, and he was running the baseball team down there. "We played in what was left of the Southern Minny League, against teams like Albert Lea, Austin, Rochester, Cannon Falls, I think, and maybe Faribault."

"I worked for the power company there, lived in Owatonna that summer, and pitched a fair amount."

"We had a special night at one of our games, and one of the things was a 'Ladies Night,' Weckman said, "so every woman who came through the gate got a pound of butter or something. Bob Anderson thought it would be a good idea to bring the school kids to the game, too."

Anderson thought the kids should get out and do something, so he loaded up a couple buses of kids and brought them to the game, according to Weckman. "It was a night game, there were a lot of people, and there were attendants who were supposed to keep track of these kids, but, anyway, there were more kids than there were attendants. We're playing our game, and the kids got a little out of control. They were climbing all over the place, climbing on the dugouts, climbing the light towers. They were trying to turn out the lights."

"We had to stop the game," Weckman said. "The players had to help round up the kids and get them back on the bus. They were just crawling everywhere–on top of the grandstand, under the grandstand, everywhere. That's one of the funniest things I've ever encountered in a ballgame."

Some of the local Jordan baseball people were critical of Weckman. They shouldn't have been, but they were. They thought he had sold out his hometown Jordan Brewers. He hadn't sold anybody out. He was reaching for his potential and listening to a very good baseball mentor in Dick Siebert, his coach. Siebert had been where none of the Jordan bench jockeys or beer stand blowhards had even had a whiff. Dick Siebert had been up with the A's and Cardinals. The only reason St. Louis traded him was because Johnny ("Big Cat") Mize had a lock on first base, Siebert's position. He would play with the Philadelphia Athletics for the next eight years. Siebert knew what he was doing and what was best for his ballplayers.

So Weckman's sophomore year, fall of 1960 and spring of 1961 was to be his breakout year in the Big Ten Conference, as the Gopher baseball team gathered to defend their conference and NCAA championships. Coach Siebert took his teams south every spring so they could get some games in while the snow melted back home in Minneapolis, Madison, and other northern cities.

Weckman was into the seventh inning in a game against the Cougars of the University of Houston in Houston, Texas. He said he was striking people out and not giving up many hits, when lightning struck.

"We were mowing 'em down," Weck said. "They had their bats stuck up their ass at that point, and then it was just like snapping a piano wire or a harp string." His arm wouldn't even hang straight at his side, he was in pain, and he left the game.

He doesn't know if the injury was to his UCL, the ulnar collateral ligament, in the elbow that would become famous years later with what became known as "Tommy John surgery," after the great lefthander's career was saved by Dr. Frank Jobe in 1974, helping to give the pitcher another 15 years in the Major Leagues and a total of 288 wins.

"Yeah, it probably was," Weckman said. "I don't know. I'm assuming it was, but, hell, I don't know. They told me it would heal with rest. They didn't do any surgery then."

He went back to Owatonna that summer, rehabilitating the elbow, he said, but didn't pitch much at all until the end of the season. "It would stiffen up," he said, holding his elbow, "and I just couldn't throw a ball."

"I didn't throw much at all for two years," he said. "I couldn't. I could go a couple innings, maybe seven innings tops, and then it would stiffen up, and I wouldn't have anything."

What he needed, the Jordan faithful thought, was some homecookin'. The hometown Brewers got their favorite son back finally in 1962. Damaged goods, to be sure, but, damn, he still *looked* good. He didn't have the pop he'd had, and he was nursing his arm yet, still tentative from over a year of rehab and too much bench time. "I could go maybe seven innings at the most," he said, "but if we had a long inning at bat, it would get so stiff I couldn't throw again."

Jordan finally unseated Shakopee that year and took high hopes of a state tournament birth into the playoffs against Miesville. But Brewer Manager Earl Dean was said to have been "saving" Weckman, along with Bob Bush and Fred Kerber, in the crucial rubber game of a three-game series. He started a draft choice, Friedges from Shakopee, instead, and the Brewers got rocked. Miesville advanced. Jordan went home for another long winter. Weckman went back to the University of Minnesota for his fourth year of college and continued arm work and rehab. He'd pitch a little bit in non-conference games the next spring, but, clearly, the sun was setting on his Gopher pitching career. Coach Siebert was re-building in 1963 for his third NCAA Championship in 1964–Weckman's graduation year with a B.A. in education. But, again, Weckman was ineligible. He'd used up his allotted eligibility.

"I looked at what teachers were getting paid," he said, "and what a truck driver was getting. The average teacher salary in Minneapolis then was $4,400 a year, so I knew I had to do something about that."

Two weeks after graduation, a letter from Eunice Schaeffer, head of his local Selective Service Board, arrived. Ms. Schaeffer had struck more fear in the hearts and lives of Scott County youth than Sister Genevieve at St. John's Parochial School and Ma Beckman at Jordan High School combined. She was so efficient at her job of rounding up wayward boys in the county, our "best and brightest" youth, and seeing to it that they became men in a hurry in Uncle Sam's army, that there were facetious rumors that she had worked the system for the other side–the Wehrmacht of Nazi Germany–during World War II.

"I got out in 1964," Weckman said, and when you're out of school, you became subject to the draft. "So I joined the reserves." But before leaving town for a six-month commitment, he thought he'd give baseball another shot. "I knew all these scouts for a number of years. Angelo Giuliani was the guy I was dealing with, and I asked him if he could get me a tryout."

"He said there was one coming up and Billy Martin's running it. 'He's coming up from the Triple-A Denver Bears. He's gonna run it. There's going to be like 40 college kids,' he said, 'from all over the United States. Coming out to Met Stadium. They're gonna be there for, like, three days. I'll make sure you get the invitation.'"

"So I hung out in the dugout with Billy Martin for three days, and I pitched the last day," Weckman said. Anxious to get in the action and show his stuff, he had sidled up to Martin on the first day and said, "'Billy, don't you wanna see what I've got. I've really got some steam,' I said to him. 'I can show you some stuff on the mound, you know, that . . .'

"'That's okay, Lefty,' Martin said, 'but here's what I'm faced with. Cal Griffith doesn't want to pay a lot of money for these guys from out of town to come and stay at a motel. I gotta get all the guys from California and Missouri looked at. I gotta get them looked at, then I gotta look at you. You just help me run the things in the dugout,' he said."

"So I ate peanuts, and drank pop with Billy Martin. It was really fun. I really liked him, and I admired his ability to deal with the talented players. Some of these guys were real prima donnas," according to Weckman, "and he had a way of dressing them down to normal human stature without embarrassing or ridiculing them."

"So I got my shot, and I think I hit the first three batters," Weckman said. "I hit the first guy in the knee, and then I hit the second guy in the back of the arm, and the third guy, I can't remember where I hit him."

"Then Billy Martin comes out to the mound, and he says, 'Lefty,' he says, 'I'm really impressed with your fastball, but a lot of your teammates are NOT!'"

"He said, 'What I think I'm gonna have you do is–I think I'm gonna have you take a shower real fast and get out of here before they heal up and come looking for you.' Billy Martin was just unbelievable."

"Anyway, so when I was leaving I asked him, 'So how much will you give me for signing?'"

"He said, 'I can give you a two thousand dollar bonus for–for mayhem or something, but that's about it.'"

"I said that wasn't going to do it, and we were out of there. It was just kind of a joke," Weckman said, "but I thanked Angelo for inviting me and giving me my shot. But from there I went right into the army. I think I was on a troop train in a matter of days."

"You're just inducted," Weckman said, "so I signed up for the reserves. I'm going in there for a minimum of six months and then I don't know how long I'm going to be there" in Ft. Jackson, South Carolina.

After intake and issuing of clothes and bunk assignments, etc., Weckman said he and the other recruits were just sitting around the barracks. "While we're sitting there, a guy comes in and says, 'Where's this guy by the name of Weckman? I heard you're a ballplayer. Are you him'? "

"'Yeah, yeah,' I answered."

"'Colonel Brown wants to see you right now,' the man said with authority."

"'What for'? I asked. 'I just got here.'"

"'Colonel Brown wants to see you *now*. I'm Major Somanovitch. You're gonna ride with me, and Sergeant Johnson is driving.'"

Weckman's paperwork had been viewed with interest at the reception center and the colonel alerted, because the 30,000-man base at Ft. Jackson had a baseball league of six to eight teams and Colonel Brown and his officer peer group were really competitive about it. Typically, the paperwork asked him to fill in name, birthdate, address, and most recent employment before you came in the service.

Since he'd just gotten out of college and had no job he said, "Well, I'd played for the Minnesota Twins for three days, so I put that down."

"'I want you to run our baseball program,' Colonel Brown said, 'and I want you to be our manager,' and he said, 'you round up everything. This is Sergeant Johnson, and Major somebody or other. They're gonna assist you in everything. You get a vehicle. You get the keys to the gymnasium. You're gonna be in charge of everything.'"

"This is in Columbia, South Carolina–Ft. Jackson," Weckman said. Hot, humid South Carolina, and it's summer. So he said he started going around the base, rounding up ballplayers. "I'd go around to all the battalions, and I'd ask if anybody was interested," he said. "Then, I conducted tryouts."

He said that he had to stay within a certain part of the military complex, but he talked to everybody there and conducted tryouts for a couple of weeks.

"I had some people who were really great and I got lucky. I found a kid from Mankato, Minnesota, who just got out of the White Sox organization, a big lefthander and he was a good pitcher."

But the year, remember, was 1964. This was The South, and it was still segregated. Jim Crow laws were still observed. That meant that Black guys didn't talk to white guys.

But Weckman was colorblind. There were no Blacks in the town of Jordan in which he'd grown up, and the Blacks at the U of M were, well, they were All Americans who had put the Gopher football team on top of the Big Ten and the nation for two years. He was from the North–a Yankee–and he was just looking for ballplayers to put a team together to help Colonel Brown win the officers' bragging rights on the base.

"I invited anybody who wanted to come. So I got a bunch of Cubans and Puerto Ricans and then, in this one battalion, there were a bunch of Black guys hanging around together. So I went over and introduced myself. Told them what I was doing and what I was looking for."

"'Oh,' a couple of guys said, 'We might be interested in playing some baseball.' But they were reluctant to talk to me, because they don't talk to white people. They were segregated at the time and it was difficult."

"So I did some inquiring. I asked them what their background was, and one guy told me, 'Well I played football for Eddie Robinson at Grambling.' Boy, my ears perked up, and I said, 'Have you ever played anything else?'"

"'Oh, yeah,' he said, 'I played some baseball.'"

"So I got a couple of these guys to try out, and, boy, were these guys good."

"I convinced these guys that I'm from Up North and I'm interested in baseball right now. Colonel Brown wants me to have a good baseball team, and I said if you want to play for me, I'll make sure you get plenty of playing time."

"After tryouts," Weckman said, "I told one guy, Jimmy Knight, who had really impressed me, 'You're batting number three.' He could pitch. He could play every position in the field. But it seemed strange that this guy was in the army, so I asked him, 'Why in the hell are you in the army? I thought you said you were a teacher. You just graduated from Grambling.'"

"'Yeah, I got a couple of girls in trouble. My first teaching job in Montgomery, Alabama,' he said. He got a couple girls in trouble, and he said they just ran him out of town. That was the quickest way they could figure to get him out of town. They submitted his name to the draft board, and he was in Fort Jackson just like that."

"Then I had some other guys that played some college ball around the grounds. One guy played for Missouri, another for maybe Texas Tech."

"The ballparks were pretty good–they supplied everything. When I had these guys playing from Cuba and particularly from Puerto Rico, they were so happy to be on the baseball team, because they got a pair of baseball shoes."

"They never had baseball shoes in their fuckin' lives," Weckman said. "They didn't have any shoes. They got *baseball* shoes."

"Yeah, the team was good," Weckman said bluntly.

"We rotated the mound duties," Weckman said. "The other lefthander from Mankato, and myself, and the kid from Grambling. That was our starting rotation. We didn't have much for relief. You pitched the whole game, and I was going the whole game again, too."

The Ft. Jackson league baseball season was over by Labor Day. Colonel Brown collected on his bets in the Officer's Club and made much of the bragging rights his team had won for him. The rumors of Weckman pitching again reached his hometown of Jordan to re-stoke the embers of hopes that had been dashed three years earlier.

"When I came back, I went out looking for a job," Weckman said. "I was living in Northeast Minneapolis with a bunch of guys I went to college with. We had like six guys in a boar's nest."

"Then I applied at and went to work for Waldorf Paper and Tom Dubbe," a Jordan legend already and future author and publisher of *Nightmares and Secrets*, a comprehensive account of the child sex abuse scandal in Jordan that would gain national attention in 1984.

"We were customer service, kind of the go-between for sales people and some of the customers," Weckman said. "We also worked with other paper companies that wanted special things. They'd go through us."

Weckman got married about the time he went to work for Waldorf Paper, which was in May of 1965, at St. Anthony of Padua, Northeast Minneapolis.

"Marlys was a flight attendant, and I had met her the year before I went into the military. I had one date with her. Then I didn't have another date with her until I got back out of the service." Today, they've got two daughters and a son, and nine grandchildren that keep both of them busy.

Weckman would leave Waldorf Paper in Minneapolis after answering an advertisement in the paper for a sales position with Pfizer Drug Company. They had an opening for a salesman in Duluth that would include a territory comprising all of northern Minnesota. He applied, was offered the job, and moved to Duluth with the beginnings of his family.

When an opening came up for a similar position in Minneapolis, he applied for and got the job. He moved his family back to more familiar and friendlier environments. He moved to Shakopee, and once again, within the 15-mile radius required by the league rules, he got a call to play ball in Jordan with the Brewers, his third go-around with the hometown in 1968.

But it wasn't the same. The old religious fervor he had known in Jordan baseball growing up was gone. The fire in the belly of Brewer baseball was out. Routine two-hop, double-play ground balls were being booted. Outfielders had trouble hitting the cutoff man. Players seemed more interested in the beer drinking after a game than they were in earning the celebration on the diamond beforehand. No longer were the stands filled with near-riotous fans, yelling and swilling beer for nine innings. Maybe 30 or 50 people would attend a game, and that was counting the two "matrons of the Mini-met," Lolly Schmidt and Hannah Deusterman popping corn in the popcorn shack and a guy or two in the beer stand. Most of the people in the park were ballplayers and their wives visiting with each other in the stands, and their kids playing beneath and behind the stands, giving chase to the inevitable foul balls. Umpires could now go an entire game without anybody questioning a call. Most of the older guys were long gone, and now, at 28, he was an elder statesman on the Jordan Brewers. The only thing that was the same was his elbow. He could be going along fine, but if his team had a long at bat, the elbow would invariably stiffen up and he'd have nothing.

He had it all going one night at LeSueur in 1968, though, when he took a one- or two-hitter, with maybe 12 strikeouts, into the seventh inning. But his Brewer teammates had scored six or seven runs in the top of the inning, and he'd cooled down. When he got to the mound to warm up for the seventh, he felt the old, familiar stiffness. He knew he was done. And he was. He wouldn't even start the inning. So he pitched a little that year, played some outfield and first base, and hung up his spikes, he thought for sure, for the last time.

Minnesota's Bob Dylan had written the title track to the album he would release in 1964, "The Times They Are a-Changin'" just a couple months before the assassination of President John Kennedy in 1963. Nothing could have been more prescient. The country was coming apart at the seams in 1968, with the assassinations of Martin Luther King, Jr., and Bobby Kennedy, and social unrest everywhere.

Meanwhile, lefty Mickey Lolich would give the Detroit Tigers the southpaw part of as strong a pitching duo as anyone had seen since Koufax and Drysdale with the Dodgers, as Denny McLain's 31-victory season would be the first of its kind since 1934 and Dizzy Dean. But it would be Lolich in the World Series who beat the great Bob Gibson and the St. Louis Cardinals in the seventh game, his third win of the series. Still, despite being called "The Year of the Pitcher," in 1968 the great left-handed pitchers, Spahn, Koufax, and Whitey Ford, were gone, gone with the slowly fading Golden Age of Baseball.

Indeed, the most iconic southpaw of the late Sixties wasn't Mickey Lolich. It wasn't even Steve Carleton of the Philadelphia Phillies, who won over 300 games in his long career, or any other pitcher anywhere. It was Jimi Hendrix. He didn't play baseball. He played the electric guitar, and his rendition of the "*Star Spangled Banner*," our national anthem played before every baseball game everywhere, would never be played before any sporting event.

The counterculture was taking root. Deep root. The fervor of the nation's pastime was on the wane; the glitter was leaving the gold. Baseball was losing its grip on a large number of the population. The national freak show was just beginning.

But baseball would provide some Old School values as a parry to the spreading cultural slime. Dunstan Tucker, O.S.B., had been the university's academic dean, professor of English, and one of a handful of recognized scholars of Dante–in the world. But this gentle, Benedictine monk, this giant of St. John's University, had one passion in life–baseball. He'd coached the school to conference championships in the 1930s and 40s with exemplary names such as Senator Eugene McCarthy and Minnesota River Valley luminaries such as Joe Schleper, Bruce Frank, and others playing for him. St. John's brought Father Dunstan back from Italy and Dante scholarship to coach baseball, again, at the age of 72.

This true priest got the kinks out in his first year back as a baseball coach since 1950. But his second year, 1969, with the aid of assistant coach Tom Hamm from St. Cloud, who was a professional player in the Twins system, Dunstan delivered what he had promised in his first meeting with his team after the intra-squad game that determined the final cut of players in his first season: "Boys," he said in a voice that creaked, "in baseball they've got what they call The Book, and I like to go against it whenever I can."

Players thought the old priest nodded off during even the most exciting parts of games. They were wrong. He was just quiet and thoughtful. In the second last doubleheader of the 1969 season and trailing St. Mary's in the conference standings, he actually called a suicide squeeze in the bottom of the seventh and final inning of a tied game–with the runner on second, not third, base! Tucker ball.

The runner scored, setting up a showdown with St. Mary's the next week in Winona. Dunstan's two pitching aces came through, with Terry Schmitz, a big lefthander from Faribault Academy High and New Market in the DRS League throwing a shutout and winning the second game, 2-0, after Denny Coleman won the first game.

The Vietnam War was in full swing in 1968, with over 500,000 troops in the Southeast Asian area of the globe. It was a good thing he'd joined the reserves,

Weckman thought, even though they were dispensing with the draft that year and going to some lottery system. There were no plans to call up the reserves, and Weckman would be out in a couple of years, his six-year commitment as a reservist in an army uniform fulfilled.

But two years later, he would return to Jordan in the colorful green and gold uniform of a Toby & Rollie's softball team. Still denigrated as a poor cousin of baseball, the slow-pitch game would take off with the old fervor Weckman once knew in baseball. T&R's would dominate league play without a loss for five years, while filling the sponsor's walls with trophies gleaned in tournaments played all over southern and western suburban communities.

Pitching in slow-pitch softball was but a fraction of the factor it was in baseball, and because everybody hit, that left only one thing with which to distinguish a team and to win. Toby and Rollie's played outstanding defense to post a winning percentage over .800 during its five-year run in the small town once ruled by baseball.

This was fun again, Weckman thought. These guys can play ball. He saw many baseball-schooled players, and even the less-talented players were great softball players, because the required skill set was a little different. Denny Personious, or "Sony," as he was affectionately known, was so strong in his forearms from working concrete and putting up hay for his friends on the farms, that he could crush even waterlogged balls over fences and carry the team on his back, with his Marine Corps-fired will to win. He really didn't have a position, Weck recalled, but he was really a tough out in the bottom half of the order, because he wanted to win so badly. He relished winning, as though it were a code of honor he'd taken out of the Marine Corps with which he'd had two tours of duty in South Vietnam between 1964 and 1967.

"The reason for the greatness of Toby and Rollie's was the defense, really," Weckman said.

"That was the difference between our team and anybody else. All the way through the whole defensive lineup. We made the putouts. We hit cutoffs. We had the double play. Guys would be used to taking the extra base in that game, because the throws would be bad. But not here. You'd hit Woody, the cutoff, and he'd wheel and crank–Bang!–you got him, and we're back in the dugout taking our rips again. It was our defense."

"I never saw another team play defense like we could," Weckman said. "That was the difference."

It wasn't baseball, we knew. It was faster, because the bases were shorter. And there was the potential and need for "the Great Play" on every single pitch in that game. He said that we made most of the plays that have to be made to be great ballplayers, and "Playing in the outfield behind Woody at shortstop was like having a front-row seat to a Baryshnikov ballet. He was quick, and he made all the plays. He could turn on a dime, and of course, he had the gun. He could play short on any team I ever played on–baseball or softball. I'd want him at short if I were pitching."

"Or Tex Erickson," Weck said, "and I would want John Freund from Shakopee, playing defense for me anywhere," Weckman said. "He could pitch, play shortstop, second base, centerfield, any position. He was just a great ballplayer."

Weckman would play the critical left field position on the softball team that could put as many as four baseball pitchers in the umbrella formation outfield the game allowed. They took homeruns away from opposing hitters, and they took line drives off their shoe tops racing in or over. Moreover, these baseball pitchers threw strikes to the bases, to home plate, cutting down base runners, or to the cutoff man.

"I'll give you an idea how good that ball club was," Weckman said. "Last week I was playing golf with some guys from Shakopee that played against us. This is July of 2013, over 40 years after we played. We're coming back from golf and somebody mentioned something about softball, and they said, 'Well, you used to play for Toby and Rollie's, didn't you?' And I said, 'Yes I did.' These guys played on different teams in Shakopee when they played against us."

"They said, 'we never came close to winning a game against Toby and Rollies.'"

With the baseball pitching they had on their tournament team, most area baseball teams then and later would have had trouble getting bats of any material on the ball. As for hitting, the team was loaded. The ability of even its so-called lightweight hitters, Fuzzy and Woody Peters, in particular, to say nothing of their bangers, Toby and Rollie's would have beaten the best baseball teams in the area just as they had beaten the best softball teams regularly. They even beat teams out of the vaunted Classic League of Minneapolis.

Weckman said, "We could have beaten most teams I ever knew of in either softball or baseball."

"The sweet spot on the aluminum bat was way bigger," Weckman said. "They were so forgiving," and the technology just kept getting better after we were done playing. "I'd watch the NCAA college scores and see games like 18 to 14, 21 to 16. That's not baseball. Once they took those bats out of it, the games are 5-3, or 3-1 again. Big, big difference," he said.

"I'm so glad they went back to wood. Now it's real baseball again."

"I root for the Twins today," Weckman said. "It's too bad they just can't compete with the big market teams of the coasts. When I was young, I liked the Cubs and Ernie Banks. I just thought he was so cool. He could play ball, and you could tell he loved it."

"But most of the time, from my earliest years, I was a Dodger fan and a big fan of their magnificent lefthander. Yeah, Koufax," he said wistfully, his voice trailing off with the memory and the promise that was oh, so close.

Jim Kubes

He was the best all-around high school baseball player I've ever seen in Minnesota.

— Dick Jonckowski, "Voice of the Gophers"

Jerry Flathman of the Los Angeles Dodgers tried to sign Jim Kubes as a third baseman just after the 36th Annual American Legion State Tournament at St. Paul's Midway Stadium in 1961. Paul Scanlon, area scout for the Detroit Tigers, had been watching Jim all summer: "I could have signed with Detroit as a catcher," Kubes recalled, "and I probably should have," he said with the 20-20 vision of 50-year-old hindsight.

Jim Kubes was a really good catcher; he could play the field, and he could really hit a baseball.

But he could also pitch, and pitching is one of the most challenging, rewarding, and satisfying endeavors in all of sports. In 1961, his high school graduation year, Jim Kubes pitched three no-hitters–one for his New Prague High School Trojans in the Minnesota River Conference, two for the summer-time American Legion team with the same coach at the helm–Tom Preston.

Jim Kubes won 18 games as a pitcher that spring and summer for his high school and American Legion baseball teams against just 2 losses, according to the August 30, 1961, *New Prague Times*. But Kubes thinks his Lonsdale DRS League games were also a part of that record, because he split the pitching duties with his Lonsdale buddy, Butch Smisek. Newspaper clippings indicate Kubes and his team played an eight-game high school schedule, with the addition of a couple of district playoff games, and their American Legion season began with just 10 league games, ending with a record of 14-4 after the run to the state tournament. Coach Preston and New Prague High School had ridden the arm and bat of Jim Kubes to three of four straight Minnesota River Conference championships between 1958 and 1961, according to a June 5, 1980 *New Prague Times* column by Mike Slavik. But Kubes, surprisingly, remembers a loss in 1959 during that phenomenal run.

"I always said that I hit a homerun off a Major League pitcher," he said, of the solo shot he got off Jordan's Lefty Weckman in what he remembers as a 2-1 loss and Jordan Yearbooks record as a 4-1 loss he took on the mound. But Kubes was a sophomore and Weckman a senior in the year that the lefthander from Jordan would own in Minnesota amateur baseball. It wasn't Kubes's turn–yet.

"He was the best all-around high school baseball player I've ever seen in Minnesota," said Dick Jonckowski, the basketball and baseball "voice of the

Gophers," and, among other things, a sports enthusiast, collector extraordinaire, and former teammate of Jim Kubes. "He was a really good catcher as well as an outstanding pitcher," Jonckowski said of Kubes. "He was good defensively wherever he played, and he knew the game so well."

"He was already good as a freshman," Jonckowski recalled, and, indeed, Jim Kubes would earn Honorable Mention his sophomore year, then All-Conference honors his junior and senior years.

You couldn't help but be impressed with Jim Kubes, just watching him. He owned the DRS League for at least 10 years. New Market and St. John's University pitcher, Terry Schmitz, an arch-rival, said of him, "Jim Kubes could take over a game, either on the mound or at bat."

"He was such a great hitter," Jonckowski said. "He never struck out very much, despite being a big power hitter." Repeatedly coming back to the American Legion State Tournament in 1961, which Jonckowski remembers with great fondness, he said, "You know, he hit two balls against the left centerfield fence in that Winona game at Midway Stadium that would have probably won the game for us had they been hit in any other ballpark." What Kubes hit at Midway Stadium would have been on or over the railroad tracks in left-center field at Jordan's Fairgrounds Park, for example. But Midway Stadium hadn't been built for high school-age kids.

Midway Stadium had been built by St. Paul business interests in the inter-city rivalry with Minneapolis in the mid-1950s as part of the effort to attract a Major League Baseball team. Minneapolis had built Metropolitan Stadium in Bloomington, opening it for the Millers in 1956. It would be the last home of the Minneapolis Millers, a good AAA team through the years in the old American Association, but it was really built, people said, to help woo Horace Stoneham, owner of the New York Giants, to move to Minnesota. St. Paul, naturally, wanted the Dodgers, its parent club, which was also in a mood to move west.

Midway Stadium was built to Major League standards, with its 10,000-seat capacity easily expanded to handle big league crowds, just as the Met was expanded in a couple of stages before being replaced by the Hubert H. Humphrey Metrodome in downtown Minneapolis. Centerfield was 410 feet from home plate; the left and right field fences were 321 feet down the lines. Gary Reierson, the former Minnesota Gopher and Edina athlete, remembers the left-centerfield power alley being 379 feet and a high fence all around. There wasn't anything cheap about a homerun at Midway Stadium–particularly for a high school age kid.

The AAA-St. Paul Saints called Midway Stadium home during their 1957 through 1960 seasons. But the stadium went without a major tenant, after both New York National League teams moved to California and the American League Washington Senators came to Minnesota and the Met as the Twins for the 1961 season.

"He just had the natural talent," Jonckowski said of Kubes. "I bet he could play anywhere." But Jim Kubes excelled as a pitcher. "He had a great curveball," Jonckowski remembered, "and his fastball was faster than most high school kids had seen then."

Jonckowski said Kubes had a beautiful pitching delivery. "He had a nice delivery and style. He threw directly overhand, and he was a great fielding pitcher, too," Jonckowski said. As great as he was, Jonckowski noted that Kubes was always shy, never liked talking about himself. He let his arm and his bat do his talking for him. Hard to say where that character quality came from, but it was a common trait during the Golden Age of Baseball. You just didn't blow your own horn too loud or too often.

Jim Kubes pitched no-hitters in each of his sophomore, junior, and senior years of high school. He added two more no-no's during that 1961 summer of American Legion ball, plus a half-dozen one-and two-hitters by rough count. Four or five more no-hitters for Lonsdale in the DRS League means a total of nine, maybe ten no-hitters, plus at least a couple more near misses among many one-hitters too numerous to count. "That's probably a good number," Kubes said in characteristic understatement of the 10 no-hitters.

In the 1961 double-elimination tournament, Jim Kubes beat unbeaten Brownton 1-0 on a one-hitter to advance to the finals of the 3rd District American Legion Championship. After breaking their heart in the first game, New Prague buried Brownton, 11-3, for the championship–a game in which Kubes remembers hitting a homerun–to advance to the state tournament at St. Paul's Midway Stadium.

Then, Kubes hurled another 1-0 gem against Edina in the opening round, limiting one of the pre-tournament favorites to two hits while striking out eight. Among its starting nine, Edina fielded three future University of Minnesota Golden Gopher football players: catcher John Hankinson would play quarterback for the Gophers; Paul Faust, at second base for Edina, would be an offensive guard for the Gophers and be drafted by the Minnesota Vikings; Gary Reierson, the third baseman batting third in the order, would play Gopher baseball and football. A linebacker on the Gopher football team, he would play one year of professional baseball, 1967, for the St. Cloud Rox in the Northern League after being drafted by the Minnesota Twins. Two years later, playing first base for highly favored Prior Lake, he would take MVP winner Jim Stoll's final pitch of the 1969 Minnesota State Amateur Baseball Championship game to what some remember as the warning track, others say was the fence, with the bases loaded at Jordan's "Mini-Met" in a 6-1 loss to Arlington.

Edina had a lot of fine athletes on its 1961 American Legion baseball team. But New Prague had Jim Kubes, and 1961 was his year.

He came closer to losing the year than he knew, because, according to Jonckowski, Kubes and Smisek "skipped practice a lot." They were the stars of the team, had been for the past two seasons. When one pitched, the other caught. Both were good hitters. But they liked to play hooky together.

"Coach Preston called a team meeting and asked us to vote on whether or not he should kick them off the team," Jonckowski recalled. "We voted unanimously to keep them on the team," he said, "because we didn't have a chance without them." But Jonckowski, over 50 years later, didn't know why Kubes and Smisek had been skipping practices. They weren't farmers with after-school chores to do, as far as he knew.

Almost as if a chapter had been lifted from a Mark Twain novel in the setting of Hannibal, Missouri, Jim Kubes said of his escapades as Tom Sawyer with sidekick Huck Finn, "We'd rather go fishing," he said, than go to practice. "We fished sunfish, bullheads, and crappies," he said, "in Shield's, Carl's, and other lakes."

Dick Siebert, University of Minnesota Gopher baseball coach, wanted Jim Kubes after the Edina game that Kubes pitched for the New Prague Legion team.

"'Why don't you come to the U'?" Kubes said Siebert asked him. "I'm sure I could've gotten a scholarship," Kubes said, "but I just didn't think college was for me."

Winona beat New Prague, 3-2, in the second round of the American Legion state tournament, thanks to six errors. But George Brophy, assistant farm director of the Minnesota Twins, had liked what he had seen in Jim Kubes on the mound against Edina. Brophy had worked in the front office of the AAA Minneapolis Millers, who were a shared farm club of the Boston Red Sox (think Ted Williams and Carl Yazstremski) and New York/San Francisco Giants (think Willie Mays, Orlando Cepeda, Felipe Alou, and Jimmy Davenport). He knew baseball talent. That's why the Minnesota Twins made him their assistant farm director. The Twins were new to Minnesota in 1961, having migrated from the East Coast where they had been franchised for years as the old Washington Senators–home of Walter ("The Big Train") Johnson, one of baseball's all-time immortals.

Brophy also knew the territory and had an established, good, local network of baseball people–coaches, scouts, and old ballplayers at every level. The Twins wanted Brophy's presence in their new Minnesota home.

George Brophy wanted Jim Kubes.

Kubes had been playing baseball since he was five years old. His father, Jim Sr., had taught him the game and had been his first coach. "I probably played baseball 250 days out of the year growing up," Kubes remembered, "and I was a batboy for the Lonsdale team when my dad was playing." He said that his father had showed him clippings of games he'd played in the old Cannon Valley League in front of as many as 1,200 to 1,500 fans in the 1940s. "I never played in front of crowds like that," he admitted.

"Every year was good," Kubes said of playing ball going back to what he called Town and Country, an organized, traveling league of youth baseball. "My dad coached," he said, "and taught me the fundamentals of the game."

Kubes said he liked catching, "because you're always in the game." He found hitting a ball was always fun. But pitching, for Jim Kubes, as it has been for nearly everybody who has ever played the game of baseball, was exhilarating. Each batter was a contest all in itself. Sometimes, it was one of cat-and-mouse in which you teased and ran away only to come back and tease again. Other times, most times, as in the case of Jim Kubes, it was a contest of wills and in-your-face power pitching. Good hitters are proud of their three or four hits in every 10 at bats. Good pitchers are never satisfied. They want goose eggs and K's filling up the scorebooks every seven-or nine-inning outing.

Kubes didn't throw any junk. No knuckleballs, screwballs, palm balls, and the like. No sidewinding submarine stuff off a double-pump windup. Just classic, over-the-top style and smart pitching. He mixed a hard fastball, curve, and changeup–like Koufax of the Dodgers. And he threw them well–like his favorite pitcher growing up, Lou Burdette, of his favorite team, the Milwaukee Braves, who, he remembered, in 1957 shocked the world by beating the almighty New York Yankees in the World Series. Burdette, a native of Nitro, West Virginia, had won 17 games that season to team up with Warren Spahn and Bob Buhl to lead the Braves to the National League pennant. He pitched three complete-game victories against the Yankees in the Series, two of them shutouts, good for MVP honors.

Like Lew Burdette, Jim Kubes worked the whole strike zone, and his father had taught him how to set up hitters with one pitch in order to take them out with another. "He had great style," Jonckowski said of Kubes. His fastball was "probably in the high 80s to low 90s," and Kubes said that he liked to get that first pitch across for a strike. It really gives the pitcher an advantage, Kubes admitted, who then liked to nip the low, outside corner with his breaking ball, or even make a good hitter chase the pitch off the plate. Then, with two strikes on a hitter, he said that he had no qualms about bringing his fastball in high and tight to take advantage of whatever it is in the heads of batters, maybe survival, to swing at a pitch that far out of the strike zone. "That high fastball with two strikes on the hitter was good for a lot of strikeouts," the right-hander mused.

It had been good enough that summer, along with the rest of his repertoire, to strike out 21 Webster hitters in a DRS league game the day before, according to the July 3, 1961, clipping from *The Minneapolis Star*. Good enough for his third no-hitter of the year and 14 strikeouts against Faribault to advance New Prague's American Legion team to the 3rd District playoffs. That was followed by a one-hitter with 11 strikeouts on August 3, less than a week after his 18th birthday, against Brownton to get to the championship game in the double-elimination tournament, which New Prague won to advance to the state tournament. Kubes was better than good enough, he was masterful, in his 1-0 defeat of Edina in the opening game at Midway Stadium. "Reierson admitted to me years later," Jonckowski said and Reierson denied, "that they laughed at us, they were so sure of an easy opening round win."

Lonsdale's amateur baseball playoffs came right on the heels of the American Legion schedule, and they were counting on Jim Kubes's bat and arm. Problem was, everybody had counted on Jim Kubes's arm, rain or shine–or cold–since April of another typical Minnesota spring. It's never good baseball weather in Minnesota when the schools are playing. Cold temperatures are never good for arms of any age.

"I pitched in a lot of really cold weather," Kubes recounted. "My arm hurt all the time," he said. "It hurt in high school already."

He would need a cortisone shot in his pitching arm, his New Prague physician, Dr. Doherty, thought, right after the Legion tournament, according to Kubes. Lonsdale's faithful thought they had a chance of winning the playoffs, but Kubes's four-hitter wasn't quite good enough this time, as they were eliminated in a no-hit 1-0 loss to St. Benedict on August 10. New Market would defeat St. Benedict to win the DRS league playoffs. Kubes said that the pain returned to his elbow about a week after the first shot of cortisone. He went back to the doctor and got another shot.

New Market needed Jim Kubes, too. They drafted him and called on him to pitch against Waseca twice–first, as a starter, then, three days later, in a relief role.

Jim Kubes pitched a lot of innings in 1961 between April of the high school season and into August of summer's American Legion and DRS League ballgames. Maybe he pitched too many innings. Remember also that Jim Kubes went behind the plate when he wasn't pitching. Catchers throw as many balls in a game as a pitcher. Sometimes more. Pitchers get knocked out of a game, or yanked from the mound by a manager or coach bent on making a move. Catchers anchor a team for the game. Base runners try to steal a base or take liberties with their leads off a base, both of which invite hard throws from the catcher. Jim Kubes was always in it to win it. He made the throws from behind the plate, too, even if he had pitched a game the day before. He threw hard, and he turned that wrist over completely with his good, hard curveball–too hard for a 17-year-old kid pitching twice a week in cold Minnesota weather.

Minnesota weather is notorious for its annual toll on the pitching arms of high school and college athletes. In an effort to "get baseball in," even high schools now take their baseball teams to warm southern states for up to two weeks. They rent or build bubbles and domed ballparks. They replace dirt and grass diamonds with expensive synthetic fields that drain water in 30 minutes. Postponed games get made up with doubleheaders and condensed schedules. But Nature cannot be defied. Baseball is a summer game. Summer means temperatures in the 70s to 90s, in general. Nature says you don't even try to throw a stone once across a frozen pond, much less a baseball 150 times in two hours, when temperatures are in the 30s to 50s, which are common in this northern state in the months of March to early May. There's nothing more disconcerting and incongruent than seeing your breath and watching nickel-sized snowflakes coming down during a baseball game.

The system of schools has insisted on their schedules, despite suggestions by baseball advocates such as Dick Siebert in the 1950s already to simply alter schedules a bit. Working with Nature, rather than trying to defy it, he and others have suggested that Minnesota and other northern-tier schools find a way to play high school and college baseball after the school year in the sport's natural season– the months of summer.

It's no coincidence that, despite a legacy of baseball talent as outstanding as has existed anywhere in the country, the only native of Minnesota in baseball's Hall of Fame until 2001 and Dave Winfield's induction, was a Native American–Charles Albert ("Chief") Bender, who was born in or near Brainerd, Minnesota, in Crow Wing County, and a member of the Hall of Fame since 1953. It's hard to know how much baseball Chief Bender actually played in Minnesota's cold spring weather, but he won 212 games in the Big Leagues, with a lifetime ERA of 2.46. He went 23-5 with an ERA of 1.58 in 1910 and is credited with six World Series wins and an ERA of 2.44 in the Fall Classic.

Ty Cobb, a charter member of baseball's Hall of Fame with the most votes in that 1936 inaugural election, feared nobody. But he respected Chief Bender, reportedly calling him "the most intelligent pitcher" he ever faced.

Some sources credit Chief Bender with inventing the slider, which was called the "nickel curve," in the early 1900s and may, in retrospect, have saved his arm the fate of many pitchers native to Minnesota because of the different mechanics involved in throwing the pitch. Instead of turning the wrist over a complete 180 degrees, as is done with a good curveball, pitchers are taught to throw the slider by turning their wrists over just 90 degrees. Less turnover of the wrist means a breaking ball that breaks less but which can be thrown harder and with ostensibly less stress on the elbow. Thus, to the hitter, a slider looks like a fastball and takes him somewhat by surprise when it does break suddenly.

Whether the slider would save the pitching arms of school-age kids is circumspect at best; however, there should be no doubt in any mind anywhere of the intuitive wisdom of pitching in warm summer months rather than cold spring weather.

High school and American Legion teams, for example, could be combined to play out schedules and tournaments between mid-May and mid-August. The quality of ball would be better, and the frequency and degree of injury would likely be reduced. Great pitching arms like those of Jim Kubes would be saved instead of added to the heap of stories of potential unrealized, careers cut short by weather, pitching too much, perhaps, and by Medicine.

Cortisone was one of many in a litany of "miracle drugs" that was introduced by Medicine with great acclaim and promise. Pioneered in its use just a dozen or so years before Jim Kubes's banner year of 1961, cortisone is a synthesized version of the body's natural hormone, cortisol, which, along with adrenaline, is released by the adrenal glands into the blood stream during times of stress. Doctors found that injections of the drug provided immediate relief of inflammatory pain in arthritic joints like the knees of the injured or aged, or in the elbows and shoulders of baseball pitchers. Rather than "read" the signal, or message, that pain is sending us within our bodies, sometimes in a whisper, oftentimes as a scream, doctors had been taught to suppress it. They had heard their patients, too: "Doc, you gotta give me something for the pain."

Indeed, the American Medical Association chartered itself long ago with its self-limiting definition: "Medicine is the diagnosis of disease and the treatment of its symptoms." In the minds of doctors everywhere, not just the country doctors like Drs. Doherty and Cervenka in New Prague, Minnesota, in the 1960s, the doctors that Jim Kubes went to with his pain, cortisone was a good drug. It quieted the screaming pain. It put out the fires of inflamed tissues. In their view, it got the job done fast. Just like the salesmen from the pharmaceutical companies had said it would. Just like the literature from these well-dressed, well-spoken young men promised. Just like the studies in the medical journals the doctors kept up with had reported.

On top of everything else, even the country doctors knew that cortisone had first been identified by a researcher, Edward Calvin Kendall, at the Mayo Clinic. He had been awarded the 1950 Nobel Prize along with two others for their discovery of adrenal cortex hormones. Moreover, the reputable Merck and Co. had first produced it commercially. So cortisone appeared to have a lot going for it in 1961. Merck had a great reputation. The Mayo Clinic's reputation was impeccable. The studies all said cortisone worked fast.

Jim Kubes would be given an injection on a Thursday. He would take the mound for Lonsdale three days later, on Sunday. No amount of ice or rubbing or stretching could have seen to that. And it was playoff season in the Dakota-Rice-Scott Baseball League. Lonsdale needed him.

But cortisone, like most drugs in the allopathic arsenal of Medicine, does nothing to address the cause of the pain. It could have been simply tendonitis, also known as "Little Leaguer's elbow," or "tennis elbow." It could have been a torn ligament–typically, the ulnar collateral ligament, or UCL. In either case, Jim Kubes in 1961 had thrown too many pitches. Too many good, hard curveballs. Too much throwing in cold weather. What he really needed at the time, from what was available, was long-term rest of up to 12 months, then gradual restoration via controlled exercise and throwing. But it was the playoffs now.

In 1961, long-term effects of the drug were still virtually unknown. Those effects included weakening of tendons, ligaments, and even bones. They might include further injury to the underlying issue, such as a torn ligament, by allowing the pitcher to throw a few more innings with the pain suppressed by the drug. The California orthopedic surgeon, Dr. Frank Jobe, would not perform the ground-breaking reconstructive surgery on the Major League pitcher, Tommy John, for another 13 years. Acupuncture might have worked, but this part of Traditional Chinese Medicine, or TCM, was at least 25 years out in its acceptance and practice in Minnesota's alternative health community. Everybody expected ballplayers to play with a little pain. It was part of the athletic ethic of the time. The good ballplayers could always be relied upon to suck it up and lay it all on the line. Coaches expected that of their players, too.

Jim Kubes accepted the offer of George Brophy and the Minnesota Twins. The September 21, 1961 issue of *The New Prague Times* reported the Twins signing Kubes to a bonus contract the previous week. Kubes said he signed a contract that paid him $400 a month to do what he loved to do–play baseball. And they gave him a bonus of $5,000 on top of it. He was assigned to the Twins' minor league team at Ft. Walton Beach in the Florida-Alabama League. Jim Kubes hunted that fall after baseball–just as he had done every fall since becoming old enough to carry a shotgun. He liked duck hunting best of all, and the Lonsdale area provided some of the best mallard shooting in southern Minnesota that you could have throughout the 1950s and into the 1960s and beyond.

But the fall of 1961 was unique. For the first time in his young life, he didn't have to worry about going to school. He would be reporting for pre-season spring practice in the following April. He had lots of time to hunt, which he knew would help keep him in shape. He jumped potholes for mallards, teal, and wood ducks. He fished the open water on nice days, then through the ice that winter on frozen lakes. And he worked out in his father's basement every day, strengthening arms, shoulders, legs, and chest.

A brief news note in *The New Prague Times* said Kubes left for spring training on April 2, 1962 after a farewell and good-luck party held for him by family and friends in Lonsdale.

"I made the team," Kubes said, but he didn't pitch much. He couldn't. His arm hurt. He needed a week or more of rest between stints of any duration. "It hurt when I threw, but I just kept throwing," Kubes said. "If I threw, I had to rest it for a week." Even from throwing batting practice, which all pitchers had to do, his arm hurt afterwards. An online source, *Baseball-Reference.com*, shows Kubes without a win or loss in just 9.1 innings of pitching. He couldn't throw. The winter rest hadn't been long enough for complete healing. Or the soft tissues that needed healing couldn't heal because the cortisone he'd been given had weakened them beyond the ability to heal completely. He said he spent a lot of time with the trainer, who applied ice packs repeatedly, but the Twins never sent their property to a doctor for orthopedic evaluation. The manager called him into his office and gave him his unconditional release. The dream for Jim Kubes had ended.

Rumors persisted for 50 years that the reason Jim Kubes "didn't make it" was because he had gotten homesick. While he no doubt missed some good Bohemian home cooking at his mother's table, and getting out on the water with his buddies or his dad for the spring run of fresh-water fish, Jim Kubes didn't wash out of professional baseball because he was homesick. He simply couldn't throw enough to keep a place on a professional team's roster.

"I couldn't keep up my turn in the rotation," Kubes said of his brief summer stint with the Twins Florida farm team. "My arm hurt."

"But I got to pitch against Tony Oliva," he said of the Major League star who was in his second year with the Twins organization in 1962. "He got a single off me," Kubes said, "but I got two strikes on him first."

George Brophy and the Twins had gotten damaged goods but didn't know it. Jim's arm could not hold up to regular pitching–starting or relieving.

"My arm hurt, and so did my knee."

Kubes said that he first hurt his knee during a high school football practice when he was a freshman in the fall of 1957. He said he was blindsided by a block during a scrimmage. "I call it a clip," he said.

"I was laying on the damned field," Kubes said, "with my leg sticking out the wrong way. The doctor came out there and gave my leg a yank and told me to come in to see him the next day."

"My femur was split just above the knee," Kubes said, "and they had to wrap the bone with wire in what was the first of three operations he's had on the knee. "My knee was bent just like my elbow," he said, and two procedures done since, in 1998 and again in 2007, were necessary to remove bone chips. In addition, the knee would blow up with retained fluid periodically, and he would have to see a doctor to have the knee drained of the water. That limited his physical capability, too.

A gifted all-around athlete, Jim Kubes would need to limit his high school sports to baseball and just two less-than-enthusiastic years of basketball. He'd had enough football.

His elbow already hurting during high school baseball, Kubes thinks that the rotator cuff in his shoulder, which he has had surgery on once, and may need again, was torn later, laying concrete block, which he started to do in 1968 after four years of working as a laborer and block tender. Rotator cuff repair surgery was even further out than Tommy John surgery on elbows.

The concrete block weren't any lighter in the 1960s than they are today. As a block tender, you carried the 12-inch, 70-pound block, two at a time, from the pallets in the center of the hole that would be a house's basement, to the footings you'd helped pour a day or two earlier. Once set up, they could support the block, and that wasn't hard on shoulders. In fact, the work undoubtedly strengthened shoulders. But once the first four or five courses of the basement's block had been put down, scaffolding was required. Lifting block onto the scaffolding, usually about eye height or so, put an additional strain on shoulders, as did laying block on courses higher than one's waist. As a block layer, you lifted, lined up with the help of a guideline, in a straight row, and placed on the cement "mud" you'd troweled in place the 70-pound blocks, one at a time, all day long. The work gave young men forearms that would make even Popeye envious. But by age 40, block layers tended to be broken down physical wrecks, with back and shoulder procedures providing annuities to orthopedic surgeons.

When you do the math, you can get an idea of what the body of Jim Kubes was going through: A union block layer laying the union-required 300 concrete blocks a day lifted and placed approximately 10 Tons a day five days a week. Jim Kubes began working construction as a block tender and concrete laborer, "graduating," he said to foreman and block layer in 1968. But he started his own company, specializing in residential concrete foundations, in 1976 and earning the nickname, "Mr. Concrete" in Lonsdale, as the small town developed into a small city of over 3,000 people. He said he built his company, J&L Concrete, up to as many as 16 to 20 employees, doing upwards of 100 residential concrete foundations a year on an ongoing subcontract for Keyland Homes of Prior Lake, Minnesota.

When you own your own company, you don't watch the clock or count the union block that you lay. You watch the sun and the clouds in the sky like a sailor for what the color at night and in the morning portend for the coming day. You don't want to pour a foundation or lay concrete block if it's going to be raining. You watch the heat and cold index, too, and you might change a workday, beginning earlier in the cool of morning during July and August, and ending before the midday crisis of heat and humidity to save your men the torture. You watch the water in the coolers onsite, and you watch the men who are working for you. You watch the consistency and density of the mortar that you mix to hold block together. You watch your costs and the invoices from suppliers, and you make sure that there's nothing anybody is doing that you haven't done or can't do yourself. Jim Kubes led his concrete company the same way he had always led his baseball teams–not with his mouth, but with his head, his heart, and his hands. He led by his example. Few ballplayers would ever outplay him on a baseball diamond. Nobody ever outworked him.

Jim Kubes kept laying block until he was 50 years old. He said that he was still doing the footings himself up until he retired and turned over the company to his sons in 2004. "You've gotta lay a good foundation, if you want a solid home," Kubes said, and he wanted the foundations done right.

"I was working too damned hard and figured if I've gotta work this hard I might as well do it for my own." But if a union block layer moved 10 Tons of concrete block a day, then a non-union layer, and a man running his own business, could probably do 15 to 20 Tons a day. There had to be more to work than just a paycheck. Doing a good job, doing it right, was important to Jim Kubes. You started earlier in the mornings and worked longer into the evenings. You worked Saturdays, too, more often than not.

"I don't know if I hurt my shoulder pitching," he said. "I suppose it didn't help any. But anytime I lifted the blocks above my waist it hurt like hell."

Construction work paid well in the 1960s. It paid better than most, if not all, blue-collar jobs. The Twin Cities housing boom that had taken off after World War II never really let up. Suburbs continued to build up and build out . . . toward Lonsdale, where Kubes made home and which was a little over 40 miles from Minneapolis and maybe 30 miles from Bloomington.

Once torn, rotator cuffs never really heal completely. Jim Kubes kept laying block, and he kept playing baseball, he said, until he was 36 years old, then squeezed another three or four years out of his body playing softball. He said he sponsored a team, making it easier to crack the lineup, which he did as both a pitcher and left fielder. "We won the "Jesse James Days" Tournament one year," he said, of a fairly competitive softball tournament held every year in Northfield during its weekend festival that recognizes a bank robbery by the Old West's gang of Jesse James and the Younger brothers.

The Kubes softball team was made up of his employees–strong, well-muscled concrete workers, most of whom were in their 20s, busting high-arced softballs up and down the order over fences at 250 to 300 feet. "I didn't hit many homeruns," he said of his own proficiency at the plate, "but I hit a lot of line drives." His swing would remain grooved for baseball. No dropping of his right shoulder for the lift. Just pure hitting–with the metal bats that had given his baseball hitting a few extra years and then gave him and his softball team, and all teams, the ability to seemingly hit homeruns at will.

Lonsdale, without Jim Kubes, dropped out of the DRS League in 1962. With Jim's return later that summer, and clear signs that he was truly "home," the players re-grouped and re-joined the league for the 1963 summer season.

Jim found work after being released by the Twins, he said, with International Harvestore in New Prague, constructing the familiar blue silos that were popular with many area farmers for a number of years. Then sales slowed with the winter, and he was out of a job, again, for the second time in less than a year. But he liked the physical work and soon found employment with Minnehaha Terrace and Cement in Bloomington–a 30-mile commute. The work–putting in curb and gutter and pouring sidewalks in Bloomington–was steady and it paid well.

More importantly, he met his first wife, Marlene, after returning to Lonsdale, and three years later they were married. They made Lonsdale their home and raised three children. But Marlene would lose a lengthy battle to cancer in 1994 at age 49. Two years later, Jim Kubes and Judy, a widow, found each other amidst their mutual losses. They have been married since 1996 and make their home today just south of Cedar Lake near the one-church, one-tavern town of St. Patrick, Minnesota.

The years, 1963 and 1964, then, were formative ones in many ways. While publication sources are incomplete and inconsistent in their coverage of Lonsdale baseball, the July 21 *Northwest Umpires Review* shows Lonsdale in third place in the DRS League behind St. Benedict and New Market with a 9-4 record. The team is hitting .299, thanks in no small part to two familiar names–Kubes and Smisek. Jim is listed as having 17 hits in 46 at bats for a .369 average. We count five homeruns among the 17 hits in five consecutive weeks.

No coverage was available for Lonsdale's season finale, nor for its first two playoff games–one a win and one a loss. Then, in the second game of the best of three game series against St. Benedict, Jim Kubes hit two homeruns, according to the Thursday, August 8 issue of *The New Prague Times*, and teammate Bill Turek hit three more to bury St. Benedict, 12-4, on Sunday afternoon. But Lonsdale's hopes for advancing were dashed in an 8-4 loss in the playoff rubber game, with no other statistics provided.

Jim Kubes was back. But he hadn't returned to the mound pitching–yet. He was Lonsdale's catcher all season. Nobody ran on Jim Kubes. His arm didn't hurt to make the throws that a catcher makes. Catchers throw baseballs like quarterbacks throw footballs. No curveballs.

Lonsdale started the 1964 season fast, and Jim Kubes started slow. The team was 7-0 after two months, with Kubes hitting just .286, according to the Sunday, June 14, 1964, *Northwest Umpires Review*. But he pitched! The next week's publication notes that Kubes scattered six hits in a 4-0 losing cause, his teammates committing three errors behind him. Lonsdale would finish the regular season tied for second place in the DRS League with a 10-4 record, then go on to win the league playoffs, and defeat Northfield in the Region 6B tournament before losing to Shakopee in the finals. Without any published records available, we can only guess that Kubes finished as strong as his team finished the 1964 season. Only his two homeruns in the final game of the regular season are listed in the *Review*. He's not included in the publication's batting averages.

The next year, 1965, would be another explosive year for Jim Kubes, after what for him had been a couple of quiet seasons. Lonsdale would open the season against Marystown on May 2 and its ace, Don Hennen. Despite being limited to just three hits, Lonsdale would prevail, 5-4. However, Don Hennen and his stuff would be figured out later in the summer.

Jim pitched a few innings in the May 9 game against St. Patrick, won by Lonsdale, 22-1, and he was on the mound with a seven-hit, 15-strikeout performance against New Market on June 6. But Terry Schmitz threw a no-hitter, winning 5-4 with four errors behind him. On July 11, Kubes beat Webster, 8-1, with a two-hitter.

Lonsdale ran away with the DRS League, finishing 13-1. Jim Kubes shows up in the July 25, 1965, *Northwest Umpires Review* with a .353 batting average (18 hits in 51 at bats) for the regular season, trailing only arch-rival Terry Schmitz of New Market, who is listed at .371 on 23 hits in 62 at bats.

Then the playoffs began and as every sports fan knows, they mean a whole new season begins. Jim Kubes got hot. Marystown, first, and Don Hennen got burned. Kubes pitched a four-hit shutout in this opening game of the best-of-three series, pitting No. 1 Lonsdale against No. 4 Marystown. What he did with his bat at Lonsdale, first, then for three more games, was unquestionably the finest hitting performance in the history of baseball anywhere in Minnesota, including Bloomington and downtown Minneapolis. He rocked Marystown's starting pitcher, Dave Bakken, then Don Hennen in relief, for four homeruns and a single that just missed, hitting the fence about a foot low. Five for five in the 20-0 rout! None were cheap. He liked the power alleys. He crushed all five of the shots he hit at Lonsdale that Sunday.

Now he was on fire. He hit three more homeruns, and we think we remember, a double in five at bats the following Sunday against Marystown, who had reverted to starting its ace, Donny Hennen, in game 2 of the playoffs. It was another whitewashing: Lonsdale over Marystown, 9-0.

That set up the championship playoff series against New Market: Kubes versus Schmitz. But Schmitz had pitched New Market into the finals with a win over Webster the week before. For some reason, he wasn't ready to go. Kubes was. He pitched a two-hitter and went five for five with a homerun in the 13-1 win. That gave Jim Kubes 14 for 15 at the plate with 8 homeruns, and two pitching gems as well. And he still wasn't done.

New Market's great lefthander, Terry Schmitz, would start the second playoff game the following Sunday but get knocked out. Kubes again. He went three for four, with a homerun, in the 14-3 win that put Lonsdale into the Region 6B playoffs.

Jim Kubes had 17 hits in 19 at bats in the DRS League playoffs. Nine of the 17 hits were homeruns. Nobody kept track of the RBIs, but he had to have had a bunch. He also pitched two masterful games, including a four-hit shutout and a two-hitter in which he gave up what was probably an unearned run. He had raised his .353 batting average to at least .500 with his playoff performance. But we think his average may have been even higher, as Lonsdale played a couple of high-scoring makeup games that had little if any coverage in either *The New Prague Times* or the *Northwest Umpires Review*. The final season batting averages posted were likely to have excluded a couple of games.

No matter–Jim Kubes was simply magnificent.

"I remember that." he said, but when we tried to talk to Don Hennen, the Marystown pitcher who had suffered the most damage in the Kubes carnage, it was as if he had PTSD–post traumatic stress disorder–nearly 50 years after the experience. He said that he had 17 strikeouts in a game against Shakopee, when we asked about the bombardment he suffered at the hands of Lonsdale and Kubes.

Lonsdale's season would end in the Region 6B playoffs to the Shakopee Indians, 4-3, after beating Northfield, 2-0, in the opening game. A pinch-hit double in the ninth inning would send Shakopee, again, not Lonsdale, to the 1965 Minnesota Amateur Baseball State Tournament at St. Cloud. But there was no disgrace in losing to the Shakopee Indians. They were 14-0 in the regular season in the River Valley League, 25-5 for the season, on the strength of a .339 team batting average. John Freund was still playing baseball, and according to the "Final 1965 Averages" in the August 1, 1965 *Northwest Umpires Review*, he batted .444 that summer, paced only by teammate Joe Schleper's .520 average.

But just as Lonsdale had run into Shakopee in region play, the Indians ran into Jim Stoll of Arlington in the state tourney. Stoll did to Shakopee what he would do to the prohibitively favored Prior Lake Jays in the state championship at Jordan four years later in 1969. According to Melchior's *Scott County Baseball*, Stoll fired a five-hitter while striking out 15 and sending Shakopee home.

The 1966 season looked eerily familiar. Through June 26, Lonsdale was atop the league with a perfect 10-0 record. Jim Kubes was hitting and pitching well. He pitched one-hitters against St. Patrick and Webster, and in the last issue of the 1966 season's *Northwest Umpires Review* his batting average was .362, with a rough count through the issues available, of about six or eight homeruns. But Shakopee had another banner year, going 29-2 on the strength of the pitching of Mike Nevin and John Freund, according to *Scott County Baseball*. Lonsdale lost to Shakopee in the Region 6B playoffs again, 7-6.

In 1967, Lonsdale beat Shakopee and Miesville in the Region 6B playoffs to advance to the state tournament at Alexandria. They had gone 13-1 again during the regular season, with Jim Kubes batting .410 on 25 hits in 61 at bats, according to the July 30 *Northwest Umpires Review*. His pitching was equally impressive, as he was part of a two-hitter against Marystown in early May, and he pitched a four-hitter to beat Shakopee, 5-3, in mid-July on the same Sunday that New Market's great lefty, Terry Schmitz, pitched another no-hitter to beat Marystown, 1-0. Jim's five-hitter beat Webster, 7-2, in the first round of the playoffs, sudden death. Then Lonsdale took the best two out of three from New Market, with Kubes pitching an 8-0 shutout in the second game to even the playoffs at a game apiece.

Lonsdale beat New Market in the rubber game, 4-3, to advance to the Region 6B playoffs. Kubes threw a three-hitter with 13 strikeouts in Lonsdale's 4-1 win over Miesville, according to the August 24 *New Prague Times*. Then Lonsdale unleashed the Doberman's on Shakopee, making up for years of frustrating losses. They brought their A-game for a change, the game that had dominated the DRS League for many years. They blasted Shakopee, 17-2, with Kubes homering in the game. Shakopee's reign was over. They would not go to the state tournament again for 13 years, according to *Scott County Baseball*. Lonsdale hadn't been to the dance since 1958. They were overdue and anxious. Even The Big Dog was tight.

"I never played very well in the state tournament," Kubes said. "I think I was trying too hard."

He was the losing pitcher in the second round of the state tournament that had Little Falls and a hot pitcher shutting out Lonsdale, 9-0. The disappointment came after an opening round shellacking of Hancock by Lonsdale, with Kubes at third base and a battery of draftees, including Terry Schmitz on the mound, who fired a four-hitter in winning 12-1. But 1967 and the state tournament at Alexandria belonged to Arlington and Jim Stoll anyway.

Jim Kubes and Lonsdale had another outstanding season in 1968. They battled Terry Schmitz and New Market for the regular season league title, and they squared off in the league playoffs again, with New Market coming out on top. Kubes was batting over .400 most of the year, slumped a bit near the end of the regular season, shows a .375 average in the July 28 edition of the *Northwest Umpires Review*, and a brief synopsis of one playoff game against New Market says he had two homeruns in the game.

But he had a hell of a good year pitching. Available published records are incomplete, but a little "reverse trend analysis" shows that Kubes probably opened the 1968 season for Lonsdale on April 27 with a two-hitter to beat Webster, 12-2. He followed that on Sunday, May 5, with a four-hitter and 18 strikeouts to beat Marystown, 7-2. Then he took a no-hitter into the last of the ninth against Veseli on the following Sunday, giving up just one hit and no runs. Kubes then pitched some relief in a Lonsdale 16-4 smashing of Elko on May 19. The entire league was rained out on May 26, according to *The New Prague Times*.

In four of the five Sundays in June of 1968, Kubes pitched a one-hit shutout, a two-hit shutout, and a four hitter to beat Union Hill, 17-2. He beat Veseli on June 30 with a one-hit shutout, and he hit two homeruns in the game, too. The next week, against Elko, Jim relieved to help preserve a 10-8 win, while Terry Schmitz of New Market was pitching yet another no-hitter against Webster.

Kubes may not have pitched another game in July. It's hard to tell because of the limited coverage. But he pitched a one-hit shutout against Elko on August 4, and he pitched a four-hitter against New Market in the second game of their best two-out-of-three playoff series, another game in which he also hit two homeruns. But New Market prevailed, winning the third and deciding playoff game, 4-1. Of course, they drafted Jim Kubes, the perfect draft choice, because only pitchers and catchers can be drafted. Kubes did both, and he hit a ton–.375 in the league, according to the July 28, 1968 *Northwest Umpires Review*.

But there was a new sheriff in town.

Whereas Shakopee had virtually dominated the River Valley League and Region 6 for years, age had quietly snuck up on them and taken its toll. Fred Kerber, Johnny Freund, Don Clemens, Howie Heller, Chuck and Butch Kreuser, and others were gone. Shakopee was in second last place in the final 1968 River Valley League standings, according to the July 28 issue of the *Northwest Umpires Review*. The list of individual batting averages was equally surprising. John Freund was in a customary position on top, leading the league with a .500 average, but with just two hits in four at bats. Joe Schleper batted an even .300 on 6 for 20. These big guns were done. Bianchi had a big year at bat, leading the league in hitting at .488, but he wasn't a banger in the tradition of Fred Kerber, John Freund, and Joe Schleper. Roger Lambrecht, one of the best bad-ball hitters the area has ever seen, was still playing and had a respectable year. He batted .283 on 15 for 53.

Prior Lake had risen like the proverbial Phoenix from its ashes. Just the year before, 1967, they finished last, again, with a mark of one win in 14 league games. Everybody was used to mopping up on them. It's not that their local ball-playing talent was that bad. It wasn't. But they had some bad chemistry going or something, and their tradition of good baseball with Pat Devitt & Co. had dissipated. Then Herb Isakson, who was an assistant baseball coach to Dick Siebert at the University of Minnesota, is quoted by Steve Schneider in Tom Melchior's *Scott County Baseball* as saying, "'I'd be interested in bringing a few of my Bloomington kids out'" to Prior Lake.

Gordie Nevers wasn't "a kid." He'd already played five years of professional baseball, as high as AAA. Gary Reierson, a former Minnesota Gopher, had signed with the Minnesota Twins and played a year of professional baseball in the Northern League for the St. Cloud Rox. Bobby Kelly was not a Minnesota Gopher, but he was a great shortstop out of the Bloomington school system, who played at Augsburg and possibly St. Cloud State. John Dill played at St. Cloud State. Fred DeGregoire, Brian Love, Steve Schneider, Don Evans, Lou Gronseth, a catcher named Walseth whom many said was actually Mike Sadek one year, a former Gopher catcher who would play for the San Francisco Giants for eight years, and others "made" the Prior Lake Jays town team. Gone were the familiar local names of the neighboring town: Felix, Snell, Devitt, the Dobles, and others.

Prior Lake was in it to win it. This Lake Conference cream of superb, talent-rich athletes, of Minnesota Gopher baseball players, had banded together for a raiding party of easy pickin's on the south side of the Minnesota River. They had tried hard to recruit Tom Hamm, a former professional with the Detroit Tiger and Minnesota Twins organizations for five years, after learning that he was living in Prior Lake. They "picked up" Joe Driscoll, a future Minnesota Hall of Fame inductee from LeSueur, later in the 1970s. As if they needed more talent. Somebody should have been paying them to play in the Northern League, or at least in a Minnesota Class-A league. They were that good.

New Market, with Kubes available to catch or pitch as a draftee, ran into that Prior Lake juggernaut in region play. But Jim Kubes, almost single handedly, would take these children of the gods to the abyss and back. According to the August 22, 1968 *New Prague Times*, Prior Lake was riding a 23-game winning streak and an undefeated season going into the regional playoffs. Jim Kubes scattered 9 hits against Prior Lake in Lonsdale's first regional game, but Prior Lake beat him, 4-3, with a run in the bottom of the ninth on a passed ball. In the double-elimination format for 1968 regional play, Lonsdale would take Prior Lake to the abyss again, losing 9-8 in 12 innings. Jim Kubes hit two homeruns in the game, including a grand slam in the first off lefty John Dill, and a solo shot in the top of the ninth that was followed on the very next pitch by a homerun by Terry Schmitz. But Prior Lake scraped up runs and tied the game in the bottom of the ninth before winning it in the 12th with a sacrifice fly.

One can surmise that only the coverage of Jim Kubes and Lonsdale baseball waned in 1969. Indeed, "The Bible" of local amateur baseball, The *Northwest Umpires Review*, ceased to include even a mention of Lonsdale after its June 29 issue in which it included only the DRS League standings: Lonsdale, again, was on top of the league with an unblemished 8-0 record, followed closely, again, by New Market at 7-1. Then "The Bible" is completely silent on Lonsdale until its first issue of the following season on May 17, 1970, in which it notes that Lonsdale finished the 1969 league season undefeated at 13-0. The weekly "Diamond Dust" summaries, with succinct line scores, are conspicuously missing. We're left with *The New Prague Times* and its brand of limited and inconsistent Lonsdale coverage.

The Times was slipping, too, publishing only the briefest of line scores in its May 1 edition. But Lonsdale beat New Market, an important win, 4-2.

It was a seminal year in baseball. The previous year, 1968, had been dubbed "The Year of the Pitcher." Only one American League player, Carl Yazstremski of the Red Sox, hit over .300. Pitchers like Koufax, Drysdale, Gibson, and Carleton had ERAs that barely moved the needle. The gods of baseball figured they had to do something to inject excitement into their game: they lowered the mound five inches, and they shrunk the strike zone to fit the batters' wheelhouse.

It didn't hurt pitchers like Jim Kubes. Nor did he and his fellow Lonsdale sluggers need the "help" at the plate. They had been putting up softball-sized scores for years. Still with wooden bats, Lonsdale, according to the May 15, 1969, *New Prague Times*, beat Webster by the score of 30-10, with Kubes pitching part of a four-hitter, the runs coming due to four errors, and his two homeruns in the game a big part of the offense that included three other homeruns by Turek and Flicek.

No, this team led by Jim Kubes didn't need the metal bats that would change the game entirely for everybody. Wood was just fine with these big sticks, among whom Kubes says he was the smallest man. "We were an all-local team, no ringers," he said. They would rack up three more consecutive wins with resounding production at the plate: 9-1 over Veseli; 18-5 over St. Benedict; then 28-9 over St. Patrick.

A close game against Shakopee, with Lonsdale winning 10-9 and in which Kubes pitched a few innings of relief, was followed the next Sunday, June 15, according to *The New Prague Times*, with a 5-1 win over Union Hill in which Jim gave up five hits. Then, Jim caught Daleiden's 8-0 shutout of Elko and Vosepka's 9-0 blanking of Webster.

A couple of July issues of *The Times* were without any coverage of the Lonsdale onslaught in the DRS League. But its July 24 issue noted that Jim Kubes had beaten Marystown, 5-1, with a three hitter.

Jordan and the state tournament were fast approaching. Things were looking up again for Lonsdale. Jim liked the Jordan ballpark and was hoping to take his game to the friendly park. He played a couple of games a year there. They had lights and it was almost a suburb of Lonsdale. "I liked the mound," he said, too, "and they always seemed to take good care of their ballpark."

He was looking forward to another shot at Prior Lake. They were running away with the River Valley League again, he noticed, and people were always talking about them. Only a 1-0 loss to Shakopee in the last game spoiled another undefeated season for the team of Olympian gods. But he knew they could be beat. Good curveball pitching, he knew, could beat Prior Lake, and both he and Daleiden could throw curveballs all day long. And if their good left-handed hitters, DeGregoire and Dill, were an unlikely problem for him, Lonsdale would bring in the Big Lefty from New Market, Terry Schmitz, to give them a lesson. But first the playoffs, which had Prior Lake in another region for some reason.

Lonsdale took two out of three each from, first, St. Benedict, then, Miesville in the playoffs. Jim started on the mound in the first game against Miesville, an 11-1 pasting, but was replaced to give some work to two other pitchers, the three scattering a total of seven hits. After losing the second game, 9-4, Lonsdale came back to beat Miesville, 6-5, in 11 innings at Jordan. Kubes started but was nicked a bit with the help of five errors, then gave way to relief help from Terry Schmitz, who got the win.

No individual pitching and hitting records are available for the 1969 season, but Jim Kubes never had an off-year. With all the runs Lonsdale put on the scoreboard that season, you have to figure he was his usual instrumental force against league pitching. That means another .400-plus season at the plate with 10 or 12 homeruns.

But it ended again for Jim and Lonsdale earlier than expected in the state tournament. Kennedy, from the far reaches of northwestern Minnesota, a town smaller than Lonsdale, with a population of maybe 200, beat Lonsdale, 3-2, in the opening round at Jordan. "We had runners at second and third with one out late in the game," Kubes said. "Somebody hit a line drive to left field. The runners had taken off, and I still say he trapped the ball. But the ump called him out, and they doubled up the base runner to end the inning."

"I watched a lot of games in that tournament," Kubes said. "I watched from the hillside and saw some good games with some nice crowds."

He said he watched Jim Stoll beat Prior Lake in the championship game before the record crowd that spilled over inside the fences down the lines. "Wasn't he something?" Kubes said of Jim Stoll's performance against Prior Lake, a 6-1 masterpiece of five-hit pitching with only an unearned run against him. Like Kubes had told a few guys on the team, these "brats of Bloomington" weren't gods from Olympus after all. They were mortal, and they could be beat. He only wished it had been him on the mound that night and not Stoll. Or wouldn't it have been great to have been catching him and calling that great stuff he showed?

Jim Kubes opened the 1970 season for Lonsdale by pitching a three-hitter on Sunday, May 3, against their big rival, New Market, winning 8-1. He took a week off from mound duty, then came back on May 19 against Elko with another three-hitter and a 3-2 win despite five errors by his teammates. A week later, he again took the mound, and according to the *Northwest Umpires Review* of June 7, 1970, he "pitched a fine 6-hitter in losing."

Jim Kubes and Lonsdale were still hitting the ball with the wooden bats, too. "The Bible" of June 14, 1970, shows Kubes on top of the league in hitting with a .636 batting average on 14 hits in 22 at bats after six games. He had taken over the lead after going 4 for 4 with two homeruns against Shakopee the week before in an 18-5 win. The team was number one in the league in team batting at .314.

No metal bats. No ringers. No Reierson, Nevers, or DeGregoire from professional and Big 10 ranks. Just local boys with names like Turek and Vosejpka, Nohava, Novak, Skluzacek, Smisek, and Kubes. If you were from Lonsdale, you played baseball, and if you played baseball, you hit the hell out of the ball on Sundays.

"Nobody partied like us either," Jim Kubes said. "Especially against New Market. Then there was always a keg of beer and really good food after the game."

The batting average of Jim Kubes in the June 28 *Northwest Umpires Review* was still above .500, although the team average had slipped below .300. But they were 6-1, atop the league's East Division after Jim handcuffed Elko on just two hits in a 4-2 win.

Lonsdale finished the regular season 10-3, and "The Bible" formally announced that Jim Kubes had led the league in hitting: "Jim Kubes is the 1970 individual batting champion in the Dakota-Rice-Scott League with an average of .467 on 21 hits in 45 at bats."

Lonsdale won the league playoffs, entered Region 6B playoffs against Prior Lake and Miesville only to be beaten by both and prevented from a return to the state tournament in 1970. Coverage is sparse and without details enough to reconstruct or report on how well Jim Kubes performed. Line box scores are not even given for most games. Individual performance is rarely mentioned. The *Northwest Umpires Review* would cease altogether its coverage of the DRS League.

But Jim Kubes and Lonsdale would keep repeating the pattern they had established in the 1960s. When scores of games are given and Lonsdale blanks another team, you're left wondering if maybe Jim Kubes had thrown yet another gem. They would usually win the DRS League title, or at least the East Division. Usually, they would win their league playoffs, but some years New Market, perhaps, would prevail. If they did, they would draft Jim Kubes, as they did in 1971, to go on to Region 6B playoffs. In the regions, Prior Lake remained strong, and they would win state championships in 1975 and 1976.

Jim Kubes said that he played regularly until around 1974, when he became player-manager, and he said that dual role gradually became more manager than player as the decade passed. He also would do less pitching and catching, spending more time on first base and then more time in the dugout. But he would always be ready for the playoffs, and Lonsdale would take good "Kubes Era" teams to Minnesota's annual state tournament again in 1973, 1976, 1978, and 1979, the year, Kubes said, "we should have won it." Down 4-3 to Granite Falls in the last inning, Darrel Vosekpka, with the bases loaded, "hit a screaming line shot at the shortstop, who made a diving catch of the ball and came up showing a 'snow cone' coming out of the end of his glove." Instead of winning the game and advancing to the championship, Arlington would beat Granite Falls. Lonsdale would go home with the loss in the semi-finals of the state tournament their only blemish on an otherwise undefeated season. They had 20 wins. It was Jim Kubes's last season of baseball.

Jim Kubes could have been on any of a number of state championship teams. He could have played for the Shakopee Indians in the 1960s. They would have loved to have had him. So also Prior Lake in the late 60s to mid-70s. Northfield and Miesville had seen enough of him to have taken him in a heartbeat in any of those years. He could have stayed closer to home and beefed up New Market and possibly given them a better chance than Lonsdale had with him.

But he chose to stay and play for his hometown. He played for Lonsdale his entire 20-year career. He stayed home, because he knew that's where he belonged.

Frank agreed that he belongs in the Minnesota State Baseball Hall of Fame.

Sherwood "Woody" Peters

If I'm pitching, I want Woody Peters playing shortstop for me.
— Lefty Weckman

Blessed with quick hands, quick feet, and the finely tuned hand-eye coordination that all good ballplayers possess, Woody Peters had as much natural ability as any athlete who ever played ball of any kind in the Minnesota River Valley. Equally quick-witted, charismatic, and fun, his infectious laughter always helped to keep things light and moving. Shooting guard on the hard court, and shortstop on a diamond of any size, suited him best. But like all shortstops, he could play any and all positions on a baseball or softball field, and he didn't have to score 25 points in a basketball game to gratify a large ego. He could be content to bring the ball up the court, play the point, find the open man, and he could bother an opposing guard with in-your-face defense like a swarming hornet on a hot, humid summer day.

Lefty Weckman would know shortstops. He pitched locally for the high school Hubmen and the Jordan Brewers. He pitched for the University of Minnesota's Golden Gophers, after turning down an offer from the Los Angeles Dodgers, and he pitched two summers for the Owatonna Aces in the Southern Minny semi-pro league. Then, he pitched in senior leagues until he was 60. Pitchers know how valuable their shortstops are in getting hitters out, and getting out of jams with the rally-killing double play. Without that, pitchers know that you give up runs and lose ballgames.

But Weckman likes Woody Peters as a shortstop–more than any other shortstop he has seen or played with–because he had a front-row seat in about 400 games over four years, playing directly behind him in the outfield for Toby and Rollie's slow-pitch softball team. "He was really quick and could turn on a dime," Weck said. "He made all the plays that good shortstops have to make–going to his left and going to his right into the hole." But maybe more than anything else, according to Weckman, "He had a gun for an arm, and he put the ball on the money every time."

You also knew that he would be right where he had to be when you made a cutoff throw from deep in the outfield. He'd take the throw from an outfielder and make the relay to the right base, making the throw when there was a chance for nailing a runner, holding the ball when the throw was useless and just a risk of another run or an advancing base runner. He continually made the right play. It's like he just knew intuitively.

Ken Hanson, the venerable basketball coach, then athletic director, at Jordan High School from 1957 to 2010, would know basketball players. He said of Woody's play for him on his 1962 District 13 Champion, a team that came just four minutes from upsetting eventual state runner-up South St. Paul in the Region 4 Tournament at Williams Arena: "Woody Peters was years ahead of his time. He was like a coach on the court," and he was as quick to spotting an open teammate as he was in taking the ball to the hoop. But his forte, his trademark, was the 20-to 25-foot jump shot. He could make the shot from the top of the key or from the corner. But he loved the wing, and in the old gymnasium, the gym that stood where the Schule House now stands on Varner Street, he would be "cocking the hammer" as he crossed mid-court and surveyed teammates moving underneath.

Hanson agreed that Woody could have averaged 45 points a game had the three-point line existed in 1962 high school basketball. "Woody Peters had no weakness," he said, and there was nothing he would have changed or improved in him if he could have. "He was an extension of you as a coach onto the court and in the game." He was a great shooter, but he didn't have to shoot. He saw the whole court and was never out of the game.

"Some guys just have it," Hanson said, "and he was one of those rare few."

The 5-9, 150-pound Peters brought the same mental acuity and game-making skills to the diamond–be it baseball, fast pitch, or slow pitch. He was a ballplayer's ballplayer, as well as a coach's dream.

"He had great peripheral vision," Ed Breimhorst, a member of Hanson's first team, said of Peters on the basketball floor, and "he had the softest hands of any infielder I've seen."

"He really did look the ball into his glove," Breimhorst said. "He was always accurate with his throws, and he was simply outstanding on either end of the double-play ball at second base." Some put Woody and Frank in the same class, maybe even better, than the great Tex Erickson-Dick Nolden keystone duo in the 1950s with the Jordan Brewers.

"All ball began in the streets," Peters reminisced. You played on a stretch of street that was long enough without a curve or a hill. You used smashed cans, flat rocks, maybe an extra, old glove for a base, and you chose sides with as much scrutiny as an NFL draft. You wanted gamers and kids who could catch and hit the ball. You had to look out for cars and stop the game when a resident in the neighborhood or just a passerby dared to invade your "ballpark." If for some reason your street was busier than usual, you moved your game and your "park" over a block. "And we would sneak into the real ballpark whenever we could," Peters said, "just like we did at the old gym" on weekends and during the summer. "We'd unlock those heavy locker room windows from the inside and open them just a crack so we could get in later from the outside to play basketball."

You could get an hour or so of play in on the hard court before somebody–a janitor maybe or a teacher or coach–would "happen" to stop by and kick you out.

Such stolen moments in the gym with a basketball were usually one-on-one, and if nothing else, you played against either the ghosts of high school athletes who had graduated a few years earlier, or you played, in Woody's case, against the likes of his favorite NBA guards, Bob Cousy of the Boston Celtics or Oscar Robertson of the Cincinnati Royals. The "game" was in the mind, but the court and the sound of the ball on the hardwood floor brought a rhythm and realism to it. He stepped to the right, took a second and third bounce, maybe feigning another step or just putting some "body English" into it to take the imaginary defender a step out of play and off balance. That's all he needed. He would blow by the defender to the bucket for a layup, or stop quickly and go up from his toes and at the top of his ascent he would release just above eye level the jump shot from the top of the key or the off-guard slot on the wing that he liked. With Woody, it was usually "all net."

He didn't see "Fanny" Busch, the janitor, leaning on his doublewide floor mop, watching from the back of the empty high school gym. Fanny had kicked a rubber stop in place on the bottom of the big metal gym door to crack the door enough to create a draft to carry the smoke from his Bel/Air cigarette outside. He took a deep drag on the menthol cigarette, then cupped it in his hand out of habit, deciding he'd watch this kid for a couple of minutes before kicking him out. Woody "saw" Cousy, the All-Star Boston Celtic guard he'd just beaten with a "J" in The Boston Garden before 16,000 fans. Cousy was reaching for the ball to make an inbounds pass. The Garden crowd, jammed to the rafters, was suddenly quiet. His 10-minute break over, Fanny Busch flicked his cigarette outside and closed the doors. Then, from the archway to the gym, the janitor mustered as much authority to his voice as he could and broke the silence with a stern warning: "Hey! You can't be in here."

Woody Peters would reluctantly grab his basketball and head for the gym's side exit door and walk home. He'd be back, though, to help fill the old gym, his gym, the house of Kerkow and Will, Haferman and the Seiferts, Busch and Coach Hanson. He would fill it to the rafters on Friday nights from 1958 through the 1961/62 basketball seasons. Indeed, Fridays were something special through the 1950s and 60s. The school and the town were turbo-charged with excitement on Game Day. For some games when Hanson's Hubmen were making a run at a conference championship or had a winning streak going, they had to close the admission doors as early as 5:30 p.m.–a full hour before the start of the preliminary B-Squad game, two hours before the opening tip of the varsity game.

"They filled the bleachers on the stage, and they crammed the aisles and the standing room-only areas," Hanson said. "It was really exciting," he said. After the game, the crowd moved uptown to Geno's on Broadway to replay the game and keep The Buzz going. "If we lost," Hanson said, "I'd get second guessed, and it could get tough in there. So I'd go out to Wagner's Supper Club to relax and unwind. It was a private club then, but they would let me in."

Bars like Geno's in small towns like Jordan were community living rooms in those days. They were gathering places for people of all walks of life, brought together by one common interest or another–like The Game. After a basketball game, Geno's would be full of patrons, sometimes hard pressed to get a drink because there were so many people inhaling the rarified air of The Game. The bar was as crowded after a Friday night game as people remember it being on the Saturday night of the Scott County Fair–when the carny desecrated the town's chapel of baseball and everybody came to town to have fun and blow off steam.

"All the referees used to stop and cash their checks," Hanson recalled, "and I could get a firsthand report of other games in the conference." He'd get more "coaching help" than he wanted, or needed, from the informal backcourt club at the bar, too. Parents of players and old alumni, excited fans, but especially parents of marginal players and the usual blowhards who didn't know anything but thought they knew it all–the "experts"–always seemed to have advice for the young coach from Melrose, Minnesota. Hanson said that they would all want to know why their son wasn't starting, wasn't playing more, or why he had called a timeout at a certain point in a game. It was all part of The Buzz–like static electricity harnessed to help generate interest and excitement.

The gym and floor were small and tight. So even high school kids could play a "run-and-gun" offense that incited the crowds to feverish pitches. "I think our gym hurt us on the road with larger courts," Hanson said, but it sure made for a great game at home, the most exciting display of offense being perhaps the 100-point plus performance of the Hubmen in a conference matchup against Le Sueur in the 1964-65 basketball season–so fitting in the old gym's last year of use, before the "new" school was opened, the school that is now the school district's middle school. "I got a call from the Le Sueur coach after that game," Hanson said, "for running up the score. But he hadn't put in his substitutes, and they scored over 80 points in the game, too!"

Something would be missing on top of the hill in the large gymnasiums that would have as many empty seats as they would patrons. Maybe what was lacking was the intimacy and intensity of competition. Maybe it was that the schoolyards and churchyards were beginning to be ignored by the school-age kids where once they served as the training grounds for young ballplayers. By at least the 1980s, the kids just didn't seem to shoot as well.

But in the 1961-'62 season, Woody Peters rained jump shots for a 20-points-per-game average. Starting the season 0-2 with losses to Prior Lake and New Prague, he led a Hubmen basketball team through a successful season of 19 wins and just four losses. They won the Conference Championship with a 12-2 record and a District 13 Championship at the Gustavus Adolphus field house in St. Peter. "We beat Le Sueur by maybe six points," Hanson recalled, and the next level–a huge step up–was the Region 4 Tournament at Williams Arena–home of the Gophers and the annual high school basketball state tournament. It was The Big Time.

Jordan would play South St. Paul, then a large metropolitan inner suburb, with a population booming because of the stockyards and meat processing industry centered there. It didn't matter. Jordan, population about 1,400, was used to "playing up." Always one of the smaller towns and smaller schools in the variously structured leagues, conferences, and districts, Jordan routinely played over the years teams from towns such as Shakopee, Prior Lake, Lakeville, New Prague, Montgomery, St. Peter, Le Sueur, and Belle Plaine. Farmington, Rosemount, and LeCenter may have been the same size, with the same kind of draw of athletes then. Cleveland and Henderson, of course, were smaller and usually patsies in the District Tournament.

Two of Hanson's first four basketball teams at Jordan got upset in district play, but the 1962 team, led by Woody Peters, kept getting better as the year wore on. Peters and the Hubmen led South St. Paul by eight points with four minutes left in the game, according to Hanson, although Woody remembered a seven-point lead. "They put a full-court press on us," Hanson said, "and we couldn't handle it." From leading by seven or eight with four minutes to go, the Hubmen lost by seven points.

"Woody had fouled out of the game," Hanson said, and nobody else could handle the ball. "They had a good team," Hanson said of the Packers, who went on to win the Region and finish second in *the* state tournament, when it was a single-class event of just eight teams, leaving no doubt for a year as to who was *champion*. Jordan, both Peters and Hanson remembered, would defeat St. Paul Wilson, another large St. Paul high school, in the Region 4 consolation game by six or eight points.

At each successive level of play, the intensity mounted with the increasing level of competition with bigger schools. Each auditorium, whether the local high school gymnasium, the field house for district tournaments at Gustavus College, or the epicenter of Minnesota basketball, Williams Arena on the campus of the University of Minnesota, was filled beyond capacity.

"But it all started on the streets then," Woody would emphasize. You could make up a "game" in your mind, shooting baskets alone or throwing a ball up against a step. You weren't organized to the point of apathy and boredom. You were engaged. Your imagination was involved. Nor were you regimented by someone other than your mother and her lunch and supper schedule. You didn't stop and head for the showers or the door after a 60-minute practice. You played until you were tired, regardless of the game. And if, by some stroke of luck, you found or were given the opportunity to shoot baskets in the gym at a real 10-foot basket, or to take an extra 15 minutes of batting practice at Fairgrounds Park, you jumped at it.

You could get enough kids up at the baseball park sometimes, at almost a moment's notice, to get a real game going. That meant nine on a side, not the creative games you made up of teams of two, five, or six. It could have been the weather of spring and summer, it could have been the "carrier pigeons" darting in and out of the old Jordan Brewery building across the creek and the highway, taking the message to kids all over town, or it could have been the non-verbal communication channels that small-town boys seemed to be tuned into during the 1950s. Word got around fast: *Ballgame. Today. Bring a bat.*

"But it all began on the streets," Woody repeated. And if you wanted to play one sport well, say basketball, you couldn't just play it in the winter. "You had to find a way to play every day," he said. You might have learned in the sense of hearing it said by a coach in an organized sport the different fundamentals, but you really learned in the street and on the yards–the playground outside the old public school building and the parking lot of St. John's Church where, first, two basketball hoops were installed, then a third added, to encourage and facilitate play. And you didn't have to be Catholic to play on the Catholic yard. Sports, remember, transcended the parochial propaganda that emanated from the two major churches, Catholic and Wisconsin Synod Lutheran, in Jordan. You didn't even have to be Catholic to play on the Knights of Columbus teams. "I got recruited for their basketball and baseball teams," Peters, a Lutheran, said.

He said that he and the Jordan kids he grew up with played catch, shot hoops, or played wiffle ball and cork ball every day. "A good park for us was where the fire station is now," he said. "Back then, there was a pump house and a back stop there." The dirt base paths were worn, and plenty of grass made for a decent field. In the near outfield, pallets of farm products stacked up to define a sort of boundary over which a homerun was declared. In the distant "outfield" a silver-gray metal building that was the Farm Bureau feed and seed store formed the "batters' eye" and a homerun of Ruthian proportions. It was a long poke, and few balls ever made it that far. Of course, "Goose" could throw a ball, any ball, over the building, just as he would throw at age 15, a baseball from the centerfield fence at Fairgrounds Park, 360 feet from home plate, over the backstop, maybe another 50 to 60 feet behind home.

"Goose had an arm," Woody laughed about his old neighborhood buddy and teammate. "He stuttered," Peters said, "but we were all so used to it that we paid no attention to it. We just accepted it and him."

"He was the strongest human being I've ever seen," Woody said of Goose Kasper. "One year he got run over by a car up on Lake Superior smelting or something," and he thought "they had to tow away the car while Goose wondered what had happened, what had hit him."

"Then he got into arm wrestling, too, and supposedly won the state tournament three years in a row." State arm wrestling champion. Strongest man. "Then he hurt his arm or something," Woody said, and took a year off to work on his other arm. "He came back and won the state championship left handed, too."

The competition on the playgrounds and the churchyard was pretty good, because you were playing against guys two and three years older. "Everything was handed down that way," Peters said. "That's how you learned."

Father Barry Schneider, a Jordan native and son of Al Schneider, used to bring a couple busloads of kids to Jordan every spring from Hales Franciscan High School, an all-Black, Catholic school on the south side of Chicago. The kids would stay in different homes in the community and put their play on at several area towns. But when they weren't performing or practicing on stage, they joined the Jordan guys on the playgrounds. "It got pretty rough sometimes," Peters said, and then one year, 1962, the running dispute as to who played better basketball–the white kids from Jordan, or the Black kids from Chicago–reached a feverish pitch. They agreed that only "a real game" would settle things.

Woody and his supporting cast from Coach Hanson's 1962 team–Sony, Steck, Rod Morlock, and Goose on the floor–took the street game indoors, with a game clock and two referees. "We took care of that, too," Peters said, bringing an end to the arguments about "Chicago-style" versus Jordan basketball. "We handled that situation pretty well," he said, with the final score readily forgotten as the difference reached more than 20 points. It's as if by the nature of the play, not the mouth, Woody Peters and a good basketball team were telling the "Chicago Invasion" something: *Look, this is our house, Jordan at the yard and in the gym. You're welcome here, but you need to remember that you're our guest.*

Anybody who tried to drive the basket and "go vertical" underneath on Goose Kasper was likely to get a bloody lip, a broken arm, or a torn rib cartilage out of it. He made everybody's game underneath ugly, including Montgomery's Joe Mucha, who would earn Little All-America honors at St. John's University.

Nobody of any ethnic background on a basketball court in the early spring of 1962 was as quick as Woody Peters. There were guys with more foot speed in longer sprints, but with those first few, critical steps, he was what was called "quick on quick."

"He didn't have a weakness," Coach Hanson said. "I can't think of a thing I'd have done to improve his game–on the diamond or the basketball court. There was only one time I was critical of him," Hanson said. "I sat him down in a basketball game against LeCenter because I didn't think he was putting out."

"There was never a problem again, after that," Hanson said, adding with a bit of laughter: "After the game, he was leaving the locker room without taking a shower and I asked him whether he had showered."

"Woody said, 'I didn't play enough to need a shower.'"

Some have said that his one weakness was with the bat. They said that because of his size, he just didn't pack the punch of bigger ballplayers. Yet, according to teammate Dick Nachbar, who said he batted behind the cleanup-hitting Peters their senior year of high school, Woody had "an outstanding season. I think he hit something like .680 that year." That's six-eight-zero for the season.

"I don't know about that," Woody said, "but it was over .500," and he said his baseball coach, John Strand, told him he should start thinking seriously about a college where he might play baseball. "'You may not like it,'" Peters said Coach Strand told him, "'but baseball's your best sport.'"

The year before, in a 1961 Region 4 high school baseball tournament game at old Midway Stadium, he burned the Anoka centerfielder with a line drive that hit the base of the centerfield fence, 410 feet from home plate. Woody stopped at third with a standup triple. He would be stranded there, as the next two batters struck out in the 5-0 loss. "I was looking for the squeeze," Woody said, "but they didn't call it."

Had he been born 20 years later and played baseball during the Go-Go years of the Easton metal bat, he'd have had 15 or 20 homeruns in as many games a year with it at the small yard in Jordan, Fairgrounds Park, where balls carried during warm summer nights as though on fair trade winds. His hand-eye coordination was that good, and that translated to good contact in nearly every at bat–be it baseball, slow-pitch, or fast-pitch softball. Moreover, he drove the ball with a ferocity that belied his 150-pound frame.

He tried to swing as hard as he saw his boyhood baseball idol, Mickey Mantle, swing the bat in the World Series games nearly every fall on the old black-and-white televisions. "He was a heckuva ballplayer," Woody exclaimed. "He hit homeruns, and he could run."

Every kid had a favorite pitcher, too, and although an American League baseball fan, Woody got a bird's eye look at two of the best pitchers of all time lock up in a classic pitchers' duel in Milwaukee's County Stadium. "We were maybe 15 or 16 years old," he remembered. "Fox had gotten the tickets and made the hotel arrangements, and we took my father's '52 Chevy over to Milwaukee"–home of the Braves and the nearest Mecca of Major League Baseball before the Twins came to Minnesota in 1961. "We had tickets right behind home plate," Peters recalled, "and we saw Warren Spahn beat Sandy Koufax, 2-1."

Warren Spahn, at age 39, would win 21 games again that year, 1960, but Koufax was still in the introductory potential part of his greatness then, at age 25, winning just 8 games against 13 losses. Still, Spahn against Koufax. If you know and love baseball, then you relish its traditions. In order to appreciate traditions, you must know history. If you know your history, then just the thought of a matchup of these two great lefthanders can still give you goose bumps over 50 years later.

Woody Peters was no Mickey Mantle with the bat. Nobody was. But he was good enough with the bat to have been recruited at the age of 17 by John Breimhorst and Larry Beckman–two veterans on the old Ruppert's Bar fast-pitch softball team of grown men that played in a good Shakopee league. They wanted him for his young legs, his glove, and the gun he had for an arm in the quickest game on a diamond of any size. They played him at the hot corner, third base. "You really had to keep your head in that game," Peters said, "and they moved me to second for the state tournament up at Hibbing."

The great Bobo Johnson of Cloquet would shut out the Ruppert's team, 1-0, on a two hitter in the first round of the tournament. One and done was the rule. But they had taken the pitcher whom many claimed was the best pitcher in the state to the ropes. The kid had the two hits. Woody said he stole second base after each single but was stranded there each time. "That's the fastest ball I've ever seen come off a pitching mound of any kind," he said. "That guy could really bring it to the plate," Woody said.

At 46 feet, rather than the 60 feet, 6 inches of distance between the mound and the plate in baseball in which amateur pitchers are throwing in the 80s, professionals in the 90s, there is precious little time for a hitter to react, swing, and connect the bat with the ball. If you can see anything other than the haze of gas or the white blur of heat, you are blessed with great vision. Getting the bat on the ball is next to impossible.

Jack Evens, retired Bloomington Jefferson High School basketball coach, grew up in Superior, Wisconsin, which had a team in the old Northern League of professional baseball. "I liked baseball," he said, "but softball was more challenging." Evens said he played with Bobo Johnson for nearly 25 years for sponsors in Cloquet and Duluth. "I played second base and batted cleanup," Evens said. "Bobo was something. He was about 6-3 and 230 to 240 pounds," with a right arm about four times the size of his left arm. "He'd cut the sleeves off his uniform tops just to intimidate hitters," Evens said.

To get on base against a pitcher like Bobo Johnson, you had to pray for a wild streak and walk, get hit by a pitch, or lay down a good bunt. But third-basemen would try to take the bunt away by playing right on top of the hitter. Larry Beckman of Ruppert's liked to play "in harm's way" on the first base line to take the bunt away there.

Despite the loss, Woody Peters said he celebrated his two hits off the great Bobo Johnson. "They put me to bed at 7 o'clock," he said. Then, the rest of the team celebrated some more without the only guy who could manage any hits that day. Sidelined for the season due to domestic and parental duties with seven kids, Harold Beckman, nonetheless, said he made the trip to Hibbing just to watch: "We closed the bar in the hotel at 1 a.m., and then a couple guys unplugged the juke box and hauled it up to the second floor." The hallway was turned into a dance floor, and the team celebrated some more, just what by now nobody was quite sure. But Sam Cooke's "Twistin' The Night Away" was nearly worn out on the 45 rpm vinyl disc on the Wurlitzer jukebox. Chubby Checker's top 10 hit, "The Twist" included lyrics about tearing the house down that concerned the hotel staff.

On the strength of his senior year of basketball, Woody Peters was recruited by a number of colleges. Coach Hanson had gone to St. Cloud State, where Red Severson's early rendition of "run-and-gun" basketball, Hanson thought, would suit his star guard. But Jordan's football coach and assistant basketball coach, Bernie Riekena, had gone to Mankato State Teachers' College and had persuaded Woody to come out for football his senior year of high school. He thought Woody should go to Mankato. It was close, an easy drive home to Jordan, and John Seifert, who had graduated a year ahead of Woody, was playing basketball at Mankato. As a junior, Woody had fed the ball to John and his brother Jerry Seifert more than he had shot it. John might be able to return some favors.

Woody Peters didn't need the favors. He was a starting guard on and leading the freshman team. He said that the varsity had "two really good senior guards" who gave the freshman a good workout every day in scrimmages. Seifert told him that the coaches liked him, and he'd picked up from others, too, that they were planning on Woody leading the backcourt the next year. "I didn't have any trouble doing what I needed to do on the basketball court," Peters said. "But the college stuff just wasn't for me." He said he wished now that he'd stuck it out and gotten a college education, but at the time he said there was no way he was going to put the kind of time needed into classes and books.

"I met a guy from Hawaii," Woody said. "We became good friends, and pretty soon I got it into my head that I wanted to go to Hawaii."

After finishing his first year of college and despite the great introduction to the game of fast pitch the previous summer with the older guys, Woody Peters would play shortstop for the 1963 Jordan Brewers. But Shakopee would resume its dominance over the league and regional teams in 1963. Weckman and other big guns were gone. It didn't feel right to the young Peters. His heart wasn't in it. He talked his mother into helping him put together enough of a grubstake to go to Hawaii. The siren song of the beach and its balmy breezes were moving Woody Peters more than ball of any kind.

He and the friend he'd made at Mankato got an apartment in Honolulu on the island of Oahu. "I worked over there," he said, "but I was really a beach bum." He said he sold shoes in a department store and managed a little miniature golf operation to make enough money to survive. Playing ball was the furthest thing from his mind. A year in paradise would erase what was left of that desire, and when he returned home a year later he knew that playing ball would never be the same again. Even basketball. He tried a couple of jobs, working for a local painter and at Rahr Malting in Shakopee. He tried college as a day student at Normandale Community College in Bloomington. But nothing was really clicking.

Then it was 1966. Lyndon Johnson was in the White House. The Vietnam War was continuously ramping up, and Woody got a letter from Eunice Schaeffer, U.S. Army Draft Headquarters for Scott County in Shakopee, Minnesota.

"It was the Vietnam Era," Peters said, "but I got sent to Germany and not Vietnam." He said that the duty he pulled was in a M60A1 tank as a gunner. Infrared sighting was just coming in, according to Peters, and the 105 mm British-designed gun, he said, "could shoot a mile down the road."

"The tank and the gun were a good match for the equivalent threats from the Soviet Union at the time," according to Retired Marine Corps Colonel Rudy Bernard. A defense industry analyst and consultant, as well as an amateur military historian, Bernard was a Marine Corps armor officer who commanded at the platoon, company, and battalion levels. He spent two tours, 1966 and 1970-'71, in Vietnam and said that the U.S. Army wisely kept its most capable armor units, equipment, and crews in Europe to face the ultimate threat to the U.S. at the time– the Soviet Union.

"A successful Soviet invasion of Europe–i.e., probably through the Fulda Gap– could have resulted in a cataclysmic world war," according to Colonel Bernard.

"The first job of our armored tank crews," Bernard said, "was to contribute to deterrence of that possibility and, second, to defeat it, if attempted."

"We trained an awful lot," Peters said.

Cold War tensions, which defined the relationship between the U.S. and Soviet Union since the end of World War II, were still running high at that time. Readiness wasn't just a buzzword. Not after the unsuccessful Bay of Pigs invasion of Cuba in 1961, and the Missile Crisis standoff with the Soviets in 1962. Moreover, we weren't even close to closure with regard to the assassination of President Kennedy in November of 1963, and some theorists had the Soviets involved in that.

"Woody could play anywhere at any time," Ed Breimhorst said. "He was a natural." He made everything look so easy, as though it were all instinct with him, not hammered out with drills and fungo shots. Yet, when you talk to him today, it's as though he's got a Ph.D. from MIT in playing shortstop.

"Knowledge of the game is the key," he said. "An awareness of the situation and an ability to react to the ball are critical." Peters said that the shortstop is moving all the time on every pitch. "You've got to be involved in it–the whole game, every pitch," he said. "You've got to be able to 'read' the pitch and the hitter, so you can anticipate, more so even in softball than baseball, because everything is so much quicker. Then it becomes second nature."

"To play shortstop," Woody Peters said, "you've got to be fairly athletic, and you've got to have an arm." Certainly, you can't hide a lame duck at shortstop. You might get by with that at the corners for a couple of games or so, or in right field, but not at shortstop.

His service duty fulfilled, Peters returned to Jordan in late 1968 and was talked into playing shortstop with the Jordan Brewers again in 1969. But he said that he'd lost the whole competitive thing. "I just could not get any enjoyment out of it anymore. It had become a chore. I lost interest. It soured me, and I knew I couldn't do it."

Woody Peters was just 25 years old in the fall of 1969. How was it possible for one of the best shortstops to ever play any summer game in any ballpark in the area to be done at that age? It didn't make any sense, but then the sense of things was getting upset in those years. Baseball was life, and life was baseball.

Baseball's grip on the society and culture would loosen slowly during the waning years of the game's Golden Age. After all, the New Age was dawning, the Age of Aquarius, with many signs of the end of The Golden Age of Baseball. Where once during the era of radio's dominance of media and colorful sports writing by the likes of Red Smith, Ring Lardner, and others, the game was engaging and exciting, television exposed the wrinkles and the weaknesses of the game. Baseball was boring, especially "good baseball." Who could wait through nine innings of a "good game" of baseball, when nothing happened? America's youth were looking for "cheap thrills" everywhere.

Janis Joplin joined Big Brother and the Holding Company as the band's lead singer in 1966. They would rapidly gain fame in 1967. The next summer was euphemistically labeled, "The Summer of Love." Big Brother, along with The Grateful Dead and The Jefferson Airplane, defined *the psychedelic sound of San Francisco*. They gained national and international acclaim for their performance at the Monterrey Pop Festival that summer of 1967 when thousands of wannabe hippies left their boring middle class homes in Minneapolis and Akron, Ames and Milwaukee, to go to the new Mecca–Haight-Ashbury in San Francisco, California. They would leave the secure, staid confines of mommy and daddy's world to join The Great Be In: "Make love, not war"; "If it feels good, do it."

The year, 1968, was dubbed "The Year of the Pitcher" by baseball, most poignantly because Detroit's Denny McLain won 30 games. Actually, he was 31–6, with an ERA of 1.96. Dizzy Dean was the last 30-game winner and that was way back in 1934. Bob Gibson had an ERA in 1968 of just 1.12. Baseball, which for years had been bringing in the fences, would respond by lowering the mound from 15 inches to just 10 inches higher than home plate, and by reducing the strike zone to fit the wheelhouse of hitters. Something had to be done to inject some excitement back into baseball for those in need of the adrenaline rush, and that meant run-scoring offense.

Carl Yastrzemski was the only American League player to bat over .300 in 1968, and while arguably a fitting tribute to the greatness of the game's icon, McLain had told his catcher in a game against the Yankees to tell Mickey Mantle he was going to get medium fastballs waist high. It was a gift. A memorial. Mantle had been McLain's idol growing up, and rumors were that this would be his last season. The Mick hit career homerun number 535, good enough for third on the all-time list behind Babe Ruth and Willie Mays.

The hippies called 1968 "The Summer of Love" because, again most poignantly, it was widely felt that love and freedom had finally been unchained from responsibility with The Pill. Sex, drugs, and rock and roll were "the real thing." It was their statement about the bombing of Hanoi, about the boredom of business and baseball. Somehow, centuries-old tribal wisdom of elders had been supplanted by the thrill-seeking expediency of youth. America was "going to pot" in more ways than the obvious. Vietnam veterans were returning home to the towns of the Minnesota River Valley with their eyes glazed over, as if they were deer caught in a car's headlights alongside the road at night. No, it wasn't combat fatigue or PTSD that was taking our ballplayers. It was speed, weed, and heroin.

Big Brother's second album was initially titled *Sex, Dope, and Cheap Thrills*, but Columbia Records, with at least one foot still in the establishment's quarter, persuaded the group to change the title to *Cheap Thrills*. The album was a critical and popular success. A couple of the songs were released as singles. Joplin would leave the group in 1969 and record "Me and Bobby McGee", written by her one-time lover, Kris Kristofferson, who had been a Rhodes Scholar. It would be her only number one hit, and it was a good one. She would perform at Woodstock in 1969. *Rolling Stone* ranked Janis Joplin 46th out of 100 all-time top singers in 2004. She was defined as "electric," as was Jimi Hendrix, another Woodstock headliner. She and Hendrix were far more electrifying to a buzzed up, turned-on crowd than any two-out walk, bases-loaded popup, or strikeout at any level of baseball.

Janis Joplin certainly wasn't the first, or the last, celebrity to flame out in an orgy of excess and self-abuse. She is just supremely emblematic–in terms of both a talent of the times, and the headlong self-destruction of a wild mare refusing to take the bit and the rein of maturity. She was reportedly a speed freak, riddled with gonorrhea, and addicted to heroin and Southern Comfort. In 1970, after a musical career of all of four years, she died of an overdose of heroin. She was 27 years old and is reported by David Comfort in a 2010 Dusty Wright *Culture Catch* biographical piece on Joplin to have "bitterly regretted" having had a Mexican abortion a year or two earlier–on her birthday, no less. Mocked and dismissed as irrelevant by the new crop of youth that thought they could ignore and defy Nature and Nature's God, The Fiddler saw it all from the shadows and corners to which He had been pushed.

"It was wrong," Comfort quoted the "Queen of Blues" after making her choice.

Comfort goes on to write that Janis Joplin over the next year "suffered six heroin overdoses, two nearly fatal." Janis Joplin was dying of despair over her choice. Yet, that crowd, the Mob that argues for choice, repeatedly warns of back alleys and clothes hangers in its unrelenting mission to ostensibly empower women. No, it's The Fiddler. He might be relegated to the shadows in times such as these, but He's always nearby, one eye intent on the dancers–even if His music is no longer desired. For, in the words of Swiss psychoanalyst Carl Jung's epitaph: "Vocatus atque non vocatus deus aderit" (Called or not called, God will be present).

"Her psychiatrist," Comfort continues, "Dr. Ed Rothschild, put her on methadone and diagnosed her as, 'Intellectually bordering on brilliant. She really could think circles around most people, but her emotions were childlike and uncontrollable.'"

A month after the death of Janis Joplin, Jimi Hendrix, who was another super-rock "free spirit" and love child, died of an overdose of sleeping pills, also at age 27. A year later, Jim Morrison of The Doors would suffer the same fate, from essentially the same cause–an alleged overdose of heroin–at the same age of 27.

While immature minds make cultural heroes of celebrities such as these, Truth is, "God is not mocked. You reap what you sow." Old and New Testaments aside, none of the Laws of Nature can be suspended because of an ideology or the infantile "I wanna." You can't piss in your own well without eventually tasting funny water at the kitchen sink. If you eat your seed corn in the winter, you won't have anything to plant in the spring, much less harvest in the fall. Instead of being a producer for your family and the world, you will have become a taker at the public trough. Sooner, rather than later, we find with the celebrity pop stars of the 60s, and far too many idolatrous fans and followers, not only do the ends not justify the means, the ends are a natural, logical consequence of those means. The New Agers call it simply, "Karma."

Maybe it was all the hubris of Shakespeare's kings. Maybe The Fiddler didn't like the new form of idolatry He witnessed in His people. But baseball was losing its hold on people and country. Baseball, indeed all ball playing, all sports and athletics, whether individual or team in orientation, is at root a dance and a celebration of life. But baseball, especially through its Golden Age, *was* life, and that direct connection was coming apart. A ghastly looking Mickey Mantle would tell us in a public statement shortly before his death at age 64 in 1995 from alcoholism and liver cancer: "Don't do what I did." The Mick would, of course, pay The Fiddler the ultimate price for the dance he danced his whole life. As good as he was, you can't help but wonder just how great Mickey Mantle would have been, not with a healthy knee, but with a healthy lifestyle.

Meanwhile, local baseball people were concerned about losing their shortstops and centerfielders to softball, which was fast becoming more fun for everybody.

While it is likely that blood alcohol levels of ballplayers were measurably higher than those of the average office worker in the nation, and that blood sugar levels were probably spiking in this cohort more than the average citizen who was not obese, it is just as likely that this correlation existed from the very beginnings of baseball. In short, like apple pie and a dollop of vanilla ice cream, baseball and beer went well together with both fans and ballplayers. It has been so since the beginnings of the game in the 1800s.

On the other hand, it is doubtful that much, if any, tetrahydrocannabinol (THC), which is the principal psychoactive constituent of the cannabis plant, could have been found in the blood of any American baseball player anywhere prior to the mid- to late-1960s. For one thing, nobody knew what it was, because it wasn't even isolated from the marijuana plant until 1964. But the point here isn't in the science, the legality, the morality, the sociology, or even in the behavioral health aspects summed up by the phrase, "drug of choice."

The point is performance. You can hustle or sweat your way out of the lethargy of alcohol's effects. At least, until a career is nearly over anyway. Recent biographies of some great ballplayers testify to that. But with the effects of weed, otherwise sure-handed infielders drop popups and boot two-hop, double-play groundballs; outfielders drop lazy fly balls and miss the cutoff man with their throws or throw to the wrong base. Hitters usually aggressive at the plate watch third strikes go by. Pitchers known to reach back for the proverbial "more," instead look for the showers. Managers and coaches can easily be affected as well in their thinking and their decision-making.

In short, there's no place for "the devil weed," or its lasting blood-stream essence, in a baseball park–on the field or in the dugout. Stoned fans, however, might boost concessions with the munchies by the fifth inning. Needless to say, other, "more advanced" street drugs have an even worse and longer-lasting effect on performance than marijuana. And if these drugs don't belong on a baseball diamond in a ballplayer, they don't belong in our doctors, lawyers, teachers, policemen, firemen, and soldiers everywhere, because of their adverse effects on physical and mental performance. If you don't want your shortstop to be a pothead, why would you put up with your children's teacher being a pothead?

Then the new game burst onto the scene everywhere–slow-pitch softball. At first, it seemed like a game for overweight, over-the-hill, and burned out baseball players, or the powder-puff set. Woody thought it might be some fun. He joined a ball club that formed around an old friend, former classmate, and ex-marine with two tours of duty in Vietnam–Denny Personius, or "Sony," as he was known. Ralph Patterson, son of long-time Ruppert's Bar owner Helen Patterson, agreed to sponsor the team in the Jordan softball league.

Something began to click again for Woody Peters. These guys were fun. This game was fun. "I got it cranked up again," he said. "We put together that team with really good ballplayers. It was fun again, and that meant something."

That first year was kind of a shakeout period. People needed to find *their* position, and "the founder" needed to be replaced as the manager of the team. Sony stepped aside without any real resistance, and Gary Steckman (i.e., "Fox") took over the helm. Woody knew both well. They had been teammates on the basketball team he'd taken to the Region 4 tournament at Williams Arena against the 1962 Minnesota State High School Basketball runner up, South St. Paul. Issues with sponsorship were bubbling up as well.

Slowly, the team found its legs, arms, and the positions for them. They began to meld. They went undefeated in the city league and even entered a few tournaments in that formative year, a year that saw an expansion of the new game. But they bowed out in the first or second rounds of each tournament. As much talent as they had, they ran into powerhouse buzz saws who showed them the game. They got beat soundly by teams like the Faribault Eagles and Snell's Bar from Prior Lake. Those teams played at a different level. They took the game seriously on the field and saved the jesting for after the games and tournaments. They didn't stop with two or three runs in a burst of offensive firepower. They would put six, eight, or a dozen runs on the board before you knew what had happened. This was all with the high-arced pitch, but still with wood bats the first year and into the second. Dick Darby from Snell's Bar in Prior Lake, in particular, literally swung out of his shoes on every pitch. He was said to have set an unverifiable Bloomington Dred Scott Fields record one year–with the wood bat.

"God, there was a lot of fun there," Woody said. "Then I got enthused again and worked at it." With the smaller diamond, the shorter bases at 60 feet rather than the 90 feet in baseball, everything is so much quicker. "There's no time for a bobble of a ball in softball," Woody said. "There's no time to get in front of a ball in the classic 1950s and 60s baseball style." He said that the shortstop has got to be able to make the backhand play deep in the hole, plant the right foot, and fire back across to second to start a double play or across the diamond to first for the putout.

In baseball, you've usually got the time that allows you to pick up a mishandled ball and still make the throw to first. You don't have that luxury in softball–either fast pitch or slow pitch. And in slow pitch, there exists the very real potential for a very good defensive play on every single pitch–because pitching is such a small factor in slow pitch and such a huge factor in baseball, and even more so in fast pitch. The truth is told by the ERAs of pitchers and the batting averages of hitters. They are both the lowest in fast-pitch softball of any of the three games. Pitching dominates. Conversely, it would be absurd to even track ERAs of pitchers or batting averages, runs batted in, and homeruns of hitters in slow-pitch softball since the development of the metal bats.

"There were some good teams out there, too," Woody said. The team under Toby and Rollie's sponsorship found it was better than it thought it was at the outset, and better than most teams it ran into. Beating Snell's Bar in the Jordan Fire Department's Sno-Flake Tournament the second winter, 1972 probably, in the same manner and result that the Prior Lake team had beaten them in a couple of previous encounters told them they had arrived. Then, Faribault Eagles, Pat's Place from Plato, Monty's Bar from Montgomery, Chaska Bell, a couple of teams in the Minneapolis Classic League, including The Press Bar, which people said was "the best team in St. Cloud," and others all went down in tournament after tournament. The wins filled Toby and Rollie's Bar with three-and four-foot high trophies that collected dust and prompted memories for years until the bar was sold and the trophies went into storage at Coach Hanson's house. Then one summer night, the last party of this team saw the distribution of a trophy to each ballplayer.

"That was it," Woody Peters remembered. It seemed like it had just begun and it was over. "Ball was life, and life was ball." But others emulated even the uniforms of this softball team. Everybody liked green and gold for a while, it seemed. They'd earned the respect from all but the diehard baseball elites. Problem there was, T&R's could have beaten most baseball teams in the area over several decades in either softball or baseball. They could hit with anybody. They played better defense than most, and they had better pitching–yes, baseball pitching–hiding up and down their tournament lineup. Four players had either signed and played some professional baseball or turned down legitimate offers from Major League Baseball teams.

This ball club had a winning ratio of something like .820 over the course of five years, playing anywhere from 70 to as many as 80 or 90 games a year. They played league games, usually on Monday nights, a beer game during the week the first year or two, then 16-and 32-team tournaments regularly, nearly every weekend through Labor Day.

They never lost a game in five years of league play. They never lost a game, beer game or tournament game, in five years of playing in at least one tournament each year in Belle Plaine.

Woody Peters was the heart of Toby and Rollie's softball team. Along with Frank Hilgers at second base, he was one-half of what might have been the best double-play combination in the area ever, certainly since Tex Erickson and Dick Nolden with the baseball Brewers in the 1950s. He hit a ton before they built the turbo-trampoline technology into the metal bats, which ensured that everybody hit a ton and that destroyed the game and made baseball a mockery of itself.

One game, perhaps more than any other out of over 400 games, defined this team and its shortstop. In 1973, T&R's had just squeaked by a team from Wolf Motors in their first of two encounters in league play. The score was something like

5-3, an unlikely and anemic offensive effort by both teams in a game where typical scores even then, prior to the advanced bat technology, were more like 17-9.

It was a Monday night after a long Sunday night celebration of another tournament championship over the weekend. Spiking blood sugar levels on Sunday had fallen precipitously all day Monday, a workday. But for two or three weeks after that game, The Buzz in Jordan was how bad Wolf Motors was going to beat T&R's the next time they met. The gold on the green and gold uniforms of Toby and Rollie's had lost its glitter, they said. It was tarnished with age and sore arms and too much beer. That team had had its run, its day in the sun. These boys were done. They were ripe to be beaten by the latest pretenders to their throne.

The league had a 15-run rule after five innings. That meant that if one team were up on another by 15 runs after five innings, the game was over. This was to prevent humiliating drubbings, but it was a rare occurrence then. Even more rare in slow-pitch softball is a shutout, because, as glorious an achievement as a shutout is in baseball, pitching is virtually nothing in the slow version of the softball game. Everybody hits. Everybody scores runs. Nobody gets shut out. Shutouts are impossible.

In the top of the fifth inning, Wolf Motors was threatening, with runners on first and third and nobody out. A sharp groundball was hit to shortstop. Woody Peters fielded it cleanly and quickly; he looked to second, then gunned a strike to home for a tag out of the runner. The next batter hit another groundball to short. Woody started the double play with precise fielding and a toss to Frank at second. Bang-bang! T&R's had shut out Wolf Motors, 20-0, in a brilliant display of defensive excellence. "I just had to preserve the shutout," Woody said later of his throw to home.

You don't poke a sharp stick into the eye of a hibernating bear. You don't arouse an old dog sleeping in the sun on the porch. You let him rest and soak up the sun. Toby and Rollie's was beginning to show some age. Key players were getting a little long in the tooth. But this old dog still had some hunt left in him.

Hard to say who it was from Wolf Motors and their followers who was doing all the talking, but they, as well as the detractors of T&R's, and the blowhards again, all ate crow for the rest of the summer and into the fall. But the game spoke volumes about the excellence and heart of a team and its shortstop. Shutouts in slow-pitch softball are impossible.

The song had been sung. The dance had been danced. The Fiddler was delighted in His boys at play.

Woody and Gini Peters have raised two athletic sons and too many Thoroughbred racehorses to count out at their ranch south of Jordan. Woody said that he retired from a 34-year career as a rural mail carrier with the U.S. Postal Service in 2004. It seems impossible that this shortstop who flitted and danced like Tinker Bell in the infields of three different summer sports could possibly have turned 70 years of age in 2014. Wasn't he, after all, who Bob Dylan had in mind when he wrote, "Forever Young"? One consolation, he notes, is that the hips that bothered him for years with their degenerative arthritis are now free of pain. Surgical replacement with titanium has been his answer.

While the hips have slowed him down to more measured movements, Woody Peters still looks like he could steal second in a fast-pitch game or make the play deep in the hole at shortstop and throw out a runner at first base. Meanwhile, his laughter comes as quickly as ever. It takes you back, too, as effortlessly as he once played the games of winter and summer. Then you're in trouble, because you begin to wish for a wiffle ball and bat or a game of H-O-R-S-E in the old gymnasium with the little guard who could shoot the lights out and the shortstop who made all the plays look so easy.

Jim "Jake" Harsh

Nobody ever hit a ball like my brother, Jim.

— Brad Harsh

Jim Harsh was a big man. Not weightlifting, gym-rat big. Not steroid-injecting, human-growth-hormone big. More like railroad-spike-driving big. With the DNA from his Dad, osmosis from his older brother, Bob, and directly from mainlining the manual labor himself. Like his father and brother, Jim Harsh worked for the railroad for a couple years. He lifted, hauled, and placed the heavy oak railroad ties and the steel rails. He drove spikes with a heavy maul into the ties to hold the rails in place.

Jake Harsh was thick. Like Mickey Mantle was thick. Only bigger. Mantle went under six feet in height and 200 pounds. Jake Harsh was big like Boog Powell was big. Belle Plaine teammates and friends even called Harsh "Boog," or "Boogie" sometimes, and he liked it, because he liked the big Baltimore first baseman. They came out of the same mold. Both were first basemen who threw right-handed and took big swings from the left side of the plate. Boog Powell with the Baltimore Orioles, Harsh with the Belle Plaine Tigers. Both were around 6-3 or 6-4 in height and 230 to 240, maybe 245 pounds, in their early 20s, according to Manley Vinkemeier, who was a classmate and teammate of Harsh's.

"We met as freshmen at Belle Plaine High School," Vinkemeier said. They played ball and ran around together, remaining friends until Harsh's tragic death in 1977. He was electrocuted while on the job, working for the Minnesota Valley Electric Cooperative, or MVEC, headquartered in Jordan, Minnesota, on Monday, August 1, 1977, according to the August 4, 1977, *Belle Plaine Herald*.

Mention Jake Harsh to anybody who's played or watched local baseball during the game's stretch run of its Golden Age that might extend into the 1970s and their eyes glaze over. Left-handed hitters lust for that short, right-field fence at Belle Plaine. But there was nothing cheap about the home runs, or the singles, that Jake hit. How could there be? He swung the bat with such tenacity that he nearly went down into the dirt from the body torque and G forces he generated with each swing. He took a rip at the ball; he wasn't "a looker." He made sure he got his money's worth with every at bat and every swing, and the fans did, too. Especially in the 1970 Belle Plaine Tiger season, which was the year that Boog Powell won the American League's MVP award, beating out the Twins' Tony Oliva and Harmon Killebrew, and Boston's Carl Yastrzemski. His numbers tell the story: a .297 batting average, with 35 homeruns and 114 runs batted in, which led the Orioles to a 108-

win season, a league championship over the Twins, and a World Series Championship over the Cincinnati Reds. Remember, too, that Baltimore Oriole team had two future Hall of Famers playing with the same last name: Robinson.

Jake Harsh batted .500 for the 1970 River Valley League season on 26 hits in 52 at bats. He smashed 15 homeruns with his heavy, whip-handled, wooden Louisville Slugger. Then he went 15 for 20 in the playoffs. "He hit everybody," Vinkemeier said, "and if we needed a run or two, he's the guy we wanted at the plate."

Jake led the league, beating out four really good hitters from Prior Lake, ballplayers with pedigrees from Dick Siebert's University of Minnesota Golden Gophers and short stints of professional baseball. Indeed, the Prior Lake Jays batted .294 as a team in 1970, with Brian Love at .462, Steve Schneider at .410, Gary Reierson at .389, and, arguably the best hitter on the team, Fred DeGregoire at .371, according to the last regular season edition, July 26, 1970, of the *Northwest Umpires Review*. John Dill and Bobby Kelly, both outstanding hitters as well, were mired in the .200s for the season. Diminutive in physical stature in comparison to Reierson, for example, "their problem was they were trying to hit homeruns all the time," the big first baseman for Prior Lake recounted. "We had a really good-hitting team," Reierson said of the 1969 and 1970 Prior Lake Jays. Good enough for the *Umpires Review* to write: "In the last two or three years when the playoffs started it was almost a foregone conclusion that Prior Lake would win and represent the league in regional and state tournament play."

But Jim Stoll–almost a local Belle Plaine boy at nearby Arlington–had stuck it to Prior Lake good in the state championship game at Jordan the previous fall, beating them 6-1 on a five-hitter with 11 strikeouts. Then the league caught Prior Lake with their hands in the cookie jar. Their talent-rich team of Lake Conference and University of Minnesota Gopher baseball players from Bloomington and Edina included at least one player whose eligibility was more than questionable.

Jake Harsh outhit them all in leading Belle Plaine to a league-best 13-3 record, a full game ahead of second-place Shakopee, according to the *Review*. But two of its wins were from Prior Lake's forfeiture of eight games for playing an ineligible player. Playoffs were the litmus test of the better ballclub: Prior Lake would prevail, beating Belle Plaine, 9-0 and 4-2, in the double-elimination format, despite Harsh's hot bat.

Harsh topped off a great 1970 summer season with his fall marriage to Peggy Elder.

"He was the team leader," Vinkemeier said, and without being a pain in the ass in the dugout, "he'd let you know if you screwed up or he saw that you were dogging it."

"He loved baseball," Vinkemeier said, "and as natural a player as he was, he liked to practice." Jake Harsh loved to take batting practice. He'd stay in the cage all afternoon if he could find somebody to throw to him and help shag balls. "Same thing at first base," Vinkemeier, a shortstop, said. "He'd ask us to throw balls over to him at first base that he'd have to dig out of the dirt on the hop." He was a natural, yet he loved to work on his game.

"He's the best natural hitter I've ever seen around here," his manager through most of the 1960s, Gerry Meyer, said. "He had that nice way of squaring up to the ball over the plate," according to Meyer, his eyes following a swing with an imaginary bat in his hand and hitting an imaginary ball at the optimum point in the swing–square to the ball over the plate, and he *drove* the ball. He didn't swat at it or patty cake it. Jake Harsh didn't "just meet" the ball. He crushed it.

Jake brought it all together with his swing: eyes–hands–stride–pull–and turn. He was power personified.

"We went down to a Twins tryout," Vinkemeier said. "Jake and I and Lefty Schultz." The Minnesota Twins must have liked something in Jim Harsh. "They called him back the second day," Vinkemeier said. He got a look, but he didn't get an offer. This was 1963, and with only 20 major league teams after the expansions in 1961 and 1962, there just weren't that many opportunities yet.

Undoubtedly, the Minnesota Twins liked Harsh's size and the potential they saw with his bat. But maybe it was the way he finished his swing one handed that dissuaded them from offering him a contract. Maybe, they felt he just wasn't agile or quick enough to play even first base. Still, he had to have been more agile than the likes of Frank Howard and Boog Powell, Major Leaguers with big time credentials. Before them, Ted Kluszewski and Johnny ("Big Cat") Mize were the prototype first basemen in whose mold Big Jake Harsh fit. You didn't play men like this for their twinkle toes or base stealing. You paid them and you played them for their slugging.

Maybe they just didn't like the way Jake Harsh moved. "He had really small feet for a big man," Brad Harsh said of his older brother, "so his ankles were always bad," adding, "I taped his ankles for him before every game." But Harsh was a good first baseman, Vinkemeier noted. "He dug everything out." And he could move pretty well for a big man. He had a handful of triples during his years of playing for Belle Plaine.

Maybe it was just a matter of numbers that day at the old Met. The Twins had a big, power-hitting first baseman in Don Mincher. At 25 years old, he promised many more years, which could only get better. They had ageless Vic Power to back him up for defensive purposes. Before the designated-hitter rule was adopted by the American League in 1973, first base was kind of reserved for the big hitters without a true position, or for aging, gimpy veterans who could still produce at the plate.

Harmon Killebrew, who didn't really have a true position, was only 27 on his way to the Hall of Fame in 1963. Bob Allison was more than adequate as a left fielder, but he was a big man with a big bat, too, and susceptible to injuries. "They made offers to six guys," Brad said, "and Jim was number seven." There's an old saying that says we're not responsible for consequences. We're responsible for the effort in the matters of our lives.

Nobody tried harder than Jake Harsh. Nobody was more careful or conscientious. He was super conscious of safety matters and the smallest of things that mattered. "He was a perfectionist," Dave Beckius, a co-worker, said of Jim Harsh. But The Fiddler is in charge of the dance and the music box. When the music stops and your number is called, no amount of design or effort on our part really matters.

"Hindsight is always 20-20," it is said, and Monday morning quarterbacks never throw an interception or call the wrong play. We all magnify the smallest of things into major significance as we seek to know why. It's natural of humans. Maybe it was the heat and humidity on a hot August day. Maybe it was receding blood sugar levels after a lunch washed down with too much cold soda pop. Maybe it was complacency from having done the same job too many times to count with the same crew. Linemen didn't do what is known as "tailgating" in 1977, a procedure in which a formal surveillance of the site is done to help identify hazards and to plan the work. Maybe it was the mainline wires hanging lower than optimum from poles settling in wet soil, rather than erect and perpendicular to the earth's plane. Maybe the yard pole was longer than the standard length of 30 feet. Maybe it was looking up into the high, blinding, early afternoon sun.

If only it hadn't been so hot that day and the crew hadn't gone to Doherty's to escape the heat but, rather, had eaten their sandwiches in the truck or sitting outside against the truck or a tree, maybe one of these three veteran linemen gazing up at the wires overhead would have noticed just how close they were. If only Jake had kept his rubber gloves on or taken his steel hooks off after cutting the wire on the mainline pole. Maybe he should have left the apprentice doing the task that he took over from him. The yard pole the crew was moving never cleared the ground.

Maybe and maybe, and too many if-only's to count.

Jake Harsh's number was up on a hot August day in 1977. He was a journeyman lineman on a three-man crew working for the electric co-op in the eastern end of Scott County in Spring Lake Township, south of Prior Lake, near St. Catherine's. The crew had eaten lunch at nearby Doherty's Tavern at noon, Dave Beckius, an apprentice lineman on the crew, remembered.

They had sandwiches along, according to Beckius, and usually ate lunch in the truck or under a shade tree on site. "But we went to Doherty's," Beckius said, "because it was so hot and they had air conditioning there." The AC was a welcome respite from a day that was already hot and would only get hotter. They ate burgers and fries, with sodas, Beckius remembered. "They only serve burgers and pizzas there," Beckius said, "and the burgers are good."

Jake was meticulous in his regard for safety, according to several men familiar with his work habits, and he even gave the lessons at safety meetings to fellow workers regularly. A six-year veteran lineman, Jake Harsh knew the hazards of his work and did his work well. But the pole with the metal meter, a metal plate, metal staples, and metal conduit with wire enclosed and the wire stubs on the top contacted the mainline wires overhead. The senior man, Pete Menke, was on the control levers on the truck that moved the boom and slowly lifted the winch attached to the pole with Jake holding on below to guide the pole as it inched upward. Dave Beckius, kneeling at Jake's feet next to the pole, had cut the copper ground wire close to the copper rod in the ground.

"It went in through his thumb," Brad Harsh said, "and came out through his feet," seeking the metal pole-climbing hooks he wore over his boots. When the pole with the wire stubs on top touched the mainline overhead, 7,200 volts of electricity shot down the length of the pole that Jake had grabbed with his leather gloves on to protect him from wood slivers.

Beckius, a volunteer fireman in Jordan, knew CPR and began the procedure immediately. He said that he even thought he had a pulse for a while. He had Menke doing the chest compressions, while he counted and cleared the throat of the partly digested food being regurgitated from the stomach. After 15 compressions, he would hold the nose with his thumb and forefinger, as he had learned in CPR class, and blow, mouth to mouth, his air into Jake, the idea being to jumpstart the lungs in the pulmonary part of the life-saving procedure known as cardio-pulmonary resuscitation.

Beckius sensed that they needed medical help fast, and he said he told Pete Menke to call for help while he continued with the CPR alone, repeating the 15 chest compressions then two breaths. "Our truck radios were our lifeline," according to Beckius. "Pete used our truck radio to call our dispatch. They, in turn, called for assistance. I don't think there was 911 back then."

But Brad Harsh, who followed his older brother into the trade and knew the physics and the mystery of electricity, too, said he believes that his brother was already dead before Beckius even began the CPR. He said he thinks that Jake's internal organs had been burned beyond life-sustaining capability.

"Ray Weierke was the line superintendent then," Beckius said, "a job I had when I retired. He made the work assignments, giving them to the crew foremen, Pete Menke in our case, every morning." Beckius said that Weierke was on the site shortly after the call was made and within 30 minutes of the call, the Prior Lake ambulance arrived. Jake Harsh was declared dead an hour later at St. Francis Hospital in Shakopee.

"I think he was gone as soon as it hit him," Brad said. "He took 7,200 volts at high amps." He said most people think that it's the voltage that kills. "But they're wrong," Brad said. "It's the amps."

When the wood yard pole's wire stubs inadvertently touched the mainline overhead, the juice jumped into the metal on the pole and ran down the stapled, conduit-enclosed wire on the pole and at lightning speed sought ground, as electricity always does. But with the No. 6 copper ground wire on the pole that led to a copper ground rod cut, and with Dave Beckius still kneeling next to the pole at Jake's legs, metal pliers in hand, the steel "hooks" on Jake's boots that linemen wear to climb poles became the ground for the electricity, and Jake's body became "the path to ground."

Jake had taken off his rubber gloves, which he'd had on when he had climbed the mainline pole minutes earlier to cut the wire from it. But he took them off as he approached Beckius at the yard pole. Nothing would have happened had he kept his rubber gloves on, according to Beckius, since, he said, "Our rubber gloves were good for 30,000 volts."

"But there was no need for the rubber gloves there," Dave said. No need that was apparent to any of these experienced linemen. The yard pole was no longer hot. So Jake switched to leather to keep from picking up slivers on the wood pole. Slivers are always a menace to a lineman's hands. A serious infection can disrupt a crew and jeopardize work and schedules.

The ground copper wire, according to Beckius, is basically protection from things like a short circuit, lightning, etc. And, yes, it serves as the path to ground. It attaches to the line neutral and any other metal parts on the pole, including the conduit that had the two 110v wires inside it. It runs from the top of the pole to the copper ground rod. Had it not been cut when the stub wire atop the pole contacted the 7,200-volt line, Jake would have been fine.

"He probably would have been extremely pissed off because we missed the hazard," Beckius said, "but he definitely would have been alive."

Beckius said that he had taken his hooks off after getting down from the yard pole. But he said that Jake had removed his body belt after cutting the wire on the mainline pole by the road, but that he still had his hooks on. His next move after the pole was removed would have been to take his hooks off. Had the staples not been popping, or had he not seen it happening, he more than likely would have been in the process of taking them off. "He just never got to do that," Beckius said.

"There are so very many reasons why it should have been me and not Jake," Beckius recounted. "There really was not a single, logical reason why he should have even got involved with Pete and I pulling the pole. It's a two-man job." Pete was on the control levers. Dave, not Jake, was on the pole.

"But like I said, the dust never settled behind Jake. He was a hard worker and fully invested in every job we did. I really wish he had sat down to take his hooks off. That also would have saved his life."

"Staples were popping off the pole," Beckius said, as Pete Menke inched it up. "Jake said to me, like he always did, 'Hey, rookie! Go get a pliers and cut that wire.'"

Beckius got a set of heavy-duty pliers from the truck and knelt down to cut the copper wire, as Jake grabbed onto the pole where Dave had been helping to guide it while Pete inched it up with the controls on the truck.

After Beckius cut the wire, "Jake said to Pete, 'Okay. Go ahead.'"

"I'm still kneeling at his feet and it seized him to the pole," Beckius said. "The guttural sounds from him lasted just seconds." Then, according to Beckius, "A down-line fuse blew, cutting the power and releasing Jake's body."

Instead of being stopped by the *rubber* gloves Jake had just taken off, the electricity passed through the *leather* gloves he'd just put on and into his thumb. It went up his arms and into his body, probably passing through his heart and taking his life instantly as it continued down through his abdomen into his legs and out his feet, seeking ground–the metal hooks on his boots.

"In my life, I've done CPR three times and the Heimlich Maneuver for choking twice," Dave Beckius winced. "Saved them all but Jake." He said that he's carried the burden of self-incriminating failure his whole life. "Did I do enough? Did I do it right?"

While CPR procedures today forego the mouth-to-mouth part, calling instead for as many as 100 chest compressions in a minute, the public's perception of the procedure's effectiveness has been unduly influenced by television shows such as *ER* and *Chicago Hope*. But television isn't reality. Even, perhaps particularly, the anomaly called "reality TV." A July 10, 2013, online article by Madeline Stix for the CNN Health website cited a 2012 study showing "that only about 2% of adults who collapse on the street and receive CPR recover." A 2009 study "showed that anywhere from 4% to 16% of patients who received bystander CPR were eventually discharged from the hospital." It's fair to say that not one of these victims had experienced 7,200 high-amped volts of electricity while being "the path to ground."

"I was really hurting," Beckius said, "but I was told by the superintendent to finish the day's work." He and Menke moved the pole with the help of the maintenance crew that had come out from the shop. The *Herald* article on Jake's death noted that the co-op had not had a fatality since 1947, and Beckius said that there hasn't been another fatality since Jake's tragedy. But he said that there were two serious 7,200-volt injuries to linemen that could easily have been fatal. "They both had angels watching over them," Beckius said.

"Jake had two or three other close calls," Beckius said, in maybe 18 months to two years prior to his death, and he'd fallen from a pole in 1973 when his hooks slipped. "It bothered him to the point where he took time off to consider whether he might be in the wrong line of work." Jake was the kind of guy, Beckius noted, who would see accidents as red flags or "early warning signs."

Harsh stayed with the co-op and by 1977 he was a journeyman lineman with six years' experience. "But it's a dangerous job," Beckius said. Indeed, citing the results of the "2012 National Census of Fatal Occupational Industries," by the U.S. Bureau of Labor Statistics, Kathy Kristoff at CBSNews.com published a story on January 16, 2014 outlining just how dangerous. In 2012, the article notes, "Powerline Installers and Maintenance Personnel"–Linemen–was the seventh-most dangerous job in the country at 23 deaths per 100,000 per capita workers. Linemen trailed loggers, commercial fishermen, aircraft pilots and flight engineers, roofers, structural iron and steel workers, and refuse and recyclable materials collectors in level of danger on the basis of fatalities measured per 100,000 workers.

"None of us noticed the proximity of the mainline and the inherent danger," Beckius said. "I've always said that complacency killed him." The mainline of three wires atop a 35-foot red cedar pole carrying 7,200 volts of power to rural Scott County residents runs along the south side of County Road 8 west of St. Catherine's and Doherty's Tavern. The wires span an average length of 300 feet between poles, and at the first place west of Doherty's Tavern, the residence in 1977 of Mrs. Leo Hesse, according to the *Herald*, a transformer on the mainline pole converts 7,200 volts into 240 volts to serve the power needs of the residence. A "yard pole," which is usually installed about 150 feet away from the mainline pole on a perpendicular line to it and the mainline, takes the 240-volt line from the transformer and passes electricity into the home. A meter connected to wires in the silver-colored conduit pipe measures customer usage.

But in this instance, at this location in 1977, the yard pole was installed, not on a line perpendicular, or 90 degrees, to the mainline and pole, but rather, only 100 feet maybe and at just a 20-degree angle from the mainline pole of 7,200-volt wires. It wasn't unusual, according to Beckius, but it was dangerously close–in hindsight. "We just didn't see the danger," Beckius said. "We do this job dozens of times a year."

The crew saw the pole that was to be pulled from the ground and moved. Looking up into a bright mid-day sun on a super-hot day in August, they just didn't see how close the pole was to the mainline wires overhead.

"Jake's prints were still on the pipe 20 years later," Beckius said, when the pole was taken out of service.

Jake Harsh was "a gentle giant," according to Beckius, "a big teddy bear." But Beckius never saw Harsh play ball. He never saw the competitiveness. He never tried to sneak a fastball by that ferocious swing. Jake Harsh was a magnificent beast with a baseball bat in the batter's box and a couple of runners on base. He saved that tenacious part of himself for the diamond.

Beckius said the two of them had become close friends during the four years they worked together. Ice fishing on Lake Waconia was a favorite pastime. "We'd put our fish houses right next to each other just north of the island," Beckius said, fishing walleyes and crappies through the winter months on the lake just west of the metro suburbs. "He was always upbeat," Beckius said.

"He was a trickster, a practical joker," Brad Harsh recalled. Harsh said his big brother let him tag along all the time when he was young, and it was obvious that he still missed him nearly 40 years after losing him. "I wasn't doing well," Brad said, "and about a month after he'd died, I woke up in the middle of the night, and he was there–at the end of my bed." It wasn't a vision, or hallucination. It was a visit from his big brother.

"He said to me, '*I'm* alright! Really! Now *you've* got to get alright.'"

"So I made up my mind that I was going to be the best ballplayer I could be, as a memorial to him," Brad said. "Because he loved playing ball so much."

Jake Harsh was 31 years old when the music stopped for him and The Fiddler called his number. The music would stop for his family, his friends, and his wife, too. It would take a long time for it to resume for them, and then it was changed forever. Everybody would dance once again, but it would be to a different tune. It would have a slower beat, the rhythm more measured, and with the depth that soul sounds have. Jake and Peggy had been married for almost eight years since 1970, and "they were so close," Dave Beckius said. So much in love.

It was so unfair. But, as every priest and minister of every flavor of faith on earth in one way or another in circumstances like this has tried to convey, "God's ways are not the ways of man." We only see the tip of the iceberg. Intuition and Faith and its practice are what inform us of the Greater Reality, the Real Mass of It All, beneath the surface of the water. Spirit lives. Bodies return to earth as ashes and dust. "We are not our bodies," prophets and gurus of spirituality have told us. Jake Harsh lives.

Jake Harsh had taken his big bat and big swing to softball in the Belle Plaine city league, playing both games at the same time, something would-be purists frowned upon, because, they said, "softball ruins your swing." On the contrary, it can teach over-anxious young hitters to wait on the ball and to "see" it better. In any event, the numbers Jake Harsh put up in baseball from 1968 through 1971 belie the truth the purists want. But Belle Plaine's baseball fortunes went as Jake Harsh's fortunes went. With a .173 batting average in 1972 for a 4-17 team, he was finished and so was the Belle Plaine Tiger town team. He was 26 years old. There would be no amateur town team baseball in Belle Plaine for the 1973 and 1974 seasons.

It's hard to pinpoint with certainty what brought an end to the Golden Age of Baseball at the local, amateur level. Some blame the arrival of the Minnesota Twins and professional baseball; others point to television coverage of baseball. Some say that people all of a sudden had so much to do that wasn't available before. Still others say that slow-pitch softball took the glitter off of baseball by "taking" all the good ballplayers. But in an increasingly fast-paced world of hyperactivity and hypertension, baseball became increasingly boring. Real baseball is a slow, cerebral game that is much closer to chess than it is to pinball or any computer game. The occasional double off the wall or homerun over it, suspends the boredom momentarily as fans and one dugout of players explode in jubilation. With the new game of high-arced softball, homeruns were hit in bunches by all teams and great defensive plays were possible on every pitch.

"Yeah, he really hit that softball," Brad Harsh said of Jake. "But they wouldn't pitch to him! They knew him." It was considered prudent to walk Jake with a couple of runners on base or even loaded. Better to give the other team a run in that game than risk the strong likelihood of a grand slam and to lose whatever wind you had left in your own sails.

Despite the high production of runs, the seven-inning softball games were over in about an hour. Contrast that with a three-hour baseball game, not including batting practice, infield practice, pitching changes, field maintenance, the National Anthem, and the seventh-inning stretch, driving time, and parking at a MLB venue, television advertising, and you begin to see why people everywhere gravitated to playing a quicker game.

Things weren't any different on the music scene. Rhythm and beat and lyrics were all quickening: The Beatles, The Stones, and Motown stole the popular charts from the likes of Buddy Holly, Bobby Darin, and the Everly Brothers. "Jake wasn't much of a party guy," Manley Vinkemeier said. "He liked the music of the old-time wedding dances at places like Hardeggers," long a popular Saturday night dance pavilion near Cleveland, Minnesota.

Camaraderie and nearly universal community competition were as much at the heart of softball as a good battery is in baseball. Lively colored uniforms, even shorts, from companies such as Sand Knit peppered the smaller diamonds. Tournaments were played every weekend that were initially for large, ostentatious trophies, then later for cash. They were fun for players and fans. Ballpark food and beer were enjoyed in prodigious amounts. Teams won and lost, then won again, there was little time to savor a victory or lament a loss. Winning a 32-team tournament meant five games in a weekend. But those five games took just five hours, roughly an hour a game, to play. There was action, and things moved along at a brisk pace rarely, if ever, matched in baseball.

The games and the weekends never seemed to stop. Winter games of slow-pitch softball were even played on frozen area lakes and snow-packed fields. Then there was the continuing evolution of the technology in the metal bats. No longer did you hear the *crack* or *whack* of wood connecting solidly with balls. The metal made an almost irritating *ping* sound that was similar in increasing frequency at golf driving ranges and tee boxes. But the metal produced homeruns with an alarming rate. At first, in the early 1970s, a good-hitting team might have three or four homeruns in a game. By the mid-70s, they were up to 8 or 10 with regularity. A good, strong hitter like Jake Harsh might hit one or two a game in 1970 with a wood bat. By 1974, he was banging three, and in 1977, the year of his death he could easily have been hitting four or five homeruns a game. But everybody on every team was doing the same. Soon, homeruns would be called outs in an attempt to govern the absurdity, and not long after that the game died.

Harsh would continue to blast many homeruns in the game that increasingly had every batter hitting many homeruns. But Harsh hadn't needed the technology that had invaded both softball and baseball, as well as golf. It was a technology that gave ordinary players the intoxicating illusions of Ruthian greatness, something Jake had earned with a wood bat playing real baseball. Then it all went too far, with the increasing springboard technology of the newer and newer bats producing too many homeruns and just too many hits. Somehow, to try to manage the absurdity of the whole comic parody of it all, homeruns became called outs in softball, and the game of baseball, which had been "good ball" forever with typical scores of 3-1 on a single homerun in the bottom of the ninth, had become a carnival sideshow of scoring affairs that rivaled the scores of typical football games and the disparaged game of softball. The games looked like gold, but the glitter, like that produced in the alchemist's lab, wasn't real. It wasn't real softball or real baseball. Too many homeruns, like a market flooded with too much of anything, even gold, and the value of each unit of the thing, homerun or gold bullion, diminishes and the producing entity shuts down. The gold-mining operation comes to a halt, and baseball loses its appeal to both players and fans.

Jake Harsh was real. If there's one important lesson to take from such a short life as his, it's just this: Step up, by God. Step up to the plate and dig in. Take your rips, and drive the ball. He hit homeruns into the horizon with a wooden bat. "He used a bat without a knob," brother Brad said, which would likely have made it a "Don Hoak" Model of probably 35 or 36 inches in length, but light at maybe 33 ounces, because he could swing a lighter bat faster than a heavier bat. He meticulously customized the handle he gripped with white athletic tape. That gave him a better grip, and he may have been the first ballplayer around the local scene to wear gloves while batting, too. "He was a really good low-ball hitter," Vinkemeier said, so young pitchers coached to the standard MO of "Keep it low" to cleanup hitters got hit hard by Jake Harsh. Veteran pitchers, ostensibly more wizened, had just as much trouble with Jake at the plate. They lacked the pop needed to get their pitches by the big hitter. Their breaking pitches weren't sharp enough to beat him. He hammered them, too.

Jake stepped up, dug in, swung his bat and hit homeruns in either game, baseball or softball, the way Dick Darby from Prior Lake's Snell's Bar in the late 1960s and early 1970s swung a bat and hit homeruns in softball. Both Darby and Harsh swung from their heels and nearly came out of their shoes, on every pitch, yet never seemed to be off balance, out of rhythm, because they made really good contact with the ball. Their bats, their swings, their power, their results were real. They were pure, 24K gold hitters with great vision and hand-eye coordination. These pure hitters like Jake Harsh, who helped to extend the Golden Age locally, were untainted by the results achieved by the alchemists in the laboratory that gave so many the illusions of being a great hitter.

Jake Harsh had been instrumental in his high school basketball team's run to the finals of the District 13 Tournament at St. Peter's Gustavus Adolphus College in 1963. The Tigers fell to Le Center in the championship game by a point after a blowout victory in the semifinals. Jake had led his team in scoring in both the semifinal and final games. He was named Honorable Mention All-Conference for the yeoman's work he did underneath as a center and forward. Then he broke out that spring, banging five homeruns in a seven-game high school baseball season that earned him All Conference honors at first base.

In the summer after his junior year in high school, 1962, Harsh began his town team play with a pinch-hit homerun. It was a false beginning, as he faltered at the plate against good veteran River Valley League pitching. These guys weren't schoolboys.

Belle Plaine was 1-10 on the season. After a few starts in the wake of the homerun, he was benched and suffered through a series of undignified losses: 25-0 at Jordan; 21-1 to Shakopee; then, the ultimate indignity in a no-hitter by Shakopee's Friedges. No wonder Jake Harsh came to hate Jordan and Shakopee, then later, Prior Lake. "He despised them," Vinkemeier said.

Then, in 1963, the Tigers won a respectable 7 games against 8 losses, with young Jake Harsh cementing his position as the club's first baseman and cleanup-hitting leader. He batted *at least* a respectable .316 with five or more homeruns on the year.

Belle Plaine hadn't had a winning season in 10 years. Not since the heady days of Class A baseball in the old Minnesota River League, with the immortal Gene O'Brien behind the plate and in his usual cleanup spot in the batting order. In O'Brien's last year, 1954, he led the Tigers as player-manager to a 13-11 record. Just two years earlier, in 1952, they won 31 games against 9 losses, the biggest disappointment being the 5-4 loss to Cannon Falls in the Class A championship game of the Minnesota State Amateur Tournament.

Just as Jake Harsh would define the end of The Golden Age of Baseball on a local level in Belle Plaine, Gene O'Brien defined its beginnings in 1947 after a two-and-a-half-year "lifetime in hell's kitchen" during World War II. O'Brien was a marine in the Pacific theatre. He had signed professional baseball contracts before the war–one while a junior at St. Thomas College in St. Paul with Fargo-Moorhead in the Northern League, then another with the New York Yankees of the DiMaggio Era in 1942. He batted as high as .299 with the Piedmont Tars, a Yankee farm team, of the Piedmont League. But The Fiddler was tapping his toes, as the drums of war beat across the world. O'Brien enlisted in the Marine Corps and would be a part of the slugfest in the South Pacific and the marines' invasion of Okinawa on the way to victory over Japan.

O'Brien and other ballplayers, who fueled the baseball boom that occurred after World War II, benefitted from the baseball seasons of 30 to 40 games, a benefit of the novelty that lighted ballparks provided beginning in 1948 in Belle Plaine, 1950 in Jordan. But Gene O'Brien didn't begin playing for the Belle Plaine Tigers until 10 years *after* graduating from high school. Yet, facing the likes of Dick Siebert at Shakopee, who had played 11 seasons in the major leagues as a first baseman, Johnny Garbett and NBA Laker star Jim Pollard at Jordan, Gene O'Brien's career batting average of .375 on 328 hits in 874 at bats, according to *Scott County Baseball*, takes on an untarnished glow when all the mitigating factors are considered. Factors such as the pitching mounds being at least five inches higher then, which made a pitcher like Jim Pollard at Jordan look like he was seven feet tall and gave him the extra leverage on a fast ball that didn't need it. He had to hit him and he had to hit Garbett, too, with that nasty curveball of his that sunk into the earth with the torque the higher mound gave him. The only question about O'Brien's greatness is why it took 40 years to be recognized by the Minnesota Amateur Baseball Hall of Fame.

Indeed, Gene O'Brien, a left-handed hitting slugger like Jake Harsh after him, batted .420 in 1948, according to Tom Melchior's *Scott County Baseball*, with 10 doubles, 2 triples, and 9 homeruns in 143 at bats. He put up similar boxcar numbers in 1952, leading the team again to a second-place finish in the state tournament at the Class-A level. O'Brien's baseball prowess helped attract as many as 2,000 people to a baseball game at Tiger Stadium. At just under 6 feet tall and listed at 192 pounds, he was Marine Corps tough-as-nails, belying a common contemporary claim that "today's ballplayers are bigger and stronger." While, in general, the claim may be true, there are enough exceptions to warrant some comparisons, but with the mitigating factors considered as well. Most Big League catchers are close to what Gene O'Brien carried in the late 1940s and into the 1950s. His record with a wood bat during The Golden Age of the game begs to differ with another contemporary claim voiced too often about today's ballplayers being better. But then again, Gene O'Brien was a professional ballplayer.

No indeed. There's a reason, or several actually, why historians, enthusiasts, and analysts of the *complete history* of the game select the players they do for their lists of All-Time Best Ballplayers. Just the fact that the New York Yankees wanted and signed Gene O'Brien in an era of only 16 major league teams and when the Yankees had the likes of catcher Yogi Berra in their system speaks volumes about Gene O'Brien's ability as a baseball player. Just the fact that O'Brien enlisted in the Marine Corps, then turned down the opportunity to play ball on a stateside service team during the war years speaks volumes about his character. Had he been born just a few decades later, he could have been a catcher in the Major Leagues, maybe even with the Yankees. The numbers alone make the case.

Character and player quality are what defined baseball at all levels during its Golden Age. Gene O'Brien tops that list. But neither Frank nor I remember seeing him play, if we did see him, so he didn't make our short list.

Belle Plaine began the 1964 season with a 3-0 record. Jake Harsh, the 18-year-old slugging first baseman, started hot. He was 9 for 12, a torrid .750 pace, after the first three games. Shakopee continued to own the league, but cracks were beginning to show in the foundation of the powerful Indian dynasty. Two familiar names were missing from the lineup: Fred Kerber and John Freund. Kerber had won eight games again on the mound for Shakopee in 1963, but his batting average had slipped to just .256, according to *Scott County Baseball*. He hung up his spikes.

But Joe Schleper had moved to Shakopee, and he hit for the next five years like Kerber had hit, or better, for the previous 10 years. Belle Plaine was a half-game behind Shakopee when the two met in a showdown at Belle Plaine on Sunday, June

7. The hometown fans were jubilant when the Tigers, according to the June 14 *Northwest Umpires Review*, "took a 5-2 lead in the fourth inning." Despite 13 hits in the game, two by Jake Harsh, Belle Plaine failed to hold the lead and lost the game, 8-6, dropping to 3-2 while the Indians remained undefeated.

Harsh cooled off and the team split its next two games. Then, "Lefty" Schultz heated up, and on the last Sunday of June at Jordan's Fairgrounds Park, he threw a one-hitter and struck out 22. Nobody on the Jordan pitching staff could stop the Tiger attack, with Jake Harsh belting two doubles and a triple, good for four RBIs. He went five for seven in the next two games to get Belle Plaine back in the hunt. They were nipping at the heels of Shakopee once again. Then, Lefty Schultz tossed another magnificent game against Prior Lake–a three-hit shutout with 18 strikeouts– and Jake went three for three with two big RBIs in the 4-0 win. A week later, Belle Plaine beat Savage, 3-2, to tie Shakopee for the league lead with 7-3 records. Jake was two for four and took a blistering bat into the Bar-B-Q-Days weekend with his .525 batting average.

According to the July 23, 1964 *Belle Plaine Herald*, 4,000 Bar-B-Q beef sandwiches were sold in 95-degree heat on Sunday, July 19. Retiring Bar-B-Q Days queen, Judi Druki, placed the 1964 crown on Joan Zellmer. Jake Harsh kept up his royal performance by going two for four at the plate, with a homerun and three RBIs. But Le Sueur disappointed a large festive crowd, winning 7-5.

Belle Plaine recovered to win two games, with Jake going two for four in the win over Le Center, with another home run and another three RBIs before getting the collar in the win over New Prague. Jake was hitless in the last game of the season–a huge win over Shakopee, 8-3. The convincing win tied Belle Plaine for first place at 10-4 in the league dominated by Shakopee forever.

Flirting with .500 all season, Jake's batting average slipped in the last two hitless games to .448 on 26 hits in 58 at bats. Belle Plaine's playoff hopes were dashed by Jordan, 5-2 and 4-1, then Shakopee's resurgence routed the Jordan Brewers, 5-3 and 18-3. Shakopee reigned once again, representing the River Valley League and Region 6B in the state tournament.

A whisker separated the 1965 Belle Plaine Tigers from a 11-3 won-loss record. No less than five one-run losses in the league kept them from improving on their great season in 1964. They finished 8-6–good enough for third place in the league that, once again, saw Shakopee dominate with a 14-0 record. John Freund was back. But the Tigers and Jake finished strong, winning their last three games, including a 26-5 pasting of Prior Lake that saw Jake Harsh with a classic day at the plate: three for five, including two homeruns and six RBIs. He would finish the regular season, according to the August 5 *Herald*, at .366, second on the team to "Lefty" Schultz's .409. Jake's six homeruns paced the team in the power category.

Belle Plaine advanced in the playoffs to the best-of-three-game series against Le Sueur. He went three for four with a double and a triple in the rubber game, but Le Sueur prevailed, 12-6, and advanced. Belle Plaine had fallen short again.

It didn't get any better the next two years either. Lyndon Johnson needed a steady stream of recruits to man up in South Vietnam. Jake Harsh was drafted and opted for the navy, getting assigned to San Diego but, nonetheless, preparing for shipping overseas at any time. It never happened. Jake played softball in San Diego. Fast-pitch softball.

When he came home in 1968 and the spring sunshine began to turn the ballpark's winter grass to summer green, Jake Harsh didn't look like Jake Harsh in the batting cage. He had developed the softball hitter's short, choppy, contact swing–if it can be called that. Jake Harsh was no contact hitter. He got Jerry Miller, his old high school baseball coach to work with him in the cage, according to Vinkemeier. Anybody in town who didn't have a sore arm was recruited to throw balls to The Big Guy. It took a thousand or more batting practice pitches and swings, but Jake would have his groove back in time for Belle Plaine baseball. A headline in the sports page of the April 4, 1968, *Belle Plaine Herald* announced, "Veterans Returning–Town Team Baseball Meeting This Saturday." Vinkemeier, Melchior, and Harsh were home–thank God.

Rainouts kept the Tigers from opening the 1968 season for three weeks. Jake was hitless in the opening 12-1 rout of Le Center. Three significant observations accompanied the return of Jake Harsh to Belle Plaine baseball in 1968: First, the team returned to its winning ways with a 9-5 River Valley League record and a second-place finish. Second, the Shakopee Indian dynasty was over; they finished second-last with a 4-10 record. Third, Jake Harsh had a new team to hate in Prior Lake. The perennial patsies of the league had undergone a complete transformation and resurrected an old definition of "town ball" made popular and successful, we might add, at Le Center in 1950 and 1951 while doing so. Gone were Prior Lake's local baseball players. In their place a galaxy of former Lake Conference greats and Minnesota Gophers from Dick Siebert's NCAA powerhouse teams took command of the River Valley League. It didn't sit well with anybody in the league. They were good. Worse, they knew it and showed it.

Belle Plaine's fortunes faded in the second half of the season. Jake missed a few games because of the job he'd taken with the Chicago-Northwestern Railroad. He batted a respectable .348, which was off of what fans had expected. But worst of all was the new menace from the East–the Prior Lake Jays. They seemed to have an inexhaustible supply of quality baseball players, none of whom had ever set foot in the Green Heights Bar on the lake, or the B&D or Snell's downtown. They were good, and they were arrogant. While their pitching wasn't world class, and hitters like Jake Harsh could get to Prior Lake's pitching, they had one solid hitter after another in their lineup. They were good defensively, and there was no easy out to be had.

Jake's season ended a game early when a ball glanced off his bat and hit him in the face in the playoff loss to Le Sueur. But the following August 8, 1968, *Belle Plaine Herald* headline told the whole story:

"Tigers Drop Two Straight In Playoffs"

The lead just clarified things: "Belle Plaine's baseball season came to an abrupt halt as the Tigers dropped two straight 10-inning ballgames in the round-robin double-elimination playoffs."

Jake Harsh batted .413 in 1969, behind Bianchi of Shakopee at .488 and the more-feared Fred DeGregoire of Prior Lake at .475, according to the *Belle Plaine*

Herald in the case of Harsh, and the *Northwest Umpires Review*'s reckoning in regard to Bianchi and DeGregoire. Belle Plaine had another good year, too, repeating their second-place finish of the previous year with a record of 11-3, which trailed Prior Lake again with their 11-1 record. Prior Lake's last game of the season saw two veteran finesse pitchers, Gordie Nevers of Prior Lake and Mike Nevin of Shakopee lock up in a classic pitchers' duel, with Nevin coming out on top, 1-0, on the strength of a four-hitter. Prior Lake would see the same kind of heady, finesse pitching in a couple weeks in the state championship game against Arlington and Jim Stoll at Jordan. With the dawn of the noisy metal bat era still only on the horizon, an old baseball truism held up in both cases: "Good pitching always beats good hitting."

Belle Plaine and Jim Harsh had wanted badly to be at Jordan for the state tournament, but, again, with Harsh relegated to just pinch-hitting roles each game because of a back problem, the Tigers were eliminated by consecutive playoff losses to Shakopee and Le Sueur.

The 1970 season, as noted above, was the height of Jake Harsh and Belle Plaine baseball as the Golden Age of the game closed out gradually. The two forfeit wins from Prior Lake as a result of the league's punitive action gave them the league championship with a 13-3 record. The team batted a strong .272 on the year, 20 points behind Prior Lake, and Jake, of course, had his banner year of .500 with 15 homeruns. But they couldn't beat Prior Lake. Not many teams could, as the Jays went 23-4 on the season, another remarkable year for a remarkable collection of baseball players in Scott County. They had so many guys that could beat you with their bat: Gary Reierson, Brian Love, John Dill, Fred DeGregoire, Bob Kelly, and others.

Gordy Nevers was a heady pitcher and no wonder: His resume included five years of professional ball, as high as AAA. Dill and DeGregoire provided more than respectable turns pitching, and others of the same pedigree showed up more sporadically, including a big left-handed pitcher, according to Manager Gerry Meyer, that "they flew in from somewhere and that nobody had heard of–just for one game with us and to stop Jake." It was too much. They had gotten greedy and gone to the well too often. They belonged in Class A, a class above Belle Plaine, Jordan, and even Shakopee the last few years.

Although an impossibility in reality, the imagination likes to play with comparisons of players and ball clubs from different eras. A mythical game, or series of games, between the best of the Shakopee Indian teams of the late 1950s to mid-60s and the Prior Lake Jays of 1968 to 1976 offers some interesting fodder for speculation. Nonetheless, the league folded in order to rid itself of the talent-bloated, over-indulgent Prior Lake Jays.

Jake Harsh married Peggy in October that fall and began looking for a new job. He liked working as his father and his brother had worked with the railroad, but he didn't like being away from Peggy and home. They lived in an apartment close to his father's house before building a new home close by, too, in 1976, according to Brad, who said Jake liked to call him up to come over and play cribbage. "We'd play for hours," Brad said.

"They'd taken out mortgage insurance," Carman Meyer, Peggy's sister said. "I don't think they made more than 10 or 11 payments. It's almost as if . . ." her voice trailed off, leaving you finish the thought yourself: "It's almost as if somebody had a premonition."

Jake Harsh was hired as an apprentice lineman with the Minnesota Valley Electric Cooperative out of Jordan the winter of 1971. He looked forward to the baseball season, as always. It would come soon enough but not until after some major changes in the composition of the league. Prior Lake, Savage, Shakopee, and New Prague were gone for a variety of reasons. Belle Plaine, Jordan, Le Sueur, Montgomery, Le Center, and St. Peter were in the league for an equal variety of reasons.

Belle Plaine and Harsh opened the 1971 season with a bang. They beat St. Peter, 15-8, on Sunday, May 30, according to the June 3 *Herald*, with Jake crushing two homeruns in a perfect day at the plate. The team matched losses with wins until the end of the month, when they shut out Montgomery, 3-0, then beat Jordan, 8-7, on Jake's slugging. He had three hits, including a triple and homerun. His batting average stood at a hefty .393 about half way through the season.

He hit another homerun the next week in the win over Le Center. Then, without Jake, Belle Plaine dropped a pair of games and their record stood at 7-5. The Tiger Story was repeating itself: As goes Jake, so go the Belle Plaine Tigers. He missed a couple more games, with the *Herald* referring to a "recuperating" period, and the team won a couple more and lost a couple more. But he was back in the lineup and hit a homerun in the 5-4 win over St. Peter to keep playoff hopes alive before bowing to Jordan with their second loss, despite another Harsh homerun.

Belle Plaine finished above .500 at 11-8, according to the *Scott County Baseball*, and Jake finished at .326, according to the August 5 *Herald*. But there was no celebration with either statistic. No feel-good moment. Worse yet, storm clouds were brewing, and the roof of the house was getting weak.

Another early fall was followed by another long winter in Belle Plaine. But hope springs eternal, and the baseball diamonds of Minnesota turn green every year with the showers of April and the sunshine of May. Those parts of the seasonal play came right on cue in 1972. But the rest of the drama failed. The power-hitting, run-scoring machine that had been a trademark of Belle Plaine baseball either ran out of gas or lost its main cog. Pat Miller summarized the season in his *Belle Plaine Herald* column, "Miller's Highlife":

> It has been a disappointing year for all, the players, the fans, and everyone connected with the team. The club had early visions of a decent season after the first four games . . . Everything collapsed at the same time and the final games were played without meaning . . . A team cannot win without runs. A team cannot score runs without hits. This year Belle Plaine lacked this quality.

He could have just printed Jake Harsh's batting average: .173. He was 26 years old. He was done with baseball. "He had the bad back," Brad Harsh said, "and everybody wanted to play softball anyway." But there was more going on, both locally and nationally, baseball signaling one and one signaling the other.

Hardegger's Dance Hall burned down in 1972, and President Nixon had taken the U.S. dollar off the gold standard a year earlier. From now on, for better or worse, the buck, too, would float freely against a group of other currencies, backed only by "the good faith and credit" of country. After intensive debate by professionals throughout 1972, homosexuality would be removed from the *DSM IV*–the psychiatric profession's Diagnostic and Statistical Manual of mental disorders, and Roe v. Wade was working its way through the U.S. courts, on its way to the landmark decision in early 1973 that made abortion on demand the law of the land. Then, too, the Watergate burglary would occur in 1972, further rendering the country apart as two investigative reporters with *The Washington Post* unraveled the clandestine activities of a paranoid White House. Baseball had always thrived during times of peace and social tranquility. Now, it was taking hits from all directions and in all levels of play. Or was it the other way around? Was it because baseball had lost its sense of direction, its grip on True North, that these other things were occurring?

"We asked Jake to play for Krantz's Bar," Gerry Meyer said, of his team in the city's slow-pitch softball league, where it was experiencing burgeoning popularity, as it was all over, because it allowed everybody to play, it was fast, and it was fun. "But he wanted to play with Huber's," Meyer said, of the local grocery store, to keep from loading up one team and making the league too unbalanced. "He thought it would be better all-around if he just stayed with Huber's."

"I took the call that day," Carman Meyer said, from the office of the co-op where Jake worked. Carman said that they told her Jake had been hurt and was at St. Francis Hospital in Shakopee. They asked me to contact my sister. So she said that she drove over to their house and just got out of the car when Peggy came running out of the house toward her.

"Before I said a word, she said to me, 'It's Jim, isn't it? He's hurt or he's dead.' She knew," Peggy said. "She knew."

Carman said she told her sister that Jake was hurt, and they headed for the Shakopee hospital, 17 miles away. "She told me that Jake was sick that morning and wasn't going to go to work. But it was payday. He decided to go in and work the day and pick up his paycheck. Peggy was going to mow the lawn, a chore that Jake usually handled."

"I think he knew something was going to happen," Brad said, "because he told me that he'd just shown Peggy where to look for things in his files in case anything happened to him."

Jim and Peggy Harsh were two months shy of their eight-year wedding anniversary. They'd built a new house and moved in less than a year earlier.

Jake's parents were devastated, according to Carman. "Russell–Jake's Dad– never recovered," she said.

"I don't think I could have either," Gerry said.

"They told us when we got to the hospital," according to Carman, "that he was dead on arrival, and that he had probably died instantly."

"We never heard the details, and Russell was beside himself wanting to know what had happened. But they wouldn't let him talk to the crew he was working with," Carman said.

"I talked to some guys from the co-op back then," Brad Harsh said. "Hey, look– it was just his time, and the Lord was bringing him home."

"Jake was a private person," Vinkemeier had said. "He liked to work, and he loved playing ball."

He really loved the right side of "Tiger Park," with a sign at the line that's probably stretched to make the 300 feet shown, to straight away center at 430 feet. But he owned the right centerfield alley with his swing. The power alley. It's marked at 350 feet and from the street side of that fence at the 350 sign, we put a Bushnell Rangefinder up to view the distances to the front doors of the last two houses, house numbers 244 and 240, across S. Eagle St. If the 350 sign at right center is accurate, then the distance to the front door of the last house, No. 244, is 461 feet from home plate, No. 240 is 440 feet. The walls and the windows of these and the other houses along S. Eagle St. have taken a pounding over the years from left-handed hitters and right-handed hitters who could handle a baseball bat the way Willie Mosconi and Minnesota Fats handled a pool cue. Gene O'Brien might have built this house, but Jake Harsh re-roofed it. He and Vinkemeier lettered as freshman on the high school varsity baseball team, when Jake started his assault of windows and siding, and porches and roofs across Eagle Street.

There was a porch on that last house in 1970 or the house the current No. 244 replaced at some time in the intervening years. We saw Jake Harsh crush a fastball in his wheelhouse that ended up in the porch, rattling around like a pinball before rolling off the edge and into a bed of flowers.

"Hell, he hit balls over those houses," Brad said in appreciation of his big brother. Whether he did or not, we don't know. But if he hit balls over, or on a line between, the last two houses along S. Eagle St., then they went 500 feet or more and Jake Harsh's homerun prowess is of the same rarified air as Babe Ruth and Jimmy Foxx, Mickey Mantle and Ted Williams. Locally, it's puts him in the same league as the likes of Gene O'Brien, Jim Pollard, Gordy Gelhaye, John Freund, and Frank Hilgers.

They all hit the long ball, and they were all authentic American heroes. Perhaps none more so than Jake Harsh. Dave Beckius knows this more than anyone. While Jake died, Dave lived to be known by his five children as father. Seven kids today call him "grampa." He says that he has kept Jake Harsh in his prayers every night since that day in August of 1977. "He saved my life," Dave Beckius said. "That juice was meant for me."

"Nobody ever hit a ball like my brother, Jim," Brad Harsh said. "He was my hero."

Mark Hess

Don't call us (ballplayers) heroes. Firemen are heroes.
— Sparky Anderson, MLB Manager

Mark Hess is a captain on the Minneapolis Fire Department, making this top rank in 10 years. He's been a fireman since 1991, so he has 25 years of service to the public in 2016, answering calls as a first responder. Like all firemen, he responds to 911 calls and people he doesn't know who are victims of shootings, stabbings, heroin overdoses, heart attacks, strokes, falls and other accidents, and fires. He hasn't cut an umbilical cord yet, but he said that he has assisted medics on the scene with the delivery of babies. He's performed CPR and used a defibrillator on people in big trouble. He gets critical help to people in crisis. He risks his health and safety, sometimes his life, to save the lives of others.

At Station 4 in North Minneapolis, where he was assigned for 10 years, Hess said, "We would have four runs on a slow day, as many as 12 on a busy day." He doesn't always like what he sees when called to respond with help. He sees the consequences of poor lifestyle choices, and he sees the results of single-parent homes. He sees neglect and abuse of self and others at too many sites to which he is called. But he cares, and he likes the team aspect of his work as a fireman. Everybody knows his and her job. It's not unlike a ball club in that sense, and Mark Hess brings the same dedication and quickness of mind and body–the athletic hand-eye coordination and the agile, supple strength of a shortstop who can make the backhanded play deep in the hole behind the third baseman, plant the right foot, and nail the runner by a heartbeat at first with the hardest throw there is in the game of baseball.

As natural of an athlete as he has been, Hess knows the value of practice and likes it. That's how the little things get done well when they really matter–when they mean a run and a ballgame, or when a life is on the line. The classic double play executed by shortstops and second basemen is high drama in a hurry. The precision required pulling it off repeatedly, consistently, and especially when the hitting team is beginning to build some scoring momentum in the late innings of a ballgame rivals that of a Russian ballet. It doesn't matter whether the action is second-to-short-to first, or short-to-second-to first. Not to Mark Hess. He knew his job and did it well at every level in which he competed.

"The double play was my home run," Mark said from the lawn chairs in his backyard, which overlooks a bay on the north end of Prior Lake. He talked about how the double play picks up your team and just sucks the wind out of the other team–just as the homerun buoys the spirits of your team and can break the back of the other team. A crisp double play inspires your team as it shuts down the other team immediately. It also plants that seed of doubt in their minds that they're not going to get it done. Not today. We own this day and this game. The double play saves pitchers. Conversely, booting a double-play groundball destroys your pitcher and will jeopardize your position in the lineup. Lots of things can go wrong on the classic double play, because the ball must be caught three times and thrown twice. Plus, runners have been programmed to "break up two" at second base, and, going back to Ty Cobb 100 years ago, rule and tradition say they own the base path. The collision at second base must be avoided, if the throw from either the shortstop or the second baseman is to have enough on it to reach first base ahead of the runner who hit the ball. Infielders learn how to jump and pivot out of harm's way while making the first putout and getting off the throw to first base.

Mark Hess worked on all the little things from the time he was old enough to play ball. He said he would find a wall and, standing maybe 20 feet or so from it, would throw to a spot on the wall that would cause the ball to carom off to one side or the other of where he was positioned. Crouched low to the ground, he would make the crossover step quickly, first to his right, and he would make the backhand catch. Then he would square up quickly and throw back to the spot on the wall, forcing himself to quickly crossover to his left, fielding the ball, then pivoting and throwing to the spot again. Back and forth . . . back and forth. He gave himself a serious workout when he couldn't find another kid around with whom to play catch or a game of wiffle ball.

But his statement–"The double play was my homerun"–speaks volumes about Mark Hess and why he's a throwback to the Golden Age of Baseball and why he's on our list. Players, along with fan interest in the game, defined what was true gold and what was fool's gold, glittering like the real thing but lacking in the inherent and sustaining value. Players like Brooks Robinson at the Major League level. One televised segment of Brooks Robinson highlights sold Mark on the legendary Baltimore Oriole third baseman and the still-critical importance of defense in a game that had gone another direction beginning with the end of the Dead Ball Era and the arrival of one George Herman Ruth as an everyday right fielder. He couldn't have picked a better ballplayer to try to emulate, because Brooks Robinson won 16 consecutive Gold Gloves. It's not that he was a poor hitter either. It's just that his sterling glove work so overshadowed his hitting that nobody talked about it.

Mark Hess is a throwback to a bygone era when pitching and defense defined America's pastime and won ballgames and titles. It's why he could play for any team at any level at any time in the history of the game. In that sense, Hess extends a remnant of the Golden Age far beyond its recognized period, and with his play in the Minnesota River Valley, from 2001 through 2007 at the end of his playing days, offered the hope of a return of the game to its Golden Age.

We saw his steady play and a few flashes of brilliance in his junior year with the University of Minnesota Gophers in 1985 when they won the Big Ten tournament but got beat in the NCAA regionals. Hess made the Gopher team and the spring trip squad as a freshman already, but he said he got in Coach John Anderson's doghouse for missing a curfew by 30 minutes. Mark's freshman year was just the second year of Anderson's long tenure at Minnesota, after replacing George Thomas, who had replaced the icon, Dick Siebert. So Anderson no doubt felt a need to make sure his players knew he meant business. Hess played just a few innings at third base that first year, getting six hits in 12 at bats. He didn't break into the starting lineup until his sophomore year. He batted nearly .300 that year and over .300 each of the next two years, earning All-Big Ten honors and All-Tournament at shortstop his senior year. With Mark starting at shortstop 1984-'86, the Gophers won 104 games against just 62 losses. They led the Big Ten's West Division in 1984 with a record of 11-5 and again in 1986 on the strength of a 10-5 record. In 1985, the Gophers finished second in the West Division at 9-7, but they won the Big Ten's coveted post-season tournament, beating Michigan and Ohio State to advance to the NCAA's regional tournament.

We saw Mark Hess again in the 1990s with Hamel and its Class-B amateur "town team" club that was loaded with ex-Gophers. Then, we were treated to seven of his last eight years of organized baseball play at Jordan. We saw Mark Hess still making all the plays at shortstop and second base at 40 years of age, doing all the little things that go unnoticed by most onlookers but which help to win ball games. Frank agreed that maybe we saw both Tex Erickson and Dick Nolden in him, and that may be why we liked him immediately. "He was a joy to watch," former Jordan High School basketball coach and athletic director Ken Hanson said of Mark Hess. Hanson worked the public address system, announcing Brewer games for many years. He saw a lot of Hess and just couldn't help being impressed.

We saw him slam a two-on, two-out triple to the right center-field wall in the 2004 Class-B State Tournament opening game win against Bemidji at Jordan, a championship won by the host team and highlighted by Trent Bohnsack's MVP award. A young Mark Hess wasn't supposed to have the leg speed for triples in a small yard, much less so on 40-year-old legs. But tournament kudos deservedly went to Manager Charlie Larca, who turned Bohnsack, a starting pitcher, into a "killer closer" for the tournament. In retrospect, the controversial manager's strategy was pure genius, and Bohnsack earned his MVP award by pitching in all five games of the tournament, winning two and gaining three saves–all in relief. He pitched 15-2/3 innings, allowed a measly six hits and no runs while striking out 17.

Mark Hess, who batted .327 for the season at age 41 in 2004 while playing a solid second base and filling in at shortstop now and then, liked playing for the late Charlie Larca at Jordan, although he admitted disliking the New York transplant while playing at Hamel. He said he liked Charlie because he was different and was always thinking ahead of the immediate. "He always had a plan," Hess said, "and it didn't matter who you were."

But baseball at Jordan in the Minnesota River Valley was the end of a long ball-playing road for Mark Hess. He was a gift to local baseball people and a young team that had undergone a transition with the end of the Metal Bat Era and the retirement of the team's nucleus of stars: Jon and Ron Beckman; Dave Hentges; Jerry Chapman; and others. They were noisy bangers with the metal bats and so was Paul Buss, who never retired. Mark Hess, on the other hand, was a ballplayer forged in the mold reserved for old gold.

"Technically, he's the best infielder I've ever coached," Assistant Gopher Baseball Coach Rob Fornasiere was overheard saying of Mark Hess while watching Jordan's T.J. Oakes hurl a perfect game for his American Legion team at Jordan's "Mini-Met in July of 2009–nearly 25 years later and 250 Gopher infielders or more, plus another cohort at Normandale Junior College where Fornasiere coached before moving up in the college baseball coaching ranks. "Fundamentally, he's as good as anyone in the country," Head Coach John Anderson said of Mark Hess in a June 20, 1986, feature article by Greg Matson in the *Minneapolis Star Tribune*.

As for T.J. Oakes, who grabbed our attention while we listened to the crowd of coaching chatter and the blowing of Mark Hess's horn, he beat Sibley East, 5-0, in his perfect game with 12 strikeouts. He went on to the University of Minnesota, where his father was the pitching coach and he pitched well for three years. He was drafted in the 41st round of the MLB June Draft of 2011, according to Jordan's Steve Beckman, second baseman for the 2014 Jordan Brewers and a former infielder at Luther College, a Division III school in Iowa. In 2012 the Colorado Rockies drafted young Oakes in the 11th round, and he signed. He was 1-2 on the mound in 49 innings of work for the Tri-City Dust Devils in the Northwest League, according to online sources. In 2013, at Class-A Asheville, T.J. Oakes was 9-8 with an ERA of 4.27 in 25 games and 139 innings.

Hess said then that his dream was to play professional baseball. "He deserves to be playing someplace," Anderson was quoted as saying in the 1986 Matson article. "Some of the scouts didn't like his pure running speed," Anderson continued, "but you can't measure his first step, his ability to play the ball and his quick release. All of them are excellent."

Mark Hess, ". . . one of the best fielding shortstops in Gopher history," wrote Greg Matson, and who batted .620 in the 1986 Big Ten Tournament on top of a solid .315 average for the year, never got the chance. None of this reckons with the Dance of Life and The Fiddler's tune. Fires would one day need to be put out. Hearts beating in a whacked-out rhythm would need to be tamed. Breathing would need to be restored in human beings on the verge of crossing over. Lives would need to be saved. Minneapolis would need the real hero to get it done. They needed a fireman, not a slick-fielding shortstop.

"'They (scouts) always seemed to have an interest in me,' Hess said," in Matson's article. "'Nothing ever happened. I'm kind of bummed out. I put in four years of hard work and I had a pretty good year. Now I see players I played against getting drafted, knowing I can play better than some of them.'"

But baseball minds and the powers that be can be strange, fickle. The critical rap on Hess, according to Tony Wakaruk, area scout for the Kansas City Royals in a May 19, 1986, article in the *Minnesota Daily*, were foot speed and an average arm. "He's quick," Wakaruk said (of Hess in the article). "If he goes to the pros, he would have to play second, maybe third. He doesn't have a shortstop's arm. His bat is good, too."

Despite his admitted weakness of power hitting, Hess hit two homeruns and a double in the 1986 Big Ten tournament, "tying a Big Ten tournament record with 10 hits." His strengths were his quickness, his dedication, and his work ethic. Mark loved baseball. If his arm was only average in strength after the injury his sophomore year, it was the arm of every great shortstop for its precision. He wore a mark on the concrete wall that he used to do his fielding drills. The mark became "the chest" for every throw he ever made. He hit the chest of his second baseman, Dan VanDehey, at the University of Minnesota and Hamel on short putouts, often from awkward positions to start double plays. He hit the chest of first baseman Alex Bauer at the U of M and at Hamel, too, making the long throws to first, and to catchers on relays home.

Mark Hess's arm was honed as a high school quarterback at St. Anthony Village on the northeast side of Minneapolis. Indeed, his 62.1 percent pass completion rate, along with 16 TD passes, and over 1,300 yards were all record-setting marks at St. Anthony Village High in 1982. He was named All-Conference his senior year in the tough Tri-Metro Conference in football, as well as in hockey and baseball.

Hess took up golf late, playing maybe twice a year until age 27, and then taking it up seriously at 28. He worked at it with the same dedication he'd given the other summer game, eventually playing to a one-handicap at The Wilds in Prior Lake and winning the club championship in 2008.

Hess's golf game, like his shortstop play in baseball, is virtually free of mistakes and so fundamentally sound you've got to cheat to beat him in a match. And he brings to golf what every hockey player brings to golf: a swing with everything in it at the moment of truth–the 10 to 20 degrees both before and after impact with the ball. Hands and forearms quickened with sinew and strength from slap shots in the hockey rink and weight work in the gym. The result is solid, consistent impact and shots that travel low, long, and on line.

Hockey, golf, and football notwithstanding, Mark Hess has baseball in his blood and his DNA. His dad, Wally Hess, who died in the hospital in 2002 at age 62, was named "Most Athletic" in his high school class of 1958 at Columbia Heights, which played then in a tough Suburban Conference. In fact, like his son Mark, the elder Hess was a multi-sport star throughout high school. He was a pitcher with several no-hitters and other outstanding gems from the mound in high school, American Legion, and amateur baseball. When he wasn't pitching, he was in the lineup, usually at third base. Wally Hess hit well, with several homeruns noted in family scrapbook newspaper clippings.

He was also a member of the 1963 Class-A State Championship Minneapolis A&B Sporting Goods team that beat unbeaten Bloomington and former five-year professional and Southern Minny ace, Gordy Nevers, 5-2, then beat them again for the championship, 7-2. Included in the team picture, but out of uniform and probably a draft choice, was one Fred Degregoire. Just two years out of high school at Minneapolis Roosevelt, Degregoire would show up two years later in 1965 on the roster of the University of Minnesota Gophers, a year after the third of three Dick Siebert NCAA national championships. Then, in 1968, Degregoire, as well as Gordy Nevers, would join Herb Isakson's Bloomington-retrofitted version of the Prior Lake Jays in the River Valley League where he chased batting titles with solid hitting while the Jays won handily.

The year, 1963, also brought the Wally Hess household in St. Anthony Village its first of five athletic sons. Wally Hess had to have been beaming on the morning of December 5, 1963, at St. Luke's Hospital in St. Paul, Minnesota, with the birth of his first child, a 7 lb. 2-1/2 oz. baby boy, then again with every cigar he proudly passed out over the next couple of weeks.

Four more sons later and the ball gaming began in earnest. The boys played hard in the house; they played hard in the front yard; they played hard in the street; and they played hard in the nearby city parks. They played baseball in the summer, football in the fall, and hockey in the winter. The bedroom shared by Mark and two of his brothers could readily turn into a "steel-cage battle royal"–even without the promotional help of Vince McMahan and the WWF.

Five boys were a load in the 1970s in St. Anthony Village, and the backyard pickup games that turned into organized ball-playing were welcome in the Hess home. Hit balls were beginning to leave the yard with regularity, and errant throws were taking out a window now and then.

Mark Hess learned "the hammerlock" and "the sleeper hold" wrestling in the brotherly bedroom brawls, and he tried amateur wrestling as well as hockey until he was forced to choose one or the other in junior high. The choice was easy. In fact, Mark stayed with a good hockey program through his senior year in high school when he was the second-leading scorer on his team, with 25 points in 12 games on 14 goals and 11 assists. In fact, Hess is still playing hockey at over 50 years of age with the informal groups of pickup players who can't give it up. "It's fun," Hess said, who admitted to usually being one of the oldest guys on the ice. "I need to skate a couple times a week," he said.

He starred in football, too, having whetted his appetite for the gridiron by watching University of Minnesota Gopher practices. The university campus was just a 15-minute bike ride for Mark and his buddies.

Mark's success in organized athletics began as early as the St. Anthony House League A Squirts hockey championship in District 10. Two good junior high football seasons, with Mark at halfback, promised St. Anthony Village High School future success. But at age 15 Mark helped to lead his Roseville Mickey Mantle League team to a state championship against Crystal in 1978. Here's Pat Fugina with his lead in the *St. Anthony Village Bulletin*:

> Eric Borg and Mark Hess hit back-to-back, two-run doubles in the eighth inning Sunday to lift the Roseville Mickey Mantle baseball team to a 5-1 win over Crystal to capture the state championship at Osseo.

Crystal had won the regular season title and had beaten Hess and his Roseville team four times that year and twice the year before in state championship finals. Fugina continues:

> But it was the play of second baseman Hess, who returned to action only recently after being sidelined by a neck injury that kept Roseville in the game in earlier innings. In the third, with Crystal runners on first and second and nobody out, Hess dove to his left to spear a line drive 'about two inches off the ground,' according to (Roseville Manager Maynard) Kelsey, got up to step on second and force one runner, and threw to first to force the other runner and complete a triple play that cut short Crystal's rally.

Fugina cites a couple of other defensive gems by the young infielder and that he went 7 for 16 at the plate in the tournament for a .438 average. The state championship sent Mark's team to the Mickey Mantle Division regional tournament at Independence, Missouri. "It was a big deal," Hess recalled. They drew an Illinois team, "but we got homered by the umpire," according to Hess, "and we got beat in the first game."

Hess said he was called upon to lay down a double-suicide squeeze bunt in the bottom of the seventh inning, trailing by a run. "I got it down the third-base line just right," Hess remembered. The third baseman fielded the ball and made the throw to first. The runner on third scored easily, but with the throw to first, the runner on second headed home, too. A double squeeze, with both runs scoring for the win. "The ump called me out for stepping on the plate," he said. "I didn't step on the plate," he vowed.

Mark and classmate Eric Borg made the St. Anthony Village baseball team as freshmen in 1979–first freshmen in the history of the school to do so. Mark cruised through high school with B's and C's in the classroom and with honors and records in football, hockey, and baseball. He batted .392 his senior year and even made the Metro All-Stars team that lost to the Out-state team, 6-5, at St. Cloud's Municipal Stadium. According to Dave Anderson in the Saturday, June 26, 1982 *Daily Times*, Hess started at shortstop, while his future Gopher teammate and a future San Francisco Giant, Bryan Hickerson of Bemidji, pitched three good innings for the Out-state team, getting the win.

Mark was a "walk-on" at the University of Minnesota, meaning that despite his significant baseball and all-around athletic skills, he got no scholarship. Coach John Anderson operated with just nine scholarships, four under the conference limit. Living just a few miles from campus, Mark would cut costs by living at home and commuting to school. His timing couldn't have been much better. Four-year starting Gopher shortstop Bill Piwnica was a senior Mark's freshman year in the spring of 1983. Piwnica made all-conference, and Hess made the team, with the senior working with Mark during winter practice and throughout the season.

The Big Ten is NCAA Division I baseball, and in the 1980s, the peak of the Metal Bat Era, which meant extra-hot balls coming off the high-tech bats, shortstops earned their keep with quickness, sure handedness, and throwing accuracy. A July 18, 1983, *Minnesota Daily* feature by Donald Coulter was headlined: "New kid Gopher shortstop Mark Hess doubles for Piwnica in style and stature."

Coulter was covering the Gopher summer league baseball team for the university's student newspaper, his story line caught in the headline. Gopher freshmen and sophomores were playing to impress Minnesota assistant coach Herb Isakson. Hess did get Isakson's eye, as Coulter relates:

> The kid at shortstop not only caught Isakson's attention, but everyone else's as well. In the first inning he made a diving snag of a grounder that seemed destined for left field. His throw from deep in the shortstop hole retired the batter at first base by half a step.
>
> The shortstop then came to bat for the first time in the third inning, and with a remarkably familiar compact swing, laced an opposite–field single for the Gophers' first of the evening.

"... In style and in stature, the shortstop was the spitting image of Bill Piwnica, the recently graduate Gopher who was an all-Big Ten shortstop as a senior in 1983." Piwnica liked Hess, too, as he was quoted by Coulter in the article as saying of Mark, 'It makes me proud,' Piwnica said of his protégé, Hess. 'He's a real good glove man and he has a strong arm.'

Herb Isakson was impressed with his new shortstop, too, and he knew shortstops well. In addition to Gopher Piwnica, Isakson coached Bobby Kelly at Bloomington High School in the 1960s and with the Prior Lake Jays in the River Valley League in the late 60s and early 70s, and Paul Molitor, too. "'Mark Hess has impressed me the most of the new guys on the summer team,' Isakson said. 'He is an excellent defensive player, with a tremendous arm. Mark just needs to work on his hitting over the summer and during practice next winter. Billy (Piwnica) is going to be a tough guy for us to replace. We're really going to miss him. But Hess will probably be our shortstop next year.'"

Mark did work on his hitting that summer, "... averaging six games a week" by playing for both the Gopher team and his Columbia Heights neighborhood town ball team. The next spring, 1984, sophomore Mark Hess was the starting shortstop for the University of Minnesota. He helped the Gophers win the Western Division championship of the Big Ten before bowing out to Michigan and Northwestern in the post-season conference tournament.

Staff writer Lisa Dillman in the *Minneapolis Star Tribune* captured the Gopher surge and Mark Hess's contribution in an early Big Ten game after the team's return from Texas–"VanDehey, Hess may be Gophers' winning combo." Dillman quoted Gopher Coach John Anderson:

> 'I would say the two of them together make the best double play combination in the conference,' Anderson said. 'They have all the skills you look for in middle infielders.'
>
> 'From what I've seen, they're as good as anybody in the country.'

The *Star Tribune* covered the Gophers' early win over Michigan State, 8-7, in the Big Ten tournament at Siebert Field. Hess was two for three with a big RBI double in the win, and "he wasn't supposed to be one of the tournament's top shortstops. Barry Larkin, Michigan's All-American, and Cordell Ross, the Big Ten's leading hitter from Michigan State, had served to steal some of the spotlight from Minnesota's Hess."

> But Hess was the most impressive in the field. In Friday's game, Hess dived to his left for a grounder behind second base and narrowly threw the runner out at first. An inning or so later, he backhanded a ball in the hole to his right and hurled the ball with that overhanded style of his– much as a quarterback would toss a football, from behind his ear–all in one motion, to throw the batter out.

Bill Wagner in a *St. Anthony Village Bulletin* feature article on Hess at the end of his sophomore year as the Gopher shortstop said Mark's high school coach, Gary Palm, watched with pride as his former star competed against the Michigan Wolverines at Siebert Field on the campus of the University of Minnesota. Wagner wrote of Hess that he was "a smooth fielder with the grace of Mark Belanger when he goes after a ground ball." And Palm noted that Mark "has no weakness as a defensive player. 'He ranges out,' said Palm. 'If he can reach the ball, he'll make the play.'"

The local writer provided high praise and an interesting comparison. Mark Belanger had a lifetime fielding average of .964 over 18 seasons, 17 of which were with the Baltimore Orioles. He won eight Gold Glove awards during that span and helped lead the Orioles to four World Series while helping, along with the likes of Brooks Robinson at third base, to make 20-game winners out of Jim Palmer, Mike Cuellar, Dave McNally, Pat Dobson, and Mike Flanagan. While Belanger is listed online at 6-1 and 170 pounds, Mark Hess says he played during his peak years at 6-0 and 175 pounds.

The two early losses in the 1984 Big Ten tournament hurt. But Mark worked on his weaknesses. In addition to the six games a week he averaged playing that summer, he lifted weights and took extra batting practice whenever he could. He vowed that he would get stronger–at the plate with a bat that he knew he could improve, and at short with his arm that he'd hurt at the beginning of his sophomore season and wasn't so sure had healed completely.

Mark's junior year, 1985, was a good one. He batted over .300 and his fielding average was .956–outstanding in any league at any level for the most demanding defensive position on a team, especially in the NCAA Division I level during the hot Metal Bat Era. Balls simply came at you faster, hot off the bat and picking up speed after first bounces, often hugging the ground after a torrid skip and suddenly taking that proverbial bad hop that bounces off the heal of your glove, or worse, your shoulder or mouth. The Gophers were 33-23 on the year, just 9-7 in the Big Ten, but still good enough for second place in the division and a berth in the tournament.

They upset a highly ranked Michigan Wolverine team, No. 3 in the nation and sporting a 51-7 won-loss record and a .373 team batting average. In a special feature to the *Minneapolis Star Tribune*, Joel Rippel reported: "The loss not only snapped Michigan's 24-game winning streak but was the first defeat the Wolverines have suffered at Fisher Stadium in the three years they have been the hosts of the playoffs."

Mark had three hits in five at bats, but more importantly, he started the rally in the top of the ninth with the Gophers trailing 10-9. He beat out an infield single and scored the tying run.

The Gophers then beat Ohio State, 8-5 and 5-3, to win the Big Ten championship and advance to the NCAA regionals. They were on a roll after nearly failing to make the post-season tournament. They smelled College World Series, but they ran into the Oklahoma State Cowboys and Pete Incaviglia, who set numerous hitting records that year. The Cowboys beat the Gophers, 6-4, Hess recalled. "He hit a shot that went by me so fast I'll never forget it. It just kept going and bounced over the fence for a ground-rule double." We clipped the following report on Incaviglia from the OK State Cowboys Hall of Fame website:

> Incaviglia is the most recognized power hitter in Oklahoma State and NCAA baseball history. He had the most impressive offensive year in NCAA history as a junior in 1985 in which he set NCAA single-season

records for home runs (48), RBIs (143), total bases (285) and slugging percentage (1.140). He set the NCAA career records for home runs (100) and slugging percentage (.915) and holds the Big Eight career records for RBIs (324) and total bases (635). . . .

On Jan. 14, 1999, Incaviglia was named college baseball's Player of the Century by Baseball America.

In 1985, Pete Incaviglia owned NCAA baseball. "You should have seen him take batting practice," Mark Hess said. "He hit one shot after another, clearing the left-center-field fence by a mile."

"He made sure everybody knew who he was," Hess said. "You couldn't miss him. He was like King-Kong out there."

Indeed, Incaviglia was inducted into the College Baseball Hall of Fame in 2007 after joining the Oklahoma State Cowboys Hall of Fame in 1992.

Oklahoma State took the wind out of the Gopher sails. Then, Oral Roberts University, ranked number 12 in the nation with 58 wins after defeating the Gophers, took them out of the tournament, 17-8, with six homeruns in the game.

Mark worked even harder in the summer of 1985 than he had the year before. Again, he played five or six games a week, for both the Gopher summer league team and the Class-A Columbia Heights town team. He wanted to finish strong his senior year and get his Gopher team back into at least the NCAA regionals. He knew they had taken the Oklahoma State Cowboys down to the wire. They could have won that game. They could have made it to Omaha and the College World Series. Nothing gets the sour taste of losing out of your mouth like winning. It's sweet. It restores the dobber and rightness in the world. The 1986 edition of the Gopher baseball team would have many returning starters in addition to Mark, particularly first baseman and cleanup hitter Alex Bauer and starting pitcher Bryan Hickerson. Michigan would again provide the biggest obstacle.

The Gophers finished with 40 wins against 19 losses in 1986. They won the Western Division of the Big Ten, and Mark hit .315 and had a fielding average of .955. Because of his quickness, he got to balls and got his glove on them, but it cost him some official errors. But nobody doubted Mark's glove work, and earning all-conference honors at shortstop merely confirmed what everybody knew and appreciated.

The Gophers won the Western Division of the Big Ten with a 10-5 conference record. But they wanted more of what they had tasted in the post season in 1985. Moreover, as hosts of the tournament at Siebert Field, they had at least a psychological advantage over their guests from Michigan, Purdue, and Wisconsin. Minnesota opened Friday night against Purdue with a 16-4 blowout, and Mark went three for four with two homeruns. "It surprised the hell out of me," he was quoted as saying in the May 19, 1986 *Minnesota Daily*. They were the only homeruns he'd hit all year, although he'd led the team with 14 doubles.

Michigan beat the Gophers 10-7 on Saturday to send them into the loser's bracket in the double-elimination tournament. They squared off with Wisconsin on Sunday and routed them 13-3 for their 40th win of the season, a school record. Mark had a perfect day at the plate, going five for five on his way to a tournament record of 10 hits.

Minnesota needed to beat undefeated Michigan twice on Sunday to win the tournament. But the *Minnesota Daily's* May 19, 1986, headline was more an undergrad student's exercise in alliteration than truth-in-journalism: "Michigan mauls Minnesota." The final score was 9-5, but with all the homeruns hit in the tournament, the Gophers blasting 17 of the 35, the game was closer to a one-run affair than a mauling. The Gophers took a 4-3 lead after three innings on the strength of three homeruns. Then (Jim) "Abbott, a left-handed pitcher born without a right hand, mowed down the Gopher hitters . . . In 6-2/3 innings, Abbott struck out 10 and allowed just one run and three hits for a 9-5 Michigan win."

"I got two hits off him in the game at the dome," Hess said, "but it seemed that he had picked up 10 mph on his fastball in the Big Ten finals." One account of the game has Mark breaking up Abbott's hitless streak with one out in the ninth–a line drive single back up the middle into centerfield. Two more hits brought him in to give the Gophers their fifth and last run in the ball game.

Abbott was superb. Again, the *Minnesota Daily* and Tom Larson of May 19, 1986:

> The freshman left-hander, 6-2 for the season, no-hit a Minnesota lineup that had hit 17 homeruns in the tournament. . . .
>
> Usually a starter, Abbott was roughed up in a 7-2 loss to Minnesota at the Metrodome earlier this season and admitted being apprehensive facing the Gophers.
>
> 'Things didn't go my way (at the Dome), but you've got to give them credit. Bauer hit one about 900 feet off me to center field, so I had that on my mind. But I thought I had good stuff, and if I'm not walking people and I'm around the plate, I think I'm doing all right.'

Jim Abbot had good stuff. He had been drafted as a high school senior in 1985, but he didn't sign. When the California Angels drafted him in the first round (Number 8 pick overall) in the 1988 draft, after his junior year, he signed. His 10-year career in Major League Baseball was highlighted by an 18-win, 2.89-ERA season in 1991 with the Angels. After six years in California, he was traded to the Yankees and won 20 games over the 1993-94 seasons. Jim Abbott could bring it. He brought the gas to the Gophers in the Big Ten tournament and to the American League hitters for 10 years. He brought home a salary of as much as $2.75 million a year as well before finishing his career with the Milwaukee Brewers in 1999.

"What a story Abbott was," Mark Hess mused. "Teams thought they could bunt on him because of that one-arm handicap. But it didn't matter. He fielded everything cleanly and as quickly as a pitcher with two arms."

A *Minnesota Daily* picture of Mark Hess in the dugout after the loss to Michigan is worth the proverbial thousand words. His hands are hanging onto a support beam overhead, batting glove on his left hand as though waiting to head to the on-deck circle for another time at bat, one foot ahead of the other, anticipating taking the step. The cutline beneath the picture tells one level of the story: "Being named to the Big Ten all-tournament team was little consolation for Gopher senior shortstop Mark Hess (above) as he watched Michigan celebrate (right) its 9-5 win over Minnesota Sunday at Siebert Field." The deeper levels of the story are etched in the expression on Mark's face. You see and you feel the intensity, the pain, and the bitter taste of defeat. Looking at the picture nearly 30 years later, Mark Hess's reaction was what it was then: "Yeah," he mumbled, "It was over. Now what?" It wasn't supposed to happen this way. Not in Mark's dream.

In Mark's dream, Hickerson beats Michigan and the Gophers knock Abbott around again like they had done at the dome earlier in the year. Then they beat them again to advance to the NCAA regionals and another shot at the Titans of Oral Roberts and the Cowboys of Oklahoma State.

But The Fiddler's in charge of the dance. He picks the tune, the time, and the beat. Hess and the Gophers would wait for an NCAA at-large bid that never came. Then Mark would wait for a professional baseball team to call. That call never came either.

A month later, Mark Hess was still waiting. Greg Matson's June 20 *Minneapolis Star Tribune* feature carried the headline, "U's Hickerson, Hess still waiting for the pros." While the left-handed pitcher was drafted by the Twins and ended up with the San Francisco Giants, "Hess' waiting game," wrote Matson, "involves no major league squad. The shortstop was by-passed all four years of his college career and will take part in free agent camps next week with the Twins and Mets."

He impressed Twins scouts at a local tryout camp, but they couldn't find room for him in their organization. He impressed New York Mets' scouts in a similar tryout camp they held at Midway Stadium for 15 or 20 Minnesota ballplayers. Jim Bass said he would sign Mark, and the Mets would assign him to their Class-A Little Falls Mets in the New York-Pennsylvania League's Yawkey Division. Mark was excited and told his family and friends about it. He ran and worked out every night. But he didn't hear from Bass and finally, after a week or more, he called Bass. The Mets' scout told Mark that another area scout at another camp had filled the slot already that he had projected for Mark.

You do a lot of waiting in a fire station. Maybe The Fiddler was preparing his captain for more important duty than professional baseball. But it was a huge disappointment for Hess at the time.

Meanwhile, Mark helped Columbia Heights win the Class-A Minnesota State Amateur Baseball Tournament in September of 1986 after waiting all summer to hear from pro scouts. With two quarters of credits needed to graduate, Mark finished up his undergraduate degree work and graduated the following spring.

He attended a tryout camp in early 1987 in Southern California and impressed the Boise Hawks manager who was looking for some infield help. Mark signed with and moved to Boise, Idaho, to play in the relatively fast Class-A Northwest League with the independent Hawks. He said he was to be paid $500 a month and $5 per meal every day. Four guys shared a hotel room. But the owner's nephew had a lock on the shortstop position. Mark rode the bench and slowly simmered as the starting shortstop butchered one ground ball after another for over a month of games. He got no opportunity to play. The manager's hands were tied. After all, he wanted to keep his job. So Mark walked away from the bad experience. "It soured me on baseball," Mark said.

He returned home to his job with the Mark 7 Beer Distributors located north of University Avenue off Hwy. 280. He also returned in time to help lead the Columbia Heights town team to another Class-A state championship. In all, between 1984 and 1991, Hess made eight trips to the state tournament with Columbia Heights, which won the state championship twice (1986 and '89) and had three second-place finishes and two third-place finishes in the eight years.

Still, it wasn't enough. Mark was bored with the merchandising work for the beer distributor, and the baseball seams were starting to unravel in Colombia Heights. Mark and his old Gopher double-play partner, Dan VanDehey, played an adventurous hunch and took a flyer down under. With six-month visas in hand, the pair booked a $1,700 round-trip flight to Brisbane, Australia. They'd heard that there was some baseball being played in Australia and that Americans were welcome. Their plan was to look for work and to use baseball as a vehicle to get it. At 26 now, Mark Hess knew his dream of playing Major League baseball had played out. But he was pragmatic and looking for honest work. Besides, he knew that he could still handle ground balls and turn a double play with the best in the business.

Australia is on the other side of the equator, so Minnesota wintertime is their summer baseball-playing time. Located on the eastern coast of Australia, Brisbane is the capital of Queensland, one of six mainland Australian states, Tasmania–the seventh–an island state located about 150 miles off the southern coast of the mainland. The city is located in the southeastern corner of the state and the distinct municipality of Gold Coast, the pair's destination, converges on it to form today a metropolitan community of about three million people. In the 1980s Gold Coast had become a tourist mecca. Surfers Paradise was a popular beach community with a hotel of the same name that had been built there in the late 1920s. It was old but elegant, and it served as the center of local action, because of its fine beach and challenging surf. That action, Hess and VanDehey soon found, included baseball– being played as a kind of club sport with the sponsorship of Surfers' Paradise. Both young men were in excellent baseball condition, having just finished play in Minnesota's amateur ball in September.

They found what they were looking for–a ballgame, or practice rather, in one of the area parks, and literally asked, like Minnesota kids used to ask at parks everywhere in the 1950s, if they could play, too. They both made the Surfers' Paradise team, with VanDehey locking up second base and Hess third base. It wasn't long before an exhibition game was scheduled with the nearby professional team–the Daikyo Dolphins, who had played the previous season as the Gold Coast Clippers in the ABL–the Australian Baseball League. Daikyo Australia, Pty. Ltd. was a real-estate development and operations company with its parent company in Tokyo, Japan. The man who everyone thought to be the owner of the business conglomerate, including the baseball team, was in all likelihood the president or CEO of Daikyo Australia, reporting to superiors in Japan. But baseball, like real estate, was big in both Japan and Australia. Both countries had participated in economic booms in the 1980s, too. Japan was really on a roll and seeking to expand the world over. Sponsorship and ownership of a baseball team was a feather in a businessman's hat. "He showed up for one game," Hess said, "and he brought along Gregg Norman–"The Shark"–to throw out the first ball."

"I made a couple of good plays at third," Hess said of the game against the Dolphins. "One was a double-play off a hard shot over the bag down the line that I dove for and backhanded," he said. But the play and the momentum of his body, Hess explained, had taken him back toward the outfield. Instead of turning forward to make the throw to his buddy at second for the putout, he spun the other way– away from the infield, clockwise, and fired a laser to "the mark" over the bag where he knew from a thousand throws just like it, VanDehey would be when he needed to be there. VanDehey, too, knew from the thousand throws he'd taken from Mark Hess that the ball would be just where it needed to be–chest high–when he crossed the bag to take out the lead runner. He timed it just right, breaking at the exactly the right moment. With the runner barreling down on him from first base, VanDehey took the throw from Mark, and in one pirouetting motion evaded the sliding runner and fired a bullet to first base to nail the runner headed for first and complete the second half of the double play. Bang-bang! It was picture perfect on both ends.

Adrian Meagher, manager of the Dolphins, had spent five years in organized baseball, four of them with the Dodger organization as high as AAA, before taking the player-manager gig with the Dolphins in Australia for the Milwaukee Brewers. He couldn't believe what he had just seen. This kid–and he wasn't a kid anymore, he reminded himself–had just made a big time play at third base. *It can't be done any better than that*, he told himself. Then Hess made another play on a dribbler down the line, picking up the ball with his free hand and throwing from underneath off his right foot in time to nail his leadoff hitter at first. *Nobody in the ABL does it any better*, Meagher thought.

"They're gonna want to sign you," Mark's teammates were telling him after the game. He didn't know what he could and couldn't do, because he had signed a contract, he thought, with the Surfers' Paradise team. "Didn't matter," they said. Sure enough, Adrian Meagher, player-manager of the Daikyo Dolphins, asked Mark if he'd play for them that season, which was just getting underway. Meagher wanted both of them, Hess and VanDehey, but he was limited to four Americans, according to the league rules. Nillson, although a professional in the Milwaukee Brewer organization, was a native Australian, which gave him an opening to sign Hess.

The Australian Baseball League's first edition had begun in 1989. It lasted for 10 years before going defunct and being replaced by a new ABL in 1999. Money, or its management, was the issue. If total league costs, underwritten by corporate sponsors such as Pepsi, Dominoes' Pizza, 4X Beer, and Easton Sporting Goods, were $6 million, the revenues from gate admissions and concession sales would come in at $4 million.

The ABL was recognized and sanctioned by important baseball bodies: the International Baseball Association; the Australian Baseball Federation; the Japan Amateur Baseball Association; and Major League Baseball in the U.S. It developed a strong relationship with the U.S. Major League teams by way of player participation in the league, with ABL clubs forming affiliations with big-league clubs in America. Some 90 Major League Baseball players have come from or through the ABL.

Attendances at ABL baseball games averaged only 1,500 in 1989 but jumped to an average of nearly 4,000 in 1993/94. Some games attracted over 10,000 fans.

But revenues were always short of costs. It's not that players were paid that much either. Mark said he only received $25 a game. But his rent, for example, was subsidized by the owner of the Dolphins. He and VanDehey had been paying $400 a week, he remembered, for the first apartment they took in Gold Coast. After signing with the Dolphins, he was paying something like $25 a week, living in an apartment building owned by Daikyo. "They gave me a check for my round-trip airfare," Mark said, "and Easton gave me two good baseball gloves, spikes, and dress attire for airplane travel."

They travelled by plane to distant league cities such as Perth, 2,700 miles away on the southwest coast of Australia, a distance comparable to that between New York and Los Angeles in the states. They would fly to Paramatta to play the Patriots; to Waverly to play the Reds; to Sydney, the country's capital, to play the Metros; to Adelaide to take on the Giants; or to Melbourne to play the Monarchs. Brisbane had a team in the ABL called the Bandits, but they were just an hour away by team bus. They would play a three-game series over the weekend, and then fly home. Travel costs were taken care of by the team, or the league, Mark didn't know which. After every game, especially the doubleheaders they played, the league sponsors treated the ballplayers of both teams to unlimited servings of pizza, beer, and Pepsi Cola. Was the food figured in the league's losses? Who knows now? Danny and Mark would take care of each other at their respective home games, and members of both teams regularly invited them to their homes for dinner. With their living costs reduced considerably, the two baseball bums from Minnesota gave up on the idea of looking for work. The baseball season went into February, and that gave them only two months left on their visas anyway.

With Hess playing regularly but never the same infield position more than two or three games in a row, the Dolphins won the nine-team regular league season outright with a record of 31 wins against just 9 losses. Then they faced second-place Perth in a five-game series to decide the national champion, what Aussies call "the premiership." Mark said that the Dolphins had their choice of either playing two games at home to start the series, then three at Perth if necessary, or they could play two games at Perth, then come home to finish with as many as three games. As many as 7,000 fans had paid to see the Dolphins play at Gold Coast, so the management thought it would be nice to win it for them at home. They opened at Perth against the Heat and got beat twice at Parry Field, 6-4 in the first game and 7-4 in the second. Back home at Gold Coast's Palm Meadows ballpark, they beat Perth 4-3 and 6-2 to knot up the series at two games apiece. In the rubber game, "Our starting pitcher got rocked, and they beat us 11-1," Mark said.

Mark Hess had played for the "Claxton Shield Premiership," the name given to both the competition and the traveling trophy, which–like the Claret Jug that goes home for a year with the winner of golf's British Open, and the Stanley Cup in North America's National Hockey League–stays with the national champion of Australian baseball until the next season. It is steeped in tradition, dating back to 1934, when Norrie Claxton, who had played for South Australia in both cricket and baseball, and who was a patron of the South Australia Baseball Association, donated a shield to be awarded to the winners of the annual carnival. The intention was to permanently award the shield to the first team to win three consecutive tournaments. Interstate baseball tournaments predate the start of the Claxton Shield. As early as 1890, Victoria and South Australia locked horns at the East Melbourne Cricket Ground in Melbourne, Australia, with South Australia the eventual winners, two games to one. A smallpox outbreak in 1913 brought an end to an annual series between New South Wales and Victoria that had begun in 1900. The series resumed in 1919 after World War I. The first "national" tournament was held in 1910 in Hobart, the capital and most populous city of Tasmania–the country's island state. It was won by New South Wales defeating Victoria and host Tasmania. New South Wales repeated the feat in 1912 in Melbourne when they won again, this time South Australia joining the tournament. The Western Australia Baseball League participated in the 1937 national tournament, and the Queensland Baseball Association made their debut for the Claxton Shield in Melbourne in 1939.

World War II interrupted baseball and tournaments. But post-war Australian baseball bloomed again, with the Victoria Aces winning three titles in a row between 1947 and 1949. Victoria holds the most Claxton Shield Premierships, with 22 going back to the inaugural year, 1934. Queensland, the state represented by Mark Hess and the Daikyo Dolphins in 1990-91, has won seven of the nation's titles. "It's a big thing. It should have been eight," Mark recalls.

The loss hurt, as all losses do, but the Dolphins also blew a promised trip to Japan by the owner of the team on top of a promised $10,000 bonus for each ballplayer. "You should have been here for the kickoff party," the Dolphin players had told Mark. No expense was spared. They had gotten ahead of themselves and paid the price.

Mark got to see a lot of Australia, which he probably would never have had an opportunity to do without baseball. But more importantly, Mark got the bad taste out of his mouth that he had carried since his experience in Boise, Idaho. "I hated baseball," Mark said, "and Australia revived my love for the game."

"It was a minor league team," Mark said. Three out of the four Class-AA ballplayers allowed made it big in the Major Leagues, according to Hess. John Jaha led the ABL in 1990-'91 with his .445 average for the Dolphins, and he played for the Milwaukee Brewers from 1992 through 1998 before finishing his career with Oakland in 2001. His career MLB batting average of .263 was highlighted by a banner year in 1996 when he batted .300, with 34 homeruns, 28 doubles, and 118 runs batted in–against American League pitchers. David Nillson, a catcher, outfielder, and first baseman, originally signed with the Brewers in 1987 and also made the big club in 1992 where he played through the 1999 season, compiling a .284 career batting average that included two seasons in which he hit over .300. He made over $5.6 million his last year, 1999. He must have saved most of it, because he returned to his native Australia and bought the financially troubled ABL for $5 million. Outfielder Troy O'Leary, beginning in 1993, spent 11 years with Milwaukee and Boston mostly. His salary in 2001 was $4.6 million. He hit 28 homeruns in 1999, with 103 RBIs. His career MLB batting average was .274.

"These guys were the real deal," Hess said, "and I went from hating baseball to loving it again, because I knew I could play with them." The Daikyo Dolphins gave Mark Hess a gold glove at their season-ending banquet with an inscription citing him as the best defensive player on the team.

"I felt good."

The Fiddler was just warming up.

The 15-hour flight home to Minneapolis from Brisbane provided more than enough time to reflect on the Australian experience. It was good to have played through the winter. It was good to have played on a good ball club with the quality of players the Dolphins had fielded. Mark Hess knew he belonged, and they had asked him to come back the next fall for the 1991-'92 season. He wanted to come back and was sure that he would play for the Dolphins again.

But Mark Hess had turned 27 years old in December. That's about the time a young man gets serious about life if he hasn't had the responsibility of maybe military service or marriage and a family. If you can't be a ballplayer, playing for pay, then what is it that you can be? What is it that you are meant to be? Until you ask the questions, you can't answer them.

Upon his return home, Mark had two things to take care of. One was to see about his old job with the Mark-7 Beer Distributors, and the other was summer baseball with Columbia Heights.

Columbia Heights has participated in the Minnesota State Amateur Baseball Tournament 17 times, going back to 1966 when they finished third in the Class-A competition. They have won eight championships, three with Hess playing shortstop. Between 1982, when Mark began playing shortstop for Columbia Heights, and 1991, his last year with them, they went to the state tournament eight times. They haven't been to the tournament since 1991–Hess's last year. They finished third in the Class-A tournament, but Mark noticed that the little things weren't getting done. When Mark chided another ballplayer for something, he got sarcasm in response. "Yeah, big-time Minnesota Gopher, telling us all what to do." He wasn't like that anyway. With his brother, this was unfinished family business– the steel-cage bedroom brawl that Mom had always decided in a draw.

Tim Olson was a teammate of Mark's on the Columbia Heights town team. He had first told Mark about baseball in Australia. He and Mark had played touch football on a team in Northeast Minneapolis the past couple of falls. He had urged Mark to think about becoming a fireman. The test was coming up. The idea had taken root, and a month after returning from Australia Hess was at the Civic Center in downtown Minneapolis, taking the test along with 1,300 other would-be firemen. "It was mostly physical then," Mark said, "timed agility drills." He finished 28th out of the 1,300 despite giving up points to military servicemen. "There was a brief psychological test and some written questions," he remembered. "But nothing like it is now."

After eight weeks of Rookie School, then toeing the line and busting his butt for a couple of years to satisfy the unwritten codes of seniority and pecking orders, Mark Hess was the real deal in responding to Minneapolis emergencies.

Mark established a residency in Plymouth over the winter to be within the 15-mile requirement he needed to play at Hamel–a western suburb of Minneapolis in the North Star League. Hamel was loading up with former Gophers, including two other infielders from his 1985 team, Dan VanDehey, who had played with the

Hawks since the early 1980s, and Alex Bauer, the cleanup-hitting first baseman who had taken Michigan's Jim Abbott as deep as it gets at the dome in downtown Minneapolis. Hamel started as many as seven former Minnesota Gophers in 1992 when they lost the state championship to Miesville at Jordan. The Hawks then got caught with an ineligible player due to a three-block infringement of the 15-mile residency rule. So they were banned from the 1993 state tournament, but managed to play in, and win, the national amateur baseball tournament held at Eau Claire, Wisconsin that year.

Hamel was loaded. Without Hess, they had won the Class-B state championship in 1987, finished third in 1988, and second in 1989. They had made the state tournament in both 1990 and 1991 but finished "out of the money" both years, despite proving the absurdity of the metal bat and the consequences of poor class qualification criteria in a 33-0 humiliation of Proctor in a 1990 state tournament baseball game. With a population of just over 3,000 people, located in northeastern Minnesota, on Hwy 2, just off Interstate 35, close to Duluth and Superior, Wisconsin, it was Proctor's first trip to the state tournament–at any level. It was also their last trip.

Perhaps the most apparently egregious example of the residency issue involving a quality baseball player involved what looked like the reincarnation of Willie Mays in centerfield for the Miesville Mudhens in 1991. The impressive-looking Harry Davis, wearing Mays's number, 24, played centerfield in the Class-B state tournament co-hosted by Red Wing and Cannon Falls. The account included in *Scott County Baseball* of the game against Jordan in the semifinals has Davis hitting a double and a single in three at-bats and figuring in both runs in Miesville's 2-1 win. But the account fails to capture "The Catch II," which was the defining moment of the ball game. Willie Mays' catch of a Vic Wertz shot in the 1954 World Series is immortalized simply as "The Catch." With his back to the plate, running full out toward the deepest centerfield fence in baseball then, at the Polo Grounds in New York, Mays caught the ball over his head and shoulders near the base of the fence.

With two on and two out at Cannon Falls, Ron Beckman was hitting in the eighth inning, Pat Pohl remembers, of the semi-final game of the 1991 Minnesota Class-B State Tournament. Harry Davis broke quickly with the solid contact of Beckman's metal bat on the ball. It was hit hard, a line shot heading into the gap, deep into right-center field. "I was thinking triple right off the bat," Beckman would say of it years later. Davis got a great jump on the scorched ball. He ran hard to his left into the power alley and angling back toward the fence. *But damn! Davis said to himself. Damn metal bats! This ball just wasn't sinking.* It seemed to jettison payload and take off with a turbo boost as it cleared the Mudhen second baseman and ripped air toward the fence. Davis would have to step on it. He would engage his own internal turbo. Then, at the very last possible instant, the moment now frozen in memory, Harry Davis, running hard, went airborne. No, not vertical. Harry Davis left his feet and propelled his body toward the cavernous gap in right centerfield and the screaming baseball that had ballgame written all over it. He reached, stretched–even farther yet–and willed his gloved hand as far out from his body as he could. Willie Mays might have caught that ball in his back pocket, but parallel to the ground and maybe four feet off it, Harry Davis was putting it all out there. Then without seeing the ball hit his glove, he felt the unmistakable thud. The next thud, he knew, would be his body hitting the ground. He instinctively tucked his shoulder, hit the ground, and rolled over and up, as if all in one calibrated gymnastic motion. Harry Davis made the best catch of a baseball we have ever seen.

It was bad enough having a game-winning, extra-base hit taken away from you, Ron Beckman recalled, bad enough losing a big ballgame. "On top of it," Beckman said, "for the next three weeks at home, my sons played *Harry Davis Live* in the living room, taking turns catching balls in midair while diving into the couch." Alex, 7, and Steven, 5, both now regulars on the Jordan Brewer team their father helped build into a powerhouse in Minnesota amateur baseball a generation ago, had witnessed the circus catch, too. They couldn't help re-enacting it for their father in the living room:

"Hey Dad! Watch this . . . Harry Davis!"

The Buzz was that Harry Davis had just gotten off an airplane in time to join the Mudhens of Miesville after his release from Class-AA professional baseball somewhere. One vocal Jordan partisan was heard saying that Harry Davis satisfied the state baseball residency requirement with his chicken ranch three miles from Weiderholt's Supper Club in downtown Miesville. The PC police would have a case with that one. Certainly worse things were said throughout the grandstands and at the beer stand. But everybody laughed, giving affirmation to the narrow minded and shortsighted, the blowhards and the bigots.

"We heard it all," Pat Pohl, former Gopher teammate of Mark Hess, a Hastings native and a longstanding Mudhen, said of the racial slurs in 1991, 45 years after Jackie Robinson took it all and worse with the Brooklyn Dodgers.

Harry Davis had signed with the San Francisco Giants in 1984. He's listed online at 5 ft. 10 in. and 165 lbs., but he looked bigger, thicker, in 1991. He played much bigger. The number on his back was unmistakable. The Giants gave up on him after five years in which the best year he had was a .296 batting average playing for Class-A Fresno in 1987. A jump to AA Shreveport in 1988 showed that he couldn't hit the better pitching at that level, batting just .222 there. His sixth and last year of professional baseball was in the Seattle organization in 1989. It was a repeat of the previous year. He hit a promising .289 at Class-A Wausau and was promoted to AA Williamsport where he managed a meager .209. In six seasons of professional baseball, Harry Davis averaged .241. But in the late summer of 1991, two years after his last game at Williamsport, Harry Davis stole a baseball game from the Jordan Brewers for his Miesville Mudhens.

He lived in Rosemount, according to Pohl, with his wife, a native of Minnesota, and, according to Brian Larson, the daughter of the principal of the Rosemount school district. They'd returned to her home after the 1989 season in the Seattle organization. Rosemount, according to MapQuest is 22.83 miles from Miesville, which, despite a population of 125, has kept alive a vibrant baseball tradition in its community with ballplayers from nearby, larger towns. "As the crow flies," downtown Rosemount is probably less than 20 miles from Miesville and well within a required 25-mile radius. City limits as the crow flies likely put him within 15 miles of Miesville. We didn't try to calculate it, but you can bet somebody did in the spring of 1990. What was good for the goose wasn't good for the gander in Jordan, where a Grandfather Clause allowed exceptions to the radius rules. That allowed the Brewers to play two Division I favorite sons who had long ago taken up residency in other communities at considerable distances from Jordan. At some time, citing fairness of all things, Jordan was allowed to extend its reach from 8 miles to 15 miles to 25 miles. Now, when they needed frontline pitching, which they couldn't come up with organically, they brought it in from across the river–in breach of long-standing unwritten rules. Tommy Smith, like Jon Beckman and Dave Hentges, had played Division I college baseball for the Minnesota Gophers, as had Jerry Chapman. Others, like native John McFarland, an outstanding centerfielder, had played at St. Cloud State, and John Dolan, a native of St. Cloud, had pitched for St. John's. There were others, too. Manager Charlie Larca knew the strengths and weaknesses of his teams, and he had contacts on the other side of the Minnesota River, some inside the 494-694 corridor, recruiting in which was also against the unwritten rules.

The residence-radius rule of 15 miles in Minnesota state baseball goes back to 1924, according to baseball historian Brian Larson, although it was just 8 miles briefly in the 1950s for Jordan and the Minnesota River League. Until the late 1990s, he said, the mileage was measured "as the crow flies," city limits to city limits. A rapidly growing community, Rosemount is likely to have annexed enough land outside of its downtown streets to be within 15 miles of a more rural Miesville in the 1990s when Harry Davis moved home with his Rosemount wife. The radius was expanded to 25 miles in the mid-to late-90s, and, according to Larson, "The radius was extended to 30 miles four years ago" in 2010. He also said that today they use a GPS to measure ballpark address to ballplayer address, "and if the ballpark in question doesn't have a street address, they use the address of the nearest house."

Fairness is always foreign to the partisan. Jordan baseball people went out and filled holes they needed to fill in order to compete at the Class-B level. But to the partisan, "competing" means only winning, not winning and losing a relatively equal number of times. Moreover, "competing" to the partisan means that the ends justify the means. Jordan, like Hamel, and probably Dundas, Miesville, and Cold Spring, invoked rules; they changed rules; they stretched rules; and they probably broke rules. They decimated the old unwritten rule about crossing the Minnesota River to recruit and what Brian Larson called "the Class-A Ring," which he explained is bounded by Highway 694 on the north end of the Twin Cities metro area, and Highway 494 on the east and west sides, with the Minnesota River the southern perimeter. The Class-A Ring, according to Larson, protected Class-B town teams like Chaska and Shakopee from losing their better players to Class-A teams playing within the ring. Similarly, it was verboten for Class-B teams located on the southern side of the river or west of Highway 494, for example, to invite and play ballplayers within the ring on their Class-B teams.

It was an old story being played out on the diamond. Baseball people wanted it both ways while wanting to play down rather than up. Smaller towns cried foul while committing the very same infractions themselves. The whining reminded us of the sandbagging that golf club members do throughout the summer in order to "compete" for the club championship.

Harry Davis, no doubt, met the letter and the spirit of the state's baseball rules. What Jordan baseball people claimed with a feverish disdain for the likes of Miesville and Hamel, they were guilty of themselves. Harry Davis was simply the best ballplayer in Cannon Falls that day and maybe the tournament in the late summer of 1991. Harry Davis had six years of pro ball on his resume, and he looked it. He was the class of the field.

In Mark Hess's first year with Hamel, reunited with many of his former Gopher teammates, the Hawks narrowly missed winning it all at Jordan in 1992, losing to Miesville in the championship game. The next year, 1993, was the year of the residency rules violation and the subsequent national amateur championship at Eau Claire, Wisconsin. They made the Minnesota Class-B State Tournament again in both 1994 and 1995, finished third overall in 1996, then won the Class-B State Championship in 1997, beating Cold Spring, the defending champions, in the title game. They made the tournament the following year, 1998, but getting long in the tooth from top to bottom in their lineup, they missed in 1999 before returning in 2000.

"It's all about making the state tournament," Hess said of Minnesota's amateur baseball. "If you don't make the tournament," he said, "it's a wasted season." So you do anything you can to make the tournament. It wasn't always that way. Over the years, what gets done to achieve a berth in the state tournament has changed considerably. Teams play hard; teams play well; teams play down. Teams with Class-A caliber ballplayers forgo the upper class for the better opportunity to win it all in Class B. Recently, Class-B teams have been playing down to Class-C level, as evidenced by the 2013 Minnesota State Amateur Baseball Tournament at Delano and Maple Lake, by the 2014 tournament at Jordan and Belle Plaine, and again in 2015 by the tournament at Cold Spring and Watkins, where 48 teams competed for the Class C championship.

As talented as the Hawks were throughout this period, other teams were loaded with Class-A baseball talent, too, playing Class-B level baseball. In fact, for 15 years from 1986 through 2000, Miesville, Dundas, Cold Spring, Jordan, and Hamel dominated their baseball leagues and the state tournament. Together, these teams finished first and second 21 out of the possible 30 times.

Miesville, a whistle stop with a gem of a baseball park on Hwy 50 east of Farmington, had 11 tournament appearances in the period, 1987 through 2000, with three state championships, two second-place finishes, and a third-place finish. Dundas, another small village located just north of Northfield, MN, was the Class-B State Champion in 1982. They were absent from the tournament a few years, then in the period we focus on–1986 through 2000–they made the state tournament 12 times, earning three more Class-B State Championships–1988, 1998, and 1999. Cold Spring, located near St. Cloud in Stearns County, has a rich amateur baseball history, as do the other towns. They won the Class-B State Championship in 1986, missed the tournament the following year, 1987, then ran the table through the rest of the 15-year period, making the tournament the 13 consecutive years while adding state championships in 1996 and 2000. They also won it the following year, in 2001.

Jordan, with a cohort of Class-A hitters from the Division I University of Minnesota Gophers and augmented by the best baseball majors from posh private colleges and local enthusiasts, won the 1986 Class-C State Championship. According to Tom Melchior in his *Scott County Baseball*, Jordan won the Carver Central League with a 20-2 record, 36-10 overall on the year. They destroyed Maple Lake 15-9 before embarrassing, in succession, the likes of Lake Wilson, 14-2; St. Nicholas, 16-6; and Flensburg, 16-4, before finally getting a game from Sleepy Eye, 4-3. But it was "a state championship."

Hitting statistics published in Melchior's book define the Jordan game. Rounding up to emphasize our point, everybody batted .300, and six Brewers batted .400 on the season. They rattled and cleared the fences, with three men belting 13 or more homeruns on the year. Class-A hitters with metal bats beat up Class-C pitching. It wasn't fair.

But with the Class-C Championship came the state's requirement to move up a class in play. Jordan would find by 1992 that they needed some Class-A pitching to go with their Class-A hitting. Town team baseball had taken on new dimensions with, first, growing populations and larger school enrollments, which meant more teachers and likely ballplayers; metal bats, expanded schedules, stretching rules to meet residency requirements, and the granddaddy of all rules, which said that regardless of how far outside the 15-mile radius a ballplayer lived he could choose to play either where he lived or in the town in which he graduated from high school. There was also the breaking of the unwritten rule of not crossing the Minnesota River for ballplayers. Prior Lake, beginning in 1968, had breached it. Now, Jordan with a new manager who had played on the other side of the river in towns like Waconia, St. Boni, and Victoria and who had to have been aware of the unwritten rule that served the river's lower basin leagues for several decades would bring players to Jordan he thought would fill holes or strengthen weak spots. Then the 15-mile radius was expanded to 25 miles to give more teams more access to metro area ballplayers. They had changed leagues, too, and maybe the thinking was that what was verboten in the old River Valley League was okay in the Carver-Central League.

You can't blame Jordan, and you can't blame the ballplayers on any of the teams. Jordan only did what everybody else was doing–everybody being Hamel, Cold Spring, Dundas, and Miesville. The ballplayers simply want to play with their buddies and on good teams. If you can't build a winning team organically–from ballplayers residing in your town, or within your organization, you go outside. If you are the New York Yankees, you simply buy the ballplayers you want. If you are St. Patrick, population 16, you have no choice. If you are Jordan or Belle Plaine, population each about 6,000, you do have a choice. You can field a team of locals, as Lonsdale did in a most competitive way throughout the 1960s and into the 70s with Kubes, Smiseks, Rezacs, Tureks, and Vosejpkas, despite a population of about 300 then, or you can go outside your city limits to get what you feel you need. You can also bang the doors down all season long with hitting, as Jordan did, then draft quality pitching needed to compete beyond league play. We take no umbrage with the choice either way. Our complaint is with those claiming the innocence of lambs while feasting like ravenous wolves in the pasture of lambs, deceiving the sleeping shepherd, and scoffing at The Fiddler at the same time.

But when Don Meyer and Herb Isakson did it with Prior Lake in the late 1960s and early 1970s, by putting a River Valley League team of former Minnesota Gophers, along with John Dill and Bobby Kelly, and one former AAA and Southern Minny pitcher on the field, all of whom lived on the other side of the Minnesota River, league officers shut down the River Valley League after a few years of the shellacking and started up anew–without the Jays. Steve Schneider, who succeeded Herb Isakson as manager of the Jays, argues with good reason in Tom Melchior's *Scott County Baseball* the letter of the league's rules–that eligibility of Prior Lake's Minnesota Gopher-rich Class-B amateur baseball team shouldn't have been a question, because they all met the 15-mile residency rule. Maybe they did and maybe they didn't. It surely was not reason to ban them from play. It could have provided the impetus around the league to man up, but it didn't. Where Prior Lake went afoul of the league was in replacing *all* the local, community players with Bloomington and Edina guys, in crossing the river for talent in the first place, violating that unwritten rule, and for the arrogance with which they took the field for every game they played "out in the country." Isakson and his ballplayers should have been playing where they belonged–Class-A. Still, there was no travesty of the game then by Prior Lake. No embarrassment and humiliation. Prior Lake won, but they didn't "Proctor" anyone. They were a Class-A team that chose to play down to feed their own narcissistic needs. Fairness wasn't in their equation. They should have been playing at a Class-A level.

Imagine the "baseball PTSD" in the community of Proctor after coming home from the state tournament on the short side of a 33-0 ball game! That score would shame a football team! The shame of a baseball game by that score rests with the governing body of the state's amateur baseball, the Minnesota State Amateur Baseball Board of Directors. Fairness ought to be at the forefront of all the class-qualifying decisions.

The Hamel humiliation of Proctor should never be allowed to happen in Minnesota amateur baseball. It happened for three reasons: (1) the metal bat; (2) the lack of strict enforcement of residency-qualifying criteria; and (3) the failure to assign teams to their appropriate class.

There is no way that the 1990 Hamel Hawks belong in the same class, Class B, as the Proctor baseball team. There is no way the 1986 Jordan Brewers belong in the same class, Class C, as Lake Wilson, St. Nicholas, and Flensburg. We couldn't find those towns with a Rand-McNally Atlas of the state and a Garmin GPS. We don't know what the solution is, but we do know that the addition of still more classes is no solution at all, because if you create, as they have done with high school basketball, for example, or professional boxing, as many as five different champions, you really have no champion. Nor is the bloating of the Class-C state tournament to a 48-team field a solution. That only dilutes the quality of the tournament, as does the addition of classes, cheapening what ought to be something really special. It's special if making the tournament has been earned. If 48 teams out of a field of 224 "make the state tournament," as was the case in the 2014 Class-C Minnesota Amateur Baseball Tournament, just what exactly has been earned?

That's better than a one-in-five chance at approximately 22 percent. Contrast that with the three-class 1950 state tournament in which 31 teams out of 800 qualified for the tournament, a four-percent chance. When outstanding and awesome are made easy and commonplace, they vanish. When they are given away, the value disappears. We can say that attendance reflects at least perceived value, and a record 35,318 fans attended the tournament so long ago.

Appeasement and ease of entry are not what *the* state baseball championship, or *the* heavyweight boxing championship is about. Joe Frazier gave up weight, size, and essential reach to Muhammed Ali in their "classic trilogy" of heavyweight boxing matches. But he gave up nothing in the way of heart. He paid the price he needed to pay in order to "get inside" where, neutralizing Ali's reach, he could do his own damage–to the body with disemboweling uppercuts from hell and to the right side of the pretty one's head with the most devastating left hook the fight game has ever seen. The point is that the physically overmatched Frazier didn't run, didn't hide; he didn't seek another division or a "championship" outside of *the* championship. He fought up.

Mark Hess played on two Class-A State Championship teams at Columbia Heights, playing in the state tournament eight times. He played on Hamel's 1997 Class-B State Championship team and on six other Hamel teams that made the Class-B State Tournament, making the Class-B All-Tournament Team three times. He also played on the 1993 National Amateur Baseball Championship team. Mark Hess made two Class-B All-Tournament teams while playing for Jordan in 2002 and 2004. He is listed in the official state tournament guide as having made the All-Tournament team seven times, one behind the record-holding Jon Beckman of Jordan, his teammate with the University of Minnesota's 1985 Big Ten Championship team. But Brian Larson, former member of the Minnesota State Baseball Board of Directors and considered "the historian" today for Minnesota baseball, explained how All-Tournament selections were made. "Fifteen players were chosen on the basis of their statistics," Larson said. "That means that you could have 15 first basemen." With those selection criteria and that MO, Brooks Robinson would have made just one or two American League All-Star teams and been shut out of Cooperstown. Like Robinson and Major League Baseball's Hall of Fame, Mark Hess belongs in the Minnesota State Baseball Hall of Fame for his glove work at the most important defensive position on the diamond.

His state tournament participation and his all-tournament selections were done with his glove. He never hurt any team with his bat, but just imagine how well a shortstop must have played to be noticed during all the noise made by the boys with their Easton metal bats. But if "community service" still ranks high on the list of criteria used by the Hall of Fame Selection Committee, then what baseball person in the state would have better credentials ever than a fireman serving the needs of the big city? He doesn't sell tickets, serve popcorn, or cut grass. He responds with care for people in dire straits. He saves lives.

Hess played the string out with Hamel in 2000, the year he met his wife, Cindy, he said, at Nye's Bar in Northeast Minneapolis. "Actually, it was at a party after the bar closed," Hess said. "I spent all night talking to the bouncer at Nye's and talked to her at the party."

The Fiddler was playing that night at Nye's, unseen and unheard by Mark, or anyone else for that matter. Now 37 years old, Mark was smitten. He stole the heart of Cindy and the heart of Cindy's dog, "Simba." He would need both hearts by the time he and Cindy married in 2002. Cindy was, and remains, an entrepreneurial businesswoman. She owns and manages *Body & Sol*, a hair, nails, and massage salon in Lakeville, where she employs 30 to 35 people, 14 of whom are full-time employees.

"She works all the time," Mark said. "It's really 24/7 when you are a small business owner," and you only get to eat what you kill. It's not drudgery, however, because, like all entrepreneurs, she loves her work. It's not just a job in that sense. It's an important part of her life that transcends a Friday paycheck, and Mark admires and respects his wife for her vocation and the diligence with which she runs her business. Hess, on the other hand, is on the other end of the employment spectrum. As a fireman–a public employee–he works continuously rotating shifts of two days on, four days off. A work shift "day" is a full 24 hours however. Mark and his crewmembers, men and women, spend two full days (48 hours) on duty at their station, responding to calls of distress and crisis. When the bell rings in a fire station in response to a 911 call, within two minutes The Big Red Machine–the fire engine–is rolling out of the garage and on its way to the scene of crisis and the purpose of the call.

The thinking and the subsequent waste, fraud, and abuse evident at the scene of many of the calls made by the first responders are enough to make you question a lot of things. Hess sees the problem playing out every day on the job, and he sees his wife working around the clock, 24/7, as a small business owner. Hess helps Cindy clean the shop on the nights he's off work, and it seems he's doing janitorial plumbing once or twice a week there. He's there for his wife every night, too, as she sometimes anguishes over the management of personnel, balancing menstrual cycles, employee day care schedules, and inevitable crises that can't be anticipated. That's on top of the normal scheduling of customers, promoting, bookkeeping, tax accounting, payroll, and civic membership duties she has as part of "her job." It's all part of being a small business owner.

But Hess said he and his wife don't complain about it. Instead, he admits, "We're lucky."

"There's no comparison," Hess said. "When I'm done with a shift at the station, I'm completely punched out. My wife never punches out. She's always working."

Hess's wife earns every buck she gets and for her hard work, including the management of people she employs, she is rewarded with the right to keep less than half of it in Minnesota. The rest goes into The Big Black Hole.

There is a spiritual danger of not playing with your own nickel, of not running your own business. Reality gets distorted. In not working for yourself in your own business, and contrary to an old axiom of wisdom, you can get the notion that there is such a thing as a free lunch. You can get the idea that just because you can figure out a way to qualify for public assistance that you are entitled to it.

Hess is thinking more and more about retirement. He wonders what it is he might like to do. He knows he wants to be able to ice skate and push a hockey puck around a little bit. But beyond that, he's not sure. At one time, he thought he would like to coach young kids, but he's changed his mind as a result of seeing the pressure put on kids by many parents.

"Cindy has no retirement program with her business," Hess said of his wife. "The house is her retirement," Hess figures. She bought what was, by today's standards on Prior Lake, a shack in the late 1990s, before she met Mark. When Mark moved in, they lived for years in literally one bedroom and the rest of the love nest a construction zone. Mark and Cindy worked tirelessly to tear down and renovate the shack, turning it into a comfortable lakefront home. He quickly noticed the "double jeopardy," however, as with each stage of improvement his assessed valuation went up along with his Scott County property taxes. He did much of the work himself, he said, with the help of fellow off-duty firemen, taking the structure down to its skeletal studs and floor supports. Mark's father-in-law re-wired the house and upped the service to handle the load of a contemporary home. He re-did all the plumbing from the bathrooms to the city sewage lines. Room by room, wall by wall, ceilings and floors, he gutted and rebuilt the home he and Cindy share.

They married in 2002 but before the gleam was even out of the eyes of this 39-year-old shortstop and his bride, they discovered they couldn't have children. "We tried to have kids," Hess said. "But we couldn't." Mark and Cindy have long ago reconciled that reality with, "It was the Big Guy upstairs, I guess."

Who knows why The Fiddler picks the tunes He does. All we know is that the recognition of Him being in charge of the music and the dance goes a long way on this earth alone. For in Bill Bonner's writing, we've read several times that shortly before her maiden voyage in 1912 the architect of the *S.S. Titanic* was heard to say, "Even God couldn't sink this ship."

Why would God deny such good people, a couple with such great parenting potential, the privilege of having *His* children? Maybe it's a good thing, they've told each other after seeing what's happened to some families and far too many children.

Moving to Prior Lake and the home with Cindy that would give him a "hobby" for the next 14 years, Mark Hess now met the 15-mile residency rule to play baseball for the Jordan Brewers with his old Gopher teammates, Jon Beckman and Dave Hentges. But when he called Beckman to tell him about his plans, he learned that all of the Old Guard of Brewers, with the exception of "Gilly" Buss, had retired. Hess would have to make new friends with new teammates in Jordan. He bonded with Charlie Larca, the manager, immediately, and although he said he wanted to play "his" position, shortstop, with the Brewers, he acceded to Larca's reasoning that he wanted a full-time guy at short to anchor the infield. Hess's fireman's duty would keep him from being available to play 100 percent of the time. It had worked at Hamel, Hess reasoned with Larca. He would make every game he wasn't on duty, and he would swap schedules when he could with other firemen to be able to make big games–the playoffs and the state tournament.

Charlie Larca wouldn't buy Hess's argument, but Larca knew when he had pure gold in his hands. At the risk of losing another aging but great ballplayer from *his* team, the team he had to have felt he built, nurtured, and led to 15 state tournaments and two state championships already at the start of the 2001 season, the late Charlie Larca convinced Mark Hess that playing second base for the 2001

Jordan Brewers would be best for everyone. Despite the turnover of Brewer stars, they made the state tournament again but lost two straight, 2-1 to eventual runner-up, Austin, then 6-5 to Prior Lake. Hess played his usual outstanding defense for the Jordan Brewers, playing mostly second base, as he had agreed to do, but also some third base as well as shortstop when regulars were absent or Larca merely felt like it. But he had problems at the plate. He batted just .207 on the year. When we inquired of Mark Hess what accounted for such a dismal year at the plate, his response reminded us of what Ty Cobb, whose lifetime batting average of .367 remains the best ever among major leaguers, supposedly told a reporter when he said that he thought he would have trouble hitting .300 against today's pitchers. "Really?" the reporter asked, "Why is that, Mr. Cobb?"

"You've got to remember–I'm seventy-three," Cobb said, in 1960, the year before he died.

A right-handed hitter, Hess had to bat left handed all season. His elbow was locking up on him, and he couldn't swing the bat right-handed. An off-season surgical procedure to remove a bone spur restored full mobility the following year, 2002, when he hit .268 and helped lead the Brewers to the state tournament, in which he was named to the All-Tournament Team again and now for the third team in the third decade of this selection. Making the All-Tournament Team as a position player so many times speaks volumes about the infield glove work of Mark Hess. Unlike many pitchers and catchers who are available as draft choices when their own team fails to advance toward tournament play, Mark's honors had to be earned with his own teams.

Mark liked playing baseball in Jordan. "There was no comparison between Hamel and Jordan," Hess said, "as far as the field and the crowds. Nobody followed us at Hamel, whereas at Jordan there were always people at the games and they adopted you as a member of the community."

"He had a real passion for the game," Cindy said, "and it was so evident in just the way he hustled between the dugout and his position in the field," when he was the old man out there among much younger players. "He was 40 years old and still stealing bases," Hess's wife said proudly, "and it was just great to hear these old men dressed in bib overalls sitting in the stands nearby talking about how good a ballplayer he was." Hess was still making tough infield plays look routine when he was 42 years old playing for the Jordan Brewers. But when Charlie Larca called it quits after the 2006 season as the manager, Hess felt it was time for him to hang up his spikes, too–in Jordan. Not many people know that he played still one more year of baseball in 2007. Mark Hess played a year with the Prior Lake Mudcats in the DRS League.

But the year, 2002, was stressful for a number of reasons. Getting married is supposed to be a big stressor for men. The sudden death of his father, at age 62, was another. Mark's father, a builders' representative for Minnegasco, the old gas utility company, had gone to the doctor with sinus and vision problems. His regular doctor was on vacation, Mark said, and the M.D. he saw gave him a prescription for sinus congestion. A week later, Wally Hess was admitted to the hospital, where he died of a stroke.

Mark was devastated by the death of his father. He said that Simba, Cindy's Golden Retriever, which had become Mark's Simba, really turned on the canine compassion and unconditional love. Dogs know the score. No dog is better at simple companionship than the Golden. Their range, Mark learned, is amazing. "They're the best," Mark said of Golden Retrievers. They are so expressive, and they have the most beautiful and engaging brown eyes of all God's creatures. One visitor to a local dog park remarked that he had read somewhere a quote, "Life is a party, and the Golden Retriever is the guest of honor." In life they delight us. In loss they comfort and console. Simba helped heal the grief Mark was living. She would continue to grace the presence of Mark and Cindy's home and lives for another 10 years, before she had to be put down at age 14. That was a sad time, too, for Mark and Cindy. They kept putting off what they knew they must do, as Simba would seem to rally one day, then slip again the next. Finally, they had no choice.

After three years without a dog, "Frankie," a cream-colored, female Golden Retriever puppy showed up with her pure gold pedigree for Mark and Cindy. "She's great for us," Mark said. "We just love her."

We had to ask Mark Hess if he was aware of how people perceive him. "You mean that quiet and shy stuff in the articles from high school?" That was it. He makes you wonder where that comes from in an age of excess, narcissism, and immediate gratification. How is it possible in an age of Bullwinkles and blowhards, who know it all and can't stop blowing their own horn? Where does the all-too-apparent modesty and humility come from in an All Big Ten shortstop?

Let's not forget the rest of the resume: a star on his Mickey Mantle State Championship team; an all-conference high school shortstop; a star shortstop on four Minnesota state amateur champions with three different teams; starting shortstop on two Big 10 West Division championship teams and a Big 10 Conference Championship his junior year; starting shortstop for the Hamel Hawks' National Amateur Baseball Championship team. And there's that gold glove award he was presented by the Daikyo Dolphins in Australia.

Mark Hess made the Minnesota state amateur all-tournament team more times with three different teams than you can count. Moreover, the elite selections were all as a position player, most of the time as a shortstop. He didn't need to bring his bat either when the metal bats made all the noise. He was a quiet glove man in whose hands "the double-play was my homerun." Like the glove of Brooks Robinson, his boyhood hero, Mark Hess's glove was pure gold. They don't have Robinson's bat on display at Cooperstown. His career batting average is .267. His bat wasn't needed to get there, and Mark Hess's bat shouldn't be needed to get to St. Cloud, MN. But where does the humility come from when the trophy case is so full?

"Well, my parents were quiet and unassuming people," Hess said. "They were never loud and boisterous. They worked their jobs, raised the family, and tried to be good neighbors."

"The apple never falls too far from the tree." Maybe character, too, resides in the DNA, waiting–like an apple seed–for the right conditions to call it forth. Conditions like the 2 a.m. first alarm response to a fire in a duplex at 2507 4th Street N. in Minneapolis when Mark Hess broke fire department protocol because his gut told him there wasn't time to wait for a line or another fireman. He went into the smoke-filled building alone, feeling the wall as he advanced into the no-man's land of a fireman. Then he felt what he instantly knew to be a body. He picked the young girl up, noting that she wasn't breathing. Then there was some panic as he sought the exit. Then lights and yelling, "Over here!" came the voices. Once outside, Mark started CPR, put his oxygen mask on her, compressing the lifeless girl's chest, and she threw up into his mask, which he knew to be a good thing–a sign of life. Then the paramedics arrived and took over and rushed the girl to a hospital. Mark got the word the next day that she had lived. "It was the most rewarding thing I've ever experienced," Hess said.

Here's the official report from John S. Fruetel, Fire Chief, Minneapolis Fire Department, dated October 11, 2013:

> When crews arrived, fire was showing from a second story window. Captain Hess was met in the front yard by several people who reported one child was still in an upper bedroom. Captain Hess met the mother, who was trying to go after her child, in the stairwell and escorted her back down and out of the building. He then went up the stairs alone, without a line, to the second floor where smoke was banked down to less than a foot. Captain Hess found the seven year old girl on the floor, unconscious. He rescued her, brought her out to the front yard, started emergency medical care and requested paramedics.
>
> Without question, the actions Captain Hess took saved the life of the seven year old child.
>
> Captain Mark Hess is therefore being awarded the Distinguished Service Medal for performing this highly unusual act of distinction while on duty as a member of Engine 4 at the aforementioned incident. His actions bring credit upon himself, the Minneapolis Fire Department and the fire service.

The Distinguished Service Medal is pure gold. It's brighter than any trophy in the Hess collection. It's more enduring than any college or Major League Baseball World Series ring. It is far more valuable than the Claxton Shield, a Big Ten Championship trophy, and a handful of state amateur baseball championships. It reflects the light of a little girl's life. It reflects, too, true heroism, and the character deep in the Hess DNA that dances to the Fiddler's tune.

AFTERWORD

They shall mount up with wings like eagles.

—-Isaiah 40:31

As we close the book that is a digestion of three years of conversations with our old friend and some supporting research, we can't say for sure that this "memory exercise" we introduced to the world of human health care has meant one iota of difference in Frank's condition. You can't measure what you've prevented, and we wouldn't know what to measure anyway. We can say with certainty, though, that it hasn't done any harm. Together with the therapeutic services of our Golden Retriever, "Nikki," who knows what we may have forestalled? Nikki lights up as we near the Lutheran Home campus. Frank lights up when we enter his Memory Care Unit or his room down the hallway.

We can't help thinking about the ballplayers here that we've gotten to know so well, to respect even more than we knew, and hopefully to have related to readers in meaningful ways. We toy with the idea from time to time of fielding this team, this "Dream Team" of the Minnesota River Valley's Lower Basin in a mythical matchup game or series against anybody of anytime. What a delight and a dilemma. We are loaded on all fronts—pitching, hitting, and defense.

We have seven pitchers, three catchers, and four shortstops on our "roster" of 11, 12 with Frank. We can put three fleet-footed, strong-armed, strike-throwing pitchers in our outfield at will, so nobody is going to run on us should they be so lucky as to get on base. Our infield is without peer. We have really good speed, and we hit the ball. Oh, Lord, do we hit.

I suppose we would play the righty-lefty thing with our starting pitcher, going with either Johnny Garbett or Lefty Weckman against a team with a lineup of strong left-handed hitters. Conversely, we would tap Jim Stoll if our opposition were a typical lineup of mostly right-handed hitters.

We have the choice of catching Stoll, Jim Kubes, or Frank himself. With "mighty mite" Tex Erickson starting at shortstop and probably leading off for us, we have the choice of three other outstanding shortstops to play third base and second base. Jim Pollard would be an excellent choice at either third or first base. If we are facing a right-handed pitcher, we like Big Jake Harsh at first and Pollard probably in the outfield flanking John Freund in center field. Okay, it's Woody at third and Mark Hess at second base. Pat Devitt fills the remaining outfield position.

We can pitch Stoll, Devitt, Freund, Pollard, or Kubes in the second and third games of a typical series, and we have whichever lefty we didn't start in the first game to go as well. If John Freund's power pitching is needed or if he is needed elsewhere, we insert Weckman or Garbett into centerfield.

If Jake's back is acting up, we move Pollard to first base. If Jim is pitching, we can play Weck at that corner as well as Harsh or Freund. If Stoll is not pitching or catching, we can play him confidently at third or on either outfield flank.

The batting order is another delightful dilemma: We'd hit Woody after Tex because he can do so much with the bat and he always gets the bat on the ball. He and Tex on the bases would drive pitchers and defenses crazy. We would bat Jim Stoll third whether he's pitching or in the field, and we like our other Jim's in the next power slots, 4, 5, and 6: Jim Pollard, Jim Kubes, and Jim Harsh. But we really like the left-handed bat of John Freund, so we'd bat him cleanup after Stoll and then follow up with the rest of our "murderers' row." How can Pat Devitt be in the bottom of a batting order? We would follow him with Mark Hess and Garbett or Weck if either one is pitching.

We have visited the catacombs. We have walked hallowed ground. Memory speaks! It merges with and morphs into dreams. The Fiddler strikes up an old tune, and Spirit lives to play another ballgame.

ACKNOWLEDGEMENTS

Most professional baseball-related statistics, records, and other facts were obtained from www.baseball-reference.com, which was also used to confirm factual information derived from other sources.

We were helped immensely by the works of Tom Melchior–*Scott County Baseball*–and Armand Peterson and Tom Tomashek–*Town Ball: The Glory Days of Minnesota Amateur Baseball*. Ed Breimhorst provided us with a stack of old *Northwest Umpires Reviews*, which he said came from Roman Dorzinski of New Prague, MN. Jim Taddei did some helpful fact-checking for us in Alexandria, MN, as did Jiv Pauly in Jordan. Families of some of our profiled ballplayers had scrapbooks with important collections of articles from various, usually unidentified, newspapers, which were really helpful. But we had to make educated guesses in many cases as to the actual publication and dates. Similarly, we were delighted by the coverage given baseball during the game's Golden Age in the *Jordan Independent*. We rely extensively on excerpts of writing we attribute to Max Casey. Although the articles and columns were usually without any byline, several senior Jordan citizens have assured us that Max Casey did, in fact, do the sports writing for his father, John E. Casey, Editor and Publisher.

Historical Societies in Scott County and Stevens County, as well as the Minnesota Historical Society at the History Center in St. Paul, and county libraries in Jordan, Le Sueur, Shakopee, Belle Plaine, Prior Lake, and Glencoe provided access to microfilm–stored and actual newspapers. Nancy Hammer helped track down Tex Erickson's son, Dwight, a classmate of hers. Brian Larson, the official historian for the Minnesota State Amateur Baseball Board of Directors, helped out with some valuable information. Director Dave Hartmann not only provided us with keen insight on many ballplayers, the difference that the metal bats made in amateur ball, and important comparisons, he put us in touch with Jim Stoll in Nevada, with whom we enjoyed hours of interviewing and conversation. Dr. Daniel A. Russell, the professor of physics who unveils the performance secrets of metal bats, shared his insights in on-line articles and private correspondence and telephone conversation.

We are indebted to Nancy Huber for her editing of the manuscript. Likewise, Dave Hartmann, Jerry Stahl, and Paul Sunder were especially helpful in various ways. Ron Bump helped come up with the title.

While Nancy closely read more than once every manuscript page for us, others who read individual chapters or introductory material and provided some valuable feedback included Mary Kay Langager, Tony Strupeck, Jim Hoesley, Bob and Vivian Freund, Gerry and Carman Meyer, Woody and Ginny Peters, Dave Beckius, Pat and Rosemary Devitt, Mark and Cindy Hess, Jim Taddei, and Manley Vinkemeier.

Subjects were interviewed directly and in person when possible. When not possible, or to get more complete profiles, teammates, coaches, friends, family, and others were interviewed directly or via telephone. We did follow-up interviews, when necessary, on the telephone or via email.

Sources—Conversations, interviews, and correspondence with many people have been invaluable. The conversations with Frank Hilgers were most important.

ACKNOWLEDGEMENTS

They set the stage, the agenda, and formed our structure as we proceeded. Subsequently, other major sources included the following:

Lefty Weckman	Tom Stoll	Dave Wagner
Ed Breimhorst	Woody Peters	Mike Petrich
Butch Kreuser	Ken Hanson	Ralph Guenzel
Fred Kerber	Dick Nachbar	John Gornick
Dick Erickson	Bobby Bolf	Babe Glumac
Howie Heller	Bob and Vivian Freund	Jack Evens
Dan Driscoll	Jack and Jerry Freund	Col. Rudy Bernard (ret.)
Gerry and Carman Meyer	Kieran O'Brien	Lee McCormick
Dave Beckius	Don Clemens	Dick Nolden
Manley Vinkemeier	Jiv Pauly	Rich Hartman
Brad Harsh	Jerry Stahl	Paul Sunder
Jim Kubes	Joe Dean	Bill Breimhorst
Terry Schmitz	Pat Devitt	Jim Taddei
Dick Jonckowski	Lowell Stark	Dwight Erickson
Patty Rezac	Dave Stock	Madelyn (Erickson) Gardner
Don Hennen	Mark and Cindy Hess	Tom Betchwars
Dave Bakken	Pat Pohl	Daniel A. Russell, Ph.D.
Glen Bauer	Brian Larson	Mark Fuhrman and his father, Ray
Jim Stoll	Harold Beckman	
Chuck Warner	Ron and Steven Beckman	Dave Hartmann and his father, Gary Hartmann
Gary Porter	Mark and Ken Beckman	
Gary Reierson	Pete Beckius	

About the Author — Doug Nachbar grew up in Jordan, Minnesota, where he enjoyed the Golden Age of Baseball, watching his boyhood heroes play ball and having the opportunity to play ball with some of them. He lives now in Bloomington, Minnesota.

BIBLIOGRAPHY

– BOOKS –

Adomites, Paul; Cassidy, Robert; Herman, Bruce; Schlossberg, Dan; Wisnia, Saul. *The Golden Age of Baseball,* Lincolnwood, Illinois: Publications International, Ltd, 2003.

Asinof, Eliot. *Eight Men Out; The Black Sox and the 1919 World Series.* New York: Henry Holt and Company, 1963.

Brokaw, Tom. *The Greatest Generation.* New York: Random House, 1998.

Brown, Dee. *Bury My Heart at Wounded Knee, An Indian History of the American West.* New York: Bantam Books, 1970.

Christgau, John. *Tricksters In The Madhouse, Lakers vs. Globetrotters, 1948.* Lincoln, Nebraska: University of Nebraska Press, 2004.

Cramer, Richard Ben. *Joe DiMaggio—The Hero's Life.* New York: Simon & Schuster, 2000.

Dodson, James. *Ben Hogan, An American Life.* New York: Broadway Books, 2004.

Einstein, Charles. *Willie's Time, Baseball's Golden Age*. New York: Penguin Books, 1979.

Grabitzke, Dwight; Nagel, Lowell; and Dooner, Mike. *The History of Arlington Baseball.* Arlington, MN: McLeod Publishing, Inc., 2008.

Graf, Gary. *And God Said, "PLAY BALL!"* Liguori, Missouri: Liguori Publications, 2005.

Grundman, Dolph. *Jim Pollard, The Kangaroo Kid*. Minneapolis: Nodin Press, 2009.

Halberstam, David. *October 1964.* New York: Random House, 1994.

Halberstam, David. *The Fifties.* New York: Random House, 1993.

Halberstam, David. *Summer of '49.* New York: Harper Perennial Modern Classics, 2006.

Halberstam, David. *The Teammates*, *A Portrait of a Friendship*. New York: Hyperion, 2003.

Halfon, Mark S. *Tales From The Deadball Era: Ty Cobb, Home Run Baker, Shoeless Joe Jackson, And The Wildest Times In Baseball History.* University of Nebraska Press: Potomac Books, 2014.

Heinz, W.C. *Once They Heard the Cheers*. Garden City, New York: Doubleday, 1979.

Heinz, W.C. *What A Time It Was, The Best of W.C. Heinz On Sports*. De Capo Press, 2001.

Kahn, Roger. *The Era, 1947 – 1957: When the Yankees, the Giants, and the Dodgers Ruled the World*. Lincoln and London: University of Nebraska Press, 1993.

Leavy, Jane. *The Last Boy, Mickey Mantle and the End of America's Childhood*. New York: HarperCollins, 2010.

Leerhsen, Charles. *Ty Cobb: A Terrible Beauty*. New York: Simon & Schuster, 2015.

Lewis, Nathan. *Gold, The Once and Future Money*. Hoboken, NJ: John Wiley & Sons, Inc., 2007

Melchior, Tom. *Scott County Baseball* with Co-Sponsor Scott County Historical Society, 2008.

Montville, Leigh. *The Big Bam—The Life and Times of Babe Ruth*. New York: Random House (Broadway Books), 2006.

Okrent, Daniel (ed.). *American Pastimes, The Very Best of Red Smith*. New York: Library of America, 2013.

Paul, Ron. *The Case for Gold, A Minority Report of the U.S. Gold Commission, 2nd Edition*. Auburn, Alabama: Ludwig von Mises Inst.; and Baltimore, Maryland: Laissez Faire Books: 2011.

Penrice, James. *Crossing Home—The Spiritual Lessons of Baseball*. New York: Society of St. Paul/Alba House, 1993.

Peterson, Armand and Tomashek, Tom. *Town Ball, The Glory Days of Minnesota Amateur Baseball*. Minneapolis: University of Minnesota Press, 2006.

Peary, Danny (ed.). *We Played the Game*. New York: Hyperion, 1994.

Ritter, Lawrence S. *The Glory of Their Times: The Story of the Early Days of Baseball Told by the Men Who Played It*. New York: HarperCollins, 1966, 1984.

Sampson, Curt. *Hogan*. Nashville, Tennessee: Rutledge Hill Press, 1996.

Sampson, Curt. *The Eternal Summer, Palmer, Nicklaus, and Hogan in 1960, Golf's Golden Year*. New York: Random House, 1992.

Sauls, J.H. *GOD and baseball*. Tate Publishing & Enterprises, 2006.

Schumacher, E.F. *Small Is Beautiful: Economics As If People Mattered*. London: Blond and Briggs, Ltd., 1973.

Sexton, John (with Thomas Oliphant and Peter J. Schwartz). *Baseball as a Road to God, Seeing Beyond the Game*. New York: Penguin Group, 2013.

Red Smith on Baseball, The Game's Greatest Writer on the Game's Greatest Years. Chicago: Ivan R. Dee, 2000.

Starr, Bill. *Clearing the Bases, Baseball Then & Now.* Hampton, New Hampshire: Curley Publishing, Inc., 1989.

Tye, Larry. *Satchel, The Life and Times of an American Legend.* New York: Random House, 2009.

Weintraub, Robert. *The Victory Season: The End of World War II and the Birth of Baseball's Golden Age.* New York: Back Bay Books/Little, Brown and Company, 2013.

White, William (ed.). *By-Line: Ernest Hemingway, Selected Articles and Dispatches of Four Decades.* New York: Simon & Schuster, 1995.

Wolfe, Tom. *The Right Stuff.* New York: Farrar, Straus, and Giroux, 1979.

Wolfe, Tom. *The Pumphouse Gang.* Toronto: Collins Publishers, 1987.

– WEBSITES –

mrbdc@mnsu.edu - Minnesota River Basin Data Center @ Minnesota State University Mankato

http://www.historyontheweb.org/minnbrew/mnbrew.html

www.history.com

www.historyorb.com

University of Minnesota Official Athletic Site — Baseball History

www.baseball-reference.com

www.baseball-almanac.com

www.wikipedia.com

www.wiki.answers.com

– NEWSPAPERS AND PERIODICALS –

The Belle Plaine Herald, Belle Plaine, MN *The Brownton Bulletin,* Brownton, MN.

The Glencoe Enterprise, Glencoe, MN. *The Jordan Independent,* Jordan, MN.

The LeSueur News Herald, LeSueur, MN.

The Minneapolis Star Tribune, Minneapolis, MN.

The Minnesota Daily, University of Minnesota, Minneapolis, MN. *The Morris Star,* Morris, MN

The Morris Tribune, Morris, MN

The Northwest Umpires Review

The New Prague Times, New Prague, MN

The New Ulm Daily Journal, New Ulm, MN

The Rochester Post-Bulletin, Rochester, MN

The St. Anthony Village Bulletin, St. Anthony Village, MN

The St. Cloud Daily Times, St. Cloud, MN

The Shakopee Argus/Shakopee Valley News, Shakopee, MN

The South Crow River News, Osseo, MN: Larson Publications *The Tulsa World,* Tulsa, Oklahoma

– MISCELLANEOUS –

Jordan Baseball Association (JBA) Archives; Created or Collected and Archived by Max Casey, circa 1949-1963. D

Doug Nachbar. Minnesota School of Journalism Submission. "The Jordan Brewery," 1976.

"Spirit of '76"—Minnesota State Baseball Tournament Program Guide, Hosted by Arlington, MN, 1976.

Sandy Dietel and Taura Sauter with the Arlington A's Hall of Fame Committee. Glencoe, MN: McLeod Publishing, Inc., 2008.

Jim Donahue. "Once Every 40 Years," Official Program of American Legion World Series, 1985 (From www.edinahistoricalsociety.org).

90th Annual Minnesota State Amateur Baseball Tournament Program Guide. Hosted by Delano & Maple Lake, MN, 2013.

Made in the USA
Monee, IL
29 June 2023